Algebra 2

Solutions Manual

Third Edition

Acknowledgments

Saxon Publishers thanks those staff members who helped this book reach its final form.

Editorial
- Brian E. Rice
- Rodney Clint Keele
- Andrew C. Kershen
- Sean G. Douglas
- Chris Davey
- Candice L. Holcombe

Production
- Eric S. Atkins
- Brenda M. Bell
- Jack W. Day
- Nick Key
- Tonea D. Morrow
- Nancy J. Rimassa
- Lois A. Rossman
- Debra Sullivan
- Eric A. Sullivan
- Darlene Terry

© 2003 Saxon Publishers, Inc.

Printed in the United States of America

ISBN: 978-1-56577-143-7

16 17 0982 16 15

4500521284

Preface

This manual contains solutions to every problem in the third edition of John Saxon's *Algebra 2* textbook. The solutions are designed to be representative of students' work, but please keep in mind that many problems will have more than one correct solution. We have attempted to stay as close as possible to the methods and procedures outlined in the textbook. Early solutions of problems of a particular type contain every step. Later solutions omit simpler steps. The final answers are set in boldface for ease of grading.

PROBLEM SET A

1. $y + 65 = 180$
   $y = 180 - 65 = \mathbf{115}$

2. $x + 40 = 90$
   $x = 90 - 40 = \mathbf{50}$

3. $x + 89 = 180$
   $x = 180 - 89$
   $x = \mathbf{91}$

   Since vertical angles are equal,
   $y = \mathbf{89}$
   $p = \mathbf{91}$

4. $z + 100 = 180$
   $z = 180 - 100 = \mathbf{80}$

   Since vertical angles are equal,
   $2x = 80$
   $x = \mathbf{40}$
   $4y = 100$
   $y = \mathbf{25}$

5. Angle + Supplement = 180°
   Angle + 40° = 180°
   Angle = 180° − 40°
   Angle = **140°**

6. Angle + Complement = 90°
   Angle + 40° = 90°
   Angle = 90° − 40°
   Angle = **50°**

7. $-2 - (-2) = -2 + 2 = \mathbf{0}$

8. $-3 - [-(-2)] = -3 - 2 = \mathbf{-5}$

9. $-2 - 3(-2 - 2) - 5(-5 + 7)$
   $= -2 - 3(-4) - 5(2)$
   $= -2 - (-12) - (10)$
   $= -2 + 12 - 10 = \mathbf{0}$

10. $-[-2(-5 + 2) - (-2 - 3)]$
    $= -[-2(-3) - (-5)]$
    $= -[6 + 5] = \mathbf{-11}$

11. $-2 + (-2)^3 = -2 + (-8)$
    $= -2 - 8 = \mathbf{-10}$

12. $-3^2 - 3 - (-3)^2$
    $= -9 - 3 - 9 = \mathbf{-21}$

13. $-3(-2 - 3 + 6) - [-5(-2) + 3(-2 - 4)]$
    $= -3(1) - [-5(-2) + 3(-6)]$
    $= -3 - [10 - 18] = -3 - [-8] = \mathbf{5}$

14. $-2 - 2^2 - 2^3 - 2^4$
    $= -2 - 4 - 8 - 16 = \mathbf{-30}$

15. $|-2| - |-4 - 2| + |8| = |-2| - |-6| + |8|$
    $= 2 - 6 + 8 = \mathbf{4}$

16. $-|-3(2) - 3| - 2^2 = -|-6 - 3| - 4$
    $= -|-9| - 4 = -9 - 4 = \mathbf{-13}$

17. $-2^2 - 2^3 - |-2| - 2 = -4 - 8 - 2 - 2$
    $= \mathbf{-16}$

18. $-3[-1 - 2(-1 - 1)][-3(-2) - 1]$
    $= -3[-1 - 2(-2)][6 - 1] = -3[-1 + 4][6 - 1]$
    $= -3[3][5] = \mathbf{-45}$

19. $-3[-3(-4 - 1) - (-3 - 4)]$
    $= -3[-3(-5) - (-7)]$
    $= -3[15 + 7] = -3[22] = \mathbf{-66}$

20. $-2[(-3 + 1) - (-2 - 2)(-1 + 3)]$
    $= -2[(-2) - (-4)(2)] = -2[-2 + 8]$
    $= -2[6] = \mathbf{-12}$

21. $-2[-2(-4) - 2^3](-|2|) = -2[8 - 8](-2)$
    $= -2[0](-2) = \mathbf{0}$

22. $-8 - 3^2 - (-2)^2 - 3(-2) + 2$
    $= -8 - 9 - 4 + 6 + 2 = \mathbf{-13}$

23. $-\{-[-5(-3 + 2)7]\} = -\{-[-5(-1)7]\}$
    $= -\{-[35]\} = \mathbf{35}$

24. $-5 - |-3 - 4| - (3)^2 - 3$
    $= -5 - |-7| - 9 - 3$
    $= -5 - 7 - 9 - 3 = \mathbf{-24}$

25. $3(-2 + 5) - 2^2(2 - 3) - |-2|$
    $= 3(3) - 4(-1) - 2$
    $= 9 + 4 - 2 = \mathbf{11}$

26. $\dfrac{-5 - (-2) + 8 - 4(5)}{6 - 4(-3)}$

$= \dfrac{-5 + 2 + 8 - 20}{6 + 12} = \dfrac{-15}{18} = -\dfrac{5}{6}$

27. $(-2)[\,|-3 - 4 - 5| - 2^3 - (-1)\,]$

$= (-2)[\,|-12| - 8 + 1\,] = (-2)[12 - 8 + 1]$

$= -2[5] = \mathbf{-10}$

28. $\dfrac{-3 - (-2) + 9 - (-5)}{7(|-3 + 4|)}$

$= \dfrac{-3 + 2 + 9 + 5}{7(1)} = \dfrac{13}{7}$

29. $4(-2)[-(7 - 3)(5 - 2)2] = -8[-(4)(3)(2)]$

$= -8[-24] = \mathbf{192}$

30. $4 - (-4) - 5(3 - 1) + 3(4)(-2)^3$

$= 4 + 4 - 5(2) + 3(4)(-8)$

$= 4 + 4 - 10 - 96 = \mathbf{-98}$

PROBLEM SET B

1. $A_{\text{Shaded}} = A_{\text{Square}} - A_{\text{Circle}}$

$= [(8)(8) - \pi(4)^2]\ \text{m}^2$

$= (64 - 16\pi)\ \text{m}^2 \approx \mathbf{13.76\ m^2}$

2. $A_{\text{Shaded}} = A_{\text{Total}} - A_{\text{Not Shaded}}$

$= \left[\dfrac{1}{2}(12)(10)\right]\text{m}^2$

$\quad - \left[(3)(4) + \dfrac{1}{2}(3)(6) + \dfrac{1}{2}(9)(4)\right]\text{m}^2$

$= 60\ \text{m}^2 - 39\ \text{m}^2 = \mathbf{21\ m^2}$

3. $A_{\text{Shaded}} = A_{\text{Circle}} - A_{\text{Triangle}}$

$= \left[\pi(8)^2 - \dfrac{1}{2}(16)(8)\right]\text{cm}^2$

$= (64\pi - 64)\ \text{cm}^2 \approx \mathbf{136.96\ cm^2}$

4. Perimeter $= \left[\dfrac{1}{2}(2)(\pi)(2) + 14\right]\text{m}$

$= (2\pi + 14)\ \text{m} \approx \mathbf{20.28\ m}$

5. Area of $40°$ sector $= \dfrac{40}{360}(A_{\text{Circle}})$

$= \dfrac{40}{360}[\pi(5)^2]\ \text{m}^2$

$= \dfrac{40}{360}(25\pi)\ \text{m}^2 \approx \mathbf{8.72\ m^2}$

6. $V_{\text{Pyramid}} = \dfrac{1}{3}V_{\text{Prism}}$

$= \dfrac{1}{3}[A_{\text{Base}} \times \text{height}]$

$= \dfrac{1}{3}\left[\dfrac{1}{2}(6)(4)\ \text{cm}^2 \times 10\ \text{cm}\right]$

$= \dfrac{1}{3}(120)\ \text{cm}^3 = \mathbf{40\ cm^3}$

7. $A_{\text{Base}} = \left[(3)(4) + \dfrac{1}{2}\pi(2)^2\right]\text{m}^2$

$= (12 + 2\pi)\ \text{m}^2 \approx \mathbf{18.28\ m^2}$

$V_{\text{Cylinder}} = A_{\text{Base}} \times \text{height}$

$= (12 + 2\pi)\ \text{m}^2 \times 8\ \text{m}$

$= (96 + 16\pi)\ \text{m}^3 \approx \mathbf{146.24\ m^3}$

8. $V_{\text{Sphere}} = \dfrac{2}{3}V_{\text{Cylinder}}$

$= \dfrac{2}{3}[A_{\text{Base}} \times \text{height}]$

$= \dfrac{2}{3}[\pi(6)^2\ \text{cm}^2 \times 12\ \text{cm}]$

$= \dfrac{2}{3}(36\pi)(12)\ \text{cm}^3 \approx \mathbf{904.32\ cm^3}$

$S.\,A. = 4\pi r^2 = 4\pi(6)^2\ \text{cm}^2 \approx \mathbf{452.16\ cm^2}$

9. Area of $72°$ sector $= \dfrac{72}{360}(A_{\text{Circle}})$

$= \dfrac{72}{360}[\pi(10)^2]\ \text{cm}^2$

$= \dfrac{72}{360}(100\pi)\ \text{cm}^2 \approx \mathbf{62.8\ cm^2}$

10. Perimeter $= \left[\dfrac{1}{2}(2)(\pi)(2) + 16 + 4\right]\text{yd}$

$\quad + \left[\dfrac{1}{2}(2)(\pi)(2)\right]\text{yd}$

$= (4\pi + 20)\ \text{yd} \approx \mathbf{32.56\ yd}$

11. $z + 70 = 180$

$z = 180 - 70$

$z = \mathbf{110}$

Since vertical angles are equal,

$2x = 70$

$x = \mathbf{35}$

$y = \mathbf{110}$

12. $5A + 40 = 90$

$5A = 90 - 40$

$5A = 50$

$A = \dfrac{50}{5} = \mathbf{10}$

13. $2B + 140 = 180$

$2B = 180 - 140$

$2B = 40$

$B = \dfrac{40}{2} = \mathbf{20}$

14. Angle + Complement = $90°$

Angle + $10° = 90°$

Angle = $90° - 10° = \mathbf{80°}$

15. Angle + Supplement = $180°$

Angle + $60° = 180°$

Angle = $180° - 60° = \mathbf{120°}$

16. $-2^2 - 2^3 - (-2)^2 - 2$

$= -4 - 8 - 4 - 2 = \mathbf{-18}$

17. $-2^2 - |-4| + |4| = -4 - 4 + 4 = \mathbf{-4}$

18. $-|-3| - 3 - 3^2 = -3 - 3 - 9 = \mathbf{-15}$

19. $-4 - (-3)^3 - 2^2 + |-4|$

$= -4 + 27 - 4 + 4 = \mathbf{23}$

20. $-3^2 - 2(-4 + 6) = -9 - 2(2) = \mathbf{-13}$

21. $-4(-2^2 - 3) - 5 + |-3| = -4(-4 - 3) - 5 + 3$

$= -4(-7) - 5 + 3 = 28 - 5 + 3 = \mathbf{26}$

22. $-2[-1 - (-5)] - [-6(-2) + 3]$

$= -2[-1 + 5] - [12 + 3]$

$= -2[4] - [15] = -8 - 15 = \mathbf{-23}$

23. $-2^2 - 2^3 - 2 - |-2| = -4 - 8 - 2 - 2 = \mathbf{-16}$

24. $-2 - |-3 - 4 + 8| - 2^2 = -2 - |1| - 4$

$= -2 - 1 - 4 = \mathbf{-7}$

25. $-|-2 - 3 - 4| - |-2| = -|-9| - |-2|$

$= -9 - 2 = \mathbf{-11}$

26. $\dfrac{-5 - (-2) + 8 - 4(5) - 3}{6 - 4(-3)}$

$= \dfrac{-5 + 2 + 8 - 20 - 3}{6 + 12} = \dfrac{-18}{18} = \mathbf{-1}$

27. $(-2)[|-3 + 4 - 5| - 2^3 - (-1)]$

$= (-2)[|-4| - 8 + 1] = (-2)[4 - 8 + 1]$

$= (-2)(-3) = \mathbf{6}$

28. $\dfrac{-|-5| - (-2) + 6 - 4(3 - |6 - 9|)}{5 - |(4)(-3)|}$

$= \dfrac{-5 + 2 + 6 - 4(3 - 3)}{5 - |-12|}$

$= \dfrac{-5 + 2 + 6 - 0}{5 - 12} = \dfrac{3}{-7} = \mathbf{-\dfrac{3}{7}}$

29. $\dfrac{-2 - (-3 - 2) - (-2 + 5)}{-4(2^2 - 3)(-2)}$

$= \dfrac{-2 - (-5) - (3)}{-4(1)(-2)} = \dfrac{-2 + 5 - 3}{8}$

$= \dfrac{0}{8} = \mathbf{0}$

30. $-2(-3 + 4 - 6) - 2^2(-2) - 3(-2) - |-5|$

$= -2(-5) - 4(-2) + 6 - 5$

$= 10 + 8 + 6 - 5 = \mathbf{19}$

PRACTICE SET 1

a. $m\angle A = m\angle C$ because they are angles opposite equal sides.

$m\angle C = \mathbf{35°}$

$m\angle B = 180° - m\angle A - m\angle C$

$m\angle B = 180° - 35° - 35°$

$m\angle B = \mathbf{110°}$

b. $x = 180 - 145$

$x = \mathbf{35}$

$y = 180 - x - 40$

$y = 180 - 35 - 40$

$y = \mathbf{105}$

c. $A = 180 - 130$

$A = \mathbf{50}$

$C = A$

$C = \mathbf{50}$

$2B = 180 - C$

$B = \dfrac{(180 - 50)}{2}$

$B = \mathbf{65}$

d. $\dfrac{3}{4}\overrightarrow{SF} = \dfrac{6}{5}$

$\overrightarrow{SF} = \dfrac{6}{5} \cdot \dfrac{4}{3} = \dfrac{24}{15} = \dfrac{8}{5}$

$x = \dfrac{5}{3}\overrightarrow{SF} = \dfrac{5}{3} \cdot \dfrac{8}{5} = \mathbf{\dfrac{8}{3}}$

PROBLEM SET 1

1. Since angles opposite equal sides are equal angles,

$x = $ **45.**

$$y + 45 + 45 = 180$$
$$y = 180 - 90 = \mathbf{90}$$

2. Since angles opposite equal sides are equal angles,

$x = $ **55.**

$$y + 55 + 55 = 180$$
$$y = 180 - 110 = \mathbf{70}$$

3.
$$2C + 70 = 180$$
$$2C = 110$$
$$C = \mathbf{55}$$

Since lines are parallel, $B = $ **110** and $A = $ **70.**

4.
$$2 \times \overrightarrow{SF} = 3$$
$$\overrightarrow{SF} = \frac{3}{2}$$
$$3 \times \overrightarrow{SF} = x$$
$$3\left(\frac{3}{2}\right) = x$$
$$x = \mathbf{\frac{9}{2}}$$

5.
$$A_{\text{Top Shaded}} = \left[\frac{1}{2}\pi(4)^2 - \frac{1}{2}(8)(4)\right] \text{cm}^2$$
$$= (8\pi - 16) \text{ cm}^2$$

$$A_{\text{Bottom Shaded}} = \frac{60}{360}\left[\pi(4)^2\right] \text{cm}^2$$
$$= \frac{60}{360}(16\pi) \text{ cm}^2$$

$$A_{\text{Shaded}} = A_{\text{Top Shaded}} + A_{\text{Bottom Shaded}}$$
$$= (8\pi - 16) \text{ cm}^2 + \frac{60}{360}(16\pi) \text{ cm}^2$$
$$= \left(8\pi + \frac{8}{3}\pi - 16\right) \text{cm}^2 \approx \mathbf{17.49 \text{ cm}^2}$$

6.
$$A_{\text{Total}} = \left[\frac{1}{2}(8)(6) + \frac{1}{2}\pi(5)^2\right.$$
$$\left. + \frac{1}{2}\pi(4)^2 + \frac{1}{2}\pi(3)^2\right] \text{cm}^2$$
$$= (24 + 25\pi) \text{ cm}^2$$

$$A_{\text{White Triangles}} = \left[\frac{1}{2}(5)(5) + \frac{1}{2}(4)(4)\right.$$
$$\left. + \frac{1}{2}(3)(3)\right] \text{cm}^2$$
$$= 25 \text{ cm}^2$$

$$A_{\text{Shaded}} = A_{\text{Total}} - A_{\text{White Triangles}}$$
$$= (24 + 25\pi) \text{ cm}^2 - 25 \text{ cm}^2$$
$$= (25\pi - 1) \text{ cm}^2 \approx \mathbf{77.5 \text{ cm}^2}$$

7.
$$\text{Perimeter} = \left[\frac{1}{2}(2)(\pi)(4) + 48\right] \text{ft}$$
$$= (4\pi + 48) \text{ ft} \approx \mathbf{60.56 \text{ ft}}$$

8.
$$V_{\text{Cylinder}} = A_{\text{Base}} \times \text{height}$$
$$= [\pi(4)^2 \text{ ft}^2 \times 8 \text{ ft}]$$
$$= 128\pi \text{ ft}^3 \approx \mathbf{401.92 \text{ ft}^3}$$

$$V_{\text{Sphere}} = \frac{2}{3}V_{\text{Cylinder}}$$
$$= \frac{2}{3}(128\pi) \text{ ft}^3 \approx \mathbf{267.95 \text{ ft}^3}$$

9.
$$p + 30 = 180$$
$$p = 180 - 30 = \mathbf{150}$$
$$2y + 30 = 90$$
$$2y = 90 - 30$$
$$y = \mathbf{30}$$

Since vertical angles are equal angles, $x = $ **30.**

10.
$$p + 60 = 180$$
$$p = 180 - 60 = \mathbf{120}$$

Since vertical angles are equal angles,

$$10x = 60$$
$$x = \mathbf{6}$$
$$4y = 120$$
$$y = \mathbf{30}$$

11.
$$\text{Angle} + \text{Complement} = 90°$$
$$\text{Angle} + 17° = 90°$$
$$\text{Angle} = 90° - 17° = \mathbf{73°}$$

12.
$$V_{\text{Cone}} = \frac{1}{3}(A_{\text{Base}} \times \text{height})$$
$$= \frac{1}{3}\left[\frac{1}{2}\pi(3)^2 + (5)(6)\right] \text{m}^2 \times 7 \text{ m}$$
$$= \frac{1}{3}\left(\frac{9}{2}\pi + 30\right)(7) \text{ m}^3 \approx \mathbf{102.97 \text{ m}^3}$$

13. $r = \frac{1}{4}$ side of square

   $A_{\text{Square}} = s^2$

   $s = 4r$

   $A_{\text{Square}} = (4r)^2 = \mathbf{16r^2}$

14. $-[-2(-3 - 2) - (-2 - 3)] = -[-2(-5) - (-5)]$

   $= -[10 + 5] = -[15] = \mathbf{-15}$

15. $-2[-2 - 3(-2 - 2)][-2(-4) - 3]$

   $= -2[-2 - 3(-4)][-2(-4) - 3]$

   $= -2[-2 + 12][8 - 3] = -2[10][5] = \mathbf{-100}$

16. $-2^2 - 2^3[-2 + 3(-2)] - |-2^3|$

   $= -4 - 8[-2 - 6] - |-8| = -4 - 8[-8] - 8$

   $= -4 + 64 - 8 = \mathbf{52}$

17. $-3 - 2^3 - 4^2 - |-2 - 3(2)|$

   $= -3 - 8 - 16 - |-2 - 6|$

   $= -3 - 8 - 16 - |-8|$

   $= -3 - 8 - 16 - 8 = \mathbf{-35}$

18. $-\{-2[(-3 + 7) - (-2)][-3(-2 + 1)]\}$

   $= -\{-2[4 + 2][-3(-1)]\} = -\{-2[6][3]\}$

   $= -\{-36\} = \mathbf{36}$

19. $3^2 - 3^3 + 3^4 - (-3)^3 - 3$

   $= 9 - 27 + 81 - (-27) - 3$

   $= 9 - 27 + 81 + 27 - 3 = \mathbf{87}$

20. $-(-4)^2 - 4|-2| - 2^3 + |-11 - 4|$

   $= -16 - 4(2) - 8 + |-15|$

   $= -16 - 8 - 8 + 15 = \mathbf{-17}$

21. $6 - \{[3^2 - 8 + (-2)][-(4 - 6)(-3)^2 + 2]2\}$

   $= 6 - \{[9 - 8 - 2][-(-2)(9) + 2]2\}$

   $= 6 - \{[9 - 8 - 2][18 + 2]2\}$

   $= 6 - \{[-1][20]2\} = 6 - \{-40\}$

   $= 6 + 40 = \mathbf{46}$

22. $-[-(-2)] - |-4 - 3|2^2 - 4$

   $= -[2] - |-7|4 - 4 = -2 - 7(4) - 4$

   $= -2 - 28 - 4 = \mathbf{-34}$

23. $(-|-3|)[(2 - 7)(-3 - 2) + (-2)^2]$

   $= -3[-5(-5) + 4] = -3[25 + 4]$

   $= -3[29] = \mathbf{-87}$

24. $\dfrac{-|-4| - (-3) + 7 - 6(4 - |7 - 11|)}{7 - |(3)(-2)|}$

   $= \dfrac{-4 + 3 + 7 - 6(4 - |-4|)}{7 - |-6|}$

   $= \dfrac{-4 + 3 + 7 - 6(4 - 4)}{7 - 6}$

   $= \dfrac{-4 + 3 + 7 - 6(0)}{1}$

   $= \dfrac{-4 + 3 + 7 - 0}{1} = \dfrac{6}{1} = \mathbf{6}$

25. $-(-3 - 2)(-7 - |-3 - 2|) - (-3)^2$

   $= -(-5)(-7 - |-5|) - 9 = 5(-7 - 5) - 9$

   $= 5(-12) - 9 = -60 - 9 = \mathbf{-69}$

26. $(-3)[|-2 - 7 - 2| - (-3)^2 - (-2)]$

   $= -3[|-11| - 9 + 2] = -3[11 - 9 + 2]$

   $= -3[4] = \mathbf{-12}$

27. $\dfrac{-4 - (-3) + 7 - 6(2)}{7 - (3)(-2)}$

   $= \dfrac{-4 + 3 + 7 - 12}{7 + 6} = \dfrac{-6}{13} = -\dfrac{6}{13}$

28. $3 - 5 - 2^2 - 4^2(-1)(-3 - |-2 - 5| - 3)$

   $= 3 - 5 - 4 - 16(-1)(-3 - |-7| - 3)$

   $= 3 - 5 - 4 - 16(-1)(-3 - 7 - 3)$

   $= 3 - 5 - 4 - 16(-1)(-13)$

   $= 3 - 5 - 4 - 208 = \mathbf{-214}$

29. $-8 + (-3)(-2)^2 + (-7) - 2(-4 - 2)$

   $= -8 + (-3)(4) - 7 - 2(-6)$

   $= -8 - 12 - 7 + 12 = \mathbf{-15}$

30. $6(-3)[-(5 - 4)(6 - 2)3] = -18[-1(4)(3)]$

   $= -18[-12] = \mathbf{216}$

PRACTICE SET 2

a. $-4^{-2} = \dfrac{1}{-4^2} = \dfrac{1}{-16} = \mathbf{-\dfrac{1}{16}}$

b. $-(-4)^{-2} = \dfrac{1}{-(-4)^2} = \dfrac{1}{-(16)} = \mathbf{-\dfrac{1}{16}}$

c. $\dfrac{(x^2y^{-2})^0(x^{-3}y)^{-2}}{y^{-8}x^4y^2x^3} = \dfrac{x^0y^0x^6y^{-2}}{y^{-8}x^4y^2x^3}$

$= \dfrac{x^6y^{-2}}{x^7y^{-6}} = \mathbf{\dfrac{y^4}{x}}$

d. $A = \pi r^2 = 49\pi \text{ cm}^2$

$r^2 = 49 \text{ cm}^2$

$r = 7 \text{ cm}$

$C = 2\pi r = 2\pi(7 \text{ cm}) = \mathbf{14\pi \text{ cm}}$

PROBLEM SET 2

1. $4 \times \overrightarrow{SF} = 6$

$\overrightarrow{SF} = \dfrac{6}{4} = \dfrac{3}{2}$

$3 \times \overrightarrow{SF} = x$

$3 \times \dfrac{3}{2} = x$

$x = \mathbf{\dfrac{9}{2}}$

2. Since angles opposite equal sides are equal angles,

$x = \mathbf{38}.$

$y + 38 + 38 = 180$

$y = 180 - 38 - 38 = \mathbf{104}$

3. $V_{\text{Cylinder}} = A_{\text{Base}} \times \text{height}$

$= \left[\dfrac{60}{360}(\pi(4)^2) + \dfrac{1}{2}(4)(7)\right] \text{m}^2 \times 8 \text{ m}$

$= \left[\dfrac{60}{360}(16\pi) + 14\right](8) \text{ m}^3 \approx \mathbf{178.99 \text{ m}^3}$

4. Since vertical angles are equal angles,

$4A = 80$

$A = \mathbf{20}$

$2B + 80 = 180$

$2B = 100$

$B = \mathbf{50}$

Since lines are parallel,

$2C = 4A$

$2C = 80$

$C = \mathbf{40}$

5. $A + 60 = 180$

$A = 180 - 60 = \mathbf{120}$

Since vertical angles are equal angles,

$2B = 60$

$B = \mathbf{30}$

$3C = 120$

$C = \mathbf{40}$

6. $A_{\text{Square}} = s^2 = 16 \text{ cm}^2$

$s = \sqrt{16 \text{ cm}^2} = \mathbf{4 \text{ cm}}$

$r = \dfrac{1}{4}(s) = \dfrac{1}{4}(4 \text{ cm}) = \mathbf{1 \text{ cm}}$

$A_{\text{Circle}} = \pi r^2 \approx 3.14(1 \text{ cm})^2 = \mathbf{3.14 \text{ cm}^2}$

7. $V_{\text{Cylinder}} = A_{\text{Base}} \times \text{height}$

$250\pi \text{ cm}^3 = [\pi(5)^2] \text{ cm}^2 \times \text{height}$

$250\pi \text{ cm}^3 = 25\pi \text{ cm}^2 \times \text{height}$

$\text{height} = \dfrac{250\pi \text{ cm}^3}{25\pi \text{ cm}^2} = \mathbf{10 \text{ cm}}$

8. $V_{\text{Cone}} = \dfrac{1}{3} \times A_{\text{Base}} \times \text{height}$

$= \dfrac{1}{3}\left[\dfrac{1}{2}(1)(2) + (2)(2)\right.$

$\left. + \dfrac{1}{2}\pi(1)^2\right] \text{m}^2 \times 4\text{m}$

$= \dfrac{1}{3}\left(5 + \dfrac{\pi}{2}\right)(4) \text{ m}^3 \approx \mathbf{8.76 \text{ m}^3}$

9. $\dfrac{xx^2(x^0y^{-1})^2}{x^2x^{-5}(y^2)^5} = \dfrac{xx^2x^0y^{-2}}{x^2x^{-5}y^{10}} = \dfrac{x^3y^{-2}}{x^{-3}y^{10}}$

$= \mathbf{x^6y^{-12}}$

10. $\dfrac{m^2p^0(m^{-2}p)^2}{m^{-2}p^{-1}(m^{-3}p^2)^3} = \dfrac{m^2p^0m^{-4}p^2}{m^{-2}p^{-1}m^{-9}p^6}$

$= \dfrac{m^{-2}p^2}{m^{-11}p^5} = \mathbf{m^9p^{-3}}$

11. $\dfrac{(x^2y)^0xy}{x^2(y^{-2})^3} = \dfrac{x^0y^0xy}{x^2y^{-6}} = \dfrac{xy}{x^2y^{-6}} = \mathbf{x^{-1}y^7}$

12. $\dfrac{(a^2 b^0)^2 \, ab^{-2}}{a^2 b^{-2} (ab^{-3})^2} = \dfrac{a^4 b^0 ab^{0-2}}{a^2 b^{-2} a^2 b^{-6}} = \dfrac{a^5 b^{-2}}{a^4 b^{-8}}$

$= \boldsymbol{ab^6}$

13. $\dfrac{(xm^{-1})^{-3} \, x^2 m^2}{(x^0 y^2)^{-2} \, xy} = \dfrac{x^{-3} m^3 x^2 m^2}{x^0 y^{-4} xy} = \dfrac{x^{-1} m^5}{xy^{-3}}$

$= \dfrac{\boldsymbol{m^5 y^3}}{\boldsymbol{x^2}}$

14. $\dfrac{(c^2 d)^{-3} \, c^{-5}}{(c^2 d^0)^{-2} \, d^3} = \dfrac{c^{-6} d^{-3} c^{-5}}{c^{-4} d^0 d^3} = \dfrac{c^{-11} d^{-3}}{c^{-4} d^3}$

$= \dfrac{\boldsymbol{1}}{\boldsymbol{c^7 d^6}}$

15. $\dfrac{(m^2 n^{-5})^{-2} \, m(n^0)^2}{(m^2 n^{-2})^{-3} \, m^2} = \dfrac{m^{-4} n^{10} mn^0}{m^{-6} n^6 m^2}$

$= \dfrac{m^{-3} n^{10}}{m^{-4} n^6} = \boldsymbol{mn^4}$

16. $\dfrac{(x^{-2} y^5)^3 (x^2)^0 \, y}{xy^{-3} x^{-2}} = \dfrac{x^{-6} y^{15} x^0 y}{xy^{-3} x^{-2}} = \dfrac{x^{-6} y^{16}}{x^{-1} y^{-3}}$

$= \dfrac{\boldsymbol{y^{19}}}{\boldsymbol{x^5}}$

17. $\dfrac{(b^2 c^{-2})^{-3} \, c^{-3}}{(b^2 c^0 b^{-2})^4} = \dfrac{b^{-6} c^6 c^{-3}}{b^8 c^0 b^{-8}} = \dfrac{b^{-6} c^3}{1}$

$= \dfrac{\boldsymbol{c^3}}{\boldsymbol{b^6}}$

18. $\dfrac{(abc)^{-3} \, c^2 b}{a^{-4} bc^2 a} = \dfrac{a^{-3} b^{-3} c^{-3} c^2 b}{a^{-4} bc^2 a} = \dfrac{a^{-3} b^{-2} c^{-1}}{a^{-3} bc^2}$

$= \boldsymbol{b^{-3} c^{-3}}$

19. $\dfrac{kL^2 k^{-2}}{(k^0 L)^2 \, L^{-3} k} = \dfrac{kL^2 k^{-2}}{k^0 L^2 L^{-3} k} = \dfrac{k^{-1} L^2}{kL^{-1}} = \dfrac{\boldsymbol{k^{-2}}}{\boldsymbol{L^{-3}}}$

20. $\dfrac{s^2 ym^{-3}}{(s^0 t^2)^{-3} \, m^{-3} st} = \dfrac{s^2 ym^{-3}}{s^0 t^{-6} m^{-3} st} = \dfrac{s^2 ym^{-3}}{sm^{-3} t^{-5}}$

$= \dfrac{\boldsymbol{1}}{\boldsymbol{s^{-1} t^{-5} y^{-1}}}$

21. $\dfrac{(x^{-3} yz^{-3})^2 \, xy^0}{(xy^0 z^{-2})^{-3} \, xy} = \dfrac{x^{-6} y^2 z^{-6} xy^0}{x^{-3} y^0 z^6 xy} = \dfrac{x^{-5} y^2 z^{-6}}{x^{-2} yz^6}$

$= \dfrac{\boldsymbol{x^{-3} z^{-12}}}{\boldsymbol{y^{-1}}}$

22. $\dfrac{x^{-3} y^2 xy^4}{(x^{-2} y)^3 \, y^{-3} x} = \dfrac{x^{-3} y^2 xy^4}{x^{-6} y^3 y^{-3} x} = \dfrac{x^{-2} y^6}{x^{-5}}$

$= \dfrac{\boldsymbol{1}}{\boldsymbol{x^{-3} y^{-6}}}$

23. $-3^{-2} = -\dfrac{1}{3^2} = \boldsymbol{-\dfrac{1}{9}}$

24. $\dfrac{1}{-2^{-3}} = -2^3 = \boldsymbol{-8}$

25. $-3^2 - [-2^0 - (3 - 2) - 2]$

$= -9 - [-1 - 1 - 2]$

$= -9 - [-4] = -9 + 4 = \boldsymbol{-5}$

26. $-2\{[-3 - 2(-2)][-2 - 3(-2)]\}$

$= -2\{[-3 + 4][-2 + 6]\} = -2\{[1][4]\} = \boldsymbol{-8}$

27. $2\{-3^0[(-5 - 2)(-3) - 2]\}$

$= 2\{-1[(-7)(-3) - 2]\} = 2\{-1[21 - 2]\}$

$= 2\{-1[19]\} = 2\{-19\} = \boldsymbol{-38}$

28. $-3[4^0 - 7(2 - 3) - 2^2] = -3[1 - 7(-1) - 4]$

$= -3[1 + 7 - 4] = -3[4] = \boldsymbol{-12}$

29. $-|2 - 3| - (-5) - 3^3 = -|-5| + 5 - 27$

$= -5 + 5 - 27 = \boldsymbol{-27}$

30. $-|-3^2 - 2| - 2^0 - (-3) = -|-9 - 2| - 1 + 3$

$= -|-11| - 1 + 3 = -11 - 1 + 3 = \boldsymbol{-9}$

PRACTICE SET 3

a. $ab^2 - b = (2)(-3)^2 - (-3) = 2(9) + 3 = \boldsymbol{21}$

b. $xy - (-xy + y) = (2)(-3) - [-(2)(-3) + (-3)]$

$= -6 - [6 - 3] = \boldsymbol{-9}$

c. $\dfrac{2a^{-3} x}{m} - \dfrac{5x}{a^3 m} + \dfrac{a^3}{m^{-1} x}$

$= \dfrac{2x}{a^3 m} - \dfrac{5x}{a^3 m} + \dfrac{a^3 m}{x} = \dfrac{a^3 m}{x} - \dfrac{3x}{a^3 m}$

PROBLEM SET 3

1. $4 \times \overrightarrow{SF} = 6$

$$\overrightarrow{SF} = \frac{6}{4} = \frac{3}{2}$$

$$5 \times \overrightarrow{SF} = x$$

$$5 \times \frac{3}{2} = x$$

$$x = \frac{15}{2}$$

Since lines are parallel,

$9z = 81$

$z = 9$

$3y + 9z = 180$

$3y + 81 = 180$

$3y = 99$

$y = 33$

2. $V_{\text{Cone}} = \frac{1}{3}(A_{\text{Base}} \times \text{height})$

$$48\pi \, \text{m}^3 = \frac{1}{3}[\pi r^2 \times 9 \, \text{m}]$$

$$144\pi \, \text{m}^3 = \pi r^2 \times 9 \, \text{m}$$

$$r = \sqrt{\frac{144\pi \, \text{m}^3}{9\pi \, \text{m}}} = 4 \, \text{m}$$

Circumference $= 2\pi r = 2\pi(4 \, \text{m}) \approx \mathbf{25.12 \, m}$

3. Since angles opposite equal sides are equal angles,
$A = \mathbf{40}.$

$B + 40 + 40 = 180$

$B = 180 - 40 - 40 = \mathbf{100}$

4. $V_{\text{Cone}} = \frac{1}{3}(A_{\text{Base}} \times \text{height})$

$$= \frac{1}{3}\left[\frac{60}{360}(\pi(5)^2) + \frac{1}{2}(5)(8)\right] \text{cm}^2 \times 10 \, \text{cm}$$

$$= \frac{1}{3}\left[\frac{60}{360}(25\pi) + 20\right](10) \, \text{cm}^3 \approx \mathbf{110.28 \, cm^3}$$

5. Perimeter $= 2r_8 + 2r_8 + 2r_6 + 2r_5$

$$= 2(8\text{cm}) + 2(8\text{cm}) + 2(6\text{cm}) + 2(5 \, \text{cm})$$

$$= 16\text{cm} + 16\text{cm} + 12\text{cm} + 10\text{cm}$$

$$= \mathbf{54 \, cm}$$

6. $x - |x|y^2 - xy = -2 - |-2|(-3)^2 - (-2)(-3)$

$= -2 - 2(9) - 6 = -2 - 18 - 6 = \mathbf{-26}$

7. $(a - b) - a(-b) = (-5 - 3) - (-5)(-3)$

$= -8 - 15 = \mathbf{-23}$

8. $-a(a - ax)(x - a)$

$= -(-2)[-2 - (-2)(4)][4 - (-2)]$

$= 2(-2 + 8)(4 + 2) = 2(6)(6) = \mathbf{72}$

9. $a^2 - y^3(a - y^2)y$

$= (-2)^2 - (-3)^3[-2 - (-3)^2](-3)$

$= 4 + 27(-2 - 9)(-3) = 4 + 27(-11)(-3)$

$= 4 + 891 = \mathbf{895}$

10. $-p^2 - p(a - p^2) = -(-3)^2 - (-3)[4 - (-3)^2]$

$= -9 + 3(4 - 9) = -9 + 3(-5) = -9 - 15$

$= \mathbf{-24}$

11. $a^2 - y^3(a - y^2)y^2 = (-2)^2 - 3^3(-2 - 3^2)3^2$

$= 4 - 27(-2 - 9)9 = 4 - 27(-11)9 = \mathbf{2677}$

12. $a^2 - a(x - ax) = 1^2 - 1[2 - 1(2)]$

$= 1 - 1(2 - 2) = 1 - 1(0) = 1 - 0 = \mathbf{1}$

13. $\dfrac{p^2 x^4}{m^5} - \dfrac{2p^4 m^5}{x^{-4}} - \dfrac{3p^2 x^2}{x^{-2}m^5} + \dfrac{7p^2 m^{-5}m^{10}x^4}{p^{-2}}$

$$= \frac{p^2 x^4}{m^5} - 2p^4 x^4 m^5 - \frac{3p^2 x^4}{m^5} + 7p^4 x^4 m^5$$

$$= 5p^4 x^4 m^5 - \frac{2p^2 x^4}{m^5}$$

14. $-\dfrac{m^4 x^5}{k^5} + \dfrac{2m^2 x^5}{k^5 m^{-2}} - \dfrac{3m^3 x^2 k}{m^{-4}x^3 k^4}$

$$= -\frac{m^4 x^5}{k^5} + \frac{2m^4 x^5}{k^5} - \frac{3m^7}{xk^3}$$

$$= \frac{m^4 x^5}{k^5} - \frac{3m^7}{xk^3}$$

15. $-2x^5 y^4 + \dfrac{3xy^3}{x^{-4}y^{-1}} + \dfrac{4x^3 y^2}{x^2 y}$

$= -2x^5 y^4 + 3x^5 y^4 + 4xy = \mathbf{x^5 y^4 + 4xy}$

16. $2xy^2 m - \dfrac{3x^2 y^2 m^4}{m^3 x} + \dfrac{2x^2 ym^3}{mx^2}$

$= 2xy^2 m - 3xy^2 m + 2ym^2 = \mathbf{2ym^2 - xy^2 m}$

17. $\dfrac{(x^0 y^2)^{-3} y^{-2} p^0}{(x^2)^{-4}(y^2)^0 (p^3)^{-2}} = \dfrac{x^0 y^{-6} y^{-2} p^0}{x^{-8} y^0 p^{-6}}$

$$= \frac{x^0 y^{-8} p^0}{x^{-8} y^0 p^{-6}} = \mathbf{x^8 y^{-8} p^6}$$

18. $\dfrac{(mxy^2p)^2\,p^{-2}x^2}{(p^0xmy^3)^{-2}\,xp^{-2}} = \dfrac{m^2x^2y^4p^2p^{-2}x^2}{p^0x^{-2}m^{-2}y^{-6}xp^{-2}}$

$\quad = \dfrac{m^2x^4y^4}{m^{-2}x^{-1}y^{-6}p^{-2}} = \mathbf{m^4x^5y^{10}p^2}$

19. $\dfrac{xx^2(x^{-2})^{-2}(mpx^2)^{-4}}{(x^0)^2(x^2)^0(x^2mp^{-2})^3} = \dfrac{xx^2x^4m^{-4}p^{-4}x^{-8}}{x^0x^0x^6m^3p^{-6}}$

$\quad = \dfrac{x^{-1}m^{-4}p^{-4}}{x^6m^3p^{-6}} = \mathbf{x^{-7}m^{-7}p^2}$

20. $\dfrac{p^2x^{-4}k^5(p^2k)^{-2}}{(p^2x^{-3})^{-2}} = \dfrac{p^2x^{-4}k^5p^{-4}k^{-2}}{p^{-4}x^6}$

$\quad = \dfrac{p^{-2}x^{-4}k^3}{p^{-4}x^6} = \mathbf{p^2x^{-10}k^3}$

21. $\dfrac{x^2xx^0(x^{-2})^2}{xx^3x^{-14}(x^{-2})^{-3}} = \dfrac{x^2xx^0x^{-4}}{xx^3x^{-14}x^6}$

$\quad = \dfrac{x^{-1}}{x^{-4}} = \mathbf{x^3}$

22. $\dfrac{(x^2y^{-2}p^0)^{-3}p^2}{x^2(x^{-4})^0(p^{-2}y^5)^{-2}} = \dfrac{x^{-6}y^6p^0p^2}{x^2x^0p^4y^{-10}}$

$\quad = \dfrac{x^{-6}y^6p^2}{x^2p^4y^{-10}} = \mathbf{x^{-8}y^{16}p^{-2}}$

23. $\dfrac{(x^{-2}y^2)^5(x^0y^{-2})^{-4}}{(x^{-4}yy^2)^2(p^{-4})^0} = \dfrac{x^{-10}y^{10}x^0y^8}{x^{-8}y^2y^4p^0}$

$\quad = \dfrac{x^{-10}y^{18}}{x^{-8}y^6} = \mathbf{x^{-2}y^{12}}$

24. $-3^{-2} + \dfrac{1}{2^{-3}} = -\dfrac{1}{3^2} + 2^3 = -\dfrac{1}{9} + 8 = \mathbf{7\dfrac{8}{9}}$

25. $-(-2)^3 - \dfrac{1}{(-3)^{-2}} = -(-8) - (-3)^2$

$\quad = 8 - 9 = \mathbf{-1}$

26. $-3[-2 - 2 - (-3)](-2 - 3)$

$\quad = -3[-2 - 2 + 3](-5) = -3[-1](-5) = \mathbf{-15}$

27. $-2(-3 + 7^0) - |(-2 - 3)| = -2(-3 + 1) - |-5|$

$\quad = -2(-2) - 5 = 4 - 5 = \mathbf{-1}$

28. $|-2| - 3^2 - (-3)^3 - 2 = 2 - 9 - (-27) - 2$

$\quad = 2 - 9 + 27 - 2 = \mathbf{18}$

29. $-2\big\{[(-3 - 2)(-2)](-2 - 3)\big\}$

$\quad = -2\big\{[-5(-2)](-5)\big\} = -2\big\{[10](-5)\big\} = \mathbf{100}$

30. $-[(-3)(-2) - (-3)(-2 + 4)] = -[6 + 3(2)]$

$\quad = -[6 + 6] = -[12] = \mathbf{-12}$

PRACTICE SET 4

a. $\dfrac{2a^{-4}b^0}{c}\left(\dfrac{2ab^2c}{x^2} - \dfrac{a^{-2}}{b^{-4}}\right)$

$\quad = \dfrac{4a^{-4}b^0ab^2c}{cx^2} - \dfrac{2a^{-4}b^0a^{-2}}{cb^{-4}}$

$\quad = \dfrac{4b^2}{a^3x^2} - \dfrac{2b^4}{a^6c}$

b. $2\left(\dfrac{1}{8} - \dfrac{3}{2}x\right) = -\left(-\dfrac{1}{4}x + 2\right)$

$\quad \dfrac{1}{4} - 3x = \dfrac{1}{4}x - 2$

$\quad 2 + \dfrac{1}{4} = 3x + \dfrac{1}{4}x$

$\quad \dfrac{9}{4} = \dfrac{13}{4}x$

$\quad \dfrac{9}{4}\cdot\dfrac{4}{13} = x$

$\quad \dfrac{9}{13} = x$

PROBLEM SET 4

1. $A_{\text{Circle}} = \pi r^2$

Radius $= r$ cm: Area $= \pi(r\text{ cm})^2 = \pi r^2\ \text{cm}^2$

Radius $= 2r$ cm: Area $= \pi(2r\text{ cm})^2 = 4\pi r^2\ \text{cm}^2$

2. Since lines are parallel, $2x = 78$

$\qquad\qquad\qquad\qquad x = \mathbf{39}$

$6z + 2x = 180$

$6z + 78 = 180$

$\quad 6z = 102$

$\quad\ z = \mathbf{17}$

$2 \times \overrightarrow{SF} = 3$

$\quad \overrightarrow{SF} = \dfrac{3}{2}$

$y = \dfrac{7}{2} \times \overrightarrow{SF}$

$y = \dfrac{7}{2} \times \dfrac{3}{2} = \mathbf{\dfrac{21}{4}}$

3. $x + y + 100 = 180$

$\qquad x + y = 80$

Since angles opposite equal sides are equal angles,

$x = y = \mathbf{40.}$

$\quad x + P = 180$

$40 + P = 180$

$\qquad P = \mathbf{140}$

$\quad Q + R + P = 180$

$Q + R + 140 = 180$

$\qquad Q + R = 40$

Since angles opposite equal sides are equal angles,

$Q = R = \mathbf{20.}$

4. $A_{\text{Square}} = s^2 = (6 \text{ cm})^2 = \mathbf{36 \text{ cm}^2}$

Radius of circle $= \dfrac{s}{6} = \dfrac{6 \text{ cm}}{6} = \mathbf{1 \text{ cm}}$

$A_{\text{Shaded}} = A_{\text{Square}} - A_{\text{All circles}}$

$\qquad = 36 \text{ cm}^2 - 9\pi(1)^2 \text{ cm}^2$

$\qquad = (36 - 9\pi) \text{ cm}^2 \approx \mathbf{7.74 \text{ cm}^2}$

5. $\quad A_{\text{Circle}} = A_{\text{Triangle}}$

$\qquad \pi r^2 = \dfrac{1}{2}bH$

$\pi(1)^2 \text{ cm}^2 = \dfrac{1}{2}(3 \text{ cm})(H)$

$\qquad H = \dfrac{2\pi}{3} \text{ cm} \approx \mathbf{2.09 \text{ cm}}$

6. $15(4 - 5b) = 16(4 - 6b) + 10$

$\quad 60 - 75b = 64 - 96b + 10$

$96b - 75b = 64 + 10 - 60$

$\qquad 21b = 14$

$\qquad b = \dfrac{14}{21} = \dfrac{\mathbf{2}}{\mathbf{3}}$

7. $3\dfrac{1}{3}x - \dfrac{5}{6} = -\dfrac{2}{3}$

$\qquad \dfrac{10}{3}x = -\dfrac{2}{3} + \dfrac{5}{6}$

$\qquad \dfrac{10}{3}x = \dfrac{-4}{6} + \dfrac{5}{6}$

$\qquad \dfrac{10}{3}x = \dfrac{1}{6}$

$\qquad x = \dfrac{1}{6} \cdot \dfrac{3}{10} = \dfrac{3}{60} = \dfrac{\mathbf{1}}{\mathbf{20}}$

8. $3(-2x - 3) - 2^2 = -(-3x - 5) - 2$

$\quad -6x - 9 - 4 = 3x + 5 - 2$

$\quad -6x - 13 = 3x + 3$

$\quad -13 - 3 = 3x + 6x$

$\qquad -16 = 9x$

$\qquad x = -\dfrac{\mathbf{16}}{\mathbf{9}}$

9. $-2(2x - 3) - 2^3 - 3 = -x - (-4)$

$\quad -4x + 6 - 8 - 3 = -x + 4$

$\qquad -4x - 5 = -x + 4$

$\qquad -4 - 5 = -x + 4x$

$\qquad -9 = 3x$

$\qquad x = \dfrac{-9}{3} = \mathbf{-3}$

10. $4\dfrac{1}{3}x - \dfrac{1}{2} = 3\dfrac{2}{5}$

$\qquad \dfrac{13}{3}x = \dfrac{17}{5} + \dfrac{1}{2}$

$\qquad \dfrac{13}{3}x = \dfrac{34}{10} + \dfrac{5}{10}$

$\qquad \dfrac{13}{3}x = \dfrac{39}{10}$

$\qquad x = \dfrac{39}{10} \cdot \dfrac{3}{13} = \dfrac{117}{130} = \dfrac{\mathbf{9}}{\mathbf{10}}$

11. $-\dfrac{3}{5}x + \dfrac{2}{7} = 4\dfrac{3}{8}$

$\qquad -\dfrac{3}{5}x = \dfrac{35}{8} - \dfrac{2}{7}$

$\qquad -\dfrac{3}{5}x = \dfrac{245}{56} - \dfrac{16}{56}$

$\qquad -\dfrac{3}{5}x = \dfrac{229}{56}$

$\qquad x = \dfrac{229}{56} \cdot -\dfrac{5}{3} = -\dfrac{\mathbf{1145}}{\mathbf{168}}$

12. $\dfrac{xy^2}{x^0 x^{-3}}\left[\dfrac{xy^{-2}}{x(y^2)^0} - \dfrac{3y^{-2}}{x^4}\right]$

$= \dfrac{xy^2 xy^{-2}}{x^0 x^{-3} x(y^2)^0} - \dfrac{3xy^2 y^{-2}}{x^0 x^{-3} x^4}$

$= \dfrac{x^2}{x^{-2}} - \dfrac{3x}{x} = \mathbf{x^4 - 3}$

13. $\dfrac{ay^{-4}}{p}\left(\dfrac{p^{-2}}{ay^2} - \dfrac{3a^{-1}y}{p^{-2}}\right)$

$= \dfrac{ay^{-4}p^{-2}}{pay^2} - \dfrac{3ay^{-4}a^{-1}y}{pp^{-2}} = \boldsymbol{y^{-6}p^{-3} - 3y^{-3}p}$

14. $\dfrac{(3x^2)^{-2}y^0y^5}{(9y)^{-2}yy^2x^{-3}} = \dfrac{81x^{-4}y^0y^5}{9y^{-2}yy^2x^{-3}} = \dfrac{81x^{-4}y^5}{9yx^{-3}}$

$= \boldsymbol{9x^{-1}y^4}$

15. $\dfrac{(2yx^{-2})^{-2}yx^2}{(x^2)^0y^{-3}x^2} = \dfrac{y^{-2}x^4yx^2}{4x^0y^{-3}x^2} = \dfrac{y^{-1}x^6}{4y^{-3}x^2}$

$= \boldsymbol{\dfrac{x^4y^2}{4}}$

16. $\dfrac{2(x^{-2})^{-2}yx^2y^{-3}}{x^0xx^2x^{-5}(x^2)^3} = \dfrac{2x^4yx^2y^{-3}}{x^0xx^2x^{-5}x^6} = \dfrac{2x^6y^{-2}}{x^4}$

$= \boldsymbol{2x^2y^{-2}}$

17. $\dfrac{(x^2y2x)^{-2}y}{(x^{-4})^0xxy^2} = \dfrac{x^{-4}y^{-2}x^{-2}y}{4x^0xxy^2} = \dfrac{x^{-6}y^{-1}}{4x^2y^2}$

$= \boldsymbol{\dfrac{x^{-8}y^{-3}}{4}}$

18. $\dfrac{3x^2xy^2x^{-4}}{(x^2y)^{-2}(-2)^{-2}} = \dfrac{12x^2xy^2x^{-4}}{x^{-4}y^{-2}} = \dfrac{12x^{-1}y^2}{x^{-4}y^{-2}}$

$= \boldsymbol{12x^3y^4}$

19. $\dfrac{2x^2xyx}{x^2y^{-1}} - \dfrac{3x^2y^4}{yy} + \dfrac{7xx^{-3}y^{-2}}{x^{-4}y^{-4}}$

$= 2x^2y^2 - 3x^2y^2 + 7x^2y^2 = \boldsymbol{6x^2y^2}$

20. $\dfrac{3x}{y} - 7x^2x^{-1}y^{-1} + 2y^2y^{-1}x^{-1}$

$= \dfrac{3x}{y} - \dfrac{7x}{y} + \dfrac{2y}{x} = \boldsymbol{\dfrac{2y}{x} - \dfrac{4x}{y}}$

21. $\dfrac{2ay^2}{x} + \dfrac{5a^2x^{-1}}{ay^{-2}} + \dfrac{2xy^2}{ay}$

$= \dfrac{2ay^2}{x} + \dfrac{5ay^2}{x} + \dfrac{2xy}{a} = \boldsymbol{\dfrac{7ay^2}{x} + \dfrac{2xy}{a}}$

22. $a^2(a - ab) = (-2)^2[-2 - (-2)(3)] = 4(-2 + 6)$

$= 4(4) = \boldsymbol{16}$

23. $x^0yx(xy - x^2) = (-3)^0(-1)(-3)[-3(-1) - (-3)^2]$

$= 3(3 - 9) = 3(-6) = \boldsymbol{-18}$

24. $a^{-2}b(a - b)(b - a)$

$= (-1)^{-2}(-2)[-1 - (-2)][-2 - (-1)]$

$= -2(-1 + 2)(-2 + 1) = -2(1)(-1) = \boldsymbol{2}$

25. $ab(a^2 - b)a - b$

$= (-3)(-1)[(-3)^2 - (-1)](-3) - (-1)$

$= 3(9 + 1)(-3) + 1 = 3(10)(-3) + 1 = \boldsymbol{-89}$

26. $-3^0 - 2^0 - 2^0(-2 - 3^2) - (-2 + 7) - |-2 - 3|$

$= -1 - 1 - 1(-11) - 5 - |-5|$

$= -1 - 1 + 11 - 5 - 5 = \boldsymbol{-1}$

27. $-2\{2[(-3 - 2^2) - (-3 + 7)] - 2\}$

$= -2\{2[(-7) - 4] - 2\} = -2\{2[-11] - 2\}$

$= -2\{-22 - 2\} = -2\{-24\} = \boldsymbol{48}$

28. $-3^0 - (-2 - 3 - 2^0)(-3) - (-2 - 4) + (-6)$

$= -1 - (-6)(-3) - (-6) - 6$

$= -1 - 18 + 6 - 6 = \boldsymbol{-19}$

29. $-2^{-2}(-16) = -\dfrac{1}{2^2}(-16) = -\dfrac{1}{4}(-16) = \dfrac{16}{4} = \boldsymbol{4}$

30. $-(-2^{-3}) - \dfrac{1}{(-2)^{-2}} = -\left(\dfrac{1}{-2^3}\right) - (-2)^2$

$= -\left(-\dfrac{1}{8}\right) - 4 = \dfrac{1}{8} - 4 = \boldsymbol{-3\dfrac{7}{8}}$

PRACTICE SET 5

a. $3(-4 + 5N) = 7N - 212$

$-12 + 15N = 7N - 212$

$8N = -200$

$N = \boldsymbol{-25}$

b. If $\dfrac{3}{8}$ were Victorian, $\dfrac{5}{8}$ were not.

$\dfrac{5}{8} \times 1624 = NV$

$5 \times 203 = NV$

$\boldsymbol{1015 \text{ pieces} = NV}$

PROBLEM SET 5

1. $(2N - 9)4 = 10N - 8$

$8N - 36 = 10N - 8$

$-36 + 8 = 10N - 8N$

$-28 = 2N$

$N = -14$

2. $3N_D + 11 = 4N_D - 13$

$11 + 13 = 4N_D - 3N_D$

24 ducks $= N_D$

3. $(5N - 8)4 = 6N - 116$

$20N - 32 = 6N - 116$

$20N - 6N = -116 + 32$

$14N = -84$

$N = -6$

4. $F \times of = is$

$\dfrac{1}{8} \times C = 12$

$C = 12 \cdot \dfrac{8}{1} = $ **96 clowns**

5. $F \times of = is$

$\dfrac{2}{7} \times 140{,}000 = N_R$

40,000 horde members $= N_R$

6. $A_{PQR} = \dfrac{1}{2}bH$

$27 \text{ in.}^2 = \dfrac{1}{2}(6 \text{ in.})(H)$

9 in. $= H$

$AQ = PQ - PA = 9 \text{ in.} - 6 \text{ in.} = $ **3 in.**

$A_{QAB} = \dfrac{1}{2}bH = \dfrac{1}{2}(2)(3) \text{ in.}^2 = $ **3 in.^{2}**

7. Since angles opposite equal sides are equal angles,

$y = $ **52.**

$x + y + 52 = 180$

$x + 52 + 52 = 180$

$x = 180 - 52 - 52 = $ **76**

8. $K + 110 = 180$

$K = 180 - 110 = $ **70**

Since lines are parallel, $Q = $ **70,** $P = $ **110,** and $D = x = $ **70.**

Since C is a straight angle, $C = $ **180.**

9. Circumference $= 2\pi r$

$16\pi \text{ in.} = 2\pi r$

8 in. $= r$

$A_{\text{Circle}} = \pi r^2 = \pi(8 \text{ in.})^2$

$= 64\pi \text{ in.}^2 \approx $ **200.96 in.^{2}**

$V_{\text{Cylinder}} = A_{\text{Base}} \times \text{height}$

$= (64\pi) \text{ in.}^2 \times 5 \text{ in.}$

$= 320\pi \text{ in.}^3 \approx $ **1004.8 in.^{3}**

10. $-3x^0(2x - 3) - (-2^0) - 2 = 5(x - 3^0)2$

$-6x + 9 + 1 - 2 = 10x - 10$

$-6x + 8 = 10x - 10$

$10 + 8 = 10x + 6x$

$18 = 16x$

$x = \dfrac{18}{16} = \dfrac{9}{8}$

11. $-2^2(-2 - x) - x^0(3 - 2) = -2(x + 3)$

$8 + 4x - 3 + 2 = -2x - 6$

$4x + 7 = -2x - 6$

$2x + 4x = -6 - 7$

$6x = -13$

$x = -\dfrac{13}{6}$

12. $3\dfrac{1}{2}x + 2\dfrac{1}{4} = -\dfrac{1}{8}$

$\dfrac{7}{2}x = -\dfrac{1}{8} - \dfrac{9}{4}$

$\dfrac{7}{2}x = -\dfrac{1}{8} - \dfrac{18}{8}$

$\dfrac{7}{2}x = \dfrac{-19}{8}$

$x = \dfrac{-19}{8} \cdot \dfrac{2}{7} = -\dfrac{38}{56} = -\dfrac{19}{28}$

13. $\dfrac{1}{2}(6 - 8x) + \dfrac{3}{4}(8x - 12) = 4x + 6$

$3 - 4x + 6x - 9 = 4x + 6$

$2x - 6 = 4x + 6$

$-6 - 6 = 4x - 2x$

$-12 = 2x$

$x = \boldsymbol{-6}$

14. $-3 - 3^0 - 3^2(2x - 5) - (-2x - 3)$

$= -x^0(x - 3)$

$-3 - 1 - 18x + 45 + 2x + 3 = -x + 3$

$-16x + 44 = -x + 3$

$-16x + x = 3 - 44$

$-15x = -41$

$x = \boldsymbol{\dfrac{41}{15}}$

15. $-2^3 - \dfrac{1}{-2^{-2}}(x + 2) - 3x = -2^0(-2x^0 - 4)$

$-8 + 4x + 8 - 3x = 2 + 4$

$x = \boldsymbol{6}$

16. $-3[x - 2 - 3(2)] + 2[x - 3(x - 2)]$

$= 7(x - 5)$

$-3x + 6 + 18 + 2x - 6x + 12 = 7x - 35$

$-7x + 36 = 7x - 35$

$-7x - 7x = -35 - 36$

$-14x = -71$

$x = \boldsymbol{\dfrac{71}{14}}$

17. $\dfrac{2ab}{c^2}\left(\dfrac{c^2a^{-1}}{b} - \dfrac{3ac}{b}\right) = \dfrac{2abc^2a^{-1}}{c^2b} - \dfrac{6abac}{c^2b}$

$= \dfrac{2bc^2}{c^2b} - \dfrac{6a^2bc}{c^2b} = \boldsymbol{2 - \dfrac{6a^2}{c}}$

18. $-\dfrac{ax^2}{b}\left(\dfrac{bax^3}{a^2} - 3ax\right) = -\dfrac{ax^2bax^3}{ba^2} + \dfrac{3ax^2ax}{b}$

$= -\dfrac{a^2bx^5}{ba^2} + \dfrac{3a^2x^3}{b} = \boldsymbol{-x^5 + \dfrac{3a^2x^3}{b}}$

19. $\dfrac{(xm^{-2})^0 x^0 m^0}{xx^2 m^0 (2x)^{-2}} = \dfrac{4\,x^0 m^0\,x^0 m^0}{xx^2 m^0 x^{-2}} = \boldsymbol{\dfrac{4}{x}}$

20. $\dfrac{4c^2dc^{-3}(2cd^{-2})^{-2}}{c^0c^{-3}(c^{-2}d)^2} = \dfrac{4c^2dc^{-3}2^{-2}c^{-2}d^4}{c^0c^{-3}c^{-4}d^2}$

$= \dfrac{c^{-3}d^5}{c^{-7}d^2} = \boldsymbol{c^4d^3}$

21. $\dfrac{p^2m^5(p^{-3})(2p)^{-3}}{m^6(m^{-2})^2mp^3} = \dfrac{p^2m^5p^{-3}2^{-3}p^{-3}}{m^6m^{-4}mp^3}$

$= \dfrac{m^5p^{-4}}{8m^3p^3} = \boldsymbol{\dfrac{m^2}{8p^7}}$

22. $\dfrac{x^2xy}{y^{-2}} - \dfrac{3x^5}{xxy^{-3}} + \dfrac{7x^7}{y^3x^4}$

$= x^3y^3 - 3x^3y^3 + 7x^3y^{-3} = \boldsymbol{-2x^3y^3 + 7x^3y^{-3}}$

23. $-\dfrac{3a^2x^4}{x} + \dfrac{2aax^2}{x} - \dfrac{5x^3}{a^{-2}}$

$= -3a^2x^3 + 2a^2x - 5a^2x^3 = \boldsymbol{2a^2x - 8a^2x^3}$

24. $mx - m(m - mx^2)$

$= -2(-1) - (-2)[-2 - (-2)(-1)^2]$

$= 2 + 2(-2 + 2) = 2 + 2(0) = 2 + 0 = \boldsymbol{2}$

25. $a^2 - b(a - b) = \left(-\dfrac{1}{2}\right)^2 - \dfrac{1}{4}\left(-\dfrac{1}{2} - \dfrac{1}{4}\right)$

$= \dfrac{1}{4} - \dfrac{1}{4}\left(-\dfrac{2}{4} - \dfrac{1}{4}\right) = \dfrac{1}{4} - \dfrac{1}{4}\left(-\dfrac{3}{4}\right)$

$= \dfrac{1}{4} + \dfrac{3}{16} = \dfrac{4}{16} + \dfrac{3}{16} = \boldsymbol{\dfrac{7}{16}}$

26. $a - ba(a^2 - b)$

$= -\dfrac{1}{2} - \left(-\dfrac{1}{4}\right)\left(-\dfrac{1}{2}\right)\left[\left(-\dfrac{1}{2}\right)^2 - \left(-\dfrac{1}{4}\right)\right]$

$= -\dfrac{1}{2} - \dfrac{1}{8}\left(\dfrac{1}{4} + \dfrac{1}{4}\right) = -\dfrac{1}{2} - \dfrac{1}{8}\left(\dfrac{2}{4}\right)$

$= -\dfrac{1}{2} - \dfrac{2}{32} = -\dfrac{8}{16} - \dfrac{1}{16} = \boldsymbol{-\dfrac{9}{16}}$

27. $-2(-2 - 3^2) - 2[-2(-3)] = -2(-2 - 9) - 2[6]$

$= -2(-11) - 2[6] = 22 - 12 = \boldsymbol{10}$

28. $-3^2 - (-3)^3 - \dfrac{1}{-2^2} = -9 + 27 + \dfrac{1}{4} = \boldsymbol{18\dfrac{1}{4}}$

29. $-3^0[-2^0 - 2^2 - 2^3(-2 - 3)]$

$= -1[-1 - 4 - 8(-5)] = -1[-1 - 4 + 40]$

$= -1[35] = \boldsymbol{-35}$

30. $-3[(-2^0 + 5) - (-3 + 7) - |-2|]$

$= -3[4 - 4 - 2] = -3[-2] = \boldsymbol{6}$

PRACTICE SET 6

a. If 0.017 were red dwarfs, then $1 - 0.017 = 0.983$ were not.

$(0.983)(29,000) = NRD$

28,507 stars $= NRD$

b. Consecutive even integers: $N, N + 2, N + 4$

$3[N + (N + 4)] = 12(N + 2) - 84$

$3[2N + 4] = 12N + 24 - 84$

$6N + 12 = 12N - 60$

$72 = 6N$

$12 = N$

The desired integers are **12, 14,** and **16.**

PROBLEM SET 6

1. $WD \times of = is$

$0.016T = 480$

$T = $ **30,000 teachers**

2. If 0.653 were prophetic, then 0.347 were not prophetic.

$WD \times of = is$

$0.347(3000) = NP$

1041 statements $= NP$

3. $-3N - 7 = -2N - 4$

$-3 = N$

4. $F \times of = is$

$2\frac{1}{2} \times BW = 175$

$BW = 175 \times \frac{2}{5} = $ **70 barge workers**

5. Odd integers: $N, N + 2, N + 4$

$6(N + N + 4) = 8(N + 2) + 28$

$12N + 24 = 8N + 44$

$4N = 20$

$N = 5$

The desired integers are **5, 7,** and **9.**

6. Integers: $N, N + 1, N + 2, N + 3$

$4(N + N + 3) = 6(N + 2) + 24$

$8N + 12 = 6N + 36$

$2N = 24$

$N = 12$

The desired integers are **12, 13, 14,** and **15.**

7. Surface area $= 4\pi r^2 = 46\pi \text{ cm}^2$

$r = \sqrt{\dfrac{46\pi \text{ cm}^2}{4\pi}}$

$r = \dfrac{\sqrt{46}}{2} \text{ cm}$

8. Since angles opposite equal sides are equal angles, $A = B = $ **34.**

$K + A = 180$

$K = 180 - 34 = $ **146**

Since angles opposite equal sides are equal angles, $M = $ **17.**

9. $3 \times \overrightarrow{SF} = \dfrac{11}{3}$

$\overrightarrow{SF} = \dfrac{11}{3} \times \dfrac{1}{3} = \dfrac{11}{9}$

$\dfrac{15}{2} \times \overrightarrow{SF} = x$

$\dfrac{15}{2} \times \dfrac{11}{9} = x$

$\dfrac{55}{6} = x$

Since lines are parallel,

$3B = 130$

$B = \dfrac{130}{3}$

$2A + 3B = 180$

$2A = 180 - 130$

$2A = 50$

$A = $ **25**

10. $A = 2(180 - A)$

$A = 360 - 2A$

$3A = 360$

$A = $ **120°**

11. $0.005x + 0.6 = 2.05$

$5x + 600 = 2050$

$5x = 1450$

$x = \mathbf{290}$

12. $3\dfrac{2}{5}x + 1\dfrac{1}{4} = 7\dfrac{1}{3}$

$\dfrac{17}{5}x = \dfrac{22}{3} - \dfrac{5}{4}$

$\dfrac{17}{5}x = \dfrac{88}{12} - \dfrac{15}{12}$

$\dfrac{17}{5}x = \dfrac{73}{12}$

$x = \dfrac{73}{12} \cdot \dfrac{5}{17} = \dfrac{\mathbf{365}}{\mathbf{204}}$

13. $-3(x - 2 + 1) - (-2)^2 - 3(x - 2)$

$= 5x^0(2 - x) - 2x$

$-3x + 6 - 3 - 4 - 3x + 6 = 10 - 5x - 2x$

$-6x + 5 = 10 - 7x$

$x = \mathbf{5}$

14. $-3 - 2^2 - 2(x - 3) = 2[(x - 5)(2 - 5)]$

$-3 - 4 - 2x + 6 = 2[-3x + 15]$

$-2x - 1 = -6x + 30$

$4x = 31$

$x = \dfrac{\mathbf{31}}{\mathbf{4}}$

15. $4(x + 3) - 2^0(-x - 3) = 2x - 4(x^0 - x) - 3^2$

$4x + 12 + x + 3 = 2x - 4 + 4x - 9$

$5x + 15 = 6x - 13$

$\mathbf{28} = x$

16. $\dfrac{xy}{p}\left(\dfrac{-3p^{-1}}{xy} + \dfrac{2p}{x^{-1}y}\right) = \dfrac{-3xyp^{-1}}{pxy} + \dfrac{2xyp}{px^{-1}y}$

$= \mathbf{-3p^{-2} + 2x^2}$

17. $-\dfrac{x^0 k}{p}\left(\dfrac{k^0 p}{x} - 2p\right) = -\dfrac{x^0 kk^0 p}{px} + \dfrac{2px^0 k}{p}$

$= -\dfrac{kp}{px} + \dfrac{2pk}{p} = \mathbf{-kx^{-1} + 2k}$

18. $\dfrac{(2x^{-2}y^0)^{-2}\, yx^{-2}}{xxxy^2(y^{-2})^2} = \dfrac{x^4 y^0 yx^{-2}}{4x^3 y^2 y^{-4}} = \dfrac{x^2 y}{4x^3 y^{-2}}$

$= \dfrac{\mathbf{y^3}}{\mathbf{4x}}$

19. $\dfrac{a^0 bc^0 (a^{-1}b^{-1})^2}{ab(ab^0)abc} = \dfrac{ba^{-2}b^{-2}}{abaabc} = \dfrac{a^{-2}b^{-1}}{a^3 b^2 c}$

$= \mathbf{a^{-5}b^{-3}c^{-1}}$

20. $\dfrac{(2x^2)^{-3}(xy^0)^{-2}}{2xx^0 x^1 xxy^2} = \dfrac{x^{-6}x^{-2}y^0}{8(2)x^4 y^2} = \dfrac{x^{-8}}{16x^4 y^2}$

$= \dfrac{\mathbf{1}}{\mathbf{16x^{12}y^2}}$

21. $-2xy + \dfrac{5x^0 xy^{-1}}{y^{-2}} - \dfrac{5xx^{-1}x^2}{(x^{-1})^{-1}}$

$= -2xy + 5xy - 5x = \mathbf{3xy - 5x}$

22. $-\dfrac{3x^2 xy^2}{y^4} + \dfrac{2xxx}{y^{-2}} - \dfrac{3xy}{x^{-2}y^{-1}}$

$= -3x^3 y^{-2} + 2x^3 y^2 - 3x^3 y^2 = \mathbf{-3x^3 y^{-2} - x^3 y^2}$

23. $xy - x^2 y - y = (-2)(-4) - (-2)^2(-4) - (-4)$

$= 8 + 16 + 4 = \mathbf{28}$

24. $a^{-2}b - a(a - b)$

$= \left(-\dfrac{1}{2}\right)^{-2}\left(\dfrac{1}{4}\right) - \left(-\dfrac{1}{2}\right)\left(-\dfrac{1}{2} - \dfrac{1}{4}\right)$

$= 1 + \left(\dfrac{1}{2}\right)\left(-\dfrac{3}{4}\right) = 1 - \dfrac{3}{8} = \dfrac{\mathbf{5}}{\mathbf{8}}$

25. $m^2 p(mp - p^2) = \left(-\dfrac{1}{4}\right)^2\left(\dfrac{1}{5}\right)\left[-\dfrac{1}{4}\left(\dfrac{1}{5}\right) - \left(\dfrac{1}{5}\right)^2\right]$

$= \dfrac{1}{80}\left(-\dfrac{1}{20} - \dfrac{1}{25}\right) = \dfrac{1}{80}\left(-\dfrac{9}{100}\right) = -\dfrac{\mathbf{9}}{\mathbf{8000}}$

26. $-3^0[-3^2 - 2(-2 - 3)][-2^0] = -1[-9 + 10][-1]$

$= -1[1][-1] = \mathbf{1}$

27. $-3 - (-3)^2 + (-3)(-6) = -3 - 9 + 18 = \mathbf{6}$

28. $-3^2 + (-3)^2 - 4^2 - |-2 - 2|$

$= -9 + 9 - 16 - 4 = \mathbf{-20}$

29. $-3^{-2} - \dfrac{2}{-2^{-3}} - 2^0 = -\dfrac{1}{9} + 16 - 1$

$= -\dfrac{1}{9} + \dfrac{135}{9} = \dfrac{134}{9} = \mathbf{14\dfrac{8}{9}}$

30. $-(-2)^{-3} - 3^{-2} - 3 = \dfrac{1}{8} - \dfrac{1}{9} - 3$

$= \dfrac{9}{72} - \dfrac{8}{72} - \dfrac{216}{72} = -\dfrac{215}{72} = \mathbf{-2\dfrac{71}{72}}$

PRACTICE SET 7

a.

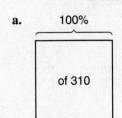

$$\frac{30}{100} \times WN = 93$$

$$\frac{100}{30} \times \frac{30}{100} WN = \frac{100}{30} \times 93$$

$$WN = \mathbf{310}$$

b.

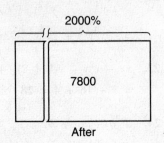

$$\frac{WP}{100} \times 390 = 7800$$

$$\frac{100}{390} \times \frac{WP}{100} \times 390 = 7800 \times \frac{100}{390}$$

$$WP = \mathbf{2000\%}$$

c. $5x - 21 = 2x + 12$

$$3x = 33$$

$$x = \mathbf{11}$$

$$B = 5x - 21$$

$$B = 5(11) - 21$$

$$B = \mathbf{34}$$

$$A = B$$

$$A = \mathbf{34}$$

PROBLEM SET 7

1. $\dfrac{P}{100} \times of = is \quad\longrightarrow\quad \dfrac{20}{100} \times WN = 26$

$$WN = 26 \cdot \frac{100}{20} = \mathbf{130}$$

Since one part of 130 is 26 for 20%, the other part must be 104 for 80%.

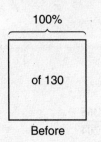

2. $\dfrac{WP}{100} \times of = is \quad\longrightarrow\quad \dfrac{WP}{100} \times 350 = 1400$

$$WP = 1400 \cdot \frac{100}{350} = \mathbf{400\%}$$

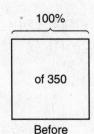
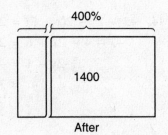

3. $\dfrac{P}{100} \times of = is \quad\longrightarrow\quad \dfrac{20}{100} \times WN = 460$

$$WN = 460 \cdot \frac{100}{20} = \mathbf{2300}$$

Since one part of 2300 is 460 for 20%, the other part must be 1840 for 80%.

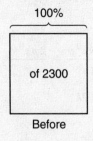
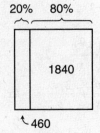

16

4. $\dfrac{WP}{100} \times of = is \longrightarrow \dfrac{WP}{100} \times 20 = 680$

$WP = 680 \cdot \dfrac{100}{20} = \mathbf{3400\%}$

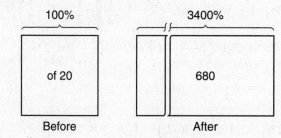

5. $\dfrac{P}{100} \times of = is \longrightarrow \dfrac{1900}{100} \times WN = 380$

$WN = 380 \cdot \dfrac{100}{1900} = \mathbf{20}$

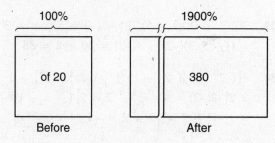

6. Odd integers: $N,\ N + 2,\ N + 4$

$7(N + N + 4) = 10(-N - 2) - 120$

$14N + 28 = -10N - 140$

$24N = -168$

$N = -7$

The desired integers are **−7, −5,** and **−3.**

7. Even integers: $N,\ N + 2,\ N + 4$

$6(N + N + 4) = 14(N + 2) - 8$

$12N + 24 = 14N + 20$

$4 = 2N$

$2 = N$

The desired integers are **2, 4,** and **6.**

8. $-2N + 5 = -N$

$5 = N$

9. $(4x + 15) + (5x + 10) + (x + 5) = 180$

$10x + 30 = 180$

$10x = 150$

$x = \mathbf{15}$

10. Since lines are parallel,

$(3x + 20) + (5x) = 180$

$8x + 20 = 180$

$8x = 160$

$x = \mathbf{20}$

11. Relabel the angles a, b, c, and d as having measures $x°$, $(3x)°$, $(6x)°$, and $(2x)°$ respectively.

$x + 3x + 6x + 2x = 180$

$12x = 180$

$x = 15$

$m\angle a = \mathbf{15°};\ m\angle b = \mathbf{45°};$

$m\angle c = \mathbf{90°};\ m\angle d = \mathbf{30°}$

12. The sum of $x°$, $y°$, $z°$, and the three $60°$ angles that touch the vertex must equal $360°$, a full circle.

$x + y + z + 60 + 60 + 60 = 360$

$x + y + z = 180$

$x° + y° + z° = \mathbf{180°}$

13. $-3p(-2 - 3) + p - 2^2 = -(2p + 4) - p^0$

$6p + 9p + p - 4 = -2p - 4 - 1$

$16p - 4 = -2p - 5$

$18p = -1$

$p = -\dfrac{1}{18}$

14. $0.005x - 0.07 = 0.02x + 0.0032$

$50x - 700 = 200x + 32$

$-732 = 150x$

$x = -\dfrac{732}{150} = -\dfrac{122}{25} = \mathbf{-4.88}$

15. $2\dfrac{1}{5} + 3\dfrac{1}{8} + 2\dfrac{1}{2}x = 4\dfrac{3}{20}$

$\dfrac{5}{2}x = \dfrac{166}{40} - \dfrac{88}{40} - \dfrac{125}{40}$

$\dfrac{5}{2}x = -\dfrac{47}{40}$

$x = -\dfrac{47}{40} \cdot \dfrac{2}{5}$

$x = -\dfrac{94}{200} = -\dfrac{47}{100}$

16. $3x - 2 - 2^0(x - 3) - 2^0 + 2^2$

$= 5(-x - 2) + 3^0$

$3x - 2 - x + 3 - 1 + 4 = -5x - 10 + 1$

$2x + 4 = -5x - 9$

$7x = -13$

$x = -\dfrac{13}{7}$

17. $\dfrac{2xyp}{y^{-2}}\left(\dfrac{x^{-1}}{y^3 p} - \dfrac{3x}{yyp^2}\right) = \dfrac{2xypx^{-1}}{y^{-2}y^3 p} - \dfrac{6xypx}{y^{-2}yyp^2}$

$= \mathbf{2 - 6x^2yp^{-1}}$

18. $\dfrac{4x^{-2}y}{k}\left(\dfrac{2kx^2}{y} - \dfrac{3xy}{k}\right)$

$= \dfrac{8x^{-2}ykx^2}{ky} - \dfrac{12x^{-2}yxy}{kk} = \mathbf{8 - 12x^{-1}y^2k^{-2}}$

19. $\dfrac{(2x^2y^3)^{-3}\,y}{(4xy)^{-2}(x^{-2}y)^3\,y} = \dfrac{16x^{-6}y^{-9}y}{8x^{-2}y^{-2}x^{-6}y^3y}$

$= \dfrac{2x^{-6}y^{-8}}{x^{-8}y^2} = \mathbf{2x^2y^{-10}}$

20. $\dfrac{xx^{-2}y(x^{-3})^2\,xy^0}{(2xy)^{-2}x^2(y^{-3})^2} = \dfrac{4xx^{-2}yx^{-6}xy^0}{x^{-2}y^{-2}x^2y^{-6}} = \dfrac{4x^{-6}y}{y^{-8}}$

$= \mathbf{4x^{-6}y^9}$

21. $-\dfrac{3x^2xy}{p} + \dfrac{7xyp^{-1}}{x^{-2}} - \dfrac{2xxp^{-1}}{y^{-1}}$

$= -\dfrac{3x^3y}{p} + \dfrac{7x^3y}{p} - \dfrac{2x^3y}{p} = \mathbf{\dfrac{2x^3y}{p}}$

22. $-4xp^2 + \dfrac{3xxp^4}{p^2x^2} - \dfrac{2xp}{p^{-1}}$

$= -4xp^2 + 3p^2 - 2xp^2$

$= \mathbf{-6xp^2 + 3p^2}$

23. $-a(a - b) = -\left(-\dfrac{1}{2}\right)\left(-\dfrac{1}{2} - \dfrac{1}{3}\right)$

$= \dfrac{1}{2}\left(-\dfrac{3}{6} - \dfrac{2}{6}\right) = \dfrac{1}{2}\left(-\dfrac{5}{6}\right) = \mathbf{-\dfrac{5}{12}}$

24. $-xy(-x^2 - y) = -\left(-\dfrac{1}{2}\right)\left(\dfrac{1}{4}\right)\left[-\left(-\dfrac{1}{2}\right)^2 - \dfrac{1}{4}\right]$

$= \dfrac{1}{8}\left(-\dfrac{1}{4} - \dfrac{1}{4}\right) = \dfrac{1}{8}\left(-\dfrac{2}{4}\right) = -\dfrac{2}{32} = \mathbf{-\dfrac{1}{16}}$

25. $x^3 - x(xy - y)$

$= (-2)^3 - (-2)[(-2)(-4) - (-4)]$

$= -8 + 2(8 + 4) = -8 + 24 = \mathbf{16}$

26. $x - a(a - xa) = 2 - \left(-\dfrac{1}{2}\right)\left[-\dfrac{1}{2} - 2\left(-\dfrac{1}{2}\right)\right]$

$= 2 + \dfrac{1}{2}\left(-\dfrac{1}{2} + 1\right) = 2 + \dfrac{1}{2}\left(\dfrac{1}{2}\right) = 2 + \dfrac{1}{4}$

$= \mathbf{2\dfrac{1}{4}}$

27. $-2\left\{[-2^0 - 3(-2)] - [-2(-3 - 2)(-2)]\right\}$

$= -2\left\{[-1 + 6] - [-2(-5)(-2)]\right\}$

$= -2\{[5] - [-20]\} = -2\{25\} = \mathbf{-50}$

28. $-2^0 - 2 - 2^2 - (-2)^3 - 2(-2 - 2) - 2$

$= -1 - 2 - 4 + 8 + 4 + 4 - 2 = \mathbf{7}$

29. $3^0(-2 - 3)(-2 + 5)(-2) - (-3 + 7)(-4^0 - 3^0)$

$= (1)(-5)(3)(-2) - 4(-2) = 30 + 8 = \mathbf{38}$

30. $2[(-2^0 - 1)(-2^0 - 15^0) - (-2)^2 - 3^0] - 2$

$= 2[-2(-2) - 4 - 1] - 2 = 2[4 - 4 - 1] - 2$

$= 2[-1] - 2 = -2 - 2 = \mathbf{-4}$

PRACTICE SET 8

$3x + 4y = 12$

$4y = -3x + 12$

$y = -\dfrac{3}{4}x + 3$

The y-intercept is at $(0, 3)$; the slope is $-\frac{3}{4}$.

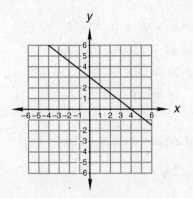

Algebra 2, **Third Edition**

PROBLEM SET 8

1. $WD \times of = is$

$0.36 \times K = 828$

$K = \dfrac{828}{0.36} = \textbf{2300 knights}$

2. Even integers: $N,\ N + 2,\ N + 4,\ N + 6$

$10(N + N + 6) = 9(N + 2 + N + 6) + 24$

$20N + 60 = 18N + 96$

$2N = 36$

$N = 18$

The desired integers are **18, 20, 22,** and **24.**

3. $3N - 7 = -2N - 72$

$5N = -65$

$N = \textbf{-13}$

4. $F \times of = is$

$\dfrac{7}{16} \times WN = 420$

$WN = 420 \times \dfrac{16}{7} = \textbf{960 warriors}$

5. Odd integers: $N,\ N + 2,\ N + 4$

$5(N + N + 4) = 2(-N - 2) + 108$

$10N + 20 = -2N + 104$

$12N = 84$

$N = 7$

The desired integers are **7, 9,** and **11.**

6. $\dfrac{P}{100} \times of = is \quad \longrightarrow \quad \dfrac{20}{100} \times WN = 86$

$WN = 86 \cdot \dfrac{100}{20} = \textbf{430}$

Since one part of 430 is 86 for 20%, the other part must be 344 for 80%.

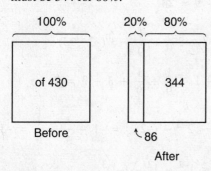

7. $\dfrac{P}{100} \times of = is \quad \longrightarrow \quad \dfrac{340}{100} \times 56 = WN$

$WN = \dfrac{340}{100} \cdot 56 = \textbf{190.4}$

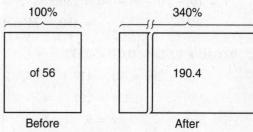

8. $A = 2(90 - A) + 3$

$A = 180 - 2A + 3$

$3A = 183$

$A = \textbf{61}°$

9. $3x + 4y = 8$

$4y = -3x + 8$

$y = -\dfrac{3}{4}x + 2$

The y-intercept is 2; the slope is $-\dfrac{3}{4}$.

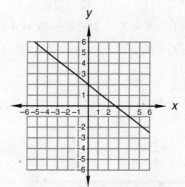

10. $(2x + 2) + (4x + 4) + (3x + 3) = 180$

$9x + 9 = 180$

$9x = 171$

$x = \textbf{19}$

11. $A_{\text{Circle}} = \pi r^2 = 25\pi\ \text{m}^2$

$r = \sqrt{\dfrac{25\pi\ \text{m}^2}{\pi}} = 5\ \text{m}$

$r = BD = AC = \textbf{5 m}$

12. Since lines are parallel,

$(5x - 19) + (3x - 1) = 180$

$8x - 20 = 180$

$8x = 200$

$x = \textbf{25}$

13. $(x + 5) + 155 = 180$

$$x = 180 - 155 - 5 = \mathbf{20}$$

$(y + 10) + (x + 5) + 40 = 180$

$y + 10 + 20 + 5 + 40 = 180$

$$y = 180 - 75 = \mathbf{105}$$

14. $0.003x + 0.02x - 0.03 = 0.177$

$$3x + 20x - 30 = 177$$

$$23x = 207$$

$$x = \mathbf{9}$$

15. $2\frac{1}{3}x + 1\frac{3}{5} = 7\frac{2}{5}$

$$\frac{7}{3}x = \frac{37}{5} - \frac{8}{5}$$

$$\frac{7}{3}x = \frac{29}{5}$$

$$x = \frac{29}{5} \cdot \frac{3}{7} = \mathbf{\frac{87}{35}}$$

16. $-3(-2 + 2x)$

$= -4^0 - 2^2 - (-2)^3 - 3 - (2 - 2x) - 4$

$6 - 6x = -1 - 4 + 8 - 3 - 2 + 2x - 4$

$6 - 6x = 2x - 6$

$8x = 12$

$$x = \frac{12}{8} = \mathbf{\frac{3}{2}}$$

17. $-\frac{1}{2} + 2\frac{3}{8} - 7\frac{1}{4} + 3\frac{1}{2}x = 4\frac{1}{16}$

$$\frac{7}{2}x = \frac{65}{16} + \frac{8}{16} - \frac{38}{16} + \frac{116}{16}$$

$$x = \frac{151}{16} \cdot \frac{2}{7} = \frac{302}{112} = \mathbf{\frac{151}{56}}$$

18. $\dfrac{x^{-2}y}{p}\left(\dfrac{-3x^2p}{y} - \dfrac{4xy^2}{p^2}\right)$

$= \dfrac{-3x^{-2}yx^2p}{py} - \dfrac{4x^{-2}yxy^2}{pp^2} = \mathbf{-3 - 4x^{-1}y^3p^{-3}}$

19. $\dfrac{-3^0x^0}{p^0}\left(-3x + \dfrac{5xy}{p^{-2}}\right) = 3x - \dfrac{5xy}{p^{-2}}$

$= \mathbf{3x - 5p^2xy}$

20. $\dfrac{(4x)^{-2}y^0(y^{-2})^2y}{32^{-1}x^2(yx^0)^{-3}} = \dfrac{32x^{-2}y^{-4}y}{16x^2y^{-3}} = \mathbf{2x^{-4}}$

21. $\dfrac{5x^{-2}(y^2x^3)^{-3}}{2^{-2}xyx^2(x^{-2}y)} = \dfrac{20x^{-2}y^{-6}x^{-9}}{xyx^2x^{-2}y}$

$= \dfrac{20x^{-11}y^{-6}}{xy^2} = \mathbf{20x^{-12}y^{-8}}$

22. $3x^{-2}y + 5x^2y^{-1} - \dfrac{3}{xxy^{-1}}$

$= 3x^{-2}y + 5x^2y^{-1} - 3x^{-2}y = \mathbf{5x^2y^{-1}}$

23. $\dfrac{2xxy^{-3}y}{xy} + \dfrac{2y^{-1}y^{-2}}{x^{-1}} - \dfrac{7xy^2}{y}$

$= 2xy^{-3} + 2xy^{-3} - 7xy = \mathbf{4xy^{-3} - 7xy}$

24. $ax - a(x^2) = -\dfrac{1}{2}\left(\dfrac{1}{4}\right) - \left(-\dfrac{1}{2}\right)\left(\dfrac{1}{4}\right)^2$

$= -\dfrac{1}{8} + \dfrac{1}{2}\left(\dfrac{1}{16}\right) = -\dfrac{1}{8} + \dfrac{1}{32} = -\dfrac{4}{32} + \dfrac{1}{32}$

$= \mathbf{-\dfrac{3}{32}}$

25. $ab^2(a - ab) = \dfrac{1}{2}\left(-\dfrac{1}{3}\right)^2\left[\dfrac{1}{2} - \dfrac{1}{2}\left(-\dfrac{1}{3}\right)\right]$

$= \dfrac{1}{18}\left(\dfrac{1}{2} + \dfrac{1}{6}\right) = \dfrac{1}{18}\left(\dfrac{3}{6} + \dfrac{1}{6}\right) = \dfrac{1}{18}\left(\dfrac{2}{3}\right)$

$= \dfrac{2}{54} = \mathbf{\dfrac{1}{27}}$

26. $mx - (m^2 - x) = -\dfrac{1}{3}\left(\dfrac{1}{2}\right) - \left[\left(-\dfrac{1}{3}\right)^2 - \dfrac{1}{2}\right]$

$= -\dfrac{1}{6} - \left(\dfrac{1}{9} - \dfrac{1}{2}\right) = -\dfrac{1}{6} - \left(\dfrac{2}{18} - \dfrac{9}{18}\right)$

$= -\dfrac{1}{6} - \left(-\dfrac{7}{18}\right) = -\dfrac{3}{18} + \dfrac{7}{18} = \dfrac{4}{18} = \mathbf{\dfrac{2}{9}}$

27. $-3\left[(-2^0 - 4) - (-2)(-3)\right]$
$- \left[(-6^0 - 2) - 2^2(-3)\right]$

$= -3[-5 - 6] - [-3 + 12]$

$= -3[-11] - [9]$

$= 33 - 9 = \mathbf{24}$

28. $-3 - 3^0 - 3^{-2} + \dfrac{1}{9} - 3^0(-3 - 3)$

$= -3 - 1 - \dfrac{1}{9} + \dfrac{1}{9} + 3 + 3 = \mathbf{2}$

29. $-|-2^0| - 2^{-2} - (-2)^{-2} = -1 - \dfrac{1}{4} - \dfrac{1}{4} = \mathbf{-1\dfrac{1}{2}}$

30. $(-1)^{-3} - 1^{-2} - 1^2 - (-1)^3$

$= -1 - 1 - 1 + 1 = \mathbf{-2}$

Practice Set 9

a. If 60% were neophytes, 40% were not.

$$\frac{40}{100} \cdot A = 200$$

$$\frac{100}{40} \cdot \frac{40}{100}A = 200 \cdot \frac{100}{40}$$

$$A = \mathbf{500 \ people}$$

b. $$\frac{245}{100} \cdot LY = 171{,}500$$

$$\frac{100}{245} \cdot \frac{245}{100} \cdot LY = 171{,}500 \cdot \frac{100}{245}$$

$$LY = \mathbf{70{,}000 \ widgets}$$

Problem Set 9

1.

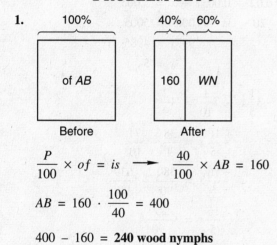

$$\frac{P}{100} \times of = is \longrightarrow \frac{40}{100} \times AB = 160$$

$$AB = 160 \cdot \frac{100}{40} = 400$$

$$400 - 160 = \mathbf{240 \ wood \ nymphs}$$

2.

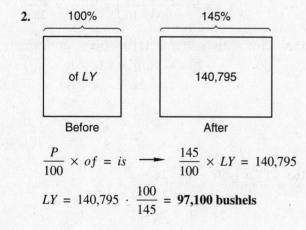

$$\frac{P}{100} \times of = is \longrightarrow \frac{145}{100} \times LY = 140{,}795$$

$$LY = 140{,}795 \cdot \frac{100}{145} = \mathbf{97{,}100 \ bushels}$$

3.

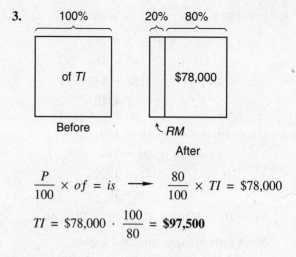

$$\frac{P}{100} \times of = is \longrightarrow \frac{80}{100} \times TI = \$78{,}000$$

$$TI = \$78{,}000 \cdot \frac{100}{80} = \mathbf{\$97{,}500}$$

4. Integers: $N, \ N + 1, \ N + 2$

$$-5(N + N + 1) = 2(N + 1) - 43$$

$$-10N - 5 = 2N - 41$$

$$36 = 12N$$

$$3 = N$$

The desired integers are **3, 4,** and **5.**

5. If 84% staggered to their feet, then 16% did not get up.

$$\frac{P}{100} \times of = is$$

$$\frac{16}{100} \times SP = 40{,}000$$

$$SP = 40{,}000 \times \frac{100}{16} = \mathbf{250{,}000 \ soldiers}$$

6. If he could not see $\frac{7}{8}$ of the Trojans, then he could see $\frac{1}{8}$ of the Trojans.

$$F \times of = is$$

$$\frac{1}{8} \times T = 1400$$

$$T = 1400 \times \frac{8}{1} = \mathbf{11{,}200 \ Trojans}$$

7.

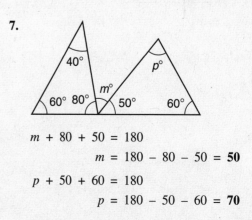

$$m + 80 + 50 = 180$$

$$m = 180 - 80 - 50 = \mathbf{50}$$

$$p + 50 + 60 = 180$$

$$p = 180 - 50 - 60 = \mathbf{70}$$

8. $y + 140 = 180 \longrightarrow y = \mathbf{40}$

$(7x + 6) + (6x + 4) + y = 180$

$13x + 10 + 40 = 180$

$13x = 130$

$x = \mathbf{10}$

9. $(5x + 10) + (7x + 50) = 180$

$12x + 60 = 180$

$12x = 120$

$x = \mathbf{10}$

$5x + 10 = 5(10) + 10 = 50 + 10 = \mathbf{60}$

Since vertical angles are equal angles,

$y + 1 = 60$

$y = \mathbf{59}$

$z + 60 = 180$

$z = \mathbf{120}$

10. $A_{\text{Circle}} = \pi r^2 = 9\pi \, \text{m}^2$

$r = \sqrt{\dfrac{9\pi \, \text{m}^2}{\pi}} = \mathbf{3\ m}$

Circumference $= 2\pi r = 2\pi(3\ \text{m}) = \mathbf{6\pi\ m}$

11. $y - 2x + 3 = 0$

$y = 2x - 3$

The y-intercept is -3; the slope is $\dfrac{2}{1}$.

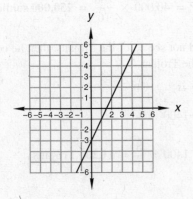

12. $3y + 6 = -x$

$y = -\dfrac{1}{3}x - 2$

The y-intercept is -2; the slope is $-\dfrac{1}{3}$.

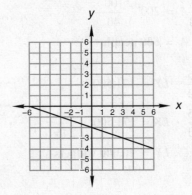

13. $0.02 - 0.003x + x = 5.005$

$20 - 3x + 1000x = 5005$

$997x = 4985$

$x = \mathbf{5}$

14. $-3\dfrac{1}{5}x + 7\dfrac{1}{10} = 4\dfrac{2}{9}$

$-\dfrac{16}{5}x = \dfrac{38}{9} - \dfrac{71}{10}$

$-\dfrac{16}{5}x = \dfrac{380}{90} - \dfrac{639}{90}$

$-\dfrac{16}{5}x = -\dfrac{259}{90}$

$x = -\dfrac{259}{90}\left(-\dfrac{5}{16}\right) = \dfrac{1295}{1440} = \mathbf{\dfrac{259}{288}}$

15. $-2\left[(2 - 3)x + 7(2^0 - 1)\right] = -3(x - 2)$

$-2[-x + 7(0)] = -3x + 6$

$2x = -3x + 6$

$5x = 6$

$x = \mathbf{\dfrac{6}{5}}$

16. $-2^0(2x - 3) - 4 = 2x - 3^0$

$-2x + 3 - 4 = 2x - 1$

$-2x - 1 = 2x - 1$

$0 = 4x$

$\mathbf{0} = x$

17. $\dfrac{x^0 y^2}{p^{-2}}\left(\dfrac{p^2}{y^2} - \dfrac{y^{-2}}{p^{-2}}\right) = \dfrac{x^0 y^2 p^2}{p^{-2} y^2} - \dfrac{x^0 y^2 y^{-2}}{p^{-2} p^{-2}}$

$= p^4 - p^4 = \mathbf{0}$

18. $\dfrac{ak^{-2}}{a^{-3}}\left(\dfrac{2k^4}{a^4} - 3k\right) = \dfrac{2ak^{-2}k^4}{a^{-3}a^4} - \dfrac{3ak^{-2}k}{a^{-3}}$

$= 2k^2 - 3a^4k^{-1}$

19. $\dfrac{(2x^2ya)^{-3}ya^3}{x^2y(ay)^{-2}y} = \dfrac{x^{-6}y^{-3}a^{-3}ya^3}{8x^2ya^{-2}y^{-2}y} = \dfrac{x^{-6}y^{-2}}{8x^2a^{-2}}$

$= \dfrac{a^2}{8x^8y^2}$

20. $\dfrac{(-2xyz)^{-3}}{(x^2z^{-3})^{-3}} = -\dfrac{x^{-3}y^{-3}z^{-3}}{8x^{-6}z^9} = -\dfrac{x^3}{8y^3z^{12}}$

21. $3x - \dfrac{2xy^2}{y} + \dfrac{4xx^{-2}}{(x^2)^{-1}} = 3x - 2xy + 4x$

$= 7x - 2xy$

22. $\dfrac{2xy}{p} - \dfrac{5xxx}{(x^{-2})^{-1}y^{-1}} + \dfrac{3xp^{-1}}{y^{-1}}$

$= \dfrac{2xy}{p} - 5xy + \dfrac{3xy}{p} = \dfrac{5xy}{p} - 5xy$

23. $-a^2b - a = -\left(-\dfrac{1}{2}\right)^2\left(\dfrac{1}{4}\right) - \left(-\dfrac{1}{2}\right)$

$= -\dfrac{1}{16} + \dfrac{1}{2} = -\dfrac{1}{16} + \dfrac{8}{16} = \dfrac{7}{16}$

24. $a(a - ab) = -\dfrac{1}{2}\left[-\dfrac{1}{2} - \left(-\dfrac{1}{2}\right)\left(-\dfrac{1}{8}\right)\right]$

$= -\dfrac{1}{2}\left(-\dfrac{1}{2} - \dfrac{1}{16}\right) = -\dfrac{1}{2}\left(-\dfrac{8}{16} - \dfrac{1}{16}\right)$

$= -\dfrac{1}{2}\left(-\dfrac{9}{16}\right) = \dfrac{9}{32}$

25. $a(a - b)(ab - b) = -2(-2 - 3)[-2(3) - 3]$

$= -2(-5)(-6 - 3) = -2(-5)(-9) = -90$

26. $a^2(x - ax^2) = (-2)^2[-4 - (-2)(-4)^2]$

$= 4(-4 + 32) = 4(28) = 112$

27. $-2(-3 - 2^0) - 2^0(-2^2 - 2) = -2(-4) - 1(-6)$

$= 8 + 6 = 14$

28. $-3\big[(-5 + 2)(-2) - (3^0 - 2) - 2\big]$

$= -3[(-3)(-2) - (-1) - 2] = -3[6 + 1 - 2]$

$= -3[5] = -15$

29. $-2^0(-2 - 3^0) - (-2)^3 - |-3|$

$= -1(-3) + 8 - 3$

$= 3 + 8 - 3 = 8$

30. $-\dfrac{1}{-2^{-3}} + \dfrac{1}{-(-2)^{-3}} - 3^2 = 8 + 8 - 9 = 7$

PRACTICE SET 10

a. $a^2 + 5^2 = 9^2$

$a^2 + 25 = 81$

$a^2 = 56$

$a = \sqrt{56}$

b.

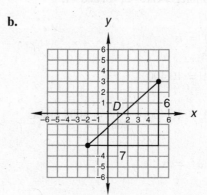

$D^2 = 6^2 + 7^2$

$D^2 = 36 + 49$

$D = \sqrt{85}$

PROBLEM SET 10

1. If 20% were in a festive mood, then 80% were not in a festive mood.

$\dfrac{P}{100} \times of = is$

$\dfrac{80}{100} \times P = 1400$

$P = 1400 \times \dfrac{100}{80} = 1750$ **people**

2. $F \times of = is$

$3\dfrac{1}{4} \times S = 26{,}000$

$S = 26{,}000 \times \dfrac{4}{13} = 8000$ **soldiers**

3. $F \times of = is$

$\dfrac{1}{10} \times M = 590$

$M = 590 \times \dfrac{10}{1} = 5900$

$Men_{After} = Men_{Total} - Men_{Killed}$

$Men_{After} = 5900 - 590 = 5310$ **men**

4. Odd integers: $N, N + 2, N + 4$

$4N = 3(N + 2 + N + 4) - 8$

$4N = 6N + 10$

$-2N = 10$

$N = -5$

The desired integers are **–5, –3,** and **–1.**

5. $\dfrac{P}{100} \times of = is$

$\dfrac{260}{100} \times OA = 10,400$

$OA = 10,400 \cdot \dfrac{100}{260} = \textbf{4000 minas}$

6. $\dfrac{P}{100} \times of = is$

$\dfrac{14}{100} \times A_{Total} = 4200$

$A_{Total} = 4200 \cdot \dfrac{100}{14} = 30,000$

$A_{Hidden} = A_{Total} - A_{Seen}$

$A_{Hidden} = 30,000 - 4200 = \textbf{25,800 Argives}$

7. Circumference $= 2\pi r = 6\pi$ cm

$r = \dfrac{6\pi}{2\pi}$ cm $= 3$ cm

Area $= \pi r^2 = \pi(3 \text{ cm})^2 = \textbf{9}\boldsymbol{\pi}\textbf{ cm}^2$

8. Since angles opposite equal sides are equal angles,

$x = \textbf{60.}$

$x + y + 60 = 180$

$y = 180 - 60 - 60 = \textbf{60}$

$y + \angle BDC = 180$

$\angle BDC = 180 - 60 = 120$

$z + 20 + 120 = 180$

$z = 180 - 20 - 120 = \textbf{40}$

9. $(17x + 20) + (20x - 25) = 180$

$37x - 5 = 180$

$37x = 185$

$x = 5$

Since vertical angles are equal angles,

$P = 17x + 20$

$P = 17(5) + 20 = 105$

Since lines are parallel,

$Q = P = \textbf{105.}$

10. $A_{Square} = 4 \times A_{Shaded}$

$= 4 \times 9 \text{ m}^2 = \textbf{36 m}^2$

$A_{Square} = s^2 = 36 \text{ m}^2$

$s = \sqrt{36 \text{ m}^2} = \textbf{6 m}$

11. $2y = 3x + 2$

$y = \dfrac{3}{2}x + 1$

The y-intercept is 1; the slope is $\dfrac{3}{2}$.

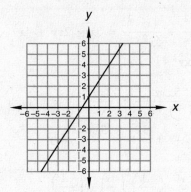

12. $y = -3$

The y-intercept is -3; the slope is 0.

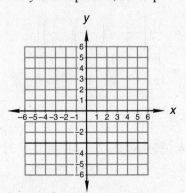

13. $c^2 = a^2 + b^2$

$7^2 = p^2 + 4^2$

$49 = p^2 + 16$

$33 = p^2$

$\sqrt{33} = p$

14.

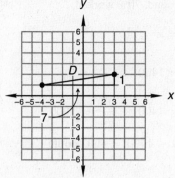

$D^2 = 1^2 + 7^2$
$D^2 = 1 + 49$
$D^2 = 50$
$D = \sqrt{50}$
$D = \mathbf{5\sqrt{2}}$

15. $\dfrac{3}{4}x - \dfrac{1}{5}x = 2\dfrac{3}{4}$

$\dfrac{15}{20}x - \dfrac{4}{20}x = \dfrac{11}{4}$

$\dfrac{11}{20}x = \dfrac{11}{4}$

$x = \dfrac{11}{4} \cdot \dfrac{20}{11} = \mathbf{5}$

16. $-5.2 + 3y = 0.2(y + 2)$
$-52 + 30y = 2y + 4$
$28y = 56$
$y = \mathbf{2}$

17. $4x(2 - 3^0) + (-2)(x - 5) = -(3x + 2)$
$8x - 4x - 2x + 10 = -3x - 2$
$2x + 10 = -3x - 2$
$5x = -12$
$x = -\dfrac{\mathbf{12}}{\mathbf{5}}$

18. $\dfrac{4xy}{m^{-2}}\left(\dfrac{3y^{-1}}{m^2 x} - \dfrac{2x}{ym}\right) = \dfrac{12xyy^{-1}}{m^{-2}m^2 x} - \dfrac{8xyx}{m^{-2}ym}$
$= \mathbf{12 - 8x^2 m}$

19. $\dfrac{2x^0 y}{p}\left(\dfrac{2p}{y} - \dfrac{3xy}{p}\right) = \dfrac{4x^0 yp}{py} - \dfrac{6x^0 yxy}{pp}$
$= \mathbf{4 - 6xy^2 p^{-2}}$

20. $\dfrac{(3x^{-2})^{-2}xy}{3^{-3}x^{-2}(yx^0)^{-3}} = \dfrac{27x^4 xy}{9x^{-2}y^{-3}x^0} = \dfrac{3x^5 y}{x^{-2}y^{-3}}$
$= \mathbf{3x^7 y^4}$

21. $\dfrac{(x^2 p^2)^{-3}x^0 p^2}{x^{-2}px^0(xp)^{-3}} = \dfrac{x^{-6}p^{-6}x^0 p^2}{x^{-2}px^0 x^{-3}p^{-3}} = \dfrac{x^{-6}p^{-4}}{x^{-5}p^{-2}}$
$= \mathbf{x^{-1}p^{-2}}$

22. $3x + \dfrac{2x^2 x^{-3}}{x^{-2}y^0} - x^0 = 3x + 2x - 1 = \mathbf{5x - 1}$

23. $\dfrac{5x^2 y}{z} - \dfrac{3z^{-1}y}{x^{-2}} + \dfrac{7xxy^2 z}{yz^2}$
$= \dfrac{5x^2 y}{z} - \dfrac{3x^2 y}{z} + \dfrac{7x^2 y}{z} = \dfrac{\mathbf{9x^2 y}}{\mathbf{z}}$

24. $(A + x + 3) + (B + x + 2) + (C + x + 1)$
$= 30 \text{ cm}$

Since $A = x + 3$; $B = x + 2$; and $C = x + 1$:
$2(x + 3) + 2(x + 2) + 2(x + 1) = 30 \text{ cm}$
$2x + 6 + 2x + 4 + 2x + 2 = 30 \text{ cm}$
$6x = 18 \text{ cm}$
$x = \mathbf{3 \text{ cm}}$

25. $b(ab - b) = -\dfrac{1}{2}\left[\left(-\dfrac{1}{3}\right)\left(-\dfrac{1}{2}\right) - \left(-\dfrac{1}{2}\right)\right]$
$= -\dfrac{1}{2}\left(\dfrac{1}{6} + \dfrac{1}{2}\right) = -\dfrac{1}{2}\left(\dfrac{1}{6} + \dfrac{3}{6}\right) = -\dfrac{1}{2}\left(\dfrac{2}{3}\right)$
$= -\dfrac{2}{6} = -\dfrac{\mathbf{1}}{\mathbf{3}}$

26. $ab - a^2 b^2 - b$
$= -\dfrac{1}{2}\left(-\dfrac{1}{2}\right) - \left(-\dfrac{1}{2}\right)^2\left(-\dfrac{1}{2}\right)^2 - \left(-\dfrac{1}{2}\right)$
$= \dfrac{1}{4} - \dfrac{1}{16} + \dfrac{1}{2} = \dfrac{4}{16} - \dfrac{1}{16} + \dfrac{8}{16} = \dfrac{\mathbf{11}}{\mathbf{16}}$

27. $a^2(b - ab)b$
$= \left(-\dfrac{1}{2}\right)^2\left[-\dfrac{1}{2} - \left(-\dfrac{1}{2}\right)\left(-\dfrac{1}{2}\right)\right]\left(-\dfrac{1}{2}\right)$
$= \dfrac{1}{4}\left(-\dfrac{1}{2} - \dfrac{1}{4}\right)\left(-\dfrac{1}{2}\right) = \dfrac{1}{4}\left(-\dfrac{2}{4} - \dfrac{1}{4}\right)\left(-\dfrac{1}{2}\right)$
$= \dfrac{1}{4}\left(-\dfrac{3}{4}\right)\left(-\dfrac{1}{2}\right) = \dfrac{\mathbf{3}}{\mathbf{32}}$

28. $-\dfrac{1}{2^{-3}} - \dfrac{1}{-2^{-3}} - (-3 - 2^0) - 2$
$= -8 + 8 + 4 - 2 = \mathbf{2}$

29. $-|-2| - |-2^0| - 3^2 - (-3)^3$
$= -2 - 1 - 9 + 27 = \mathbf{15}$

30. $-\dfrac{1}{2} - \left(\dfrac{1}{2}\right)^2 - \left(-\dfrac{1}{2}\right)^3 - \dfrac{1}{2}$
$= -\dfrac{1}{2} - \dfrac{1}{4} + \dfrac{1}{8} - \dfrac{1}{2} = -\dfrac{4}{8} - \dfrac{2}{8} + \dfrac{1}{8} - \dfrac{4}{8}$
$= -\dfrac{\mathbf{9}}{\mathbf{8}}$

PRACTICE SET 11

a. $\dfrac{m}{3b} + \dfrac{ak}{bz^3} - \dfrac{y}{bz^4} = \dfrac{mz^4}{3bz^4} + \dfrac{3akz}{3bz^4} - \dfrac{3y}{3bz^4}$

$= \dfrac{mz^4 + 3akz - 3y}{3bz^4}$

b. $\dfrac{z}{b} - k + \dfrac{2mn}{ab^3} = \dfrac{ab^2z}{ab^3} - \dfrac{ab^3k}{ab^3} + \dfrac{2mn}{ab^3}$

$= \dfrac{ab^2z - ab^3k + 2mn}{ab^3}$

c. $y = 2(40)$

$y = \mathbf{80}$

$(4x + 20) + (5x + 80) = 360 - 80$

$9x + 100 = 280$

$9x = 180$

$x = \mathbf{20}$

PROBLEM SET 11

1. If 13% believed, 87% did not believe.

$\dfrac{P}{100} \times of = is$

$\dfrac{87}{100} \times L_{\text{Total}} = 5220$

$L_{\text{Total}} = 5220 \times \dfrac{100}{87} = 6000$

$L_{\text{Believed}} = L_{\text{Total}} - L_{\text{Not believed}}$

$L_{\text{Believed}} = 6000 - 5220 = \mathbf{780\ people}$

2. Even integers: $N,\ N + 2,\ N + 4,\ N + 6$

$-2(N + N + 6) = -N - 4 - 20$

$-4N - 12 = -N - 24$

$-3N = -12$

$N = 4$

The desired integers are **4, 6, 8,** and **10.**

3. $\dfrac{P}{100} \times of = is$

$\dfrac{220}{100} \times OP = \$5599$

$OP = \$5599 \times \dfrac{100}{220} = \$2545$

Increase = $\$5599 - \$2545 = \mathbf{\$3054}$

4. If 30% sat around, 70% worked.

$\dfrac{P}{100} \times of = is$

$\dfrac{70}{100} \times P = 1400$

$P = 1400 \times \dfrac{100}{70} = 2000$

$P_{\text{Sat}} = 2000 - 1400 = \mathbf{600\ people}$

5. $\dfrac{P}{100} \times of = is$

$\dfrac{340}{100} \times RP = 6800$

$RP = 6800 \times \dfrac{100}{340} = 2000$

Total = $6800 + 2000 = \mathbf{8800\ plums}$

6. Odd integers: $N,\ N + 2,\ N + 4,\ N + 6$

$-4(N + N + 6) = 10(-N - 4) + 10$

$-8N - 24 = -10N - 30$

$2N = -6$

$N = -3$

The desired integers are **–3, –1, 1,** and **3.**

7. Since angles opposite equal sides are equal angles, $z = \mathbf{32}$.

$y + z + 32 = 180$

$y = 180 - 32 - 32 = \mathbf{116}$

$x + y = 180$

$x + 116 = 180$

$x = \mathbf{64}$

Since the measure of an arc of a circle equals the measure of the central angle, $p = \mathbf{64}$.

8. $A_{\text{Shaded}} = A_{\text{Square}} - A_{\text{3 Triangles}}$

$= (4)(4) - \dfrac{1}{2}(2)(1) - \dfrac{1}{2}(2)(3) - \dfrac{1}{2}(4)(1)$

$= 16 - 1 - 3 - 2$

$= \mathbf{10\ units^2}$

9. $A_{\text{Circle}} = A_{\text{Triangle}}$

$\pi r^2 = \dfrac{1}{2}bH$

$\pi(\pi\ \text{cm})^2 = \dfrac{1}{2}(\pi\ \text{cm})(H)$

$H = \dfrac{2\pi^3\ \text{cm}^2}{\pi\ \text{cm}} = \mathbf{2\pi^2\ cm}$

10. $2(3x + 2) + 2(4x - 2) + 2(3x - 2) = 36 \text{ m}$

$6x + 4 + 8x - 4 + 6x - 4 = 36 \text{ m}$

$20x - 4 = 36 \text{ m}$

$20x = 40 \text{ m}$

$x = 2 \text{ m}$

$3x + 2 = 3(2 \text{ m}) + 2 = \mathbf{8 \text{ m}}$

11. $\dfrac{k}{ax} + \dfrac{bc}{x^2} - \dfrac{m}{ax^3} = \dfrac{kx^2}{ax^3} + \dfrac{abcx}{ax^3} - \dfrac{m}{ax^3}$

$= \dfrac{\mathbf{kx^2 + abcx - m}}{\mathbf{ax^3}}$

12. $\dfrac{p}{ak} - c + \dfrac{3a}{4k} = \dfrac{4p}{4ak} - \dfrac{4ack}{4ak} + \dfrac{3a^2}{4ak}$

$= \dfrac{\mathbf{4p - 4ack + 3a^2}}{\mathbf{4ak}}$

13. $\dfrac{m^2}{p} - \dfrac{3p}{cx} - \dfrac{5}{4c^2x}$

$= \dfrac{4c^2m^2x}{4c^2px} - \dfrac{12cp^2}{4c^2px} - \dfrac{5p}{4c^2px}$

$= \dfrac{\mathbf{4c^2m^2x - 12cp^2 - 5p}}{\mathbf{4c^2px}}$

14. $c^2 = a^2 + b^2$

$11^2 = 4^2 + x^2$

$121 = 16 + x^2$

$105 = x^2$

$\sqrt{105} = x$

15.

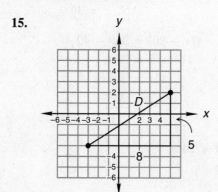

$D^2 = 5^2 + 8^2$

$D^2 = 25 + 64$

$D^2 = 89$

$D = \sqrt{\mathbf{89}}$

16. (a) $4x + 3y - 6 = 0$

$3y = -4x + 6$

$y = -\dfrac{4}{3}x + 2$

(b) $x = -3$

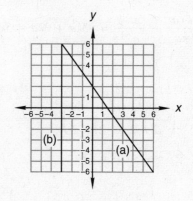

17. $3\dfrac{1}{2} - 2\dfrac{1}{3}x = 3\dfrac{1}{4}$

$-\dfrac{7}{3}x = \dfrac{13}{4} - \dfrac{14}{4}$

$-\dfrac{7}{3}x = -\dfrac{1}{4}$

$x = -\dfrac{1}{4}\left(-\dfrac{3}{7}\right) = \dfrac{\mathbf{3}}{\mathbf{28}}$

18. $0.03x - x + 2 = -0.91$

$3x - 100x + 200 = -91$

$-97x = -291$

$x = 3$

19. $3x(2 - 3^0) - 7^0 = -2x(3 - 7^0) + 2$

$3x - 1 = -4x + 2$

$7x = 3$

$x = \dfrac{\mathbf{3}}{\mathbf{7}}$

20. $\dfrac{a^{-2}}{y}\left(3a^2y - \dfrac{2y}{a^2}\right) = \dfrac{3a^{-2}a^2y}{y} - \dfrac{2a^{-2}y}{ya^2}$

$= \mathbf{3 - 2a^{-4}}$

21. $\dfrac{2x^0yp}{k}\left(\dfrac{3k}{yp} - \dfrac{2yk}{p}\right) = \dfrac{6x^0ypk}{kyp} - \dfrac{4x^0ypyk}{kp}$

$= \mathbf{6 - 4y^2}$

22. $\dfrac{2p^2a^{-2}ap^0p^4}{(2pa^{-2})^{-3}ap^0} = \dfrac{16p^6a^{-1}}{p^{-3}a^7} = \mathbf{16p^9a^{-8}}$

23. $\dfrac{xym^2m^{-4}xm}{(2x^2y)^{-3}xy^0x^{-3}y} = \dfrac{8x^2ym^{-1}}{x^{-8}y^{-2}} = \mathbf{8x^{10}y^3m^{-1}}$

24. $\dfrac{xp^{-3}}{y} - \dfrac{3y^{-1}}{x^{-1}p^3} + \dfrac{2x}{ppy} = \dfrac{x}{yp^3} - \dfrac{3x}{yp^3} + \dfrac{2x}{yp^3}$

$= \mathbf{0}$

25. $-3ka + \dfrac{3k^2a^2}{ka} - \dfrac{5a^0k}{a^{-1}} = -3ka + 3ka - 5ka$

$= \mathbf{-5ka}$

26. $-a - ax(a - x)$

$= -\left(-\dfrac{1}{2}\right) - \left(-\dfrac{1}{2}\right)\left(\dfrac{3}{2}\right)\left(-\dfrac{1}{2} - \dfrac{3}{2}\right)$

$= \dfrac{1}{2} + \dfrac{3}{4}(-2) = \dfrac{1}{2} - \dfrac{3}{2} = \mathbf{-1}$

27. $-a^2(b - a) = -\left(-\dfrac{1}{2}\right)^2\left[\dfrac{3}{2} - \left(-\dfrac{1}{2}\right)\right] = -\dfrac{1}{4}(2)$

$= -\dfrac{2}{4} = \mathbf{-\dfrac{1}{2}}$

28. $-2(-3 - 2^0 - 2)(-2 + 5)(-2) = -2(-6)(3)(-2)$

$= \mathbf{-72}$

29. $-\dfrac{1}{-2^0} - \dfrac{1}{-2^2} - \dfrac{1}{-2^{-2}} = 1 + \dfrac{1}{4} + 4 = \mathbf{5\dfrac{1}{4}}$

30. $\left|-3^0\right| - \left|-2 - 3\right| + (-2^0)(-2 - 5)$

$= 1 - 5 + 7 = \mathbf{3}$

PRACTICE SET 12

a. Every point on this line is 5 units below the *x*-axis, so the equation is $\mathbf{y = -5}$.

b. The *y*-intercept is -1. The slope is negative with a rise over the run of $\frac{1}{2}$ for any triangle drawn. The equation is $\mathbf{y = -\frac{1}{2}x - 1}$.

PROBLEM SET 12

1. If 40% were monochromatic, 60% were variegated.

$\dfrac{P}{100} \times of = is$

$\dfrac{60}{100} \times V = 2400$

$V = 2400 \times \dfrac{100}{60} = 4000$

Monochromatic $= 4000 - 2400 = \mathbf{1600\ vases}$

2. Integers: $N,\ N + 1,\ N + 2,\ N + 3$

$2(N + N + 1 + N + 3) = 3(-N - 2) - 40$

$6N + 8 = -3N - 46$

$9N = -54$

$N = -6$

The desired integers are **−6, −5, −4,** and **−3.**

3. $F \times of = is$

$4\dfrac{1}{4} \times S = 5100$

$S = 5100 \times \dfrac{4}{17} = \mathbf{1200}$

4. $F \times of = is$

$2\dfrac{1}{5} \times N = 1$

$N = 1 \times \dfrac{5}{11} = \mathbf{\dfrac{5}{11}}$

5. $5(-N) + 25 = 8N + 90$

$-13N = 65$

$N = \mathbf{-5}$

6. If the train completed 30%, then 70% remained.

$\dfrac{P}{100} \times of = is$

$\dfrac{70}{100} \times TL = 6300$

$TL = 6300 \times \dfrac{100}{70} = \mathbf{9000\ miles}$

7. $z + (180 - 140) + (180 - 70) = 180$

$z + 40 + 110 = 180$

$z = \mathbf{30}$

8. $(4x + 25) + (7x - 20) = 360 - 40$

$11x + 5 = 320$

$11x = 315$

$x = \mathbf{\dfrac{315}{11}}$

$y = \dfrac{1}{2}(40) = \mathbf{20}$

9. $A_{\text{Sector}} = \dfrac{60}{360}(\pi r^2) = 36\pi\ \text{cm}^2$

$r^2 = \dfrac{6(36\pi)\ \text{cm}^2}{\pi}$

$r = \sqrt{216}\ \text{cm} = 6\sqrt{6}\ \text{cm}$

Diameter $= 2r = 2(6\sqrt{6})\ \text{cm} = \mathbf{12\sqrt{6}\ cm}$

10. Relabel angles A, B, and C as having measures of $3x$, $2x$, and x respectively.

$$3x + 2x + x = 180$$
$$6x = 180$$
$$x = 30$$

$$A = 90; \; B = 60; \; C = 30$$

11. $m + \dfrac{x}{c} + \dfrac{c}{x^2 b} = \dfrac{mbcx^2}{bcx^2} + \dfrac{bx^3}{bcx^2} + \dfrac{c^2}{bcx^2}$

$$= \dfrac{mbcx^2 + bx^3 + c^2}{bcx^2}$$

12. $\dfrac{a}{b} - \dfrac{3b}{a^2} - \dfrac{2}{abc} = \dfrac{a^3 c}{a^2 bc} - \dfrac{3b^2 c}{a^2 bc} - \dfrac{2a}{a^2 bc}$

$$= \dfrac{a^3 c - 3b^2 c - 2a}{a^2 bc}$$

13. $1 + \dfrac{a}{b} = \dfrac{b}{b} + \dfrac{a}{b} = \dfrac{b + a}{b}$

14. $c^2 = a^2 + b^2$
$$13^2 = 5^2 + k^2$$
$$169 = 25 + k^2$$
$$144 = k^2$$
$$12 = k$$

15.

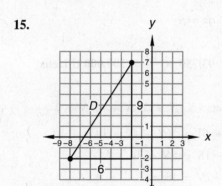

$$D^2 = 9^2 + 6^2$$
$$D^2 = 81 + 36$$
$$D^2 = 117$$
$$D = \sqrt{117}$$
$$D = 3\sqrt{13}$$

16. (a) $3y + x - 9 = 0$
$$3y = -x + 9$$
$$y = -\dfrac{1}{3}x + 3$$

(b) $x = 2$

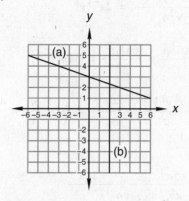

17. (a) The y-intercept is $+2$. The slope is positive and the rise over the run for any triangle drawn is $\frac{1}{3}$.

$$y = \dfrac{1}{3}x + 2$$

(b) Every point is 2 units below the x-axis.
$$y = -2$$

18. $8\dfrac{1}{4} + 2\dfrac{1}{2}x = \dfrac{1}{8}$

$$\dfrac{5}{2}x = \dfrac{1}{8} - \dfrac{66}{8}$$
$$\dfrac{5}{2}x = -\dfrac{65}{8}$$
$$x = -\dfrac{65}{8} \cdot \dfrac{2}{5} = -\dfrac{130}{40} = -\dfrac{13}{4}$$

19. $0.001 + 0.02x - 0.1 = 0.002x$
$$1 + 20x - 100 = 2x$$
$$18x = 99$$
$$x = \dfrac{11}{2} = 5.5$$

20. $-3(-2 - 2^0 x) - (-2) - 2(-2 - 3x) = -2(x + 4)$
$$6 + 3x + 2 + 4 + 6x = -2x - 8$$
$$9x + 12 = -2x - 8$$
$$11x = -20$$
$$x = -\dfrac{20}{11}$$

21. $\dfrac{a^{-3} x}{y^{-3}} \left(\dfrac{xxx^{-2}}{y^{-2} yy} - 3 \right) = \dfrac{a^{-3} xxxx^{-2}}{y^{-3} y^{-2} yy} - \dfrac{3 a^{-3} x}{y^{-3}}$

$$= a^{-3} x y^3 - 3 a^{-3} x y^3$$
$$= -2 a^{-3} x y^3$$

22. $\dfrac{x^0 x^{-2}}{y} \left(x^2 y - \dfrac{2 x^2 y}{x^4} \right)$

$$= \dfrac{x^0 x^{-2} x^2 y}{y} - \dfrac{2 x^0 x^{-2} x^2 y}{y x^4} = 1 - 2 x^{-4}$$

23. $\dfrac{x^{-2}(2x^{-3})y^2y^0}{x^{-3}yx^2y^{-7}} = \mathbf{2x^{-4}y^8}$

24. $\dfrac{a^0ba^2a^{-1}a}{(2^2b^{-2})^{-3}} = \dfrac{64ba^2}{b^6} = \mathbf{64a^2b^{-5}}$

25. $\dfrac{a}{x} - \dfrac{3a^2y^0x^{-1}}{a} + \dfrac{4x^{-1}}{aa^{-2}} = \dfrac{a}{x} - \dfrac{3a}{x} + \dfrac{4a}{x}$

$= \mathbf{2ax^{-1}}$

26. $abc - \dfrac{5a^2c^3}{ab^{-1}c^2} - \dfrac{3}{a^{-1}b^{-1}c^{-1}}$

$= abc - 5abc - 3abc = \mathbf{-7abc}$

27. $a^2(a^0 - ab) = \left(-\dfrac{1}{2}\right)^2\left[\left(-\dfrac{1}{2}\right)^0 - \left(-\dfrac{1}{2}\right)\left(\dfrac{3}{4}\right)\right]$

$= \dfrac{1}{4}\left(1 + \dfrac{3}{8}\right) = \dfrac{1}{4}\left(\dfrac{11}{8}\right) = \mathbf{\dfrac{11}{32}}$

28. $x(x^2 - x^2y) = -\dfrac{1}{2}\left[\left(-\dfrac{1}{2}\right)^2 - \left(-\dfrac{1}{2}\right)^2\left(\dfrac{1}{2}\right)\right]$

$= -\dfrac{1}{2}\left(\dfrac{1}{4} - \dfrac{1}{8}\right) = -\dfrac{1}{2}\left(\dfrac{1}{8}\right) = \mathbf{-\dfrac{1}{16}}$

29. $-ab(a - a^2b - b)$

$= -2(-3)[2 - (2)^2(-3) - (-3)]$

$= 6(2 + 12 + 3) = 6(17) = \mathbf{102}$

30. $-2^0(-2^0 - 3^0 - |-2|) - (-2)(-3)$

$- \dfrac{1}{3^{-2}} - 3^2 - 3$

$= -1(-1 - 1 - 2) - 6 - 9 - 9 - 3$

$= -1(-4) - 6 - 9 - 9 - 3$

$= 4 - 6 - 9 - 9 - 3 = \mathbf{-23}$

PRACTICE SET 13

a. $2(y + 7) + 3y = 4$

$2y + 14 + 3y = 4$

$5y = -10$

$y = -2$

$x = y + 7 = (-2) + 7 = 5$

The solution is **(5, –2)**.

b.

$H^2 + 2^2 = 3^2$

$H^2 + 4 = 9$

$H^2 = 5$

$H = \sqrt{5}$

Area $= \dfrac{1}{2}BH = \dfrac{1}{2}(4)(\sqrt{5}) = \mathbf{2\sqrt{5}\ m^2}$

PROBLEM SET 13

1. If 60% had blue sails, 40% did not have blue sails.

$\dfrac{P}{100} \times of = is$

$\dfrac{40}{100} \times B = 300$

$B = 300 \times \dfrac{100}{40} = 750$

Blue sails $= 750 - 300 = \mathbf{450\ boats}$

2. $F \times of = is$

$\dfrac{3}{16} \times C = 93{,}750$

$C = 93{,}750 \times \dfrac{16}{3} = \mathbf{500{,}000\ citizens}$

3. Even integers: $N,\ N + 2,\ N + 4,\ N + 6$

$3(N + N + 6) = 5(N + 4) + 14$

$6N + 18 = 5N + 34$

$N = 16$

The desired integers are **16, 18, 20,** and **22**.

4. $3(N + 14) = 2(-N) + 67$

$3N + 42 = -2N + 67$

$5N = 25$

$N = \mathbf{5}$

5. $A_{\text{Shaded}} = A_{\text{Rectangle}} + A_{\text{Triangle}}$

$= (1)(4) + \dfrac{1}{2}(4)(3)$

$= 4 + 6 = \mathbf{10\ units^2}$

6. $(10x + 10) + (6x + 10) = 180$

$$16x + 20 = 180$$
$$16x = 160$$
$$x = \mathbf{10}$$

$$4 \times \overrightarrow{SF} = \frac{9}{2}$$

$$\overrightarrow{SF} = \frac{9}{2} \cdot \frac{1}{4} = \frac{9}{8}$$

$$5 \times \overrightarrow{SF} = y$$

$$5 \cdot \frac{9}{8} = y$$

$$\frac{\mathbf{45}}{\mathbf{8}} = y$$

Since lines are parallel,

$$P = 10x + 10$$
$$P = 10(10) + 10$$
$$P = \mathbf{110}$$

7. $5^2 = (AB)^2 + 4^2$

$$25 = (AB)^2 + 16$$
$$9 = (AB)^2$$
$$\mathbf{3} = AB$$

$$AC - AB = BC$$
$$12 - 3 = BC$$
$$9 = BC$$

$$(DC)^2 = 9^2 + 4^2$$
$$(DC)^2 = 81 + 16$$
$$DC = \sqrt{\mathbf{97}}$$

8. (a) $x = y + 1$

(b) $3x + 2y = 8$

Substitute (a) into (b) and get:

(b) $3(y + 1) + 2y = 8$
$$3y + 3 + 2y = 8$$
$$5y = 5$$
$$y = 1$$

(a) $x = y + 1$
$$x = (1) + 1 = 2$$

(2, 1)

9. (a) $3x - y = 22$

(a') $y = 3x - 22$

(b) $2x + 3y = -11$

Substitute (a') into (b) and get:

(b) $2x + 3(3x - 22) = -11$
$$11x - 66 = -11$$
$$11x = 55$$
$$x = 5$$

(a') $y = 3(5) - 22 = -7$

(5, –7)

10. (a) $x + y = 20$

(a') $y = -x + 20$

(b) $5x + 10y = 200$

Substitute (a') into (b) and get:

(b) $5x + 10(-x + 20) = 200$
$$-5x + 200 = 200$$
$$-5x = 0$$
$$x = 0$$

(a') $y = -(0) + 20 = 20$

(0, 20)

11. (a) $x + y = 20$

(a') $y = -x + 20$

(b) $25x + 10y = 395$

Substitute (a') into (b) and get:

(b) $25x + 10(-x + 20) = 395$
$$15x + 200 = 395$$
$$15x = 195$$
$$x = 13$$

(a') $y = -(13) + 20 = 7$

(13, 7)

12. $4 + \dfrac{2}{a} = \dfrac{4a}{a} + \dfrac{2}{a} = \dfrac{\mathbf{4a + 2}}{\mathbf{a}}$

13. $\dfrac{a^2}{k} + k + \dfrac{k}{4} = \dfrac{4a^2}{4k} + \dfrac{4k^2}{4k} + \dfrac{k^2}{4k}$

$$= \dfrac{\mathbf{4a^2 + 5k^2}}{\mathbf{4k}}$$

14. $m^2 + \dfrac{m}{p} + \dfrac{m}{ap^2} = \dfrac{am^2p^2}{ap^2} + \dfrac{amp}{ap^2} + \dfrac{m}{ap^2}$

$$= \dfrac{\mathbf{am^2p^2 + amp + m}}{\mathbf{ap^2}}$$

15.

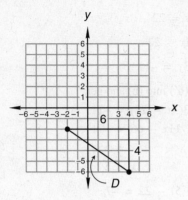

$$D^2 = 6^2 + 4^2$$
$$D^2 = 36 + 16$$
$$D^2 = 52$$
$$D = \sqrt{52}$$
$$\mathbf{D = 2\sqrt{13}}$$

16. (a) $y = -3$

(b) $2x - 3y = 9$
$$-3y = -2x + 9$$
$$y = \frac{2}{3}x - 3$$

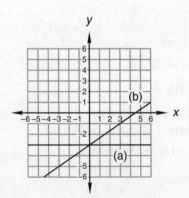

17. (a) Every point is 5 units to the right of the y-axis.
$$\mathbf{x = 5}$$

(b) The y-intercept is -2. The slope is negative and the rise over the run for any triangle drawn is $-\frac{2}{3}$.
$$\mathbf{x = -\frac{2}{3}x - 2}$$

18. $3\frac{1}{2}x + 4\frac{1}{3} = 7\frac{2}{9}$
$$\frac{7}{2}x = \frac{65}{9} - \frac{39}{9}$$
$$x = \frac{26}{9} \cdot \frac{2}{7} = \mathbf{\frac{52}{63}}$$

19. $0.03 + 0.03x = 0.003$
$$30 + 30x = 3$$
$$30x = -27$$
$$x = -\frac{27}{30} = \mathbf{-0.9}$$

20. $-3^0 - 3^2 - (-2x - |2|) = 7x$
$$-1 - 9 + 2x + 2 = 7x$$
$$-8 = 5x$$
$$\mathbf{-\frac{8}{5} = x}$$

21. $\dfrac{x^2 a}{3}\left(\dfrac{9a^{-1}}{x^2} - \dfrac{2xa^2}{xa}\right) = \dfrac{3x^2 aa^{-1}}{x^2} - \dfrac{2x^2 axa^2}{3xa}$
$$= \mathbf{3 - \frac{2x^2 a^2}{3}}$$

22. $\dfrac{-2a^0 p}{m}\left(\dfrac{mp}{a^{-2}} - \dfrac{2a^{-4}a}{p^2 m}\right)$
$$= \frac{-2a^0 pmp}{ma^{-2}} + \frac{4a^0 pa^{-4}a}{mp^2 m}$$
$$= \mathbf{-2a^2 p^2 + 4a^{-3}m^{-2}p^{-1}}$$

23. $\dfrac{xa^2(x^0 a^{-2})^4}{(2x^{-2})^{-2}} = \dfrac{4xa^{-6}}{x^4} = \mathbf{4x^{-3}a^{-6}}$

24. $\dfrac{m^2 pxx^{-4}(x^{-2})^2}{(3p^{-2})^{-2}xpx} = \dfrac{9m^2 px^{-7}}{p^5 x^2} = \mathbf{9m^2 p^{-4}x^{-9}}$

25. $xa - \dfrac{3x^2 a^3}{xa^2} + \dfrac{2x}{a^{-1}} = xa - 3xa + 2xa = \mathbf{0}$

26. $\dfrac{amp^{-1}}{m^{-1}} - \dfrac{3a^2 m^2}{pa} + \dfrac{5pa}{m^2}$
$$= am^2 p^{-1} - 3am^2 p^{-1} + 5pam^{-2}$$
$$= \mathbf{-2am^2 p^{-1} + 5pam^{-2}}$$

27. $-x^3 - x^2 - x(a - x)$
$$= -\left(-\frac{1}{2}\right)^3 - \left(-\frac{1}{2}\right)^2 - \left(-\frac{1}{2}\right)\left[2 - \left(-\frac{1}{2}\right)\right]$$
$$= \frac{1}{8} - \frac{1}{4} + \frac{1}{2}\left(2 + \frac{1}{2}\right) = \frac{1}{8} - \frac{1}{4} + \frac{1}{2}\left(\frac{5}{2}\right)$$
$$= \frac{1}{8} - \frac{2}{8} + \frac{10}{8} = \mathbf{\frac{9}{8}}$$

28. $a^2 - ax(x - ax) = 4^2 - 4(-3)[-3 - (4)(-3)]$
$$= 16 + 12(-3 + 12)$$
$$= 16 + 12(9) = \mathbf{124}$$

29. $\dfrac{1}{2^{-3}} - \dfrac{2}{-2^{-2}} - \dfrac{1}{(-2)^{-2}} - 2^0 = 8 + 8 - 4 - 1$

$\qquad = \mathbf{11}$

30. $3^0 - 2(-2) - |-2 - 4^0 - 3| = 1 + 4 - 6 = \mathbf{-1}$

PRACTICE SET 14

a.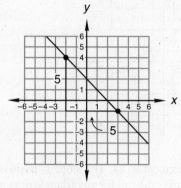

Slope $= -\dfrac{5}{5} = -1 \longrightarrow y = -x + b$

Using $(-2, 4),\qquad (4) = -(-2) + b$

$\qquad\qquad\qquad 4 = 2 + b$

$\qquad\qquad\qquad 2 = b$

The equation is $y = -x + 2.$

b. $\quad y = -\dfrac{2}{3}x + b$

$(6) = -\dfrac{2}{3}(-3) + b$

$\quad 6 = 2 + b$

$\quad 4 = b$

The equation is $y = -\dfrac{2}{3}x + 4.$

PROBLEM SET 14

1. $\dfrac{P}{100} \times of = is$

$\dfrac{260}{100} \times R = 6578$

$R = 6578 \times \dfrac{100}{260} = \mathbf{2530\ rats}$

2. $\dfrac{P}{100} \times of = is$

$\dfrac{350}{100} \times 4900 = S$

$S = \dfrac{350}{100} \times 4900 = \mathbf{17{,}150\ sheep}$

3. $\quad -3(2N + 7) = 3(-N) + 9$

$\qquad -6N - 21 = -3N + 9$

$\qquad\qquad -3N = 30$

$\qquad\qquad\quad N = \mathbf{-10}$

4. Odd integers: $N,\ N + 2,\ N + 4$

$4(N + 2 + N + 4) = 10N + 2$

$\qquad 8N + 24 = 10N + 2$

$\qquad\qquad -2N = -22$

$\qquad\qquad\quad N = 11$

The desired integers are **11, 13,** and **15.**

5. (a) $3x - 3y = 21$

(b) $2x - y = 12$

(b′) $y = 2x - 12$

Substitute (b′) into (a) and get:

(a) $3x - 3(2x - 12) = 21$

$\qquad 3x - 6x + 36 = 21$

$\qquad\qquad\quad -3x = -15$

$\qquad\qquad\qquad x = 5$

(b′) $y = 2(5) - 12 = -2$

(5, −2)

6. (a) $4x - y = 22$

(a′) $y = 4x - 22$

(b) $2x + 3y = 4$

Substitute (a′) into (b) and get:

(b) $2x + 3(4x - 22) = 4$

$\qquad 2x + 12x - 66 = 4$

$\qquad\qquad\qquad 14x = 70$

$\qquad\qquad\qquad\quad x = 5$

(a′) $y = 4(5) - 22 = -2$

(5, −2)

7. (a) $x + y = 28$

(a′) $y = -x + 28$

(b) $5x + 10y = 230$

Substitute (a′) into (b) and get:

(b) $5x + 10(-x + 28) = 230$

$\qquad 5x - 10x + 280 = 230$

$\qquad\qquad\qquad -5x = -50$

$\qquad\qquad\qquad\quad x = 10$

(a′) $y = -(10) + 28 = 18$

(10, 18)

8. (a) $x + y = 22$

    (a') $x = -y + 22$

    (b) $100x + 25y = 2050$

    Substitute (a') into (b) and get:

    (b) $100(-y + 22) + 25y = 2050$

    $-100y + 2200 + 25y = 2050$

    $-75y = -150$

    $y = 2$

    (a') $x = -(2) + 22 = 20$

    (20, 2)

9. $x + \dfrac{x^2}{y} - \dfrac{3x}{cy^2} = \dfrac{cy^2 x}{cy^2} + \dfrac{cyx^2}{cy^2} - \dfrac{3x}{cy^2}$

    $= \dfrac{cy^2 x + cyx^2 - 3x}{cy^2}$

10. $\dfrac{m}{x} + 4 = \dfrac{m}{x} + \dfrac{4x}{x} = \dfrac{\boldsymbol{m + 4x}}{\boldsymbol{x}}$

11. $4 + \dfrac{c}{x} - cxy = \dfrac{4x}{x} + \dfrac{c}{x} - \dfrac{cx^2 y}{x}$

    $= \dfrac{\boldsymbol{4x + c - cx^2 y}}{\boldsymbol{x}}$

12. $9^2 = H^2 + 2^2$

    $81 = H^2 + 4$

    $77 = H^2$

    $\sqrt{77} = H$

    $\text{Area} = \dfrac{B \times H}{2} = \dfrac{(4 \times \sqrt{77})}{2} = \boldsymbol{2\sqrt{77} \text{ cm}^2}$

13.

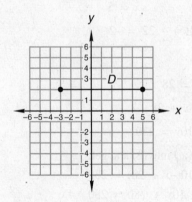

$D^2 = 8^2 + 0^2$

$D^2 = 64$

$D = \sqrt{64}$

$D = 8$

14. (a) $x = -4$

    (b) $3y + 2x = 6$

    $3y = -2x + 6$

    $y = -\dfrac{2}{3}x + 2$

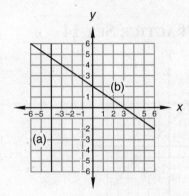

15. (a) The y-intercept is $+4$. The slope is positive and the rise over the run for any triangle drawn is $\frac{2}{3}$.

    $y = \dfrac{2}{3}x + 4$

    (b) Every point on this line is 4 units below the x-axis.

    $y = -4$

16. Graph the line to find the slope.

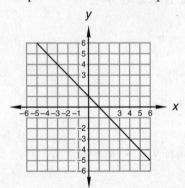

    $\text{Slope} = \dfrac{-1}{1} = -1$

    $y = -1x + b$

    $4 = -1(-3) + b$

    $1 = b$

    Since $m = -1$ and $b = 1$, $y = -x + 1$.

17. $y = -\dfrac{3}{4}x + b$

    $6 = -\dfrac{3}{4}(-4) + b$

    $3 = b$

    Since $m = -\dfrac{3}{4}$ and $b = 3$, $y = -\dfrac{3}{4}x + 3$.

18. $A + 134 = 180$

$\quad\quad\quad A = \textbf{46}$

$\quad B + 46 + 90 = 180$

$\quad\quad\quad\quad\quad B = \textbf{44}$

$\quad C + 44 = 180$

$\quad\quad\quad C = \textbf{136}$

19. $A = B = \dfrac{1}{2} \cdot 30 = 15$

$\quad A = B = \textbf{15}$

$\quad C + 150 = 180$

$\quad\quad\quad C = \textbf{30}$

Since the measure of an arc of a circle is the same as the measure of the central angle, $D = C = \textbf{30}$.

20. $2\dfrac{1}{4}x - \dfrac{3}{5} = -1\dfrac{1}{20}$

$\quad\quad\quad \dfrac{9}{4}x = -\dfrac{21}{20} + \dfrac{12}{20}$

$\quad\quad\quad x = -\dfrac{9}{20} \cdot \dfrac{4}{9} = -\dfrac{36}{180} = -\dfrac{\textbf{1}}{\textbf{5}}$

21. $0.005x - 0.05 = 0.5$

$\quad\quad 5x - 50 = 500$

$\quad\quad\quad 5x = 550$

$\quad\quad\quad\quad x = \textbf{110}$

22. $-2^0 - 3^2 = -2(x - 3^0) - 4(2x - 5)$

$\quad -1 - 9 = -2x + 2 - 8x + 20$

$\quad\quad -10 = -10x + 22$

$\quad\quad -32 = -10x$

$\quad\quad\quad x = \dfrac{\textbf{16}}{\textbf{5}}$

23. $\dfrac{-3^{-2}x}{y}\left(\dfrac{9y^0x}{-x} - \dfrac{3x}{y}\right) = \dfrac{xy^0x}{yx} + \dfrac{3xx}{9yy}$

$\quad = \dfrac{\textbf{x}}{\textbf{y}} + \dfrac{\textbf{x}^2}{\textbf{3y}^2}$

24. $\dfrac{(-2x)^{-2}xy^0y^2(x)^{-2}}{(x^2y)^{-2}xyxy^{-2}} = \dfrac{x^{-2}xy^2x^{-2}}{4x^{-4}y^{-2}xyxy^{-2}}$

$\quad = \dfrac{x^{-3}y^2}{4x^{-2}y^{-3}} = \dfrac{\textbf{y}^5}{\textbf{4x}}$

25. $mp^2\left(m^{-1}p^{-2} - \dfrac{4m}{p^2}\right) = mp^2m^{-1}p^{-2} - \dfrac{4mp^2m}{p^2}$

$\quad = \textbf{1} - \textbf{4m}^2$

26. $-\dfrac{3xy}{m} + \dfrac{7x^2x^{-1}m^{-1}}{y} - \dfrac{8m^{-1}x^{-1}}{x^{-2}y^{-1}}$

$\quad = -\dfrac{3xy}{m} + \dfrac{7x}{ym} - \dfrac{8xy}{m} = -\dfrac{\textbf{11xy}}{\textbf{m}} + \dfrac{\textbf{7x}}{\textbf{ym}}$

27. $x^2 - y - xy^2 = \left(-\dfrac{1}{3}\right)^2 - \dfrac{1}{2} - \left(-\dfrac{1}{3}\right)\left(\dfrac{1}{2}\right)^2$

$\quad = \dfrac{1}{9} - \dfrac{1}{2} + \dfrac{1}{12}$

$\quad = \dfrac{4}{36} - \dfrac{18}{36} + \dfrac{3}{36} = -\dfrac{\textbf{11}}{\textbf{36}}$

28. $a^2x - a(xa - a)$

$\quad = (-1)^2(-3) - (-1)[-3(-1) - (-1)]$

$\quad = -3 + 1(3 + 1) = -3 + 4 = \textbf{1}$

29. $-5^0(-2 - 3^0) - 2^2 - \dfrac{1}{(-2)^{-2}} = 3 - 4 - 4$

$\quad = \textbf{-5}$

30. $5 - |-2 - 3| - 4^0 - 2|-2^0| - 3$

$\quad = 5 - 5 - 1 - 2 - 3 = \textbf{-6}$

Practice Set 15

(a) $4x + 3y = 17$

(b) $-3x + 4y = 6$

$3(a)\quad 12x + 9y = 51$

$4(b)\quad \underline{-12x + 16y = 24}$

$\quad\quad\quad\quad\quad\quad 25y = 75$

$\quad\quad\quad\quad\quad\quad\quad y = 3$

$4x + 3(3) = 17$

$\quad\quad\quad 4x = 8$

$\quad\quad\quad\quad x = 2$

The solution is the ordered pair **(2, 3)**.

Check: $\quad -3x + 4y = 6$

$\quad\quad -3(2) + 4(3) = 6$

$\quad\quad\quad -6 + 12 = 6$

$\quad\quad\quad\quad\quad\quad 6 = 6$

Problem Set 15

1. $\dfrac{P}{100} \times of = is$

$\quad \dfrac{20}{100} \times P = 1400$

$\quad\quad\quad P = 1400 \times \dfrac{100}{20} = \textbf{7000 people}$

2. $\dfrac{WP}{100} \times of = is$

$\dfrac{WP}{100} \times 1000 = 200$

$WP = 200 \times \dfrac{100}{1000} = \mathbf{20\ percent}$

3. $5(-N) - 7 = 2N - 35$

$-5N - 7 = 2N - 35$

$-7N = -28$

$N = \mathbf{4}$

4. Integers: $N,\ N + 1,\ N + 2$

$-4(N + N + 2) = 7(-N - 1) + 12$

$-8N - 8 = -7N + 5$

$-N = 13$

$N = -13$

The desired integers are **–13, –12,** and **–11.**

5. (a) $3x + y = 11$

(b) $3x - 2y = 2$

2(a) $6x + 2y = 22$

 (b) $\underline{3x - 2y = 2}$

$9x \qquad = 24$

$x = \dfrac{8}{3}$

(a) $3\left(\dfrac{8}{3}\right) + y = 11$

$8 + y = 11$

$y = 3$

$\left(\dfrac{8}{3}, 3\right)$

6. (a) $3x + 4y = 20$

(b) $-4x + 3y = 15$

4(a) $12x + 16y = 80$

3(b) $\underline{-12x + 9y = 45}$

$25y = 125$

$y = 5$

(a) $3x + 4(5) = 20$

$3x + 20 = 20$

$3x = 0$

$x = 0$

(0, 5)

7. (a) $3x + y = 16$

(a′) $y = -3x + 16$

(b) $2x - 3y = -4$

Substitute (a′) into (b) and get:

(b) $2x - 3(-3x + 16) = -4$

$2x + 9x - 48 = -4$

$11x = 44$

$x = 4$

(a′) $y = -3(4) + 16 = 4$

(4, 4)

8. (a) $x + 3y = -9$

(a′) $x = -3y - 9$

(b) $5x - 2y = 23$

Substitute (a′) into (b) and get:

(b) $5(-3y - 9) - 2y = 23$

$-15y - 45 - 2y = 23$

$-17y = 68$

$y = -4$

(a′) $x = -3(-4) - 9 = 3$

(3, –4)

9. $y + \dfrac{x}{a^2} - \dfrac{mx}{3y^2} = \dfrac{3a^2y^3}{3a^2y^2} + \dfrac{3xy^2}{3a^2y^2} - \dfrac{a^2mx}{3a^2y^2}$

$= \dfrac{3a^2y^3 + 3xy^2 - a^2mx}{3a^2y^2}$

10. $4 - \dfrac{3a}{x} = \dfrac{4x}{x} - \dfrac{3a}{x} = \dfrac{4x - 3a}{x}$

11. $c + \dfrac{c^2}{x} + ac^2 = \dfrac{cx}{x} + \dfrac{c^2}{x} + \dfrac{ac^2x}{x}$

$= \dfrac{cx + c^2 + ac^2x}{x}$

12. $c^2 = a^2 + b^2$

$m^2 = 4^2 + 8^2$

$m^2 = 16 + 64$

$m^2 = 80$

$m = \sqrt{80} = \mathbf{4\sqrt{5}}$

13.

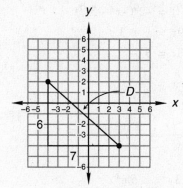

$D^2 = 6^2 + 7^2$

$D^2 = 36 + 49$

$D^2 = 85$

$D = \sqrt{85}$

14. (a) $y = -3$

(b) $3x - 4y = 8$

$-4y = -3x + 8$

$y = \dfrac{3}{4}x - 2$

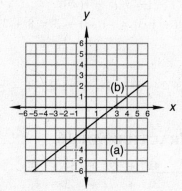

15. (a) Every point on this line is $\frac{9}{2}$ units above the x-axis.

$y = \dfrac{9}{2}$

(b) The y-intercept is -1. The slope is negative and the rise over the run for any triangle drawn is $-\frac{2}{3}$.

$y = -\dfrac{2}{3}x - 1$

16. Graph the line to find the slope.

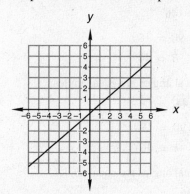

$\text{Slope} = \dfrac{-5}{-6} = \dfrac{5}{6}$

$y = \dfrac{5}{6}x + b$

$-2 = \dfrac{5}{6}(-2) + b$

$-2 = \dfrac{-10}{6} + b$

$\dfrac{5}{3} - \dfrac{6}{3} = b$

$-\dfrac{1}{3} = b$

Since $m = \dfrac{5}{6}$ and $b = -\dfrac{1}{3}$,

$y = \dfrac{5}{6}x - \dfrac{1}{3}$

17. $y = -\dfrac{1}{7}x + b$

$5 = -\dfrac{1}{7}(-2) + b$

$5 = \dfrac{2}{7} + b$

$-\dfrac{2}{7} + \dfrac{35}{7} = b$

$\dfrac{33}{7} = b$

Since $m = -\dfrac{1}{7}$ and $b = \dfrac{33}{7}$,

$y = -\dfrac{1}{7}x + \dfrac{33}{7}$

18. $A + 134 = 180$

$A = \textbf{46}$

$B + 46 + 90 = 180$

$B = \textbf{44}$

Since vertical angles are equal angles,

$C = B = \textbf{44.}$

$k + 44 + 90 = 180$

$k = \textbf{46}$

Since vertical angles are equal angles,

$y = k = \textbf{46.}$

19. $A + B + 140 = 180$

$A + B = 40$

Since angles opposite equal sides are equal angles,

$A = B = \textbf{20.}$

$C + 140 = 180$

$C = \textbf{40}$

Since the measure of an arc of a circle is the same as the measure of the central angle, $D = C = \textbf{40.}$

20. $3x + 2 = \dfrac{9x - 17}{2}$

$6x + 4 = 9x - 17$

$-3x = -21$

$x = \textbf{7}$

$P = 3(7) + 2 = \textbf{23}$

21. $\dfrac{-3x^{-1}y^2}{p}\left(\dfrac{-px}{y^2} - \dfrac{3x^2 y}{p^{-3}}\right)$

$= \dfrac{3x^{-1}y^2 px}{py^2} + \dfrac{9x^{-1}y^2 x^2 y}{pp^{-3}} = \textbf{3} + \textbf{9}xy^3p^2$

22. $3\dfrac{2}{5}x - \dfrac{4}{5} = 7\dfrac{3}{10}$

$\dfrac{17}{5}x = \dfrac{73}{10} + \dfrac{8}{10}$

$\dfrac{17}{5}x = \dfrac{81}{10}$

$x = \dfrac{81}{10} \cdot \dfrac{5}{17} = \dfrac{405}{170} = \dfrac{\textbf{81}}{\textbf{34}}$

23. $0.07x - 0.02 = 0.4$

$7x - 2 = 40$

$7x = 42$

$x = \textbf{6}$

24. $-3x(-2 - 3^0) = -2^0(-x - 3x^0)$

$9x = x + 3$

$8x = 3$

$x = \dfrac{\textbf{3}}{\textbf{8}}$

25. $\dfrac{x^2 y^{-2} x^0(y^{-1})}{x^2 y^2(x^0)^2} = \dfrac{x^2 y^{-3}}{x^2 y^2} = \textbf{\textit{y}}^{-5}$

26. $\dfrac{8x^2 yy}{m^{-2}x^2} + \dfrac{3y^2}{m^{-2}} - \dfrac{5m^2 x^{-2}}{x^{-2}y^{-2}}$

$= 8m^2 y^2 + 3m^2 y^2 - 5m^2 y^2 = \textbf{6}m^2 y^2$

27. $axy - a^2 x = \left(-\dfrac{1}{2}\right)(3)\left(-\dfrac{1}{3}\right) - \left(-\dfrac{1}{2}\right)^2 (3)$

$= \dfrac{1}{2} - \dfrac{3}{4} = \dfrac{2}{4} - \dfrac{3}{4} = -\dfrac{\textbf{1}}{\textbf{4}}$

28. $a^0(a^0 x - ax) = (-2)^0[(-2)^0(-3) - (-2)(-3)]$

$= 1(-3 - 6) = \textbf{--9}$

29. $-2^0(2^0 - 3^2) - [-2 - 3 - (-2)]$

$= -1(1 - 9) - [-3] = -1(-8) + 3 = 8 + 3$

$= \textbf{11}$

30. $3^0 - \dfrac{3}{3^{-2}} + 2 - 5^0 = 1 - 27 + 2 - 1 = \textbf{--25}$

PRACTICE SET 16

$$x - 3 \overline{)\,4x^3 - 3x^2 + 7x + 3} \quad\begin{array}{r} 4x^2 + 9x + 34 + \frac{105}{x-3} \end{array}$$

$\underline{4x^3 - 12x^2}$

$9x^2 + 7x$

$\underline{9x^2 - 27x}$

$34x + 3$

$\underline{34x - 102}$

105

Check:

$\dfrac{4x^2(x - 3)}{x - 3} + \dfrac{9x(x - 3)}{x - 3} + \dfrac{34(x - 3)}{x - 3}$

$+ \dfrac{105}{x - 3}$

$= \dfrac{4x^3 - 12x^2 + 9x^2}{x - 3}$

$+ \dfrac{-27x + 34x - 102 + 105}{x - 3}$

$= \dfrac{4x^3 - 3x^2 + 7x + 3}{x - 3}$

PROBLEM SET 16

1. $F \times of = is$

$$2\frac{1}{7} \times AN = 900$$

$$AN = 900 \times \frac{7}{15} = \textbf{420}$$

2. $WD \times of = is$

$$0.016 \times 420{,}000 = D$$

6720 microbes $= D$

3. If 14% were uninvited, 86% had been invited.

$$\frac{P}{100} \times of = is$$

$$\frac{86}{100} \times GA = 903$$

$$GA = 903 \times \frac{100}{86} = \textbf{1050 guests}$$

4. $\dfrac{P}{100} \times of = is$

$$\frac{40}{100} \times C = 8600$$

$$C = 8600 \times \frac{100}{40} = 21{,}500$$

$$N_P = 21{,}500 - N_M = 21{,}500 - 8600$$

$$= \textbf{12,900}$$

5. (a) $4x - 3y = -1$

(b) $2x + 5y = 19$

$\begin{array}{ll} 1(a) & 4x - 3y = -1 \\ -2(b) & \underline{-4x - 10y = -38} \\ & -13y = -39 \\ & y = 3 \end{array}$

(b) $2x + 5(3) = 19$

$$2x = 4$$

$$x = 2$$

(2, 3)

6. (a) $7x - 2y = 13$

(b) $4x + 7y = 40$

$\begin{array}{ll} 7(a) & 49x - 14y = 91 \\ 2(b) & \underline{8x + 14y = 80} \\ & 57x = 171 \\ & x = 3 \end{array}$

(b) $4(3) + 7y = 40$

$$7y = 28$$

$$y = 4$$

(3, 4)

7. (a) $3x + y = 2$

(a') $y = -3x + 2$

(b) $2x - 5y = 7$

Substitute (a') into (b) and get:

(b) $2x - 5(-3x + 2) = 7$

$$2x + 15x - 10 = 7$$

$$17x = 17$$

$$x = 1$$

(a') $y = -3(1) + 2 = -1$

(1, –1)

8. (a) $x - 3y = 4$

(a') $x = 3y + 4$

(b) $4x - 7y = 16$

Substitute (a') into (b) and get:

(b) $4(3y + 4) - 7y = 16$

$$12y + 16 - 7y = 16$$

$$5y = 0$$

$$y = 0$$

(a') $x = 3(0) + 4 = 4$

(4, 0)

9. $(2x + 3)(2x^2 - 4x + 3)$

$$= 4x^3 - 8x^2 + 6x + 6x^2 - 12x + 9$$

$$= \textbf{4x}^{\textbf{3}} - \textbf{2x}^{\textbf{2}} - \textbf{6x} + \textbf{9}$$

10.

$$x - 3 \overline{\smash{\big)}\, 4x^3 - 2x^2 + 4x + 2} \quad \frac{4x^2 + 10x + 34}{} + \frac{104}{x-3}$$

$$\underline{4x^3 - 12x^2}$$
$$10x^2 + 4x$$
$$\underline{10x^2 - 30x}$$
$$34x + 2$$
$$\underline{34x - 102}$$
$$104$$

Check:

$$\frac{4x^2(x-3)}{x-3} + \frac{10x(x-3)}{x-3} + \frac{34(x-3)}{x-3}$$

$$+ \frac{104}{x-3} = \frac{4x^3 - 2x^2 + 4x + 2}{x-3}$$

11.

$$x - 4 \overline{\smash{\big)}\, x^3 + 0x^2 + 0x - 8} \quad \frac{x^2 + 4x + 16}{} + \frac{56}{x-4}$$

$$\underline{x^3 - 4x^2}$$
$$4x^2 + 0x$$
$$\underline{4x^2 - 16x}$$
$$16x - 8$$
$$\underline{16x - 64}$$
$$56$$

Check:

$$\frac{x^2(x-4)}{x-4} + \frac{4x(x-4)}{x-4}$$

$$+ \frac{16(x-4)}{x-4} + \frac{56}{x-4}$$

$$= \frac{x^3 - 4x^2 + 4x^2 - 16x + 16x - 8}{x-4}$$

$$= \frac{x^3 - 8}{x-4}$$

12. $2 + \dfrac{a}{2x^2} = \dfrac{4x^2}{2x^2} + \dfrac{a}{2x^2} = \dfrac{4x^2 + a}{2x^2}$

13. $\dfrac{4}{cx} + c - \dfrac{3}{4c^2x} = \dfrac{16c}{4c^2x} + \dfrac{4c^3x}{4c^2x} - \dfrac{3}{4c^2x}$

$$= \frac{16c + 4c^3x - 3}{4c^2x}$$

14. $2^2 = H^2 + 1^2$

$$4 = H^2 + 1$$
$$3 = H^2$$
$$\sqrt{3} = H$$

Area $= \dfrac{b \times H}{2} = \dfrac{2 \times \sqrt{3}}{2} = \sqrt{3}$ **in.^{2}**

15.

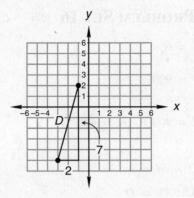

$$D^2 = 7^2 + 2^2$$
$$D^2 = 49 + 4$$
$$D^2 = 53$$
$$D = \sqrt{53}$$

16. (a) $x = -2\dfrac{1}{2}$

(b) $x - 3y = 6$

$$-3y = -x + 6$$
$$y = \frac{1}{3}x - 2$$

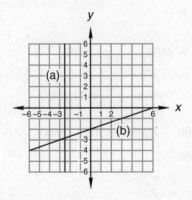

17. (a) Every point on this line is 4 units below the x-axis.

$$y = -4$$

(b) The y-intercept is $+3$. The slope is negative and the rise over the run for any triangle drawn is $-\frac{1}{2}$.

$$y = -\frac{1}{2}x + 3$$

18. Graph the line to find the slope.

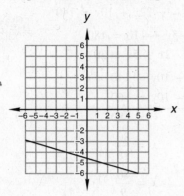

$$\text{Slope} = \frac{+2}{-7} = -\frac{2}{7}$$

$$y = -\frac{2}{7}x + b$$

$$-4 = -\frac{2}{7}(-2) + b$$

$$-4 = \frac{4}{7} + b$$

$$-\frac{28}{7} - \frac{4}{7} = b$$

$$-\frac{32}{7} = b$$

Since $m = -\frac{2}{7}$ and $b = -\frac{32}{7}$,

$$y = -\frac{2}{7}x - \frac{32}{7}.$$

19.
$$y = \frac{3}{5}x + b$$

$$1 = \frac{3}{5}(-4) + b$$

$$1 = -\frac{12}{5} + b$$

$$\frac{5}{5} + \frac{12}{5} = b$$

$$\frac{17}{5} = b$$

Since $m = \frac{3}{5}$ and $b = \frac{17}{5}$,

$$y = \frac{3}{5}x + \frac{17}{5}.$$

20. $\text{Area}_S = \pi r_S^2 = \pi \text{ cm}^2$

$r_S = \mathbf{1\ cm}$

$r_L = 2r_S = \mathbf{2\ cm}$

$\text{Area}_L = \pi r_L^2 = \pi(2 \text{ cm})^2 = \mathbf{4\pi\ cm^2}$

21. *S*ince angles opposite equal sides are equal angles,

$A = \mathbf{30.}$

$B + 30 + 30 = 180$
$\quad B = \mathbf{120}$

$C + 120 = 180$
$\quad C = \mathbf{60}$

Since the measure of an arc of a circle is the same as the measure of the central angle, $D = C = \mathbf{60.}$

22. $3\frac{1}{2}x - \frac{1}{5} = 3\frac{3}{20}$

$$\frac{7}{2}x = \frac{63}{20} + \frac{4}{20}$$

$$\frac{7}{2}x = \frac{67}{20}$$

$$x = \frac{67}{20} \cdot \frac{2}{7} = \frac{134}{140} = \mathbf{\frac{67}{70}}$$

23. $0.05m - 0.05 = 0.5$

$5m - 5 = 50$

$5m = 55$

$m = \mathbf{11}$

24. $-4(-x - 2) - 3(-2 - 4) = -4^0(x - 2)$

$4x + 8 + 18 = -x + 2$

$5x = -24$

$x = \mathbf{-\frac{24}{5}}$

25.
$$\frac{3^{-2}x^{-2}y}{z}\left(\frac{18x^2z}{y} - \frac{3xyz^2}{x}\right)$$
$$= \frac{2x^{-2}yx^2z}{zy} - \frac{x^{-2}yxyz^2}{3xz} = \mathbf{2 - \frac{y^2z}{3x^2}}$$

26.
$$\frac{3^{-2}x^0(x^{-2}y^4)^{-3}}{xxy^2y^0(y^3)^{-4}} = \frac{x^6y^{-12}}{9x^2y^{-10}} = \mathbf{\frac{x^4}{9y^2}}$$

27.
$$\frac{3x^2xxy}{y^{-4}} - \frac{2x^2}{(x^{-1})^2y^{-5}} - \frac{7xxyx^2}{(y^{-2})^2}$$
$$= 3x^4y^5 - 2x^4y^5 - 7x^4y^5 = \mathbf{-6x^4y^5}$$

28. $p^2 - xp - x(p - x)$

$= \left(\dfrac{1}{2}\right)^2 - (-2)\left(\dfrac{1}{2}\right) - (-2)\left(\dfrac{1}{2} - (-2)\right)$

$= \dfrac{1}{4} + 1 + 2\left(\dfrac{5}{2}\right) = \dfrac{1}{4} + \dfrac{4}{4} + \dfrac{20}{4} = \dfrac{\mathbf{25}}{\mathbf{4}}$

29. $-2^0(-2 - 3) - (-2)^0$
$\quad - 2[-1 - (-3 - 7) - 2(-5 + 3)]$

$= 5 - 1 - 2[-1 + 10 + 4]$

$= 5 - 1 - 2[13] = 5 - 1 - 26 = \mathbf{-22}$

30. $2^0 - \dfrac{27}{3^2} - 3^1 - 3^0 - |-3^0 - 2| - (-3)$

$= 1 - 3 - 3 - 1 - 3 + 3 = \mathbf{-6}$

PRACTICE SET 17

a. $-5\text{(a)}\quad -5N_N - 5N_O = -300$
$\quad\ \ \text{(b)}\quad \underline{\ 5N_N + 10N_O = \ \ 310\ }$
$\qquad\qquad\qquad\quad 5N_O = \ \ 10$
$\qquad\qquad\qquad\qquad N_O = 2$

$N_N + (2) = 60$
$\qquad N_N = \mathbf{58}$

b. $R_M = 50$

$R_W = 70$

$T_M = 5 - T_W$

$\qquad R_M T_M + R_W T_W = 380$

$(50)(5 - T_W) + (70)T_W = 380$

$\quad 250 - 50T_W + 70T_W = 380$

$\qquad\qquad\qquad 20T_W = 130$

$\qquad\qquad\qquad\quad T_W = \dfrac{\mathbf{13}}{\mathbf{2}}$

$T_M = 5 - \left(\dfrac{13}{2}\right)$

$T_M = \dfrac{10}{2} - \dfrac{13}{2}$

$T_M = -\dfrac{\mathbf{3}}{\mathbf{2}}$

c. $20x + 5y + 40 + 2x + 5y = 180$
$\qquad\qquad 22x + 10y = 140$
$\quad 40 + 2x + 5y + 110 = 180$
$\qquad\qquad\quad 2x + 5y = 30$

$\quad\ \text{(a)}\ \ 22x + 10y = 140$
$-2\text{(b)}\ \ \underline{-4x - 10y = -60\ }$
$\qquad\quad 18x \qquad\quad = \ \ 80$

$\qquad\qquad x = \dfrac{80}{18}$

$\qquad\qquad x = \dfrac{\mathbf{40}}{\mathbf{9}}$

$2\left(\dfrac{40}{9}\right) + 5y = 30$

$\qquad\qquad 5y = 30 - \dfrac{80}{9}$

$\qquad\qquad\ y = \dfrac{190}{9} \cdot \dfrac{1}{5}$

$\qquad\qquad\ y = \dfrac{\mathbf{38}}{\mathbf{9}}$

PROBLEM SET 17

1. If $\frac{2}{5}$ doubted, then $\frac{3}{5}$ were nondoubters.
$\quad F \times of = is$

$\qquad \dfrac{3}{5} \times S = 600$

$\qquad S = 600 \times \dfrac{5}{3} = \mathbf{1000\ students}$

2. $F \times of = is$

$\qquad \dfrac{7}{13} \times T = 210$

$\qquad T = 210 \times \dfrac{13}{7} = \mathbf{390\ teachers}$

3. $\dfrac{P}{100} \times of = is$

$\qquad \dfrac{360}{100} \times 400 = S$

$\qquad\qquad S = \mathbf{1440\ skeptics}$

4. Integers: $N, N + 1, N + 2$

$\quad 7(N + 1 + N + 2) = 10N + 109$

$\qquad\quad 14N + 21 = 10N + 109$

$\qquad\qquad\quad 4N = 88$

$\qquad\qquad\quad\ N = 22$

The desired integers are **22, 23,** and **24.**

5. (a) $N_N + N_D = 150$

(b) $5N_N + 10N_D = 450$

$-5(a)$ $-5N_N - 5N_D = -750$

$1(b)$ $\underline{5N_N + 10N_D = 450}$

$5N_D = -300$

$N_D = \mathbf{-60}$

(a) $N_N + (-60) = 150$

$N_N = \mathbf{210}$

6. (a) $N_P + N_D = 50$

(b) $N_P + 10N_D = 140$

(b') $N_P = -10N_D + 140$

Substitute (b') into (a) and get:

(a) $(-10N_D + 140) + N_D = 50$

$-9N_D = -90$

$N_D = \mathbf{10}$

(a) $N_P + (10) = 50$

$N_P = \mathbf{40}$

7. $(2x + 3)(2x^2 + 2x + 2)$

$= 4x^3 + 4x^2 + 4x + 6x^2 + 6x + 6$

$= \mathbf{4x^3 + 10x^2 + 10x + 6}$

8.
$$
x + 1 \overline{\smash{\big)}\,\begin{aligned}3x^2 - 3x + 3 - \tfrac{5}{x+1}\\[2pt] 3x^3 + 0x^2 + 0x - 2\end{aligned}}
$$

$\underline{3x^3 + 3x^2}$

$-3x^2 + 0x$

$\underline{-3x^2 - 3x}$

$3x - 2$

$\underline{3x + 3}$

-5

Check:

$\dfrac{3x^2(x+1)}{x+1} - \dfrac{3x(x+1)}{x+1}$

$+ \dfrac{3(x+1)}{x+1} - \dfrac{5}{x+1}$

$= \dfrac{3x^3 + 3x^2 - 3x^2 - 3x + 3x - 2}{x+1}$

$= \dfrac{3x^3 - 2}{x+1}$

9. (a) $R_M T_M + R_W T_W = 250$

(b) $R_M = 50$

(c) $R_W = 80$

(d) $T_M + T_W = 5$

$T_M = 5 - T_W$

Substitute (b) and (c) into (a) and get:

(a') $50T_M + 80T_W = 250$

Substitute $T_M = 5 - T_W$ into (a') and get:

(a'') $50(5 - T_W) + 80T_W = 250$

$250 - 50T_W + 80T_W = 250$

$30T_W = 0$

$T_W = \mathbf{0}$

$T_M = 5 - T_W$

$T_M = \mathbf{5}$

10. (a) $R_E T_E = R_W T_W$

(b) $R_E = 200$

(c) $R_W = 250$

(d) $9 - T_E = T_W$

Substitute (b) and (c) into (a) and get:

(a') $200T_E = 250T_W$

Substitute (d) into (a') and get:

(a'') $200T_E = 250(9 - T_E)$

$200T_E = 2250 - 250T_E$

$450T_E = 2250$

$T_E = \mathbf{5}$

$T_W = 9 - T_E$

$T_W = \mathbf{4}$

11. (a) $R_M T_M = R_R T_R$

(b) $R_M = 8$

(c) $R_R = 2$

(d) $5 - T_M = T_R$

Substitute (b) and (c) into (a) and get:

(a') $8T_M = 2T_R$

Substitute (d) into (a') and get:

(a'') $8T_M = 2(5 - T_M)$

$8T_M = 10 - 2T_M$

$10T_M = 10$

$T_M = \mathbf{1}$

$T_R = 5 - T_M$

$T_R = \mathbf{4}$

12. $4x + \dfrac{3x}{a} = \dfrac{4ax}{a} + \dfrac{3x}{a} = \boxed{\dfrac{4ax + 3x}{a}}$

13. $-\dfrac{2x}{y} - cx + \dfrac{7x^2 y}{np^2}$

$= \dfrac{-2np^2 x}{np^2 y} - \dfrac{cnp^2 xy}{np^2 y} + \dfrac{7x^2 y^2}{np^2 y}$

$= \boxed{\dfrac{-2np^2 x - cnp^2 xy + 7x^2 y^2}{np^2 y}}$

14. $7^2 = H^2 + 6^2$

$49 = H^2 + 36$

$13 = H^2$

$\sqrt{13} = H$

Area $= \dfrac{b \times H}{2} = \dfrac{12 \text{ m} \times \sqrt{13} \text{ m}}{2}$

$= \mathbf{6\sqrt{13} \text{ m}^2}$

15.

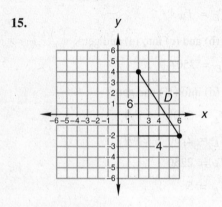

$D^2 = 6^2 + 4^2$

$D^2 = 36 + 16$

$D^2 = 52$

$D = \sqrt{52}$

$D = \mathbf{2\sqrt{13}}$

16. (a) $y = -3$

(b) $3x - 5y = 10$

$y = \dfrac{3}{5}x - 2$

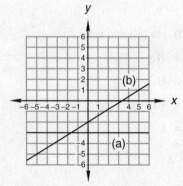

17. (a) The y-intercept is –2. The slope is negative and the rise over the run for any triangle drawn is –2.

$\mathbf{y = -2x - 2}$

(b) Every point on this line is 4 units to the right of the y-axis.

$\mathbf{x = 4}$

18. Graph the line to find the slope.

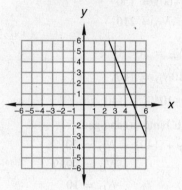

Slope $= \dfrac{-5}{+2} = -\dfrac{5}{2}$

$y = -\dfrac{5}{2}x + b$

$2 = -\dfrac{5}{2}(4) + b$

$12 = b$

Since $m = -\dfrac{5}{2}$ and $b = 12$, $\mathbf{y = -\dfrac{5}{2}x + 12.}$

19. $y = -\dfrac{2}{7}x + b$

$5 = -\dfrac{2}{7}(-3) + b$

$b = -\dfrac{6}{7} + \dfrac{35}{7} = \dfrac{29}{7}$

Since $m = -\dfrac{2}{7}$ and $b = \dfrac{29}{7}$, $\mathbf{y = -\dfrac{2}{7}x + \dfrac{29}{7}.}$

20. $(2x + 10y) + (-2x + 6y) + 60 = 180$

$16y = 120$

$y = \dfrac{15}{2}$

Since vertical angles are equal angles,

$-2x + 6y = 50$

$-2x + 6\left(\dfrac{15}{2}\right) = 50$

$-2x = 5$

$x = -\dfrac{5}{2}$

$$z = 2x + 10y$$
$$z = 2\left(-\frac{5}{2}\right) + 10\left(\frac{15}{2}\right)$$
$$z = -5 + 75 = \mathbf{70}$$

21. Volume $= \pi r^2 l = 245\pi \text{ cm}^3$
$$l = \frac{245\pi \text{ cm}^3}{(5 \text{ cm})^2 \pi}$$
$$l = \frac{\mathbf{49}}{\mathbf{5}} \text{ cm}$$

22. $2\frac{1}{5}x - 3\frac{1}{4} = \frac{7}{20}$
$$\frac{11}{5}x = \frac{7}{20} + \frac{65}{20}$$
$$x = \frac{72}{20} \cdot \frac{5}{11} = \frac{360}{220} = \frac{\mathbf{18}}{\mathbf{11}}$$

23. $0.003 - 0.03 + 0.3x = 3.3$
$$3 - 30 + 300x = 3300$$
$$300x = 3327$$
$$x = \frac{1109}{100} = \mathbf{11.09}$$

24. $3^0(2x - 5) + (-x - 5) = -3(x^0 - 2)$
$$2x - 5 - x - 5 = -3 + 6$$
$$x = \mathbf{13}$$

25. $\dfrac{x^0 y^{-2} x}{x^3 y}\left(\dfrac{x^2 y}{m} - \dfrac{3x^4 y^2}{m^{-2}}\right)$
$$= \frac{x^3 y^{-1}}{x^3 ym} - \frac{3x^5}{x^3 ym^{-2}} = \frac{\mathbf{1}}{\mathbf{y^2 m}} - \frac{\mathbf{3x^2 m^2}}{\mathbf{y}}$$

26. $\dfrac{2^{-3} x^0 (x^2)}{x^{-3} x y^{-3} y} = \dfrac{x^2}{8x^{-2} y^{-2}} = \dfrac{\mathbf{x^4 y^2}}{\mathbf{8}}$

27. $\dfrac{xy}{y^{-2}} - \dfrac{3x^4 y^4}{x^3 y} + \dfrac{7xy^{-2}}{xy^{-3}} = xy^3 - 3xy^3 + 7y$
$$= \mathbf{-2xy^3 + 7y}$$

28. $xy - x(x - y^0) = 2\left(-\dfrac{1}{2}\right) - 2\left(2 - \left(-\dfrac{1}{2}\right)^0\right)$
$$= -1 - 2(1) = \mathbf{-3}$$

29. $-(-3 - 2) + 4(-2) + \dfrac{1}{-2^{-3}} - (-2)^{-3}$
$$= 5 - 8 - 8 + \frac{1}{8} = \mathbf{-10\frac{7}{8}}$$

30. $-|-2 - 7| - |-2 - 4| - 3|-2 + 7|$
$$= -9 - 6 - 3(5) = \mathbf{-30}$$

PRACTICE SET 18

a. Total $= 3 + 11 = 14$
$$\frac{3}{14} = \frac{M}{350}$$
$$14M = 1050$$
$$M = \mathbf{75 \text{ malefactors}}$$

b. $NS = 4000 - 800 = 3200$
$$\frac{3200}{4000} = \frac{NS}{5000}$$
$$4000NS = 16,000,000$$
$$NS = \mathbf{4000 \text{ kg}}$$

c. $4\overrightarrow{SF} = 9$
$$\overrightarrow{SF} = \frac{9}{4}$$
$$a = 5\left(\frac{9}{4}\right)$$
$$a = \frac{\mathbf{45}}{\mathbf{4}}$$
$$b = 6\left(\frac{9}{4}\right)$$
$$b = \frac{\mathbf{27}}{\mathbf{2}}$$

PROBLEM SET 18

1.
$$\frac{2}{21} = \frac{A}{420}$$
$$2 \cdot 420 = 21A$$
$$840 = 21A$$
$$\mathbf{40 \text{ Arabians}} = A$$

2.
$$\frac{2500}{3000} = \frac{NS}{6000}$$
$$2500 \cdot 6000 = 3000NS$$
$$\mathbf{5000 \text{ kg}} = NS$$

3. $\dfrac{P}{100} \times of = is$
$$\frac{27}{100} \times N = 54,000$$
$$N = 54,000 \times \frac{100}{27} = \mathbf{200,000 \text{ natives}}$$

4. $\dfrac{P}{100} \times of = is$

$\dfrac{0.004}{100} \times TP = 40$

$TP = 40 \times \dfrac{100}{0.004} = \mathbf{1{,}000{,}000}$

5. (a) $N_D + N_Q = 200$

(b) $10N_D + 25N_Q = 2750$

-10(a) $\quad -10N_D - 10N_Q = -2000$

1(b) $\quad\underline{10N_D + 25N_Q = 2750}$

$15N_Q = 750$

$N_Q = \mathbf{50}$

(a) $N_D + (50) = 200$

$N_D = \mathbf{150}$

6. (a) $N_P + N_D = 30$

(b) $N_P + 10N_D = 291$

Substitute $N_P = 30 - N_D$ into (b) and get:

(b′) $(30 - N_D) + 10N_D = 291$

$9N_D = 261$

$N_D = \mathbf{29}$

(a) $N_P + (29) = 30$

$N_P = \mathbf{1}$

7. $(2x + 4)(3x^2 - 2x - 10)$

$= 6x^3 - 4x^2 - 20x + 12x^2 - 8x - 40$

$= \mathbf{6x^3 + 8x^2 - 28x - 40}$

8.
$$x - 2 \overline{\smash{\big)}\,5x^3 + 0x^2 + 0x - 1} \quad \frac{5x^2 + 10x + 20}{} + \frac{39}{x-2}$$

$\underline{5x^3 - 10x^2}$

$10x^2 + 0x$

$\underline{10x^2 - 20x}$

$20x - 1$

$\underline{20x - 40}$

39

Check:

$\dfrac{5x^2(x - 2)}{x - 2} + \dfrac{10x(x - 2)}{x - 2} + \dfrac{20(x - 2)}{x - 2}$

$+ \dfrac{39}{x - 2} = \dfrac{5x^3 - 10x^2 + 10x^2}{x - 2}$

$+ \dfrac{-20x + 20x - 40 + 39}{x - 2} = \dfrac{5x^3 - 1}{x - 2}$

9. (a) $R_F T_F = R_S T_S$

(b) $T_S = 6$

(c) $T_F = 5$

(d) $R_F - 16 = RS$

Substitute (b) and (c) into (a) and get:

(a′) $5R_F = 6R_S$

Substitute (d) into (a′) and get:

(a″) $5R_F = 6(R_F - 16)$

$5R_F = 6R_F - 96$

$R_F = \mathbf{96}$

(d) $(96) - 16 = R_S = \mathbf{80}$

10. (a) $R_M T_M = R_R T_R$

(b) $R_M = 8$

(c) $R_R = 2$

(d) $T_R = 5 - T_M$

Substitute (b) and (c) into (a) and get:

(a′) $8T_M = 2T_R$

Substitute (d) into (a′) and get:

(a″) $8T_M = 2(5 - T_M)$

$8T_M = 10 - 2T_M$

$10T_M = 10$

$T_M = \mathbf{1}$

(d) $T_R = 5 - T_M$

$T_R = \mathbf{4}$

11. (a) $R_G T_G + R_B T_B = 100$

(b) $R_G = 4$

(c) $R_B = 10$

(d) $T_B = T_G + 3$

Substitute (b) and (c) into (a) and get:

(a′) $4T_G + 10T_B = 100$

Substitute (d) into (a′) and get:

(a″) $4T_G + 10(T_G + 3) = 100$

$4T_G + 10T_G + 30 = 100$

$14T_G = 70$

$T_G = \mathbf{5}$

(d) $T_B = T_G + 3$

$T_B = \mathbf{8}$

12. $7xyz + \dfrac{1}{xyz} = \dfrac{7x^2y^2z^2}{xyz} + \dfrac{1}{xyz}$

$= \dfrac{7x^2y^2z^2 + 1}{xyz}$

13. $-\dfrac{3x}{y} - c + \dfrac{7c}{xy^3} = \dfrac{-3x^2y^2}{xy^3} - \dfrac{cxy^3}{xy^3} + \dfrac{7c}{xy^3}$

$= \dfrac{-3x^2y^2 - cxy^3 + 7c}{xy^3}$

14. $\qquad 6^2 = H^2 + 5$

$\qquad 36 = H^2 + 25$

$\qquad 11 = H^2$

$\sqrt{11}\ \text{cm} = H$

$\text{Area} = \dfrac{b \times H}{2} = \dfrac{10\ \text{cm} \times \sqrt{11}\ \text{cm}}{2}$

$\qquad = \mathbf{5\sqrt{11}\ cm^2}$

15.

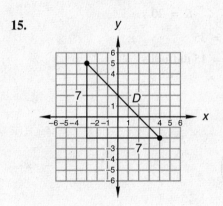

$D^2 = 7^2 + 7^2$

$D^2 = 49 + 49$

$D^2 = 98$

$\ D = \sqrt{98} = \mathbf{7\sqrt{2}}$

16. (a) $y = 2$

(b) $y = 2x$

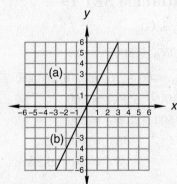

17. (a) Every point on this line is 3 units below the x-axis.

$\mathbf{y = -3}$

(b) The y-intercept is 0. The slope is negative and the rise over the run for any triangle drawn is -3.

$\mathbf{y = -3x}$

18. Graph the line to find the slope.

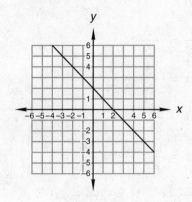

$\text{Slope} = \dfrac{-1}{1} = -1$

$y = -x + b$

$5 = -(-3) + b$

$2 = b$

Since $m = -1$ and $b = 2$, $\mathbf{y = -x + 2.}$

19. $\qquad\qquad y = \dfrac{5}{3}x + b$

$\qquad -2 = \dfrac{5}{3}(4) + b$

$\qquad -2 = \dfrac{20}{3} + b$

$-\dfrac{20}{3} - \dfrac{6}{3} = b$

$\qquad -\dfrac{26}{3} = b$

Since $m = \dfrac{5}{3}$ and $b = -\dfrac{26}{3}$, $\mathbf{y = \dfrac{5}{3}x - \dfrac{26}{3}.}$

20. $3 \times \overrightarrow{SF} = 9$

$\qquad \overrightarrow{SF} = 3$

$a = 4 \times \overrightarrow{SF}$

$a = 4(3) = \mathbf{12}$

$b = 5 \times \overrightarrow{SF}$

$b = 5(3) = \mathbf{15}$

21. $3x + 2 = \dfrac{5x + 10}{2}$

$6x + 4 = 5x + 10$

$x = \mathbf{6}$

$P = 3(6) + 2 = \mathbf{20}$

22. Area $= \dfrac{120}{360}(\pi r^2) = \dfrac{\pi(15\text{ ft})^2}{3} \approx \mathbf{235.5\ ft^2}$

23. $4\dfrac{1}{6}x - 2\dfrac{1}{12} = -\dfrac{5}{24}$

$\dfrac{25}{6}x = -\dfrac{5}{24} + \dfrac{50}{24}$

$\dfrac{25}{6}x = \dfrac{45}{24}$

$x = \dfrac{15}{8} \cdot \dfrac{6}{25} = \dfrac{90}{200} = \dfrac{\mathbf{9}}{\mathbf{20}}$

24. $-2\big[(x - 2) - 4x - 3\big] = -(-4 - 2x)$

$-2[-3x - 5] = 4 + 2x$

$6x + 10 = 4 + 2x$

$4x = -6$

$x = -\dfrac{\mathbf{3}}{\mathbf{2}}$

25. $\dfrac{3x^0 y^{-2}}{z^2}\left(\dfrac{2xyz^{-1}}{p} - \dfrac{y^2}{(3x)^{-2}}\right)$

$= \dfrac{6xy^{-1}z^{-1}}{z^2 p} - \dfrac{27}{z^2 x^{-2}} = \dfrac{\mathbf{6x}}{\mathbf{pyz^3}} - \dfrac{\mathbf{27x^2}}{\mathbf{z^2}}$

26. $\dfrac{a^0 xy^2 (a^2)^{-2} (xy^{-2})^2}{ax^0 (y^{-2})^2} = \dfrac{xy^2 a^{-4} x^2 y^{-4}}{ay^{-4}}$

$= \dfrac{\mathbf{x^3 y^2}}{\mathbf{a^5}}$

27. $-\dfrac{2x^2}{y^2} - \dfrac{5y^{-2}p^0}{x^{-2}} + \dfrac{7xxy}{y^3}$

$= -\dfrac{2x^2}{y^2} - \dfrac{5x^2}{y^2} + \dfrac{7x^2}{y^2} = \mathbf{0}$

28. $ax - a(a - x) = -\dfrac{1}{2}\left(\dfrac{1}{4}\right) - \left(-\dfrac{1}{2}\right)\left(-\dfrac{1}{2} - \dfrac{1}{4}\right)$

$= -\dfrac{1}{8} + \dfrac{1}{2}\left(-\dfrac{3}{4}\right) = -\dfrac{1}{8} - \dfrac{3}{8} = -\dfrac{4}{8} = -\dfrac{\mathbf{1}}{\mathbf{2}}$

29. $-2|-2 - 5| + (-3)|-2(-2) - 3| + 7$

$= -2(7) + (-3)(1) + 7 = -14 - 3 + 7 = \mathbf{-10}$

30. $-\dfrac{1}{(-2)^{-3}} + \dfrac{3}{-3^{-2}} = 8 - 27 = \mathbf{-19}$

PRACTICE SET 19

a. (a) $N + D = 80$

(b) $0.05N + 0.10D = 6.50$

$$
\begin{array}{ll}
-5\text{(a)} & -5N - 5D = -400 \\
100\text{(b)} & \underline{5N + 10D = 650} \\
 & 5D = 250 \\
 & D = \mathbf{50\ dimes}
\end{array}
$$

$N + (50) = 80$

$N = \mathbf{30\ nickels}$

b. (a) $R + D = 35$

(b) $12R + 4D = 300$

$$
\begin{array}{ll}
-4\text{(a)} & -4R - 4D = -140 \\
\text{(b)} & \underline{12R + 4D = 300} \\
 & 8R = 160 \\
 & R = 20
\end{array}
$$

$(20) + D = 35$

$D = \mathbf{15\ daffodils}$

c. $3\overrightarrow{SF} = 5$

$\overrightarrow{SF} = \dfrac{5}{3}$

$x = 5\left(\dfrac{5}{3}\right)$

$x = \dfrac{25}{3}$

$y = 4\left(\dfrac{5}{3}\right)$

$y = \dfrac{20}{3}$

PROBLEM SET 19

1. (a) $N_N + N_D = 60$

(b) $5N_N + 10N_D = 500$

Substitute $N_D = 60 - N_N$ into (b) and get:

(b′) $5N_N + 10(60 - N_N) = 500$

$5N_N + 600 - 10N_N = 500$

$-5N_N = -100$

$N_N = \mathbf{20\ nickels}$

(a) $(20) + N_D = 60$

$N_D = \mathbf{40\ dimes}$

2. (a) $N_C + N_M = 26$

(b) $7N_C + N_M = 86$

Substitute $N_M = 26 - N_C$ into (b) and get:

(b') $7N_C + (26 - N_C) = 86$

$$6N_C = 60$$

$$N_C = \textbf{10 codfish}$$

3. $\dfrac{33}{49} = \dfrac{NS}{294}$

$$49NS = 294(33)$$

$$NS = \textbf{198 tons}$$

4. If 19% was used, 81% remained.

$$\frac{P}{100} \times of = is$$

$$\frac{81}{100} \times NA = 1134$$

$$NA = 1134 \times \frac{100}{81}$$

$$NA = 1400$$

Beginning amount = **1400 liters**

Amount used = $1400 - 1134$

Amount used = **266 liters**

5. $(-7N - 7)2 = -5N + 4$

$$-14N - 14 = -5N + 4$$

$$-9N = 18$$

$$N = \textbf{-2}$$

6. (a) $5x + 25y = -160$

(b) $-3x + 2y = -23$

3(a) $\quad 15x + 75y = -480$

5(b) $\dfrac{-15x + 10y = -115}{}$

$$85y = -595$$

$$y = -7$$

(b) $-3x + 2(-7) = -23$

$$-3x = -9$$

$$x = 3$$

(3, –7)

7. $(x^2 - 2)(x^3 - 2x^2 - 2x + 4)$

$= x^5 - 2x^4 - 2x^3 + 4x^2 - 2x^3 + 4x^2$
$\quad + 4x - 8$

$= \textbf{x}^5 - \textbf{2x}^4 - \textbf{4x}^3 + \textbf{8x}^2 + \textbf{4x} - \textbf{8}$

8.

$$x - 2 \overline{)\,-3x^3 + 0x^2 + 0x - 2}\qquad \begin{array}{r} -3x^2 - 6x - 12 - \frac{26}{x-2} \end{array}$$

$$\underline{-3x^3 + 6x^2}$$
$$-6x^2 + 0x$$
$$\underline{-6x^2 + 12x}$$
$$-12x - 2$$
$$\underline{-12x + 24}$$
$$-26$$

Check:

$$\frac{-3x^2(x-2)}{x-2} - \frac{6x(x-2)}{x-2} - \frac{12(x-2)}{x-2}$$

$$-\frac{26}{x-2} = \frac{-3x^3 + 6x^2 - 6x^2 + 12x}{x-2}$$

$$+ \frac{-12x + 24 - 26}{x-2} = \frac{-3x^3 - 2}{x-2}$$

9. (a) $R_H T_H + R_S T_S = 180$

(b) $R_H = 70$

(c) $R_S = 20$

(d) $T_H = T_S$

Substitute (b) and (c) into (a) and get:

(a') $70T_H + 20T_S = 180$

Substitute (d) into (a') and get:

(a'') $70T_H + 20(T_H) = 180$

$$90T_H = 180$$

$$T_H = \textbf{2}$$

(d) $T_S = \textbf{2}$

10. (a) $R_F T_F = R_S T_S$

(b) $T_S = 6$

(c) $T_F = 5$

(d) $R_F - 10 = R_S$

Substitute (b) and (c) into (a) and get:

(a') $5R_F = 6R_S$

Substitute (d) into (a') and get:

(a'') $5R_F = 6(R_F - 10)$

$$5R_F = 6R_F - 60$$

$$R_F = \textbf{60}$$

(d) $R_S = (60) - 10 = \textbf{50}$

11. (a) $R_M T_M = R_R T_R$

(b) $R_M = 8$

(c) $R_R = 2$

(d) $T_R = 5 - T_M$

Substitute (b) and (c) into (a) and get:

(a′) $8T_M = 2T_R$

Substitute (d) into (a′) and get:

(a″) $8T_M = 2(5 - T_M)$

$8T_M = 10 - 2T_M$

$10T_M = 10$

$T_M = \mathbf{1}$

(d) $T_R = 5 - (1) = \mathbf{4}$

12. $4 + \dfrac{3x^2}{7y^2z} = \dfrac{28y^2z}{7y^2z} + \dfrac{3x^2}{7y^2z}$

$= \dfrac{\mathbf{28y^2z + 3x^2}}{\mathbf{7y^2z}}$

13. $\dfrac{a}{2x^2} - \dfrac{b}{x^2y} - c = \dfrac{ay}{2x^2y} - \dfrac{2b}{2x^2y} - \dfrac{2cx^2y}{2x^2y}$

$= \dfrac{\mathbf{ay - 2b - 2cx^2y}}{\mathbf{2x^2y}}$

14. $10^2 = z^2 + 8^2$

$100 = z^2 + 64$

$36 = z^2$

$\mathbf{6} = z$

$10\overleftrightarrow{SF} = 7$

$\overleftrightarrow{SF} = \dfrac{7}{10}$

$x = 6\left(\dfrac{7}{10}\right) = \dfrac{42}{10} = \dfrac{\mathbf{21}}{\mathbf{5}}$

$y = 8\left(\dfrac{7}{10}\right) = \dfrac{56}{10} = \dfrac{\mathbf{28}}{\mathbf{5}}$

15.

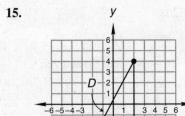

$D^2 = 9^2 + 5^2$

$D^2 = 81 + 25$

$D^2 = 106$

$D = \sqrt{\mathbf{106}}$

16. (a) $x = -3$

(b) $5x - 3y = 9$

$-3y = -5x + 9$

$y = \dfrac{5}{3}x - 3$

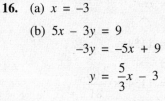

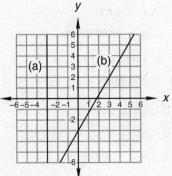

17. (a) Every point on this line is 2 units above the x-axis.

$\mathbf{y = 2}$

(b) The y-intercept is 0. The slope is positive and the rise over the run for any triangle drawn is 2.

$\mathbf{y = 2x}$

18. Graph the line to find the slope.

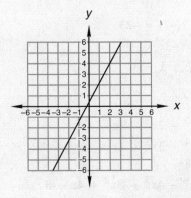

Slope $= \dfrac{+9}{+5} = \dfrac{9}{5}$

$$y = \dfrac{9}{5}x + b$$

$$-5 = \dfrac{9}{5}(-3) + b$$

$$-5 = -\dfrac{27}{5} + b$$

$$\dfrac{27}{5} - \dfrac{25}{5} = b$$

$$\dfrac{2}{5} = b$$

Since $m = \dfrac{9}{5}$ and $b = \dfrac{2}{5}$, $y = \dfrac{9}{5}x + \dfrac{2}{5}$.

19.

$$y = \dfrac{2}{7} + b$$

$$-5 = \dfrac{2}{7}(-3) + b$$

$$-5 = -\dfrac{6}{7} + b$$

$$-\dfrac{35}{7} + \dfrac{6}{7} = b$$

$$-\dfrac{29}{7} = b$$

Since $m = \dfrac{2}{7}$ and $b = -\dfrac{29}{7}$, $y = \dfrac{2}{7}x - \dfrac{29}{7}$.

20. $5x + 15 = 6x - 5$

$$-x = -20$$

$$x = \mathbf{20}$$

$$3 \times \overrightarrow{SF} = \dfrac{11}{3}$$

$$\overrightarrow{SF} = \dfrac{11}{9}$$

$$5 \times \dfrac{11}{9} = y$$

$$\dfrac{\mathbf{55}}{\mathbf{9}} = y$$

$$k = 6x - 5 = 6(20) - 5 = \mathbf{115}$$

21. Since the measure of an arc of a circle is the same as the measure of the central angle, $A = \mathbf{50}$.

$$B + 50 = 180$$

$$B = \mathbf{130}$$

Since angles opposite equal sides are equal angles, $C = D$.

$$C + D + (130) = 180$$

$$C + D = 50$$

$$C = D = \mathbf{25}$$

$$\text{Area} = \dfrac{50}{360} \cdot \pi r^2 = \dfrac{50}{360} \cdot \pi(3 \text{ cm})^2$$

$$\approx \mathbf{3.93 \text{ cm}^2}$$

22. $3\dfrac{1}{4}p - \dfrac{7}{3} = -\dfrac{5}{12}$

$$\dfrac{13}{4}p = -\dfrac{5}{12} + \dfrac{28}{12}$$

$$p = \dfrac{23}{12} \cdot \dfrac{4}{13} = \dfrac{92}{156} = \dfrac{\mathbf{23}}{\mathbf{39}}$$

23. $0.07x - 0.7 = -7.7$

$$7x - 70 = -770$$

$$7x = -700$$

$$x = \mathbf{-100}$$

24. $-[(-2 - 6)(-2) - 2]$

$$= -2[(x - 2)2 - (2x - 3)3]$$

$$-[4 + 12 - 2] = -2[2x - 4 - 6x + 9]$$

$$-14 = -2[-4x + 5]$$

$$-14 = 8x - 10$$

$$-4 = 8x$$

$$-\dfrac{\mathbf{1}}{\mathbf{2}} = x$$

25. $-\dfrac{3x^0y^2}{p^{-2}}\left(\dfrac{x}{p^2y^2} - \dfrac{3xy}{x^2p}\right) = -\dfrac{3xy^2}{y^2} + \dfrac{9xy^3}{p^{-1}x^2}$

$$= \mathbf{-3x} + \dfrac{\mathbf{9py^3}}{\mathbf{x}}$$

26. $\dfrac{x^2x^0(xx^{-3})}{x(y^0y^2)^{-2}} = \dfrac{1}{xy^{-4}} = \dfrac{\mathbf{y^4}}{\mathbf{x}}$

27. $\dfrac{2x^2a}{y} - \dfrac{3xy^{-2}a}{y^{-1}x^{-1}} + \dfrac{4x^0y^{-1}}{x^{-2}a^{-1}}$

$$= \dfrac{2x^2a}{y} - \dfrac{3x^2a}{y} + \dfrac{4x^2a}{y} = \dfrac{\mathbf{3x^2a}}{\mathbf{y}}$$

28. $m - m^2y(m - y)$

$$= -\dfrac{1}{3} - \left(-\dfrac{1}{3}\right)^2\left(\dfrac{1}{6}\right)\left(-\dfrac{1}{3} - \dfrac{1}{6}\right)$$

$$= -\dfrac{1}{3} - \dfrac{1}{54}\left(-\dfrac{1}{2}\right) = -\dfrac{1}{3} + \dfrac{1}{108} = -\dfrac{\mathbf{35}}{\mathbf{108}}$$

29. $-4^0\big[(-5 + 2) - |-3 + 7| - 3(-1 - (-2)^0)\big]$

$= -1[-3 - 4 - 3(-2)] = -1[-3 - 4 + 6]$

$= -1[-1] = \mathbf{1}$

30. $-\dfrac{-1}{-(-2)^{-2}} + \dfrac{3}{-(-2)^{-2}} = -4 - 12 = \mathbf{-16}$

PRACTICE SET 20

a. $4\sqrt{40} - 3\sqrt{140}$

$= 4\sqrt{2 \cdot 2 \cdot 2 \cdot 5} - 3\sqrt{2 \cdot 2 \cdot 5 \cdot 7}$

$= 4\sqrt{2}\sqrt{2}\sqrt{2}\sqrt{5} - 3\sqrt{2}\sqrt{2}\sqrt{5}\sqrt{7}$

$= \mathbf{8\sqrt{10} - 6\sqrt{35}}$

b. $3\sqrt{2}(3\sqrt{2} - \sqrt{8}) = 9\sqrt{2}\sqrt{2} - 3\sqrt{2}\sqrt{8}$

$= 18 - 3\sqrt{2}\sqrt{2}\sqrt{2}\sqrt{2} = 18 - 12 = \mathbf{6}$

c. $3y - x = 5$

$3y = x + 5$

$y = \dfrac{1}{3}x + \dfrac{5}{3}$

For the parallel line

$y = \dfrac{1}{3}x + b$

$(3) = \dfrac{1}{3}(3) + b$

$3 = 1 + b$

$2 = b$

$y = \dfrac{1}{3}x + 2$

PROBLEM SET 20

1. $\dfrac{140}{160} = \dfrac{NC}{640}$

$160NC = 640(140)$

$NC = \mathbf{560\ kg}$

2. If $\frac{3}{10}$ were virtuosos, $\frac{7}{10}$ were not virtuosos.

$F \times of = is$

$\dfrac{7}{10} \times P = 28$

$P = 28 \times \dfrac{10}{7} = \mathbf{40\ performers}$

$N_V = 40 - 28 = \mathbf{12\ virtuosos}$

3. (a) $N_E = N_W + 3$

(b) $7N_E + 2N_W = 111$

Substitute $N_E = N_W + 3$ into (b) and get:

(b') $7(N_W + 3) + 2N_W = 111$

$9N_W = 90$

$N_W = \mathbf{10\ worthless\ ones}$

(a) $N_E = (10) + 3$

$N_E = \mathbf{13\ expensive\ ones}$

4. $\dfrac{P}{100} \times of = is$

$\dfrac{40}{100} \times C = 240$

$C = 240 \times \dfrac{100}{40} = 600$

$N_{NB} = 600 - 240 = \mathbf{360\ tons}$

5. Even integers: $N,\ N + 2,\ N + 4,\ N + 6$

$-4(N + N + 6) = -(N + 2 + N + 4) + 6$

$-8N - 24 = -2N$

$-6N = 24$

$N = -4$

The desired integers are **−4, −2, 0,** and **2.**

6. (a) $y - 2x = 8$

(b) $2y + 2x = 40$

Substitute $y = 2x + 8$ into (b) and get:

(b') $2(2x + 8) + 2x = 40$

$6x + 16 = 40$

$6x = 24$

$x = 4$

(a) $y - 2(4) = 8$

$y = 16$

(4, 16)

7.

$$
\begin{array}{r}
-2x^2 - 2x - 3 - \frac{1}{x-1} \\
x-1\overline{)-2x^3 - 0x^2 - x + 2} \\
\underline{-2x^3 + 2x^2} \\
-2x^2 - x \\
\underline{-2x^2 + 2x} \\
-3x + 2 \\
\underline{-3x + 3} \\
-1
\end{array}
$$

Check:

$$\frac{-2x^2(x-1)}{x-1} - \frac{2x(x-1)}{x-1} - \frac{3(x-1)}{x-1}$$

$$-\frac{1}{x-1} = \frac{-2x^3 + 2x^2 - 2x^2 + 2x}{x-1}$$

$$+ \frac{-3x+3-1}{x-1} = \frac{-2x^3 - x + 2}{x-1}$$

8. (a) $R_G T_G + R_B T_B = 100$

(b) $R_G = 4$

(c) $R_B = 10$

(d) $T_B = T_G + 3$

Substitute (b) and (c) into (a) and get:

(a′) $4T_G + 10T_B = 100$

Substitute (d) into (a′) and get:

(a″) $4T_G + 10(T_G + 3) = 100$

$$14T_G = 70$$

$$T_G = 5$$

(d) $T_B = (5) + 3$

$$T_B = 8$$

9. $3\sqrt{3} \cdot 4\sqrt{12} - 5\sqrt{300}$

$$= 3\sqrt{3} \cdot 4\sqrt{2 \cdot 2 \cdot 3} - 5\sqrt{2 \cdot 2 \cdot 3 \cdot 5 \cdot 5}$$

$$= 3\sqrt{3} \cdot 4\sqrt{2}\sqrt{2}\sqrt{3} - 5\sqrt{2}\sqrt{2}\sqrt{3}\sqrt{5}\sqrt{5}$$

$$= 3\sqrt{3} \cdot 8\sqrt{3} - 50\sqrt{3} = \mathbf{72 - 50\sqrt{3}}$$

10. $4\sqrt{3}(2\sqrt{3} - \sqrt{6}) = 8\sqrt{3}\sqrt{3} - 4\sqrt{3}\sqrt{3}\sqrt{2}$

$$= \mathbf{24 - 12\sqrt{2}}$$

11. $5\sqrt{5}(2\sqrt{5} - 3\sqrt{10}) = 10\sqrt{5}\sqrt{5} - 15\sqrt{5}\sqrt{5}\sqrt{2}$

$$= \mathbf{50 - 75\sqrt{2}}$$

12. $\dfrac{m^2}{x^2 a} + \dfrac{5}{ax} - \dfrac{m}{a} = \dfrac{m^2}{ax^2} + \dfrac{5x}{ax^2} - \dfrac{mx^2}{ax^2}$

$$= \frac{\mathbf{m^2 + 5x - mx^2}}{\mathbf{ax^2}}$$

13. $\dfrac{a}{x^2} - a - \dfrac{3x}{2a^4}$

$$= \frac{2a^5}{2a^4 x^2} - \frac{2a^5 x^2}{2a^4 x^2} - \frac{3x^3}{2a^4 x^2}$$

$$= \frac{2a^5 - 2a^5 x^2 - 3x^3}{2a^4 x^2}$$

14. $4^2 = H^2 + 3^2$

$$16 = H^2 + 9$$

$$7 = H^2$$

$$\sqrt{7} = H$$

Area $= \dfrac{b \times H}{2} = \dfrac{6 \text{ ft} \times \sqrt{7} \text{ ft}}{2} = \mathbf{3\sqrt{7} \text{ ft}^2}$

15. $5 \times \overrightarrow{SF} = 4$

$$\overrightarrow{SF} = \frac{4}{5}$$

$$z = 6\left(\frac{4}{5}\right) = \frac{24}{5}$$

$$A = 7\left(\frac{4}{5}\right) = \frac{28}{5}$$

16. (a) $y = -2$

(b) $y = -2x - 2$

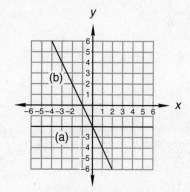

17. (a) Every point on this line is 1 unit above the x-axis.

$$\mathbf{y = 1}$$

(b) The y-intercept is 0. The slope is negative and the rise over the run for any triangle drawn is −1.

$$\mathbf{y = -x}$$

18. Write the equation of the given line in slope-intercept form.

$$3y - x = 3$$

$$3y = x + 3$$

$$y = \frac{1}{3}x + 1$$

Since parallel lines have the same slope,

$$y = \frac{1}{3}x + b$$

$$-1 = \frac{1}{3}(2) + b$$

$$-\frac{3}{3} - \frac{2}{3} = b$$

$$-\frac{5}{3} = b$$

Since $m = \frac{1}{3}$ and $b = -\frac{5}{3}$, $y = \frac{1}{3}x - \frac{5}{3}$.

19.

$$y = -\frac{1}{12}x + b$$

$$5 = -\frac{1}{12}(2) + b$$

$$5 = -\frac{1}{6} + b$$

$$\frac{30}{6} + \frac{1}{6} = b$$

$$\frac{31}{6} = b$$

Since $m = -\frac{1}{12}$ and $b = \frac{31}{6}$, $y = -\frac{1}{12}x + \frac{31}{6}$.

20. $A + 140 = 180$

$$A = \mathbf{40}$$

$$B + 40 + 90 = 180$$

$$B = \mathbf{50}$$

Since vertical angles are equal angles,

$C = B = \mathbf{50.}$

$$P + 50 + 90 = 180$$

$$P = \mathbf{40}$$

Since vertical angles are equal angles,

$y = P = \mathbf{40.}$

21. $3\frac{1}{12} - \frac{1}{6}x = 2\frac{1}{24}$

$$-\frac{1}{6}x = \frac{49}{24} - \frac{74}{24}$$

$$x = -\frac{25}{24} \cdot -\frac{6}{1} = \frac{150}{24} = \frac{\mathbf{25}}{\mathbf{4}}$$

22. $-0.04x - x - 0.2x = 6.2$

$$-4x - 100x - 20x = 620$$

$$x = \mathbf{-5}$$

23. $-2\big[(-3)(-2 - x) + 2(x - 3)\big] = -2x$

$$-2[6 + 3x + 2x - 6] = -2x$$

$$-10x = -2x$$

$$x = \mathbf{0}$$

24. $\dfrac{-x^0 y}{y^2 y^{-2}}\left(\dfrac{x}{y} - \dfrac{3xy^2}{y^3}\right) = \dfrac{-xy}{y} + \dfrac{3xy^3}{y^3} = \mathbf{2x}$

25. $\dfrac{(-2x^0)^{-3} x^2 yy^0 y^3}{(xy^{-2})^2 (-2x^{-1})^{-2}} = \dfrac{4x^2 y^4}{-8x^4 y^{-4}} = -\dfrac{y^8}{2x^2}$

26. $-\dfrac{3x}{a} + \dfrac{(a^0)a}{aax^{-1}} - \dfrac{5x^{-1}}{a} = -\dfrac{3x}{a} + \dfrac{x}{a} - \dfrac{5}{xa}$

$$= -\frac{2x}{a} - \frac{5}{xa}$$

27. $k - kx(k^2 - x)$

$$= -\frac{1}{4} - \left(-\frac{1}{4}\right)\left(\frac{1}{8}\right)\left[\left(-\frac{1}{4}\right)^2 - \frac{1}{8}\right]$$

$$= -\frac{1}{4} + \frac{1}{32}\left(\frac{1}{16} - \frac{2}{16}\right) = -\frac{1}{4} + \frac{1}{32}\left(-\frac{1}{16}\right)$$

$$= -\frac{1}{4} - \frac{1}{512} = -\frac{128}{512} - \frac{1}{512} = -\frac{\mathbf{129}}{\mathbf{512}}$$

28. $-2^0\big\{(-7 + 3) - |-2 + 9| - 2[-2^0 - (-5)]\big\}$

$$= -1\{-4 - 7 - 2[4]\} = -1\{-19\} = \mathbf{19}$$

29. $-2^0|-3 - 7| + |(-5^0)| - 2(-5) + 2$

$$= -10 + 1 + 10 + 2 = \mathbf{3}$$

30. $-\dfrac{1}{-(-3)^{-3}} + \dfrac{2}{-(-3)^{-3}} = -27 + 54 = \mathbf{27}$

PRACTICE SET 21

a. (a) $\dfrac{N}{D} = \dfrac{4}{5} \longrightarrow 4D = 5N$

(b) $N + D = 108 \longrightarrow D = 108 - N$

Substitute $D = 108 - N$ into (a) and get:

(a′) $4(108 - N) = 5N$

$432 - 4N = 5N$

$432 = 9N$

$\mathbf{48} = N$

(b) $D = 108 - (48)$

$D = \mathbf{60}$

b. $\quad A + B = 136$

$\underline{A - B = \;\;\;50}$

$2A \qquad = 186$

$A = \mathbf{93}$

$(93) + B = 136$

$B = \mathbf{43}$

PROBLEM SET 21

1. (a) $\dfrac{N}{D} = \dfrac{3}{5} \longrightarrow 5N = 3D$

(b) $N + D = 96 \longrightarrow D = 96 - N$

Substitute $D = 96 - N$ into (a) and get:

(a′) $5N = 3(96 - N)$

$8N = 288$

$N = \mathbf{36}$

(b) $(36) + D = 96$

$D = \mathbf{60}$

2. (a) $L + S = 200$

(b) $\underline{L - S = \;\;66}$

$2L \quad\;\; = 266$

$L = \mathbf{133}$

(a) $(133) + S = 200$

$S = \mathbf{67}$

3. $\dfrac{1500}{2400} = \dfrac{NA}{3600} \longrightarrow 2400NA = 3600(1500)$

$NA = \mathbf{2250\ kg}$

4. If 20% combined, 80% did not combine.

$\dfrac{80}{100} \times N = 740$

$N = 740 \times \dfrac{100}{80} = 925$

$N_C = 925 - 740 = \mathbf{185\ kg}$

5. (a) $5N_N + 10N_D = 575$

(b) $N_N + N_D = 70$

$\;\;1(a) \quad\;\; 5N_N + 10N_D = 575$

$-10(b) \;\; \underline{-10N_N - 10N_D = -700}$

$-5N_N \qquad\qquad = -125$

$N_N = \mathbf{25}$

6. Integers: $N,\ N + 1,\ N + 2$

$-5(N + N + 2) = 4(-N - 1) + 24$

$-10N - 10 = -4N + 20$

$-6N = 30$

$N = -5$

The desired integers are **−5, −4,** and **−3.**

7. (a) $8y - 3x = 22$

(b) $2y + 4x = 34$

$\;\;1(a) \quad\;\; 8y - \;\;3x = \;\;\;\;22$

$-4(b) \;\; \underline{-8y - 16x = -136}$

$-19x = -114$

$x = 6$

(b) $2y + 4(6) = 34$

$2y = 10$

$y = 5$

(6, 5)

8. $(4x^2 - 2x + 2)(2x - 3)$

$= 8x^3 - 4x^2 + 4x - 12x^2 + 6x - 6$

$= \mathbf{8x^3 - 16x^2 + 10x - 6}$

9. (a) $R_K T_K = R_N T_N$

(b) $R_K = 6$

(c) $R_N = 3$

(d) $T_N - T_K = 8$

Substitute (b) and (c) into (a) and get:

(a′) $6T_K = 3T_N$

Substitute $T_N = T_K + 8$ into (a′) and get:

(a″) $6T_K = 3(T_K + 8)$

$6T_K = 3T_K + 24$

$3T_K = 24$

$T_K = \mathbf{8}$

(d) $T_N - (8) = 8$

$T_N = \mathbf{16}$

10. $3\sqrt{200} - 5\sqrt{18} + 7\sqrt{50}$

$= 3\sqrt{2}\sqrt{2}\sqrt{2}\sqrt{5}\sqrt{5} - 5\sqrt{2}\sqrt{3}\sqrt{3}$

$\quad + 7\sqrt{2}\sqrt{5}\sqrt{5}$

$= 30\sqrt{2} - 15\sqrt{2} + 35\sqrt{2} = \mathbf{50\sqrt{2}}$

11. $2\sqrt{3} \cdot 2\sqrt{2}(6\sqrt{6} - 3\sqrt{2})$
$= 2\sqrt{3} \cdot 2\sqrt{2}(6\sqrt{2}\sqrt{3} - 3\sqrt{2})$
$= 4\sqrt{2}\sqrt{3}(6\sqrt{2}\sqrt{3} - 3\sqrt{2})$
$= 24\sqrt{2}\sqrt{2}\sqrt{3}\sqrt{3} - 12\sqrt{2}\sqrt{2}\sqrt{3}$
$= \mathbf{144 - 24\sqrt{3}}$

12. $4x + \dfrac{1}{p} = \dfrac{4px}{p} + \dfrac{1}{p} = \dfrac{\mathbf{4px + 1}}{\mathbf{p}}$

13. $\dfrac{m^2}{a^2x^2} - \dfrac{3}{ax} - \dfrac{m}{x} = \dfrac{m^2}{a^2x^2} - \dfrac{3ax}{a^2x^2} - \dfrac{a^2mx}{a^2x^2}$

$= \dfrac{\mathbf{m^2 - 3ax - a^2mx}}{\mathbf{a^2x^2}}$

14. $\dfrac{(0.0003 \times 10^8)(6000)}{(0.006 \times 10^{15})(2000 \times 10^5)}$

$= \dfrac{(3 \times 10^4)(6 \times 10^3)}{(6 \times 10^{12})(2 \times 10^8)} = \dfrac{18 \times 10^7}{12 \times 10^{20}}$

$= \mathbf{1.5 \times 10^{-13}}$

15.

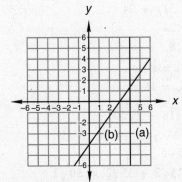

$D^2 = 7^2 + 0^2$
$D^2 = 49$
$D = \mathbf{7}$

16. (a) $x = 4$

(b) $4x - 3y = 12$

$y = \dfrac{4}{3}x - 4$

17. (a) Every point on this line is 2 units below the x-axis.

$\mathbf{y = -2}$

(b) The y-intercept is 0. The slope is negative and the rise over the run for any triangle drawn is -2.

$\mathbf{y = -2x}$

18. Graph the line to find the slope.

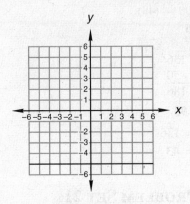

Slope $= \dfrac{0}{7} = 0$

$y = 0x + b$

$-5 = 0(-3) + b$

$-5 = b$

Since $m = 0$ and $b = -5$, $\mathbf{y = -5}$.

19. Since parallel lines have the same slope,

$y = -\dfrac{3}{7}x + b$

$2 = -\dfrac{3}{7}(2) + b$

$\dfrac{14}{7} + \dfrac{6}{7} = b$

$\dfrac{20}{7} = b$

Since $m = -\dfrac{3}{7}$ and $b = \dfrac{20}{7}$, $\mathbf{y = -\dfrac{3}{7}x + \dfrac{20}{7}}$.

20. $x + 4 = 6$

$x = \mathbf{2}$

$x + y = 10$

$y = 10 - (2) = \mathbf{8}$

21. $A + 130 = 180$
$$A = 50$$

$B + 50 + 90 = 180$
$$B = 40$$

Since vertical angles are equal angles,
$C = B = 40$.

$D + 40 + 90 = 180$
$$D = 50$$

Since vertical angles are equal angles,
$y = D = 50$.

22. $5\dfrac{1}{3}x - \dfrac{3}{4} = \dfrac{7}{8}$

$$\dfrac{16}{3}x = \dfrac{7}{8} + \dfrac{6}{8}$$

$$\dfrac{16}{3}x = \dfrac{13}{8}$$

$$x = \dfrac{13}{8} \cdot \dfrac{3}{16} = \mathbf{\dfrac{39}{128}}$$

23. $0.03(x - 4) = 0.02(x + 6)$

$$3(x - 4) = 2(x + 6)$$
$$3x - 12 = 2x + 12$$
$$x = \mathbf{24}$$

24. $-[(-4 - 1)(-3) - 6^0]$
$$= -2[(y - 4)3 - (2y - 5)]$$
$$-[15 - 1] = -2[3y - 12 - 2y + 5]$$
$$-[14] = -2[y - 7]$$
$$-14 = -2y + 14$$
$$-28 = -2y$$
$$\mathbf{14} = y$$

25. $\dfrac{5y^0 p^{-2}}{x^2}\left(-\dfrac{2p^2}{x^2} - \dfrac{p^2}{x}\right) = -\dfrac{\mathbf{10}}{x^4} - \dfrac{\mathbf{5}}{x^3}$

26. $\dfrac{x^2(y^{-2})^2(y^0)^2}{(2x^2y^3)^{-2}} = \dfrac{4x^2y^{-4}}{x^{-4}y^{-6}} = \mathbf{4x^6y^2}$

27. $\dfrac{3x^2a}{x} - 5xa + \dfrac{7x^{-2}}{x^{-3}a^{-1}} = 3xa - 5xa + 7xa$
$$= \mathbf{5xa}$$

28. $x(x - ax)x = -\dfrac{1}{2}\left(-\dfrac{1}{2} - \dfrac{1}{3}\left(-\dfrac{1}{2}\right)\right)\left(-\dfrac{1}{2}\right)$

$$= \dfrac{1}{4}\left(-\dfrac{1}{2} + \dfrac{1}{6}\right) = \dfrac{1}{4}\left(-\dfrac{3}{6} + \dfrac{1}{6}\right) = \dfrac{1}{4}\left(-\dfrac{1}{3}\right)$$

$$= \mathbf{-\dfrac{1}{12}}$$

29. $-7^0[(-2 + 3) - |-4 + 3|] = -1[1 - 1]$
$$= -1[0] = \mathbf{0}$$

30. $-\dfrac{1}{-2^{-2}} - \dfrac{1}{-(-2)^0} = 4 + 1 = \mathbf{5}$

Practice Set 22

a.

$R_E = 14$

$R_D = 21$

$R_E T_E = R_D T_D$

$T_D = T_E - 3$

$(14)T_E = (21)(T_E - 3)$

$14T_E = 21T_E - 63$

$7T_E = 63$

$T_E = 9$ hours

$D = R_E T_E = (14)(9) = \mathbf{126 \text{ miles}}$

b. $\dfrac{x}{7} = \dfrac{5}{6}$

$6x = 35$

$$x = \dfrac{\mathbf{35}}{\mathbf{6}}$$

$\dfrac{y}{9} = \dfrac{5}{6}$

$6y = 45$

$$y = \dfrac{\mathbf{15}}{\mathbf{2}}$$

Problem Set 22

1.

$D_E = D_C$ so $R_E T_E = R_C T_C$

$R_E = 15;\ R_C = 30;\ T_C = T_E - 3$

$15T_E = 30(T_E - 3)$

$15T_E = 30T_E - 90$

$-15T_E = -90$

$T_E = 6$

$D_C = D_E = R_E T_E = (15)(6) = \mathbf{90 \text{ miles}}$

2.

$$D_A = D_W \quad \text{so} \quad R_A T_A = R_W T_W$$
$$R_A = 9; \ T_A = 4; \ T_W = 2$$
$$9(4) = R_W(2)$$
18 kph $= R_W$

3. (a) $\dfrac{N}{D} = \dfrac{7}{5} \longrightarrow 5N = 7D$

(b) $N + D = 960 \longrightarrow D = 960 - N$

Substitute $D = 960 - N$ into (a) and get:

(a') $5N = 7(960 - N)$
$$12N = 6720$$
$$N = \mathbf{560}$$

(b) $(560) + D = 960$
$$D = \mathbf{400}$$

4. (a) $T_F = T_S + 500$

(b) $T_F + T_S = 6900$

Substitute (a) into (b) and get:

(b') $(T_S + 500) + T_S = 6900$
$$2T_S = 6400$$
$$T_S = \$3200$$

(a) $T_F = (3200) + 500 = \mathbf{\$3700}$

5. (a) $5P_H + 13P_W = 109$

(b) $P_H + P_W = 9$

$$\begin{array}{r} 1(a) \quad 5P_H + 13P_W = 109 \\ -5(b) \ \underline{-5P_H - 5P_W = -45} \\ 8P_W = 64 \\ P_W = \textbf{8 pecks} \end{array}$$

6. $\dfrac{570}{600} = \dfrac{NI}{5000} \longrightarrow 600NI = 5000(570)$

$$NI = \textbf{4750 grams}$$

7. (a) $5x + y = 24$

(b) $7x - 2y = 20$

Substitute $y = 24 - 5x$ into (b) and get:

(b') $7x - 2(24 - 5x) = 20$
$$7x - 48 + 10x = 20$$
$$17x = 68$$
$$x = 4$$

(a) $5(4) + y = 24$
$$y = 4$$

(4, 4)

8.

$$\begin{array}{r} x^2 + x - 3 - \frac{1}{x-1} \\ x - 1 \overline{)\ x^3 + 0x^2 - 4x + 2} \\ \underline{x^3 - x^2} \\ x^2 - 4x \\ \underline{x^2 - x} \\ -3x + 2 \\ \underline{-3x + 3} \\ -1 \end{array}$$

Check:

$$\frac{x^2(x-1)}{x-1} + \frac{x(x-1)}{x-1} - \frac{3(x-1)}{x-1} - \frac{1}{x-1}$$

$$= \frac{x^3 - x^2 + x^2 - x - 3x + 3 - 1}{x-1}$$

$$= \frac{x^3 - 4x + 2}{x-1}$$

9. $\dfrac{x}{12} = \dfrac{15}{10} \longrightarrow 10x = 180 \longrightarrow x = \mathbf{18}$

$\dfrac{y}{11} = \dfrac{15}{10} \longrightarrow 10y = 165 \longrightarrow y = \dfrac{\mathbf{33}}{\mathbf{2}}$

10. $2\sqrt{27} - 3\sqrt{75} = 2\sqrt{3}\sqrt{3}\sqrt{3} - 3\sqrt{3}\sqrt{5}\sqrt{5}$

$$= 6\sqrt{3} - 15\sqrt{3} = \mathbf{-9\sqrt{3}}$$

11. $3\sqrt{2}(2\sqrt{2} - \sqrt{6}) \cdot 4\sqrt{3} + 2$

$$= 3\sqrt{2}(2\sqrt{2} - \sqrt{2}\sqrt{3}) \cdot 4\sqrt{3} + 2$$

$$= 12\sqrt{2}\sqrt{3}(2\sqrt{2} - \sqrt{2}\sqrt{3}) + 2$$

$$= 24\sqrt{2}\sqrt{2}\sqrt{3} - 12\sqrt{2}\sqrt{2}\sqrt{3}\sqrt{3} + 2$$

$$= 48\sqrt{3} - 72 + 2 = \mathbf{48\sqrt{3} - 70}$$

12. $2\sqrt{3}(5\sqrt{3} - 2\sqrt{6}) = 2\sqrt{3}(5\sqrt{3} - 2\sqrt{2}\sqrt{3})$

$$= 10\sqrt{3}\sqrt{3} - 4\sqrt{2}\sqrt{3}\sqrt{3} = \mathbf{30 - 12\sqrt{2}}$$

13. $2 + \dfrac{1}{x} = \dfrac{2x}{x} + \dfrac{1}{x} = \dfrac{\mathbf{2x+1}}{\mathbf{x}}$

14. $\dfrac{5x^2}{y} + p^2 - \dfrac{3x}{py} = \dfrac{5x^2 p}{py} + \dfrac{p^3 y}{py} - \dfrac{3x}{py}$

$$= \dfrac{\mathbf{5x^2 p + p^3 y - 3x}}{\mathbf{py}}$$

15. $\dfrac{(0.0035 \times 10^{-4})(200 \times 10^6)}{(700 \times 10^5)(0.00005)}$

$$= \dfrac{(3.5 \times 10^{-7})(2 \times 10^8)}{(7 \times 10^7)(5 \times 10^{-5})} = \dfrac{7 \times 10^1}{35 \times 10^2}$$

$$= \mathbf{2 \times 10^{-2}}$$

16. (a) $x = -5$

(b) $2x - y = 4$

$$-y = -2x + 4$$

$$y = 2x - 4$$

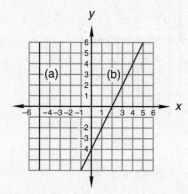

17. (a) Every point on this line is 4 units to the left of the y-axis.

$$x = -4$$

(b) The y-intercept is $+3$. The slope is negative and the rise over the run for any triangle drawn is $-\frac{3}{2}$.

$$y = -\frac{3}{2}x + 3$$

18. Graph the line to find the slope.

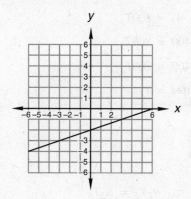

Slope $= \dfrac{+1}{+3} = \dfrac{1}{3}$

$$y = \frac{1}{3}x + b$$

$$0 = \frac{1}{3}(6) + b$$

$$-2 = b$$

Since $m = \dfrac{1}{3}$ and $b = -2$, $y = \dfrac{1}{3}x - 2.$

19. $D^2 = 9^2 + 3^2$

$$D^2 = 81 + 9$$

$$D^2 = 90$$

$$D = \sqrt{90}$$

$$D = 3\sqrt{10}$$

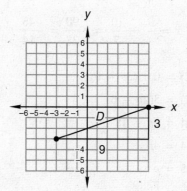

20. $y = \dfrac{2}{5}x + b$

$$-5 = \frac{2}{5}(3) + b$$

$$-5 = \frac{6}{5} + b$$

$$-\frac{25}{5} - \frac{6}{5} = b$$

$$-\frac{31}{5} = b$$

Since $m = \dfrac{2}{5}$ and $b = -\dfrac{31}{5}$, $y = \dfrac{2}{5}x - \dfrac{31}{5}.$

21. $A + 140 = 180$

$$A = 40$$

$$B + 40 + 90 = 180$$

$$B = 50$$

Since vertical angles are equal angles,

$C = B = 50.$

$$k + 50 + 90 = 180$$

$$k = 40$$

$$M + 90 + 40 = 180$$

$$M = 50$$

22. $3\dfrac{2}{5}x - 4\dfrac{1}{10}x = 2\dfrac{1}{4}$

$\dfrac{34}{10}x - \dfrac{41}{10}x = \dfrac{9}{4}$

$-\dfrac{7}{10}x = \dfrac{9}{4}$

$x = \dfrac{9}{4} \cdot -\dfrac{10}{7} = -\dfrac{90}{28} = -\dfrac{45}{14}$

23. $0.02(p - 2) = 0.03(2p - 6)$

$2(p - 2) = 3(2p - 6)$

$2p - 4 = 6p - 18$

$14 = 4p$

$\mathbf{3.5} = p$

24. $-[(-3 - 6)(-1^0) - 6^0] = -4[(x - 3)2]$

$-[9 - 1] = -4[2x - 6]$

$-8 = -8x + 24$

$8x = 32$

$x = \mathbf{4}$

25. $\dfrac{xy^{-2}}{z^0 p}\left(\dfrac{py^2}{x} - \dfrac{3xy^{-4}}{py}\right) = \dfrac{xp}{xp} - \dfrac{3x^2y^{-6}}{p^2 y}$

$= \mathbf{1 - 3x^2y^{-7}p^{-2}}$

26. $\dfrac{(x^{-2}yp)^{-3}(x^0yp)^2}{(2x^2)^{-2}} = \dfrac{4x^6 y^{-1}p^{-1}}{x^{-4}}$

$= \mathbf{4x^{10}y^{-1}p^{-1}}$

27. $-\dfrac{3x^2y}{xx} + \dfrac{2x^{-2}x^4}{y^{-1}x^2} - \dfrac{5xy^2}{xy} = -3y + 2y - 5y$

$= \mathbf{-6y}$

28. $ya(y - a)y = -\dfrac{1}{2}\left(\dfrac{1}{5}\right)\left(-\dfrac{1}{2} - \dfrac{1}{5}\right)\left(-\dfrac{1}{2}\right)$

$= \dfrac{1}{20}\left(-\dfrac{5}{10} - \dfrac{2}{10}\right) = \dfrac{1}{20}\left(-\dfrac{7}{10}\right) = -\dfrac{7}{200}$

29. $-2^0[(5 - 7 - 2) - |-2 - 7| - 2^0] + 2$

$= -1[-4 - 9 - 1] + 2$

$= -1[-14] + 2 = 14 + 2 = \mathbf{16}$

30. $\dfrac{-3}{-3^{-2}} - \dfrac{2}{-2^{-3}} = 27 + 16 = \mathbf{43}$

PRACTICE SET 23

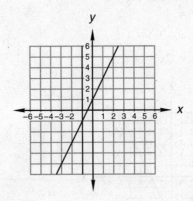

$(-1, -1)$

Check: $(-1) = 2(-1) + 1$

$-1 = -2 + 1$

$-1 = -1$

PROBLEM SET 23

1.

$\begin{array}{c} D_M \\ \longrightarrow \\ \hline D_J \\ \longrightarrow \end{array}$

$D_M = D_J$ so $R_M T_M = R_J T_J$

$R_M = 600;\ R_J = 800;\ T_M = T_J + 4$

$600(T_J + 4) = 800T_J$

$600T_J + 2400 = 800T_J$

$2400 = 200T_J$

$\mathbf{12\ minutes} = T_J$

2.

$\begin{array}{c} D_F \\ \longrightarrow \\ \hline D_S \\ \longrightarrow \end{array}$

$D_F = D_S$ so $R_F T_F = R_S T_S$

$T_F = 10;\ T_S = 12;\ R_F = R_S + 10$

$(R_S + 10)(10) = R_S(12)$

$10R_S + 100 = 12R_S$

$100 = 2R_S$

$50 = R_S$

$D_F = D_S = (50)(12) = \mathbf{600\ kilometers}$

3. (a) $\dfrac{N}{D} = \dfrac{11}{12}$ $\longrightarrow$ $12N = 11D$

   (b) $N + D = 230$ $\longrightarrow$ $D = 230 - N$

   $12N = 11(230 - N)$

   $12N = 2530 - 11N$

   $23N = 2530$

   $\quad N = 110$

   $D = 230 - 110 = 120$

   Fraction $= \dfrac{\mathbf{110}}{\mathbf{120}}$

4. (a) $N_V + N_S = 300$

   (b) $\dfrac{N_V - N_S = \ \ 50}{2N_V \quad\quad = 350}$

   $\quad\quad N_V = \mathbf{175\ viands}$

   (b) $(175) - N_S = 50$

   $\quad\quad N_S = \mathbf{125\ sandwiches}$

5. (a) $5N_N + 25N_Q = 500$

   (b) $N_N - N_Q = 40$

   1(a) $\quad 5N_N + 25N_Q = \ \ 500$

   25(b) $\dfrac{25N_N - 25N_Q = 1000}{30N_N \quad\quad\quad = 1500}$

   $\quad\quad\quad N_N = \mathbf{50\ nickels}$

   (b) $(50) - N_Q = 40$

   $\quad\quad N_Q = \mathbf{10\ quarters}$

6. If 20% was copper sulfate, 80% was not copper sulfate.

   $\dfrac{P}{100} \times of = is$

   $\dfrac{80}{100} \times 400 = NC$

   $\quad NC = \mathbf{320\ tons}$

7. (a) $5x + 2y = 70$

   (b) $\dfrac{3x - 2y = 10}{8x \quad\quad = 80}$

   $\quad\quad x = 10$

   (b) $3(10) - 2y = 10$

   $\quad\quad -2y = -20$

   $\quad\quad\quad y = 10$

   $\mathbf{(10, 10)}$

8. $(3x^3 - 2x)(2x^2 - x - 4)$

   $= 6x^5 - 3x^4 - 12x^3 - 4x^3 + 2x^2 + 8x$

   $= \mathbf{6x^5 - 3x^4 - 16x^3 + 2x^2 + 8x}$

9. $4\sqrt{3} \cdot 3\sqrt{12} \cdot 2\sqrt{3} = 4\sqrt{3} \cdot 3\sqrt{2}\sqrt{2}\sqrt{3} \cdot 2\sqrt{3}$

   $= 24\sqrt{2}\sqrt{2}\sqrt{3}\sqrt{3}\sqrt{3} = \mathbf{144\sqrt{3}}$

10. $3\sqrt{75} - 4\sqrt{48}$

    $= 3\sqrt{3}\sqrt{5}\sqrt{5} - 4\sqrt{2}\sqrt{2}\sqrt{2}\sqrt{2}\sqrt{3}$

    $= 15\sqrt{3} - 16\sqrt{3} = \mathbf{-\sqrt{3}}$

11. $2\sqrt{5}(5\sqrt{5} - 3\sqrt{15}) = 2\sqrt{5}(5\sqrt{5} - 3\sqrt{3}\sqrt{5})$

    $= 10\sqrt{5}\sqrt{5} - 6\sqrt{3}\sqrt{5}\sqrt{5} = \mathbf{50 - 30\sqrt{3}}$

12. $3xy^2m + \dfrac{4}{x} = \dfrac{3x^2y^2m}{x} + \dfrac{4}{x}$

    $= \dfrac{\mathbf{3x^2y^2m + 4}}{\mathbf{x}}$

13. $\dfrac{5x^2}{pm} - 4 + \dfrac{c}{p^2m} = \dfrac{5x^2p}{p^2m} - \dfrac{4p^2m}{p^2m} + \dfrac{c}{p^2m}$

    $= \dfrac{\mathbf{5x^2p - 4p^2m + c}}{\mathbf{p^2m}}$

14. $\dfrac{(0.00003)(0.006 \times 10^{-6})}{(1800 \times 10^{15})(100,000)}$

    $= \dfrac{(3 \times 10^{-5})(6 \times 10^{-9})}{(1.8 \times 10^{18})(1 \times 10^5)} = \dfrac{18 \times 10^{-14}}{18 \times 10^{22}}$

    $= \mathbf{1 \times 10^{-36}}$

15. (a) $2y - 2x = 8$

    $\quad\quad 2y = 2x + 8$

    $\quad\quad\quad y = x + 4$

    (b) $y + x = -2$

    $\quad\quad y = -x - 2$

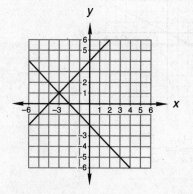

    (a) $2y - 2x = \ \ 8$

    2(b) $\dfrac{2y + 2x = -4}{4y \quad\quad = \ \ 4}$

    $\quad\quad\quad y = 1$

    (b) $(1) + x = -2$

    $\quad\quad\quad x = -3$

    $\mathbf{(-3, 1)}$

16. (a) $y - 2x = 1$

$y = 2x + 1$

(b) $y = -2$

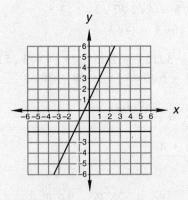

Substitute (b) into (a) and get:

(a') $(-2) - 2x = 1$

$-2x = 3$

$x = -\dfrac{3}{2}$

$\left(-\dfrac{3}{2}, -2\right)$

17. Graph the line to find the slope.

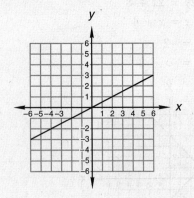

Slope $= \dfrac{+1}{+2} = \dfrac{1}{2}$

$y = \dfrac{1}{2}x + b$

$0 = \dfrac{1}{2}(0) + b$

$0 = b$

Since $m = \dfrac{1}{2}$ and $b = 0$, $y = \dfrac{1}{2}x.$

18.

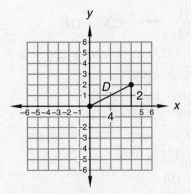

$D^2 = 4^2 + 2^2$

$D^2 = 16 + 4$

$D^2 = 20$

$D = \sqrt{20}$

$D = 2\sqrt{5}$

19. $y = -\dfrac{3}{8}x + b$

$4 = -\dfrac{3}{8}(4) + b$

$4 = -\dfrac{12}{8} + b$

$\dfrac{8}{2} + \dfrac{3}{2} = b$

$\dfrac{11}{2} = b$

Since $m = -\dfrac{3}{8}$ and $b = \dfrac{11}{2}$, $y = -\dfrac{3}{8}x + \dfrac{11}{2}.$

20. $13^2 = (BC)^2 + 5^2$

$169 = (BC)^2 + 25$

$144 = (BC)^2$

$\mathbf{12\ m} = BC$

$CM = \dfrac{1}{2}BC = \dfrac{1}{2}(12\ m) = \mathbf{6\ m}$

$\text{Area}_{ACM} = \dfrac{6\ m \times 5\ m}{2} = \mathbf{15\ m^2}$

21. $\dfrac{x}{4} = \dfrac{7}{3} \longrightarrow 3x = 28 \longrightarrow x = \dfrac{28}{3}$

$\dfrac{y}{6} = \dfrac{3}{7} \longrightarrow 7y = 18 \longrightarrow y = \dfrac{18}{7}$

22. $3\frac{1}{4}x + 5\frac{1}{3} = 2\frac{1}{6}$

$$\frac{13}{4}x = \frac{13}{6} - \frac{32}{6}$$

$$\frac{13}{4}x = -\frac{19}{6}$$

$$x = -\frac{19}{6} \cdot \frac{4}{13} = -\frac{76}{78} = -\frac{38}{39}$$

23. $0.3(2p - 4) = 0.1(p + 3)$

$$3(2p - 4) = 1(p + 3)$$

$$6p - 12 = p + 3$$

$$5p = 15$$

$$p = 3$$

24. $-[(-4 - 6)(-4) - 2] = -2^0(x - 4)$

$$-[40 - 2] = -x + 4$$

$$-38 = -x + 4$$

$$x = 42$$

25. $xy^{-2}\left(\dfrac{x^0 y^2}{x} - \dfrac{3x^0 y^2}{x^2}\right) = \dfrac{x}{x} - \dfrac{3x}{x^2}$

$$= 1 - 3x^{-1}$$

26. $\dfrac{(-3xy)^{-2} x^2 y^2}{(x^{-3})^2 yx^2} = \dfrac{x^{-2} y^{-2} x^2 y^2}{9x^{-6} yx^2} = \dfrac{x^4}{9y}$

27. $\dfrac{3m}{x} - \dfrac{2x^{-1}}{m^0 m^{-1}} + \dfrac{5x^2 m^2}{x^3 m} = \dfrac{3m}{x} - \dfrac{2m}{x} + \dfrac{5m}{x}$

$$= \dfrac{6m}{x}$$

28. $xy - (x - y) = -\dfrac{1}{2}(2) - \left(-\dfrac{1}{2} - 2\right)$

$$= -1 - \left(-\dfrac{1}{2} - \dfrac{4}{2}\right) = -\dfrac{2}{2} + \dfrac{5}{2} = \dfrac{3}{2}$$

29. $-3^0[(-2 - 3 + 8) - |-3 - 5| - 5^0]$

$$= -1[3 - 8 - 1] = -1[-6] = 6$$

30. $\dfrac{-2^0}{-2^2} - \dfrac{(-2)^0}{(-2)^{-3}} = \dfrac{1}{4} + 8 = 8\dfrac{1}{4}$

PRACTICE SET 24

a. $\dfrac{2x + 3}{4} - \dfrac{4}{3} = \dfrac{1}{4}$

$$12 \cdot \dfrac{2x + 3}{4} - 12 \cdot \dfrac{4}{3} = 12 \cdot \dfrac{1}{4}$$

$$6x + 9 - 16 = 3$$

$$6x = 10$$

$$x = \dfrac{5}{3}$$

b. $\dfrac{4x}{3} + \dfrac{7 - 2x}{5} = 2$

$$15 \cdot \dfrac{4x}{3} + 15 \cdot \dfrac{7 - 2x}{5} = 15 \cdot 2$$

$$20x + 21 - 6x = 30$$

$$14x = 9$$

$$x = \dfrac{9}{14}$$

c. $\dfrac{x}{3} = \dfrac{3}{2}$

$$2x = 9$$

$$x = \dfrac{9}{2}$$

$$\dfrac{y}{4} = \dfrac{5}{2}$$

$$2y = 20$$

$$y = 10$$

PROBLEM SET 24

1.

$D_F = D_S$ so $R_F T_F = R_S T_S$

$T_F = 6$; $T_S = 8$; $R_F = 60$

$$60(6) = R_S(8)$$

$$45 \text{ mph} = R_S$$

2.

$D_1 = D_2$ so $R_1 T_1 = R_2 T_2$

$R_1 = 4$; $R_2 = 5$; $T_1 = T_2 + 1$

$$4(T_2 + 1) = 5T_2$$

$$4T_2 + 4 = 5T_2$$

$$4 = T_2$$

$$D_1 = D_2 = 4(5) = 20 \text{ miles}$$

3. (a) $\dfrac{N}{D} = \dfrac{5}{7} \longrightarrow 7N = 5D$

(b) $N + D = 120$

Substitute $D = 120 - N$ into (a) and get:

(a′) $7N = 5(120 - N)$

$12N = 600$

$N = 50$

(b) $(50) + D = 120$

$D = 70$

The fraction was $\dfrac{\mathbf{50}}{\mathbf{70}}$.

4. (a) $Q_C + Q_N = 173$

(b) $\dfrac{Q_C - Q_N = \ \ 11}{2Q_C \ \ \ \ \ \ \ \ = 184}$

$Q_C = \mathbf{92 \ quarts}$

(b) $(92) - Q_N = 11$

$Q_N = \mathbf{81 \ quarts}$

5. (a) $700M_R + 900M_P = 41,000$

(b) $M_R + M_P = 50$

$\begin{array}{lrr} 1\text{(a)} & 700M_R + 900M_P = & 41,000 \\ -900\text{(b)} & \underline{-900M_R - 900M_P =} & \underline{-45,000} \\ & -200M_R \ \ \ \ \ \ \ \ \ \ = & -4,000 \end{array}$

$M_R = \mathbf{20 \ measures}$

6. $\dfrac{48,300}{49,000} = \dfrac{NP}{4200}$

$49,000NP = 4200(48,300)$

$NP = \mathbf{4140 \ kilograms}$

7. (a) $7x + 9y = 119$

(b) $2x + y = 23 \longrightarrow y = 23 - 2x$

Substitute $y = 23 - 2x$ into (a) and get:

(a′) $7x + 9(23 - 2x) = 119$

$7x + 207 - 18x = 119$

$-11x = -88$

$x = 8$

(b) $2(8) + y = 23$

$y = 7$

(8, 7)

8.

$$-x - 2 \ \overline{)\ 3x^3 + 0x^2 + \ 0x \ - \ 3} \quad \dfrac{-3x^2 + \ 6x \ - 12 - \frac{27}{-x-2}}{}$$

$$\begin{array}{r} \underline{3x^3 + 6x^2} \\ -6x^2 + \ 0x \\ \underline{-6x^2 - 12x} \\ 12x - \ 3 \\ \underline{12x + 24} \\ -27 \end{array}$$

Check:

$-\dfrac{3x^2(-x - 2)}{-x - 2} + \dfrac{6x(-x - 2)}{-x - 2} - \dfrac{12(-x - 2)}{-x - 2}$

$-\dfrac{27}{-x - 2}$

$= \dfrac{3x^3 + 6x^2 - 6x^2 - 12x + 12x + 24 - 27}{-x - 2}$

$= \dfrac{3x^3 - 3}{-x - 2}$

9. $4\sqrt{3} \cdot 5\sqrt{2} \cdot 6\sqrt{12} = 4\sqrt{3} \cdot 5\sqrt{2} \cdot 6\sqrt{2}\sqrt{2}\sqrt{3}$

$= 120\sqrt{2}\sqrt{2}\sqrt{2}\sqrt{3}\sqrt{3} = \mathbf{720\sqrt{2}}$

10. $4\sqrt{63} - 3\sqrt{28} = 4\sqrt{3}\sqrt{3}\sqrt{7} - 3\sqrt{2}\sqrt{2}\sqrt{7}$

$= 12\sqrt{7} - 6\sqrt{7} = \mathbf{6\sqrt{7}}$

11. $3\sqrt{2}(5\sqrt{2} - 6\sqrt{12}) = 3\sqrt{2}(5\sqrt{2} - 6\sqrt{2}\sqrt{2}\sqrt{3})$

$= 15\sqrt{2}\sqrt{2} - 18\sqrt{2}\sqrt{2}\sqrt{2}\sqrt{3} = \mathbf{30 - 36\sqrt{6}}$

12. $2\sqrt{2}(5\sqrt{10} - 3\sqrt{2}) = 2\sqrt{2}(5\sqrt{2}\sqrt{5} - 3\sqrt{2})$

$= 10\sqrt{2}\sqrt{2}\sqrt{5} - 6\sqrt{2}\sqrt{2} = \mathbf{20\sqrt{5} - 12}$

13. $4m^2yp + \dfrac{6}{m^2y} = \dfrac{4m^4y^2p}{m^2y} + \dfrac{6}{m^2y}$

$= \dfrac{\mathbf{4m^4y^2p + 6}}{\mathbf{m^2y}}$

14. $\dfrac{k^2}{2p} + c - \dfrac{4}{p^2c} = \dfrac{k^2pc}{2p^2c} + \dfrac{2p^2c^2}{2p^2c} - \dfrac{8}{2p^2c}$

$= \dfrac{\mathbf{k^2pc + 2p^2c^2 - 8}}{\mathbf{2p^2c}}$

15. $\dfrac{(0.0007 \times 10^{-23})(4000 \times 10^6)}{(0.00004)(7,000,000)}$

$= \dfrac{(7 \times 10^{-27})(4 \times 10^9)}{(4 \times 10^{-5})(7 \times 10^6)} = \dfrac{28 \times 10^{-18}}{28 \times 10^1}$

$= \mathbf{1 \times 10^{-19}}$

16. (a) $3x + 2y = 12$

$$2y = -3x + 12$$

$$y = -\frac{3}{2}x + 6$$

(b) $5x - 4y = 8$

$$-4y = -5x + 8$$

$$y = \frac{5}{4}x - 2$$

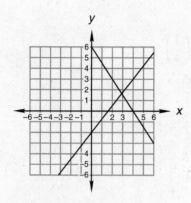

2(a) $6x + 4y = 24$

(b) $\dfrac{5x - 4y = 8}{11x = 32}$

$$x = \frac{32}{11}$$

(a) $3\left(\dfrac{32}{11}\right) + 2y = 12$

$$2y = \frac{132}{11} - \frac{96}{11}$$

$$y = \frac{36}{11} \cdot \frac{1}{2} = \frac{18}{11}$$

$$\left(\frac{32}{11}, \frac{18}{11}\right)$$

17. (a) The y-intercept is +2. The slope is positive and the rise over the run for any triangle drawn is $\frac{5}{6}$.

$$y = \frac{5}{6}x + 2$$

(b) Every point on this line is 4 units below the x-axis.

$$y = -4$$

18. Since the measure of a central angle is the same as the measure of an arc of a circle,

$A = \mathbf{70}.$

$B + 70 = 180$

$B = \mathbf{110}$

Since angles opposite equal sides are equal angles,

$C = D = \mathbf{35}.$

$$\text{Area} = \frac{70}{360}\pi r^2 = \frac{70}{360}(\pi)(4 \text{ cm})^2 \approx \mathbf{9.77 \text{ cm}^2}$$

19. $(\sqrt{21})^2 = H^2 + 2^2$

$$21 = H^2 + 4$$

$$17 = H^2$$

$$\sqrt{17} = H$$

$$\text{Area} = \frac{4 \text{ in.} \times \sqrt{17} \text{ in.}}{2} = \mathbf{2\sqrt{17} \text{ in.}^2}$$

20. Graph the line to find the slope.

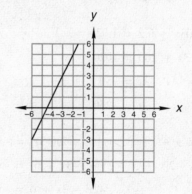

$$\text{Slope} = \frac{+2}{+1} = 2$$

$$y = 2x + b$$

$$5 = 2(-2) + b$$

$$9 = b$$

Since $m = 2$ and $b = 9$, $\mathbf{y = 2x + 9.}$

21. $y = \dfrac{2}{9}x + b$

$$-3 = \frac{2}{9}(5) + b$$

$$-3 = \frac{10}{9} + b$$

$$-\frac{37}{9} = b$$

Since $m = \dfrac{2}{9}$ and $b = -\dfrac{37}{9}$, $\mathbf{y = \dfrac{2}{9}x - \dfrac{37}{9}.}$

22. $\dfrac{k + 3}{3} = \dfrac{9}{4} \longrightarrow 4k + 12 = 27$

$$4k = 15$$

$$k = \frac{15}{4}$$

23. $\dfrac{4x + 2}{3} - \dfrac{3}{4} = \dfrac{1}{2}$

$16x + 8 - 9 = 6$

$16x = 7$

$x = \dfrac{7}{16}$

24. $\dfrac{3x}{2} + \dfrac{8 - 4x}{7} = 3$

$21x + 16 - 8x = 42$

$13x = 26$

$x = \mathbf{2}$

25. $0.07 - 0.003x + 0.2 = 1.02$

$70 - 3x + 200 = 1020$

$-3x = 750$

$x = \mathbf{-250}$

26. $-2[x - (-2 - 4^0) - 3] + [(x - 2)(-3)] = -x$

$-2[x + 3 - 3] + [-3x + 6] = -x$

$-2x - 3x + 6 = -x$

$-4x = -6$

$x = \dfrac{\mathbf{3}}{\mathbf{2}}$

27. $\dfrac{xy^{-2}}{p^2}\left(\dfrac{p^2 y^2}{x} + \dfrac{5x^2 y^3}{p^{-2}}\right) = \dfrac{xp^2}{p^2 x} + 5x^3 y$

$= \mathbf{1 + 5x^3 y}$

28. $\dfrac{4x^2 y^{-2} x}{(-2x^0)^{-3}} = -\dfrac{32x^3 y^{-2}}{x^0} = \mathbf{-32x^3 y^{-2}}$

29. $\dfrac{3p^2 x^2}{xy} - \dfrac{5ppy^{-1}}{x^{-1}} - \dfrac{5p^2 x^2 x^2}{x^{-3} y}$

$= \dfrac{3p^2 x}{y} - \dfrac{5p^2 x}{y} - \dfrac{5p^2 x^7}{y}$

$= \dfrac{\mathbf{-2p^2 x}}{\mathbf{y}} - \dfrac{\mathbf{5p^2 x^7}}{\mathbf{y}}$

30. $xa(ax - a) = \dfrac{1}{2}\left(-\dfrac{1}{3}\right)\left(-\dfrac{1}{3}\left(\dfrac{1}{2}\right) - \left(-\dfrac{1}{3}\right)\right)$

$= -\dfrac{1}{6}\left(-\dfrac{1}{6} + \dfrac{2}{6}\right) = -\dfrac{1}{6}\left(\dfrac{1}{6}\right) = -\dfrac{\mathbf{1}}{\mathbf{36}}$

PRACTICE SET 25

a. $8m^2 xy^5 + 6yx^2 m^3 - 2xym^2$
$= \mathbf{2m^2 xy(4y^4 + 3mx - 1)}$

b. $\dfrac{4m^5 + m^2}{m^2} = \mathbf{4m^3 + 1}$

c. $4\overrightarrow{SF} = 7$

$\overrightarrow{SF} = \dfrac{7}{4}$

$5 + x = 5\left(\dfrac{7}{4}\right)$

$5 + x = \dfrac{35}{4}$

$x = \dfrac{35}{4} - 5$

$x = \dfrac{\mathbf{15}}{\mathbf{4}}$

$y = 7\left(\dfrac{7}{4}\right)$

$y = \dfrac{\mathbf{49}}{\mathbf{4}}$

d. $\dfrac{M}{6} = \dfrac{4}{7}$

$7M = 24$

$M = \dfrac{\mathbf{24}}{\mathbf{7}}$

$\dfrac{N}{3} = \dfrac{7}{4}$

$4N = 21$

$N = \dfrac{\mathbf{21}}{\mathbf{4}}$

PROBLEM SET 25

1. $\dfrac{38}{14,440} = \dfrac{D}{36,100}$

$14,440D = 38(36,100)$

$D = \mathbf{95\ days}$

2.

$$\begin{array}{c} D_B \\ \longmapsto\!\!\longrightarrow \\ \longrightarrow \\ D_F \end{array}$$

$D_B = D_F \quad \text{so} \quad R_B T_B = R_F T_F$

$T_B = 40; \ T_F = 30; \ R_F = R_B + 6$

$40R_B = (R_B + 6)30$

$40R_B = 30R_B + 180$

$10R_B = 180$

$R_B = 18 \text{ kph}$

$D_F = D_B = 18(40) = \textbf{720 kilometers}$

3. (a) $N_B = 5N_G$

(b) $N_B = 15N_G - 100$

Substitute (a) into (b) and get:

(b′) $(5N_G) = 15N_G - 100$

$-10N_G = -100$

$N_G = \textbf{10 girls}$

(a) $N_B = 5(10) = \textbf{50 boys}$

4. (a) $\dfrac{D_I}{D_A} = \dfrac{5}{2} \longrightarrow 2D_I = 5D_A$

(b) $D_I + D_A = 980 \longrightarrow D_A = 980 - D_I$

Substitute (b) into (a) and get:

(a′) $2D_I = 5(980 - D_I)$

$7D_I = 4900$

$D_I = \textbf{700 minor disasters}$

5. (a) $N_Q + N_H = 200$

(b) $25N_Q + 50N_H = 7500$

$\begin{array}{ll} -50\text{(a)} & -50N_Q - 50N_H = -10,000 \\ 1\text{(b)} & \underline{25N_Q + 50N_H = 7,500} \\ & -25N_Q = -2,500 \end{array}$

$N_Q = \textbf{100 quarters}$

(a) $(100) + N_H = 200$

$ N_H = \textbf{100 half-dollars}$

6. If 70% was sodium chloride, 30% was other chemicals.

$\dfrac{P}{100} \times of = is$

$\dfrac{30}{100} \times TW = 660$

$TW = 660 \times \dfrac{100}{30} = \textbf{2200 grams}$

7.

$$x - 5 \overline{\smash{\big)}\ x^3 + 0x^2 + 0x - 2} \qquad \dfrac{x^2 + 5x + 25 + \frac{123}{x-5}}{}$$

$\underline{x^3 - 5x^2}$

$5x^2 + 0x$

$\underline{5x^2 - 25x}$

$25x - 2$

$\underline{25x - 125}$

123

Check:

$\dfrac{x^2(x-5)}{x-5} + \dfrac{5x(x-5)}{x-5} + \dfrac{25(x-5)}{x-5} + \dfrac{123}{x-5}$

$= \dfrac{x^3 - 5x^2 + 5x^2 - 25x + 25x - 2}{x-5}$

$= \dfrac{x^3 - 2}{x-5}$

8. $5x^2y^2 - 2xy + 10xy^2 = \textbf{\textit{xy}(5\textit{xy} - 2 + 10\textit{y})}$

9. $x^2y^3m^5 + 12x^3ym^4 - 3x^2y^2m^2$
$= \textbf{\textit{x}}^2\textbf{\textit{ym}}^2(\textbf{\textit{y}}^2\textbf{\textit{m}}^3 + \textbf{12\textit{xm}}^2 - \textbf{3\textit{y}})$

10. $16m^2p^3y - 8y^4mp^3 + 4m^2p^2y^2$
$= \textbf{4\textit{mp}}^2\textbf{\textit{y}}(\textbf{4\textit{mp}} - \textbf{2\textit{py}}^3 + \textbf{\textit{my}})$

11. $x^3y^2z^3 + x^2yz^2 - 3x^3yz = \textbf{\textit{x}}^2\textbf{\textit{yz}}(\textbf{\textit{xyz}}^2 + \textbf{\textit{z}} - \textbf{3\textit{x}})$

12. $p^5x^3 + p^4x^2 - p^3x = \textbf{\textit{p}}^3\textbf{\textit{x}}(\textbf{\textit{p}}^2\textbf{\textit{x}}^2 + \textbf{\textit{px}} - \textbf{1})$

13. $2\sqrt{3} \cdot 3\sqrt{6} \cdot 5\sqrt{12}$
$= 2\sqrt{3} \cdot 3\sqrt{2}\sqrt{3} \cdot 5\sqrt{2}\sqrt{2}\sqrt{3}$
$= 30\sqrt{2}\sqrt{2}\sqrt{2}\sqrt{3}\sqrt{3}\sqrt{3} = \textbf{180}\sqrt{\textbf{6}}$

14. $6\sqrt{18} + 5\sqrt{8} - 3\sqrt{50}$
$= 6\sqrt{2}\sqrt{3}\sqrt{3} + 5\sqrt{2}\sqrt{2}\sqrt{2} - 3\sqrt{2}\sqrt{5}\sqrt{5}$
$= 18\sqrt{2} + 10\sqrt{2} - 15\sqrt{2} = \textbf{13}\sqrt{\textbf{2}}$

15. $2\sqrt{5}(3\sqrt{15} - 2\sqrt{5}) = 2\sqrt{5}(3\sqrt{3}\sqrt{5} - 2\sqrt{5})$
$= 6\sqrt{3}\sqrt{5}\sqrt{5} - 4\sqrt{5}\sqrt{5} = \textbf{30}\sqrt{\textbf{3}} - \textbf{20}$

16. $a + \dfrac{a}{b} = \dfrac{ab}{b} + \dfrac{a}{b} = \dfrac{\textbf{\textit{ab}} + \textbf{\textit{a}}}{\textbf{\textit{b}}}$

17. $\dfrac{ax^2}{m^2p} - c + \dfrac{2}{m} = \dfrac{ax^2}{m^2p} - \dfrac{cm^2p}{m^2p} + \dfrac{2mp}{m^2p}$

$= \dfrac{\textbf{\textit{ax}}^2 - \textbf{\textit{cm}}^2\textbf{\textit{p}} + \textbf{2\textit{mp}}}{\textbf{\textit{m}}^2\textbf{\textit{p}}}$

18. $\dfrac{(38{,}000 \times 10^3)(300 \times 10^{-4})}{0.00019 \times 10^{-5}}$

$= \dfrac{(38 \times 10^6)(3 \times 10^{-2})}{19 \times 10^{-10}} = \dfrac{114 \times 10^4}{19 \times 10^{-10}}$

$= \textbf{6} \times \textbf{10}^{\textbf{14}}$

19. (a) $3x - 2y = 10$

$$-2y = -3x + 10$$

$$y = \frac{3}{2}x - 5$$

(b) $y = -\frac{1}{2}$

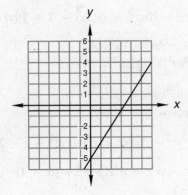

Substitute (b) into (a) and get:

(a') $3x - 2\left(-\frac{1}{2}\right) = 10$

$$3x + 1 = 10$$

$$3x = 9$$

$$x = 3$$

$$\left(3, -\frac{1}{2}\right)$$

20. Since parallel lines have the same slope,

$$y = \frac{1}{6}x + b$$

$$5 = \frac{1}{6}(3) + b$$

$$\frac{9}{2} = b$$

Since $m = \frac{1}{6}$ and $b = \frac{9}{2}$, $y = \frac{1}{6}x + \frac{9}{2}$.

21. (a) $6x - 2y = 100$

(b) $\underline{3x + 2y = 80}$

$9x = 180$

$$x = 20$$

(b) $3(20) + 2y = 80$

$$2y = 20$$

$$y = 10$$

$7 \times \overrightarrow{SF} = 11$

$$\overrightarrow{SF} = \frac{11}{7}$$

$9 \times \frac{11}{7} = P$

$$\frac{99}{7} = P$$

22. Arc length $= \frac{280}{360} \cdot 2\pi r = \frac{280}{360} \cdot 2\pi(12 \text{ cm})$

$$\approx \textbf{58.61 cm}$$

23. $\frac{x + 1}{4} - \frac{3}{2} = \frac{2x - 9}{10}$

$$5x + 5 - 30 = 4x - 18$$

$$x = 7$$

24. $\frac{4x - 8}{5} + \frac{2x - 4}{2} = 9$

$$8x - 16 + 10x - 20 = 90$$

$$18x = 126$$

$$x = 7$$

25. $\frac{n + 3}{6} - \frac{1}{3} = \frac{2n - 2}{5}$

$$5n + 15 - 10 = 12n - 12$$

$$-7n = -17$$

$$n = \frac{17}{7}$$

26. $\frac{5x + 3}{2} - \frac{3}{4} = \frac{5}{2}$

$$10x + 6 - 3 = 10$$

$$10x = 7$$

$$x = \frac{7}{10}$$

27. $\frac{8x^5 + 12x^3}{4x^3} = \frac{4x^3(2x^2 + 3)}{4x^3} = 2x^2 + 3$

28. $\frac{x^2 y^{-2}}{z^2}\left(\frac{z^2}{y^2(2x^{-2})^{-1}} - \frac{4x^2 y^0}{z^{-2}}\right)$

$$= \frac{2x^2 y^{-2} z^2}{z^2 y^2 x^2} - 4x^4 y^{-2} = 2y^{-4} - 4x^4 y^{-2}$$

29. $-3^0\left[(-2 - 4 - 2^2 - 2^0) - |-3 - 2|\right]$

$$= -1[-11 - 5] = -1[-16] = \textbf{16}$$

30. $km(m^2 k - k) = \frac{1}{3}\left(-\frac{1}{4}\right)\left(\left(-\frac{1}{4}\right)^2\left(\frac{1}{3}\right) - \frac{1}{3}\right)$

$$= -\frac{1}{12}\left(\frac{1}{48} - \frac{16}{48}\right) = -\frac{1}{12}\left(-\frac{5}{16}\right) = \frac{5}{192}$$

PRACTICE SET 26

a. $x^2 - 7 - 6x = x^2 - 6x - 7 = (x - 7)(x + 1)$

b. $-x^2 + 6x + 16 = (-1)(x^2 - 6x - 16)$

$\quad = (-1)(x - 8)(x + 2)$

c. $24x^2 + 21x^3 - 3x^4 = -3x^2(x^2 - 7x - 8)$

$\quad = -3x^2(x - 8)(x + 1)$

d. $A^2 = 4^2 + 5^2$

$\quad A^2 = 16 + 25$

$\quad A^2 = 41$

$\quad A = \sqrt{41}$

$\quad \dfrac{C}{8} = \dfrac{4}{5}$

$\quad 5C = 32$

$\quad C = \dfrac{32}{5}$

$\quad \dfrac{B + \sqrt{41}}{\sqrt{41}} = \dfrac{8}{5}$

$\quad 5B + 5\sqrt{41} = 8\sqrt{41}$

$\quad 5B = 3\sqrt{41}$

$\quad B = \dfrac{3}{5}\sqrt{41}$

PROBLEM SET 26

1.

$D_S = D_O$ so $R_S T_S = R_O T_O$

$T_S = 20;\ T_O = 8;\ R_O = R_S + 60$

$20R_S = (R_S + 60)8$

$20R_S = 8R_S + 480$

$12R_S = 480$

$R_S = 40$

$D_S = D_O = (40)(20) = $ **800 miles**

2. (a) $N_B = 5N_R + 50$

(b) $N_R = N_B - 210$

Substitute (a) into (b) and get:

(b′) $\quad N_R = (5N_R + 50) - 210$

$\quad -4N_R = -160$

$\quad N_R = $ **40 reds**

(a) $N_B = 5(40) + 50 = $ **250 blues**

3. (a) $5N_F + 10N_T = 7000$

(b) $N_F + N_T = 1200$

$\begin{array}{ll} 1(a) & 5N_F + 10N_T = \ \ \ 7{,}000 \\ -10(b) & -10N_F - 10N_T = -12{,}000 \\ \hline & -5N_F \qquad\ = -5{,}000 \end{array}$

$N_F = $ **1000 fives**

(b) $(1000) + N_T = 1200$

$\quad N_T = $ **200 tens**

4. If 14% were belligerent, 86% were eristic.

$\dfrac{P}{100} \times of = is$

$\dfrac{86}{100} \times N_T = 4300$

$\quad N_T = 4300 \times \dfrac{100}{86} = 5000$

$N_B = 5000 - 4300 = $ **700**

5. $\dfrac{1820}{1960} = \dfrac{N\text{Ca}}{2240}$

$1960 N\text{Ca} = 1820(2240)$

$\quad N\text{Ca} = $ **2080 grams**

6. If 10% were nonabsorbent, 90% were absorbent.

$\dfrac{P}{100} \times of = is$

$\dfrac{90}{100} \times C = 7290$

$\quad C = 7290 \times \dfrac{100}{90} = $ **8100 chemicals**

7.

$$x + 1\ \overline{)\,x^4 + 0x^3 + 0x^2 + 0x - 2}\qquad x^3 - x^2 + x - 1 - \dfrac{1}{x+1}$$

$\quad \underline{x^4 + \ x^3}$

$\quad\quad -x^3 + 0x^2$

$\quad\quad \underline{-x^3 - \ x^2}$

$\quad\quad\quad\ x^2 + 0x$

$\quad\quad\quad\ \underline{x^2 + \ x}$

$\quad\quad\quad\quad\ -x - 2$

$\quad\quad\quad\quad\ \underline{-x - 1}$

$\quad\quad\quad\quad\quad\quad -1$

Check:

$\dfrac{x^3(x+1)}{x+1} - \dfrac{x^2(x+1)}{x+1} + \dfrac{x(x+1)}{x+1}$

$- \dfrac{1(x+1)}{x+1} - \dfrac{1}{x+1}$

$= \dfrac{x^4 + x^3 - x^3 - x^2 + x^2 + x - x - 1 - 1}{x+1}$

$= \dfrac{x^4 - 2}{x+1}$

8. $35x^7y^5m - 7x^5m^2y^2 + 14y^7x^4m^2$
$= 7x^4y^2m(5x^3y^3 - xm + 2y^5m)$

9. $6x^2ym^5 - 2x^2ym + 4xym$
$= 2xym(3xm^4 - x + 2)$

10. $4x^2y^4p^6 - 2xp^5y^7 + 8x^4p^5y^5$
$= 2xy^4p^5(2xp - y^3 + 4x^3y)$

11. $x^2 + x - 6 = (x + 3)(x - 2)$

12. $x^2 - 6x + 8 = (x - 4)(x - 2)$

13. $-2ab + abx + abx^2 = ab(x + 2)(x - 1)$

14. $\dfrac{6x^2y - xy}{xy} = \dfrac{xy(6x - 1)}{xy} = 6x - 1$

15. $3\sqrt{2} \cdot 2\sqrt{6} \cdot 3\sqrt{6} = 3\sqrt{2} \cdot 2\sqrt{2}\sqrt{3} \cdot 3\sqrt{2}\sqrt{3}$
$= 18\sqrt{2}\sqrt{2}\sqrt{2}\sqrt{3}\sqrt{3}$
$= \mathbf{108\sqrt{2}}$

16. $-3\sqrt{12} + 5\sqrt{27} - 8\sqrt{25}$
$= -3\sqrt{2}\sqrt{2}\sqrt{3} + 5\sqrt{3}\sqrt{3}\sqrt{3} - 8\sqrt{5}\sqrt{5}$
$= -6\sqrt{3} + 15\sqrt{3} - 40 = \mathbf{9\sqrt{3} - 40}$

17. $3\sqrt{2}(5\sqrt{3} - 2\sqrt{2}) = 15\sqrt{2}\sqrt{3} - 6\sqrt{2}\sqrt{2}$
$= \mathbf{15\sqrt{6} - 12}$

18. $\dfrac{a^2m}{x^2} - x^2 - \dfrac{x^2}{c} = \dfrac{a^2cm}{cx^2} - \dfrac{cx^4}{cx^2} - \dfrac{x^4}{cx^2}$
$= \dfrac{a^2cm - cx^4 - x^4}{cx^2}$

19. $\dfrac{(3000 \times 10^{-14})(0.00008)}{(0.0002 \times 10^5)(200{,}000)}$
$= \dfrac{(3 \times 10^{-11})(8 \times 10^{-5})}{(2 \times 10^1)(2 \times 10^5)} = \dfrac{24 \times 10^{-16}}{4 \times 10^6}$
$= \mathbf{6 \times 10^{-22}}$

20. (a) $2y - x = 6$
$2y = x + 6$
$y = \dfrac{1}{2}x + 3$

(b) $y - 2x = -3$
$y = 2x - 3$

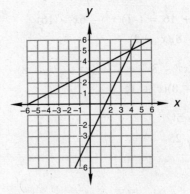

Substitute $y = 2x - 3$ into (a) and get:

(a') $2(2x - 3) - x = 6$
$4x - 6 - x = 6$
$3x = 12$
$x = 4$

(b) $y - 2(4) = -3$
$y = 5$

(4, 5)

21.

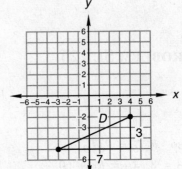

$D^2 = 7^2 + 3^2$
$D^2 = 49 + 9$
$D^2 = 58$
$D = \sqrt{\mathbf{58}}$

22. $A^2 = 5^2 + 4^2$
$A^2 = 25 + 16$
$A^2 = 41$
$A = \sqrt{\mathbf{41}}$
$4 \cdot \overrightarrow{SF} = 7$
$\overrightarrow{SF} = \dfrac{7}{4}$

$$\sqrt{41} \cdot \frac{7}{4} = B + \sqrt{41}$$

$$7\sqrt{41} = 4B + 4\sqrt{41}$$

$$3\sqrt{41} = 4B$$

$$\frac{3\sqrt{41}}{4} = B$$

$$5 \cdot \frac{7}{4} = C$$

$$\frac{35}{4} = C$$

23. $x + 10 = 90$

$$x = \mathbf{80}$$

$$y + 80 + 70 = 180$$

$$y = \mathbf{30}$$

$$m + 30 = 180$$

$$m = \mathbf{150}$$

$$z + 10 + 150 = 180$$

$$z = \mathbf{20}$$

24. (a) $4x + y = 70$

(b) $2x + 6y - 1 = 115$

(b′) $2x + 6y = 116$

-6(a) $-24x - 6y = -420$

(b′) $\underline{2x + 6y = 116}$

$$-22x = -304$$

$$x = \frac{\mathbf{152}}{\mathbf{11}}$$

(a) $4\left(\dfrac{152}{11}\right) + y = 70$

$$y = \frac{770}{11} - \frac{608}{11} = \frac{\mathbf{162}}{\mathbf{11}}$$

25. $A_{\text{Triangle}} = \dfrac{b \times H}{2} = 54 \text{ m}^2$

$$b = \frac{54(2) \text{ m}^2}{9 \text{ m}}$$

$$b = \mathbf{12 \text{ m}} = BC$$

$A_{\text{Circle}} = \pi r^2 = \pi(12 \text{ m})^2 \approx \mathbf{452.16 \text{ m}^2}$

26. $\dfrac{2x}{3} + \dfrac{6 - 3x}{4} = 7$

$$8x + 18 - 9x = 84$$

$$-x = 66$$

$$x = \mathbf{-66}$$

27. $\dfrac{4 - x}{3} + \dfrac{1}{6} = 5$

$$8 - 2x + 1 = 30$$

$$-2x = 21$$

$$x = -\frac{\mathbf{21}}{\mathbf{2}}$$

28. $-2x - \dfrac{3^0 - x}{2} + \dfrac{x - 5^0}{7} = 2$

$$-28x - 7 + 7x + 2x - 2 = 28$$

$$-19x = 37$$

$$x = -\frac{\mathbf{37}}{\mathbf{19}}$$

29. $\dfrac{x^2(yz^0)^{-2}}{(-2x^2y)^{-3}} = \dfrac{-8x^2y^{-2}}{x^{-6}y^{-3}} = \mathbf{-8x^8y}$

30. $-\dfrac{1}{-(-3)^{-2}} + \dfrac{1}{-2^{-3}}(a - ba)$

$$= 9 - 8\left(-\frac{1}{2} - 3\left(-\frac{1}{2}\right)\right) = 9 - 8\left(-\frac{1}{2} + \frac{3}{2}\right)$$

$$= 9 - 8(1) = 9 - 8 = \mathbf{1}$$

PRACTICE SET 27

a. $\dfrac{m + 3}{m + 4} + 5 + \dfrac{2}{m^2}$

$$= \frac{m^2(m + 3)}{m^2(m + 4)} + \frac{m^2(m + 4)5}{m^2(m + 4)} + \frac{(m + 4)2}{m^2(m + 4)}$$

$$= \frac{m^3 + 3m^2 + 5m^3 + 20m^2 + 2m + 8}{m^2(m + 4)}$$

$$= \frac{\mathbf{6m^3 + 23m^2 + 2m + 8}}{\mathbf{m^2(m + 4)}}$$

b. $\dfrac{z + 3}{z^2 + 5z + 4} - \dfrac{1}{z(z + 4)}$

$$= \frac{z + 3}{(z + 4)(z + 1)} - \frac{1}{z(z + 4)}$$

$$= \frac{z(z + 3)}{z(z + 4)(z + 1)} - \frac{(z + 1)}{z(z + 4)(z + 1)}$$

$$= \frac{\mathbf{z^2 + 2z - 1}}{\mathbf{z(z + 4)(z + 1)}}$$

Problem Set 27

1.

$D_H = D_T$ so $R_H T_H = R_T T_T$

$R_H = 4$; $R_T = 20$; $T_H + T_T = 18$

$4T_H = 20(18 - T_H)$

$4T_H = 360 - 20T_H$

$24T_H = 360$

$T_H = 15$

$D_T = D_H = 15(4) = $ **60 miles**

2.

$D_H = D_R$ so $R_H T_H = R_R T_R$

$R_H = 5$; $R_R = 20$; $T_H + T_R = 10$

$5T_H = 20(10 - T_H)$

$5T_H = 200 - 20T_H$

$25T_H = 200$

$T_H = 8$

$D_H = D_R = 5(8) = $ **40 kilometers**

3. (a) $N_G = 2N_B + 6$

(b) $N_G + N_B = 36$

Substitute (a) into (b) and get:

(b′) $(2N_B + 6) + N_B = 36$

$3N_B = 30$

$N_B = $ **10 boys**

(b) $N_G + (10) = 36$

$N_G = $ **26 girls**

4. Multiples of 7: $7N$, $7N + 7$, $7N + 14$

$-3(7N + 7N + 14) = 5(-7N - 7) - 21$

$-42N - 42 = -35N - 56$

$-7N = -14$

$N = 2$

The desired integers are **14**, **21**, and **28**.

5. $\dfrac{600}{3000} = \dfrac{Ba}{9000}$

$3000Ba = 600(9000)$

$Ba = $ **1800 grams**

6. If 70% was silver iodide, 30% was not silver iodide.

$\dfrac{P}{100} \times of = is$

$\dfrac{30}{100} \times 2000 = NS$

$NS = $ **600 grams**

7.

$$x - 2 \overline{\smash{\big)}\ x^3 + 0x^2 + 0x - 6} \quad \rightarrow \quad x^2 + 2x + 4 + \dfrac{2}{x-2}$$

$$\underline{x^3 - 2x^2}$$
$$2x^2 + 0x$$
$$\underline{2x^2 - 4x}$$
$$4x - 6$$
$$\underline{4x - 8}$$
$$2$$

Check:

$\dfrac{x^2(x-2)}{x-2} + \dfrac{2x(x-2)}{x-2} + \dfrac{4(x-2)}{x-2} + \dfrac{2}{x-2}$

$= \dfrac{x^3 - 2x^2 + 2x^2 - 4x + 4x - 8 + 2}{x-2}$

$= \dfrac{x^3 - 6}{x-2}$

8. $9m^2x^4p^2 + 3x^2p^6m^4 - 6x^4m^3p^2$
$= 3m^2x^2p^2(3x^2 + p^4m^2 - 2x^2m)$

9. $mx^4y - mx^2y^3 - 4mx^2y = mx^2y(x^2 - y^2 - 4)$

10. $a^2x^3p - 4a^3x^3p - a^2x^4p = a^2x^3p(1 - 4a - x)$

11. $4ax + ax^2 - 5a = a(x + 5)(x - 1)$

12. $8x^2 - x^3 - 15x = -x(x - 5)(x - 3)$

13. $24ax - 5ax^2 - ax^3 = -ax(x + 8)(x - 3)$

14. $-ax^4 + 4ax^3 + 5ax^2 = -ax^2(x - 5)(x + 1)$.

15. $56p - 15px + px^2 = p(x - 8)(x - 7)$

16. $\dfrac{4xa + 4x}{4x} = \dfrac{4x(a + 1)}{4x} = a + 1$

17. $3\sqrt{2} - 2\sqrt{3} \cdot 3\sqrt{12} = 3\sqrt{2} - 2\sqrt{3} \cdot 3\sqrt{2}\sqrt{2}\sqrt{3}$
$= 3\sqrt{2} - 6\sqrt{2}\sqrt{2}\sqrt{3}\sqrt{3}$
$= 3\sqrt{2} - 36$

18. $-3\sqrt{20} + 2\sqrt{125} + 5\sqrt{45}$
$= -3\sqrt{2}\sqrt{2}\sqrt{5} + 2\sqrt{5}\sqrt{5}\sqrt{5} + 5\sqrt{3}\sqrt{3}\sqrt{5}$
$= -6\sqrt{5} + 10\sqrt{5} + 15\sqrt{5} = 19\sqrt{5}$

19. $2\sqrt{3}(3\sqrt{2} - 3\sqrt{3}) = 6\sqrt{2}\sqrt{3} - 6\sqrt{3}\sqrt{3}$
$= \mathbf{6\sqrt{6} - 18}$

20. $\dfrac{2}{x} + \dfrac{3}{x + p} = \dfrac{2(x + p)}{x(x + p)} + \dfrac{3(x)}{x(x + p)}$

$= \dfrac{2x + 2p + 3x}{x(x + p)} = \dfrac{\mathbf{5x + 2p}}{\mathbf{x(x + p)}}$

21. $\dfrac{x + 3}{x + 6} + 5 + \dfrac{3}{x^2}$

$= \dfrac{x^2(x + 3)}{x^2(x + 6)} + \dfrac{5x^2(x + 6)}{x^2(x + 6)} + \dfrac{3(x + 6)}{x^2(x + 6)}$

$= \dfrac{x^3 + 3x^2 + 5x^3 + 30x^2 + 3x + 18}{x^2(x + 6)}$

$= \dfrac{\mathbf{6x^3 + 33x^2 + 3x + 18}}{\mathbf{x^2(x + 6)}}$

22. $\dfrac{(0.00056 \times 10^4)(7 \times 10^3)}{(0.00049 \times 10^{16})(0.00002 \times 10^{-5})}$

$= \dfrac{(56 \times 10^{-1})(7 \times 10^3)}{(49 \times 10^{11})(2 \times 10^{-10})} = \dfrac{392 \times 10^2}{98 \times 10^1}$

$= \mathbf{4 \times 10^1}$

23. (a) $3x + 2y = 12$
$2y = -3x + 12$
$y = -\dfrac{3}{2}x + 6$

(b) $8x - 2y = 10$
$-2y = -8x + 10$
$y = 4x - 5$

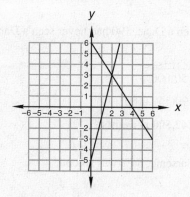

(a) $3x + 2y = 12$
(b) $\dfrac{8x - 2y = 10}{}$
$\overline{11x \qquad = 22}$
$x = 2$

(a) $3(2) + 2y = 12$
$2y = 6$
$y = 3$

$\mathbf{(2, 3)}$

24. Since parallel lines have the same slope,

$y = -\dfrac{3}{8}x + b$

$-3 = -\dfrac{3}{8}(-3) + b$

$-3 = \dfrac{9}{8} + b$

$-\dfrac{33}{8} = b$

Since $m = -\dfrac{3}{8}$ and $b = -\dfrac{33}{8}$,

$\mathbf{y = -\dfrac{3}{8}x - \dfrac{33}{8}.}$

25. $A^2 = 7^2 + 4^2$
$A^2 = 49 + 16$
$A^2 = 65$
$A = \sqrt{65}$

$7 \cdot \overrightarrow{SF} = 12$
$\overrightarrow{SF} = \dfrac{12}{7}$

$\sqrt{65} \cdot \dfrac{12}{7} = B + \sqrt{65}$

$12\sqrt{65} = 7B + 7\sqrt{65}$

$5\sqrt{65} = 7B$

$\dfrac{\mathbf{5\sqrt{65}}}{\mathbf{7}} = B$

$4 \cdot \dfrac{12}{7} = C$

$\dfrac{\mathbf{48}}{\mathbf{7}} = C$

26. $\dfrac{x}{6} = \dfrac{3}{5} \longrightarrow 5x = 18 \longrightarrow x = \dfrac{\mathbf{18}}{\mathbf{5}}$

$\dfrac{5}{8} = \dfrac{7}{y} \longrightarrow 5y = 56 \longrightarrow y = \dfrac{\mathbf{56}}{\mathbf{5}}$

27. $\dfrac{6 + x}{5} + \dfrac{1}{3} = 8$

$18 + 3x + 5 = 120$

$3x = 97$

$x = \dfrac{\mathbf{97}}{\mathbf{3}}$

28. $\dfrac{3x - 2}{3} + 4 = \dfrac{1}{6}$

$6x - 4 + 24 = 1$

$6x = -19$

$x = -\dfrac{19}{6}$

29. $\dfrac{3a^{-2}y}{b} + 7b^{-1}ya^{-2} - \dfrac{5b^{-1}}{a^2y^{-1}}$

$= \dfrac{3y}{a^2b} + \dfrac{7y}{a^2b} - \dfrac{5y}{a^2b} = \dfrac{5y}{a^2b}$

30. $-3^0(-3 - 2^2) - 4(-2)ax - a$

$= -(-7) + 8(-2)(4) - (-2)$

$= 7 - 64 + 2 = -55$

PRACTICE SET 28

a. $\dfrac{\dfrac{m}{p}}{\dfrac{z+x}{p}} \cdot \dfrac{\dfrac{p}{z+x}}{\dfrac{p}{z+x}} = \dfrac{m}{z+x}$

b. $\dfrac{\dfrac{m}{x+y}}{\dfrac{z}{x+y}} \cdot \dfrac{\dfrac{x+y}{z}}{\dfrac{x+y}{z}} = \dfrac{m}{z}$

c. $\dfrac{4}{3\sqrt{2}} \cdot \dfrac{\sqrt{2}}{\sqrt{2}} = \dfrac{4\sqrt{2}}{6} = \dfrac{2\sqrt{2}}{3}$

PROBLEM SET 28

1.

$D_R = D_P$ so $R_RT_R = R_PT_P$

$R_R = 60;\ R_P = 3;\ T_R + T_P = 21$

$60(21 - T_P) = 3T_P$

$1260 - 60T_P = 3T_P$

$1260 = 63T_P$

$20 = T_P$

$D_P = 3(20) =$ **60 miles**

2. Multiples of 3: $3N,\ 3N + 3,\ 3N + 6,\ 3N + 9$

$5(3N + 3N + 9) = 13(3N + 6) - 6$

$30N + 45 = 39N + 72$

$-9N = 27$

$N = -3$

The desired integers are **–9, –6, –3,** and **0.**

3. (a) $N_G = 3N_B - 1$

(b) $N_G + N_B = 15$

Substitute (a) into (b) and get:

(b′) $(3N_B - 1) + N_B = 15$

$4N_B = 16$

$N_B =$ **4 boys**

(a) $N_G = 3(4) - 1 =$ **11 girls**

4. (a) $5N_N + 10N_D = 3000$

(b) $N_N + N_D = 500$

$\begin{array}{rl} 1(a) & 5N_N + 10N_D = 3000 \\ -10(b) & -10N_N - 10N_D = -5000 \\ \hline & -5N_N = -2000 \end{array}$

$N_N =$ **400 nickels**

(b) $(400) + N_D = 500$

$N_D =$ **100 dimes**

5. If 10 had seen a Dane, 190 had never seen a Dane.

$\dfrac{190}{200} = \dfrac{NS}{150{,}000}$

$200NS = 190(150{,}000)$

$NS =$ **142,500 peasants**

6. If 16% was arsenic, 84% was silicon.

$\dfrac{P}{100} \times of = is$

$\dfrac{84}{100} \times EM = 7350$

$EM = 7350 \times \dfrac{100}{84}$

Entire mixture = **8750 kg**

$M_A = 8750 - 7350 =$ **1400 kg of arsenic**

7.
$$x - 5 \overline{) x^3 + 0x^2 + 0x - 7} \quad \frac{x^2 + 5x + 25 + \frac{118}{x-5}}{}$$

$$\underline{x^3 - 5x^2}$$
$$5x^2 + 0x$$
$$\underline{5x^2 - 25x}$$
$$25x - 7$$
$$\underline{25x - 125}$$
$$118$$

Check:

$$\frac{x^2(x-5)}{x-5} + \frac{5x(x-5)}{x-5} + \frac{25(x-5)}{x-5} + \frac{118}{x-5}$$

$$= \frac{x^3 - 5x^2 + 5x^2 - 25x + 25x - 125 + 118}{x - 5}$$

$$= \frac{x^3 - 7}{x - 5}$$

8. $2x^2y - 8x^4y^4 = 2x^2y(1 - 4x^2y^3)$

9. $4x^2y^3p^3 - 16x^2y^3p - x^4y^3p^4$
$= x^2y^3p(4p^2 - 16 - x^2p^3)$

10. $-35xy + 2x^2y + x^3y = xy(x + 7)(x - 5)$

11. $-8a - 7ax + ax^2 = a(x - 8)(x + 1)$

12. $2m^2 + 3xm^2 + m^2x^2 = m^2(x + 2)(x + 1)$

13. $-a^2 - a^2x^2 - 2xa^2 = -a^2(x + 1)(x + 1)$

14. $\frac{4x^2 + x}{x} = \frac{x(4x + 1)}{x} = 4x + 1$

15. $4\sqrt{27} - 3\sqrt{48} + 2\sqrt{75}$
$= 4\sqrt{3}\sqrt{3}\sqrt{3} - 3\sqrt{2}\sqrt{2}\sqrt{2}\sqrt{2}\sqrt{3} + 2\sqrt{3}\sqrt{5}\sqrt{5}$
$= 12\sqrt{3} - 12\sqrt{3} + 10\sqrt{3} = 10\sqrt{3}$

16. $3\sqrt{5}(\sqrt{15} - 2\sqrt{5}) = 3\sqrt{5}(\sqrt{3}\sqrt{5} - 2\sqrt{5})$
$= 3\sqrt{3}\sqrt{5}\sqrt{5} - 6\sqrt{5}\sqrt{5}$
$= 15\sqrt{3} - 30$

17. $\frac{(0.00077 \times 10^{-3})(40 \times 10^6)}{(0.00011 \times 10^5)(140,000)}$

$= \frac{(77 \times 10^{-8})(4 \times 10^7)}{(11)(14 \times 10^4)} = \frac{308 \times 10^{-1}}{154 \times 10^4}$

$= 2 \times 10^{-5}$

18. $\dfrac{\dfrac{x}{m + p}}{\dfrac{y}{m + p}} \cdot \dfrac{\dfrac{m + p}{y}}{\dfrac{m + p}{y}} = \dfrac{x}{y}$

19. $\frac{3}{4\sqrt{15}} \cdot \frac{\sqrt{15}}{\sqrt{15}} = \frac{3\sqrt{15}}{60} = \frac{\sqrt{15}}{20}$

20. $\frac{4a}{a + x} + \frac{6}{a} = \frac{4a(a)}{a(a + x)} + \frac{6(a + x)}{a(a + x)}$

$= \frac{4a^2 + 6(a + x)}{a(a + x)}$

21. $\frac{2x}{x^2 + 2x + 1} + \frac{3}{x + 1}$

$= \frac{2x}{(x + 1)(x + 1)} + \frac{3(x + 1)}{(x + 1)(x + 1)}$

$= \frac{2x + 3x + 3}{(x + 1)(x + 1)} = \frac{5x + 3}{(x + 1)^2}$

22. (a) $5x + 2y = 6$
$$2y = -5x + 6$$
$$y = -\frac{5}{2}x + 3$$

(b) $y = \frac{1}{2}x$

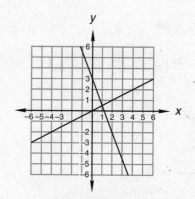

Substitute (b) into (a) and get:

(a) $5x + 2\left(\frac{1}{2}x\right) = 6$
$$6x = 6$$
$$x = 1$$

(b) $y = \frac{1}{2}(1) = \frac{1}{2}$

$\left(1, \dfrac{1}{2}\right)$

23. (a) Every point on this line is 4 units below the x-axis.
$$y = -4$$

(b) The y-intercept is +2. The slope is negative and the rise over the run for any triangle drawn is $-\frac{1}{3}$.

$$y = -\frac{1}{3}x + 2$$

24. $A + 150 = 180$

$A = \mathbf{30}$

$B + 30 + 90 = 180$

$B = \mathbf{60}$

$C = B = \mathbf{60}$

$D + 60 + 90 = 180$

$D = \mathbf{30}$

$E + 30 + 90 = 180$

$E = \mathbf{60}$

$F + 60 + 40 = 180$

$F = \mathbf{80}$

25. $3x + 90 = 180$

$3x = 90$

$x = \mathbf{30}$

$2x = 2(30) = \mathbf{60}$

$A_{\text{Shaded}} = \dfrac{60}{360}(\pi(2\text{ m})^2) \approx \mathbf{2.09 \text{ m}^2}$

Length of $\overset{\frown}{BC} = \dfrac{60}{360}(2\pi(2\text{ m})) \approx \mathbf{2.09 \text{ m}}$

26. $\dfrac{2x}{3} + \dfrac{x-3}{5} = 1$

$10x + 3x - 9 = 15$

$13x = 24$

$x = \dfrac{\mathbf{24}}{\mathbf{13}}$

27. $4\dfrac{1}{3} - 2\dfrac{1}{5}x = -\dfrac{3}{10}$

$-\dfrac{11}{5}x = -\dfrac{9}{30} - \dfrac{130}{30}$

$x = -\dfrac{139}{30} \cdot -\dfrac{5}{11} = \dfrac{\mathbf{139}}{\mathbf{66}}$

28.

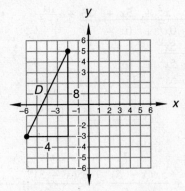

$D^2 = 8^2 + 4^2$

$D^2 = 64 + 16$

$D^2 = 80$

$D = \sqrt{80}$

$D = \mathbf{4\sqrt{5}}$

29. $\dfrac{3x^{-2}y^2}{z}\left(\dfrac{x^2 z}{3y^2} - \dfrac{4x^{-2}y}{z^{-3}}\right) = \dfrac{3y^2 z}{3y^2 z} - \dfrac{12\,x^{-4}y^3}{z^{-2}}$

$= \mathbf{1 - 12x^{-4}y^3 z^2}$

30. $x^0 - xy^0(x - y)$

$= \left(-\dfrac{1}{3}\right)^0 - \left(-\dfrac{1}{3}\right)\left(-\dfrac{1}{4}\right)^0\left(\left(-\dfrac{1}{3}\right) - \left(-\dfrac{1}{4}\right)\right)$

$= 1 - \left(-\dfrac{1}{3}\right)\left(-\dfrac{4}{12} + \dfrac{3}{12}\right) = 1 - \left(-\dfrac{1}{3}\right)\left(-\dfrac{1}{12}\right)$

$= \dfrac{36}{36} - \dfrac{1}{36} = \dfrac{\mathbf{35}}{\mathbf{36}}$

PRACTICE SET 29

$\overset{D_C}{\longrightarrow} \quad \overset{D_M}{\longleftarrow}$
$\underset{66}{\rule{2cm}{0pt}}$

$T_C = 8; \ T_M = 7$

$D_C + D_M = 66$

$R_C T_C + R_M T_M = 66$

$R_C(8) + (2R_C)(7) = 66$

$8R_C + 14R_C = 66$

$22R_C = 66$

$R_C = \mathbf{3 \text{ mph}}$

$R_M = 2R_C$

$R_M = \mathbf{6 \text{ mph}}$

PROBLEM SET 29

1.

$R_W T_W + R_R T_R = 76;\ R_W = 4;$

$R_R = 15;\ T_W + T_R = 8$

$4T_W + 15(8 - T_W) = 76$

$4T_W + 120 - 15T_W = 76$

$\qquad\qquad -11T_W = -44$

$\qquad\qquad\quad T_W = \textbf{4 hr}$

2.

$R_C T_C + R_D T_D = 63;$

$R_C = 3;\ T_C = 9;\ T_D = 6$

$3(9) + 6R_D = 63$

$\qquad 6R_D = 36$

$\qquad\ R_D = \textbf{6 mph}$

3.

$R_R T_R + R_M T_M = 7900;$

$R_M = R_R - 400;\ T_R = 6;\ T_M = 5$

$6R_R + (R_R - 400)5 = 7900$

$6R_R + 5R_R - 2000 = 7900$

$\qquad\qquad 11R_R = 9900$

$\qquad\qquad\ \ R_R = \textbf{900 kph}$

$R_M = (900) - 400$

$R_M = \textbf{500 kph}$

4. (a) $N_R = 2N_P + 15$

(b) $N_R + N_P = 255$

Substitute (a) into (b) and get:

(b′) $(2N_P + 15) + N_P = 255$

$\qquad\qquad\quad 3N_P = 240$

$\qquad\qquad\quad\ N_P = 80$

(a) $N_R = 2(80) + 15 = \textbf{175 roses}$

5. $\dfrac{130}{156,000} = \dfrac{3250}{H}$

$130H = 3250(156,000)$

$H = \textbf{3,900,000 places}$

6. If 17% contained xenophobes, then 83% did not contain xenophobes.

$\dfrac{P}{100} \times of = is$

$\dfrac{83}{100} \times HP = 116,200$

$HP = 116,200 \times \dfrac{100}{83}$

$= \textbf{140,000 hiding places}$

7.

$$
\begin{array}{r}
x^2 + 2x + 5 \\
x+1\overline{\smash{)}\,x^3 + 3x^2 + 7x + 5} \\
\underline{x^3 + \ x^2} \qquad\qquad\quad \\
2x^2 + 7x \qquad\ \\
\underline{2x^2 + 2x} \qquad\ \\
5x + 5 \\
\underline{5x + 5} \\
0
\end{array}
$$

Check:

$\dfrac{x^2(x+1)}{x+1} + \dfrac{2x(x+1)}{x+1} + \dfrac{5(x+1)}{x+1}$

$= \dfrac{x^3 + x^2 + 2x^2 + 2x + 5x + 5}{x+1}$

$= \dfrac{x^3 + 3x^2 + 7x + 5}{x+1}$

8. $16x^3y^2z^3 - 8x^2y^2z^2 = \mathbf{8x^2y^2z^2(2xz - 1)}$

9. $2x^2yp^4 - 6x^3yp^3 - 2x^2yp^2$
$= \mathbf{2x^2yp^2(p^2 - 3xp - 1)}$

10. $12a^2x + a^2x^2 + 35a^2 = \mathbf{a^2(x + 7)(x + 5)}$

11. $-2m^2x - m^2 - m^2x^2 = \mathbf{-m^2(x + 1)(x + 1)}$

12. $x^2k + 3kx - 40k = \mathbf{k(x + 8)(x - 5)}$

13. $\dfrac{x^2 + ax^2}{x^2} = \dfrac{x^2(1 + a)}{x^2} = \mathbf{1 + a}$

14. $2\sqrt{75} - 5\sqrt{48} + 2\sqrt{12}$
$= 2\sqrt{3}\sqrt{5}\sqrt{5} - 5\sqrt{2}\sqrt{2}\sqrt{2}\sqrt{2}\sqrt{3} + 2\sqrt{2}\sqrt{2}\sqrt{3}$
$= 10\sqrt{3} - 20\sqrt{3} + 4\sqrt{3} = \mathbf{-6\sqrt{3}}$

15. $2\sqrt{3}(3\sqrt{6} - 4\sqrt{3}) = 2\sqrt{3}(3\sqrt{2}\sqrt{3} - 4\sqrt{3})$
$= 6\sqrt{2}\sqrt{3}\sqrt{3} - 8\sqrt{3}\sqrt{3}$
$= \mathbf{18\sqrt{2} - 24}$

16. $\dfrac{(0.00052 \times 10^{-4})(5000 \times 10^{7})}{(0.0026 \times 10^{21})(10{,}000 \times 10^{-42})}$

$= \dfrac{(52 \times 10^{-9})(5 \times 10^{10})}{(26 \times 10^{17})(1 \times 10^{-38})} = \dfrac{260 \times 10^{1}}{26 \times 10^{-21}}$

$= \mathbf{1 \times 10^{23}}$

17. $\dfrac{\dfrac{\frac{m}{x}}{\frac{m+x}{x}}}{} \cdot \dfrac{\dfrac{x}{m+x}}{\frac{x}{m+x}} = \dfrac{\boldsymbol{m}}{\boldsymbol{m+x}}$

18. $\dfrac{\dfrac{\frac{a}{m+x}}{b}}{m+x} \cdot \dfrac{\dfrac{m+x}{b}}{\frac{m+x}{b}} = \dfrac{\boldsymbol{a}}{\boldsymbol{b}}$

19. $\dfrac{3}{5\sqrt{12}} \cdot \dfrac{\sqrt{12}}{\sqrt{12}} = \dfrac{3\sqrt{12}}{60} = \dfrac{\boldsymbol{\sqrt{3}}}{\boldsymbol{10}}$

20. $\dfrac{14}{3\sqrt{75}} \cdot \dfrac{\sqrt{75}}{\sqrt{75}} = \dfrac{14\sqrt{75}}{225} = \dfrac{70\sqrt{3}}{225} = \dfrac{\boldsymbol{14\sqrt{3}}}{\boldsymbol{45}}$

21. $\dfrac{4x}{x+4} + \dfrac{6}{x+2}$

$= \dfrac{4x(x+2)}{(x+4)(x+2)} + \dfrac{6(x+4)}{(x+4)(x+2)}$

$= \dfrac{4x^2 + 8x + 6x + 24}{(x+4)(x+2)} = \dfrac{\boldsymbol{4x^2 + 14x + 24}}{\boldsymbol{(x+4)(x+2)}}$

22. $\dfrac{3m}{m^2 + 3m + 2} - \dfrac{5m}{m+1}$

$= \dfrac{3m}{(m+2)(m+1)} - \dfrac{5m(m+2)}{(m+2)(m+1)}$

$= \dfrac{3m - 5m^2 - 10m}{(m+2)(m+1)} = \dfrac{\boldsymbol{-5m^2 - 7m}}{\boldsymbol{(m+2)(m+1)}}$

23. (a) $y - x = 3$

$\quad\quad y = x + 3$

(b) $y + 2x = 6$

$\quad\quad y = -2x + 6$

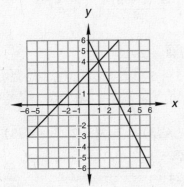

Substitute $y = x + 3$ into (b) and get:

(b) $(x + 3) + 2x = 6$

$\quad\quad\quad 3x = 3$

$\quad\quad\quad\ \ x = 1$

(a) $y - (1) = 3$

$\quad\quad\ \ y = 4$

(1, 4)

24. Since parallel lines have the same slope,

$y = -\dfrac{3}{8}x + b$

$-3 = -\dfrac{3}{8}(2) + b$

$-3 = -\dfrac{3}{4} + b$

$-\dfrac{9}{4} = b$

Since $m = -\dfrac{3}{8}$ and $b = -\dfrac{9}{4}$,

$\boldsymbol{y = -\dfrac{3}{8}x - \dfrac{9}{4}}.$

25. Area $= \pi r^2 = 2500\pi \text{ m}^2$

$r = \sqrt{\dfrac{2500\pi \text{ m}^2}{\pi}}$

$r = \boldsymbol{50 \text{ m}}$

Arc length $= \dfrac{36}{360}[2\pi(50 \text{ m})]$

Arc length $= \boldsymbol{10\pi \text{ m} \approx 31.4 \text{ m}}$

26. $A^2 = 9^2 + 6^2$

$A^2 = 81 + 36$

$A^2 = 117$

$A = \sqrt{117} = \boldsymbol{3\sqrt{13}}$

$9 \cdot \overrightarrow{SF} = 13$

$\overrightarrow{SF} = \dfrac{13}{9}$

$3\sqrt{13} \cdot \dfrac{13}{9} = B + 3\sqrt{13}$

$\dfrac{\boldsymbol{4\sqrt{13}}}{\boldsymbol{3}} = B$

$C = 6 \cdot \dfrac{13}{9} = \dfrac{\boldsymbol{26}}{\boldsymbol{3}}$

27. $\dfrac{3x}{2} - \dfrac{5}{7} = \dfrac{x+2}{3}$

$63x - 30 = 14x + 28$

$49x = 58$

$x = \dfrac{58}{49}$

28. $2\dfrac{1}{5} - \dfrac{1}{10}x = \dfrac{3}{15}$

$-\dfrac{1}{10}x = \dfrac{3}{15} - \dfrac{33}{15}$

$x = -2 \cdot -\dfrac{10}{1} = \mathbf{20}$

29. $\dfrac{(x^2 y^{-2} z)^{-3} x^0}{(x^0 y^{-3} z^2)^3} = \dfrac{x^{-6} y^6 z^{-3}}{y^{-9} z^6} = \boldsymbol{x^{-6} y^{15} z^{-9}}$

30. $x^2 - y^2(x - y) = \left(\dfrac{1}{2}\right)^2 - \left(\dfrac{1}{3}\right)^2\left(\dfrac{1}{2} - \dfrac{1}{3}\right)$

$= \dfrac{1}{4} - \dfrac{1}{9}\left(\dfrac{1}{6}\right) = \dfrac{1}{4} - \dfrac{1}{54}$

$= \dfrac{27}{108} - \dfrac{2}{108} = \dfrac{\mathbf{25}}{\mathbf{108}}$

Practice Set 30

a. This is a valid argument because the conclusion follows directly from the major premise.

b. This is not valid, because we have reversed the order of the major premise (scholar $\longrightarrow$ poor) in the conclusion (poor $\longrightarrow$ scholar).

Problem Set 30

1. $\dfrac{40}{280} = \dfrac{S}{3360}$

$280S = 40(3360)$

$S = \mathbf{480\ grams}$

2. $\dfrac{P}{100} \times of = is$

$\dfrac{86}{100} \times M = 430$

$M = 430 \times \dfrac{100}{86} = \mathbf{500\ grams}$

3.

$R_F T_F + R_B T_B = 68;$

$R_F = 6;\ T_F = 6;\ T_B = 4$

$6(6) + 4R_B = 68$

$4R_B = 32$

$R_B = \mathbf{8\ mph}$

4. (a) $5N_D = 2N_P$

(b) $N_D + N_P = 35$

Substitute $N_P = 35 - N_D$ into (a) and get:

(a') $5N_D = 2(35 - N_D)$

$5N_D = 70 - 2N_D$

$7N_D = 70$

$N_D = \mathbf{10\ daisies}$

(b) $(10) + N_P = 35$

$N_P = \mathbf{25\ prunes}$

5. (a) $N_D + N_Q = 15$

(b) $10N_D + 25N_Q = 225$

$-10\text{(a)} \quad -10N_D - 10N_Q = -150$

$\underline{\text{(b)} \quad 10N_D + 25N_Q = 225}$

$15N_Q = 75$

$N_Q = \mathbf{5\ quarters}$

(a) $N_D + (5) = 15$

$N_D = \mathbf{10\ dimes}$

6. $120\ \text{in.} = 10\ \text{ft}$

(a) Area $= l \times w = 40\ \text{ft} \times 10\ \text{ft} = \mathbf{400\ ft^2}$

(b) Perimeter $= 40\ \text{ft} + 40\ \text{ft} + 10\ \text{ft} + 10\ \text{ft}$

$= \mathbf{100\ ft}$

7.
$$
\begin{array}{r}
x^2 - x + 1 + \frac{1}{x+1} \\
x+1\overline{)x^3 + 0x^2 + 0x + 2} \\
\underline{x^3 + x^2} \\
-x^2 + 0x \\
\underline{-x^2 - x} \\
x + 2 \\
\underline{x + 1} \\
1
\end{array}
$$

Check:

$\dfrac{x^2(x+1)}{x+1} - \dfrac{x(x+1)}{x+1} + \dfrac{1(x+1)}{x+1} + \dfrac{1}{x+1}$

$= \dfrac{x^3 + x^2 - x^2 - x + x + 1 + 1}{x+1} = \dfrac{x^3 + 2}{x+1}$

8. $35a^2 + 2a^2x - a^2x^2 = -a^2(x - 7)(x + 5)$

9. $30 + 3x^2 - 21x = 3(x - 5)(x - 2)$

10. $-x^2ab - 25ab + 10axb = -ab(x - 5)(x - 5)$

11. $14a^2b^2 + 9a^2xb^2 + x^2a^2b^2$
$= a^2b^2(x + 7)(x + 2)$

12. $\dfrac{p - 4px}{p} = \dfrac{p(1 - 4x)}{p} = 1 - 4x$

13. $5\sqrt{18} - 10\sqrt{50} + 3\sqrt{72}$
$= 5\sqrt{2}\sqrt{3}\sqrt{3} - 10\sqrt{2}\sqrt{5}\sqrt{5} + 3\sqrt{2}\sqrt{6}\sqrt{6}$
$= 15\sqrt{2} - 50\sqrt{2} + 18\sqrt{2} = -17\sqrt{2}$

14. $3\sqrt{18}(4\sqrt{2} - 2\sqrt{3})$
$= 3\sqrt{3}\sqrt{3}\sqrt{2}(4\sqrt{2} - 2\sqrt{3})$
$= 12\sqrt{3}\sqrt{3}\sqrt{2}\sqrt{2} - 6\sqrt{3}\sqrt{3}\sqrt{2}\sqrt{3}$
$= 72 - 18\sqrt{6}$

15. $\dfrac{(0.00035)(5000 \times 10^{42})}{0.00025 \times 10^{-4}}$
$= \dfrac{(35 \times 10^{-5})(5 \times 10^{45})}{25 \times 10^{-9}} = \dfrac{175 \times 10^{40}}{25 \times 10^{-9}}$
$= 7 \times 10^{49}$

16. $\dfrac{\dfrac{\frac{x}{y}}{\frac{x+y}{y}}}{} \cdot \dfrac{\dfrac{y}{x+y}}{\dfrac{y}{x+y}} = \dfrac{x}{x+y}$

17. $\dfrac{\dfrac{a}{a+b}}{\dfrac{p}{a+b}} \cdot \dfrac{\dfrac{a+b}{p}}{\dfrac{a+b}{p}} = \dfrac{a}{p}$

18. $\dfrac{2}{3\sqrt{6}} \cdot \dfrac{\sqrt{6}}{\sqrt{6}} = \dfrac{2\sqrt{6}}{18} = \dfrac{\sqrt{6}}{9}$

19. $\dfrac{2}{5\sqrt{18}} \cdot \dfrac{\sqrt{18}}{\sqrt{18}} = \dfrac{2\sqrt{18}}{90} = \dfrac{6\sqrt{2}}{90} = \dfrac{\sqrt{2}}{15}$

20. $\dfrac{4a}{a+4} + \dfrac{a+2}{2a}$
$= \dfrac{4a(2a)}{2a(a+4)} + \dfrac{(a+2)(a+4)}{2a(a+4)}$
$= \dfrac{8a^2 + a^2 + 6a + 8}{2a(a+4)} = \dfrac{9a^2 + 6a + 8}{2a(a+4)}$

21. $\dfrac{4x}{x^2 + 5x + 6} + \dfrac{2}{x + 2}$
$= \dfrac{4x}{(x+2)(x+3)} + \dfrac{2(x+3)}{(x+2)(x+3)}$
$= \dfrac{4x + 2x + 6}{(x+2)(x+3)} = \dfrac{6x + 6}{(x+2)(x+3)}$

22. (a) $3x + 2y = 8$
$y = -\dfrac{3}{2}x + 4$

(b) $2x + 3y = 6$
$y = -\dfrac{2}{3}x + 2$

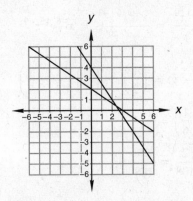

$\begin{array}{rl} 3\text{(a)} & 9x + 6y = 24 \\ -2\text{(b)} & \underline{-4x - 6y = -12} \\ & 5x = 12 \\ & x = \dfrac{12}{5} \end{array}$

(a) $y = -\dfrac{3}{2}\left(\dfrac{12}{5}\right) + 4 = -\dfrac{36}{10} + \dfrac{40}{10} = \dfrac{2}{5}$

$\left(\dfrac{12}{5}, \dfrac{2}{5}\right)$

23. Graph the line to find the slope.

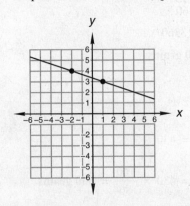

Slope $= \dfrac{-1}{+3} = -\dfrac{1}{3}$

$y = -\dfrac{1}{3}x + b$

$4 = -\dfrac{1}{3}(-2) + b$

$\dfrac{10}{3} = b$

Since $m = -\dfrac{1}{3}$ and $b = \dfrac{10}{3}$, $\boldsymbol{y = -\dfrac{1}{3}x + \dfrac{10}{3}}$.

24. Lateral Surface Area = Perimeter × Height

$= \left[3\left(\dfrac{2\pi(1 \text{ m})}{2}\right) + 2 \text{ m}\right] \times 10 \text{ m}$

$= (3\pi + 2)(10) \text{ m}^2 \approx \boldsymbol{114.2 \text{ m}^2}$

25. (A) $\angle 1 + \angle 2 = 180°$; True.

$\overline{(AB}$ is a straight angle.)

(B) $\angle 4 = \angle 7$; True.

(Alternate interior angles are equal.)

(C) $\angle 2 + \angle 3 = 180°$; **False.**

(It is not shown that $\angle 6 = \angle 7$.)

(D) $\angle 2 = \angle 6$; True.

(Corresponding angles are equal.)

26. $\dfrac{2x}{3} - \dfrac{2}{5} = \dfrac{x - 5}{2}$

$20x - 12 = 15x - 75$

$5x = -63$

$x = -\dfrac{\boldsymbol{63}}{\boldsymbol{5}}$

27. $3\dfrac{2}{3} + \dfrac{1}{5}x = \dfrac{1}{15}$

$\dfrac{1}{5}x = \dfrac{1}{15} - \dfrac{55}{15}$

$x = -\dfrac{54}{15} \cdot \dfrac{5}{1} = \boldsymbol{-18}$

28. $\dfrac{2x - 3}{2} = -\dfrac{2}{5}$

$10x - 15 = -4$

$10x = 11$

$x = \dfrac{\boldsymbol{11}}{\boldsymbol{10}}$

29. $\dfrac{4a^2x^2y}{p} - \dfrac{3p^{-1}x^4y}{a^{-2}x^2} + \dfrac{2xa}{a^{-1}y^{-1}p} - \dfrac{2a^2yx^2}{p}$

$= \dfrac{4a^2x^2y}{p} - \dfrac{3a^2x^2y}{p} + \dfrac{2a^2xy}{p} - \dfrac{2a^2x^2y}{p}$

$= \dfrac{\boldsymbol{2a^2xy}}{\boldsymbol{p}} - \dfrac{\boldsymbol{a^2x^2y}}{\boldsymbol{p}}$

30. $x^2 - y(x - y) = \left(-\dfrac{1}{2}\right)^2 - \dfrac{1}{4}\left(-\dfrac{1}{2} - \dfrac{1}{4}\right)$

$= \dfrac{1}{4} - \dfrac{1}{4}\left(-\dfrac{3}{4}\right) = \dfrac{4}{16} + \dfrac{3}{16}$

$= \dfrac{\boldsymbol{7}}{\boldsymbol{16}}$

PRACTICE SET 31

$y = -4x + b$

at $(1, 2)$ $(2) = -4(1) + b$

$2 = -4 + b$

$6 = b$

$\boldsymbol{y = -4x + 6}$

PROBLEM SET 31

1. Multiples of 5:

$5N, \ 5N + 5, \ 5N + 10, \ 5N + 15$

$6(5N) = 2(5N + 5 + 5N + 15) + 40$

$30N = 20N + 80$

$10N = 80$

$N = 8$

The desired integers are **40, 45, 50,** and **55.**

2.

$$\overset{\displaystyle D_B \qquad\qquad D_O}{\underset{960}{\longleftarrow\!\!\!\bullet\!\!\!\longrightarrow}}$$

$R_BT_B + R_OT_O = 960$; $R_B = 40$;

$R_O = 70$; $T_B = T_O + 2$

$40(T_O + 2) + 70T_O = 960$

$110T_O = 880$

$T_O = 8 \text{ hr}$

Since the *Orange Blossom Special* left at noon, it was **8 p.m.** when it and the bus were 960 miles apart.

3.

$$R_J T_J = R_R T_R; \quad R_J = 6;$$
$$R_R = 30; \quad T_J + T_R = 12$$
$$6T_J = 30(12 - T_J)$$
$$36T_J = 360$$
$$T_J = 10$$

Distance $= R_J T_J = 6(10) = $ **60 miles**

4. (a) $N_P + N_T = 70$

(b) $4N_P + 6N_T = 360$

Substitute $N_T = 70 - N_P$ into (b) and get:

(b$'$) $4N_P + 6(70 - N_P) = 360$
$$-2N_P = -60$$
$$N_P = \textbf{30 pansy plants}$$

(a) $N_T = 70 - (30)$
$$N_T = \textbf{40 tomato plants}$$

5. $\dfrac{P}{100} \times of = is$

$$\dfrac{10}{100} \times N = 1200$$

$$N = 1200 \times \dfrac{100}{10} = \textbf{12,000 kilograms}$$

6. $\dfrac{40}{1440} = \dfrac{P}{4320}$
$$1440P = 40(4320)$$
$$P = \textbf{120 grams}$$

7. Since the slopes of perpendicular lines are negative reciprocals of each other,

$$y = -3x + b$$
$$-3 = -3(2) + b$$
$$3 = b$$

Since $m = -3$ and $b = 3$, $y = \textbf{-3x + 3.}$

8. $\dfrac{(0.0006 \times 10^{-42})(2000 \times 10^{-4})}{(0.004 \times 10^{-13})}$

$$= \dfrac{(6 \times 10^{-46})(2 \times 10^{-1})}{4 \times 10^{-16}} = \textbf{3} \times \textbf{10}^{-31}$$

9. $\dfrac{\frac{a}{b}}{\frac{a+b}{b}} \cdot \dfrac{\frac{b}{a+b}}{\frac{b}{a+b}} = \dfrac{a}{a+b}$

10. $\dfrac{\frac{4}{x+y}}{\frac{m}{x+y}} \cdot \dfrac{\frac{x+y}{m}}{\frac{x+y}{m}} = \dfrac{4}{m}$

11. $\dfrac{3}{2\sqrt{5}} \cdot \dfrac{\sqrt{5}}{\sqrt{5}} = \dfrac{3\sqrt{5}}{10}$

12. $\dfrac{7}{3\sqrt{2}} \cdot \dfrac{\sqrt{2}}{\sqrt{2}} = \dfrac{7\sqrt{2}}{6}$

13. $5\sqrt{75} - 3\sqrt{300} + 2\sqrt{27}$
$$= 5\sqrt{3}\sqrt{5}\sqrt{5} - 3\sqrt{2}\sqrt{2}\sqrt{3}\sqrt{5}\sqrt{5} + 2\sqrt{3}\sqrt{3}\sqrt{3}$$
$$= 25\sqrt{3} - 30\sqrt{3} + 6\sqrt{3} = \sqrt{\textbf{3}}$$

14. $3\sqrt{2}(5\sqrt{2} - 4\sqrt{6}) = 3\sqrt{2}(5\sqrt{2} - 4\sqrt{2}\sqrt{3})$
$$= \textbf{30 - 24}\sqrt{\textbf{3}}$$

15. $\dfrac{x + 4x^2}{x} = \dfrac{x(1 + 4x)}{x} = \textbf{1 + 4x}$

16. $\dfrac{x}{x+2} + \dfrac{3+x}{x^2 + 4x + 4}$

$$= \dfrac{x(x+2)}{(x+2)(x+2)} + \dfrac{3+x}{(x+2)(x+2)}$$

$$= \dfrac{\textbf{x}^2 + \textbf{3x + 3}}{(\textbf{x + 2})^2}$$

17. $\dfrac{x}{x-3} + \dfrac{2x}{x^2 - 3x} = \dfrac{x^2}{x(x-3)} + \dfrac{2x}{x(x-3)}$

$$= \dfrac{x^2 + 2x}{x(x-3)} = \dfrac{x(x+2)}{x(x-3)} = \dfrac{\textbf{x + 2}}{\textbf{x - 3}}$$

18. $-x^3 + 5x^2 - 6x = \textbf{-x(x - 3)(x - 2)}$

19. $2ax^3 - 18ax^2 + 40ax = \textbf{2ax(x - 5)(x - 4)}$

20. $-3pax + pax^2 + 2pa = \textbf{pa(x - 2)(x - 1)}$

21. $-10mc + 3mxc + mx^2c = \textbf{mc(x + 5)(x - 2)}$

22. $\dfrac{2x + 3}{6} - \dfrac{x}{2} = 1$
$$2x + 3 - 3x = 6$$
$$-x = 3$$
$$x = \textbf{-3}$$

23. $\dfrac{3x + 2}{3} - \dfrac{2}{5} = \dfrac{x + 2}{6}$
$$30x + 20 - 12 = 5x + 10$$
$$25x = 2$$
$$x = \dfrac{\textbf{2}}{\textbf{25}}$$

24. (a) $2x + 3y = 18$

$$y = -\frac{2}{3}x + 6$$

(b) $-12x + 6y = -18$

$$y = 2x - 3$$

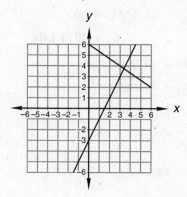

Substitute $y = 2x - 3$ into (a) and get:

(a') $2x + 3(2x - 3) = 18$

$$8x = 27$$

$$x = \frac{27}{8}$$

(b) $y = 2\left(\frac{27}{8}\right) - \frac{24}{8} = \frac{15}{4}$

$$\left(\frac{27}{8}, \frac{15}{4}\right)$$

25.

$$
\begin{array}{r}
x^3 - x^2 + x - 1 - \frac{1}{x+1} \\
x + 1 \overline{)\, x^4 + 0x^3 + 0x^2 + 0x - 2} \\
\underline{x^4 + x^3} \\
-x^3 + 0x^2 \\
\underline{-x^3 - x^2} \\
x^2 + 0x \\
\underline{x^2 + x} \\
-x - 2 \\
\underline{-x - 1} \\
-1
\end{array}
$$

26. (a) $6x + 4y = 11$

(b) $2x - 3y = -5$

1(a)　$6x + 4y = 11$

-3(b)　$\underline{-6x + 9y = 15}$

$$13y = 26$$

$$y = 2$$

(b) $2x - 3(2) = -5$

$$2x = 1$$

$$x = \frac{1}{2}$$

$$\left(\frac{1}{2}, 2\right)$$

27. $a^2 = 24^2 + 7^2$

$$a^2 = 625$$

$$a = 25$$

$$24 \times \overrightarrow{SF} = 30$$

$$\overrightarrow{SF} = \frac{5}{4}$$

$$25 \times \frac{5}{4} = 25 + c$$

$$125 = 100 + 4c$$

$$\frac{25}{4} = c$$

28. $-2(-x^0 - 3) + 4(-x - 5^0) = -3^0(2x - 5)$

$$2 + 6 - 4x - 4 = -2x + 5$$

$$-2x = 1$$

$$x = -\frac{1}{2}$$

29. $B = 180 - 30 = 150$

$$F + 150 = 180$$

$$F = 30$$

$$P + 30 + 90 = 180$$

$$P = 60$$

$$A + 60 = 180$$

$$A = 120$$

$$C + 60 + 90 = 180$$

$$C = 30$$

$$D = C = 30$$

$$E + 30 + 90 = 180$$

$$E = 60$$

$A = \mathbf{120};\ B = \mathbf{150};\ C = \mathbf{30};\ D = \mathbf{30};$

$E = \mathbf{60};\ F = \mathbf{30};\ P = \mathbf{60}$

30. $A_{\text{Circle}} = \dfrac{36\pi\,\text{m}^2}{4} = \mathbf{9\pi\,m^2}$

$$d = 2r = 2\left(\sqrt{\frac{9\pi}{\pi}\,\text{m}^2}\right) = \mathbf{6\ m}$$

$$A_{\text{Square}} = (2d)^2 = (12\,\text{m})^2 = \mathbf{144\ m^2}$$

PRACTICE SET 32

a. $\sqrt{\dfrac{3}{5}} + \sqrt{\dfrac{5}{3}} = \dfrac{\sqrt{3}}{\sqrt{5}} \cdot \dfrac{\sqrt{5}}{\sqrt{5}} + \dfrac{\sqrt{5}}{\sqrt{3}} \cdot \dfrac{\sqrt{3}}{\sqrt{3}}$

$= \dfrac{\sqrt{15}}{5} + \dfrac{\sqrt{15}}{3} = \dfrac{3\sqrt{15}}{15} + \dfrac{5\sqrt{15}}{15} = \dfrac{\mathbf{8\sqrt{15}}}{\mathbf{15}}$

b. $2\sqrt{\dfrac{2}{7}} - 3\sqrt{\dfrac{7}{2}} = 2\dfrac{\sqrt{2}}{\sqrt{7}} \cdot \dfrac{\sqrt{7}}{\sqrt{7}} - 3\dfrac{\sqrt{7}}{\sqrt{2}} \cdot \dfrac{\sqrt{2}}{\sqrt{2}}$

$= \dfrac{2\sqrt{14}}{7} - \dfrac{3\sqrt{14}}{2} = \dfrac{4\sqrt{14}}{14} - \dfrac{21\sqrt{14}}{14}$

$= -\dfrac{\mathbf{17\sqrt{14}}}{\mathbf{14}}$

c. $4x + 1 = 12x - 7$

$8 = 8x$

$\mathbf{1} = x$

$p = 4x - 1$

$p = 4(1) - 1$

$p = \mathbf{3}$

PROBLEM SET 32

1.

$R_W T_W + R_J T_J = 56; \ R_W = 4;$

$R_J = 8; \ T_W + T_J = 10$

$4T_W + 8(10 - T_W) = 56$

$\qquad\qquad -4T_W = -24$

$\qquad\qquad\quad T_W = 6$

$D_W = 4(6) = \mathbf{24 \ miles}$

$D_J = 8(4) = \mathbf{32 \ miles}$

2. (a) $N_L = 3N_S + 30$

(b) $\dfrac{N_S}{N_L} = \dfrac{1}{6} \longrightarrow 6N_S = N_L$

Substitute $6N_S = N_L$ into (a) and get:

(a') $(6N_S) = 3N_S + 30$

$\qquad\quad 3N_S = 30$

$\qquad\quad N_S = \mathbf{10 \ small \ ones}$

(a) $N_L = 3(10) + 30 = \mathbf{60 \ large \ ones}$

3. (a) $5N_N + 10N_D = 900$

(b) $N_D - N_N = 30$

Substitute $N_D = N_N + 30$ into (a) and get:

(a') $5N_N + 10(N_N + 30) = 900$

$\qquad\qquad\qquad 15N_N = 600$

$\qquad\qquad\qquad\quad N_N = \mathbf{40 \ nickels}$

(b) $N_D - 40 = 30$

$\qquad N_D = \mathbf{70 \ dimes}$

4. $\dfrac{P}{100} \times of = is$

$\dfrac{60}{100} \times M = 300$

$M = 300 \times \dfrac{100}{60} = \mathbf{500 \ kilograms}$

5. $\dfrac{20}{24} = \dfrac{NM}{1440}$

$24NM = 20(1440)$

$NM = \mathbf{1200 \ grams}$

6. $WD \times of = is$

$0.87 \times S = 1914$

$S = \dfrac{1914}{0.87} = \mathbf{2200 \ students}$

7. $\sqrt{\dfrac{2}{3}} + \sqrt{\dfrac{3}{2}} = \dfrac{\sqrt{2}}{\sqrt{3}}\dfrac{\sqrt{3}}{\sqrt{3}} + \dfrac{\sqrt{3}}{\sqrt{2}}\dfrac{\sqrt{2}}{\sqrt{2}} = \dfrac{\sqrt{6}}{3} + \dfrac{\sqrt{6}}{2}$

$= \dfrac{2\sqrt{6}}{6} + \dfrac{3\sqrt{6}}{6} = \dfrac{\mathbf{5\sqrt{6}}}{\mathbf{6}}$

8. $2\sqrt{\dfrac{5}{7}} - 3\sqrt{\dfrac{7}{5}} = \dfrac{2\sqrt{5}}{\sqrt{7}}\dfrac{\sqrt{7}}{\sqrt{7}} - \dfrac{3\sqrt{7}}{\sqrt{5}}\dfrac{\sqrt{5}}{\sqrt{5}}$

$= \dfrac{2\sqrt{35}}{7} - \dfrac{3\sqrt{35}}{5} = \dfrac{10\sqrt{35}}{35} - \dfrac{21\sqrt{35}}{35}$

$= -\dfrac{\mathbf{11\sqrt{35}}}{\mathbf{35}}$

9. $2\sqrt{\dfrac{3}{5}} - 5\sqrt{\dfrac{5}{3}} = \dfrac{2\sqrt{3}}{\sqrt{5}}\dfrac{\sqrt{5}}{\sqrt{5}} - \dfrac{5\sqrt{5}}{\sqrt{3}}\dfrac{\sqrt{3}}{\sqrt{3}}$

$= \dfrac{2\sqrt{15}}{5} - \dfrac{5\sqrt{15}}{3} = \dfrac{6\sqrt{15}}{15} - \dfrac{25\sqrt{15}}{15}$

$= -\dfrac{\mathbf{19\sqrt{15}}}{\mathbf{15}}$

10. $A_{\text{Square}} = s^2 = 64 \text{ m}^2$

$$s = \mathbf{8 \text{ m}}$$

$$r = \frac{1}{4}(8 \text{ m}) = \mathbf{2 \text{ m}}$$

$$A_{\text{Circle}} = \pi(2 \text{ m})^2 \approx \mathbf{12.56 \text{ m}^2}$$

11. $(180 - A) = 3(90 - A) - 30$

$$180 - A = 270 - 3A - 30$$

$$2A = 60$$

$$A = \mathbf{30°}$$

12. Since the slopes of perpendicular lines are negative reciprocals of each other,

$$y = -\frac{1}{3}x + b$$

$$2 = -\frac{1}{3}(2) + b$$

$$\frac{6}{3} = -\frac{2}{3} + b$$

$$\frac{8}{3} = b$$

Since $m = -\frac{1}{3}$ and $b = \frac{8}{3}$, $\mathbf{y = -\dfrac{1}{3}x + \dfrac{8}{3}}$.

13. $\dfrac{(0.0035 \times 10^{15})(0.002 \times 10^{17})}{7000 \times 10^{33}}$

$$= \frac{(3.5 \times 10^{12})(2 \times 10^{14})}{7 \times 10^{36}} = \frac{7 \times 10^{26}}{7 \times 10^{36}}$$

$$= \mathbf{1 \times 10^{-10}}$$

14. $\dfrac{\dfrac{x + 4y}{y}}{\dfrac{x + y}{y}} \cdot \dfrac{\dfrac{y}{x + y}}{\dfrac{y}{x + y}} = \dfrac{x + 4y}{x + y}$

15. $\dfrac{xy + 4x^2y^2}{xy} = \dfrac{xy(1 + 4xy)}{xy} = \mathbf{1 + 4xy}$

16. $3\sqrt{125} - 2\sqrt{45} + 3\sqrt{20}$

$$= 3\sqrt{5}\sqrt{5}\sqrt{5} - 2\sqrt{3}\sqrt{3}\sqrt{5} + 3\sqrt{2}\sqrt{2}\sqrt{5}$$

$$= 15\sqrt{5} - 6\sqrt{5} + 6\sqrt{5} = \mathbf{15\sqrt{5}}$$

17. $4\sqrt{5}(2\sqrt{10} - 3\sqrt{5}) = 4\sqrt{5}(2\sqrt{2}\sqrt{5} - 3\sqrt{5})$

$$= \mathbf{40\sqrt{2} - 60}$$

18. $\dfrac{x}{x + 3} - \dfrac{2x - 2}{x^2 + 5x + 6}$

$$= \frac{x(x + 2)}{(x + 3)(x + 2)} - \frac{2x - 2}{(x + 3)(x + 2)}$$

$$= \frac{x^2 + 2x - 2x + 2}{(x + 3)(x + 2)}$$

$$= \mathbf{\frac{x^2 + 2}{(x + 3)(x + 2)}}$$

19. $\dfrac{m}{m - 5} - \dfrac{2}{m^2 - 5m} = \dfrac{m^2}{m(m - 5)} - \dfrac{2}{m(m - 5)}$

$$= \mathbf{\frac{m^2 - 2}{m(m - 5)}}$$

20. $-2x^3 + 8x^2 - 6x = \mathbf{-2x(x - 3)(x - 1)}$

21. $-14x^3 + 5x^4 + x^5 = \mathbf{x^3(x + 7)(x - 2)}$

22. $7ax + ax^3 - 8ax^2 = \mathbf{ax(x - 7)(x - 1)}$

23. $-12py + px^2y + 4xpy = \mathbf{py(x + 6)(x - 2)}$

24. $\dfrac{x + 2}{5} - \dfrac{3x - 3}{2} = 4$

$$2x + 4 - 15x + 15 = 40$$

$$-13x = 21$$

$$x = \mathbf{-\frac{21}{13}}$$

25. $\dfrac{x}{2} - \dfrac{3x + 2}{4} = 7$

$$2x - 3x - 2 = 28$$

$$-x = 30$$

$$x = \mathbf{-30}$$

26. (a) $-x + 2y = 4$

$$y = \frac{1}{2}x + 2$$

(b) $x + y = -2$

$$y = -x - 2$$

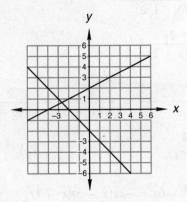

Substitute $y = (-x - 2)$ into (a) and get:

(a') $-x + 2(-x - 2) = 4$

$$-3x = 8$$

$$x = -\frac{8}{3}$$

(b) $y = -\left(-\dfrac{8}{3}\right) - \dfrac{6}{3} = \dfrac{2}{3}$

$$\left(-\frac{8}{3}, \frac{2}{3}\right)$$

27. $(4x + 2)(x^3 - 2x + 4)$

$$= 4x^4 - 8x^2 + 16x + 2x^3 - 4x + 8$$

$$= \mathbf{4x^4 + 2x^3 - 8x^2 + 12x + 8}$$

28. (a) $x + 2y = 5$

(b) $3x - y = 7$

(b') $y = 3x - 7$

Substitute $y = 3x - 7$ into (a) and get:

(a') $x + 2(3x - 7) = 5$

$$7x = 19$$

$$x = \frac{19}{7}$$

(b') $y = 3\left(\dfrac{19}{7}\right) - \dfrac{49}{7} = \dfrac{8}{7}$

$$\left(\frac{19}{7}, \frac{8}{7}\right)$$

29.

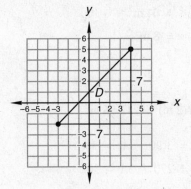

$$D^2 = 7^2 + 7^2$$

$$D^2 = 49 + 49$$

$$D = \sqrt{98}$$

$$D = \mathbf{7\sqrt{2}}$$

30. $-3\left[(-2^0 - 3^0 - 2)(-3^0) - 2^2\right] - \left|3 - 2^0\right|$

$$= -3[(-4)(-1) - 4] - 2 = -3[0] - 2 = \mathbf{-2}$$

PRACTICE SET 33

a. $\dfrac{\dfrac{m}{p} + \dfrac{3}{zp}}{\dfrac{s}{p}} = \dfrac{\dfrac{m}{p} \cdot \dfrac{z}{z} + \dfrac{3}{zp}}{\dfrac{s}{p}} = \dfrac{\dfrac{mz + 3}{pz}}{\dfrac{s}{p}} \cdot \dfrac{\dfrac{p}{s}}{}$

$$= \frac{mz + 3}{sz}$$

b. $\dfrac{\dfrac{y}{a + m} + \dfrac{s}{m}}{\dfrac{a}{y + s}} = \dfrac{\dfrac{y}{a + m} \cdot \dfrac{m}{m} + \dfrac{s}{m} \cdot \dfrac{a + m}{a + m}}{\dfrac{a}{y + s}}$

$$= \dfrac{\dfrac{my}{m(a + m)} + \dfrac{as + ms}{m(a + m)}}{\dfrac{a}{y + s}}$$

$$= \dfrac{\dfrac{as + ms + my}{m(a + m)}}{\dfrac{a}{y + s}} \cdot \dfrac{\dfrac{y + s}{a}}{}$$

$$= \frac{(as + ms + my)(y + s)}{am(a + m)}$$

PROBLEM SET 33

1. $\dfrac{4}{17} = \dfrac{104}{H}$

$4H = 17(104)$

$H = $ **442 hedonists**

2. $\dfrac{7}{9} = \dfrac{M}{3600}$

$9M = 7(3600)$

$M = $ **2800 grams**

3. $\dfrac{P}{100} \times of = is$

$\dfrac{80}{100} \times L = 1620$

$L = 1620 \times \dfrac{100}{80} = $ **2025 grams**

4. (a) $N_R = 8N_B + 10$

(b) $N_R = 11N_B - 5$

Substitute (b) into (a) and get:

(a′) $11N_B - 5 = 8N_B + 10$

$3N_B = 15$

$N_B = $ **5 blues**

(a) $N_R = 8(5) + 10 = $ **50 reds**

5.

$$\xrightarrow{\;\;D_M\;\;}\xrightarrow{\;\;D_C\;\;}$$
$$\underset{540}{\rule{4cm}{0.4pt}}$$

$R_M T_M + R_C T_C = 540;\; R_M = 40;$

$R_C = 60;\; T_M + T_C = 11$

$40T_M + 60(11 - T_M) = 540$

$-20T_M = -120$

$T_M = 6$

$D_M = 40(6) = $ **240 miles**

6. $\dfrac{\dfrac{m}{p} + \dfrac{3}{xp}}{\dfrac{y}{p}} = \dfrac{\dfrac{m}{p}\left(\dfrac{x}{x}\right) + \dfrac{3}{xp}}{\dfrac{y}{p}} = \dfrac{\dfrac{mx + 3}{xp}}{\dfrac{y}{p}} \cdot \dfrac{\dfrac{p}{y}}{\;}$

$= \dfrac{mx + 3}{xy}$

7. $\dfrac{\dfrac{s}{a + b} + \dfrac{x}{b}}{\dfrac{a}{s + x}} = \dfrac{\dfrac{s}{a + b}\left(\dfrac{b}{b}\right) + \dfrac{x}{b}\left(\dfrac{a + b}{a + b}\right)}{\dfrac{a}{s + x}}$

$= \dfrac{\dfrac{bs + ax + bx}{ab + b^2}}{\dfrac{a}{s + x}} \cdot \dfrac{\dfrac{s + x}{a}}{\;}$

$= \dfrac{(s + x)(bs + ax + bx)}{ab(a + b)}$

8. $x + 40 = 180$

$x = $ **140**

$2y + 140 = 180$

$2y = 40$

$y = $ **20**

$z = $ **40**

Arc length $= \dfrac{40}{360} \cdot 2(\pi)(6\text{ cm}) \approx $ **4.19 cm**

9. $z = 360 - 150 - 70$

$z = $ **140**

$x = \dfrac{150}{2} = $ **75**

$y = \dfrac{140}{2} = $ **70**

10. Since the slopes of perpendicular lines are negative reciprocals of each other,

$2 = \dfrac{5}{3}(-4) + b$

$\dfrac{26}{3} = b$

Since $m = \dfrac{5}{3}$ and $b = \dfrac{26}{3}$, $y = \dfrac{5}{3}x + \dfrac{26}{3}$.

11. $3\sqrt{\dfrac{5}{2}} - 2\sqrt{\dfrac{2}{5}} = \dfrac{3\sqrt{5}}{\sqrt{2}} - \dfrac{2\sqrt{2}}{\sqrt{5}}$

$= \dfrac{3\sqrt{5}}{\sqrt{2}}\dfrac{\sqrt{2}}{\sqrt{2}} - \dfrac{2\sqrt{2}}{\sqrt{5}}\dfrac{\sqrt{5}}{\sqrt{5}} = \dfrac{3\sqrt{10}}{2} - \dfrac{2\sqrt{10}}{5}$

$= \dfrac{15\sqrt{10}}{10} - \dfrac{4\sqrt{10}}{10} = \dfrac{\mathbf{11\sqrt{10}}}{\mathbf{10}}$

12. $4\sqrt{\dfrac{5}{6}} - 2\sqrt{\dfrac{6}{5}} = \dfrac{4\sqrt{5}}{\sqrt{6}} - \dfrac{2\sqrt{6}}{\sqrt{5}}$

$= \dfrac{4\sqrt{5}}{\sqrt{6}}\dfrac{\sqrt{6}}{\sqrt{6}} - \dfrac{2\sqrt{6}}{\sqrt{5}}\dfrac{\sqrt{5}}{\sqrt{5}} = \dfrac{4\sqrt{30}}{6} - \dfrac{2\sqrt{30}}{5}$

$= \dfrac{20\sqrt{30}}{30} - \dfrac{12\sqrt{30}}{30} = \dfrac{8\sqrt{30}}{30} = \dfrac{\mathbf{4\sqrt{30}}}{\mathbf{15}}$

13. Perimeter $= 11.28 \text{ cm} + 6 \text{ cm} + 6 \text{ cm}$
$= \mathbf{23.28 \text{ cm}}$

14. $3(90 - A) = (180 - A) + 50$
$270 - 3A = 230 - A$
$-2A = -40$
$A = \mathbf{20°}$

15. $\dfrac{(0.0027 \times 10^{15})(500 \times 10^{-20})}{900 \times 10^{14}}$

$= \dfrac{(2.7 \times 10^{12})(5 \times 10^{-18})}{9 \times 10^{16}} = \dfrac{13.5 \times 10^{-6}}{9 \times 10^{16}}$

$= \mathbf{1.5 \times 10^{-22}}$

16. $\dfrac{x + \dfrac{4xy}{x}}{\dfrac{1}{x} - y} = \dfrac{\dfrac{x^2 + 4xy}{x}}{\dfrac{1 - xy}{x}} \cdot \dfrac{\dfrac{x}{1 - xy}}{\dfrac{x}{1 - xy}} = \dfrac{\mathbf{x^2 + 4xy}}{\mathbf{1 - xy}}$

17. $3\sqrt{18} + 2\sqrt{50} - \sqrt{98}$
$= 3\sqrt{2}\sqrt{3}\sqrt{3} + 2\sqrt{2}\sqrt{5}\sqrt{5} - \sqrt{2}\sqrt{7}\sqrt{7}$
$= 9\sqrt{2} + 10\sqrt{2} - 7\sqrt{2} = \mathbf{12\sqrt{2}}$

18. $\dfrac{4x + 4xy}{4x} = \dfrac{4x(1 + y)}{4x} = \mathbf{1 + y}$

19. $\dfrac{a}{x(x + y)} + \dfrac{b}{x^2} + \dfrac{cx + 4}{x + y}$

$= \dfrac{ax}{x^2(x + y)} + \dfrac{b(x + y)}{x^2(x + y)} + \dfrac{x^2(cx + 4)}{x^2(x + y)}$

$= \dfrac{\mathbf{ax + b(x + y) + x^2(cx + 4)}}{\mathbf{x^2(x + y)}}$

20. $\dfrac{4}{x + 4} - \dfrac{6x - 2}{x^2 + 2x - 8}$

$= \dfrac{4(x - 2)}{(x + 4)(x - 2)} - \dfrac{6x - 2}{(x + 4)(x - 2)}$

$= \dfrac{4x - 8 - 6x + 2}{(x + 4)(x - 2)} = \dfrac{\mathbf{-2x - 6}}{\mathbf{(x + 4)(x - 2)}}$

21. $5x^2 + 4x^3 - x^4 = \mathbf{-x^2(x - 5)(x + 1)}$

22. $10k^2 - 7k^2x + k^2x^2 = \mathbf{k^2(x - 5)(x - 2)}$

23. $apx^2 - 20ap - apx = \mathbf{ap(x - 5)(x + 4)}$

24. $\dfrac{x + 2}{3} - \dfrac{2x - 2}{4} = 5$
$4x + 8 - 6x + 6 = 60$
$-2x = 46$
$x = \mathbf{-23}$

25. $\dfrac{3x - 2}{2} - \dfrac{2x + 3}{3} = 4$
$9x - 6 - 4x - 6 = 24$
$5x = 36$
$x = \dfrac{\mathbf{36}}{\mathbf{5}}$

26. (a) $2x - y = -5$
$y = 2x + 5$

(b) $x + y = 1$
$y = -x + 1$

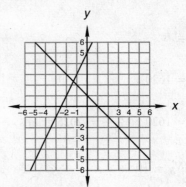

Substitute $y = -x + 1$ into (a) and get:

(a') $2x - (-x + 1) = -5$
$3x = -4$
$x = -\dfrac{4}{3}$

(b) $y = -\left(-\dfrac{4}{3}\right) + \dfrac{3}{3} = \dfrac{7}{3}$

$\left(-\dfrac{4}{3}, \dfrac{7}{3}\right)$

27. Divide $2x^4 - x$ by $x - 2$:

$$
\begin{array}{r}
2x^3 + 4x^2 + 8x + 15 + \frac{30}{x-2} \\
x - 2 \overline{)2x^4 + 0x^3 + 0x^2 - x + 0} \\
\underline{2x^4 - 4x^3} \\
4x^3 + 0x^2 \\
\underline{4x^3 - 8x^2} \\
8x^2 - x \\
\underline{8x^2 - 16x} \\
15x + 0 \\
\underline{15x - 30} \\
30
\end{array}
$$

Check:

$\dfrac{2x^3(x - 2)}{x - 2} + \dfrac{4x^2(x - 2)}{x - 2} + \dfrac{8x(x - 2)}{x - 2}$

$+ \dfrac{15(x - 2)}{x - 2} + \dfrac{30}{x - 2} = \dfrac{2x^4 - x}{x - 2}$

28. $-3^0 - x - y^0 - y^2(-2^0 - 3) - |-2 - x|$

$= -3^0 - (-2) - (-3)^0 - (-3)^2(-4) - |-2 - (-2)|$

$= -1 + 2 - 1 - 9(-4) - 0$

$= -1 + 2 - 1 + 36 = \mathbf{36}$

29. Perimeter $= 2(2 \text{ ft}) + 2(4 \text{ ft}) = \mathbf{12 \text{ ft}}$

30. Area $= l \times w = 2 \text{ ft} \times 4 \text{ ft} = \mathbf{8 \text{ ft}^2}$

PRACTICE SET 34

$R_Z = 30; \ R_T = 40; \ T_Z = T_T + 2$

$R_T T_T + 20 = R_Z T_Z$

$(40)T_T + 20 = (30)(T_T + 2)$

$40T_T + 20 = 30T_T + 60$

$10T_T = 40$

$T_T = 4$

Time $= 7 \text{ a.m.} + 4 \text{ hours} = \mathbf{11 \text{ a.m.}}$

PROBLEM SET 34

1.

$R_B T_B + 60 = R_E T_E; \ R_E = 40;$

$R_B = 50; \ T_E = T_B + 3$

$50T_B + 60 = 40(T_B + 3)$

$10T_B = 60$

$T_B = 6 \text{ hr}$

Since Benita left at 11 a.m. and traveled for 6 hours, she got within 60 kilometers of Elliot by **5 p.m.**

2.

$R_R T_R + 14 = R_C T_C; \ R_R = 7.5;$

$R_C = 11; \ T_R = T_C$

$7.5(T_C) + 14 = 11T_C$

$-3.5T_C = -14$

$T_C = \mathbf{4 \text{ hr}}$

3.

$R_K T_K = R_Y T_Y; \ R_K = 10;$

$R_Y = 3; \ T_K + T_Y = 13$

$10T_K = 3(13 - T_K)$

$13T_K = 39$

$T_K = 3$

$D_K = 10(3) = \mathbf{30 \text{ miles}}$

4. $\dfrac{P}{100} \times of = is$

$\dfrac{70}{100} \times S = 42$

$S = 42 \times \dfrac{100}{70} = \mathbf{60 \text{ tons}}$

5. $\dfrac{50}{100} = \dfrac{S}{300}$

$100S = 50(300)$

$S = \mathbf{150 \text{ grams}}$

6. Integers: $N, \ N + 1, \ N + 2$

$5(N + N + 2) = 8(N + 1) + 14$

$10N + 10 = 8N + 22$

$2N = 12$

$N = 6$

The desired integers are **6, 7,** and **8.**

7. $\dfrac{\dfrac{y}{ab} - ab}{\dfrac{1}{a} - \dfrac{a}{b}} = \dfrac{\dfrac{y - a^2 b^2}{ab}}{\dfrac{b - a^2}{ab}} \cdot \dfrac{\dfrac{ab}{b - a^2}}{\dfrac{ab}{b - a^2}} = \dfrac{y - a^2 b^2}{b - a^2}$

8. $\dfrac{\dfrac{1}{x} - b}{x} = \dfrac{\dfrac{1 - bx}{x}}{x} \cdot \dfrac{\dfrac{1}{x}}{\dfrac{1}{x}} = \dfrac{1 - bx}{x^2}$

9. $V_{\text{Cone}} = \dfrac{1}{3}(A_{\text{Base}} \times \text{Height})$

$= \dfrac{1}{3}\Big[(2)(4) + (4)(4) + (12)(4)$

$+ \dfrac{1}{2}(\pi)(4)^2 \Big] \text{m}^2 \times 8 \text{ m}$

$= \dfrac{1}{3}(72 + 8\pi)(8) \text{ m}^3 \approx \mathbf{258.99 \text{ m}^3}$

10. $(4x + 20) = 2(x + 20)$
    $4x + 20 = 2x + 40$
    $2x = 20$
    $x = \mathbf{10}$

11. Since the slopes of perpendicular lines are negative reciprocals of each other,

    $y = \dfrac{1}{2}x + b$

    $-1 = \dfrac{1}{2}(-2) + b$

    $0 = b$

    Since $m = \dfrac{1}{2}$ and $b = 0$, $y = \dfrac{1}{2}x$.

12. $2\sqrt{\dfrac{2}{9}} - 3\sqrt{\dfrac{9}{2}} = \dfrac{2\sqrt{2}}{\sqrt{9}}\dfrac{\sqrt{9}}{\sqrt{9}} - \dfrac{3\sqrt{9}}{\sqrt{2}}\dfrac{\sqrt{2}}{\sqrt{2}}$

    $= \dfrac{2\sqrt{18}}{9} - \dfrac{3\sqrt{18}}{2} = \dfrac{4\sqrt{18}}{18} - \dfrac{27\sqrt{18}}{18}$

    $= -\dfrac{23\sqrt{18}}{18} = -\dfrac{\mathbf{23\sqrt{2}}}{\mathbf{6}}$

13. $-3\sqrt{\dfrac{2}{3}} + 2\sqrt{\dfrac{3}{2}} = -\dfrac{3\sqrt{2}}{\sqrt{3}}\dfrac{\sqrt{3}}{\sqrt{3}} + \dfrac{2\sqrt{3}}{\sqrt{2}}\dfrac{\sqrt{2}}{\sqrt{2}}$

    $= -\dfrac{3\sqrt{6}}{3} + \dfrac{2\sqrt{6}}{2} = -\sqrt{6} + \sqrt{6} = \mathbf{0}$

14. $A_{\text{Shaded}} = A_{\text{Circle, 22}} - A_{\text{Circle, 16}} - A_{\text{Circle, 6}}$
    $= \pi(22\text{ cm})^2 - \pi(16\text{ cm})^2 - \pi(6\text{ cm})^2$
    $= (484\pi - 256\pi - 36\pi)\text{ cm}^2$
    $\approx \mathbf{602.88\ 1\text{-cm-square floor tiles}}$

15. $\dfrac{(0.000032 \times 10^4)(700 \times 10^{-14})}{16,000}$

    $= \dfrac{(3.2 \times 10^{-1})(7 \times 10^{-12})}{1.6 \times 10^4}$

    $= \dfrac{2.24 \times 10^{-12}}{1.6 \times 10^4} = \mathbf{1.4 \times 10^{-16}}$

16. $\dfrac{4 + \dfrac{x}{y^2}}{3 - \dfrac{1}{y^2}} = \dfrac{\dfrac{4y^2 + x}{y^2}}{\dfrac{3y^2 - 1}{y^2}} \cdot \dfrac{\dfrac{y^2}{3y^2 - 1}}{\dfrac{y^2}{3y^2 - 1}} = \dfrac{\mathbf{4y^2 + x}}{\mathbf{3y^2 - 1}}$

17. $8\sqrt{27} - 2\sqrt{75} + 2\sqrt{147}$
    $= 8\sqrt{3}\sqrt{3}\sqrt{3} - 2\sqrt{3}\sqrt{5}\sqrt{5} + 2\sqrt{3}\sqrt{7}\sqrt{7}$
    $= 24\sqrt{3} - 10\sqrt{3} + 14\sqrt{3} = \mathbf{28\sqrt{3}}$

18. $\dfrac{x^2 y - 5x^2 y^2}{x^2 y} = \dfrac{x^2 y(1 - 5y)}{x^2 y} = \mathbf{1 - 5y}$

19. $\dfrac{a}{x(x + y)} + \dfrac{bx}{x^2(x + y)} + \dfrac{cx}{x^3}$

    $= \dfrac{ax^2}{x^3(x + y)} + \dfrac{bx^2}{x^3(x + y)} + \dfrac{cx(x + y)}{x^3(x + y)}$

    $= \dfrac{\mathbf{ax^2 + bx^2 + cx(x + y)}}{\mathbf{x^3(x + y)}}$

20. $\dfrac{x - 4}{x - 3} - \dfrac{2x - 1}{x^2 - 6x + 9}$

    $= \dfrac{(x - 4)(x - 3)}{(x - 3)(x - 3)} - \dfrac{2x - 1}{(x - 3)(x - 3)}$

    $= \dfrac{x^2 - 7x + 12 - 2x + 1}{(x - 3)^2}$

    $= \dfrac{\mathbf{x^2 - 9x + 13}}{\mathbf{(x - 3)^2}}$

21. $-4x^2 + 2x^3 + 2x^4 = \mathbf{2x^2(x + 2)(x - 1)}$

22. $ax^2 p - 8pa - 2axp = \mathbf{ap(x - 4)(x + 2)}$

23. $yx^2 - 4xy + 4y = \mathbf{y(x - 2)(x - 2)}$

24. $\dfrac{x - 3}{2} - \dfrac{3x + 4}{2} = 3$

    $x - 3 - 3x - 4 = 6$

    $-2x = 13$

    $x = -\dfrac{\mathbf{13}}{\mathbf{2}}$

25. $\dfrac{x}{3} - \dfrac{2x - 4}{2} = 5$

    $2x - 6x + 12 = 30$

    $-4x = 18$

    $x = -\dfrac{\mathbf{9}}{\mathbf{2}}$

26. (a) $x - 3y = 6$

    $y = \dfrac{1}{3}x - 2$

    (b) $2x + y = 2$

    $y = -2x + 2$

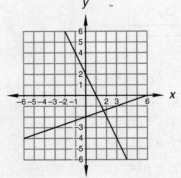

Substitute $y = -2x + 2$ into (a) and get:

(a') $x - 3(-2x + 2) = 6$

$$7x = 12$$

$$x = \frac{12}{7}$$

(b) $y = -2\left(\dfrac{12}{7}\right) + \dfrac{14}{7} = -\dfrac{10}{7}$

$$\left(\frac{12}{7}, -\frac{10}{7}\right)$$

27. $(x^2 + x)(x^2 + 2x + 3)$

$= x^4 + 2x^3 + 3x^2 + x^3 + 2x^2 + 3x$

$= x^4 + 3x^3 + 5x^2 + 3x$

28. (a) $3x - 2y = 2$

(b) $x - 3y = 4$

(b') $x = 3y + 4$

Substitute $x = 3y + 4$ into (a) and get:

(a') $3(3y + 4) - 2y = 2$

$$7y = -10$$

$$y = -\frac{10}{7}$$

(b') $x = 3\left(-\dfrac{10}{7}\right) + \dfrac{28}{7} = -\dfrac{2}{7}$

$$\left(-\frac{2}{7}, -\frac{10}{7}\right)$$

29. $(\sqrt{17})^2 = H^2 + 3^2$

$$17 - 9 = H^2$$

$$8 = H^2$$

$$2\sqrt{2} = H$$

Area $= \dfrac{6 \text{ cm} \times 2\sqrt{2} \text{ cm}}{2} = \mathbf{6\sqrt{2} \text{ cm}^2}$

30. $-2^0[-2^0 - 2^2 - (-2)^3 - 2](-2^0 - 2) + x - xy$

$= -1[-1 - 4 + 8 - 2](-3) + (-3) - (-3)(-4)$

$= -1[1](-3) - 3 - 12 = 3 - 3 - 12 = \mathbf{-12}$

PRACTICE SET 35

a. $(14 - 2) \times 180° = 12 \times 180° = \mathbf{2160°}$

b. The sum of the measures of the exterior angles of any polygon is always **360°**.

c. $64^{-1/2} = \dfrac{1}{64^{1/2}} = \dfrac{1}{\sqrt{64}} = \dfrac{1}{8}$

d. $64^{2/3} = (64^2)^{1/3} = \sqrt[3]{64^2} = \sqrt[3]{8 \cdot 8 \cdot 8 \cdot 8}$

$= 8\sqrt[3]{8} = 8\sqrt[3]{2 \cdot 2 \cdot 2} = \mathbf{16}$

e. $-125^{-2/3} = -\dfrac{1}{125^{2/3}} = -\dfrac{1}{\sqrt[3]{125^2}}$

$= -\dfrac{1}{\sqrt[3]{5 \cdot 5 \cdot 5 \cdot 5 \cdot 5 \cdot 5}} = -\dfrac{1}{25}$

PROBLEM SET 35

1.

$R_M T_M + 1200 = R_L T_L$; $R_L = 3R_M$;

$T_M = T_L = 30$

$30R_M + 1200 = 3R_M(30)$

$$-60R_M = -1200$$

$R_M = \mathbf{20 \text{ yards per minute}}$

$R_L = 3(20) = \mathbf{60 \text{ yards per minute}}$

2.

$R_T T_T + R_W T_W = 56$; $R_T = 4$;

$R_W = 6$; $T_T + T_W = 12$

$4T_T + 6(12 - T_T) = 56$

$$-2T_T = -16$$

$$T_T = 8$$

$T_W = 12 - (8) = 4$

They trudged for **8 hours** and walked briskly for **4 hours**.

3.

$R_D T_D = R_B T_B$; $T_D = 12$;

$T_B = 4$; $R_B = R_D + 6$

$12R_D = 4(R_D + 6)$

$$8R_D = 24$$

$$R_D = 3$$

$D_D = D_B = 3(12) = \mathbf{36 \text{ miles}}$

4. (a) $5N_B + 8N_Y = 82$

(b) $N_B = 2N_Y + 2$

Substitute (b) into (a) and get:

(a′) $5(2N_Y + 2) + 8N_Y = 82$

$$10N_Y + 10 + 8N_Y = 82$$

$$18N_Y = 72$$

$$N_Y = \textbf{4 yellows}$$

(b) $N_B = 2(4) + 2 = \textbf{10 blues}$

5. $\dfrac{P}{100} \times of = is$

$$\dfrac{40}{100} \times A = 40$$

$$A = 40 \times \dfrac{100}{40} = \textbf{100 tons}$$

6. $\dfrac{20}{20} = \dfrac{V}{400}$

$$20V = 20(400)$$

$$V = \textbf{400 grams}$$

7. Lateral $S.A. = $ Perimeter $\times$ Height

$$= \left[\left(\dfrac{1}{2}(2)(\pi)(2)\right) + \left(\dfrac{1}{2}(2)(\pi)(2)\right) + 20\right] \text{m}$$

$$\times\ 10\ \text{m}$$

$$= (4\pi + 20)(10)\ \text{m}^2 \approx \textbf{325.6 m}^2$$

8. $16^{-1/2} = \dfrac{1}{16^{1/2}} = \dfrac{\textbf{1}}{\textbf{4}}$

9. $27^{-1/3} = \dfrac{1}{27^{1/3}} = \dfrac{\textbf{1}}{\textbf{3}}$

10. $9^{3/2} = (9^{1/2})^3 = 3^3 = \textbf{27}$

11. $-64^{-2/3} = -\dfrac{1}{64^{2/3}} = -\dfrac{1}{(64^{1/3})^2} = -\dfrac{\textbf{1}}{\textbf{16}}$

12. (a) $3x - 4y = 84$

(b) $x + 10y = 96$

$$
\begin{array}{rl}
1(a) & 3x - 4y = 84 \\
-3(b) & \underline{-3x - 30y = -288} \\
& -34y = -204 \\
& y = \textbf{6}
\end{array}
$$

(b) $x + 10(6) = 96$

$$x = \textbf{36}$$

$$5 \times \overrightarrow{SF} = 9$$

$$\overrightarrow{SF} = \dfrac{9}{5}$$

$$7 \times \dfrac{9}{5} = A$$

$$\dfrac{\textbf{63}}{\textbf{5}} = A$$

13. $3\sqrt{\dfrac{7}{5}} + 2\sqrt{\dfrac{5}{7}} = \dfrac{3\sqrt{7}}{\sqrt{5}}\dfrac{\sqrt{5}}{\sqrt{5}} + \dfrac{2\sqrt{5}}{\sqrt{7}}\dfrac{\sqrt{7}}{\sqrt{7}}$

$$= \dfrac{3\sqrt{35}}{5} + \dfrac{2\sqrt{35}}{7} = \dfrac{21\sqrt{35}}{35} + \dfrac{10\sqrt{35}}{35}$$

$$= \dfrac{\textbf{31}\sqrt{\textbf{35}}}{\textbf{35}}$$

14. $2\sqrt{\dfrac{2}{5}} - 9\sqrt{\dfrac{5}{2}} = \dfrac{2\sqrt{2}}{\sqrt{5}}\dfrac{\sqrt{5}}{\sqrt{5}} - \dfrac{9\sqrt{5}}{\sqrt{2}}\dfrac{\sqrt{2}}{\sqrt{2}}$

$$= \dfrac{2\sqrt{10}}{5} - \dfrac{9\sqrt{10}}{2} = \dfrac{4\sqrt{10}}{10} - \dfrac{45\sqrt{10}}{10}$$

$$= -\dfrac{\textbf{41}\sqrt{\textbf{10}}}{\textbf{10}}$$

15. $\dfrac{\dfrac{a}{b} - 4}{\dfrac{xy}{b}} = \dfrac{\dfrac{a - 4b}{b}}{\dfrac{xy}{b}} \cdot \dfrac{\dfrac{b}{xy}}{\dfrac{b}{xy}} = \dfrac{\textbf{a} - \textbf{4b}}{\textbf{xy}}$

16. $\dfrac{\dfrac{x}{x+y} + 6}{\dfrac{4}{x+y}} = \dfrac{\dfrac{x + 6(x+y)}{x+y}}{\dfrac{4}{x+y}} \cdot \dfrac{\dfrac{x+y}{4}}{\dfrac{x+y}{4}}$

$$= \dfrac{x + 6(x+y)}{4} = \dfrac{\textbf{7x} + \textbf{6y}}{\textbf{4}}$$

17. $2x + 10 = 80$

$$2x = 70$$

$$x = \textbf{35}$$

$$3y + 40 = 130$$

$$3y = 90$$

$$y = \textbf{30}$$

$$k = 360 - 130 - 80 = \textbf{150}$$

18. $2x + 332 = 360$

$\qquad 2x = 28$

$\qquad\ x = \mathbf{14}$

$y + 40 + 14 = 180$

$\qquad\qquad y = \mathbf{126}$

19. $x = 2(105) - 112 = \mathbf{98}$

$y = \dfrac{x + 88}{2} = \dfrac{98 + 88}{2} = \mathbf{93}$

$p = \dfrac{88 + 62}{2} = \mathbf{75}$

20. Graph the line to find the slope.

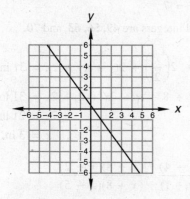

Slope $= \dfrac{-4}{+3} = -\dfrac{4}{3}$

$y = -\dfrac{4}{3}x + b$

$\dfrac{9}{3} = -\dfrac{4}{3}(-2) + b$

$\dfrac{1}{3} = b$

Since $m = -\dfrac{4}{3}$ and $b = \dfrac{1}{3}$, $\mathbf{y = -\dfrac{4}{3}x + \dfrac{1}{3}}$.

21. $\dfrac{4}{x^2(x + y)} + \dfrac{2x - 2}{x(x + y)}$

$= \dfrac{4}{x^2(x + y)} + \dfrac{2x^2 - 2x}{x^2(x + y)} = \mathbf{\dfrac{2x^2 - 2x + 4}{x^2(x + y)}}$

22. $\dfrac{3x}{x - 2} - \dfrac{2x}{x^2 + x - 6}$

$= \dfrac{3x(x + 3)}{(x - 2)(x + 3)} - \dfrac{2x}{(x - 2)(x + 3)}$

$= \mathbf{\dfrac{x(3x + 7)}{(x - 2)(x + 3)}}$

23. $35a - ax^2 - 2xa = \mathbf{-a(x + 7)(x - 5)}$

24. $8x^2 - 2x^3 - x^4 = \mathbf{-x^2(x + 4)(x - 2)}$

25. $2\sqrt{3} \cdot \sqrt{12} - 3\sqrt{2} \cdot \sqrt{6} + 4\sqrt{2}(3\sqrt{2} - \sqrt{6})$

$= 2\sqrt{3}\sqrt{2}\sqrt{2}\sqrt{3} - 3\sqrt{2}\sqrt{2}\sqrt{3} + 12\sqrt{2}\sqrt{2}$
$\quad - 4\sqrt{2}\sqrt{2}\sqrt{3}$

$= 12 - 6\sqrt{3} + 24 - 8\sqrt{3} = \mathbf{36 - 14\sqrt{3}}$

26. $\dfrac{(7000 \times 10^{14})(0.0002 \times 10^{-11})}{1400 \times 10^{-10}}$

$= \dfrac{(7 \times 10^{17})(2 \times 10^{-15})}{14 \times 10^{-8}} = \dfrac{14 \times 10^2}{14 \times 10^{-8}}$

$= \mathbf{1 \times 10^{10}}$

27. $\dfrac{x - 3}{7} - \dfrac{2x}{4} = 5$

$4x - 12 - 14x = 140$

$\qquad\quad -10x = 152$

$\qquad\qquad\quad x = \mathbf{-\dfrac{76}{5}}$

28. $0.002x = 0.02 + 0.04$

$\quad\ 2x = 20 + 40$

$\qquad x = \mathbf{30}$

29. $2\dfrac{1}{3}x - 2x^0 = 3\dfrac{1}{4}$

$\dfrac{7}{3}x = \dfrac{13}{4} + \dfrac{8}{4}$

$\quad\ x = \dfrac{21}{4} \cdot \dfrac{3}{7} = \mathbf{\dfrac{9}{4}}$

30.

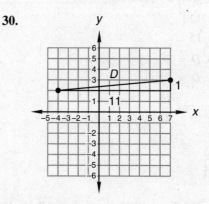

$D^2 = 11^2 + 1^2$

$D^2 = 121 + 1$

$D^2 = 122$

$D = \mathbf{\sqrt{122}}$

PRACTICE SET 36

a. $\dfrac{x^2 - 6x + 9}{x^2 + 5x - 24} \div \dfrac{x^2 - 5x + 6}{x^2 - x - 72}$

$= \dfrac{(x-3)(x-3)}{(x+8)(x-3)} \cdot \dfrac{(x-9)(x+8)}{(x-3)(x-2)} = \dfrac{x-9}{x-2}$

b. $\dfrac{x^2 + 2x - 8}{x^3 - 4x^2 - 21x} \div \dfrac{x-2}{x^2 - 7x}$

$= \dfrac{(x+4)(x-2)}{x(x-7)(x+3)} \cdot \dfrac{x(x-7)}{(x-2)} = \dfrac{x+4}{x+3}$

PROBLEM SET 36

1. $\dfrac{P}{100} \times of = is$

$\dfrac{340}{100} \times 400 = W$

$W = \textbf{1360 words}$

2. (a) $4N_F + 21N_L = 290$

(b) $N_F + N_L = 30$

Substitute $N_L = 30 - N_F$ into (a) and get:

(a′) $4N_F + 21(30 - N_F) = 290$

$-17N_F = -340$

$N_F = \textbf{20 fats}$

(b) $(20) + N_L = 30$

$N_L = \textbf{10 leans}$

3. (a) $\dfrac{N}{D} = \dfrac{3}{5} \longrightarrow 5N = 3D$

(b) $N + D = 40$

Substitute $D = 40 - N$ into (a) and get:

(a′) $5N = 3(40 - N)$

$8N = 120$

$N = 15$

(b) $(15) + D = 40$

$D = 25$

The fraction was $\dfrac{\textbf{15}}{\textbf{25}}$.

4.

$R_D T_D = R_H T_H;\ T_D = 10;\ T_H = 8;\ R_H = R_D + 10$

$10R_D = 8(R_D + 10)$

$2R_D = 80$

$R_D = 40$

$D_D = D_H = 40(10) = \textbf{400 miles}$

5.

$R_J T_J + 80 = R_B T_B;\ T_J = T_B = 4;\ R_J = 30$

$30(4) + 80 = 4R_B$

$200 = 4R_B$

$\textbf{50 mph} = R_B$

6. Multiples of 7: $7N,\ 7N + 7,\ 7N + 14,$

$7N + 21$

$4(7N + 2) = 3(7N + 14) + 15$

$28N + 8 = 21N + 57$

$7N = 49$

$N = 7$

The desired integers are **49, 56, 63,** and **70.**

7. $2(x + 4) + 2\left(\dfrac{x}{2}\right) + 2(x + 1) + 2x = 31$ in.

$2x + 8 + x + 2x + 2 + 2x = 31$ in.

$7x = 21$ in.

$x = \textbf{3 in.}$

8. $\dfrac{(x + 5)(x - 4)}{(x - 2)(x + 1)} \cdot \dfrac{(x + 8)(x + 2)}{(x + 8)(x - 5)}$

$= \dfrac{(x + 5)(x - 4)(x + 2)}{(x - 2)(x + 1)(x - 5)}$

9. $\dfrac{(x - 6)(x + 3)}{(x - 8)(x + 4)} \cdot \dfrac{(x - 5)(x + 4)}{(x - 6)(x + 4)}$

$= \dfrac{(x + 3)(x - 5)}{(x - 8)(x + 4)}$

10. $\dfrac{1}{-3^{-2}} = -3^2 = \textbf{-9}$

11. $-27^{-2/3} = \dfrac{1}{-27^{2/3}} = -\dfrac{1}{(27^{1/3})^2} = -\dfrac{\textbf{1}}{\textbf{9}}$

12. $\dfrac{1}{81^{-3/4}} = 81^{3/4} = (81^{1/4})^3 = \textbf{27}$

13. $(-27)^{-2/3} = \dfrac{1}{(-27)^{2/3}} = \dfrac{1}{((-27)^{1/3})^2} = \dfrac{\textbf{1}}{\textbf{9}}$

14. $\dfrac{\dfrac{1}{x} + \dfrac{4}{y}}{3 + \dfrac{1}{xy}} = \dfrac{\dfrac{y + 4x}{xy}}{\dfrac{3xy + 1}{xy}} \cdot \dfrac{\dfrac{xy}{3xy + 1}}{\dfrac{xy}{3xy + 1}}$

$= \dfrac{\textbf{y + 4x}}{\textbf{3xy + 1}}$

15. $\dfrac{\dfrac{4}{x} - 3}{\dfrac{7}{x} + 2} = \dfrac{\dfrac{4 - 3x}{x}}{\dfrac{7 + 2x}{x}} \cdot \dfrac{\dfrac{7 + 2x}{x}}{\dfrac{7 + 2x}{x}} = \dfrac{\mathbf{4 - 3x}}{\mathbf{7 + 2x}}$

16. $3\sqrt{\dfrac{5}{3}} - 2\sqrt{\dfrac{3}{5}} = \dfrac{3\sqrt{5}}{\sqrt{3}}\dfrac{\sqrt{3}}{\sqrt{3}} - \dfrac{2\sqrt{3}}{\sqrt{5}}\dfrac{\sqrt{5}}{\sqrt{5}}$

$= \dfrac{3\sqrt{15}}{3} - \dfrac{2\sqrt{15}}{5} = \dfrac{15\sqrt{15}}{15} - \dfrac{6\sqrt{15}}{15}$

$= \dfrac{\mathbf{3\sqrt{15}}}{\mathbf{5}}$

17. $\dfrac{(6 \times 10^{17})(3 \times 10^{-20})}{18 \times 10^{-10}} = \dfrac{18 \times 10^{-3}}{18 \times 10^{-10}}$

$= \mathbf{1 \times 10^7}$

18. $2\sqrt{\dfrac{7}{3}} - 3\sqrt{\dfrac{3}{7}} = \dfrac{2\sqrt{7}}{\sqrt{3}}\dfrac{\sqrt{3}}{\sqrt{3}} - \dfrac{3\sqrt{3}}{\sqrt{7}}\dfrac{\sqrt{7}}{\sqrt{7}}$

$= \dfrac{2\sqrt{21}}{3} - \dfrac{3\sqrt{21}}{7} = \dfrac{14\sqrt{21}}{21} - \dfrac{9\sqrt{21}}{21}$

$= \dfrac{\mathbf{5\sqrt{21}}}{\mathbf{21}}$

19. $4\sqrt{12}(3\sqrt{2} - 4\sqrt{3}) = 4\sqrt{2}\sqrt{2}\sqrt{3}(3\sqrt{2} - 4\sqrt{3})$

$= \mathbf{24\sqrt{6} - 96}$

20. $2\sqrt{28} - 3\sqrt{63} + 2\sqrt{175}$

$= 2\sqrt{2}\sqrt{2}\sqrt{7} - 3\sqrt{3}\sqrt{3}\sqrt{7} + 2\sqrt{5}\sqrt{5}\sqrt{7}$

$= 4\sqrt{7} - 9\sqrt{7} + 10\sqrt{7} = \mathbf{5\sqrt{7}}$

21. $\dfrac{6}{x^2(x + 2)} - \dfrac{3}{x^2 + 3x + 2}$

$= \dfrac{6(x + 1)}{x^2(x + 2)(x + 1)} - \dfrac{3x^2}{x^2(x + 2)(x + 1)}$

$= \dfrac{\mathbf{-3x^2 + 6x + 6}}{\mathbf{x^2(x + 2)(x + 1)}}$

22. $\dfrac{p}{ax^2} + \dfrac{cx + a}{ax^3} + \dfrac{mx + b}{a^2 x^4}$

$= \dfrac{pax^2}{a^2 x^4} + \dfrac{ax(cx + a)}{a^2 x^4} + \dfrac{mx + b}{a^2 x^4}$

$= \dfrac{\mathbf{pax^2 + ax(cx + a) + mx + b}}{\mathbf{a^2 x^4}}$

23. $\dfrac{3x - 2}{7} - \dfrac{x}{4} - \dfrac{x - 3}{2} = 1$

$12x - 8 - 7x - 14x + 42 = 28$

$-9x = -6$

$x = \dfrac{\mathbf{2}}{\mathbf{3}}$

24. $3x^0 - 2(x - 3^0) - |-11 - 2|$

$= 4x(2 - 5^0) - 7x$

$3 - 2x + 2 - 13 = 8x - 4x - 7x$

$-2x - 8 = -3x$

$x = \mathbf{8}$

25. (a) Every point on this line is 2 units above the x-axis.

$y = \mathbf{2}$

(b) The y-intercept is -2. The slope is positive and the rise over the run for any triangle drawn is $\frac{1}{3}$.

$y = \dfrac{\mathbf{1}}{\mathbf{3}}x - \mathbf{2}.$

26. $A = 180 - 140 = \mathbf{40}$

$B = 180 - 40 - 100 = \mathbf{40}$

$C = 180 - 100 = \mathbf{80}$

$D = B = \mathbf{40}$

$E = 180 - 90 - 40 = \mathbf{50}$

$M = 180 - 80 - 50 = \mathbf{50}$

27.
$$
\begin{array}{r}
x^3 - x^2 + x - 1 - \frac{1}{x+1} \\
x + 1{\overline{\smash{\big)}\,x^4 + 0x^3 + 0x^2 + 0x - 2}} \\
\underline{x^4 + x^3} \\
-x^3 + 0x^2 \\
\underline{-x^3 - x^2} \\
x^2 + 0x \\
\underline{x^2 + x} \\
-x - 2 \\
\underline{-x - 1} \\
-1
\end{array}
$$

Check:

$\dfrac{x^3(x + 1)}{x + 1} - \dfrac{x^2(x + 1)}{x + 1} + \dfrac{x(x + 1)}{x + 1}$

$- \dfrac{1(x + 1)}{x + 1} - \dfrac{1}{x + 1} = \dfrac{x^4 - 2}{x + 1}$

28.

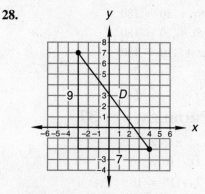

$D^2 = 9^2 + 7^2$

$D^2 = 81 + 49$

$D^2 = 130$

$D = \sqrt{\mathbf{130}}$

29. $\dfrac{x^{-2}y}{zx^4}\left(3x^6y^{-1}z - \dfrac{3x^{-3}y^2}{z^{-1}x^{-4}}\right) = \dfrac{3x^4z}{x^4z} - 3x^{-5}y^3$

$= \mathbf{3 - 3x^{-5}y^3}$

30. $-3^0(2 - 4^0) - |-3| - 2 - 4^2 - (-2)^3 - 2$

$= -1 - 3 - 2 - 16 + 8 - 2 = \mathbf{-16}$

PRACTICE SET 37

a. Carbon: $\quad 12 \times 1 = 12$

Chlorine: $\quad 35 \times 2 = 70$

Fluorine: $\quad 19 \times 2 = 38$

Total: $\quad 12 + 70 + 38 = 120$

$\dfrac{C}{Total} = \dfrac{12}{120}$

$\dfrac{C}{1200} = \dfrac{12}{120}$

$120C = 14,400$

$C = \mathbf{120 \text{ grams}}$

b. $m\angle ABC + m\angle BCD = 180°$

$(125°) + m\angle BCD = 180°$

$m\angle BCD = \mathbf{55°}$

$m\angle DAB = m\angle BCD$

$m\angle DAB = \mathbf{55°}$

$x + 2 = 6$

$x = \mathbf{4}$

$2y - 4 = 8$

$y = \mathbf{6}$

c. $8y + 20 + 10y + 70 = 180$

$18y = 90$

$y = \mathbf{5}$

$x + 50 + 8y + 20 = 180$

$x + 8(5) + 70 = 180$

$x + 110 = 180$

$x = \mathbf{70}$

PROBLEM SET 37

1. Hydrogen: $\quad 2 \times 1 = 2$

Oxygen: $\quad 1 \times 16 = 16$

Total: $\quad 2 + 16 = 18$

$\dfrac{16}{18} = \dfrac{Oxygen}{5400}$

$18(Oxygen) = 16(5400)$

$Oxygen = \mathbf{4800 \text{ grams}}$

2. Nitrogen: $\quad 1 \times 14 = 14$

Hydrogen: $\quad 3 \times 1 = 3$

Total: $\quad 14 + 3 = 17$

$\dfrac{14}{17} = \dfrac{N}{850}$

$17N = 14(850)$

$N = \mathbf{700 \text{ grams}}$

3. Nitrogen: $\quad 1 \times 14 = 14$

Hydrogen: $\quad 4 \times 1 = 4$

Chlorine: $\quad 1 \times 35 = 35$

Total: $\quad 14 + 4 + 35 = 53$

$\dfrac{35}{53} = \dfrac{Cl}{795}$

$53Cl = 35(795)$

$Cl = \mathbf{525 \text{ grams}}$

4.

$R_BT_B + 100 = R_TT_T; \ T_B = T_T = 4; \ R_T = 2R_B$

$4R_B + 100 = 4(2R_B)$

$-4R_B = -100$

$R_B = 25$

$R_T = 2(25) = 50$

$D_B = 25(4) = \mathbf{100 \text{ miles}}$

$D_T = 50(4) = \mathbf{200 \text{ miles}}$

5. $\quad F \times of = is$

$2\dfrac{3}{4} \times GR = 550$

$GR = 550 \times \dfrac{4}{11} = \mathbf{200 \text{ gestures}}$

6. $\dfrac{(x + 3)(x - 2)}{x(x + 4)(x + 3)} \cdot \dfrac{x(x + 4)(x + 1)}{(x + 4)(x - 2)} = \dfrac{x + 1}{x + 4}$

7. $\dfrac{ax(x - 4)(x + 3)}{(x + 4)(x + 3)} \cdot \dfrac{(x + 4)(x - 2)}{ax(x - 4)} = x - 2$

8. $-8^{-4/3} = -\dfrac{1}{8^{4/3}} = -\dfrac{1}{(8^{1/3})^4} = -\dfrac{1}{16}$

9. $(-27)^{-4/3} = \dfrac{1}{(-27)^{4/3}} = \dfrac{1}{((-27)^{1/3})^4} = \dfrac{1}{81}$

10. $-27^{-4/3} = -\dfrac{1}{27^{4/3}} = -\dfrac{1}{(27^{1/3})^4} = -\dfrac{\mathbf{1}}{\mathbf{81}}$

11. $\dfrac{-3}{-9^{-3/2}} = (-3)(-9^{3/2}) = (-3)(-9^{1/2})^3 = \mathbf{81}$

12. $m\angle PON = 180 - 85 = \mathbf{95°}$

$x - 3 = 11$
$\quad x = \mathbf{14}$

$y + 4 = 9$
$\quad y = \mathbf{5}$

13. $x = 2(90) - 80 = \mathbf{100}$

$y = \dfrac{360 - 180}{2} = \dfrac{180}{2} = \mathbf{90}$

$z = \dfrac{100 + 60}{2} = \dfrac{160}{2} = \mathbf{80}$

14. $\dfrac{x + \dfrac{1}{x^2}}{x^2 - \dfrac{2}{x^2}} = \dfrac{\dfrac{x^3 + 1}{x^2}}{\dfrac{x^4 - 2}{x^2}} \cdot \dfrac{\dfrac{x^2}{x^4 - 2}}{\dfrac{x^2}{x^4 - 2}} = \dfrac{\mathbf{x^3 + 1}}{\mathbf{x^4 - 2}}$

15. $\dfrac{a + \dfrac{y}{x}}{a - \dfrac{my}{x}} = \dfrac{\dfrac{ax + y}{x}}{\dfrac{ax - my}{x}} \cdot \dfrac{\dfrac{x}{ax - my}}{\dfrac{x}{ax - my}} = \dfrac{\mathbf{ax + y}}{\mathbf{ax - my}}$

16. $\dfrac{3\sqrt{2}}{\sqrt{7}} \dfrac{\sqrt{7}}{\sqrt{7}} - \dfrac{5\sqrt{7}}{\sqrt{2}} \dfrac{\sqrt{2}}{\sqrt{2}} = \dfrac{3\sqrt{14}}{7} - \dfrac{5\sqrt{14}}{2}$

$= \dfrac{6\sqrt{14}}{14} - \dfrac{35\sqrt{14}}{14} = -\dfrac{\mathbf{29\sqrt{14}}}{\mathbf{14}}$

17. $\dfrac{2\sqrt{11}}{\sqrt{3}} \dfrac{\sqrt{3}}{\sqrt{3}} - \dfrac{5\sqrt{3}}{\sqrt{11}} \dfrac{\sqrt{11}}{\sqrt{11}} = \dfrac{2\sqrt{33}}{3} - \dfrac{5\sqrt{33}}{11}$

$= \dfrac{22\sqrt{33}}{33} - \dfrac{15\sqrt{33}}{33} = \dfrac{\mathbf{7\sqrt{33}}}{\mathbf{33}}$

18. Graph the line to find the slope.

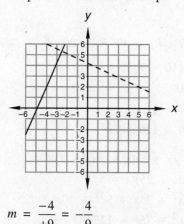

$m = \dfrac{-4}{+9} = -\dfrac{4}{9}$

Since the slopes of perpendicular lines are negative reciprocals of each other,

$m_\perp = \dfrac{9}{4}$

$y = \dfrac{9}{4}x + b$

$2 = \dfrac{9}{4}(-4) + b$

$11 = b$

Since $m_\perp = \dfrac{9}{4}$ and $b = 11$, $y = \dfrac{\mathbf{9}}{\mathbf{4}}x + \mathbf{11}.$

19. $2x + 280 = 360$
$\quad 2x = 80$
$\quad\; x = \mathbf{40}$

$y + (40 + 30) = 180$
$\qquad\qquad y = \mathbf{110}$

20. (a) $3x - 3y = -6$
$\qquad\quad y = x + 2$

(b) $3x + y = 6$
$\qquad\; y = -3x + 6$

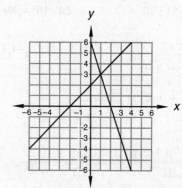

Substitute $y = -3x + 6$ into (a) and get:

(a′) $3x - 3(-3x + 6) = -6$
$\qquad\qquad\quad 12x = 12$
$\qquad\qquad\quad\; x = 1$

(a) $y = (1) + 2 = 3$

(1, 3)

21. $\dfrac{x}{x + 5} - \dfrac{3x}{x^2 + 4x - 5}$

$= \dfrac{x(x - 1)}{(x + 5)(x - 1)} - \dfrac{3x}{(x + 5)(x - 1)}$

$= \dfrac{\mathbf{x^2 - 4x}}{\mathbf{(x + 5)(x - 1)}}$

22. $\dfrac{4}{x(x+2)} + \dfrac{6}{x} = \dfrac{4}{x(x+2)} + \dfrac{6(x+2)}{x(x+2)}$

$\quad = \dfrac{6x+16}{x(x+2)}$

23. $\dfrac{3x+2}{5} - \dfrac{x-3}{7} = 2$

$\quad 21x + 14 - 5x + 15 = 70$

$\quad\quad\quad\quad\quad\quad 16x = 41$

$\quad\quad\quad\quad\quad\quad\quad x = \dfrac{41}{16}$

24. $\dfrac{4x}{3} - \dfrac{2x}{4} + x = 5$

$\quad 16x - 6x + 12x = 60$

$\quad\quad\quad\quad 22x = 60$

$\quad\quad\quad\quad\quad x = \dfrac{30}{11}$

25. $3\sqrt{2}(5\sqrt{12} - 2\sqrt{2})$

$\quad = 3\sqrt{2}(5\sqrt{2}\sqrt{2}\sqrt{3} - 2\sqrt{2}) = \mathbf{30\sqrt{6} - 12}$

26. $4\sqrt{20}(3\sqrt{2} - 2\sqrt{5})$

$\quad = 4\sqrt{2}\sqrt{2}\sqrt{5}(3\sqrt{2} - 2\sqrt{5}) = \mathbf{24\sqrt{10} - 80}$

27. $\dfrac{(x^{-2})^{-1}(y^{-2}x)^{-3}x^0 y}{(x^{-2})^2 x^4 xx^0 y^0 x^2} = \dfrac{x^2 y^6 x^{-3} y}{x^3} = \mathbf{x^{-4}y^7}$

28. $-2^2 - (-2)^3 - (-2) - 2^0 - 2$

$\quad = -4 + 8 + 2 - 1 - 2 = \mathbf{3}$

29. $\dfrac{(3.5 \times 10^{-18})(3 \times 10^2)}{2.1 \times 10^{-36}} = \dfrac{10.5 \times 10^{-16}}{2.1 \times 10^{-36}}$

$\quad = \mathbf{5 \times 10^{20}}$

30. $\dfrac{4x^{-2}y^{-2}}{z^2}\left(\dfrac{x^2 y}{z^{-2}} - \dfrac{3x^2 y^2 z^2}{p}\right) = \mathbf{4y^{-1} - 12p^{-1}}$

PRACTICE SET 38

a. $(x+2)^3 = (x+2)(x+2)(x+2)$

$\quad = (x+2)(x^2 + 4x + 4)$

$\quad\quad x^2 + 4x + 4$

$\quad\quad \underline{x\ \ + 2}$

$\quad\quad x^3 + 4x^2 + 4x$

$\quad\quad\quad \underline{2x^2 + 8x + 8}$

$\quad\quad x^3 + 6x^2 + 12x + 8$

b. $-36x = 16x^2 - x^3$

$\longrightarrow \quad x^3 - 16x^2 - 36x = 0$

$\quad\quad x(x^2 - 16x - 36) = 0$

$\quad\quad x(x - 18)(x + 2) = 0$

$\quad\quad\quad\quad\quad x = \mathbf{0, 18, -2}$

PROBLEM SET 38

1. $3N_P = -4(-N_P) - 15$

$\quad N_P = \mathbf{15\ protrusions}$

2. $\dfrac{2}{9} = \dfrac{Fe}{1440}$

$\quad 9Fe = 2(1440)$

$\quad Fe = \mathbf{320\ kilograms}$

3. Hydrogen: $\quad\quad 2 \times 1 = 2$

Sulfur: $\quad\quad\quad 1 \times 32 = 32$

Oxygen: $\quad\quad\quad 4 \times 16 = 64$

Total: $\quad\quad 2 + 32 + 64 = 98$

$\quad \dfrac{32}{98} = \dfrac{S}{196}$

$\quad 98S = 32(196)$

$\quad\quad S = \mathbf{64\ grams}$

4. (a) $\dfrac{N}{D} = \dfrac{7}{2} \quad\longrightarrow\quad 2N = 7D$

(b) $10D = 2N + 84 \quad\longrightarrow\quad N = 5D - 42$

Substitute (b) into (a) and get:

(a′) $2(5D - 42) = 7D$

$\quad\quad\quad 3D = 84$

$\quad\quad\quad\ D = \mathbf{28}$

(b) $N = 5(28) - 42 = \mathbf{98}$

5.

$R_C T_C = R_T T_T;\ R_C = 30;\ R_T = 20;\ T_C + T_T = 10$

$30T_C = 20(10 - T_C)$

$50T_C = 200$

$\quad T_C = 4$

$D_C = 30(4) = \mathbf{120\ miles}$

6. $(x+5)^3 = (x+5)(x+5)(x+5)$

$\quad = (x^2 + 10x + 25)(x + 5)$

$\quad = x^3 + 10x^2 + 25x + 5x^2 + 50x + 125$

$\quad = \mathbf{x^3 + 15x^2 + 75x + 125}$

7. $(x + 4)^3 = (x + 4)(x + 4)(x + 4)$

$= (x^2 + 8x + 16)(x + 4)$

$= x^3 + 8x^2 + 16x + 4x^2 + 32x + 64$

$= \mathbf{x^3 + 12x^2 + 48x + 64}$

8. $-x + x^2 = 12$

$x^2 - x - 12 = 0$

$(x - 4)(x + 3) = 0$

$x = \mathbf{4, -3}$

9. $-48x = -2x^2 - x^3$

$x^3 + 2x^2 - 48x = 0$

$x(x + 8)(x - 6) = 0$

$x = \mathbf{0, -8, 6}$

10. $2x^2 + 2x - 112 = 0$

$2(x + 8)(x - 7) = 0$

$x = \mathbf{-8, 7}$

11. $\dfrac{(x + 5)(x + 2)}{x(x + 7)(x + 2)} \cdot \dfrac{x(x + 7)(x + 4)}{(x + 5)(x - 3)}$

$= \dfrac{\mathbf{x + 4}}{\mathbf{x - 3}}$

12. $-16^{-1/4} = -\dfrac{1}{16^{1/4}} = -\dfrac{\mathbf{1}}{\mathbf{2}}$

13. $-16^{-3/4} = -\dfrac{1}{16^{3/4}} = -\dfrac{1}{(16^{1/4})^3} = -\dfrac{\mathbf{1}}{\mathbf{8}}$

14. $8^{2/3} = (8^{1/3})^2 = \mathbf{4}$

15. $(-8)^{1/3} = \mathbf{-2}$

16. $(\sqrt{11})^2 = H^2 + \left(\dfrac{3}{2}\right)^2$

$11 = H^2 + \dfrac{9}{4}$

$\dfrac{35}{4} = H^2$

$\dfrac{\sqrt{35}}{2} = H$

$\text{Area} = \dfrac{3 \text{ in.} \times \dfrac{\sqrt{35}}{2} \text{ in.}}{2} = \dfrac{\mathbf{3\sqrt{35}}}{\mathbf{4}} \text{ in.}^2$

17. $\text{Length } \widehat{DEF} = \dfrac{320}{360} \cdot 2(\pi)(20 \text{ m}) \approx \mathbf{111.64 \text{ m}}$

18. $\dfrac{x^2 - \dfrac{a}{x}}{a^2 - \dfrac{a}{x}} = \dfrac{\dfrac{x^3 - a}{x}}{\dfrac{a^2x - a}{x}} \cdot \dfrac{\dfrac{x}{a^2x - a}}{\dfrac{x}{a^2x - a}} = \dfrac{\mathbf{x^3 - a}}{\mathbf{a^2x - a}}$

19. $\dfrac{\dfrac{mp^2}{4} - 5}{4p^2 - \dfrac{p^2}{4}} = \dfrac{\dfrac{mp^2 - 20}{4}}{\dfrac{16p^2 - p^2}{4}} \cdot \dfrac{\dfrac{4}{16p^2 - p^2}}{\dfrac{4}{16p^2 - p^2}}$

$= \dfrac{\mathbf{mp^2 - 20}}{\mathbf{15p^2}}$

20. $\dfrac{(7 \times 10^{-28})(3 \times 10^{-7})}{7 \times 10^{-25}} = \mathbf{3 \times 10^{-10}}$

21. $\dfrac{3\sqrt{2}}{\sqrt{11}} \dfrac{\sqrt{11}}{\sqrt{11}} + \dfrac{5\sqrt{11}}{\sqrt{2}} \dfrac{\sqrt{2}}{\sqrt{2}} = \dfrac{3\sqrt{22}}{11} + \dfrac{5\sqrt{22}}{2}$

$= \dfrac{6\sqrt{22}}{22} + \dfrac{55\sqrt{22}}{22} = \dfrac{\mathbf{61\sqrt{22}}}{\mathbf{22}}$

22. $-\dfrac{2\sqrt{11}}{\sqrt{3}} \dfrac{\sqrt{3}}{\sqrt{3}} + \dfrac{7\sqrt{3}}{\sqrt{11}} \dfrac{\sqrt{11}}{\sqrt{11}} = -\dfrac{2\sqrt{33}}{3} + \dfrac{7\sqrt{33}}{11}$

$= -\dfrac{22\sqrt{33}}{33} + \dfrac{21\sqrt{33}}{33} = -\dfrac{\mathbf{\sqrt{33}}}{\mathbf{33}}$

23. $3\sqrt{24}(2\sqrt{6} - 3\sqrt{12})$

$= 3\sqrt{2}\sqrt{2}\sqrt{2}\sqrt{3}(2\sqrt{2}\sqrt{3} - 3\sqrt{2}\sqrt{2}\sqrt{3})$

$= \mathbf{72 - 108\sqrt{2}}$

24. Graph the line to find the slope.

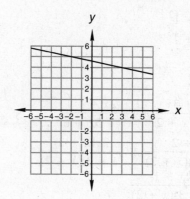

$\text{Slope} = \dfrac{-1}{+5} = -\dfrac{1}{5}$

$y = -\dfrac{1}{5}x + b$

$\dfrac{25}{5} = -\dfrac{1}{5}(-2) + b$

$\dfrac{23}{5} = b$

Since $m = -\dfrac{1}{5}$ and $b = \dfrac{23}{5}$, $y = -\dfrac{1}{5}x + \dfrac{23}{5}$.

25. $\dfrac{5x-2}{3} - \dfrac{x}{4} = 7$

$20x - 8 - 3x = 84$

$17x = 92$

$x = \dfrac{92}{17}$

26.
$$
\begin{array}{r}
x^3 - x^2 + x - 1 \\
x+1\overline{)x^4 + 0x^3 + 0x^2 + 0x - 1} \\
\underline{x^4 + x^3} \\
-x^3 + 0x^2 \\
\underline{-x^3 - x^2} \\
x^2 + 0x \\
\underline{x^2 + x} \\
-x - 1 \\
\underline{-x - 1} \\
0
\end{array}
$$

27.

$D^2 = 5^2 + 1^2$

$D^2 = 25 + 1$

$D^2 = 26$

$D = \sqrt{26}$

28. $\dfrac{1}{x+3} + \dfrac{3x}{x+2} + \dfrac{2x+1}{x^2+5x+6}$

$= \dfrac{x+2}{(x+3)(x+2)} + \dfrac{3x(x+3)}{(x+3)(x+2)}$

$\quad + \dfrac{2x+1}{(x+3)(x+2)}$

$= \dfrac{x + 2 + 3x^2 + 9x + 2x + 1}{(x+3)(x+2)}$

$= \dfrac{3x^2 + 12x + 3}{(x+3)(x+2)}$

29. $\dfrac{(p^2 y^{-2})^{-3}\, p^{-2}\, (y^0)^{-2}}{(p^{-2} p^0 py)^{-3}\, (yp^{-2})^{-4}\, p} = \dfrac{p^{-6} y^6 p^{-2}}{p^6\, p^{-3}\, y^{-3}\, y^{-4}\, p^8\, p}$

$= p^{-20} y^{13}$

30. $|3^0 - 3^2| - \dfrac{1}{2^{-2}} - 3^0(-3^3 - 3^2)$

$= 8 - 4 + 36 = \mathbf{40}$

a. $144s^2 - 36 = 0$

$(12s - 6)(12s + 6) = 0$

$12s - 6 = 0$

$12s = 6$

$s = \dfrac{1}{2}$

$12s + 6 = 0$

$12s = -6$

$s = -\dfrac{1}{2}$

$s = -\dfrac{1}{2}, \dfrac{1}{2}$

b. $121m^2 - 64 = 0$

$(11m - 8)(11m + 8) = 0$

$11m - 8 = 0$

$11m = 8$

$m = \dfrac{8}{11}$

$11m + 8 = 0$

$11m = -8$

$m = -\dfrac{8}{11}$

$m = -\dfrac{8}{11}, \dfrac{8}{11}$

c. $X + B = 360 - 306$

$X + B = 54$

$X = B = \dfrac{54}{2}$

Thus $X = \mathbf{27}$

$X + B + 2A = 180$

$(27) + (27) + 2A = 180$

$2A = 126$

$A = 63$

$Z = \mathbf{90}$ because the diagonals of a rhombus are perpendicular.

PROBLEM SET 39

1. $F \times of = is$

$$\frac{3}{16} \times S = 420$$

$$S = 420 \times \frac{16}{3} = 2240$$

Number with ulterior motives = 2240 − 420
= **1820 sophomores**

2. $\frac{P}{100} \times of = is$

$$\frac{28}{100} \times P = 9576$$

$$P = 9576 \times \frac{100}{28} = 34,200$$

Ukases = 34,200 − 9576 = **24,624**

3. Carbon: $1 \times 12 = 12$
Oxygen: $2 \times 16 = 32$
Total: $12 + 32 = 44$

$$\frac{12}{44} = \frac{C}{528}$$

$44C = 12(528)$

$C =$ **144 grams**

4. $\frac{P}{100} \times of = is$

$$\frac{86}{100} \times M = 688$$

$$M = 688 \times \frac{100}{86} = 800$$

Sr = 800 − 688 = **112 grams**

5.

$R_R T_R = R_W T_W;\ R_R = 5;\ R_W = 3;\ T_R + T_W = 8$

$5T_R = 3(8 - T_R)$

$8T_R = 24$

$T_R = 3$

$D_R = 5(3) =$ **15 miles**

6. $7(90 - A) = 2(180 - A) + 110$

$630 - 7A = 360 - 2A + 110$

$-5A = -160$

$A = \mathbf{32°}$

7. Area $= \frac{bh}{2} = 52\ \text{ft}^2$

$$h = MP = \frac{2(52\ \text{ft}^2)}{13\ \text{ft}} = \mathbf{8\ ft}$$

Area$_{\text{Circle}} = \pi r^2 = (\pi)(8\ \text{ft})^2 \approx \mathbf{200.96\ ft^2}$

8. $x^2 - 9 = 0$

$(x - 3)(x + 3) = 0$

$x = \mathbf{3, -3}$

9. $36x^2 - 36 = 0$

$36(x^2 - 1) = 0$

$36(x - 1)(x + 1) = 0$

$x = \mathbf{1, -1}$

10. $24x = -11x^2 - x^3$

$x^3 + 11x^2 + 24x = 0$

$x(x + 8)(x + 3) = 0$

$x = \mathbf{0, -3, -8}$

11. $(x - 1)^3 = (x - 1)(x - 1)(x - 1)$

$= (x^2 - 2x + 1)(x - 1)$

$= x^3 - 2x^2 + x - x^2 + 2x - 1$

$= \mathbf{x^3 - 3x^2 + 3x - 1}$

12. $\dfrac{x(x + 5)(x + 1)}{(x + 5)(x - 3)} \cdot \dfrac{(x + 7)(x - 2)}{x(x + 7)(x + 1)} = \dfrac{\mathbf{x - 2}}{\mathbf{x - 3}}$

13. $\dfrac{2^0}{-4^{-3/2}} = -2^0 4^{3/2} = -(4^{1/2})^3 = \mathbf{-8}$

14. $\dfrac{-3^0}{-27^{-2/3}} = -1[-27^{2/3}] = (27^{1/3})^2 = \mathbf{9}$

15. $\dfrac{ax^2 - \dfrac{4}{a}}{\dfrac{x^2}{a} + 6} = \dfrac{\dfrac{a^2 x^2 - 4}{a}}{\dfrac{x^2 + 6a}{a}} \cdot \dfrac{\dfrac{a}{x^2 + 6a}}{\dfrac{a}{x^2 + 6a}}$

$= \dfrac{a^2 x^2 - 4}{x^2 + 6a}$

16. $\dfrac{\dfrac{m^2 p}{x} - 6}{m^2 p - \dfrac{4}{x}} = \dfrac{\dfrac{m^2 p - 6x}{x}}{\dfrac{m^2 px - 4}{x}} \cdot \dfrac{\dfrac{x}{m^2 px - 4}}{\dfrac{x}{m^2 px - 4}}$

$= \dfrac{m^2 p - 6x}{m^2 px - 4}$

17. $\dfrac{(3 \times 10^{-38})(8 \times 10^6)}{2.4 \times 10^{14}} = \dfrac{2.4 \times 10^{-31}}{2.4 \times 10^{14}}$

$= 1 \times 10^{-45}$

18. $\dfrac{2\sqrt{3}}{\sqrt{13}} \dfrac{\sqrt{13}}{\sqrt{13}} - \dfrac{5\sqrt{13}}{\sqrt{3}} \dfrac{\sqrt{3}}{\sqrt{3}} = \dfrac{2\sqrt{39}}{13} - \dfrac{5\sqrt{39}}{3}$

$= \dfrac{6\sqrt{39}}{39} - \dfrac{65\sqrt{39}}{39} = -\dfrac{59\sqrt{39}}{39}$

19. $\dfrac{5\sqrt{3}}{\sqrt{2}} \dfrac{\sqrt{2}}{\sqrt{2}} - \dfrac{2\sqrt{2}}{\sqrt{3}} \dfrac{\sqrt{3}}{\sqrt{3}} = \dfrac{5\sqrt{6}}{2} - \dfrac{2\sqrt{6}}{3}$

$= \dfrac{15\sqrt{6}}{6} - \dfrac{4\sqrt{6}}{6} = \dfrac{11\sqrt{6}}{6}$

20. $5\sqrt{45} - 2\sqrt{75} + 2\sqrt{108}$

$= 5\sqrt{3}\sqrt{3}\sqrt{5} - 2\sqrt{3}\sqrt{5}\sqrt{5} + 2\sqrt{2}\sqrt{2}\sqrt{3}\sqrt{3}\sqrt{3}$

$= 15\sqrt{5} - 10\sqrt{3} + 12\sqrt{3} = \mathbf{15\sqrt{5} + 2\sqrt{3}}$

21. (a) $2x + 4y = 120$

(b) $3x - 2y = 60$

1(a) $2x + 4y = 120$

2(b) $\dfrac{6x - 4y = 120}{8x \qquad = 240}$

$x = \mathbf{30}$

(a) $2(30) + 4y = 120$

$4y = 60$

$y = \mathbf{15}$

22. $m\angle WXY = m\angle YZW = \mathbf{68°}$

$2x + 3 = 13$

$2x = 10$

$x = \mathbf{5}$

$3y + 4 = 11$

$3y = 7$

$y = \dfrac{\mathbf{7}}{\mathbf{3}}$

23. $3\sqrt{12}(4\sqrt{3} - 3\sqrt{3}) = 3\sqrt{2}\sqrt{2}\sqrt{3}(4\sqrt{3} - 3\sqrt{3})$

$= 72 - 54 = \mathbf{18}$

24. Graph the line to find the slope.

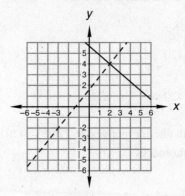

$m = \dfrac{+6}{+5} = \dfrac{6}{5}$

Since the slopes of perpendicular lines are negative reciprocals of each other,

$m_\perp = -\dfrac{5}{6}$

$y = -\dfrac{5}{6}x + b$

$\dfrac{24}{6} = -\dfrac{5}{6}(2) + b$

$\dfrac{17}{3} = b$

Since $m_\perp = -\dfrac{5}{6}$ and $b = \dfrac{17}{3}$,

$\mathbf{y = -\dfrac{5}{6}x + \dfrac{17}{3}}$

25. $2\dfrac{1}{4}x - 3\dfrac{1}{2} = -\dfrac{1}{16}$

$\dfrac{9}{4}x = -\dfrac{1}{16} + \dfrac{56}{16}$

$x = \dfrac{55}{16} \cdot \dfrac{4}{9} = \dfrac{\mathbf{55}}{\mathbf{36}}$

26. $0.002x - 0.02 = 6.6$

$2x - 20 = 6600$

$2x = 6620$

$x = \mathbf{3310}$

27. $\dfrac{3}{x + 1} + \dfrac{2x}{y(x + 1)} + \dfrac{3x + 2}{x^2 + 2x + 1}$

$= \dfrac{3y(x + 1)}{y(x + 1)^2} + \dfrac{2x(x + 1)}{y(x + 1)^2} + \dfrac{y(3x + 2)}{y(x + 1)^2}$

$= \dfrac{3xy + 3y + 2x^2 + 2x + 3xy + 2y}{y(x + 1)^2}$

$= \dfrac{\mathbf{2x^2 + 2x + 5y + 6xy}}{\mathbf{y(x + 1)^2}}$

28. $\dfrac{4xy + 4x^2y^2}{4xy} = \dfrac{4xy(1 + xy)}{4xy} = 1 + xy$

29. $\dfrac{4x^{-2}y^{-2}}{z^2}\left(\dfrac{3x^2y^2z^2}{4} + \dfrac{2x^0y^{-2}}{z^2y^2}\right)$

$= 3 + 8x^{-2}y^{-6}z^{-4}$

30. $-2^0 - 3^0(-2 - 5^0) - \dfrac{1}{-2^{-2}} + x^2y - xy$

$= -1 + 3 + 4 + (-2)^2(3) - (-2)(3)$

$= -1 + 3 + 4 + 12 + 6 = \textbf{24}$

PRACTICE SET 40

a. $\dfrac{5}{m} - ay = \dfrac{p}{x} + s$

$\dfrac{5}{m} \cdot mx - ay \cdot mx = \dfrac{p}{x} \cdot mx + s \cdot mx$

$5x - amxy = mp + msx$

$5x = amxy + mp + msx$

$5x = m(axy + p + sx)$

$\dfrac{5x}{axy + p + sx} = m$

b. $\dfrac{m}{x} + \dfrac{p}{m} = z$

$\dfrac{m}{x} \cdot mx + \dfrac{p}{m} \cdot mx = z \cdot mx$

$m^2 + px = mxz$

$m^2 = mxz - px$

$m^2 = x(mz - p)$

$\dfrac{m^2}{mz - p} = x$

PROBLEM SET 40

1. $\dfrac{P}{100} \times of = is$

$\dfrac{164}{100} \times 1{,}200{,}000 = ME$

$ME = \textbf{\$1,968,000}$

2. $\dfrac{P}{100} \times of = is$

$\dfrac{380}{100} \times 4800 = MS$

$MS = \textbf{18,240 words}$

3. Iron: $\quad 1 \times 56 = 56$

Sulfur: $\quad 1 \times 32 = 32$

Total: $\quad 56 + 32 = 88m$

$\dfrac{56}{88} = \dfrac{448}{\text{FeS}}$

$56\text{FeS} = 88(448)$

$\text{FeS} = \textbf{704 grams}$

4. (a) $20N_S + 60N_B = 8000$

(b) $N_B = 3N_S$

Substitute (b) into (a) and get:

(a′) $20N_S + 60(3N_S) = 8000$

$200N_S = 8000$

$N_S = \textbf{40 pairs of shoes}$

(b) $N_B = 3(40) = \textbf{120 pairs of boots}$

5.

$R_A T_A + 120 = R_K T_K; \quad R_K = 15; \quad R_A = 3;$

$T_A = T_K$

$3T_K + 120 = 15T_K$

$120 = 12T_K$

$10 = T_K$

$D_K = 15(10) = \textbf{150 miles}$

6. $\dfrac{c}{x} + \dfrac{m}{a} = c$

$ac + mx = acx$

$mx = acx - ac$

$mx = a(cx - c)$

$\dfrac{mx}{cx - c} = a$

7. $\dfrac{x}{m} + c = \dfrac{y}{a}$

$ax + acm = my$

$a(x + cm) = my$

$a = \dfrac{my}{x + cm}$

8. $\dfrac{6}{p} - ax = \dfrac{m}{y} + k$

$6y - apxy = mp + kpy$

$6y - apxy - kpy = mp$

$y(6 - apx - kp) = mp$

$y = \dfrac{mp}{6 - apx - kp}$

9.　$\dfrac{a}{c} - b = \dfrac{m}{k}$

$ak - bck = cm$

$k(a - bc) = cm$

$k = \dfrac{cm}{a - bc}$

10.　$(x - 3)^3 = (x - 3)(x - 3)(x - 3)$

$= (x^2 - 6x + 9)(x - 3)$

$= x^3 - 6x^2 + 9x - 3x^2 + 18x - 27$

$= \mathbf{x^3 - 9x^2 + 27x - 27}$

11.　$X = \dfrac{360 - 318}{2} = \mathbf{21}$

Since diagonal bisectors of a rhombus are perpendicular, $Z = \mathbf{90}$.

$Y + 21 + 90 = 180$

$Y = \mathbf{69}$

12.　$4x^2 - 49 = 0$

$(2x - 7)(2x + 7) = 0$

$x = \mathbf{\dfrac{7}{2}, -\dfrac{7}{2}}$

13.　$x^3 + 3x^2 = 18x$

$x^3 + 3x^2 - 18x = 0$

$x(x + 6)(x - 3) = 0$

$x = \mathbf{0, 3, -6}$

14.　$\dfrac{x(x - 5)(x - 2)}{(x + 6)(x - 2)} \cdot \dfrac{(x + 6)(x - 3)}{x(x - 5)(x - 3)} = \mathbf{1}$

15.　$\dfrac{(-4^0)^2}{4^{-3/2}} = (1)(4^{3/2}) = (4^{1/2})^3 = \mathbf{8}$

16.　$\dfrac{1}{16^{-1/4}} = 16^{1/4} = \mathbf{2}$

17.　$\dfrac{\dfrac{4x^2 a}{y^2} + \dfrac{1}{a^2}}{2 - \dfrac{2}{y^2 a^2}}$

$= \dfrac{\dfrac{4x^2 a^3 + y^2}{y^2 a^2}}{\dfrac{2y^2 a^2 - 2}{y^2 a^2}} \cdot \dfrac{\dfrac{y^2 a^2}{2y^2 a^2 - 2}}{\dfrac{y^2 a^2}{2y^2 a^2 - 2}}$

$= \dfrac{\mathbf{4x^2 a^3 + y^2}}{\mathbf{2y^2 a^2 - 2}}$

18.　$\dfrac{\dfrac{xy^2}{p} - 4}{a^2 y - \dfrac{1}{p}} = \dfrac{\dfrac{xy^2 - 4p}{p}}{\dfrac{a^2 py - 1}{p}} \cdot \dfrac{\dfrac{p}{a^2 py - 1}}{\dfrac{p}{a^2 py - 1}}$

$= \dfrac{\mathbf{xy^2 - 4p}}{\mathbf{a^2 py - 1}}$

19.　$\dfrac{(4 \times 10^{17})(7 \times 10^{-26})}{1.4 \times 10^{-16}} = \dfrac{2.8 \times 10^{-8}}{1.4 \times 10^{-16}}$

$= \mathbf{2 \times 10^8}$

20.　$3\sqrt{50} - 2\sqrt{72} + 3\sqrt{162}$

$= 3\sqrt{2}\sqrt{5}\sqrt{5} - 2\sqrt{2}\sqrt{6}\sqrt{6} + 3\sqrt{2}\sqrt{3}\sqrt{3}\sqrt{3}\sqrt{3}$

$= 15\sqrt{2} - 12\sqrt{2} + 27\sqrt{2} = \mathbf{30\sqrt{2}}$

21.　$\dfrac{3\sqrt{3}}{\sqrt{7}}\dfrac{\sqrt{7}}{\sqrt{7}} + \dfrac{2\sqrt{7}}{\sqrt{3}}\dfrac{\sqrt{3}}{\sqrt{3}} = \dfrac{3\sqrt{21}}{7} + \dfrac{2\sqrt{21}}{3}$

$= \dfrac{9\sqrt{21}}{21} + \dfrac{14\sqrt{21}}{21} = \dfrac{\mathbf{23\sqrt{21}}}{\mathbf{21}}$

22.　$A = \mathbf{30}$

$B + 30 = 180$

$B = \mathbf{150}$

$2C + 150 = 180$

$2C = 30$

$C = \mathbf{15}$

23.　$\text{Volume}_{\text{Cylinder}} = \pi r^2 \times h = 32\pi \text{ cm}^3$

$r^2 = \dfrac{32\pi \text{ cm}^3}{8\pi \text{ cm}}$

$r = \sqrt{4 \text{ cm}^2} = \mathbf{2 \text{ cm}}$

24.　(a) Every point on this line is 1 unit to the left of the y-axis.

$\mathbf{x = -1}$

(b) The y-intercept is –2. The slope is positive and the rise over the run for any triangle drawn is +1.

$\mathbf{y = x - 2}$

25.　$\dfrac{3 - 2x}{4} + \dfrac{x}{3} = 5$

$9 - 6x + 4x = 60$

$-2x = 51$

$x = -\dfrac{\mathbf{51}}{\mathbf{2}}$

26. $0.004x - 0.02 = 2.02$

$$4x - 20 = 2020$$
$$4x = 2040$$
$$x = \mathbf{510}$$

27. $\dfrac{3}{x} + \dfrac{2}{x + 2} + \dfrac{3x}{x^2 + 3x + 2}$

$= \dfrac{3(x + 1)(x + 2)}{x(x + 1)(x + 2)} + \dfrac{2x(x + 1)}{x(x + 1)(x + 2)}$

$\quad + \dfrac{3x^2}{x(x + 1)(x + 2)}$

$= \dfrac{3x^2 + 9x + 6 + 2x^2 + 2x + 3x^2}{x(x + 1)(x + 2)}$

$= \dfrac{\mathbf{8x^2 + 11x + 6}}{\mathbf{x(x + 1)(x + 2)}}$

28. $\dfrac{x + 4x}{x} = \dfrac{x(1 + 4)}{x} = \mathbf{5}$

29. $\dfrac{x^{-2}y}{p}\left(\dfrac{x^2 p}{y} - \dfrac{3x^2 y}{p}\right) = \mathbf{1 - 3y^2 p^{-2}}$

30. $x^2 - xy - x^3 = \left(\dfrac{1}{2}\right)^2 - \dfrac{1}{2}\left(\dfrac{1}{3}\right) - \left(\dfrac{1}{2}\right)^3$

$= \dfrac{1}{4} - \dfrac{1}{6} - \dfrac{1}{8} = \dfrac{6}{24} - \dfrac{4}{24} - \dfrac{3}{24} = \mathbf{-\dfrac{1}{24}}$

PRACTICE SET 41

a. $840 \ \cancel{\text{in.}} \times \dfrac{1 \text{ ft}}{12 \ \cancel{\text{in.}}} = \dfrac{\mathbf{840}}{\mathbf{12}} \text{ ft} = \mathbf{70 \text{ ft}}$

b. $90 \ \cancel{\text{ft}^2} \times \dfrac{12 \text{ in.}}{1 \ \cancel{\text{ft}}} \times \dfrac{12 \text{ in.}}{1 \ \cancel{\text{ft}}} = \mathbf{90(12)(12) \text{ in.}^2}$

c. $30 \ \cancel{\text{mi}^3} \times \dfrac{5280 \ \cancel{\text{ft}}}{1 \ \cancel{\text{mi}}} \times \dfrac{5280 \ \cancel{\text{ft}}}{1 \ \cancel{\text{mi}}} \times \dfrac{5280 \ \cancel{\text{ft}}}{1 \ \cancel{\text{mi}}}$

$\times \dfrac{12 \text{ in.}}{1 \ \cancel{\text{ft}}} \times \dfrac{12 \text{ in.}}{1 \ \cancel{\text{ft}}} \times \dfrac{12 \text{ in.}}{1 \ \cancel{\text{ft}}}$

$= \mathbf{30(5280)(5280)(5280)(12)(12)(12) \text{ in.}^3}$

PROBLEM SET 41

1. Odd integers: $N, N + 2, N + 4, N + 6$

$$4(N + N + 6) = 3(N + 2 + N + 4) + 12$$
$$8N + 24 = 6N + 30$$
$$2N = 6$$
$$N = 3$$

The desired integers are **3, 5, 7,** and **9.**

2. Chromium: $\quad 1 \times 52 = 52$

Chlorine: $\quad 3 \times 35 = 105$

Total: $\quad 52 + 105 = 157$

$\dfrac{105}{157} = \dfrac{\text{Cl}}{1256}$

$157\text{Cl} = 105(1256)$

$\text{Cl} = \mathbf{840 \text{ grams}}$

3. $\dfrac{284}{100} \times TR = 1136$

$TR = 1136 \times \dfrac{100}{284} = \mathbf{400 \text{ tons}}$

4. (a) $5N_N + 10N_D = 700$

(b) $N_N + N_D = 100$

Substitute $N_D = 100 - N_N$ into (a) and get:

(a') $5N_N + 10(100 - N_N) = 700$

$$-5N_N = -300$$
$$N_N = \mathbf{60 \text{ nickels}}$$

(b) $N_D = 100 - (60) = \mathbf{40 \text{ dimes}}$

5.

$R_R T_R + R_W T_W = 76; \ R_R = 16;$

$R_W = 4; \ T_R + T_W = 7$

$16(7 - T_W) + 4T_W = 76$

$$-12T_W = -36$$
$$T_W = 3$$

$T_R = 4$

$D_W = 4(3) = \mathbf{12 \text{ miles}}$

$D_R = 16(4) = \mathbf{64 \text{ miles}}$

6. $87 \text{ ft}^2 \times \dfrac{12 \text{ in.}}{1 \text{ ft}} \times \dfrac{12 \text{ in.}}{1 \text{ ft}} = \mathbf{87(12)(12) \text{ in.}^2}$

7. $61 \text{ yd}^2 \times \dfrac{3 \text{ ft}}{1 \text{ yd}} \times \dfrac{3 \text{ ft}}{1 \text{ yd}} \times \dfrac{12 \text{ in.}}{1 \text{ ft}} \times \dfrac{12 \text{ in.}}{1 \text{ ft}}$

$= \mathbf{61(3)(3)(12)(12) \text{ in.}^2}$

8. $32 \text{ mi}^3 \times \dfrac{5280 \text{ ft}}{1 \text{ mi}} \times \dfrac{5280 \text{ ft}}{1 \text{ mi}} \times \dfrac{5280 \text{ ft}}{1 \text{ mi}}$

$\times \dfrac{12 \text{ in.}}{1 \text{ ft}} \times \dfrac{12 \text{ in.}}{1 \text{ ft}} \times \dfrac{12 \text{ in.}}{1 \text{ ft}}$

$= \mathbf{32(5280)(5280)(5280)(12)(12)(12) \text{ in.}^3}$

9. $\dfrac{x}{p} - \dfrac{k}{m} = c$

$mx - kp = cmp$

$mx = cmp + kp$

$\dfrac{mx}{cm + k} = p$

10. $\dfrac{xy}{p} - \dfrac{k}{c} = m$

$cxy - kp = cmp$

$cxy = cmp + kp$

$\dfrac{cxy}{cm + k} = p$

11. $\dfrac{4p}{x} - \dfrac{xk}{c} = \dfrac{y}{m}$

$4cmp - x^2km = cxy$

$4cmp - cxy = x^2km$

$c = \dfrac{x^2 km}{4mp - xy}$

12. $8 \times \overrightarrow{SF} = 20$

$\overrightarrow{SF} = \dfrac{5}{2}$

$17 \times \dfrac{5}{2} = m + 17$

$\dfrac{51}{2} = m$

$15 \times \dfrac{5}{2} = p$

$\dfrac{75}{2} = p$

13. $2x + 40 = 180$

$2x = 140$

$x = \mathbf{70}$

Since $\triangle DEF$ is equilateral, $y = \mathbf{60}$.

$k + 70 + 50 = 180$

$k = \mathbf{60}$

14. $16x = -x^3 + 10x^2$

$x^3 - 10x^2 + 16x = 0$

$x(x - 8)(x - 2) = 0$

$x = \mathbf{0, 2, 8}$

15. $4x^2 - 9x = 0$

$x(4x - 9) = 0$

$x = \mathbf{0,\ \dfrac{9}{4}}$

16.
$$\require{enclose}
\begin{array}{r}
2x^2 + 4x + 8 + \frac{15}{x-2} \\[2pt]
x - 2 \enclose{longdiv}{2x^3 + 0x^2 + 0x - 1} \\
\underline{2x^3 - 4x^2} \\
4x^2 + 0x \\
\underline{4x^2 - 8x} \\
8x - 1 \\
\underline{8x - 16}\\
15
\end{array}$$

17. $4^2 = H^2 + \left(\dfrac{3}{2}\right)^2$

$16 = H^2 + \dfrac{9}{4}$

$\dfrac{55}{4} = H^2$

$\dfrac{\sqrt{55}}{2} = H$

$\text{Area} = \dfrac{3 \times \frac{\sqrt{55}}{2}}{2} + \dfrac{\pi(2)^2}{2} \approx \mathbf{11.84 \text{ units}^2}$

18. $\dfrac{x(x + 5)(x + 3)}{(x - 2)(x - 2)} \cdot \dfrac{(x + 4)(x - 2)}{x(x + 4)(x + 3)}$

$= \dfrac{x + 5}{x - 2}$

19. $32^{-2/5} = \dfrac{1}{32^{2/5}} = \dfrac{1}{(32^{1/5})^2} = \dfrac{1}{4}$

20. $\dfrac{a^2x - \dfrac{a}{x}}{ax - \dfrac{4}{x}} = \dfrac{\dfrac{a^2x^2 - a}{x}}{\dfrac{ax^2 - 4}{x}} \cdot \dfrac{\dfrac{x}{ax^2 - 4}}{\dfrac{x}{ax^2 - 4}}$

$= \dfrac{a^2x^2 - a}{ax^2 - 4}$

21. $\dfrac{(2.1 \times 10^{-38})(5 \times 10^5)}{1.5 \times 10^{-11}} = \dfrac{1.05 \times 10^{-32}}{1.5 \times 10^{-11}}$

$= \mathbf{7 \times 10^{-22}}$

22. $\dfrac{3\sqrt{5}}{\sqrt{7}}\dfrac{\sqrt{7}}{\sqrt{7}} - \dfrac{6\sqrt{7}}{\sqrt{5}}\dfrac{\sqrt{5}}{\sqrt{5}} = \dfrac{3\sqrt{35}}{7} - \dfrac{6\sqrt{35}}{5}$

$= \dfrac{15\sqrt{35}}{35} - \dfrac{42\sqrt{35}}{35} = -\dfrac{27\sqrt{35}}{35}$

23. $4\sqrt{24}(2\sqrt{6} - 3\sqrt{2})$

$= 4\sqrt{2}\sqrt{2}\sqrt{2}\sqrt{3}(2\sqrt{2}\sqrt{3} - 3\sqrt{2})$

$= \mathbf{96 - 48\sqrt{3}}$

24. Write the equation of the given line in slope-intercept form.

$y = -\dfrac{1}{3}x - \dfrac{2}{3}$

Since the slopes of perpendicular lines are negative reciprocals of each other,

$y = 3x + b$

$-5 = 3(-2) + b$

$1 = b$

$\mathbf{y = 3x + 1}$

25. $\dfrac{-3 - x}{2} - \dfrac{x}{2} = 7$

$-3 - x - x = 14$

$-2x = 17$

$x = -\dfrac{\mathbf{17}}{\mathbf{2}}$

26. $2\dfrac{1}{3}x - \dfrac{1}{9} = -\dfrac{1}{18}$

$\dfrac{7}{3}x = -\dfrac{1}{18} + \dfrac{2}{18}$

$x = \dfrac{1}{18} \cdot \dfrac{3}{7}$

$x = \dfrac{\mathbf{1}}{\mathbf{42}}$

27. $\dfrac{2}{x^2(x - 2)} - \dfrac{2x + 2}{(x^2 - 4)}$

$= \dfrac{2(x + 2)}{x^2(x - 2)(x + 2)}$

$- \dfrac{x^2(2x + 2)}{x^2(x - 2)(x + 2)}$

$= \dfrac{2x + 4 - 2x^3 - 2x^2}{x^2(x - 2)(x + 2)}$

$= \dfrac{-2x^3 - 2x^2 + 2x + 4}{x^2(x - 2)(x + 2)}$

28. $\dfrac{4x + 8x^2}{4x} = \dfrac{4x(1 + 2x)}{4x} = \mathbf{1 + 2x}$

29. $\dfrac{x^2 x^0 x^{-1}(x^{-2})^2 yx^{-3}}{(x^2 y)^{-3} xyx^{-2} x^2} = \dfrac{x^{-6}y}{x^{-5}y^{-2}} = \dfrac{\mathbf{y^3}}{\mathbf{x}}$

30. $x^3 - xy + x^2 = \left(\dfrac{1}{2}\right)^3 - \dfrac{1}{2}\left(\dfrac{1}{3}\right) + \left(\dfrac{1}{2}\right)^2$

$= \dfrac{3}{24} - \dfrac{4}{24} + \dfrac{6}{24} = \dfrac{\mathbf{5}}{\mathbf{24}}$

PRACTICE SET 42

a. $13(5280)(5280)(12)(12)$

$\approx (1 \times 10^1)(5 \times 10^3)(5 \times 10^3)$
$\quad (1 \times 10^1)(1 \times 10^1)$

$= \mathbf{25 \times 10^9 = 2.5 \times 10^{10}}$

b. $\dfrac{(4353)(933,216 \times 10^{-11})}{(319,214)(0.01603 \times 10^{-31})}$

$\approx \dfrac{(4 \times 10^3)(9 \times 10^{-6})}{(3 \times 10^5)(2 \times 10^{-33})} = \dfrac{36}{6} \times \dfrac{10^{-3}}{10^{-28}}$

$= \mathbf{6 \times 10^{25}}$

c. $\dfrac{(0.013926 \times 10^{-12})(27,153 \times 10^{21})}{6354 \times 10^{-31}}$

$\approx \dfrac{(1 \times 10^{-14})(3 \times 10^{25})}{6 \times 10^{-28}}$

$= \dfrac{3 \times 10^{11}}{6 \times 10^{-28}} = \mathbf{0.5 \times 10^{39} = 5 \times 10^{38}}$

PROBLEM SET 42

1. $\dfrac{3}{17} \cdot 2244 = P$

$\mathbf{396\ fish = P}$

2. $\dfrac{80}{100} \times S = 4800$

$S = 4800 \times \dfrac{100}{80} = \mathbf{6000\ students}$

3. $\dfrac{600}{3600} = \dfrac{P}{43,200}$

$3600P = 600(43,200)$

$P = \mathbf{7200\ grams}$

4. Potassium: $1 \times 39 = 39$
Chlorine: $1 \times 35 = 35$
Oxygen: $3 \times 16 = 48$
Total: $39 + 35 + 48 = 122$

$$\frac{39}{122} = \frac{K}{488}$$

$$122K = 39(488)$$

$$K = \textbf{156 grams}$$

5. (a) $N_L = 4N_S + 2$

(b) $N_L = 8N_S - 6$

Substitute (b) into (a) and get:

(a′) $(8N_S - 6) = 4N_S + 2$

$$4N_S = 8$$

$$N_S = \textbf{2}$$

(a) $N_L = 4(2) + 2 = \textbf{10}$

6. $(24)(5280)(5280)(5280)(12)(12)(12)$

$\approx (2 \times 10^1)(5 \times 10^3)(5 \times 10^3)(5 \times 10^3)$
$\quad (1 \times 10^1)(1 \times 10^1)(1 \times 10^1)$

$= 250 \times 10^{13} \approx \textbf{3} \times \textbf{10}^{\textbf{15}}$

7. $\dfrac{(2472)(570{,}185 \times 10^{-12})}{(243{,}195)(0.0003128 \times 10^{-6})}$

$\approx \dfrac{(2 \times 10^3)(6 \times 10^{-7})}{(2 \times 10^5)(3 \times 10^{-10})} = \textbf{2} \times \textbf{10}^{\textbf{1}}$

8. $\dfrac{(0.0319743 \times 10^{-15})(61{,}853 \times 10^{37})}{6934 \times 10^{-29}}$

$\approx \dfrac{(3 \times 10^{-17})(6 \times 10^{41})}{7 \times 10^{-26}} \approx \textbf{3} \times \textbf{10}^{\textbf{50}}$

9. $40 \text{ yd}^3 \times \dfrac{3 \text{ ft}}{1 \text{ yd}} \times \dfrac{3 \text{ ft}}{1 \text{ yd}} \times \dfrac{3 \text{ ft}}{1 \text{ yd}}$

$\times \dfrac{12 \text{ in.}}{1 \text{ ft}} \times \dfrac{12 \text{ in.}}{1 \text{ ft}} \times \dfrac{12 \text{ in.}}{1 \text{ ft}}$

$= \textbf{40(3)(3)(3)(12)(12)(12) in.}^{\textbf{3}}$

10. $\dfrac{m}{c} - x = \dfrac{p}{m}$

$$m^2 - cmx = cp$$

$$m^2 = cp + cmx$$

$$\frac{m^2}{p + mx} = c$$

11. $\dfrac{ax}{y} + m = \dfrac{pc}{d}$

$$adx + dmy = pcy$$

$$adx = pcy - dmy$$

$$\frac{adx}{pc - dm} = y$$

12.

$$x + 2 \overline{)4x^3 + 0x^2 + 0x - 1} \quad \begin{matrix} 4x^2 - 8x + 16 - \frac{33}{x+2} \end{matrix}$$

$\quad \quad \underline{4x^3 + 8x^2}$
$\quad \quad -8x^2 + 0x$
$\quad \quad \underline{-8x^2 - 16x}$
$\quad \quad \quad 16x - 1$
$\quad \quad \quad \underline{16x + 32}$
$\quad \quad \quad \quad -33$

13. Area $= \dfrac{240}{360} \cdot \pi(2 \text{ cm})^2 \approx \textbf{8.37 cm}^2$

14. $\qquad -20x = x^3 - 9x^2$

$$x^3 - 9x^2 + 20x = 0$$

$$x(x - 5)(x - 4) = 0$$

$$x = \textbf{0, 4, 5}$$

15. $\qquad 4x^2 - 25 = 0$

$$(2x - 5)(2x + 5) = 0$$

$$x = \frac{5}{2}, -\frac{5}{2}$$

16. $\dfrac{x(x - 2)(x - 1)}{(x + 4)(x - 1)} \cdot \dfrac{(x + 5)(x + 3)}{x(x + 3)(x - 2)}$

$= \dfrac{x + 5}{x + 4}$

17. $-81^{-3/4} = -\dfrac{1}{81^{3/4}} = -\dfrac{1}{(81^{1/4})^3} = -\dfrac{1}{27}$

18. $\dfrac{\dfrac{m}{x} - 4}{6 - \dfrac{1}{x}} = \dfrac{\dfrac{m - 4x}{x}}{\dfrac{6x - 1}{x}} \cdot \dfrac{\dfrac{x}{6x - 1}}{\dfrac{x}{6x - 1}}$

$= \dfrac{m - 4x}{6x - 1}$

19. $\dfrac{2\sqrt{3}}{\sqrt{11}} \dfrac{\sqrt{11}}{\sqrt{11}} - \dfrac{5\sqrt{11}}{\sqrt{3}} \dfrac{\sqrt{3}}{\sqrt{3}} = \dfrac{2\sqrt{33}}{11} - \dfrac{5\sqrt{33}}{3}$

$= \dfrac{6\sqrt{33}}{33} - \dfrac{55\sqrt{33}}{33} = -\dfrac{49\sqrt{33}}{33}$

20. $3\sqrt{6}(2\sqrt{6} - 4\sqrt{2}) = 3\sqrt{2}\sqrt{3}(2\sqrt{2}\sqrt{3} - 4\sqrt{2})$
$= \mathbf{36 - 24\sqrt{3}}$

21. $3\sqrt{20} + 2\sqrt{45} - \sqrt{245}$
$= 3\sqrt{2}\sqrt{2}\sqrt{5} + 2\sqrt{3}\sqrt{3}\sqrt{5} - \sqrt{5}\sqrt{7}\sqrt{7}$
$= 6\sqrt{5} + 6\sqrt{5} - 7\sqrt{5} = \mathbf{5\sqrt{5}}$

22. $16 \cdot \overrightarrow{SF} = 24$

$\overrightarrow{SF} = \dfrac{3}{2}$

$30 \cdot \dfrac{3}{2} = a$

$\mathbf{45 = a}$

$34 \cdot \dfrac{3}{2} = b$

$\mathbf{51 = b}$

23. (a) $3x + 2y = 80$

(b) $4x - 4y = 100$

2(a) $6x + 4y = 160$

(b) $\underline{4x - 4y = 100}$

$10x = 260$

$x = \mathbf{26}$

(b) $4(26) - 4y = 100$

$y = \mathbf{1}$

24. Graph the line to find the slope.

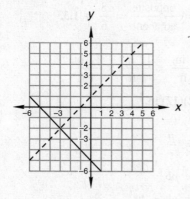

$m = \dfrac{+1}{+1} = 1$

Since the slopes of perpendicular lines are negative reciprocals of each other,

$m_\perp = -1$

$y = -x + b$

$-2 = -(-3) + b$

$-5 = b$

$\mathbf{y = -x - 5}$

25. $\dfrac{-2x - 4}{2} - \dfrac{x}{3} = 5$

$-6x - 12 - 2x = 30$

$-8x = 42$

$x = -\dfrac{21}{4}$

26. $3\dfrac{1}{4}x - \dfrac{1}{8} = \dfrac{3}{16}$

$\dfrac{13}{4}x = \dfrac{3}{16} + \dfrac{2}{16}$

$x = \dfrac{5}{16} \cdot \dfrac{4}{13} = \dfrac{5}{52}$

27. $\dfrac{3}{x + 2} - \dfrac{4}{x^2 - 4} - \dfrac{3}{x - 2}$

$= \dfrac{3(x - 2)}{(x - 2)(x + 2)} - \dfrac{4}{(x - 2)(x + 2)}$

$ - \dfrac{3(x + 2)}{(x - 2)(x + 2)}$

$= \dfrac{3x - 6 - 4 - 3x - 6}{(x - 2)(x + 2)}$

$= \dfrac{-16}{(x - 2)(x + 2)}$

28. $-\dfrac{x^{-2}}{y^2}\left(y^2 x^2 - \dfrac{3x^{-2}}{y^{-2}}\right) = -1 + 3x^{-4}$

29. $\dfrac{4x^2 - 4x^4}{4x^2} = \dfrac{4x^2(1 - x^2)}{4x^2} = 1 - x^2$

30. $-3x - x^{-2} - x^{-3} = -3\left(\dfrac{1}{2}\right) - \dfrac{1}{\left(\dfrac{1}{2}\right)^2} - \dfrac{1}{\left(\dfrac{1}{2}\right)^3}$

$= -\dfrac{3}{2} - 4 - 8 = -\dfrac{3}{2} - \dfrac{8}{2} - \dfrac{16}{2} = -\dfrac{27}{2}$

PRACTICE SET 43

a. $4 \cos 75.8° \approx$ **0.98**

b. $6 \sin 37.42° \approx$ **3.65**

c. $\sin C = \dfrac{3.61}{7.52} \approx$ **0.48**

d. $\cos D = \dfrac{3.63}{4.76} \approx$ **0.76**

e. $\tan E = \dfrac{8.73}{11.30} \approx$ **0.77**

f. Inverse tangent of $0.405 \approx$ **22.05°**

g. Inverse sine of $0.794 \approx$ **52.56°**

PROBLEM SET 43

1. $0.0032 \times TP = 1280$

$$TP = \dfrac{1280}{0.0032} = \textbf{400,000 people}$$

2. $\dfrac{232}{100} \times LM = 9280$

$$LM = 9280 \times \dfrac{100}{232} = \textbf{4000 boys}$$

3. Sodium: $\quad 1 \times 23 = 23$

Oxygen: $\quad 1 \times 16 = 16$

Hydrogen: $\quad 1 \times 1 = 1$

Total: $\quad 23 + 16 + 1 = 40$

$$\dfrac{23}{40} = \dfrac{\text{Na}}{320}$$

$40\text{Na} = 23(320)$

$\text{Na} = $ **184 grams**

4. $\dfrac{77}{100} \cdot 3000 = NC$

$$NC = \textbf{2310 grams}$$

5.

$R_C T_C + 20 = R_L T_L$;

$T_C = T_L = 5$; $R_L = 2R_C$

$\dfrac{1}{2} R_L (5) + 20 = 5R_L$

$$20 = \dfrac{5}{2} R_L$$

$$8 = R_L$$

$D_L = 8(5) = $ **40 miles**

6. $\text{sine } A = \dfrac{\textbf{opposite}}{\textbf{hypotenuse}}$; $\text{cosine } A = \dfrac{\textbf{adjacent}}{\textbf{hypotenuse}}$;

$\text{tangent } A = \dfrac{\textbf{opposite}}{\textbf{adjacent}}$

7. (a) $417 \cos 51.5° \approx$ **259.59**

(b) $32.6 \tan 86.3° \approx$ **504.12**

8. (a) $\sin A = \dfrac{\text{opposite}}{\text{hypotenuse}} = \dfrac{5}{7.6} = $ **0.66**

(b) $\cos B = \dfrac{\text{adjacent}}{\text{hypotenuse}} = \dfrac{7}{9.2} = $ **0.76**

(c) $\tan C = \dfrac{\text{opposite}}{\text{adjacent}} = \dfrac{8}{6} = $ **1.33**

9. $4 \text{ ft}^3 \times \dfrac{12 \text{ in.}}{1 \text{ ft}} \times \dfrac{12 \text{ in.}}{1 \text{ ft}} \times \dfrac{12 \text{ in.}}{1 \text{ ft}}$

$= \textbf{4(12)(12)(12) in.}^3$

10. $\dfrac{a}{b} - x = \dfrac{p}{z}$

$az - bxz = pb$

$az = pb + bxz$

$$\dfrac{az}{p + xz} = b$$

11. $\dfrac{xz}{p} - k = \dfrac{m}{c}$

$cxz - ckp = mp$

$cxz = mp + ckp$

$$\dfrac{cxz}{m + ck} = p$$

12.
$$\frac{x}{m} - \frac{k}{c} = \frac{p}{z}$$
$$cxz - kmz = cmp$$
$$cxz = cmp + kmz$$
$$\frac{cxz}{cp + kz} = m$$

13.
$$a^2 = 4^2 + \left(\frac{7}{2}\right)^2$$
$$a^2 = 16 + \frac{49}{4}$$
$$a^2 = \frac{113}{4}$$
$$a = \frac{\sqrt{113}}{2}$$
$$4 \cdot \overrightarrow{SF} = 6$$
$$\overrightarrow{SF} = \frac{3}{2}$$
$$\frac{7}{2} \cdot \frac{3}{2} = b$$
$$\frac{21}{4} = b$$
$$\frac{\sqrt{113}}{2} \cdot \frac{3}{2} = c + \frac{\sqrt{113}}{2}$$
$$3\sqrt{113} = 4c + 2\sqrt{113}$$
$$\sqrt{113} = 4c$$
$$\frac{\sqrt{113}}{4} = c$$

14.
$$-x^3 - 9x^2 = 20x$$
$$x^3 + 9x^2 + 20x = 0$$
$$x(x + 5)(x + 4) = 0$$
$$x = 0, -5, -4$$

15.
$$4x^2 - 81 = 0$$
$$(2x - 9)(2x + 9) = 0$$
$$x = \frac{9}{2}, -\frac{9}{2}$$

16. $(x - 3)^3 = (x - 3)(x - 3)(x - 3)$
$$= (x^2 - 6x + 9)(x - 3)$$
$$= x^3 - 6x^2 + 9x - 3x^2 + 18x - 27$$
$$= x^3 - 9x^2 + 27x - 27$$

17. $\dfrac{x(x - 5)(x - 1)}{(x + 3)(x - 1)} \cdot \dfrac{(x - 3)(x + 3)}{x(x - 5)(x - 3)} = 1$

18. $16^{-3/4} = \dfrac{1}{16^{3/4}} = \dfrac{1}{(16^{1/4})^3} = \dfrac{1}{8}$

19.
$$\frac{4x + \dfrac{1}{x}}{\dfrac{ay^2}{x} - 4} = \frac{\dfrac{4x^2 + 1}{x}}{\dfrac{ay^2 - 4x}{x}} \cdot \frac{\dfrac{x}{ay^2 - 4x}}{\dfrac{x}{ay^2 - 4x}}$$
$$= \frac{4x^2 + 1}{ay^2 - 4x}$$

20.
$$\sqrt{\frac{3}{7}} - 4\sqrt{\frac{7}{3}} = \frac{\sqrt{3}}{\sqrt{7}}\frac{\sqrt{7}}{\sqrt{7}} - \frac{4\sqrt{7}}{\sqrt{3}}\frac{\sqrt{3}}{\sqrt{3}}$$
$$= \frac{\sqrt{21}}{7} - \frac{4\sqrt{21}}{3} = \frac{3\sqrt{21}}{21} - \frac{28\sqrt{21}}{21}$$
$$= -\frac{25\sqrt{21}}{21}$$

21. $3\sqrt{2}(5\sqrt{12} - \sqrt{2}) = 3\sqrt{2}(5\sqrt{2}\sqrt{2}\sqrt{3} - \sqrt{2})$
$$= 30\sqrt{6} - 6$$

22. Since the triangle is isosceles, $A = B$.
$$A^2 = 2^2 + 4^2$$
$$A^2 = 4 + 16$$
$$A = \sqrt{20} = 2\sqrt{5}$$
$$A = B = 2\sqrt{5}$$

23.
$$y = -\frac{1}{7}x + b$$
$$-5 = -\frac{1}{7}(-2) + b$$
$$-\frac{37}{7} = b$$
$$y = -\frac{1}{7}x - \frac{37}{7}$$

24.
$$\frac{5x - 7}{2} - \frac{3x - 2}{5} = 4$$
$$25x - 35 - 6x + 4 = 40$$
$$19x = 71$$
$$x = \frac{71}{19}$$

25.
$$\frac{(47,816 \times 10^5)(4923 \times 10^{-14})}{403,000}$$
$$\approx \frac{(5 \times 10^9)(5 \times 10^{-11})}{4 \times 10^5} = 6.25 \times 10^{-7}$$
$$\approx 6 \times 10^{-7}$$

26. (a) $2x - 3y = -9$

$$-3y = -2x - 9$$

$$y = \frac{2}{3}x + 3$$

(b) $x + y = 2$

$$y = -x + 2$$

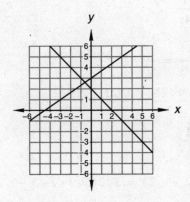

Substitute $y = -x + 2$ into (a) and get:

(a') $2x - 3(-x + 2) = -9$

$$5x = -3$$

$$x = -\frac{3}{5}$$

(b) $y = -\left(-\frac{3}{5}\right) + 2 = \frac{13}{5}$

$$\left(-\frac{3}{5}, \frac{13}{5}\right)$$

27. $\dfrac{3}{x + 1} - \dfrac{2}{x^2(x + 1)} + \dfrac{3x + 2}{(x^2 - 1)}$

$$= \frac{3x^2(x - 1)}{x^2(x + 1)(x - 1)} - \frac{2(x - 1)}{x^2(x + 1)(x - 1)}$$

$$+ \frac{x^2(3x + 2)}{x^2(x + 1)(x - 1)}$$

$$= \frac{3x^3 - 3x^2 - 2x + 2 + 3x^3 + 2x^2}{x^2(x + 1)(x - 1)}$$

$$= \frac{6x^3 - x^2 - 2x + 2}{x^2(x + 1)(x - 1)}$$

28. $\dfrac{4x^{-2}y}{p^{-2}}\left(\dfrac{2p^{-2}x^2}{y} - \dfrac{4x^{-2}y}{p^2}\right) = 8 - 16x^{-4}y^2$

29.

$$D^2 = 6^2 + 1^2$$

$$D^2 = 36 + 1$$

$$D = \sqrt{37}$$

30. $x^2 - yx - (x - y)$

$$= \left(\frac{1}{2}\right)^2 - \frac{1}{4}\left(\frac{1}{2}\right) - \left(\frac{1}{2} - \frac{1}{4}\right)$$

$$= \frac{1}{4} - \frac{1}{8} - \frac{1}{4} = -\frac{1}{8}$$

PRACTICE SET 44

a. $\tan 21° = \dfrac{y}{6.4}$

$$y = 6.4 \tan 21°$$

$$y \approx \mathbf{2.46}$$

$$H^2 = y^2 + 6.4^2$$

$$H^2 = (2.46)^2 + 6.4^2$$

$$H = \sqrt{47.0116}$$

$$H \approx \mathbf{6.86}$$

b. $p^2 = 12^2 + 8^2$

$$p = \sqrt{208}$$

$$p = \mathbf{4\sqrt{13}}$$

$$\tan x = \frac{12}{8}$$

$$x \approx \mathbf{56.31}$$

$$\tan y = \frac{8}{12}$$

$$y \approx \mathbf{33.69}$$

Problem Set 44

1. $-2(N + 5) = 6(-N) + 18$
$$4N = 28$$
$$N = \mathbf{7}$$

2. Odd integers: $N, N + 2, N + 4, N + 6$
$$5(N + N + 4) = 8(N + 2 + N + 6) + 22$$
$$10N + 20 = 16N + 86$$
$$-6N = 66$$
$$N = -11$$

The desired integers are **–11, –9, –7,** and **–5.**

3. $\dfrac{270}{700} = \dfrac{T}{2800}$
$$700T = 270(2800)$$
$$T = \mathbf{1080\ tons}$$

4. Carbon: $1 \times 12 = 12$
Chlorine: $2 \times 35 = 70$
Flourine: $2 \times 19 = 38$
Total: $12 + 70 + 38 = 120$

$$\dfrac{12}{120} = \dfrac{C}{550}$$
$$120C = 12(550)$$
$$C = \mathbf{55\ grams}$$

5.

$$\begin{array}{ccc} D_R & & D_D \\ \xrightarrow{\qquad} & & \\ \vert\!\!-\!\!-\!\!-\!\!-\!\!-\!\!-\!\!-\!\!-\!\!-\!\!\vert \\ & 200 & \end{array}$$

$$R_R T_R + R_D T_D = 200;\ R_R = 25;$$
$$R_D = 50;\ T_R + T_D = 5$$
$$25T_R + 50(5 - T_R) = 200$$
$$-25T_R = -50$$
$$T_R = 2$$
$$D_R = 25(2) = \mathbf{50\ miles}$$

6. $B + 28 + 90 = 180$
$$B = \mathbf{62}$$

$$\cos 28° = \dfrac{9.5}{H}$$
$$H = \dfrac{9.5}{\cos 28°} \approx \mathbf{10.76}$$

$$\tan 28° = \dfrac{y}{9.5}$$
$$y = 9.5 \tan 28° \approx \mathbf{5.05}$$

7. $B + 31 + 90 = 180$
$$B = \mathbf{59}$$

$$\cos 31° = \dfrac{m}{14}$$
$$m = 14 \cos 31° \approx \mathbf{12.00}$$

$$\sin 31° = \dfrac{x}{14}$$
$$x = 14 \sin 31° \approx \mathbf{7.21}$$

8. $\cos A = \dfrac{4}{7}$
$$A \approx \mathbf{55.15}$$
$$B + 55.15 + 90 \approx 180$$
$$B \approx \mathbf{34.85}$$

$$\sin 55.15° = \dfrac{x}{7}$$
$$x = 7 \sin 55.15° \approx \mathbf{5.74}$$

9. $4 \text{ mi}^2 \times \dfrac{5280 \text{ ft}}{1 \text{ mi}} \times \dfrac{5280 \text{ ft}}{1 \text{ mi}} = \mathbf{4(5280)(5280)\ ft^2}$

10. $\dfrac{k}{m} - c = \dfrac{p}{d}$
$$dk - cdm = pm$$
$$dk = pm + cdm$$
$$\dfrac{dk}{p + cd} = m$$

11. $\dfrac{3k}{m} - \dfrac{d}{p} = \dfrac{l}{c}$
$$3ckp - cdm = lmp$$
$$3ckp = lmp + cdm$$
$$\dfrac{3ckp}{lp + cd} = m$$

12. $\dfrac{a}{c} + d = \dfrac{x}{m}$
$$am + cdm = cx$$
$$am = cx - cdm$$
$$\dfrac{am}{x - dm} = c$$

13. If $m\angle BAD = K°$, then $m\angle ABC = \mathbf{(180 - K)°}$.

(a) $4x + 2y = 8$
(b) $4x + y = 6$

$$\begin{array}{rrcr} \text{(a)} & 4x + 2y &=& 8 \\ -1\text{(b)} & -4x - y &=& -6 \\ \hline & y &=& \mathbf{2} \end{array}$$

(a) $4x + 2(2) = 8$
$$x = \mathbf{1}$$

14.
$$24x = -x^3 + 10x^2$$
$$x^3 - 10x^2 + 24x = 0$$
$$x(x - 6)(x - 4) = 0$$
$$x = \mathbf{0, 4, 6}$$

15.
$$25p^2 - 81 = 0$$
$$(5p - 9)(5p + 9) = 0$$
$$p = \frac{\mathbf{9}}{\mathbf{5}}, -\frac{\mathbf{9}}{\mathbf{5}}$$

16.

$$
\begin{array}{r}
x^3 - 4x^2 + 16x - 64 + \frac{255}{x+4} \\
x + 4 \overline{)x^4 + 0x^3 + 0x^2 + 0x - 1} \\
\underline{x^4 + 4x^3} \\
-4x^3 + 0x^2 \\
\underline{-4x^3 - 16x^2} \\
16x^2 + 0x \\
\underline{16x^2 + 64x} \\
-64x - 1 \\
\underline{-64x - 256} \\
255
\end{array}
$$

17.
$$\frac{x(x + 7)(x + 2)}{(x - 3)(x + 2)} \cdot \frac{(x + 5)(x + 5)}{x(x + 7)(x + 5)}$$
$$= \frac{\mathbf{x + 5}}{\mathbf{x - 3}}$$

18.
$$\frac{1}{-32^{4/5}} = -\frac{1}{(32^{1/5})^4} = -\frac{\mathbf{1}}{\mathbf{16}}$$

19. Height $= 4 \text{ ft} \times \dfrac{12 \text{ in.}}{1 \text{ ft}} = 48 \text{ in.}$

$$V_{\text{Cone}} = \frac{1}{3}(A_{\text{Base}} \times \text{height})$$

$$= \frac{1}{3}\left(\frac{1}{2}\pi(4)^2 + \frac{1}{2}(12)(8)\right.$$

$$\left. - \frac{1}{2}\pi(2)^2\right)(48) \text{ in.}^3$$

$$= \frac{1}{3}(6\pi + 48)(48) \text{ in.}^3 \approx \mathbf{1069.44 \text{ in.}^3}$$

20.
$$\frac{5x^2 + \dfrac{1}{x}}{\dfrac{pm^2}{x} + 5} = \frac{\dfrac{5x^3 + 1}{x}}{\dfrac{pm^2 + 5x}{x}} \cdot \frac{\dfrac{x}{pm^2 + 5x}}{\dfrac{x}{pm^2 + 5x}}$$

$$= \frac{\mathbf{5x^3 + 1}}{\mathbf{pm^2 + 5x}}$$

21. $3\sqrt{\dfrac{2}{17}} - 5\sqrt{\dfrac{17}{2}} = \dfrac{3\sqrt{2}}{\sqrt{17}}\dfrac{\sqrt{17}}{\sqrt{17}} - \dfrac{5\sqrt{17}}{\sqrt{2}}\dfrac{\sqrt{2}}{\sqrt{2}}$

$$= \frac{3\sqrt{34}}{17} - \frac{5\sqrt{34}}{2} = \frac{6\sqrt{34}}{34} - \frac{85\sqrt{34}}{34}$$

$$= -\frac{\mathbf{79\sqrt{34}}}{\mathbf{34}}$$

22. $3\sqrt{6}(2\sqrt{6} - \sqrt{12})$
$$= 3\sqrt{2}\sqrt{3}(2\sqrt{2}\sqrt{3} - \sqrt{2}\sqrt{2}\sqrt{3})$$
$$= \mathbf{36 - 18\sqrt{2}}$$

23. (a) Every point on this line is 2 units above the x-axis.
$$y = \mathbf{2}$$

(b) The y-intercept is -4. The slope is positive and the rise over the run for any triangle drawn is $\frac{1}{2}$.
$$y = \frac{\mathbf{1}}{\mathbf{2}}x - \mathbf{4}$$

24.
$$\frac{5x - 2}{3} - \frac{2x - 4}{2} = 6$$
$$10x - 4 - 6x + 12 = 36$$
$$4x = 28$$
$$x = \mathbf{7}$$

25.
$$3\frac{1}{5}k + \frac{2}{5} = \frac{1}{10}$$
$$\frac{16}{5}k = \frac{1}{10} - \frac{4}{10}$$
$$k = -\frac{3}{10} \cdot \frac{5}{16} = -\frac{\mathbf{3}}{\mathbf{32}}$$

26. (a) $2x - y = 5$
$$y = 2x - 5$$

(b) $4x + 3y = 9$
$$y = -\frac{4}{3}x + 3$$

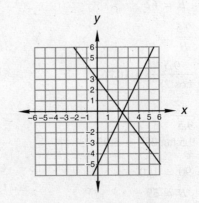

Solve the equations by elimination:

-2(a) $\quad -4x + 2y = -10$

(b) $\quad \dfrac{4x + 3y = \quad 9}{5y = \quad -1}$

$$y = -\dfrac{1}{5}$$

(a) $\quad 2x - \left(-\dfrac{1}{5}\right) = 5$

$$x = \dfrac{24}{5} \cdot \dfrac{1}{2} = \dfrac{12}{5}$$

$$\left(\dfrac{12}{5}, -\dfrac{1}{5}\right)$$

27. $\dfrac{x}{x + 2} - \dfrac{2}{x^2 - 4}$

$= \dfrac{x(x - 2)}{x^2 - 4} - \dfrac{2}{x^2 - 4} = \dfrac{x^2 - 2x - 2}{x^2 - 4}$

28. $\dfrac{(51{,}463 \times 10^{-14})(748{,}600 \times 10^{-21})}{7{,}861{,}523}$

$\approx \dfrac{(5 \times 10^{-10})(7 \times 10^{-16})}{8 \times 10^6} \approx 4 \times 10^{-32}$

29. $a^2 - ab^2 = \left(\dfrac{1}{2}\right)^2 - \dfrac{1}{2}\left(-\dfrac{1}{2}\right)^2 = \dfrac{1}{4} - \dfrac{1}{8} = \dfrac{1}{8}$

30. $-2^0 - 2^2 - (-2)^3 - |-2 - 3^0| - (-2)^3$

$= -1 - 4 + 8 - 3 + 8 = 8$

PRACTICE SET 45

a. $\quad x^2 = 14$

$\sqrt{x^2} = \pm\sqrt{14}$

$x = \pm\sqrt{14}$

Check $\sqrt{14}$: $(\sqrt{14})^2 = 14$

$14 = 14$

Check $-\sqrt{14}$: $(-\sqrt{14})^2 = 14$

$14 = 14$

b. $\quad (x + 9)^2 = 11$

$\sqrt{(x + 9)^2} = \pm\sqrt{11}$

$x + 9 = \pm\sqrt{11}$

$x = -9 \pm \sqrt{11}$

Check $-9 + \sqrt{11}$: $(-9 + \sqrt{11} + 9)^2 = 11$

$(\sqrt{11})^2 = 11$

$11 = 11$

Check $-9 - \sqrt{11}$: $(-9 - \sqrt{11} + 9)^2 = 11$

$(-\sqrt{11})^2 = 11$

$11 = 11$

c. $\quad \left(x + \dfrac{1}{7}\right)^2 = 8$

$\sqrt{\left(x + \dfrac{1}{7}\right)^2} = \pm\sqrt{8}$

$x + \dfrac{1}{7} = \pm\sqrt{8}$

$x = -\dfrac{1}{7} \pm 2\sqrt{2}$

Check $-\dfrac{1}{7} + \sqrt{8}$: $\left(-\dfrac{1}{7} + \sqrt{8} + \dfrac{1}{7}\right)^2 = 8$

$(\sqrt{8})^2 = 8$

$8 = 8$

Check $-\dfrac{1}{7} - \sqrt{8}$: $\left(-\dfrac{1}{7} - \sqrt{8} + \dfrac{1}{7}\right)^2 = 8$

$(-\sqrt{8})^2 = 8$

$8 = 8$

PROBLEM SET 45

1. $\dfrac{62}{100} \times S = 248$

$S = 248 \times \dfrac{100}{62} = 400$ **students**

2. Phosphorus: $1 \times 31 = 31$

Hydrogen: $\quad 3 \times 1 = 3$

Total: $\quad\quad 31 + 3 = 34$

$\dfrac{3}{34} = \dfrac{24}{T}$

$T = 272$ **grams**

3. $\dfrac{64}{100} \times T = 5376$

$T = 5376 \times \dfrac{100}{64} = 8400$

Bromides = $8400 - 5376 =$ **3024 bottles**

4. (a) $12N_R + 14N_C = 138$

(b) $N_R + N_C = 11$

Substitute $N_C = 11 - N_R$ into (a) and get:

(a′) $12N_R + 14(11 - N_R) = 138$

$N_R =$ **8 bunches of roses**

(b) $N_C = 11 - (8) =$ **3 bunches of carnations**

5.

$R_B T_B + 80 = R_T T_T;\ T_T = 8;$

$T_B = 12;\ R_T = R_B + 30$

$12R_B + 80 = 8(R_B + 30)$

$4R_B = 160$

$R_B =$ **40 mph**

$R_T = (40) + 30 =$ **70 mph**

6. $x^2 = 5$

$x = \pm\sqrt{5}$

7. $(x + 7)^2 = 11$

$x + 7 = \pm\sqrt{11}$

$x = \mathbf{-7 \pm \sqrt{11}}$

8. $(x + 12)^2 = 2$

$x + 12 = \pm\sqrt{2}$

$x = \mathbf{-12 \pm \sqrt{2}}$

9. $\left(x + \dfrac{3}{4}\right)^2 = 13$

$x + \dfrac{3}{4} = \pm\sqrt{13}$

$x = \mathbf{-\dfrac{3}{4} \pm \sqrt{13}}$

10. $\sin 33° = \dfrac{x}{10}$

$x = 10 \sin 33° \approx$ **5.45**

11. $\sin 38° = \dfrac{4}{p}$

$p = \dfrac{4}{\sin 38°} \approx$ **6.50**

12. $\cos A = \dfrac{8}{12}$

$A \approx$ **48.19**

$B \approx 180 - 90 - 48.19 \approx$ **41.81**

13. $100{,}000\ \text{mi}^2 \times \dfrac{5280\ \text{ft}}{1\ \text{mi}} \times \dfrac{5280\ \text{ft}}{1\ \text{mi}}$

$\times\ \dfrac{12\ \text{in.}}{1\ \text{ft}} \times \dfrac{12\ \text{in.}}{1\ \text{ft}}$

$= \mathbf{100{,}000(5280)(5280)(12)(12)\ in.^2}$

14. $\dfrac{(571{,}652)(40{,}316)}{214{,}000 \times 10^6} \approx \dfrac{(6 \times 10^5)(4 \times 10^4)}{2 \times 10^{11}}$

$= 1.2 \times 10^{-1} \approx \mathbf{1 \times 10^{-1}}$

15. $8 \times \overrightarrow{SF} = 12$

$\overrightarrow{SF} = \dfrac{3}{2}$

$x \times \dfrac{3}{2} = 5$

$x = \dfrac{10}{3}$

$c^2 = 8^2 + \left(\dfrac{10}{3}\right)^2$

$c^2 = \dfrac{676}{9}$

$c = \dfrac{26}{3}$

$\dfrac{26}{3} \times \dfrac{3}{2} = d + \dfrac{26}{3}$

$13 = d + \dfrac{26}{3}$

$\dfrac{39}{3} - \dfrac{26}{3} = d$

$\mathbf{\dfrac{13}{3}} = d$

16. $\dfrac{mx}{4} + \dfrac{y}{p} = c$

$mxp + 4y = 4cp$

$4y = 4cp - mxp$

$\mathbf{\dfrac{4y}{4c - mx}} = p$

17. $\dfrac{5x}{p} - k = \dfrac{m}{c}$

$5xc - ckp = mp$

$5xc = mp + ckp$

$\dfrac{5xc}{m + ck} = p$

18. $x^3 = -5x^2 + 50x$

$x^3 + 5x^2 - 50x = 0$

$x(x + 10)(x - 5) = 0$

$x = \mathbf{0, -10, 5}$

19. $36x^2 - 25 = 0$

$(6x - 5)(6x + 5) = 0$

$x = \dfrac{\mathbf{5}}{\mathbf{6}}, -\dfrac{\mathbf{5}}{\mathbf{6}}$

20. $\dfrac{x(x + 7)(x - 1)}{(x + 7)(x - 3)} \cdot \dfrac{(x + 5)(x - 3)}{x(x + 2)(x - 1)}$

$= \dfrac{\mathbf{x + 5}}{\mathbf{x + 2}}$

21. $-(-27)^{-5/3} = -\dfrac{1}{(-27)^{5/3}} = -\dfrac{1}{((-27)^{1/3})^5}$

$= \dfrac{\mathbf{1}}{\mathbf{243}}$

22. Perimeter $= (24 + 4\pi)$ cm

Circumference$_{\text{Semicircle}} = 24 + 4\pi - 12 - 6$
$\qquad\qquad\qquad - 4 - 2$

$\qquad\qquad = 4\pi$ cm

Circumference$_{\text{Semicircle}} = \dfrac{2\pi r}{2} = 4\pi$ cm

$r = 4$ cm

Area$_{\text{Semicircle}} = \dfrac{\pi(4\text{ cm})^2}{2} \approx \mathbf{25.12\ cm^2}$

23. $\dfrac{4xp - \dfrac{1}{x}}{6p - \dfrac{p^2}{x}} = \dfrac{\dfrac{4x^2 p - 1}{x}}{\dfrac{6px - p^2}{x}} \cdot \dfrac{\dfrac{x}{6px - p^2}}{\dfrac{x}{6px - p^2}}$

$= \dfrac{\mathbf{4x^2 p - 1}}{\mathbf{6px - p^2}}$

24. $5\sqrt{\dfrac{2}{5}} + 3\sqrt{\dfrac{5}{2}} = \dfrac{5\sqrt{2}}{\sqrt{5}}\dfrac{\sqrt{5}}{\sqrt{5}} + \dfrac{3\sqrt{5}}{\sqrt{2}}\dfrac{\sqrt{2}}{\sqrt{2}}$

$= \dfrac{5\sqrt{10}}{5} + \dfrac{3\sqrt{10}}{2} = \dfrac{10\sqrt{10}}{10} + \dfrac{15\sqrt{10}}{10}$

$= \dfrac{25\sqrt{10}}{10} = \dfrac{\mathbf{5\sqrt{10}}}{\mathbf{2}}$

25. $2\sqrt{5}(3\sqrt{15} - 2\sqrt{10})$

$= 2\sqrt{5}(3\sqrt{3}\sqrt{5} - 2\sqrt{2}\sqrt{5})$

$= \mathbf{30\sqrt{3} - 20\sqrt{2}}$

26. $y = -\dfrac{2}{3}x + b$

$-5 = -\dfrac{2}{3}(-2) + b$

$-\dfrac{19}{3} = b$

$y = -\dfrac{\mathbf{2}}{\mathbf{3}}x - \dfrac{\mathbf{19}}{\mathbf{3}}$

27. $\dfrac{5x - 2}{7} - \dfrac{x - 3}{5} = 4$

$25x - 10 - 7x + 21 = 140$

$18x = 129$

$x = \dfrac{\mathbf{43}}{\mathbf{6}}$

28. (a) $2x + 3y = 3$

$y = -\dfrac{2}{3}x + 1$

(b) $x - 5y = 20$

$y = \dfrac{1}{5}x - 4$

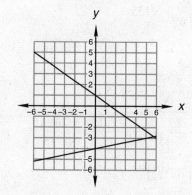

(a) $2x + 3y = 3$

-2(b) $\dfrac{-2x + 10y = -40}{13y = -37}$

$y = -\dfrac{37}{13}$

(b) $x - 5\left(-\dfrac{37}{13}\right) = 20$

$x = \dfrac{260}{13} - \dfrac{185}{13} = \dfrac{75}{13}$

$\left(\dfrac{\mathbf{75}}{\mathbf{13}}, -\dfrac{\mathbf{37}}{\mathbf{13}}\right)$

29. $\dfrac{2}{x-2} - \dfrac{3}{x+2} - \dfrac{2x}{x^2-4}$

$= \dfrac{2(x+2)}{x^2-4} - \dfrac{3(x-2)}{x^2-4} - \dfrac{2x}{x^2-4}$

$= \dfrac{2x+4-3x+6-2x}{x^2-4}$

$= \dfrac{-3x+10}{x^2-4}$

30. $a^2 - ab^3 = \left(-\dfrac{1}{2}\right)^2 - \left(-\dfrac{1}{2}\right)\left(\dfrac{1}{2}\right)^3 = \dfrac{1}{4} + \dfrac{1}{16}$

$= \dfrac{4}{16} + \dfrac{1}{16} = \dfrac{5}{16}$

PRACTICE SET 46

a. $3\sqrt{\dfrac{7}{3}} + 5\sqrt{\dfrac{3}{7}} - \sqrt{84}$

$= 3\dfrac{\sqrt{7}}{\sqrt{3}} \cdot \dfrac{\sqrt{3}}{\sqrt{3}} + \dfrac{5\sqrt{3}}{\sqrt{7}} \cdot \dfrac{\sqrt{7}}{\sqrt{7}} - \sqrt{4}\sqrt{21}$

$= \dfrac{3\sqrt{21}}{3} + \dfrac{5\sqrt{21}}{7} - 2\sqrt{21}$

$= \dfrac{7\sqrt{21}}{7} + \dfrac{5\sqrt{21}}{7} - \dfrac{14\sqrt{21}}{7} = \dfrac{-2\sqrt{21}}{7}$

b. $2\sqrt{\dfrac{3}{5}} - 5\sqrt{\dfrac{5}{3}} + \sqrt{135}$

$= \dfrac{2\sqrt{3}}{\sqrt{5}} \cdot \dfrac{\sqrt{5}}{\sqrt{5}} - \dfrac{5\sqrt{5}}{\sqrt{3}} \cdot \dfrac{\sqrt{3}}{\sqrt{3}} + \sqrt{9}\sqrt{15}$

$= \dfrac{2\sqrt{15}}{5} - \dfrac{5\sqrt{15}}{3} + 3\sqrt{15}$

$= \dfrac{6\sqrt{15}}{15} - \dfrac{25\sqrt{15}}{15} + \dfrac{45\sqrt{15}}{15} = \dfrac{26\sqrt{15}}{15}$

c. $\sqrt{7\sqrt{7}} = \left[7(7)^{1/2}\right]^{1/2} = 7^{1/2}7^{1/4} = 7^{3/4}$

PROBLEM SET 46

1. $\dfrac{240}{100} \times T = 1440$

$T = 1440 \times \dfrac{100}{240} = \mathbf{600}$

2. $\dfrac{1000}{4000} = \dfrac{B}{24{,}000}$

$4000B = 24{,}000(1000)$

$B = \mathbf{6000 \ kilograms}$

3. Nitrogen: $1 \times 14 = 14$
Hydrogen: $4 \times 1 = 4$
Chlorine: $1 \times 35 = 35$
Total: $14 + 4 + 35 = 53$

$\dfrac{35}{53} = \dfrac{140}{NH_4Cl}$

$35NH_4Cl = 53(140)$

$NH_4Cl = \mathbf{212 \ grams}$

4. (a) $\dfrac{N_F}{N_E} = \dfrac{7}{2} \longrightarrow 2N_F = 7N_E$

(b) $N_F = 3N_E + 11$

Substitute (b) into (a) and get:

(a′) $2(3N_E + 11) = 7N_E$

$N_E = \mathbf{22 \ elves}$

(b) $N_F = 3(22) + 11 = \mathbf{77 \ fairies}$

5.

$R_MT_M + 16 = R_BT_B; \ T_M = T_B = 4; \ R_M = 16$

$16(4) + 16 = 4R_B$

$80 = 4R_B$

$\mathbf{20 \ mph} = R_B$

6. $5\sqrt{\dfrac{3}{2}} + 2\sqrt{\dfrac{2}{3}} - \sqrt{600}$

$= \dfrac{5\sqrt{3}}{\sqrt{2}}\dfrac{\sqrt{2}}{\sqrt{2}} + \dfrac{2\sqrt{2}}{\sqrt{3}}\dfrac{\sqrt{3}}{\sqrt{3}} - 10\sqrt{6}$

$= \dfrac{5\sqrt{6}}{2} + \dfrac{2\sqrt{6}}{3} - 10\sqrt{6}$

$= \dfrac{15\sqrt{6}}{6} + \dfrac{4\sqrt{6}}{6} - \dfrac{60\sqrt{6}}{6} = -\dfrac{41\sqrt{6}}{6}$

7. $3\sqrt{\dfrac{5}{7}} - 5\sqrt{\dfrac{7}{5}} + 3\sqrt{140}$

$= \dfrac{3\sqrt{5}}{\sqrt{7}}\dfrac{\sqrt{7}}{\sqrt{7}} - \dfrac{5\sqrt{7}}{\sqrt{5}}\dfrac{\sqrt{5}}{\sqrt{5}} + 6\sqrt{35}$

$= \dfrac{3\sqrt{35}}{7} - \dfrac{5\sqrt{35}}{5} + 6\sqrt{35}$

$= \dfrac{15\sqrt{35}}{35} - \dfrac{35\sqrt{35}}{35} + \dfrac{210\sqrt{35}}{35} = \dfrac{38\sqrt{35}}{7}$

8. $\sqrt{5\sqrt{5}} = \left[5(5^{1/2})\right]^{1/2} = 5^{1/2}5^{1/4} = \mathbf{5^{3/4}}$

9. $\sqrt[3]{6\sqrt{6}} = \left[6(6^{1/2})\right]^{1/3} = 6^{1/3}6^{1/6} = \mathbf{6^{1/2}}$

10. $\sqrt{x^3 y^3}\sqrt[4]{xy} = (x^3 y^3)^{1/2}(xy)^{1/4}$

$= x^{3/2}y^{3/2}x^{1/4}y^{1/4}$

$= \mathbf{x^{7/4}y^{7/4}}$

11. $\sqrt[4]{x^5 y^3}\sqrt[3]{xy^5} = (x^5 y^3)^{1/4}(xy^5)^{1/3}$

$= x^{5/4}y^{3/4}x^{1/3}y^{5/3} = \mathbf{x^{19/12}y^{29/12}}$

12. $\left(x - \dfrac{2}{5}\right)^2 = 7$

$\qquad x - \dfrac{2}{5} = \pm\sqrt{7}$

$\qquad x = \mathbf{\dfrac{2}{5} \pm \sqrt{7}}$

13. $\left(x - \dfrac{1}{4}\right)^2 = 5$

$\qquad x - \dfrac{1}{4} = \pm\sqrt{5}$

$\qquad x = \mathbf{\dfrac{1}{4} \pm \sqrt{5}}$

14. $B + 24 + 90 = 180$

$\qquad B = \mathbf{66}$

$\cos 24° = \dfrac{7}{y}$

$\qquad y = \dfrac{7}{\cos 24°} \approx \mathbf{7.66}$

15. $\cos A = \dfrac{4}{7}$

$\qquad A \approx \mathbf{55.15}$

$\sin 55.15° \approx \dfrac{C}{7}$

$\qquad C \approx 7\sin 55.15° \approx \mathbf{5.74}$

16. $\dfrac{(476,800)(9,016,423 \times 10^4)}{408 \times 10^{10}}$

$\approx \dfrac{(5 \times 10^5)(9 \times 10^{10})}{4 \times 10^{12}} \approx \mathbf{1 \times 10^4}$

17. $\dfrac{ax}{b} - c = \dfrac{k}{m}$

$axm - bcm = kb$

$\qquad m = \mathbf{\dfrac{kb}{ax - bc}}$

18. $\dfrac{x}{m} - \dfrac{yb}{c} = p$

$cx - ybm = cmp$

$cx - cmp = ybm$

$\qquad c = \mathbf{\dfrac{ybm}{x - mp}}$

19. $6 \cdot \overrightarrow{SF} = \dfrac{7}{2} \longrightarrow \overrightarrow{SF} = \dfrac{7}{12}$

$4 \cdot \dfrac{7}{12} = x$

$\qquad \dfrac{7}{3} = x$

$5 \cdot \dfrac{7}{12} = y$

$\qquad \dfrac{35}{12} = y$

20. $\qquad -40x = 13x^2 + x^3$

$x^3 + 13x^2 + 40x = 0$

$x(x + 8)(x + 5) = 0$

$\qquad x = \mathbf{0, -8, -5}$

21. $\dfrac{(x + 9)(x + 5)}{x(x + 9)(x + 1)} \cdot \dfrac{x(x - 2)(x + 1)}{(x - 7)(x + 5)}$

$= \mathbf{\dfrac{x - 2}{x - 7}}$

22. $8^{-4/3} = \dfrac{1}{8^{4/3}} = \dfrac{1}{(8^{1/3})^4} = \mathbf{\dfrac{1}{16}}$

23. $x = 2(105) - 40 = \mathbf{170}$

$y = \dfrac{360 - 210}{2} = \mathbf{75}$

$z = \dfrac{360 - 2(65)}{2} = \mathbf{115}$

24. $\dfrac{\dfrac{m^2}{x} - x}{\dfrac{p^2}{x} + 2x} = \dfrac{\dfrac{m^2 - x^2}{x}}{\dfrac{p^2 + 2x^2}{x}} \cdot \dfrac{\dfrac{x}{p^2 + 2x^2}}{\dfrac{x}{p^2 + 2x^2}}$

$= \mathbf{\dfrac{m^2 - x^2}{p^2 + 2x^2}}$

25. $3\sqrt{7}(2\sqrt{14} - \sqrt{7}) = 3\sqrt{7}(2\sqrt{2}\sqrt{7} - \sqrt{7})$

$= \mathbf{42\sqrt{2} - 21}$

26. Graph the line to find the slope.

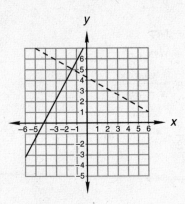

$$m = \frac{-5}{+9} = -\frac{5}{9}$$

Since the slopes of perpendicular lines are negative reciprocals of each other,

$$m_\perp = \frac{9}{5}$$

$$y = \frac{9}{5}x + b$$

$$4 = \frac{9}{5}(-2) + b$$

$$\frac{38}{5} = b$$

$$y = \frac{9}{5}x + \frac{38}{5}$$

27.
$$\frac{-x + 3}{2} - \frac{2x + 4}{3} = 5$$

$$-3x + 9 - 4x - 8 = 30$$

$$x = -\frac{29}{7}$$

28.
$$\frac{-2x - 5}{4} - \frac{x - 2}{3} = 7$$

$$-6x - 15 - 4x + 8 = 84$$

$$x = -\frac{91}{10}$$

29. (a) $x - y = -3$

$$y = x + 3$$

(b) $x + 2y = -2$

$$y = -\frac{1}{2}x - 1$$

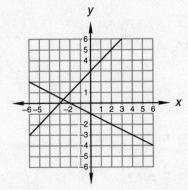

Substitute $y = x + 3$ into (b) and get:

(b') $x + 2(x + 3) = -2$

$$3x = -8$$

$$x = -\frac{8}{3}$$

(a) $y = \left(-\frac{8}{3}\right) + \frac{9}{3} = \frac{1}{3}$

$$\left(-\frac{8}{3}, \frac{1}{3}\right)$$

30. $a^2 - a^3b - ab$

$$= \left(-\frac{1}{2}\right)^2 - \left(-\frac{1}{2}\right)^3\left(-\frac{1}{4}\right) - \left(-\frac{1}{2}\right)\left(-\frac{1}{4}\right)$$

$$= \frac{1}{4} - \frac{1}{32} - \frac{1}{8} = \frac{3}{32}$$

PRACTICE SET 47

a. First method:
$$\sqrt[3]{64\sqrt{4}} = \sqrt[3]{4^3\sqrt{4}} = [4^3(4^{1/2})]^{1/3} = 4^{3/3}4^{1/6}$$
$$= 4^{6/6}4^{1/6} = \mathbf{4^{7/6}}$$

Second method:
$$\sqrt[3]{64\sqrt{4}} = \sqrt[3]{2^6\sqrt{2^2}} = [2^6(2^2)^{1/2}]^{1/3}$$
$$= 2^{6/3}2^{2/2 \cdot 1/3} = 2^2 2^{1/3} = \mathbf{2^{7/3}}$$

b. $\sqrt[6]{9\sqrt{3}} = \sqrt[6]{3^2\sqrt{3}} = [3^2(3)^{1/2}]^{1/6}$
$$= 3^{2/6}3^{1/12} = \mathbf{3^{5/12}}$$

c. $\dfrac{85 \text{ mi}}{s} \cdot \dfrac{60 \text{ s}}{1 \text{ min}} \cdot \dfrac{60 \text{ min}}{1 \text{ hr}} = 85(60)(60) \dfrac{\text{mi}}{\text{hr}}$

d. $\dfrac{207 \text{ mi}}{\text{hr}} \cdot \dfrac{1 \text{ hr}}{60 \text{ min}} \cdot \dfrac{1 \text{ min}}{60 \text{ s}} \cdot \dfrac{5280 \text{ ft}}{1 \text{ mi}}$

$$= \frac{207(5280)}{(60)(60)} \frac{\text{ft}}{\text{s}}$$

PROBLEM SET 47

1. $\dfrac{4}{7} \times T = 2800$

$T = 2800 \times \dfrac{7}{4} = \mathbf{4900 \ people}$

2. Odd integers: $N, \ N + 2, \ N + 4, \ N + 6$

$5(N + N + 2) = 7(N + 2 + N + 6) - 10$

$10N + 10 = 14N + 46$

$N = -9$

The desired integers are **–9, –7, –5,** and **–3.**

3. $\dfrac{70}{100} \times G = 1400$

$G = 1400 \cdot \dfrac{100}{70} = \mathbf{2000 \ girls}$

4. Hydrogen: $2 \times 1 = 2$

Sulfur: $1 \times 32 = 32$

Oxygen: $3 \times 16 = 48$

Total: $2 + 32 + 48 = 82$

$\dfrac{48}{82} = \dfrac{192}{H_2SO_3}$

$48 H_2SO_3 = 82(192)$

$H_2SO_3 = \mathbf{328 \ grams}$

5.

$$\begin{array}{c} \overset{D_R \qquad D_W}{\vdash\!\!\longrightarrow\!\!\dashv} \\ 48 \end{array}$$

$R_R T_R + R_W T_W = 48$

$R_R = 8; \ R_W = 4$

$T_R + T_W = 7$

$8(7 - T_W) + 4T_W = 48$

$-4T_W = -8$

$T_W = 2$

$T_R = 7 - (2) = 5$

$D_W = 4(2) = \mathbf{8 \ kilometers}$

$D_R = 8(5) = \mathbf{40 \ kilometers}$

6. $\dfrac{52 \text{ in.}}{s} \times \dfrac{1 \text{ ft}}{12 \text{ in.}} \times \dfrac{1 \text{ mi}}{5280 \text{ ft}} \times \dfrac{60 \text{ s}}{1 \text{ min}} \times \dfrac{60 \text{ min}}{1 \text{ hr}}$

$= \dfrac{52(60)(60)}{(12)(5280)} \dfrac{\text{mi}}{\text{hr}}$

7. $\dfrac{805 \text{ mi}}{\text{hr}} \times \dfrac{5280 \text{ ft}}{1 \text{ mi}} \times \dfrac{1 \text{ hr}}{60 \text{ min}} \times \dfrac{1 \text{ min}}{60 \text{ s}}$

$= \dfrac{805(5280)}{(60)(60)} \dfrac{\text{ft}}{\text{s}}$

8. $\dfrac{13 \text{ in.}}{s} \times \dfrac{1 \text{ ft}}{12 \text{ in.}} \times \dfrac{1 \text{ yd}}{3 \text{ ft}} \times \dfrac{60 \text{ s}}{1 \text{ min}} \times \dfrac{60 \text{ min}}{1 \text{ hr}}$

$= \dfrac{13(60)(60)}{(12)(3)} \dfrac{\text{yd}}{\text{hr}}$

9. $\sqrt[3]{25\sqrt{5}} = \sqrt[3]{5^2 \sqrt{5}} = \left[5^2(5^{1/2})\right]^{1/3} = 5^{2/3} 5^{1/6}$

$= \mathbf{5^{5/6}}$

10. $\sqrt[7]{9\sqrt{3}} = \sqrt[7]{3^2 \sqrt{3}} = \left[3^2(3^{1/2})\right]^{1/7} = 3^{2/7} 3^{1/14}$

$= \mathbf{3^{5/14}}$

11. $\sqrt{x^2 y} \sqrt[3]{y^2 x} = (x^2 y)^{1/2} (y^2 x)^{1/3} = xy^{1/2} y^{2/3} x^{1/3}$

$= \mathbf{x^{4/3} y^{7/6}}$

12. $\sqrt{2 \sqrt[3]{2}} = \left[2(2^{1/3})\right]^{1/2} = 2^{1/2} 2^{1/6} = \mathbf{2^{2/3}}$

13. $3\sqrt{\dfrac{2}{3}} - 5\sqrt{\dfrac{3}{2}} + 2\sqrt{24}$

$= \dfrac{3\sqrt{2}}{\sqrt{3}} \dfrac{\sqrt{3}}{\sqrt{3}} - \dfrac{5\sqrt{3}}{\sqrt{2}} \dfrac{\sqrt{2}}{\sqrt{2}} + 4\sqrt{6}$

$= \dfrac{2\sqrt{6}}{2} - \dfrac{5\sqrt{6}}{2} + \dfrac{8\sqrt{6}}{2} = \mathbf{\dfrac{5\sqrt{6}}{2}}$

14. $3\sqrt{\dfrac{5}{7}} - 2\sqrt{\dfrac{7}{5}} - \sqrt{315}$

$= \dfrac{3\sqrt{5}}{\sqrt{7}} \dfrac{\sqrt{7}}{\sqrt{7}} - \dfrac{2\sqrt{7}}{\sqrt{5}} \dfrac{\sqrt{5}}{\sqrt{5}} - 3\sqrt{35}$

$= \dfrac{15\sqrt{35}}{35} - \dfrac{14\sqrt{35}}{35} - \dfrac{105\sqrt{35}}{35} = \mathbf{-\dfrac{104\sqrt{35}}{35}}$

15. $\sin 19° = \dfrac{x}{7}$

$x = 7 \sin 19° \approx \mathbf{2.28}$

16. $\cos 15° = \dfrac{9}{x}$

$x = \dfrac{9}{\cos 15°} \approx \mathbf{9.32}$

17. $(x - 3)^2 = 5$

$x - 3 = \pm\sqrt{5}$

$x = \mathbf{3 \pm \sqrt{5}}$

18. $\left(x + \dfrac{2}{7}\right)^2 = \dfrac{4}{49}$

$x + \dfrac{2}{7} = \pm\dfrac{2}{7}$

$x = -\dfrac{2}{7} \pm \dfrac{2}{7}$

$x = \mathbf{0}, -\dfrac{\mathbf{4}}{\mathbf{7}}$

19. $\dfrac{(36{,}421 \times 10^5)(493{,}025)}{40{,}216 \times 10^7}$

$\approx \dfrac{(4 \times 10^9)(5 \times 10^5)}{4 \times 10^{11}} = \mathbf{5 \times 10^3}$

20. $\dfrac{ay}{x} + p = \dfrac{m}{c}$

$acy + cpx = mx$

$acy = mx - cpx$

$\dfrac{\boldsymbol{acy}}{\boldsymbol{m - cp}} = x$

21. $\dfrac{a}{x} - \dfrac{c}{p} = b$

$ap - cx = bpx$

$ap - bpx = cx$

$p = \dfrac{\boldsymbol{cx}}{\boldsymbol{a - bx}}$

22. $B^2 = 4^2 + 3^2$

$B^2 = 25$

$B = 5$

$4 \times \overrightarrow{SF} = 6$

$\overrightarrow{SF} = \dfrac{3}{2}$

$5 \times \dfrac{3}{2} = C + 5$

$\dfrac{15}{2} = C + \dfrac{10}{2}$

$\dfrac{\mathbf{5}}{\mathbf{2}} = C$

23. $x = 180 - 150 = \mathbf{30}$

$y = 180 - 90 - 30 = \mathbf{60}$

$z = y = \mathbf{60}$

$s = 180 - 90 - 60 = \mathbf{30}$

$p = 180 - 90 - 30 = \mathbf{60}$

$m = 180 - 90 - 60 = \mathbf{30}$

24. $\dfrac{\dfrac{x^2 p}{m} - m}{\dfrac{x}{m} - p} = \dfrac{\dfrac{x^2 p - m^2}{m}}{\dfrac{x - pm}{m}} \cdot \dfrac{\dfrac{m}{x - pm}}{\dfrac{m}{x - pm}}$

$= \dfrac{\boldsymbol{x^2 p - m^2}}{\boldsymbol{x - pm}}$

25. $\dfrac{x(x + 7)(x - 2)}{(x + 7)(x + 5)} \cdot \dfrac{(x + 5)(x + 3)}{x(x - 5)(x + 3)}$

$= \dfrac{\boldsymbol{x - 2}}{\boldsymbol{x - 5}}$

26. $-27^{-4/3} = -\dfrac{1}{27^{4/3}} = -\dfrac{1}{(27^{1/3})^4} = -\dfrac{\mathbf{1}}{\mathbf{81}}$

27. (a) $x - 4y = 8$

$y = \dfrac{1}{4}x - 2$

(b) $2x - 3y = 9$

$y = \dfrac{2}{3}x - 3$

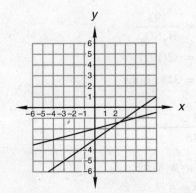

Solve the equations by elimination:

-2(a) $\quad -2x + 8y = -16$

(b) $\quad \underline{2x - 3y = 9}$

$5y = -7$

$y = -\dfrac{7}{5}$

(a) $x - 4\left(-\dfrac{7}{5}\right) = 8$

$x = \dfrac{12}{5}$

$\left(\dfrac{\mathbf{12}}{\mathbf{5}}, -\dfrac{\mathbf{7}}{\mathbf{5}}\right)$

28. $y = \dfrac{2}{5}x + b$

$5 = \dfrac{2}{5}(-2) + b$

$\dfrac{29}{5} = b$

$y = \dfrac{2}{5}x + \dfrac{29}{5}$

29. $20x = -12x^2 - x^3$

$x^3 + 12x^2 + 20x = 0$

$x(x + 10)(x + 2) = 0$

$x = \mathbf{0, -2, -10}$

30. $-a - a^2 - a^3 - ab$

$= -\left(-\dfrac{1}{2}\right) - \left(-\dfrac{1}{2}\right)^2 - \left(-\dfrac{1}{2}\right)^3 - \left(-\dfrac{1}{2}\right)\left(\dfrac{1}{5}\right)$

$= \dfrac{1}{2} - \dfrac{1}{4} + \dfrac{1}{8} + \dfrac{1}{10} = \dfrac{\mathbf{19}}{\mathbf{40}}$

PRACTICE SET 48

a. $\sqrt{x - 5} - 3 = 7$

$\sqrt{x - 5} = 10$

$x - 5 = 100$

$x = \mathbf{105}$

Check: $\sqrt{(105) - 5} - 3 = 7$

$10 - 3 = 7$

$7 = 7$

b. $\sqrt{x + 5} + 1 = -11$

$\sqrt{x + 5} = -12$

$x + 5 = 144$

$x = 139$

Check: $\sqrt{(139) + 5} + 1 = -11$

$\sqrt{144} + 1 = -11$

$12 + 1 \neq 11$

No real number solution exists.

c. $\sqrt{x^2 + 3x - 10} + 2 = x$

$\sqrt{x^2 + 3x - 10} = x - 2$

$x^2 + 3x - 10 = x^2 - 4x + 4$

$7x - 14 = 0$

$7x = 14$

$x = \mathbf{2}$

Check: $\sqrt{(2)^2 + 3(2) - 10} + 2 = (2)$

$\sqrt{4 + 6 - 10} + 2 = 2$

$2 = 2$

PROBLEM SET 48

1. $0.32 \times F = 512$

$F = \dfrac{512}{0.32} = \mathbf{1600 \text{ frontiersmen}}$

2. $\dfrac{1400}{1540} = \dfrac{NG}{6160}$

$1540NG = 1400(6160)$

$NG = \mathbf{5600 \text{ grams}}$

3. Iron: $\quad 1 \times 56 = 56$

Bromine: $\quad 2 \times 80 = 160$

Total: $\quad 56 + 160 = 216$

$\dfrac{56}{216} = \dfrac{\text{Fe}}{972}$

$216\text{Fe} = 56(972)$

$\text{Fe} = \mathbf{252 \text{ grams}}$

4. (a) $5N_B = 3N_G + 17$

(b) $6N_G = N_B + 2 \longrightarrow N_B = 6N_G - 2$

Substitute $N_B = 6N_G - 2$ into (a) and get:

(a′) $5(6N_G - 2) = 3N_G + 17$

$27N_G = 27$

$N_G = \mathbf{1 \text{ girl}}$

(b) $N_B = 6(1) - 2 = \mathbf{4 \text{ boys}}$

5.

$R_F T_F = R_E T_E; \ T_F = 20;$

$T_E = 10; \ R_E = R_F + 30$

$20R_F = 10(R_F + 30)$

$10R_F = 300$

$R_F = \mathbf{30 \text{ mph}}$

$R_E = (30) + 30 = \mathbf{60 \text{ mph}}$

6. $\sqrt{x - 3} - 3 = 4$

$\sqrt{x - 3} = 7$

$x - 3 = 49$

$x = \mathbf{52}$

Check: $\sqrt{52 - 3} - 3 = 4$

$7 - 3 = 4$

7. $\sqrt{x + 5} + 3 = -4$

$\qquad \sqrt{x + 5} = -7$

$\qquad x + 5 = 49$

$\qquad x = 44$

Check: $\sqrt{44 + 5} + 3 = -4$

$\qquad 7 + 3 = -4$

The last statement is not true, so no real number solution exists.

8. $\sqrt{x^2 + 8x + 15} - 5 = x$

$\qquad x^2 + 8x + 15 = x^2 + 10x + 25$

$\qquad -2x = 10$

$\qquad x = -5$

Check: $\sqrt{(-5)^2 + 8(-5) + 15} - 5 = -5$

$\qquad -5 = -5$

9. $\dfrac{60 \text{ mi}}{\text{hr}} \times \dfrac{5280 \text{ ft}}{1 \text{ mi}} \times \dfrac{1 \text{ hr}}{60 \text{ min}} \times \dfrac{1 \text{ min}}{60 \text{ s}}$

$= \dfrac{60(5280)}{(60)(60)} \dfrac{\text{ft}}{\text{s}}$

10. $\sqrt{2\sqrt[3]{2}} = [2(2^{1/3})]^{1/2} = 2^{1/2}2^{1/6} = \mathbf{2^{2/3}}$

11. $\sqrt{m^2 y} \sqrt[3]{m^4 y} = (m^2 y)^{1/2}(m^4 y)^{1/3}$

$= my^{1/2}m^{4/3}y^{1/3} = \mathbf{m^{7/3}y^{5/6}}$

12. $\sqrt{8\sqrt[3]{2}} = \sqrt{2^3 \sqrt[3]{2}} = [2^3(2^{1/3})]^{1/2} = 2^{3/2}2^{1/6}$

$= \mathbf{2^{5/3}}$

13. $3\sqrt{\dfrac{2}{5}} - \sqrt{\dfrac{5}{2}} + 2\sqrt{40}$

$= \dfrac{3\sqrt{2}}{\sqrt{5}}\dfrac{\sqrt{5}}{\sqrt{5}} - \dfrac{\sqrt{5}}{\sqrt{2}}\dfrac{\sqrt{2}}{\sqrt{2}} + 4\sqrt{10}$

$= \dfrac{6\sqrt{10}}{10} - \dfrac{5\sqrt{10}}{10} + \dfrac{40\sqrt{10}}{10} = \mathbf{\dfrac{41\sqrt{10}}{10}}$

14. $2\sqrt{\dfrac{7}{11}} - \sqrt{\dfrac{11}{7}} + 2\sqrt{308}$

$= \dfrac{2\sqrt{7}}{\sqrt{11}}\dfrac{\sqrt{11}}{\sqrt{11}} - \dfrac{\sqrt{11}}{\sqrt{7}}\dfrac{\sqrt{7}}{\sqrt{7}} + 4\sqrt{77}$

$= \dfrac{14\sqrt{77}}{77} - \dfrac{11\sqrt{77}}{77} + \dfrac{308\sqrt{77}}{77} = \mathbf{\dfrac{311\sqrt{77}}{77}}$

15. $\left(x - \dfrac{2}{7}\right)^2 = 4$

$\qquad x - \dfrac{2}{7} = \pm 2$

$\qquad x = \dfrac{2}{7} \pm \dfrac{14}{7}$

$\qquad x = \mathbf{\dfrac{16}{7}, -\dfrac{12}{7}}$

16. $(x - 3)^2 = 16$

$\qquad x - 3 = \pm 4$

$\qquad x = 3 \pm 4$

$\qquad x = \mathbf{7, -1}$

17. $C = 180 - 90 - 63 = \mathbf{27}$

$\sin 63° = \dfrac{b}{5}$

$\qquad b = 5 \sin 63° \approx \mathbf{4.46}$

18. $\cos A = \dfrac{4}{6}$

$\qquad A \approx \mathbf{48.19}$

19. $\dfrac{(4{,}071{,}623)(51{,}642 \times 10^5)}{200{,}000 \times 10^{-13}}$

$\approx \dfrac{(4 \times 10^6)(5 \times 10^9)}{2 \times 10^{-8}} = \mathbf{1 \times 10^{24}}$

20. $\qquad \dfrac{b}{x} - \dfrac{c}{p} + k = \dfrac{m}{y}$

$bpy - cxy + kpxy = mxp$

$bpy + kpxy - mxp = cxy$

$\qquad p = \dfrac{cxy}{by + kxy - mx}$

21. $2(180 - A)° = 4(90 - A)° + 40°$

$\qquad 360 - 2A = 400 - 4A$

$\qquad 2A = 40$

$\qquad A = \mathbf{20°}$

22.

$$x + 1 \overline{)\,3x^3 + 0x^2 + 0x - 2} \quad \mathbf{3x^2 - 3x + 3} - \dfrac{5}{x+1}$$

$\qquad \underline{3x^3 + 3x^2}$

$\qquad \quad -3x^2 + 0x$

$\qquad \quad \underline{-3x^2 - 3x}$

$\qquad \qquad \quad 3x - 2$

$\qquad \qquad \quad \underline{3x + 3}$

$\qquad \qquad \qquad \quad -5$

23.

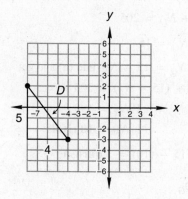

$$D^2 = 5^2 + 4^2$$
$$D^2 = 25 + 16$$
$$D^2 = 41$$
$$D = \sqrt{41}$$

24. $\dfrac{(x-2)(x-1)}{x(x+5)(x-1)} \cdot \dfrac{x(x+7)(x+5)}{(x+3)(x-2)}$

$$= \dfrac{x+7}{x+3}$$

25. $-16^{-3/4} = -\dfrac{1}{16^{3/4}} = -\dfrac{1}{(16^{1/4})^3} = -\dfrac{1}{8}$

26. $V_{\text{Cone}} = \dfrac{1}{3}(A_{\text{Base}} \times \text{height})$

$$= \dfrac{1}{3}\left(12(8) - \dfrac{1}{2}\pi(4)^2\right)(4) \text{ in.}^3$$

$$= \dfrac{1}{3}(96 - 8\pi)(4) \text{ in.}^3 \approx \textbf{94.51 in.}^3$$

27.

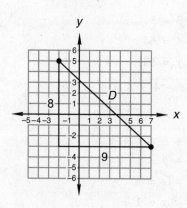

$$D^2 = 8^2 + 9^2$$
$$D^2 = 64 + 81$$
$$D^2 = 145$$
$$D = \sqrt{145}$$

28. $\dfrac{\dfrac{x-1}{x} - \dfrac{1}{x^2}}{\dfrac{x+2}{x^2} - 4}$

$$= \dfrac{\dfrac{x^2 - x - 1}{x^2}}{\dfrac{x + 2 - 4x^2}{x^2}} \cdot \dfrac{\dfrac{x^2}{x + 2 - 4x^2}}{\dfrac{x^2}{x + 2 - 4x^2}}$$

$$= \dfrac{x^2 - x - 1}{-4x^2 + x + 2}$$

29. Graph the line to find the slope.

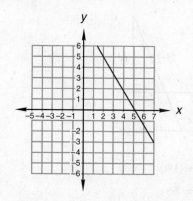

$$\text{Slope} = \dfrac{-8}{+5} = -\dfrac{8}{5}$$

$$y = -\dfrac{8}{5}x + b$$

$$5 = -\dfrac{8}{5}(2) + b$$

$$\dfrac{41}{5} = b$$

$$y = -\dfrac{8}{5}x + \dfrac{41}{5}$$

30. $\dfrac{2x-3}{2} - \dfrac{x}{2} = \dfrac{5}{3}$

$$6x - 9 - 3x = 10$$
$$3x = 19$$
$$x = \dfrac{19}{3}$$

PRACTICE SET 49

a. $y = mx + b$

$m = \dfrac{5}{2}$

Use $(2, -6)$ for (x, y).

$-6 = \dfrac{5}{2}(2) + b$

$b = -11$

$y = \dfrac{5}{2}x - 11$

b.

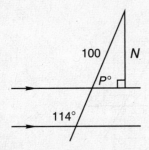

$114 + P = 180$

$P = 66$

$\sin 66° = \dfrac{N}{100}$

$N = 100 \sin 66° \approx \mathbf{91.35}$

PROBLEM SET 49

1. $5(N - 13) = 4(-N) - 92$

$\qquad 9N = -27$

$\qquad N = \mathbf{-3}$

2. $\dfrac{260}{100} \times CB = 1092$

$\qquad CB = 1092 \times \dfrac{100}{260} = \mathbf{420\ celebrants}$

3. Beryllium: $1 \times 9 = 9$

Fluoride: $2 \times 19 = 38$

Total: $9 + 38 = 47$

$\dfrac{38}{47} = \dfrac{95}{BeF_2}$

$38BeF_2 = 47(95)$

$BeF_2 = \mathbf{117.5\ grams}$

4. (a) $20N_R + N_Q = 205$

(b) $N_R + N_Q = 15$

Substitute $N_Q = 15 - N_R$ into (a) and get:

(a') $20N_R + (15 - N_R) = 205$

$\qquad 19N_R = 190$

$\qquad N_R = \mathbf{10\ riyals}$

(b) $N_Q = 15 - (10) = \mathbf{5\ qurush}$

5.

$R_B T_B + 200 = R_G T_G$

$T_B = T_G = 10;\ R_G = 240$

$10R_B + 200 = 10(240)$

$\qquad 10R_B = 2200$

$\qquad R_B = \mathbf{220\ yards\ per\ minute}$

6. $y = -6x + b$

Use the point $(3, 0)$ for x and y.

$\quad 0 = -6(3) + b$

$18 = b$

$y = \mathbf{-6x + 18}$

7. $B = 180 - 160 = 20$

$A = B = 20$

$\sin 20° = \dfrac{N}{40}$

$N = 40 \sin 20° \approx \mathbf{13.68}$

8. $\sqrt{x - 4} - 3 = 5$

$\qquad x - 4 = 64$

$\qquad x = \mathbf{68}$

Check: $\sqrt{68 - 4} - 3 = 5$

$\qquad\qquad 5 = 5$

9. $\sqrt{x^2 - 2x + 5} = x + 1$

$\quad x^2 - 2x + 5 = x^2 + 2x + 1$

$\qquad\quad 4x = 4$

$\qquad\quad x = \mathbf{1}$

Check: $\sqrt{1 - 2 + 5} = 2$

$\qquad\qquad 2 = 2$

10. $\dfrac{200\ in.}{min} \times \dfrac{1\ ft}{12\ in.} \times \dfrac{1\ min}{60\ s} = \dfrac{\mathbf{200}}{\mathbf{(12)(60)}} \dfrac{ft}{s}$

11. $\sqrt[3]{9\sqrt{3}} = \sqrt[3]{3^2\sqrt{3}} = [3^2(3^{1/2})]^{1/3} = 3^{2/3}3^{1/6}$
$= \mathbf{3^{5/6}}$

12. $\sqrt[4]{2}\sqrt[3]{2} = 2^{1/4}2^{1/3} = \mathbf{2^{7/12}}$

13. $\sqrt{x^2y^3}\sqrt{xy^4} = (x^2y^3)^{1/2}(xy^4)^{1/2} = xy^{3/2}x^{1/2}y^2$
$= \mathbf{x^{3/2}y^{7/2}}$

14. $\sqrt[3]{xy}\sqrt{xy} = (xy)^{1/3}(xy)^{1/2} = x^{1/3}y^{1/3}x^{1/2}y^{1/2}$
$= \mathbf{x^{5/6}y^{5/6}}$

15. $3\sqrt{\dfrac{7}{2}} + 2\sqrt{\dfrac{2}{7}} - 3\sqrt{56}$

$= \dfrac{3\sqrt{7}}{\sqrt{2}}\dfrac{\sqrt{2}}{\sqrt{2}} + \dfrac{2\sqrt{2}}{\sqrt{7}}\dfrac{\sqrt{7}}{\sqrt{7}} - 6\sqrt{14}$

$= \dfrac{21\sqrt{14}}{14} + \dfrac{4\sqrt{14}}{14} - \dfrac{84\sqrt{14}}{14} = \mathbf{-\dfrac{59\sqrt{14}}{14}}$

16. $5\sqrt{\dfrac{2}{9}} + 3\sqrt{\dfrac{9}{2}} + \sqrt{162}$

$= \dfrac{5\sqrt{2}}{\sqrt{9}}\dfrac{\sqrt{9}}{\sqrt{9}} + \dfrac{3\sqrt{9}}{\sqrt{2}}\dfrac{\sqrt{2}}{\sqrt{2}} + 3\sqrt{18}$

$= \dfrac{10\sqrt{18}}{18} + \dfrac{27\sqrt{18}}{18} + \dfrac{54\sqrt{18}}{18}$

$= \dfrac{91\sqrt{18}}{18} = \mathbf{\dfrac{91\sqrt{2}}{6}}$

17. $\left(x - \dfrac{5}{3}\right)^2 = 5$

$x - \dfrac{5}{3} = \pm\sqrt{5}$

$x = \dfrac{5}{3} \pm \sqrt{5}$

18. $(x + 2)^2 = 16$
$x + 2 = \pm 4$
$x = -2 \pm 4$
$x = \mathbf{2, -6}$

19. $\dfrac{(517{,}832 \times 10^{-14})(80{,}123)}{200{,}000 \times 10^{-42}}$

$\approx \dfrac{(5 \times 10^{-9})(8 \times 10^4)}{2 \times 10^{-37}} = \mathbf{2 \times 10^{33}}$

20. $\dfrac{x}{y} + c = \dfrac{m}{x} - d$

$x^2 + cxy = my - dxy$

$x^2 = my - dxy - cxy$

$\dfrac{x^2}{m - dx - cx} = y$

21. $\dfrac{2}{x} - \dfrac{3}{y} = \dfrac{m}{p}$

$2py - 3px = mxy$

$p = \dfrac{mxy}{2y - 3x}$

22. $(x + 1)^3 = (x + 1)(x + 1)(x + 1)$
$= (x^2 + 2x + 1)(x + 1)$
$= x^3 + 2x^2 + x + x^2 + 2x + 1$
$= \mathbf{x^3 + 3x^2 + 3x + 1}$

23. $\dfrac{(x - 5)(x - 1)}{x(x - 5)(x - 4)} \cdot \dfrac{x(x - 4)(x - 3)}{(x - 2)(x - 1)}$

$= \dfrac{x - 3}{x - 2}$

24.

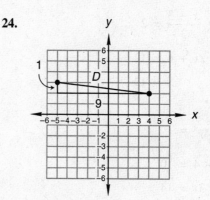

$D^2 = 9^2 + 1^2$
$D^2 = 81 + 1$
$D^2 = 82$
$D = \sqrt{82}$

25. Use the graph in the solution for problem 24 to find the slope as follows:

Slope $= \dfrac{-1}{+9} = -\dfrac{1}{9}$

$y = -\dfrac{1}{9}x + b$

$2 = -\dfrac{1}{9}(4) + b$

$\dfrac{22}{9} = b$

$y = -\dfrac{1}{9}x + \dfrac{22}{9}$

26. Number of sides $= \dfrac{360°}{12°} = \mathbf{30}$

27. $\dfrac{x}{ay^2} - \dfrac{3x}{a^2y^3} - \dfrac{5}{y^4}$

$= \dfrac{xay^2}{a^2y^4} - \dfrac{3xy}{a^2y^4} - \dfrac{5a^2}{a^2y^4}$

$= \dfrac{xay^2 - 3xy - 5a^2}{a^2y^4}$

28. $\dfrac{-3}{x + 3} - \dfrac{3x + 2}{x^2 - 9}$

$= \dfrac{-3(x - 3)}{x^2 - 9} - \dfrac{3x + 2}{x^2 - 9}$

$= \dfrac{-3x + 9 - 3x - 2}{x^2 - 9} = \dfrac{-6x + 7}{x^2 - 9}$

29. $\dfrac{x - 2}{2} - \dfrac{x - 3}{3} = 2$

$3x - 6 - 2x + 6 = 12$

$x = 12$

30. $\dfrac{x}{2} - \dfrac{x + 2}{5} = 1$

$5x - 2x - 4 = 10$

$3x = 14$

$x = \dfrac{14}{3}$

PRACTICE SET 50

$x^2 = 9x - 7$

$\left(x^2 - 9x + \phantom{\dfrac{81}{4}}\right) = -7$

$\left(x^2 - 9x + \dfrac{81}{4}\right) = -7 + \dfrac{81}{4}$

$\left(x - \dfrac{9}{2}\right)^2 = \dfrac{53}{4}$

$x - \dfrac{9}{2} = \pm\sqrt{\dfrac{53}{4}}$

$x = \dfrac{9}{2} \pm \dfrac{\sqrt{53}}{2}$

PROBLEM SET 50

1. (a) $N_T = 5N_W + 10$

(b) $N_T = 10N_W$

Substitute (b) into (a) and get:

(a') $10N_W = 5N_W + 10$

$5N_W = 10$

$N_W = $ **2 Waltzers**

(b) $N_T = 10(2) = $ **20 Two-Steppers**

2.

$$\overset{D_S \qquad\quad D_B}{\underset{104}{\vdash\!\!\longrightarrow\!\!\longrightarrow\!\!\dashv}}$$

$R_S T_S + R_B T_B = 104; \; R_S = 8;$

$R_B = 12; \; T_S + T_B = 10$

$8T_S + 12(10 - T_S) = 104$

$-4T_S = -16$

$T_S = 4$

$T_B = 10 - (4) = 6$

$D_S = 8(4) = $ **32 miles**

$D_B = 12(6) = $ **72 miles**

3. Sodium: $\quad 1 \times 23 = 23$

Chlorine: $\quad 1 \times 35 = 35$

Total: $\quad\; 23 + 35 = 58$

$\dfrac{23}{58} = \dfrac{\text{Na}}{348}$

$58\text{Na} = 23(348)$

$\text{Na} = $ **138 grams**

4. Even integers: $N, \; N + 2, \; N + 4$

$7(N + N + 4) = 10(N + 2) - 48$

$14N + 28 = 10N - 28$

$4N = -56$

$N = -14$

The desired integers are **−14, −12,** and **−10.**

5. $\dfrac{240}{100} \times OS = 432$

$OS = 432 \times \dfrac{100}{240} = $ **180 inches per day**

6.
$$x^2 + 8x - 4 = 0$$
$$(x^2 + 8x + \quad) = 4$$
$$x^2 + 8x + 16 = 4 + 16$$
$$(x + 4)^2 = 20$$
$$x + 4 = \pm 2\sqrt{5}$$
$$x = \mathbf{-4 \pm 2\sqrt{5}}$$

7.
$$12x + x^2 - 5 = 0$$
$$(x^2 + 12x + \quad) = 5$$
$$x^2 + 12x + 36 = 5 + 36$$
$$(x + 6)^2 = 41$$
$$x + 6 = \pm\sqrt{41}$$
$$x = \mathbf{-6 \pm \sqrt{41}}$$

8.
$$x^2 = 7x - 3$$
$$\left(x^2 - 7x + \quad\right) = -3$$
$$x^2 - 7x + \frac{49}{4} = -3 + \frac{49}{4}$$
$$\left(x - \frac{7}{2}\right)^2 = \frac{37}{4}$$
$$x - \frac{7}{2} = \pm\frac{\sqrt{37}}{2}$$
$$x = \mathbf{\frac{7}{2} \pm \frac{\sqrt{37}}{2}}$$

9. $y = 3x + b$

Use the point $(-3, 0)$ for x and y.
$$0 = 3(-3) + b$$
$$9 = b$$
$$\mathbf{y = 3x + 9}$$

10. $B = 180 - 120 = 60$

$C = 180 - 90 - 60 = \mathbf{30}$

$$\tan 60° = \frac{M}{10}$$
$$M = 10 \tan 60° \approx \mathbf{17.32}$$

11. $\sqrt{x^2 - 4x + 20} = x + 2$
$$x^2 - 4x + 20 = x^2 + 4x + 4$$
$$8x = 16$$
$$x = \mathbf{2}$$

Check: $\sqrt{4 - 8 + 20} = 4$
$$4 = 4$$

12.
$$-5 = -\sqrt{x + 5} + 1$$
$$6 = \sqrt{x + 5}$$
$$36 = x + 5$$
$$\mathbf{31 = x}$$

Check: $-5 = -\sqrt{31 + 5} + 1$
$$-5 = -5$$

13. $\dfrac{400 \text{ yd}}{\text{s}} \times \dfrac{3 \text{ ft}}{1 \text{ yd}} \times \dfrac{1 \text{ mi}}{5280 \text{ ft}} \times \dfrac{60 \text{ s}}{1 \text{ min}} \times \dfrac{60 \text{ min}}{1 \text{ hr}}$

$$= \mathbf{\frac{400(3)(60)(60)}{(5280)}} \frac{\mathbf{mi}}{\mathbf{hr}}$$

14. $\sqrt[5]{2\sqrt[3]{2}} = \left[2(2^{1/3})\right]^{1/5} = 2^{1/5}2^{1/15} = \mathbf{2^{4/15}}$

15. $\sqrt{9\sqrt{3}} = \sqrt{3^2\sqrt{3}} = \left[3^2(3^{1/2})\right]^{1/2} = 3 \cdot 3^{1/4}$

$= \mathbf{3^{5/4}}$

16. $\sqrt{m^3 y^5}\sqrt[3]{m^2 y^2} = (m^3 y^5)^{1/2}(m^2 y^2)^{1/3}$

$= m^{3/2}y^{5/2}m^{2/3}y^{2/3} = \mathbf{m^{13/6}y^{19/6}}$

17. $5\sqrt{\dfrac{3}{11}} + 2\sqrt{\dfrac{11}{3}} - \sqrt{297}$

$= \dfrac{5\sqrt{3}}{\sqrt{11}}\dfrac{\sqrt{11}}{\sqrt{11}} + \dfrac{2\sqrt{11}}{\sqrt{3}}\dfrac{\sqrt{3}}{\sqrt{3}} - 3\sqrt{33}$

$= \dfrac{15\sqrt{33}}{33} + \dfrac{22\sqrt{33}}{33} - \dfrac{99\sqrt{33}}{33} = \mathbf{-\dfrac{62\sqrt{33}}{33}}$

18. $\dfrac{(746,800 \times 10^{14})(703,916 \times 10^4)}{500,000}$

$\approx \dfrac{(7 \times 10^{19})(7 \times 10^9)}{5 \times 10^5} = 9.8 \times 10^{23}$

$\approx \mathbf{1 \times 10^{24}}$

19. $\dfrac{mxc}{p} - k = \dfrac{2}{r}$

$mxcr - kpr = 2p$

$mxcr = 2p + kpr$

$c = \mathbf{\dfrac{2p + kpr}{mxr}}$

20. $\dfrac{4}{x} - \dfrac{3x}{p} = \dfrac{c}{m}$

$4pm - 3x^2m = cpx$

$4pm - cpx = 3x^2m$

$p = \mathbf{\dfrac{3x^2 m}{4m - cx}}$

21. $a^2 = 24^2 + 7^2$

$a^2 = 576 + 49$

$a^2 = 625$

$a = \sqrt{625} = 25$

$24 \times \overrightarrow{SF} = 30$

$\overrightarrow{SF} = \dfrac{30}{24} = \dfrac{5}{4}$

$25 \times \dfrac{5}{4} = c + 25$

$\dfrac{125}{4} = c + \dfrac{100}{4}$

$\dfrac{25}{4} = c$

22.
$$2x - 3 \overline{)\,4x^3 + 0x^2 + 3x + 5\,} \quad 2x^2 + 3x + 6 + \tfrac{23}{2x-3}$$

$\underline{4x^3 - 6x^2}$

$\quad 6x^2 + 3x$

$\quad \underline{6x^2 - 9x}$

$\qquad 12x + 5$

$\qquad \underline{12x - 18}$

$\qquad\qquad 23$

23. $\qquad x^3 - 28x = 3x^2$

$x^3 - 3x^2 - 28x = 0$

$x(x - 7)(x + 4) = 0$

$\qquad x = \mathbf{0, -4, 7}$

24. $\dfrac{(x - 7)(x - 7)}{x(x - 7)(x - 6)} \cdot \dfrac{x(x - 6)(x + 2)}{(x - 7)(x + 5)}$

$= \dfrac{x + 2}{x + 5}$

25. $-49^{3/2} = -(49^{1/2})^3 = \mathbf{-343}$

26. $V_{\text{Prism}} = A_{\text{Base}} \times \text{height}$

$\text{height} = \dfrac{V_{\text{Prism}}}{A_{\text{Base}}}$

$= \dfrac{(600 - 50\pi)\ \text{cm}^3}{\left[\frac{1}{2}(10)(10) + (10)(10) - \frac{1}{2}\pi(5)^2\right]\ \text{cm}^2}$

$= \dfrac{(600 - 50\pi)\ \text{cm}^3}{\left(150 - \frac{25}{2}\pi\right)\ \text{cm}^2} = \mathbf{4\ cm}$

27. Write the equation of the given line in slope-intercept form.

$-5y = -3x + 2$

$y = \dfrac{3}{5}x - \dfrac{2}{5}$

Since the slopes of perpendicular lines are negative reciprocals of each other,

$m_\perp = -\dfrac{5}{3}$

$y = -\dfrac{5}{3}x + b$

$5 = -\dfrac{5}{3}(-2) + b$

$\dfrac{5}{3} = b$

$y = -\dfrac{5}{3}x + \dfrac{5}{3}$

28.

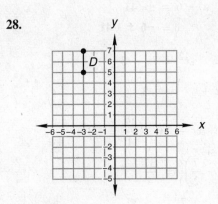

$D^2 = 2^2 + 0^2$

$D^2 = 4$

$D = \sqrt{4} = \mathbf{2}$

29. $-2(x^0 - x - 3) - |-2^0 - 3| = x - 2(-2 - 4)$

$-2(-x - 2) - 4 = x + 4 + 8$

$2x + 4 - 4 = x + 12$

$x = \mathbf{12}$

30. $\dfrac{x^2 y^{-2}}{z^2 p^0}\left(\dfrac{4p^0 x^{-5} z^2}{y^{-2}} - \dfrac{3x^{-4} y^2}{z^{-2} p}\right)$

$= \mathbf{4x^{-3} - 3x^{-2}p^{-1}}$

PRACTICE SET 51

a. $2ii - 7iii + 2i - 4 - \sqrt{-3}$

$= 2(ii) - 7i(ii) + 2i - 4 - \sqrt{-3}$

$= 2(-1) - 7i(-1) + 2i - 4 - \sqrt{-3}$

$= -2 + 7i + 2i - 4 - \sqrt{3}i$

$= \mathbf{-6 + (9 - \sqrt{3})i}$

b. $3i^3 + 5i^2 + 5i + 7 + 2i^5$

$= 3i(ii) + 5(ii) + 5i + 7 + 2i(ii)(ii)$

$= 3i(-1) + 5(-1) + 5i + 7 + 2i(-1)(-1)$

$= -3i - 5 + 5i + 7 + 2i = \mathbf{2 + 4i}$

PROBLEM SET 51

1. $\dfrac{3}{17} \times K = 72$

$$K = 72 \times \dfrac{17}{3} = \textbf{408 knights}$$

2. $\dfrac{22}{100} \times S = 528$

$$S = 528 \times \dfrac{100}{22} = \textbf{2400 students}$$

3.
Sodium: $2 \times 23 = 46$
Sulfur: $1 \times 32 = 32$
Oxygen: $4 \times 16 = 64$
Total: $46 + 32 + 64 = 142$

$$\dfrac{46}{142} = \dfrac{115}{Na_2SO_4}$$

$$46Na_2SO_4 = 115(142)$$

$$Na_2SO_4 = \textbf{355 grams}$$

4. (a) $10N_D + 25N_Q = 650$

(b) $N_D + N_Q = 35$

Substitute $N_Q = 35 - N_D$ into (a) and get:

(a') $10N_D + 25(35 - N_D) = 650$

$$-15N_D = -225$$

$$N_D = \textbf{15 dimes}$$

(b) $N_Q = 35 - (15) = \textbf{20 quarters}$

5.

$R_B T_B = R_J T_J;\ R_B = 40;\ R_J = 50;\ T_B = T_J + 2$

$$40(T_J + 2) = 50T_J$$

$$80 = 10T_J$$

$$8 = T_J$$

$$D_J = D_B = 50(8) = \textbf{400 miles}$$

6. $5 + 6i - 3i - 2 = \textbf{3 + 3i}$

7. $5ii - 8iii + 2i - 4 - \sqrt{-5}$

$= 5(ii) - 8(ii)i + 2i - 4 - \sqrt{5}i$

$= 5(-1) - 8(-1)i + 2i - 4 - \sqrt{5}i$

$= -5 + 8i + 2i - 4 - \sqrt{5}i$

$= \textbf{-9} + \textbf{(10} - \sqrt{\textbf{5}}\,\textbf{)}\textbf{\textit{i}}$

8. $5i^3 + 3i^2 + 7ii + 4 + 2i^7$

$= 5(ii)i + 3(ii) + 7(ii) + 4 + 2(ii)(ii)(ii)i$

$= 5(-1)i + 3(-1) + 7(-1) + 4 + 2(-1)(-1)(-1)i$

$= -5i - 3 - 7 + 4 - 2i$

$= \textbf{-6} - \textbf{7i}$

9. $-3i^2 - 2i + i^3 - 3 = -3(ii) - 2i + i(ii) - 3$

$= -3(-1) - 2i + i(-1) - 3 = 3 - 2i - i - 3$

$= \textbf{-3i}$

10.
$$x^2 = -x + 1$$

$$\left(x^2 + x + \phantom{\dfrac{1}{4}}\right) = 1$$

$$\left(x^2 + x + \dfrac{1}{4}\right) = 1 + \dfrac{1}{4}$$

$$\left(x + \dfrac{1}{2}\right)^2 = \dfrac{5}{4}$$

$$x + \dfrac{1}{2} = \pm\dfrac{\sqrt{5}}{2}$$

$$x = -\dfrac{\textbf{1}}{\textbf{2}} \pm \dfrac{\sqrt{\textbf{5}}}{\textbf{2}}$$

11.
$$-4 = -x^2 - 3x$$

$$\left(x^2 + 3x + \phantom{\dfrac{9}{4}}\right) = 4$$

$$\left(x^2 + 3x + \dfrac{9}{4}\right) = 4 + \dfrac{9}{4}$$

$$\left(x + \dfrac{3}{2}\right)^2 = \dfrac{25}{4}$$

$$x + \dfrac{3}{2} = \pm\dfrac{5}{2}$$

$$x = -\dfrac{3}{2} \pm \dfrac{5}{2}$$

$$x = \textbf{1, -4}$$

12. $y = -4x + b$

Use the point $(2, 2)$ for x and y.

$2 = -4(2) + b$

$10 = b$

$$\textbf{\textit{y}} = \textbf{-4\textit{x}} + \textbf{10}$$

13. $\cos 30° = \dfrac{2}{m}$

$$m = \dfrac{2}{\cos 30°} \approx \textbf{2.31}$$

14. $\sqrt{x-3}+5=2$

$\quad\quad\sqrt{x-3}=-3$

$\quad\quad\quad x-3=9$

$\quad\quad\quad\quad\quad x=12$

Check: $\sqrt{12-3}+5=2$

$\quad\quad\quad\quad\quad\quad 8=2$

The statement is not true, so no real number solution exists.

15. $\dfrac{20\text{ in.}}{\text{hr}}\times\dfrac{1\text{ ft}}{12\text{ in.}}\times\dfrac{1\text{ mi}}{5280\text{ ft}}\times\dfrac{1\text{ hr}}{60\text{ min}}$

$=\dfrac{20}{(12)(5280)(60)}\ \dfrac{\textbf{mi}}{\textbf{min}}$

16. $\sqrt[5]{3\sqrt{3}}=\left[3(3^{1/2})\right]^{1/5}=3^{1/5}3^{1/10}=\mathbf{3^{3/10}}$

17. $\sqrt{9\sqrt[3]{3}}=\sqrt{3^2\sqrt[3]{3}}=\left[3^2(3^{1/3})\right]^{1/2}$

$=3\cdot3^{1/6}=\mathbf{3^{7/6}}$

18. $\sqrt{x^2y^2m}\sqrt[4]{xym^2}=(x^2y^2m)^{1/2}(xym^2)^{1/4}$

$=xym^{1/2}x^{1/4}y^{1/4}m^{1/2}=\mathbf{x^{5/4}y^{5/4}m}$

19. $3\sqrt{\dfrac{2}{13}}+3\sqrt{\dfrac{13}{2}}+3\sqrt{104}$

$=\dfrac{3\sqrt{2}}{\sqrt{13}}\dfrac{\sqrt{13}}{\sqrt{13}}+\dfrac{3\sqrt{13}}{\sqrt{2}}\dfrac{\sqrt{2}}{\sqrt{2}}+6\sqrt{26}$

$=\dfrac{6\sqrt{26}}{26}+\dfrac{39\sqrt{26}}{26}+\dfrac{156\sqrt{26}}{26}=\mathbf{\dfrac{201\sqrt{26}}{26}}$

20. $(-27)^{-5/3}=\dfrac{1}{(-27)^{5/3}}=\dfrac{1}{((-27)^{1/3})^5}=\mathbf{-\dfrac{1}{243}}$

21. $\dfrac{(4{,}941{,}625)(7{,}041{,}683)}{0.00007142\times10^{-5}}$

$\approx\dfrac{(5\times10^6)(7\times10^6)}{7\times10^{-10}}=\mathbf{5\times10^{22}}$

22. $\dfrac{x}{p}-c=\dfrac{k}{m}$

$mx-cmp=kp$

$\quad\quad mx=kp+cmp$

$\dfrac{\textbf{\textit{mx}}}{\textbf{\textit{k}}+\textbf{\textit{cm}}}=\textbf{\textit{p}}$

23. $\dfrac{3}{p}-\dfrac{x}{R_1}=\dfrac{1}{R_2}$

$3R_1R_2-xpR_2=pR_1$

$R_2=\mathbf{\dfrac{pR_1}{3R_1-xp}}$

24. $x=\dfrac{50}{2}=\mathbf{25}$

$y=180-120-25=\mathbf{35}$

$m=x=\mathbf{25}$

$z=y=\mathbf{35}$

25. Write the equation of the given line in slope-intercept form.

$y=-\dfrac{3}{2}x+\dfrac{5}{2}$

Since the slopes of perpendicular lines are negative reciprocals of each other,

$m_\perp=\dfrac{2}{3}$

$y=\dfrac{2}{3}x+b$

$-2=\dfrac{2}{3}(-4)+b$

$\dfrac{2}{3}=b$

$y=\mathbf{\dfrac{2}{3}x+\dfrac{2}{3}}$

26.

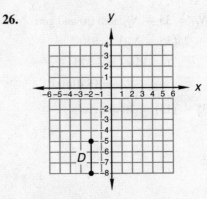

$D^2=3^2+0^2$

$D^2=9$

$D=\sqrt{9}=\mathbf{3}$

27. $\dfrac{x^{-2}y}{p^0}\left(\dfrac{4p^2}{x^{-2}y}-\dfrac{2px^2y}{y^2}\right)=\mathbf{4p^2-2p}$

28.
$$x+2\ \overline{)\ 2x^3+0x^2-2x+4}$$

quotient: $\mathbf{2x^2-4x+6-\dfrac{8}{x+2}}$

$\quad\underline{2x^3+4x^2}$

$\quad\quad -4x^2-2x$

$\quad\quad \underline{-4x^2-8x}$

$\quad\quad\quad\quad 6x+4$

$\quad\quad\quad\quad \underline{6x+12}$

$\quad\quad\quad\quad\quad\quad -8$

29. $\dfrac{-x-2}{4} - \dfrac{x+2}{3} = 3$

$-3x - 6 - 4x - 8 = 36$

$-7x = 50$

$x = -\dfrac{50}{7}$

30. $-2(x^0 - x - 2) - |-2| + 30(-x - x^0) = -x$

$-2(-x - 1) - 2 + 30(-x - 1) = -x$

$2x + 2 - 2 - 30x - 30 = -x$

$-27x = 30$

$x = -\dfrac{10}{9}$

PRACTICE SET 52

$P_N + D_N = 1600 \longrightarrow P_N = 1600 - D_N$

$0.75(P_N) + 0.95(D_N) = 0.85(1600)$

$0.75(1600 - D_N) + 0.95D_N = 1360$

$1200 - 0.75D_N + 0.95D_N = 1360$

$0.2D_N = 160$

$D_N = 800 \text{ mL}$

$P_N = 1600 - 800 = 800 \text{ mL}$

800 mL 25%, 800 mL 5%

PROBLEM SET 52

1. Iodine P_N + Iodine D_N = Iodine Total

$0.1(P_N) + 0.4(D_N) = 0.25(100)$

(a) $0.1P_N + 0.4D_N = 25$

(b) $P_N + D_N = 100$

Substitute $D_N = 100 - P_N$ into (a) and get:

(a′) $0.1P_N + 0.4(100 - P_N) = 25$

$-0.3P_N = -15$

$P_N = 50$

(b) $(50) + D_N = 100$

$D_N = 50$

50 mL 10%, 50 mL 40%

2. Salt P_N + Salt D_N = Salt Total

$0.25(P_N) + 0.05(D_N) = 0.1(1400)$

(a) $0.25P_N + 0.05D_N = 140$

(b) $P_N + D_N = 1400$

Substitute $D_N = 1400 - P_N$ into (a) and get:

(a′) $0.25P_N + 0.05(1400 - P_N) = 140$

$0.2P_N = 70$

$P_N = 350$

(b) $(350) + D_N = 1400$

$D_N = 1050$

350 mL 25%, 1050 mL 5%

3. Sodium: $\quad 2 \times 23 = 46$

Sulfur: $\quad 2 \times 32 = 64$

Oxygen: $\quad 3 \times 16 = 48$

Total: $\quad 46 + 64 + 48 = 158$

$\dfrac{46}{158} = \dfrac{\text{Na}}{1580}$

$158\text{Na} = 46(1580)$

$\text{Na} = \textbf{460 grams}$

4. (a) $4N_Y = 76 - 6N_R$

(b) $N_Y = N_R + 4$

Substitute (b) into (a) and get:

(a′) $4(N_R + 4) = 76 - 6N_R$

$10N_R = 60$

$N_R = \textbf{6 reds}$

(b) $N_Y = (6) + 4 = \textbf{10 yellows}$

5.

$$\overset{D_L \qquad D_C}{\underset{28}{\vdash\!\!\longrightarrow\!\!\longrightarrow\!\!\dashv}}$$

$R_L T_L + R_C T_C = 28; \ R_L = 2;$

$R_C = 8; \ T_L + T_C = 8$

$2T_L + 8(8 - T_L) = 28$

$-6T_L = -36$

$T_L = 6$

$T_C = 8 - (6) = 2$

$D_L = 2(6) = \textbf{12 kilometers}$

$D_C = 8(2) = \textbf{16 kilometers}$

6. $4i^2 - 3i + 2 = 4(ii) - 3i + 2$

$= 4(-1) - 3i + 2 = -4 - 3i + 2 = \textbf{-2 - 3i}$

7. $3i^5 - i + 5 - \sqrt{-9} = 3i(ii)(ii) - i + 5 - 3i$

$= 3i - i + 5 - 3i = \textbf{5 - i}$

8. $\sqrt{-16} - 2i^2 - 2i = 4i - 2(ii) - 2i$

$= 4i + 2 - 2i = \textbf{2 + 2i}$

9. $2i^4 + \sqrt{-9} - 3i^3 = 2(ii)(ii) + 3i - 3i(ii)$

$= 2 + 3i + 3i = \mathbf{2 + 6i}$

10.

$2x + 5 = x^2$

$(x^2 - 2x + \quad) = 5$

$x^2 - 2x + 1 = 5 + 1$

$(x - 1)^2 = 6$

$x - 1 = \pm\sqrt{6}$

$x = \mathbf{1 \pm \sqrt{6}}$

11.

$x^2 - 5x = 2$

$x^2 - 5x + \dfrac{25}{4} = 2 + \dfrac{25}{4}$

$\left(x - \dfrac{5}{2}\right)^2 = \dfrac{33}{4}$

$x - \dfrac{5}{2} = \pm\dfrac{\sqrt{33}}{2}$

$x = \mathbf{\dfrac{5}{2} \pm \dfrac{\sqrt{33}}{2}}$

12. $y = 2x + b$

Use the point $(4, 0)$ for x and y.

$0 = 2(4) + b$

$-8 = b$

$\mathbf{y = 2x - 8}$

13. $B = 180 - 165 = 15$

$\sin 15° = \dfrac{7}{P}$

$P = \dfrac{7}{\sin 15°} \approx \mathbf{27.05}$

14. $\sqrt{x^2 + 2x + 10} = x + 2$

$x^2 + 2x + 10 = x^2 + 4x + 4$

$2x = 6$

$x = \mathbf{3}$

Check: $\sqrt{9 + 6 + 10} = 5$

$5 = 5$

15.

$3 = -5 + \sqrt{x - 3}$

$8 = \sqrt{x - 3}$

$64 = x - 3$

$\mathbf{67} = x$

Check: $3 = -5 + \sqrt{67 - 3}$

$3 = -5 + 8$

16. $\dfrac{200 \text{ in.}}{\text{hr}} \times \dfrac{1 \text{ ft}}{12 \text{ in.}} \times \dfrac{1 \text{ mi}}{5280 \text{ ft}} \times \dfrac{1 \text{ hr}}{60 \text{ min}}$

$= \dfrac{\mathbf{200}}{\mathbf{(12)(5280)(60)}} \dfrac{\mathbf{mi}}{\mathbf{min}}$

17. $2\sqrt{2\sqrt[4]{2}} = 2[2(2^{1/4})]^{1/2} = 2 \cdot 2^{1/2} \cdot 2^{1/8}$

$= \mathbf{2^{13/8}}$

18. $3\sqrt{9\sqrt[4]{3}} = 3\sqrt{3^2\sqrt[4]{3}} = 3[3^2(3^{1/4})]^{1/2}$

$= 3 \cdot 3 \cdot 3^{1/8} = \mathbf{3^{17/8}}$

19. $\sqrt{4x^3y^5}\sqrt[3]{8xy^2} = (2^2x^3y^5)^{1/2}(2^3xy^2)^{1/3}$

$= 2x^{3/2}y^{5/2}2x^{1/3}y^{2/3} = \mathbf{4x^{11/6}y^{19/6}}$

20. $3\sqrt{\dfrac{2}{13}} - 5\sqrt{\dfrac{13}{2}} + \sqrt{104}$

$= \dfrac{3\sqrt{2}}{\sqrt{13}}\dfrac{\sqrt{13}}{\sqrt{13}} - \dfrac{5\sqrt{13}}{\sqrt{2}}\dfrac{\sqrt{2}}{\sqrt{2}} + 2\sqrt{26}$

$= \dfrac{6\sqrt{26}}{26} - \dfrac{65\sqrt{26}}{26} + \dfrac{52\sqrt{26}}{26} = \mathbf{-\dfrac{7\sqrt{26}}{26}}$

21. $\dfrac{(987,612 \times 10^5)(413,280)}{(74,630)(400)}$

$\approx \dfrac{(1 \times 10^{11})(4 \times 10^5)}{(7 \times 10^4)(4 \times 10^2)} \approx \mathbf{1 \times 10^9}$

22.

$\dfrac{x}{p} - c + \dfrac{a}{b} = m$

$bx - bcp + ap = bmp$

$bx = bmp + bcp - ap$

$x = \mathbf{\dfrac{bmp + bcp - ap}{b}}$

23. $\dfrac{x^2 + 3x - 28}{21x + 10x^2 + x^3} = \dfrac{(x + 7)(x - 4)}{x(x + 7)(x + 3)}$

$= \mathbf{\dfrac{x - 4}{x(x + 3)}}$

24. $-16^{5/4} = -(16^{1/4})^5 = \mathbf{-32}$

25. $\dfrac{\dfrac{x^2y}{p^2} - p}{\dfrac{m}{p} - \dfrac{1}{p^2}} = \dfrac{\dfrac{x^2y - p^3}{p^2}}{\dfrac{mp - 1}{p^2}} \cdot \dfrac{\dfrac{p^2}{mp - 1}}{\dfrac{p^2}{mp - 1}}$

$= \mathbf{\dfrac{x^2y - p^3}{mp - 1}}$

26. $z = \dfrac{60}{2} = 30$

$p = z = \mathbf{30}$

$x = 180 - 100 - 30 = \mathbf{50}$

$y = x = \mathbf{50}$

27. $-\dfrac{3}{x-3} + \dfrac{2x+4}{x^2-9}$

$= \dfrac{-3(x+3)}{x^2-9} + \dfrac{2x+4}{x^2-9}$

$= \dfrac{-3x-9+2x+4}{x^2-9} = \dfrac{\mathbf{-x-5}}{\mathbf{x^2-9}}$

28. Write the equation of the given line in slope-intercept form.

$y = -\dfrac{2}{3}x + \dfrac{4}{3}$

Since parallel lines have the same slope,

$y = -\dfrac{2}{3}x + b$

$-7 = -\dfrac{2}{3}(-2) + b$

$-\dfrac{25}{3} = b$

$y = -\dfrac{2}{3}x - \dfrac{25}{3}$

29.

$$x-4 \,\overline{\smash{\big)}\, 3x^3 + 0x^2 - x + 0} \quad \dfrac{3x^2 + 12x + 47 + \frac{188}{x-4}}{}$$

$\underline{3x^3 - 12x^2}$

$\quad\;\; 12x^2 - x$

$\quad\;\; \underline{12x^2 - 48x}$

$\qquad\qquad 47x + 0$

$\qquad\qquad \underline{47x - 188}$

$\qquad\qquad\qquad\;\; 188$

30. $\dfrac{3x+4}{2} - \dfrac{2x-5}{3} = 4$

$9x + 12 - 4x + 10 = 24$

$5x = 2$

$x = \dfrac{2}{5}$

PRACTICE SET 53

a. Carbon (C): $1 \times 12 = 12$

Chloride (Cl): $4 \times 35 = 140$

Total: $12 + 140 = 152$

Carbon: $\dfrac{12}{152} \times 100\% \approx \mathbf{7.89\%}$

b. $0.073 \text{ km}^2 \times \dfrac{1000 \text{ m}}{1 \text{ km}} \times \dfrac{1000 \text{ m}}{1 \text{ km}} \times \dfrac{100 \text{ cm}}{1 \text{ m}}$

$\times \dfrac{100 \text{ cm}}{1 \text{ m}} \times \dfrac{1 \text{ in.}}{2.54 \text{ cm}} \times \dfrac{1 \text{ in.}}{2.54 \text{ cm}} \times \dfrac{1 \text{ ft}}{12 \text{ in.}}$

$\times \dfrac{1 \text{ ft}}{12 \text{ in.}} \times \dfrac{1 \text{ mi}}{5280 \text{ ft}} \times \dfrac{1 \text{ mi}}{5280 \text{ ft}}$

$= \dfrac{0.073(1000)(1000)(100)(100)}{(2.54)(2.54)(12)(12)(5280)(5280)} \text{ mi}^2$

PROBLEM SET 53

1. Sodium: $2 \times 23 = 46$

Sulfur: $2 \times 32 = 64$

Oxygen: $3 \times 16 = 48$

Total: $46 + 64 + 48 = 158$

Sodium: $\dfrac{46}{158} \times 100\% \approx \mathbf{29.11\%}$

2. Alcohol P_N + Alcohol D_N = Alcohol Total

$\quad 0.2P_N + 0.6D_N = 0.52(100)$

(a) $0.2P_N + 0.6D_N = 52$

(b) $P_N + D_N = 100$

Substitute $D_N = 100 - P_N$ into (a) and get:

(a′) $0.2P_N + 0.6(100 - P_N) = 52$

$\qquad\qquad\qquad -0.4P_N = -8$

$\qquad\qquad\qquad\quad P_N = 20$

(b) $(20) + D_N = 100$

$\qquad\quad D_N = 80$

20 mL 20%, 80 mL 60%

3. Iodine P_N + Iodine D_N = Iodine Total

$\quad 0.4(P_N) + 0.8(D_N) = 0.72(250)$

(a) $0.4P_N + 0.8D_N = 180$

(b) $P_N + D_N = 250$

Substitute $D_N = 250 - P_N$ into (a) and get:

(a′) $0.4P_N + 0.8(250 - P_N) = 180$

$\qquad\qquad\qquad -0.4P_N = -20$

$\qquad\qquad\qquad\quad P_N = 50$

(b) $(50) + D_N = 250$

$\qquad\quad D_N = 200$

50 mL 40%, 200 mL 80%

4. (a) $N_G + N_B = 80$

(b) $N_G = 5N_B + 8$

Substitute (b) into (a) and get:

(a') $(5N_B + 8) + N_B = 80$

$$6N_B = 72$$

$$N_B = \textbf{12 results}$$

(b) $N_G = 5(12) + 8 = \textbf{68 results}$

5.

$R_M T_M + 200 = R_P T_P$; $R_M = 50$; $T_M = T_P = 4$

$$50(4) + 200 = 4R_P$$

$$400 = 4R_P$$

$$\textbf{100 mph} = R_P$$

6. $9350 \text{ cm} \times \dfrac{1 \text{ m}}{100 \text{ cm}} \times \dfrac{1 \text{ km}}{1000 \text{ m}}$

$= \dfrac{\textbf{9350}}{\textbf{(100)(1000)}} \textbf{ km}$

7. $32 \text{ m} \times \dfrac{100 \text{ cm}}{1 \text{ m}} \times \dfrac{1 \text{ in.}}{2.54 \text{ cm}} \times \dfrac{1 \text{ ft}}{12 \text{ in.}} \times \dfrac{1 \text{ yd}}{3 \text{ ft}}$

$= \dfrac{\textbf{32(100)}}{\textbf{(2.54)(12)(3)}} \textbf{ yd}$

8. $16{,}480{,}000 \text{ mi}^2 \times \dfrac{5280 \text{ ft.}}{1 \text{ mi}} \times \dfrac{5280 \text{ ft.}}{1 \text{ mi}} \times \dfrac{12 \text{ in}}{1 \text{ ft}}$

$\times \dfrac{12 \text{ in.}}{1 \text{ ft}} \times \dfrac{2.54 \text{ cm}}{1 \text{ in.}} \times \dfrac{2.54 \text{ cm}}{1 \text{ in.}}$

$= \textbf{16,480,000(5280)(5280)(12)(12)(2.54)(2.54) cm}^2$

9. $0.063 \text{ km}^2 \times \dfrac{1000 \text{ m}}{1 \text{ km}} \times \dfrac{1000 \text{ m}}{1 \text{ km}} \times \dfrac{100 \text{ cm}}{1 \text{ m}}$

$\times \dfrac{100 \text{ cm}}{1 \text{ m}} \times \dfrac{1 \text{ in.}}{2.54 \text{ cm}} \times \dfrac{1 \text{ in.}}{2.54 \text{ cm}} \times \dfrac{1 \text{ ft}}{12 \text{ in.}}$

$\times \dfrac{1 \text{ ft}}{12 \text{ in.}} \times \dfrac{1 \text{ mi}}{5280 \text{ ft}} \times \dfrac{1 \text{ mi}}{5280 \text{ ft}}$

$= \dfrac{\textbf{0.063(1000)(1000)(100)(100)}}{\textbf{(2.54)(2.54)(12)(12)(5280)(5280)}} \textbf{ mi}^2$

10. $-\sqrt{-4} + 2 + 2i^5 = -2i + 2 + 2i(ii)(ii)$

$= -2i + 2 + 2i = \textbf{2}$

11. $2i^2 + 5i + 4 + \sqrt{-9} = 2(ii) + 5i + 4 + 3i$

$= \textbf{2 + 8}\boldsymbol{i}$

12. $-4i^5 + 2\sqrt{-16} = -4i(ii)(ii) + 2(4i)$

$= -4i + 8i = \textbf{4}\boldsymbol{i}$

13. $2i^3 - i^4 + 3i^2 = 2i(ii) - (ii)(ii) + 3(ii)$

$= -2i - 1 - 3 = \textbf{-4 - 2}\boldsymbol{i}$

14. $$x^2 - 5 = 5x$$

$$\left(x^2 - 5x + \quad\right) = 5$$

$$x^2 - 5x + \frac{25}{4} = 5 + \frac{25}{4}$$

$$\left(x - \frac{5}{2}\right)^2 = \frac{45}{4}$$

$$x - \frac{5}{2} = \pm\frac{3\sqrt{5}}{2}$$

$$x = \boldsymbol{\frac{5}{2} \pm \frac{3\sqrt{5}}{2}}$$

15. $$-x^2 = -6x - 6$$

$$(x^2 - 6x + \quad) = 6$$

$$x^2 - 6x + 9 = 6 + 9$$

$$(x - 3)^2 = 15$$

$$x - 3 = \pm\sqrt{15}$$

$$x = \boldsymbol{3 \pm \sqrt{15}}$$

16. $A = 180 - 120 = 60$

$$\cos 60° = \frac{10}{m}$$

$$m = \frac{10}{\cos 60°} = \textbf{20}$$

17. $$\sqrt{x - 11} - 1 = 16$$

$$\sqrt{x - 11} = 17$$

$$x - 11 = 289$$

$$x = \textbf{300}$$

Check: $\sqrt{300 - 11} - 1 = 16$

$$17 - 1 = 16$$

18. $$\sqrt{x^2 + 2x + 5} - 3 = x$$

$$x^2 + 2x + 5 = x^2 + 6x + 9$$

$$-4x = 4$$

$$x = \textbf{-1}$$

Check: $\sqrt{1 - 2 + 5} - 3 = -1$

$$2 - 3 = -1$$

19. $\sqrt[5]{2\sqrt[3]{2}} = \left[2(2^{1/3})\right]^{1/5} = 2^{1/5}2^{1/15} = \textbf{2}^{\textbf{4/15}}$

Problem Set 53

20. $\sqrt{81\sqrt[4]{3}} = \sqrt{3^4\sqrt[4]{3}} = \left[3^4(3^{1/4})\right]^{1/2}$
$= 3^2 3^{1/8} = \mathbf{3^{17/8}}$

21. $\sqrt[5]{x^2 y}\sqrt[3]{xy^2} = (x^2 y)^{1/5}(xy^2)^{1/3}$
$= x^{2/5}y^{1/5}x^{1/3}y^{2/3} = \mathbf{x^{11/15}y^{13/15}}$

22. $-4^{-5/2} = -\dfrac{1}{(4^{1/2})^5} = -\dfrac{\mathbf{1}}{\mathbf{32}}$

23. $3\sqrt{\dfrac{2}{9}} - 2\sqrt{\dfrac{9}{2}} - 2\sqrt{50}$

$= \dfrac{3\sqrt{2}}{\sqrt{9}}\dfrac{\sqrt{9}}{\sqrt{9}} - \dfrac{2\sqrt{9}}{\sqrt{2}}\dfrac{\sqrt{2}}{\sqrt{2}} - 10\sqrt{2}$

$= \sqrt{2} - 3\sqrt{2} - 10\sqrt{2} = \mathbf{-12\sqrt{2}}$

24. $\dfrac{(2{,}135{,}820)(4{,}913{,}562)}{801{,}394{,}026}$

$\approx \dfrac{(2 \times 10^6)(5 \times 10^6)}{8 \times 10^8} \approx \mathbf{1 \times 10^4}$

25. $\dfrac{x}{y} - \dfrac{m}{p} + \dfrac{k}{c} = 0$

$cpx - cmy + kpy = 0$

$cpx + kpy = cmy$

$p = \dfrac{\mathbf{cmy}}{\mathbf{cx + ky}}$

26. $\dfrac{p}{x} + c = d$

$p + cx = dx$

$p = dx - cx$

$\dfrac{\mathbf{p}}{\mathbf{d - c}} = x$

27. $5 \times \overline{SF} = 10$

$\overline{SF} = 2$

$C \times 2 = 12$

$C = 6$

$A^2 = 5^2 + 6^2$

$A^2 = 25 + 36$

$A = \sqrt{61}$

$\sqrt{61} \times 2 = \sqrt{61} + B$

$2\sqrt{61} = \sqrt{61} + B$

$\sqrt{61} = B$

28. $y = \dfrac{80}{2} = \mathbf{40}$

$x = 180 - 90 - 40 = \mathbf{50}$

$P = y = \mathbf{40}$

$Q = x = \mathbf{50}$

$R = 2(50) = \mathbf{100}$

29.
$$
\begin{array}{r}
x^2 - x - 1 + \frac{3}{x+1} \\
x+1\overline{)x^3 + 0x^2 - 2x + 2} \\
\underline{x^3 + x^2} \\
-x^2 - 2x \\
\underline{-x^2 - x} \\
-x + 2 \\
\underline{-x - 1} \\
3
\end{array}
$$

30. (a) $2x - 3y = -9$

$-3y = -2x - 9$

$y = \dfrac{2}{3}x + 3$

(b) $5x + 3y = 3$

$3y = -5x + 3$

$y = -\dfrac{5}{3}x + 1$

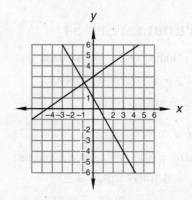

Solve the equations by elimination:

(a) $2x - 3y = -9$
(b) $\dfrac{5x + 3y = 3}{7x = -6}$

$x = -\dfrac{6}{7}$

(a) $y = \dfrac{2}{3}\left(-\dfrac{6}{7}\right) + 3 = \dfrac{17}{7}$

$\left(-\dfrac{\mathbf{6}}{\mathbf{7}}, \dfrac{\mathbf{17}}{\mathbf{7}}\right)$

PRACTICE SET 54

a.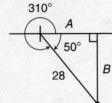

$$\sin 50° = \frac{B}{28}$$

$$28 \sin 50° = B$$

$$21.45 \approx B$$

$$\cos 50° = \frac{A}{28}$$

$$28 \cos 50° = A$$

$$18.00 \approx A$$

18.00R − 21.45U

b. $\dfrac{R}{S} = \dfrac{T}{V}$

$$RV = ST$$

$$R = \frac{ST}{V}$$

PROBLEM SET 54

1. Iodine P_N + Iodine D_N = Iodine Total

$$0.2P_N + 0.7D_N = 0.575(400)$$

(a) $0.2P_N + 0.7D_N = 230$

(b) $P_N + D_N = 400$

Substitute $D_N = 400 − P_N$ into (a) and get:

(a′) $0.2P_N + 0.7(400 − P_N) = 230$

$$-0.5P_N = -50$$

$$P_N = 100$$

(b) $(100) + D_N = 400$

$$D_N = 300$$

100 liters 20%, 300 liters 70%

2. Glycerine P_N + Glycerine D_N = Glycerine Total

$$0.1(P_N) + 0.4(D_N) = 0.3(150)$$

(a) $0.1P_N + 0.4D_N = 45$

(b) $P_N + D_N = 150$

Substitute $D_N = 150 − P_N$ into (a) and get:

(a′) $0.1P_N + 0.4(150 − P_N) = 45$

$$-0.3P_N = -15$$

$$P_N = 50$$

(b) $(50) + D_N = 150$

$$D_N = 100$$

50 mL 10%, 100 mL 40%

3. Potassium: $1 \times 39 = 39$
   Chlorine: $1 \times 35 = 35$
   Oxygen: $3 \times 16 = 48$
   Total: $39 + 35 + 48 = 122$

Potassium: $\dfrac{39}{122} \times 100\% \approx \mathbf{31.97\%}$

4. (a) $\dfrac{N_D}{N_G} = \dfrac{5}{4} \longrightarrow 4N_D = 5N_G$

(b) $4N_D = 3N_G + 40$

-1(a) $\quad -4N_D + 5N_G = 0$

(b) $\quad \underline{4N_D - 3N_G = 40}$

$$2N_G = 40$$

$$N_G = \mathbf{20 \ geese}$$

(b) $4N_D = 3(20) + 40$

$$N_D = \mathbf{25 \ ducks}$$

5.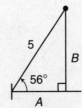

$$R_C T_C = R_T T_T; \ R_C = 2R_T$$

$$T_C = T_T - 3; \ R_T = 50$$

$$100(T_T - 3) = 50T_T$$

$$50T_T = 300$$

$$T_T = 6$$

$$D_T = D_C = 50(6) = \mathbf{300 \ miles}$$

6.

$A = 5 \cos 56° \approx 2.80$

$B = 5 \sin 56° \approx 4.15$

2.80R + 4.15U

7.

$A = 8 \cos 32° \approx 6.78$

$B = 8 \sin 32° \approx 4.24$

$-6.78R - 4.24U$

8. $\dfrac{T}{V} = \dfrac{R}{S} \longrightarrow ST = RV \longrightarrow T = \dfrac{RV}{S}$

9. $100 \text{ km}^2 \times \dfrac{1000 \text{ m}}{1 \text{ km}} \times \dfrac{1000 \text{ m}}{1 \text{ km}} \times \dfrac{100 \text{ cm}}{1 \text{ m}}$

$\times \dfrac{100 \text{ cm}}{1 \text{ m}} = \mathbf{100(1000)(1000)(100)(100) \text{ cm}^2}$

10. $100 \text{ ft}^2 \times \dfrac{12 \text{ in.}}{1 \text{ ft}} \times \dfrac{12 \text{ in.}}{1 \text{ ft}} \times \dfrac{2.54 \text{ cm}}{1 \text{ in.}}$

$\times \dfrac{2.54 \text{ cm}}{1 \text{ in.}} = \mathbf{100(12)(12)(2.54)(2.54) \text{ cm}^2}$

11. $\dfrac{60 \text{ mi}}{\text{hr}} \times \dfrac{5280 \text{ ft}}{1 \text{ mi}} \times \dfrac{12 \text{ in.}}{1 \text{ ft}} \times \dfrac{2.54 \text{ cm}}{1 \text{ in.}}$

$\times \dfrac{1 \text{ m}}{100 \text{ cm}} \times \dfrac{1 \text{ km}}{1000 \text{ m}} \times \dfrac{1 \text{ hr}}{60 \text{ min}} \times \dfrac{1 \text{ min}}{60 \text{ s}}$

$= \mathbf{\dfrac{60(5280)(12)(2.54)}{(100)(1000)(60)(60)} \dfrac{\text{km}}{\text{s}}}$

12. $-\sqrt{-4} - 2i^3 + 4i^4 = -2i - 2i(ii) + 4(ii)(ii)$

$= -2i + 2i + 4 = \mathbf{4}$

13. $3i^3 + 2i - 4i^2 + \sqrt{-9}$

$= 3i(ii) + 2i - 4(ii) + 3i$

$= -3i + 2i + 4 + 3i = \mathbf{4 + 2i}$

14. $-3i + 2i^2 - 2 + i = -3i + 2(ii) - 2 + i$

$= -3i - 2 - 2 + i = \mathbf{-4 - 2i}$

15. $2i^2 + 2i - 2\sqrt{-25} = 2(ii) + 2i - 10i$

$= \mathbf{-2 - 8i}$

16.
$$x^2 = 7 + 3x$$
$$\left(x^2 - 3x + \phantom{\dfrac{9}{4}}\right) = 7$$
$$x^2 - 3x + \dfrac{9}{4} = 7 + \dfrac{9}{4}$$
$$\left(x - \dfrac{3}{2}\right)^2 = \dfrac{37}{4}$$
$$x - \dfrac{3}{2} = \pm\dfrac{\sqrt{37}}{2}$$
$$x = \dfrac{3}{2} \pm \dfrac{\sqrt{37}}{2}$$

17.
$$-7x = -x^2 + 3$$
$$\left(x^2 - 7x + \phantom{\dfrac{49}{4}}\right) = 3$$
$$x^2 - 7x + \dfrac{49}{4} = 3 + \dfrac{49}{4}$$
$$\left(x - \dfrac{7}{2}\right)^2 = \dfrac{61}{4}$$
$$x - \dfrac{7}{2} = \pm\dfrac{\sqrt{61}}{2}$$
$$x = \dfrac{7}{2} \pm \dfrac{\sqrt{61}}{2}$$

18. $y = \dfrac{3}{2}x + b$

Use the point $(6, 0)$ for x and y.

$0 = \dfrac{3}{2}(6) + b$

$-9 = b$

$\mathbf{y = \dfrac{3}{2}x - 9}$

19. $\dfrac{4x - 2}{5} - \dfrac{x - 3}{2} = 7$

$8x - 4 - 5x + 15 = 70$

$3x = 59$

$x = \mathbf{\dfrac{59}{3}}$

20. $\sqrt{x^2 - x - 5} + 1 = x$

$x^2 - x - 5 = x^2 - 2x + 1$

$x = \mathbf{6}$

Check: $\sqrt{36 - 6 - 5} + 1 = 6$

$5 + 1 = 6$

21. $\sqrt{x - 2} - 11 = 1$

$x - 2 = 144$

$x = \mathbf{146}$

Check: $\sqrt{146 - 2} - 11 = 1$

$12 - 11 = 1$

22. $\dfrac{x}{k} - cm = \dfrac{p}{c}$

$cx - c^2km = kp$

$cx = kp + c^2km$

$\dfrac{cx}{p + c^2m} = k$

23.

$$\frac{a}{p} - x + \frac{c}{m} = y$$

$$am - mpx + cp = mpy$$

$$cp = mpy + mpx - am$$

$$\frac{cp}{py + px - a} = m$$

24. $\sqrt[3]{4\sqrt{2}} = \sqrt[3]{2^2\sqrt{2}} = \left[2^2(2^{1/2})\right]^{1/3}$

$= 2^{2/3}2^{1/6} = \mathbf{2^{5/6}}$

25. $\sqrt[5]{9\sqrt[3]{3}} = \sqrt[5]{3^2\sqrt[3]{3}} = \left[3^2(3^{1/3})\right]^{1/5}$

$= 3^{2/5}3^{1/15} = \mathbf{3^{7/15}}$

26. $\sqrt[6]{xy}\sqrt[3]{xy^2} = (xy)^{1/6}(xy^2)^{1/3}$

$= x^{1/6}y^{1/6}x^{1/3}y^{2/3} = \mathbf{x^{1/2}y^{5/6}}$

27. $-81^{1/4} = \mathbf{-3}$

28. $2\sqrt{\dfrac{3}{7}} - 5\sqrt{\dfrac{7}{3}} + 2\sqrt{84}$

$= \dfrac{2\sqrt{3}}{\sqrt{7}}\dfrac{\sqrt{7}}{\sqrt{7}} - \dfrac{5\sqrt{7}}{\sqrt{3}}\dfrac{\sqrt{3}}{\sqrt{3}} + 4\sqrt{21}$

$= \dfrac{6\sqrt{21}}{21} - \dfrac{35\sqrt{21}}{21} + \dfrac{84\sqrt{21}}{21} = \mathbf{\dfrac{55\sqrt{21}}{21}}$

29. $\dfrac{x^2p - \dfrac{x}{p^2}}{\dfrac{x^2y}{p^2} - x} = \dfrac{\dfrac{x^2p^3 - x}{p^2}}{\dfrac{x^2y - xp^2}{p^2}} \cdot \dfrac{\dfrac{p^2}{x^2y - xp^2}}{\dfrac{p^2}{x^2y - xp^2}}$

$= \dfrac{x^2p^3 - x}{x^2y - xp^2} = \mathbf{\dfrac{xp^3 - 1}{xy - p^2}}$

30. $\dfrac{4x^{-2}yp}{m^2y^{-1}}\left(\dfrac{p^{-1}m^2y}{16x^{-2}y} - \dfrac{2x^2y^0p}{m^{-2}}\right) = \mathbf{\dfrac{y^2}{4} - 8y^2p^2}$

PRACTICE SET 55

a.

$$\frac{m + s}{p} + \frac{a}{x} = t$$

$$\frac{(m + s)}{p}px + \frac{a}{x}px = tpx$$

$$xm + xs + pa = tpx$$

$$xm + xs = tpx - pa$$

$$\frac{x(m + s)}{tx - a} = p$$

b.

$$\frac{ay}{x} + \frac{c}{m + z} = s$$

$$\frac{ay}{x}x(m + z) + \frac{c}{(m + z)}x(m + z) = xs(m + z)$$

$$aym + ayz + cx = xsm + xsz$$

$$ayz + cx - xsz = xsm - aym$$

$$\frac{ayz + cx - xsz}{xs - ay} = m$$

c. Consecutive integers: $N,\ N + 1,\ N + 2$

$$N(N + 2) = 5 + 5(N + 1)$$

$$N^2 + 2N = 5 + 5N + 5$$

$$N^2 - 3N - 10 = 0$$

$$(N - 5)(N + 2) = 0$$

$$N = 5, -2$$

The desired integers are **5, 6, 7** and **-2, -1, 0.**

PROBLEM SET 55

1. Integers: $N,\ N + 1,\ N + 2$

$$N(N + 1) = -6(N + 2)$$

$$N^2 + N = -6N - 12$$

$$N^2 + 7N + 12 = 0$$

$$(N + 4)(N + 3) = 0$$

$$N = -4, -3$$

The desired integers are **-4, -3, -2** and **-3, -2, -1.**

2. Even integers: $N,\ N + 2,\ N + 4$

$$N(N + 4) = 9(N + 2) - 24$$

$$N^2 + 4N = 9N - 6$$

$$N^2 - 5N + 6 = 0$$

$$(N - 3)(N - 2) = 0$$

$$N = 3, 2$$

Since the problem asks only for even integers, the desired integers are **2, 4,** and **6.**

3. Bromide P_N + Bromide D_N = Bromide Total

$$0.05(P_N) + 0.4(D_N) = 0.12(60)$$

(a) $0.05P_N + 0.4D_N = 7.2$

(b) $P_N + D_N = 60$

Substitute $D_N = 60 - P_N$ into (a) and get:

(a′) $0.05P_N + 0.4(60 - P_N) = 7.2$

$$-0.35P_N = -16.8$$

$$P_N = 48$$

(b) $(48) + D_N = 60$

$$D_N = 12$$

48 mL 5%, 12 mL 40%

4. Carbon: $1 \times 12 = 12$

Chlorine: $4 \times 35 = 140$

Total: $12 + 140 = 152$

$$\frac{12}{152} = \frac{C}{1368}$$

$152C = 12(1368)$

$C = \textbf{108 grams}$

5. Multiples of 3: $3N, \ 3N + 3, \ 3N + 6$

$6(3N) = 4(3N + 6) + 48$

$18N = 12N + 72$

$6N = 72$

$N = 12$

The desired integers are **36, 39,** and **42.**

6. $$\frac{a + b}{x} + \frac{y}{m} = k$$

$ma + mb + xy = kmx$

$ma + mb = kmx - xy$

$$\boldsymbol{\frac{ma + mb}{km - y} = x}$$

7. $$\frac{mp}{c} + \frac{d + e}{x} = d$$

$mpx + cd + ce = cdx$

$ce = cdx - mpx - cd$

$$e = \boldsymbol{\frac{cdx - mpx - cd}{c}}$$

8. $$\frac{mx}{y} + \frac{d}{a + b} = p$$

$amx + bmx + dy = apy + bpy$

$amx + dy - apy = bpy - bmx$

$$\boldsymbol{\frac{amx + dy - apy}{py - mx} = b}$$

9.

$A = 40 \cos 35°$

$A \approx 32.77$

$B = 40 \sin 35°$

$B \approx 22.94$

$\boldsymbol{32.77R - 22.94U}$

10.

$A = 10 \cos 20°$

$A \approx 9.40$

$B = 10 \sin 20°$

$B \approx 3.42$

$\boldsymbol{-9.40R - 3.42U}$

11. $4 \text{ yd}^3 \times \dfrac{3 \text{ ft}}{1 \text{ yd}} \times \dfrac{3 \text{ ft}}{1 \text{ yd}} \times \dfrac{3 \text{ ft}}{1 \text{ yd}} \times \dfrac{12 \text{ in.}}{1 \text{ ft}}$

$\times \dfrac{12 \text{ in.}}{1 \text{ ft}} \times \dfrac{12 \text{ in.}}{1 \text{ ft}} \times \dfrac{2.54 \text{ cm}}{1 \text{ in.}} \times \dfrac{2.54 \text{ cm}}{1 \text{ in.}}$

$\times \dfrac{2.54 \text{ cm}}{1 \text{ in.}} \times \dfrac{1 \text{ m}}{100 \text{ cm}} \times \dfrac{1 \text{ m}}{100 \text{ cm}} \times \dfrac{1 \text{ m}}{100 \text{ cm}}$

$= \dfrac{4(3)(3)(3)(12)(12)(12)(2.54)(2.54)(2.54)}{(100)(100)(100)} \text{ m}^3$

12. $\dfrac{1000 \text{ ft}}{s} \times \dfrac{12 \text{ in.}}{1 \text{ ft}} \times \dfrac{2.54 \text{ cm}}{1 \text{ in.}} \times \dfrac{1 \text{ m}}{100 \text{ cm}}$

$\times \dfrac{1 \text{ km}}{1000 \text{ m}} \times \dfrac{60 \text{ s}}{1 \text{ min}}$

$= \dfrac{1000(12)(2.54)(600)}{(100)(1000)} \dfrac{\text{km}}{\text{min}}$

13. $4i^5 - 2\sqrt{-9} - 2i^4 = 4i(ii)(ii) - 6i - 2(ii)(ii)$

$= 4i - 6i - 2 = \boldsymbol{-2 - 2i}$

14. $4 + 2i^2 + 3i - \sqrt{-4} = 4 + 2(ii) + 3i - 2i$

$= 4 - 2 + 3i - 2i = \boldsymbol{2 + i}$

15. $2i^3 + 2i^4 + 2 - 2i = 2i(ii) + 2(ii)(ii) + 2 - 2i$

$= -2i + 2 + 2 - 2i = \boldsymbol{4 - 4i}$

16. $-3i^6 - 2i - 2 - 2i^2$

$= -3(ii)(ii)(ii) - 2i - 2 - 2(ii)$

$= 3 - 2i - 2 + 2 = \boldsymbol{3 - 2i}$

17. $$x^2 = 5x + 5$$

$$\left(x^2 - 5x + \right) = 5$$

$$x^2 - 5x + \frac{25}{4} = 5 + \frac{25}{4}$$

$$\left(x - \frac{5}{2}\right)^2 = \frac{45}{4}$$

$$x - \frac{5}{2} = \pm\frac{3\sqrt{5}}{2}$$

$$x = \frac{5}{2} \pm \frac{3\sqrt{5}}{2}$$

18.
$$x^2 - 6 = 6x$$
$$(x^2 - 6x + \quad) = 6$$
$$x^2 - 6x + 9 = 6 + 9$$
$$(x - 3)^2 = 15$$
$$x - 3 = \pm\sqrt{15}$$
$$x = \mathbf{3 \pm \sqrt{15}}$$

19.
$$\sqrt{x - 2} + 4 = 2$$
$$x - 2 = 4$$
$$x = 6$$
Check: $\sqrt{6 - 2} + 4 = 2$
$$2 + 4 = 2$$

The statement is not true, so no real number solution exists.

20.
$$\sqrt{x^2 - 2x + 14} - 12 = x$$
$$x^2 - 2x + 14 = x^2 + 24x + 144$$
$$-26x = 130$$
$$x = -5$$
Check: $\sqrt{25 + 10 + 14} - 12 = -5$
$$7 - 12 = -5$$

21. $\sqrt{16\sqrt{2}} = \sqrt{2^4\sqrt{2}} = \left[2^4(2^{1/2})\right]^{1/2}$
$$= 2^2 2^{1/4} = \mathbf{2^{9/4}}$$

22. $\sqrt[4]{27\sqrt[3]{3}} = \sqrt[4]{3^3\sqrt[3]{3}} = \left[3^3(3^{1/3})\right]^{1/4}$
$$= 3^{3/4}3^{1/12} = \mathbf{3^{5/6}}$$

23. $\sqrt[4]{x^2 y}\sqrt{x^5 y^2} = (x^2 y)^{1/4}(x^5 y^2)^{1/2}$
$$= x^{1/2}y^{1/4}x^{5/2}y = \mathbf{x^3 y^{5/4}}$$

24. $-81^{5/4} = -(81^{1/4})^5 = \mathbf{-243}$

25. $4\sqrt{\dfrac{2}{11}} + 2\sqrt{\dfrac{11}{2}} - 4\sqrt{198}$

$$= \frac{4\sqrt{2}}{\sqrt{11}}\frac{\sqrt{11}}{\sqrt{11}} + \frac{2\sqrt{11}}{\sqrt{2}}\frac{\sqrt{2}}{\sqrt{2}} - 12\sqrt{22}$$

$$= \frac{8\sqrt{22}}{22} + \frac{22\sqrt{22}}{22} - \frac{264\sqrt{22}}{22} = \mathbf{-\frac{117\sqrt{22}}{11}}$$

26. $\dfrac{(4{,}183{,}256)(704{,}185 \times 10^{-42})}{802{,}164 \times 10^{30}}$

$$\approx \frac{(4 \times 10^6)(7 \times 10^{-37})}{8 \times 10^{35}} \approx \mathbf{4 \times 10^{-66}}$$

27. $4 \times \overrightarrow{SF} = 8$
$$\overrightarrow{SF} = 2$$
$$C \times 2 = 6$$
$$C = 3$$
$$A^2 = 4^2 + 3^2$$
$$A^2 = 25$$
$$A = 5$$
$$5 \times 2 = 5 + B$$
$$10 = 5 + B$$
$$\mathbf{5} = B$$

28. $\dfrac{x}{y} = \dfrac{m}{p}$

$$px = ym$$

$$\boldsymbol{x = \frac{ym}{p}}$$

29. $V_{\text{Prism}} = A_{\text{Base}} \times \text{height}$

$$= \left[(8)(6) + \frac{1}{2}(8)(6) + \frac{1}{2}\pi(5)^2\right.$$
$$\left. + \frac{1}{2}\pi(6)^2\right]\text{ft}^2 \times 8\text{ ft}$$

$$= \left(72 + \frac{61}{2}\pi\right)(8)\text{ ft}^3 \approx \mathbf{1342.16\ ft^3}$$

30. $\dfrac{ap(x + 5)(x - 2)}{(x + 7)(x - 2)} \cdot \dfrac{(x + 7)(x - 3)}{ap(x + 5)(x - 4)}$

$$= \boldsymbol{\frac{x - 3}{x - 4}}$$

PRACTICE SET 56

a. $x = \dfrac{80 + 60}{2} = \dfrac{140}{2} = \mathbf{70}$

b. $x = \dfrac{80 - 60}{2} = \dfrac{20}{2} = \mathbf{10}$

c. $x = \dfrac{70 - 20}{2} = \dfrac{50}{2} = \mathbf{25}$

d. $x = \dfrac{280 - 80}{2} = \dfrac{200}{2} = \mathbf{100}$

PROBLEM SET 56

1. Even integers: N, $N + 2$, $N + 4$

$$N(N + 2) = -10(N + 4) + 8$$
$$N^2 + 2N = -10N - 32$$
$$N^2 + 12N + 32 = 0$$
$$(N + 8)(N + 4) = 0$$
$$N = -8, -4$$

The desired integers are **−8, −6, −4** and **−4, −2, 0.**

2. Carbon: $1 \times 12 = 12$

Hydrogen: $2 \times 1 = 2$

Bromine: $2 \times 80 = 160$

Total: $12 + 2 + 160 = 174$

$$\frac{160}{174} = \frac{320}{CH_2Br_2}$$

$$160 \, CH_2Br_2 = 174(320)$$

$$CH_2Br_2 = \textbf{348 grams}$$

Bromine: $\frac{160}{174} \times 100\% \approx \textbf{91.95\%}$

3.

$$\begin{array}{c} D_W \\ \hline \longleftarrow \\ D_R \end{array}$$

$$R_W T_W = R_R T_R$$
$$R_W = 4; \ R_R = 20$$
$$T_W + T_R = 12$$
$$4T_W = 20(12 - T_W)$$
$$24T_W = 240$$
$$T_W = 10$$

$$D_W = 4(10) = \textbf{40 miles}$$

4. Fluorine P_N + Fluorine D_N = Fluorine Total

$$0.2(P_N) + 0.8(D_N) = 0.56(1000)$$

(a) $0.2P_N + 0.8D_N = 560$

(b) $P_N + D_N = 1000$

Substitute $D_N = 1000 - P_N$ into (a) and get:

(a′) $0.2P_N + 0.8(1000 - P_N) = 560$

$$-0.6P_N = -240$$
$$P_N = 400$$

(b) $(400) + D_N = 1000$

$$D_N = 600$$

400 gallons 20%, 600 gallons 80%

5. $3\dfrac{3}{5} \times D = 1440$

$$D = 1440 \times \frac{5}{18} = \textbf{400 were desired}$$

6. $x + 10 \doteq 46$

$$x = \textbf{36}$$

$$y + 20 = 30$$

$$y = \textbf{10}$$

7. (a) $x = \dfrac{120 + 100}{2} = \textbf{110}$

(b) $x = \dfrac{180 - 60}{2} = \textbf{60}$

8. $\dfrac{x + 1}{y} = \dfrac{m}{p}$

$$xp + p = ym$$
$$xp = ym - p$$
$$x = \frac{ym - p}{p}$$

9. $\dfrac{a + x}{b} - \dfrac{c}{m} = \dfrac{p}{k}$

$$akm + kmx - bck = bmp$$
$$kmx = bmp + bck - akm$$
$$x = \frac{bmp + bck - akm}{km}$$

10. $\dfrac{m}{a + c} - \dfrac{x}{m} = p$

$$m^2 - ax - cx = amp + cmp$$
$$m^2 - ax - amp = cmp + cx$$
$$\frac{m^2 - ax - amp}{mp + x} = c$$

11.

$$\begin{array}{c} 210° \\ A \\ 30° \quad B \\ 10 \end{array}$$

$A = 10 \cos 30°$

$A \approx 8.66$

$B = 10 \sin 30°$

$B = 5$

$-8.66R - 5U$

12.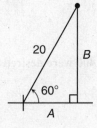

$A = 20 \cos 60°$

$A = 10$

$B = 20 \sin 60°$

$B \approx 17.32$

$10R + 17.32U$

13. $\dfrac{60 \text{ km}}{\text{hr}} \times \dfrac{1000 \text{ m}}{1 \text{ km}} \times \dfrac{100 \text{ cm}}{1 \text{ m}} \times \dfrac{1 \text{ in.}}{2.54 \text{ cm}}$

$\times \dfrac{1 \text{ hr}}{60 \text{ min}} \times \dfrac{1 \text{ min}}{60 \text{ s}}$

$= \dfrac{60(1000)(100)}{(2.54)(60)(60)} \dfrac{\text{in.}}{\text{s}}$

14. $400 \text{ yd}^3 \times \dfrac{3 \text{ ft}}{1 \text{ yd}} \times \dfrac{3 \text{ ft}}{1 \text{ yd}} \times \dfrac{3 \text{ ft}}{1 \text{ yd}}$

$\times \dfrac{12 \text{ in.}}{1 \text{ ft}} \times \dfrac{12 \text{ in.}}{1 \text{ ft}} \times \dfrac{12 \text{ in.}}{1 \text{ ft}}$

$\times \dfrac{2.54 \text{ cm}}{1 \text{ in.}} \times \dfrac{2.54 \text{ cm}}{1 \text{ in.}} \times \dfrac{2.54 \text{ cm}}{1 \text{ in.}}$

$= \mathbf{400(3)(3)(3)(12)(12)(12)(2.54)(2.54)(2.54) \text{ cm}^3}$

15. $3i^5 + 2\sqrt{-25} - 3i^2 = 3i(ii)(ii) + 10i - 3(ii)$

$= 3i + 10i + 3 = \mathbf{3 + 13i}$

16. $2i^4 - 3i^3 + 2i + 4$

$= 2(ii)(ii) - 3i(ii) + 2i + 4$

$= 2 + 3i + 2i + 4 = \mathbf{6 + 5i}$

17. $\sqrt[6]{4\sqrt[5]{2}} = \sqrt[6]{2^2 \sqrt[5]{2}} = \left[2^2(2^{1/5})\right]^{1/6}$

$= 2^{1/3} 2^{1/30} = \mathbf{2^{11/30}}$

18. $\sqrt{y^4}\sqrt{xy^2} = (y^4)^{1/2}(xy^2)^{1/2} = y^2 x^{1/2} y = \mathbf{x^{1/2} y^3}$

19. $\sqrt{25\sqrt[3]{5}} = \sqrt{5^2 \sqrt[3]{5}} = \left[5^2(5^{1/3})\right]^{1/2}$

$= 5 \cdot 5^{1/6} = \mathbf{5^{7/6}}$

20. $4\sqrt{\dfrac{3}{4}} - 2\sqrt{\dfrac{4}{3}} - 2\sqrt{27}$

$= \dfrac{4\sqrt{3}}{2} - \dfrac{4}{\sqrt{3}}\dfrac{\sqrt{3}}{\sqrt{3}} - 6\sqrt{3}$

$= \dfrac{12\sqrt{3}}{6} - \dfrac{8\sqrt{3}}{6} - \dfrac{36\sqrt{3}}{6} = \mathbf{-\dfrac{16\sqrt{3}}{3}}$

21. $x^2 = 7x + 7$

$\left(x^2 - 7x + \quad\right) = 7$

$x^2 - 7x + \dfrac{49}{4} = 7 + \dfrac{49}{4}$

$\left(x - \dfrac{7}{2}\right)^2 = \dfrac{77}{4}$

$x - \dfrac{7}{2} = \pm\dfrac{\sqrt{77}}{2}$

$\mathbf{x = \dfrac{7}{2} \pm \dfrac{\sqrt{77}}{2}}$

22. $-8x - 8 = -x^2$

$(x^2 - 8x + \quad) = 8$

$x^2 - 8x + 16 = 8 + 16$

$(x - 4)^2 = 24$

$x - 4 = \pm\sqrt{6}$

$\mathbf{x = 4 \pm 2\sqrt{6}}$

23. $\sqrt{x + 1} + 1 = 1$

$x + 1 = 0$

$\mathbf{x = -1}$

Check: $\sqrt{-1 + 1} + 1 = 1$

$0 + 1 = 1$

24. $\sqrt{x^2 - 2x + 21} - 1 = x$

$x^2 - 2x + 21 = x^2 + 2x + 1$

$-4x = -20$

$\mathbf{x = 5}$

Check: $\sqrt{25 - 10 + 21} - 1 = 5$

$6 - 1 = 5$

25. $\begin{array}{r} 4x^3 + 12x^2 + 36x + 108 + \frac{323}{x-3} \\ \hline x - 3 \, \overline{)\, 4x^4 + 0x^3 + 0x^2 - 0x - 1} \end{array}$

$\underline{4x^4 - 12x^3}$

$12x^3 + 0x^2$

$\underline{12x^3 - 36x^2}$

$36x^2 + 0x$

$\underline{36x^2 - 108x}$

$108x - 1$

$\underline{108x - 324}$

323

26. $\dfrac{\dfrac{ax}{y^2} - \dfrac{yp}{x}}{\dfrac{yp}{xy} - \dfrac{1}{y^2}} = \dfrac{\dfrac{ax^2 - y^3 p}{xy^2}}{\dfrac{y^2 p - x}{xy^2}} \cdot \dfrac{\dfrac{xy^2}{y^2 p - x}}{\dfrac{xy^2}{y^2 p - x}}$

$= \mathbf{\dfrac{ax^2 - y^3 p}{y^2 p - x}}$

27. Graph the line to find the slope.

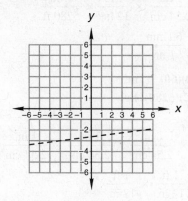

$$m = \frac{+1}{+8} = \frac{1}{8}$$

Since the slopes of perpendicular lines are negative reciprocals of each other,

$$m_\perp = -8$$

$$y = -8x + b$$

$$-5 = -8(-5) + b$$

$$-45 = b$$

$$\mathbf{y = -8x - 45}$$

28. $\dfrac{x-3}{4} - \dfrac{2-x}{8} = 6$

$$2x - 6 - 2 + x = 48$$

$$3x = 56$$

$$x = \frac{56}{3}$$

29. $\dfrac{a-5}{2} - \dfrac{3-a}{4} = 1$

$$2a - 10 - 3 + a = 4$$

$$3a = 17$$

$$a = \frac{17}{3}$$

30. $\dfrac{x}{a^2 y} - \dfrac{3x+2}{a^2 y(x-1)} - \dfrac{4}{x^2-1}$

$$= \frac{x(x^2-1)}{a^2 y(x^2-1)} - \frac{(3x+2)(x+1)}{a^2 y(x^2-1)}$$

$$- \frac{4a^2 y}{a^2 y(x^2-1)}$$

$$= \frac{x^3 - x - 3x^2 - 5x - 2 - 4a^2 y}{a^2 y(x^2-1)}$$

$$= \frac{x^3 - 3x^2 - 6x - 4a^2 y - 2}{a^2 y(x^2-1)}$$

Practice Set 57

a.
$$\frac{P_1 V_1}{T_1} = \frac{P_2 V_2}{T_2}$$

$$\frac{(200)(8)}{(1000)} = \frac{P_2(10)}{(800)}$$

$$\frac{800}{10} \cdot \frac{(200)(8)}{(1000)} = P_2$$

$$128 = P_2$$

$P_2 = \mathbf{128}$ **newtons per square meter**

b.
$$P_1 V_1 = P_2 V_2$$

$$(11)(44) = P_2(4.4)$$

$$\frac{(11)(44)}{4.4} = P_2$$

$$110 = P_2$$

$P_2 = \mathbf{110}$ **atmospheres**

Problem Set 57

1.
$$\frac{P_1 V_1}{T_1} = \frac{P_2 V_2}{T_2}$$

$$\frac{100(4)}{800} = \frac{P_2(12)}{600}$$

$$P_2 = \mathbf{25 \ N/m^2}$$

2. $P_1 V_1 = P_2 V_2$

$$7(42) = P_2(49)$$

$$P_2 = \mathbf{6 \ atmospheres}$$

3.
$$\frac{P_1}{T_1} = \frac{P_2}{T_2}$$

$$\frac{400}{1200} = \frac{P_2}{300}$$

$$P_2 = \mathbf{100 \ N/m^2}$$

4. Alcohol P_N + Alcohol D_N = Alcohol Total

$$0.2(P_N) + 0.4(D_N) = 0.352(1000)$$

(a) $0.2P_N + 0.4D_N = 352$

(b) $P_N + D_N = 1000$

Substitute $D_N = 1000 - P_N$ into (a) and get:

(a′) $0.2P_N + 0.4(1000 - P_N) = 352$

$$-0.2P_N = -48$$

$$P_N = 240$$

(b) $(240) + D_N = 1000$

$$D_N = 760$$

240 gallons 20%, 760 gallons 40%

5. Odd integers: $N, N + 2, N + 4, N + 6$

$(N + 4)(N + 6) = 10N + 49$

$N^2 + 10N + 24 = 10N + 49$

$N^2 - 25 = 0$

$(N - 5)(N + 5) = 0$

$N = 5, -5$

The desired integers are **5, 7, 9, 11** and **−5, −3, −1, 1.**

6. (a) $x = \dfrac{80 - 15}{2} = \mathbf{32.5}$

(b) $x = \dfrac{210 + 48}{2} = \mathbf{129}$

7. $\dfrac{a}{x - y} - \dfrac{c}{p} = m$

$ap - cx + cy = mpx - mpy$

$mpy + cy = mpx + cx - ap$

$y = \dfrac{mpx + cx - ap}{mp + c}$

8. $\dfrac{x - a}{p} - c = \dfrac{k}{d}$

$dx - ad - cdp = kp$

$dx - cdp - kp = ad$

$\dfrac{dx - cdp - kp}{d} = a$

9.

$A = 4 \cos 40°$

$A \approx 3.06$

$B = 4 \sin 40°$

$B \approx 2.57$

3.06R + 2.57U

10.

$A = 40 \cos 30°$

$A \approx 34.64$

$B = 40 \sin 30°$

$B \approx 20$

34.64R − 20U

11. $\dfrac{40 \text{ cm}}{\text{s}} \times \dfrac{1 \text{ in.}}{2.54 \text{ cm}} \times \dfrac{1 \text{ ft}}{12 \text{ in.}} \times \dfrac{1 \text{ mi}}{5280 \text{ ft}}$

$\times \dfrac{60 \text{ s}}{1 \text{ min}} \times \dfrac{60 \text{ min}}{1 \text{ hr}}$

$= \dfrac{40(60)(60)}{(2.54)(12)(5280)} \dfrac{\text{mi}}{\text{hr}}$

12. $1000 \text{ cm}^3 \times \dfrac{1 \text{ in.}}{2.54 \text{ cm}} \times \dfrac{1 \text{ in.}}{2.54 \text{ cm}} \times \dfrac{1 \text{ in.}}{2.54 \text{ cm}}$

$\times \dfrac{1 \text{ ft}}{12 \text{ in.}} \times \dfrac{1 \text{ ft}}{12 \text{ in.}} \times \dfrac{1 \text{ ft}}{12 \text{ in.}}$

$= \dfrac{1000}{(2.54)(2.54)(2.54)(12)(12)(12)} \text{ ft}^3$

13. $3i^3 - 2i^2 + i^4 - 5$

$= 3i(ii) - 2(ii) + (ii)(ii) - 5$

$= -3i + 2 + 1 - 5 = \mathbf{-2 - 3i}$

14. $-2\sqrt{-9} - 3i^2 + 2i - 2$

$= -6i - 3(ii) + 2i - 2$

$= -6i + 3 + 2i - 2 = \mathbf{1 - 4i}$

15. $-5x - 6 = -x^2$

$\left(x^2 - 5x + \right) = 6$

$x^2 - 5x + \dfrac{25}{4} = 6 + \dfrac{25}{4}$

$\left(x - \dfrac{5}{2}\right)^2 = \dfrac{49}{4}$

$x - \dfrac{5}{2} = \pm\dfrac{7}{2}$

$x = \dfrac{5}{2} \pm \dfrac{7}{2}$

$x = \mathbf{6, -1}$

16. $-6x + x^2 = -5$

$\left(x^2 - 6x + \right) = -5$

$x^2 - 6x + 9 = -5 + 9$

$(x - 3)^2 = 4$

$x - 3 = \pm 2$

$x = 3 \pm 2$

$x = \mathbf{5, 1}$

17. Use the graph to find the slope.

$y = \dfrac{11}{5}x + b$

Use the point $(-1, 6)$ for x and y.

$6 = \dfrac{11}{5}(-1) + b$

$\dfrac{41}{5} = b$

$y = \dfrac{11}{5}x + \dfrac{41}{5}$

18. $\sqrt{x - 2} + 2 = 3$

$x - 2 = 1$

$x = \mathbf{3}$

Check: $\sqrt{3 - 2} + 2 = 3$

$1 + 2 = 3$

19. $\sqrt{x^2 - x + 13} - 1 = x$

$x^2 - x + 13 = x^2 + 2x + 1$

$-3x = -12$

$x = \mathbf{4}$

Check: $\sqrt{16 - 4 + 13} - 1 = 4$

$5 - 1 = 4$

20. $\dfrac{x - 2}{4} - \dfrac{x}{3} = 5$

$3x - 6 - 4x = 60$

$-x = 66$

$x = \mathbf{-66}$

21. $\dfrac{x}{4} - \dfrac{3x + 1}{2} = 3$

$x - 6x - 2 = 12$

$-5x = 14$

$x = \mathbf{-\dfrac{14}{5}}$

22. $\sqrt{9\sqrt[3]{3}} = \sqrt{3^2\sqrt[3]{3}} = \left[3^2(3^{1/3})\right]^{1/2}$

$= 3 \cdot 3^{1/6} = \mathbf{3^{7/6}}$

23. $\sqrt{x^4\sqrt[3]{x^2 y}} = \left[x^4(x^2 y)^{1/3}\right]^{1/2}$

$= x^2 x^{1/3} y^{1/6} = \mathbf{x^{7/3} y^{1/6}}$

24. $\sqrt[3]{4}\sqrt[5]{2} = \sqrt[3]{2^2}\sqrt[5]{2} = 2^{2/3}2^{1/5} = \mathbf{2^{13/15}}$

25. $3\sqrt{\dfrac{2}{5}} + 7\sqrt{\dfrac{5}{2}} - 2\sqrt{40}$

$= \dfrac{3\sqrt{2}}{\sqrt{5}}\dfrac{\sqrt{5}}{\sqrt{5}} + \dfrac{7\sqrt{5}}{\sqrt{2}}\dfrac{\sqrt{2}}{\sqrt{2}} - 4\sqrt{10}$

$= \dfrac{6\sqrt{10}}{10} + \dfrac{35\sqrt{10}}{10} - \dfrac{40\sqrt{10}}{10} = \mathbf{\dfrac{\sqrt{10}}{10}}$

26. $16^{-5/4} = \dfrac{1}{16^{5/4}} = \dfrac{1}{(16^{1/4})^5} = \mathbf{\dfrac{1}{32}}$

27. $\dfrac{\dfrac{x^2 y}{p^5 z} - 1}{\dfrac{x}{p^5} - \dfrac{4}{z}} = \dfrac{\dfrac{x^2 y - p^5 z}{p^5 z}}{\dfrac{xz - 4p^5}{p^5 z}} \cdot \dfrac{\dfrac{p^5 z}{xz - 4p^5}}{\dfrac{p^5 z}{xz - 4p^5}}$

$= \mathbf{\dfrac{x^2 y - p^5 z}{xz - 4p^5}}$

28. $-2(-x^0 - 4^0) - 3x(2 - 6^0)$

$= (x)(-2 - 3^2 - 2) - x(-2 - 2^0)$

$4 - 6x + 3x = -13x + 3x$

$4 = -7x$

$\mathbf{-\dfrac{4}{7}} = x$

29. $-28x + x^3 = 3x^2$

$x^3 - 3x^2 - 28x = 0$

$x(x - 7)(x + 4) = 0$

$x = \mathbf{0, 7, -4}$

30. $\dfrac{x}{a^2} - \dfrac{x + 2}{a(a + 2)}$

$= \dfrac{x(a + 2)}{a^2(a + 2)} - \dfrac{a(x + 2)}{a^2(a + 2)}$

$= \dfrac{ax + 2x - ax - 2a}{a^2(a + 2)} = \mathbf{\dfrac{2x - 2a}{a^2(a + 2)}}$

PRACTICE SET 58

a. $3x^2 + 5x - 6 = 0$

$$x^2 + \frac{5}{3}x - 2 = 0$$

$$\left(x^2 + \frac{5}{3}x \qquad \right) = 2$$

$$\left(x^2 + \frac{5}{3}x + \frac{25}{36}\right) = 2 + \frac{25}{36}$$

$$\left(x + \frac{5}{6}\right)^2 = \frac{97}{36}$$

$$x + \frac{5}{6} = \pm\sqrt{\frac{97}{36}}$$

$$x = -\frac{5}{6} \pm \frac{\sqrt{97}}{6}$$

b. $3x^2 - x - 1 = 0$

$$x^2 - \frac{1}{3}x - \frac{1}{3} = 0$$

$$\left(x^2 - \frac{1}{3}x \qquad \right) = \frac{1}{3}$$

$$\left(x^2 - \frac{1}{3}x + \frac{1}{36}\right) = \frac{1}{3} + \frac{1}{36}$$

$$\left(x - \frac{1}{6}\right)^2 = \frac{13}{36}$$

$$x - \frac{1}{6} = \pm\sqrt{\frac{13}{36}}$$

$$x = \frac{1}{6} \pm \frac{\sqrt{13}}{6}$$

PROBLEM SET 58

1. $\dfrac{P_1 V_1}{T_1} = \dfrac{P_2 V_2}{T_2}$

$$\frac{4(6)}{600} = \frac{3(8)}{T_2}$$

$$T_2 = \textbf{600 K}$$

2. Carbon: $6 \times 12 = 72$
    Hydrogen: $8 \times 1 = 8$
    Nitrogen: $1 \times 14 = 14$
    Chlorine: $1 \times 35 = 35$
    Total: $72 + 8 + 14 + 35 = 129$

$$\frac{72}{129} = \frac{360}{C_6H_8NCl}$$

$$72C_6H_8NCl = 129(360)$$

$$C_6H_8NCl = \textbf{645 grams}$$

3. Chlorine: $\dfrac{35}{129} \times 100\% \approx \textbf{27.13\%}$

4. Bromine P_N + Bromine D_N = Bromine Total

$$0.1(P_N) + 0.4(D_N) = 0.16(50)$$

(a) $0.1P_N + 0.4D_N = 8$

(b) $P_N + D_N = 50$

Substitute $D_N = 50 - P_N$ into (a) and get:

(a′) $0.1P_N + 0.4(50 - P_N) = 8$

$$-0.3P_N = -12$$

$$P_N = 40$$

(b) $(40) + D_N = 50$

$$D_N = 10$$

40 mL 10%, 10 mL 40%

5.

$R_T T_T + 15 = R_R T_R;\ T_T = T_R = 3;$

$R_R = 20$

$3R_T + 15 = 20(3)$

$$3R_T = 45$$

$$R_T = 15$$

$D_T = 15(3) = \textbf{45 miles}$

6. $3x^2 + 4x - 3 = 0$

$$x^2 + \frac{4}{3}x - 1 = 0$$

$$\left(x^2 + \frac{4}{3}x + \qquad \right) = 1$$

$$x^2 + \frac{4}{3}x + \frac{4}{9} = 1 + \frac{4}{9}$$

$$\left(x + \frac{2}{3}\right)^2 = \frac{13}{9}$$

$$x + \frac{2}{3} = \pm\frac{\sqrt{13}}{3}$$

$$x = -\frac{2}{3} \pm \frac{\sqrt{13}}{3}$$

7.
$$4x^2 - x - 5 = 0$$
$$x^2 - \frac{1}{4}x - \frac{5}{4} = 0$$
$$\left(x^2 - \frac{1}{4}x + \right) = \frac{5}{4}$$
$$x^2 - \frac{1}{4} + \frac{1}{64} = \frac{5}{4} + \frac{1}{64}$$
$$\left(x - \frac{1}{8}\right)^2 = \frac{81}{64}$$
$$x - \frac{1}{8} = \pm\frac{9}{8}$$
$$x = \frac{1}{8} \pm \frac{9}{8}$$
$$x = \mathbf{\frac{5}{4}, -1}$$

8.
$$3x^2 - 4 = -2x$$
$$x^2 + \frac{2}{3}x - \frac{4}{3} = 0$$
$$\left(x^2 + \frac{2}{3}x + \right) = \frac{4}{3}$$
$$x^2 + \frac{2}{3}x + \frac{1}{9} = \frac{4}{3} + \frac{1}{9}$$
$$\left(x + \frac{1}{3}\right)^2 = \frac{13}{9}$$
$$x + \frac{1}{3} = \pm\frac{\sqrt{13}}{3}$$
$$x = -\frac{1}{3} \pm \frac{\sqrt{13}}{3}$$

9. $x = 176 - 100 = \mathbf{76}$
$$y = \frac{360 - 176}{2} = \mathbf{92}$$
$$z = \frac{100 + 76}{2} = \mathbf{88}$$

10.
$$\frac{x - a}{p} - c = \frac{y}{k}$$
$$kx - ak - ckp = py$$
$$kx - ak = py + ckp$$
$$\mathbf{\frac{kx - ak}{y + ck} = p}$$

11.
$$\frac{a}{x - p} - c = \frac{y}{k}$$
$$ak - ckx + ckp = xy - py$$
$$ckp + py = xy + ckx - ak$$
$$p = \mathbf{\frac{xy + ckx - ak}{ck + y}}$$

12.

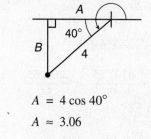

$A = 4 \cos 40°$
$A \approx 3.06$
$B = 4 \sin 40°$
$B \approx 2.57$

–3.06R – 2.57U

13.

$A = 10 \cos 45°$
$A \approx 7.07$
$B = 10 \sin 45°$
$B \approx 7.07$

7.07R – 7.07U

14.
$$\frac{70 \text{ m}}{\text{s}} \times \frac{100 \text{ cm}}{1 \text{ m}} \times \frac{1 \text{ in.}}{2.54 \text{ cm}} \times \frac{1 \text{ ft}}{12 \text{ in.}}$$
$$\times \frac{1 \text{ mi}}{5280 \text{ ft}} \times \frac{60 \text{ s}}{1 \text{ min}} \times \frac{60 \text{ min}}{1 \text{ hr}}$$
$$= \mathbf{\frac{70(100)(60)(60)}{(2.54)(12)(5280)}} \frac{\mathbf{mi}}{\mathbf{hr}}$$

15. $40 \text{ ft}^3 \times \dfrac{12 \text{ in.}}{1 \text{ ft}} \times \dfrac{12 \text{ in.}}{1 \text{ ft}} \times \dfrac{12 \text{ in.}}{1 \text{ ft}}$
$$\times \frac{2.54 \text{ cm}}{1 \text{ in.}} \times \frac{2.54 \text{ cm}}{1 \text{ in.}} \times \frac{2.54 \text{ cm}}{1 \text{ in.}}$$
$$= \mathbf{40(12)(12)(12)(2.54)(2.54)(2.54) \text{ cm}^3}$$

16. $\sqrt[4]{9}\sqrt[5]{3} = \sqrt[4]{3^2}\sqrt[5]{3} = (3^2)^{1/4}3^{1/5}$
$$= 3^{1/2}3^{1/5} = \mathbf{3^{7/10}}$$

17. $\sqrt[7]{4\sqrt{2}} = \sqrt[7]{2^2\sqrt{2}} = [2^2(2^{1/2})]^{1/7}$
$= 2^{2/7}2^{1/14} = \mathbf{2^{5/14}}$

18. $\sqrt{x^2y^3}\sqrt[3]{xy^5} = (x^2y^3)^{1/2}(xy^5)^{1/3}$
$= xy^{3/2}x^{1/3}y^{5/3} = \mathbf{x^{4/3}y^{19/6}}$

19. $-16^{-3/4} = -\dfrac{1}{16^{3/4}} = -\dfrac{1}{(16^{1/4})^3} = \mathbf{-\dfrac{1}{8}}$

20. $5\sqrt{\dfrac{5}{11}} - 2\sqrt{\dfrac{11}{5}} + 3\sqrt{220}$

$= \dfrac{5\sqrt{5}}{\sqrt{11}}\dfrac{\sqrt{11}}{\sqrt{11}} - \dfrac{2\sqrt{11}}{\sqrt{5}}\dfrac{\sqrt{5}}{\sqrt{5}} + 6\sqrt{55}$

$= \dfrac{25\sqrt{55}}{55} - \dfrac{22\sqrt{55}}{55} + \dfrac{330\sqrt{55}}{55} = \mathbf{\dfrac{333\sqrt{55}}{55}}$

21. $5i^3 - 6i^8 + 2\sqrt{-25} - 4i^2$
$= 5i(ii) - 6(ii)(ii)(ii)(ii) + 10i - 4(ii)$
$= -5i - 6 + 10i + 4 = \mathbf{-2 + 5i}$

22. $\dfrac{(40,621,857)(6,031,824)}{19,610 \times 10^{-24}}$

$\approx \dfrac{(4 \times 10^7)(6 \times 10^6)}{2 \times 10^{-20}} \approx \mathbf{1 \times 10^{34}}$

23. $\dfrac{(x+8)(x+2)}{(x+8)(x+3)} \cdot \dfrac{(x+5)(x+3)}{(x+5)(x-5)}$

$= \mathbf{\dfrac{x+2}{x-5}}$

24. $V_{\text{Cylinder}} = A_{\text{Base}} \times \text{height}$
$A_{\text{Base}} \times 3\text{ cm} = (72 - 6\pi)\text{ cm}^3$

$A_{\text{Base}} = \dfrac{(72 - 6\pi)\text{ cm}^3}{3\text{ cm}}$

$(6)(4) - \dfrac{1}{2}\pi r^2 = (24 - 2\pi)\text{ cm}^2$

$\dfrac{1}{2}\pi r^2 = 2\pi\text{ cm}^2$

$r^2 = 4\text{ cm}^2$

$r = \mathbf{2\text{ cm}}$

25. $\dfrac{\dfrac{x^2a^2}{m} - \dfrac{4}{p^3}}{\dfrac{xa}{mp^3} - 5}$

$= \dfrac{\dfrac{x^2a^2p^3 - 4m}{mp^3}}{\dfrac{xa - 5mp^3}{mp^3}} \cdot \dfrac{\dfrac{mp^3}{xa - 5mp^3}}{\dfrac{mp^3}{xa - 5mp^3}}$

$= \mathbf{\dfrac{x^2a^2p^3 - 4m}{xa - 5mp^3}}$

26. (a) $3x + 4y = -4$
$4y = -3x - 4$
$y = -\dfrac{3}{4}x - 1$

(b) $x - 5y = 10$
$-5y = -x + 10$
$y = \dfrac{1}{5}x - 2$

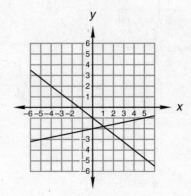

Solve the equations by elimination:

(a) $\quad 3x + 4y = -4$
$-3\text{(b)}\ \underline{-3x + 15y = -30}$
$\qquad\qquad 19y = -34$

$\qquad\qquad y = -\dfrac{34}{19}$

(b) $x = 5\left(-\dfrac{34}{19}\right) + 10 = \dfrac{20}{19}$

$\left(\mathbf{\dfrac{20}{19}, -\dfrac{34}{19}}\right)$

27.
$$x+2\,)\overline{\,4x^3 + 0x^2 + 0x - 5\,}\quad \mathbf{4x^2 - 8x + 16} - \tfrac{37}{x+2}$$
$\underline{4x^3 + 8x^2}$
$\quad -8x^2 + 0x$
$\quad \underline{-8x^2 - 16x}$
$\qquad\quad 16x - 5$
$\qquad\quad \underline{16x + 32}$
$\qquad\qquad -37$

28. $\dfrac{3-x}{2} - \dfrac{4x}{3} = 7$

$9 - 3x - 8x = 42$

$-11x = 33$

$x = \mathbf{-3}$

29. $x^0 - 2x - 5(x - 3^0) = -2x^0 - 7$

$$1 - 2x - 5x + 5 = -2 - 7$$

$$-7x = -15$$

$$x = \frac{15}{7}$$

30. $\dfrac{b}{a(y + 1)} + \dfrac{cx}{a^2(y + 1)}$

$$= \frac{ab}{a^2(y + 1)} + \frac{cx}{a^2(y + 1)} = \frac{ab + cx}{a^2(y + 1)}$$

PRACTICE SET 59

a. N = mF + b

Use the graph to find the slope.

Slope = $\dfrac{250}{3} \approx 83.33$

N = 83.33F + b

Use the point (32,200) for F and N.

$$(200) = 83.33(32) + b.$$

$$-2466.56 = b$$

N = 83.33F − 2466.56

b. (a) $\dfrac{x}{3} + \dfrac{2y}{7} = -\dfrac{3}{7}$

(b) $0.01x - 0.6y = 3.03$

21(a) = (a′) $7x + 6y = -9$

100(b) = (b′) $x - 60y = 303$

(a′) $7x + 6y = -9$

-7(b′) $\dfrac{-7x + 420y = -2121}{426y = -2130}$

$$y = -5$$

(b′) $x - 60y = 303$

$$x - 60(-5) = 303$$

$$x + 300 = 303$$

$$x = 3$$

c.

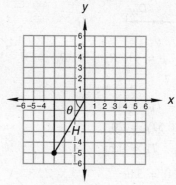

$\tan \theta = \dfrac{5}{3}$

$\theta \approx 59.04°$

Since θ is a third-quadrant angle,

$\theta = 59.04° + 180° = 239.04°$

$H = \sqrt{3^2 + 5^2} = \sqrt{34}$

$\underline{\sqrt{34}/239.04°}$

PROBLEM SET 59

1. Integers: $N,\ N + 1,\ N + 2,\ N + 3$

$$N(N + 3) = 10(-N - 2) - 22$$

$$N^2 + 3N = -10N - 42$$

$$N^2 + 13N + 42 = 0$$

$$(N + 7)(N + 6) = 0$$

$$N = -7, -6$$

The desired integers are **−7, −6, −5, −4** and **−6, −5, −4, −3.**

2. Carbon: $2 \times 12 = 24$

Hydrogen: $6 \times 1 = 6$

Oxygen: $1 \times 16 = 16$

Total: $24 + 6 + 16 = 46$

$$\frac{16}{46} = \frac{\text{Oxygen}}{460}$$

46Oxygen = $16(460)$

Oxygen = **160 grams**

3.

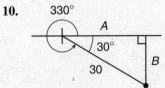

$R_R T_R + R_W T_W = 41;\ R_R = 8;\ R_W = 3;$

$T_R + T_W = 7$

$8T_R + 3(7 - T_R) = 41$

$5T_R = 20$

$T_R = 4\ hr$

$T_W = 7 - (4) = 3\ hr$

$D_R = 4(8) =$ **32 miles**

$D_W = 3(3) =$ **9 miles**

4. Iodine P_N + Iodine D_N = Iodine Total

$0.9(P_N) + 0.7(D_N) = 0.78(100)$

(a) $0.9P_N + 0.7D_N = 78$

(b) $P_N + D_N = 100$

Substitute $D_N = 100 - P_N$ into (a) and get:

(a') $0.9P_N + 0.7(100 - P_N) = 78$

$0.2P_N = 8$

$P_N = 40$

(b) $(40) + D_N = 100$

$D_N = 60$

40 liters 90%, 60 liters 70%

5. $P_1V_1 = P_2V_2$

$(14)(10) = (20)V_2$

$V_2 =$ **7 liters**

6. $Zr = mCa + b$

Use the graph to find the slope.

Slope $= \dfrac{-10}{7} = -1.43$

$Zr = -1.43Ca + b$

Use the point (100, 18) for Ca and Zr.

$18 = -1.43(100) + b$

$161 = b$

$Zr = -1.43Ca + 161$

7. (a) $x = \dfrac{78 + 42}{2} =$ **60**

(b) $x = \dfrac{258 - 102}{2} =$ **78**

8. (a) $\dfrac{x}{3} + \dfrac{3y}{4} = -\dfrac{1}{4}$

(b) $0.04x - 0.2y = 1.13$

(a') $4x + 9y = -3$

(b') $4x - 20y = 113$

$\begin{array}{r} (a')\quad 4x + 9y = -3 \\ -1(b')\ \underline{-4x + 20y = -113} \\ 29y = -116 \\ y = -4 \end{array}$

(a') $4x + 9(-4) = -3$

$4x = 33$

$x = \dfrac{33}{4}$

$\left(\dfrac{33}{4}, -4\right)$

9.

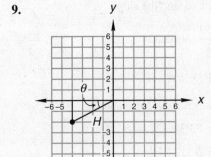

$\tan \theta = \dfrac{2}{4}$

$\theta = 26.57°$

Since θ is a third-quadrant angle,

$\theta = 26.57° + 180° = 206.57°$

$H = \sqrt{2^2 + 4^2} = 2\sqrt{5}$

$2\sqrt{5}/206.57°$

10.

$A = 30 \cos 30°$

$A \approx 25.98$

$B = 30 \sin 30°$

$B = 15$

$25.98R - 15U$

11. $\qquad 2x^2 = x + 5$

$$\left(x^2 - \frac{1}{2}x + \quad\right) = \frac{5}{2}$$

$$x^2 - \frac{1}{2}x + \frac{1}{16} = \frac{5}{2} + \frac{1}{16}$$

$$\left(x - \frac{1}{4}\right)^2 = \frac{41}{16}$$

$$x - \frac{1}{4} = \pm\frac{\sqrt{41}}{4}$$

$$x = \mathbf{\frac{1}{4} \pm \frac{\sqrt{41}}{4}}$$

12. $\qquad 3x^2 - 5 = 2x$

$$\left(x^2 - \frac{2}{3}x + \quad\right) = \frac{5}{3}$$

$$x^2 - \frac{2}{3}x + \frac{1}{9} = \frac{5}{3} + \frac{1}{9}$$

$$\left(x - \frac{1}{3}\right)^2 = \frac{16}{9}$$

$$x - \frac{1}{3} = \pm\frac{4}{3}$$

$$x = \frac{1}{3} \pm \frac{4}{3}$$

$$x = \mathbf{\frac{5}{3}, -1}$$

13. $\qquad 3x^2 - 4 = x$

$$\left(x^2 - \frac{1}{3}x + \quad\right) = \frac{4}{3}$$

$$x^2 - \frac{1}{3}x + \frac{1}{36} = \frac{4}{3} + \frac{1}{36}$$

$$\left(x - \frac{1}{6}\right)^2 = \frac{49}{36}$$

$$x - \frac{1}{6} = \pm\frac{7}{6}$$

$$x = \frac{1}{6} \pm \frac{7}{6}$$

$$x = \mathbf{\frac{4}{3}, -1}$$

14. $\qquad 3^2 = \left(\frac{\sqrt{11}}{2}\right)^2 + H^2$

$$9 = \frac{11}{4} + H^2$$

$$\frac{25}{4} = H^2$$

$$\frac{5}{2} = H$$

$$\text{Area} = \frac{(b \times H)}{2}$$

$$\text{Area} = \frac{\sqrt{11} \times \frac{5}{2}}{2} \text{ cm}^2 = \mathbf{\frac{5\sqrt{11}}{4}}\text{ cm}^2$$

15. $\qquad \frac{p - s}{m} - \frac{c}{4} + x = 0$

$$4p - 4s - cm + 4mx = 0$$

$$4p - 4s = cm - 4mx$$

$$\mathbf{\frac{4p - 4s}{c - 4x} = m}$$

16. $\qquad \frac{m}{p + s} - \frac{c}{x} + 4 = 0$

$$mx - cp - cs + 4px + 4sx = 0$$

$$4px - cp = cs - mx - 4sx$$

$$p = \mathbf{\frac{cs - mx - 4sx}{4x - c}}$$

17. $\dfrac{40 \text{ in.}}{\text{s}} \times \dfrac{2.54 \text{ cm}}{1 \text{ in.}} \times \dfrac{1 \text{ m}}{100 \text{ cm}} \times \dfrac{60 \text{ s}}{1 \text{ min}}$

$\times \dfrac{60 \text{ min}}{1 \text{ hr}}$

$= \mathbf{\dfrac{40(2.54)(60)(60)}{(100)}} \dfrac{\mathbf{m}}{\mathbf{hr}}$

18. $18{,}000 \text{ cm}^3 \times \dfrac{1 \text{ in.}}{2.54 \text{ cm}} \times \dfrac{1 \text{ in.}}{2.54 \text{ cm}} \times \dfrac{1 \text{ in.}}{2.54 \text{ cm}}$

$\times \dfrac{1 \text{ ft}}{12 \text{ in.}} \times \dfrac{1 \text{ ft}}{12 \text{ in.}} \times \dfrac{1 \text{ ft}}{12 \text{ in.}}$

$= \mathbf{\dfrac{18{,}000}{(2.54)(2.54)(2.54)(12)(12)(12)}} \text{ ft}^3$

19. $i^4 + 5 + 3\sqrt{-9} - 2\sqrt{-4}$

$= (ii)(ii) + 5 + 9i - 4i$

$= 1 + 5 + 9i - 4i = \mathbf{6 + 5i}$

20. $3i^5 - 2i^2 - 4 - i = 3i(ii)(ii) - 2(ii) - 4 - i$

$= 3i + 2 - 4 - i = \mathbf{-2 + 2i}$

21. $\sqrt{x^2 - 4x + 39} + 1 = x + 4$

$\qquad x^2 - 4x + 39 = x^2 + 6x + 9$

$\qquad\qquad\qquad -10x = -30$

$\qquad\qquad\qquad\qquad x = \mathbf{3}$

Check: $\sqrt{9 - 12 + 39} + 1 = 3 + 4$

$\qquad\qquad\qquad 6 + 1 = 3 + 4$

22. $\sqrt{x - 3} + 2 = -4$

$\qquad\qquad x - 3 = 36$

$\qquad\qquad\quad x = 39$

Check: $\sqrt{39 - 3} + 2 = -4$

$\qquad\qquad\quad 6 + 2 = -4$

The statement is not true, so no real number solution exists.

23. $\sqrt[5]{3\sqrt{3}} = \left[3(3^{1/2})\right]^{1/5} = 3^{1/5}3^{1/10} = \mathbf{3^{3/10}}$

24. $\sqrt[4]{4\sqrt{2}} = \sqrt[4]{2^2\sqrt{2}} = \left[2^2(2^{1/2})\right]^{1/4}$

$\quad = 2^{1/2}2^{1/8} = \mathbf{2^{5/8}}$

25. $-16^{-3/4} = -\dfrac{1}{16^{3/4}} = -\dfrac{1}{(16^{1/4})^3} = -\dfrac{\mathbf{1}}{\mathbf{8}}$

26. $\sqrt{x^2 y}\,\sqrt[3]{y^5 x^4} = (x^2 y)^{1/2}(y^5 x^4)^{1/3}$

$\quad = x y^{1/2} y^{5/3} x^{4/3} = \mathbf{x^{7/3}y^{13/6}}$

27. $\sqrt{\dfrac{2}{13}} - 4\sqrt{\dfrac{13}{2}} + 3\sqrt{234}$

$\quad = \dfrac{\sqrt{2}}{\sqrt{13}}\dfrac{\sqrt{13}}{\sqrt{13}} - \dfrac{4\sqrt{13}}{\sqrt{2}}\dfrac{\sqrt{2}}{\sqrt{2}} + 9\sqrt{26}$

$\quad = \dfrac{2\sqrt{26}}{26} - \dfrac{52\sqrt{26}}{26} + \dfrac{234\sqrt{26}}{26} = \dfrac{\mathbf{92\sqrt{26}}}{\mathbf{13}}$

28. $\dfrac{x - 4}{2} - \dfrac{x}{3} - 2 = \dfrac{5}{2}$

$\quad 3x - 12 - 2x - 12 = 15$

$\qquad\qquad\qquad\quad x = \mathbf{39}$

29. $\dfrac{x}{y} + \dfrac{x^2 + 2}{y^2 a} + \dfrac{x^3}{y(a + y)}$

$\quad = \dfrac{axy(a + y)}{y^2 a(a + y)} + \dfrac{(x^2 + 2)(a + y)}{y^2 a(a + y)}$

$\qquad + \dfrac{ax^3 y}{y^2 a(a + y)}$

$\quad = \dfrac{\mathbf{axy(a + y) + (x^2 + 2)(a + y) + ax^3 y}}{\mathbf{y^2 a(a + y)}}$

30. $\dfrac{(x^0 y p)^{-3} x^3 y p^0 p^{-2}}{x^2 p^2 y^0 (y^{-3} p)^2 x^{-3} y^0 p^2}$

$\quad = \dfrac{y^{-3} p^{-3} x^3 y p^{-2}}{x^2 p^2 y^{-6} p^2 x^{-3} p^2}$

$\quad = \dfrac{p^{-5} x^3 y^{-2}}{x^{-1} p^6 y^{-6}} = \dfrac{\mathbf{x^4 y^4}}{\mathbf{p^{11}}}$

PRACTICE SET 60

a. $\quad B = kR$

$\quad (12) = k(3)$

$\qquad 4 = k$

$\quad B = 4R$

$\quad B = 4(6) = \mathbf{24\ bluebirds}$

b. $\quad RPM = \dfrac{k}{N_T}$

$\quad (150) = \dfrac{k}{(60)}$

$\quad 9000 = k$

$\quad RPM = \dfrac{9000}{N_T} = \dfrac{9000}{(100)} = \mathbf{90}$

PROBLEM SET 60

1. $\quad B = kG$

$\quad (8) = k(2)$

$\qquad 4 = k$

$\quad B = 4(7) = \mathbf{28\ boys}$

2. RPM $= \dfrac{k}{N_t}$

$\quad 100 = \dfrac{k}{40}$

$\quad 4000 = k$

$\quad RPM = \dfrac{4000}{25} = \mathbf{160}$

3. $\quad C = kP$

$\quad 40 = k(20{,}000)$

$\quad 0.002 = k$

$\quad C = 0.002(8000) = \mathbf{16\ clowns}$

4.
$$\frac{P_1}{T_1} = \frac{P_2}{T_2}$$

$$\frac{400}{500} = \frac{P_2}{1000}$$

$$P_2(500) = 400(1000)$$

$$P_2 = \textbf{800 N/m}^2$$

5. (a) $N_P = N_T + 50$

(b) $2N_P = 3N_T + 60$

Substitute (a) into (b) and get:

(b') $2(N_T + 50) = 3N_T + 60$

$$N_T = \textbf{40 trepid students}$$

(a) $N_P = (40) + 50 = \textbf{90 pugnacious students}$

6.

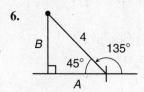

$A = 4 \cos 45°$

$A \approx 2.83$

$B = 4 \sin 45°$

$B \approx 2.83$

$\textbf{-2.83R + 2.83U}$

7.

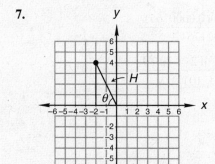

$$\tan \theta = \frac{4}{2}$$

$$\theta = 63.43°$$

Since θ is a second-quadrant angle,

$$\theta = 180° - 63.43° = 116.57°$$

$$H = \sqrt{2^2 + 4^2} = 2\sqrt{5}$$

$$\underline{\textbf{2}\sqrt{\textbf{5}}\underline{/\textbf{116.57}°}}$$

8. (a) $\frac{2}{5}x + \frac{3}{2}y = 34$

(b) $0.02x + 0.3y = 6.2$

(a') $4x + 15y = 340$

(b') $2x + 30y = 620$

-2(a') $-8x - 30y = -680$

$\quad$ (b') $\underline{\quad 2x + 30y = \quad 620}$

$$-6x \qquad = -60$$

$$x = 10$$

(a') $4(10) + 15y = 340$

$$y = 20$$

(10, 20)

9.
$$4x^2 - 3 = x$$

$$\left(x^2 - \frac{1}{4}x + \quad\right) = \frac{3}{4}$$

$$x^2 - \frac{1}{4}x + \frac{1}{64} = \frac{3}{4} + \frac{1}{64}$$

$$\left(x - \frac{1}{8}\right)^2 = \frac{49}{64}$$

$$x - \frac{1}{8} = \pm\frac{7}{8}$$

$$x = \frac{1}{8} \pm \frac{7}{8}$$

$$x = \textbf{1}, -\frac{\textbf{3}}{\textbf{4}}$$

10.
$$3x^2 = 2x + 1$$

$$\left(x^2 - \frac{2}{3}x + \quad\right) = \frac{1}{3}$$

$$x^2 - \frac{2}{3}x + \frac{1}{9} = \frac{1}{3} + \frac{1}{9}$$

$$\left(x - \frac{1}{3}\right)^2 = \frac{4}{9}$$

$$x - \frac{1}{3} = \pm\frac{2}{3}$$

$$x = \frac{1}{3} \pm \frac{2}{3}$$

$$x = \textbf{1}, -\frac{\textbf{1}}{\textbf{3}}$$

11. $Na = mC + b$

Use the graph to find the slope.

$m = \dfrac{3}{80} = 0.0375$

$Na = 0.0375C + b$

By inspection $b = 3.9$.

$Na = 0.0375C + 3.9$

12.   (a) $6x + 10y + 30 = 110$

(b) $4x + 10y + 10 = 70$

$\begin{array}{rrr} 1(a) & 6x + 10y = & 80 \\ -1(b) & -4x - 10y = & -60 \\ \hline & 2x = & 20 \\ & x = & \mathbf{10} \end{array}$

(a) $6(10) + 10y = 80$

$ y = \mathbf{2}$

13.
$$\dfrac{a}{x + y} = c + \dfrac{m}{d}$$
$$ad = cdx + cdy + mx + my$$
$$ad - cdy - my = cdx + mx$$
$$\mathbf{\dfrac{ad - cdy - my}{cd + m} = x}$$

14.
$$\dfrac{xy + c}{m} + d = \dfrac{k}{z}$$
$$xyz + cz + dmz = km$$
$$cz = km - xyz - dmz$$
$$c = \dfrac{km - xyz - dmz}{z}$$

15. $3i^3 - \sqrt{-4} + 3\sqrt{-9} - 2 + i^2$

$= 3i(ii) - 2i + 9i - 2 + (ii)$

$= -3i - 2i + 9i - 2 - 1 = \mathbf{-3 + 4i}$

16. $3i^4 - 2i^2 + 2 - 3\sqrt{-25}$

$= 3(ii)(ii) - 2(ii) + 2 - 15i$

$= 3 + 2 + 2 - 15i = \mathbf{7 - 15i}$

17. $\dfrac{60 \text{ cm}}{\text{s}} \times \dfrac{1 \text{ in.}}{2.54 \text{ cm}} \times \dfrac{1 \text{ ft}}{12 \text{ in.}} \times \dfrac{1 \text{ mi}}{5280 \text{ ft}}$

$\times \dfrac{60 \text{ s}}{1 \text{ min}} \times \dfrac{60 \text{ min}}{1 \text{ hr}}$

$= \dfrac{\mathbf{60(60)(60)}}{\mathbf{(2.54)(12)(5280)}} \dfrac{\mathbf{mi}}{\mathbf{hr}}$

18. $1{,}400{,}000 \text{ cm}^3 \times \dfrac{1 \text{ in.}}{2.54 \text{ cm}} \times \dfrac{1 \text{ in.}}{2.54 \text{ cm}} \times \dfrac{1 \text{ in.}}{2.54 \text{ cm}}$

$\times \dfrac{1 \text{ ft}}{12 \text{ in.}} \times \dfrac{1 \text{ ft}}{12 \text{ in.}} \times \dfrac{1 \text{ ft}}{12 \text{ in.}} \times \dfrac{1 \text{ yd}}{3 \text{ ft}} \times \dfrac{1 \text{ yd}}{3 \text{ ft}} \times \dfrac{1 \text{ yd}}{3 \text{ ft}}$

$= \dfrac{\mathbf{1{,}400{,}000}}{\mathbf{(2.54)(2.54)(2.54)(12)(12)(12)(3)(3)(3)}} \text{ yd}^3$

19. $\sqrt[3]{27\sqrt{3}} = \sqrt[3]{3^3\sqrt{3}} = \left[3^3(3^{1/2})\right]^{1/3}$

$= 3 \cdot 3^{1/6} = \mathbf{3^{7/6}}$

20. $\sqrt[4]{81}\sqrt[3]{3} = \sqrt[4]{3^4}\sqrt[3]{3} = (3^4)^{1/4}(3^{1/3})$

$= 3 \cdot 3^{1/3} = \mathbf{3^{4/3}}$

21. $81^{-3/4} = \dfrac{1}{81^{3/4}} = \dfrac{1}{(81^{1/4})^3} = \mathbf{\dfrac{1}{27}}$

22. $\sqrt{m^2 p}\sqrt[3]{m^5 p^4} = (m^2 p)^{1/2}(m^5 p^4)^{1/3}$

$= mp^{1/2}m^{5/3}p^{4/3} = \mathbf{m^{8/3}p^{11/6}}$

23. $5\sqrt{\dfrac{2}{9}} + 3\sqrt{\dfrac{9}{2}} - 5\sqrt{8}$

$= \dfrac{5\sqrt{2}}{3} + \dfrac{9}{\sqrt{2}}\dfrac{\sqrt{2}}{\sqrt{2}} - 10\sqrt{2}$

$= \dfrac{10\sqrt{2}}{6} + \dfrac{27\sqrt{2}}{6} - \dfrac{60\sqrt{2}}{6} = \mathbf{-\dfrac{23\sqrt{2}}{6}}$

24. $\dfrac{(5{,}162{,}348)(0.0000165)}{0.003217642}$

$\approx \dfrac{(5 \times 10^6)(2 \times 10^{-5})}{3 \times 10^{-3}} \approx \mathbf{3 \times 10^4}$

25. $15 \times \overrightarrow{SF} = 20$

$\overrightarrow{SF} = \dfrac{4}{3}$

$8 \times \dfrac{4}{3} = K$

$\dfrac{32}{3} = K$

26. $x = 180 - 90 - 40 = \mathbf{50}$

$k = 180 - 90 - 50 = \mathbf{40}$

$s = 180 - 90 - 40 = \mathbf{50}$

27. (a) $2x - 3y = -3$

(b) $2x + y = 8$

Substitute $y = -2x + 8$ into (a) and get:

(a') $2x - 3(-2x + 8) = -3$

$$8x = 21$$

$$x = \frac{21}{8}$$

(b) $y = -2\left(\dfrac{21}{8}\right) + 8 = \dfrac{11}{4}$

$$\left(\frac{21}{8}, \frac{11}{4}\right)$$

28. $x^3 + 50x = 15x^2$

$x^3 - 15x^2 + 50x = 0$

$x(x - 10)(x - 5) = 0$

$$x = \mathbf{0, 5, 10}$$

29. $y = \dfrac{2}{5}x + b$

Use the point $(-40, 2)$ for x and y.

$$2 = \frac{2}{5}(-40) + b$$

$$18 = b$$

$$y = \frac{2}{5}x + 18$$

30. $\dfrac{3x^{-4}y^0y^2}{x^2x}\left(\dfrac{2x^2y^2}{y^4} - \dfrac{y^0x^0p^{-2}}{x^4y^4}\right)$

$= \dfrac{6x^{-2}y^4}{x^3y^4} - \dfrac{3x^{-4}p^{-2}y^2}{x^7y^4}$

$= \mathbf{6x^{-5} - 3x^{-11}p^{-2}y^{-2}}$

PRACTICE SET 61

Water one $-$ water evaporated $=$ water final

$$(400) - (E_W) = (400 - E_W)$$

$$0.85(400) - 1.00E_W = 0.60(400 - E_W)$$

$$340 - E_W = 240 - 0.6E_W$$

$$100 = 0.4E_W$$

$$\mathbf{250 \text{ gallons}} = E_W$$

PROBLEM SET 61

1. $R_D = kS$

$0.005 = k(5)$

$0.001 = k$

$R_D = 0.001(0.3) = \mathbf{0.0003 \text{ kg per second}}$

2. $\dfrac{P_1}{T_1} = \dfrac{P_2}{T_2}$

$\dfrac{P_1}{1000} = \dfrac{300}{600}$

$P_1 = \dfrac{300(1000)}{600}$

$P_1 = \mathbf{500 \text{ N/m}^2}$

3. Water one $-$ water out $=$ water final

$$W_1 - W_O = W_F$$

$$(100) - (E) = (100 - E)$$

$$0.9(100) - (E) = 0.8(100 - E)$$

$$90 - E = 80 - 0.8E$$

$$-0.2E = -10$$

$$E = \mathbf{50 \text{ gallons}}$$

4. Butterfat one $+$ butterfat added $=$ butterfat final

$$B_1 + B_A = B_F$$

$$(900) + (P_N) = (900 + P_N)$$

$$0.02(900) + (P_N) = 0.1(900 + P_N)$$

$$18 + P_N = 90 + 0.1P_N$$

$$0.9P_N = 72$$

$$P_N = \mathbf{80 \text{ pounds}}$$

5. Glycol$_1$ $+$ glycol added $=$ glycol final

$$(100) + (P_N) = (100 + P_N)$$

$$0.2(100) + 0.3(P_N) = 0.25(100 + P_N)$$

$$20 + 0.3P_N = 25 + 0.25P_N$$

$$0.05P_N = 5$$

$$P_N = \mathbf{100 \text{ kilograms}}$$

6.

$A = 20 \cos 15°$

$A \approx 19.32$

$B = 20 \sin 15°$

$B \approx 5.18$

$\mathbf{-19.32R + 5.18U}$

7.

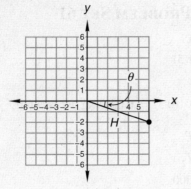

$$\tan \theta = \frac{2}{6}$$

$$\theta \approx 18.43°$$

Since θ is a fourth-quadrant angle,

$$\theta = 360 - 18.43 = 341.57°$$

$$H = \sqrt{6^2 + 2^2} = 2\sqrt{10}$$

$$\mathbf{2\sqrt{10}/341.57°}$$

8. (a) $\frac{2}{3}x - \frac{2}{5}y = -4$

(b) $0.2x + 0.9y = 19.2$

(a') $10x - 6y = -60$

(b') $2x + 9y = 192$

$$\begin{array}{rl} (a') & 10x - 6y = -60 \\ -5(b') & -10x - 45y = -960 \\ \hline & -51y = -1020 \\ & y = 20 \end{array}$$

(a') $10x - 6(20) = -60$

$$x = 6$$

(6, 20)

9.
$$-4x - 4 = -5x^2$$

$$\left(x^2 - \frac{4}{5}x + \right) = \frac{4}{5}$$

$$x^2 - \frac{4}{5}x + \frac{4}{25} = \frac{4}{5} + \frac{4}{25}$$

$$\left(x - \frac{2}{5}\right)^2 = \frac{24}{25}$$

$$x - \frac{2}{5} = \pm\frac{2\sqrt{6}}{5}$$

$$x = \frac{2}{5} \pm \frac{2\sqrt{6}}{5}$$

10.
$$-x = 7 - 2x^2$$

$$\left(x^2 - \frac{1}{2}x + \right) = \frac{7}{2}$$

$$x^2 - \frac{1}{2}x + \frac{1}{16} = \frac{7}{2} + \frac{1}{16}$$

$$\left(x - \frac{1}{4}\right)^2 = \frac{57}{16}$$

$$x - \frac{1}{4} = \pm\frac{\sqrt{57}}{4}$$

$$x = \frac{1}{4} \pm \frac{\sqrt{57}}{4}$$

11. $Pb = mSb + b$

Use the graph to find the slope.

$$m = \frac{100}{2.35} \approx 42.6$$

$Pb = (42.6)Sb + b$

Use the point (0.75, 0) for Sb and Pb.

$$0 = 42.6(0.75) + b$$

$$-32 \approx b$$

$$\mathbf{Pb = 42.6Sb - 32}$$

12. $x + 3 = 68$

$$x = \mathbf{65}$$

$$360 = y - 12 + 30 + 68 + 62 + 78 + 32 + 54$$

$$\mathbf{48} = y$$

13.
$$\frac{(m + c + x)b}{k} + \frac{a}{d} = p$$

$$bdm + bcd + bdx + ka = dkp$$

$$dkp - bdm - bdx - ka = bcd$$

$$\mathbf{\frac{dkp - bdm - bdx - ka}{bd} = c}$$

14.
$$\frac{4y}{2a + x} + \frac{m}{c} = d$$

$$4cy + 2am + mx = 2acd + cdx$$

$$2am - 2acd = cdx - 4cy - mx$$

$$a = \mathbf{\frac{cdx - 4cy - mx}{2m - 2cd}}$$

15. $-2i^2 - 3i - 4 - 2\sqrt{-4} = -2(ii) - 3i - 4 - 4i$

$$= 2 - 3i - 4 - 4i = \mathbf{-2 - 7i}$$

16. $8i^4 - 2i^3 - 6 - 4\sqrt{-16}$

$$= 8(ii)(ii) - 2i(ii) - 6 - 16i$$

$$= 8 + 2i - 6 - 16i = \mathbf{2 - 14i}$$

17. $\dfrac{40 \text{ cm}^3}{s} \times \dfrac{1 \text{ in.}}{2.54 \text{ cm}} \times \dfrac{1 \text{ in.}}{2.54 \text{ cm}} \times \dfrac{1 \text{ in.}}{2.54 \text{ cm}}$

$\times \dfrac{60 \text{ s}}{1 \text{ min}} \times \dfrac{60 \text{ min}}{1 \text{ hr}}$

$= \dfrac{40(60)(60)}{(2.54)(2.54)(2.54)} \dfrac{\text{in.}^3}{\text{hr}}$

18. $4 \text{ ft}^3 \times \dfrac{12 \text{ in.}}{1 \text{ ft}} \times \dfrac{12 \text{ in.}}{1 \text{ ft}} \times \dfrac{12 \text{ in.}}{1 \text{ ft}} \times \dfrac{2.54 \text{ cm}}{1 \text{ in.}}$

$\times \dfrac{2.54 \text{ cm}}{1 \text{ in.}} \times \dfrac{2.54 \text{ cm}}{1 \text{ in.}}$

$= \mathbf{4(12)(12)(12)(2.54)(2.54)(2.54) \text{ cm}^3}$

19. $\sqrt{32\sqrt{2}} = \sqrt{2^5 \sqrt{2}} = \left[2^5(2^{1/2})\right]^{1/2} = 2^{5/2}2^{1/4}$
$= \mathbf{2^{11/4}}$

20. $\sqrt[3]{8\sqrt[3]{2}} = \sqrt[3]{2^3 \sqrt[3]{2}} = \left[2^3(2^{1/3})\right]^{1/3} = 2 \cdot 2^{1/9}$
$= \mathbf{2^{10/9}}$

21. $-8^{-5/3} = -\dfrac{1}{8^{5/3}} = -\dfrac{1}{(8^{1/3})^5} = -\dfrac{1}{32}$

22. $\sqrt{x^5 y}\sqrt[4]{y^2 xv} = (x^5 y)^{1/2}(y^2 x)^{1/4} = x^{5/2}y^{1/2}y^{1/2}x^{1/4}$
$= \mathbf{x^{11/4}y}$

23. $3\sqrt{\dfrac{2}{3}} - 4\sqrt{\dfrac{3}{2}} + 8\sqrt{24}$

$= \dfrac{3\sqrt{2}}{\sqrt{3}} \dfrac{\sqrt{3}}{\sqrt{3}} - \dfrac{4\sqrt{3}}{\sqrt{2}} \dfrac{\sqrt{2}}{\sqrt{2}} + 16\sqrt{6}$

$= \dfrac{6\sqrt{6}}{6} - \dfrac{12\sqrt{6}}{6} + \dfrac{96\sqrt{6}}{6} = \mathbf{15\sqrt{6}}$

24. $\dfrac{(41,685,231)(0.0012846 \times 10^{-14})}{0.001998 \times 10^{-10}}$

$\approx \dfrac{(4 \times 10^7)(1 \times 10^{-17})}{2 \times 10^{-13}} = \mathbf{2 \times 10^3}$

25. $A^2 = 5^2 + 12^2$

$A^2 = 169$

$A = 13$

$5 \times \overrightarrow{SF} = 4$

$\overrightarrow{SF} = \dfrac{4}{5}$

$13 \times \dfrac{4}{5} = C$

$\dfrac{52}{5} = C$

26. $\dfrac{r+1}{s} = \dfrac{t-1}{v}$

$rv + v = st - s$

$rv = st - s - v$

$r = \dfrac{st - s - v}{v}$

27. (a) $x - 2y = -6$

$-2y = -x - 6$

$y = \dfrac{1}{2}x + 3$

(b) $x + y = -1$

$y = -x - 1$

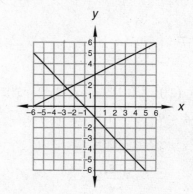

Substitute $y = -x - 1$ into (a) and get:

(a′) $x - 2(-x - 1) = -6$

$x = -\dfrac{8}{3}$

(b) $\left(-\dfrac{8}{3}\right) + y = -1$

$y = \dfrac{5}{3}$

$\left(-\dfrac{8}{3}, \dfrac{5}{3}\right)$

28. $-15x = -x^3 + 2x^2$

$x^3 - 2x^2 - 15x = 0$

$x(x - 5)(x + 3) = 0$

$x = \mathbf{0, 5, -3}$

29. Write the equation of the given line in slope-intercept form.

$$2x + 3y = 5$$

$$y = -\frac{2}{3}x + \frac{5}{3}$$

Since the slopes of perpendicular lines are negative reciprocals of each other,

$$m_\perp = \frac{3}{2}$$

$$y = \frac{3}{2}x + b$$

$$4 = \frac{3}{2}(-2) + b$$

$$7 = b$$

$$y = \frac{3}{2}x + 7$$

30. $-2^2 - 3^2 - (2^0)^2 - (-2)^0 = -x(-2x^0 - 5^0)2^2$

$$-4 - 9 - 1 - 1 = (2x + x)4$$

$$-15 = 12x$$

$$-\frac{5}{4} = x$$

PRACTICE SET 62

$$-x + 5x^2 + 3 = 0$$

$$5x^2 - x + 3 = 0$$

$$x^2 - \frac{1}{5}x + \frac{3}{5} = 0$$

$$\left(x^2 - \frac{1}{5}x \qquad\right) = -\frac{3}{5}$$

$$\left(x^2 - \frac{1}{5}x + \frac{1}{100}\right) = -\frac{3}{5} + \frac{1}{100}$$

$$\left(x - \frac{1}{10}\right)^2 = -\frac{59}{100}$$

$$x - \frac{1}{10} = \pm\sqrt{\frac{-59}{100}}$$

$$x = \frac{1}{10} \pm \frac{\sqrt{59}}{10}i$$

PROBLEM SET 62

1. $N_V = \dfrac{k}{S}$

$$8 = \frac{k}{2}$$

$$16 = k$$

$$N_V = \frac{16}{8} = \textbf{2 victories}$$

2. $\dfrac{P_1 V_1}{T_1} = \dfrac{P_2 V_2}{T_2}$

$$\frac{(600)(2)}{(300)} = \frac{(400)(4)}{T_2}$$

$$T_2 = \textbf{400 K}$$

3. $S_1 + S_A = S_T$

$$(40) + (P_N) = (40 + P_N)$$

$$0.05(40) + 0.2(P_N) = 0.1(40 + P_N)$$

$$2 + 0.2P_N = 4 + 0.1P_N$$

$$0.1P_N = 2$$

$$P_N = \textbf{20 liters}$$

4.

D_S	D_T

$$\text{152}$$

$R_S T_S + R_T T_T = 152; \; R_S = 8;$

$R_T = 20; \; T_S + T_T = 10$

$8T_S + 20(10 - T_S) = 152$

$$-12T_S = -48$$

$$T_S = 4$$

$D_S = 8(4) = \textbf{32 miles}$

5.

Carbon:	$1 \times 12 = 12$
Hydrogen:	$4 \times 1 = 4$
Oxygen:	$1 \times 16 = 16$
Nitrogen:	$2 \times 14 = 28$
Total:	$12 + 4 + 16 + 28 = 60$

Nitrogen: $\dfrac{28}{60} \times 100\% \approx \textbf{46.78\%}$

6.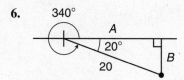

$A = 20 \cos 20°$

$A \approx 18.79$

$B = 20 \sin 20°$

$B \approx 6.84$

18.79R − 6.84U

7.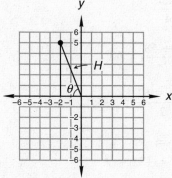

$\tan \theta = \dfrac{5}{2}$

$\theta \approx 68.20°$

Since θ is a second-quadrant angle,

$\theta = 180 - 68.20 = 111.80°$

$H = \sqrt{5^2 + 2^2} = \sqrt{29}$

$\sqrt{29}\underline{/111.80°}$

8. (a) $\dfrac{1}{3}x - \dfrac{2}{3}y = -1$

(b) $0.02x + 0.4y = 2.58$

(a') $x - 2y = -3$

(b') $2x + 40y = 258$

$\begin{array}{l} -2(a')\ -2x + 4y = 6 \\ \ \ (b')\ \underline{\ 2x + 40y = 258} \\ \qquad\qquad 44y = 264 \\ \qquad\qquad\ \ y = 6 \end{array}$

(a') $x - 2(6) = -3$

$x = 9$

(9, 6)

9. $-x + 2x^2 + 3 = 0$

$\left(x^2 - \dfrac{1}{2}x + \ \ \right) = -\dfrac{3}{2}$

$x^2 - \dfrac{1}{2}x + \dfrac{1}{16} = -\dfrac{3}{2} + \dfrac{1}{16}$

$\left(x - \dfrac{1}{4}\right)^2 = -\dfrac{23}{16}$

$x - \dfrac{1}{4} = \pm\dfrac{\sqrt{23}}{4}i$

$x = \dfrac{1}{4} \pm \dfrac{\sqrt{23}}{4}i$

10. $-5x + 6x^2 = -3$

$\left(x^2 - \dfrac{5}{6}x + \ \ \right) = -\dfrac{1}{2}$

$x^2 - \dfrac{5}{6}x + \dfrac{25}{144} = -\dfrac{1}{2} + \dfrac{25}{144}$

$\left(x - \dfrac{5}{12}\right)^2 = -\dfrac{47}{144}$

$x - \dfrac{5}{12} = \pm\dfrac{\sqrt{47}}{12}i$

$x = \dfrac{5}{12} \pm \dfrac{\sqrt{47}}{12}i$

11. $\text{Bi} = m\text{Hg} + b$

Use the graph to find the slope.

$m = \dfrac{24}{1.5} = 16$

$\text{Bi} = 16\text{Hg} + b$

Use the point (6, 24) for Hg and Bi.

$24 = 16(6) + b$

$-72 = b$

Bi = 16Hg − 72

12. Volume $= \pi r^2 h = 11{,}520\pi$ in.^{3}

$r^2 = \dfrac{11{,}520\pi \text{ in.}^3}{20\pi \text{ in.}}$

$r = \sqrt{576 \text{ in.}^2} =$ **24 in.**

13. $\dfrac{(a + b)m}{c} - k = \dfrac{p}{r}$

$amr + bmr - ckr = cp$

$bmr = cp + ckr - amr$

$b = \dfrac{cp + ckr - amr}{mr}$

14.
$$\frac{6x}{2y + 4a} - c = \frac{p}{r}$$

$$6xr - 2cry - 4acr = 2py + 4ap$$

$$6xr - 4acr - 4ap = 2py + 2cry$$

$$\frac{3xr - 2acr - 2ap}{p + cr} = y$$

15. $3i^3 - \sqrt{-4} - 2 - \sqrt{9} + 3$

$= 3i(ii) - 2i - 2 - 3 + 3$

$= -2 - 5i$

16. $-3i^3 + 2i - 4 - 3i^2 - 2\sqrt{9}$

$= -3i(ii) + 2i - 4 - 3(ii) - 6$

$= -7 + 5i$

17. $\dfrac{600 \text{ cm}^3}{\text{min}} \times \dfrac{1 \text{ in.}}{2.54 \text{ cm}} \times \dfrac{1 \text{ in.}}{2.54 \text{ cm}} \times \dfrac{1 \text{ in.}}{2.54 \text{ cm}}$

$\times \dfrac{1 \text{ ft}}{12 \text{ in.}} \times \dfrac{1 \text{ ft}}{12 \text{ in.}} \times \dfrac{1 \text{ ft}}{12 \text{ in.}} \times \dfrac{1 \text{ min}}{60 \text{ s}}$

$= \dfrac{600}{(2.54)(2.54)(2.54)(12)(12)(12)(60)} \dfrac{\text{ft}^3}{\text{s}}$

18. $20 \text{ yd}^3 \times \dfrac{3 \text{ ft}}{1 \text{ yd}} \times \dfrac{3 \text{ ft}}{1 \text{ yd}} \times \dfrac{3 \text{ ft}}{1 \text{ yd}}$

$\times \dfrac{12 \text{ in.}}{1 \text{ ft}} \times \dfrac{12 \text{ in.}}{1 \text{ ft}} \times \dfrac{12 \text{ in.}}{1 \text{ ft}}$

$\times \dfrac{2.54 \text{ cm}}{1 \text{ in.}} \times \dfrac{2.54 \text{ cm}}{1 \text{ in.}} \times \dfrac{2.54 \text{ cm}}{1 \text{ in.}}$

$= 20(3)(3)(3)(12)(12)(12)(2.54)(2.54)(2.54) \text{ cm}^3$

19. $\sqrt{16\sqrt{2}} = \sqrt{2^4\sqrt{2}} = \left[2^4(2^{1/2})\right]^{1/2} = 2^2(2^{1/4})$

$= 2^{9/4}$

20. $\sqrt[4]{4}\sqrt[5]{2} = \sqrt[4]{2^2}\sqrt[5]{2} = (2^2)^{1/4}2^{1/5} = 2^{1/2}2^{1/5}$

$= 2^{7/10}$

21. $-4^{5/2} = -(4^{1/2})^5 = -32$

22. $\sqrt{xy^7}\sqrt[3]{x^5y} = (xy^7)^{1/2}(x^5y)^{1/3} = x^{1/2}y^{7/2}x^{5/3}y^{1/3}$

$= x^{13/6}y^{23/6}$

23. $3\sqrt{\dfrac{2}{5}} - 5\sqrt{\dfrac{5}{2}} - 3\sqrt{40}$

$= \dfrac{3\sqrt{2}}{\sqrt{5}}\dfrac{\sqrt{5}}{\sqrt{5}} - \dfrac{5\sqrt{5}}{\sqrt{2}}\dfrac{\sqrt{2}}{\sqrt{2}} - 6\sqrt{10}$

$= \dfrac{6\sqrt{10}}{10} - \dfrac{25\sqrt{10}}{10} - \dfrac{60\sqrt{10}}{10} = -\dfrac{79\sqrt{10}}{10}$

24. $\dfrac{(0.000618427 \times 10^{14})(7,891,642)}{3,728,196,842}$

$\approx \dfrac{(6 \times 10^{10})(8 \times 10^6)}{4 \times 10^9} \approx 1 \times 10^8$

25. $C^2 = 24^2 + 7^2$

$C^2 = 625$

$C = 25$

$24 \times \overrightarrow{SF} = 30$

$\overrightarrow{SF} = \dfrac{5}{4}$

$B + 25 = 25 \times \overrightarrow{SF}$

$B = 25 \times \dfrac{5}{4} - 25$

$B = \dfrac{125}{4} - \dfrac{100}{4}$

$B = \dfrac{25}{4}$

26. (a) $x = \dfrac{68 + 58}{2} = 63°$

(b) $x = \dfrac{160 - 52}{2} = 54°$

27. (a) $2x - 3y = -9$

$-3y = -2x - 9$

$y = \dfrac{2}{3}x + 3$

(b) $2x + 3y = -3$

$3y = -2x - 3$

$y = -\dfrac{2}{3}x - 1$

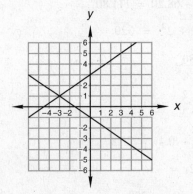

Substitute $y = -\dfrac{2}{3}x - 1$ into (a) and get:

(a′) $2x - 3\left(-\dfrac{2}{3}x - 1\right) = -9$

$4x = -12$

$x = -3$

(b) $y = -\dfrac{2}{3}(-3) - 1 = 1$

(−3, 1)

28.
$$50x + x^3 = 15x^2$$
$$x^3 - 15x^2 + 50x = 0$$
$$x(x - 10)(x - 5) = 0$$
$$x = \mathbf{0, 5, 10}$$

29.
$$y = -\frac{2}{7}x + b$$
$$-7 = -\frac{2}{7}(-5) + b$$
$$-\frac{59}{7} = b$$
$$y = -\frac{2}{7}x - \frac{59}{7}$$

30.
$$\frac{3 + x}{2} - \frac{2}{7} = 4$$
$$21 + 7x - 4 = 56$$
$$7x = 39$$
$$x = \frac{39}{7}$$

PRACTICE SET 63

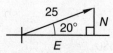

$$N = 25 \sin 20°$$
$$N \approx 25(0.34) = 8.5$$
$$E = 25 \cos 20°$$
$$E \approx 25(0.94) = 23.5$$

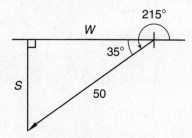

$$S = 50 \sin 35°$$
$$S \approx 50(0.57) = 28.5$$
$$W = 50 \cos 35°$$
$$W \approx 50(0.82) = 41$$

$$\begin{array}{r} 23.5R + 8.5U \\ -41\ R - 28.5U \\ \hline -17.5R + 20U \end{array}$$

Tracker was **17.5 miles west** and **20 miles south** of the cabin.

PROBLEM SET 63

1.
$$T = kD$$
$$20 = k(400)$$
$$\frac{1}{20} = k$$
$$T = \frac{1}{20}(60) = \mathbf{3\ troubles}$$

2.
$$\frac{V_1}{T_1} = \frac{V_2}{T_2}$$
$$\frac{20}{800} = \frac{12}{T_2}$$
$$T_2 = \mathbf{480\ K}$$

3.
$$W_1 + W_A = W_T$$
$$(50) + (P_N) = (50 + P_N)$$
$$0.96(50) + (P_N) = 0.99(50 + P_N)$$
$$48 + P_N = 49.5 + 0.99P_N$$
$$0.01P_N = 1.5$$
$$P_N = \mathbf{150\ gallons}$$

4.

$$R_R T_R + 4000 = R_O T_O; \ R_R = 20;$$
$$R_O = 40; \ T_R = T_O$$
$$20T + 4000 = 40T$$
$$20T = 4000$$
$$T = 200\ seconds$$

Length $= D_O = 40(200) = \mathbf{8000\ feet}$

5. Carbon: $\quad 3 \times 12 = 36$
Hydrogen: $\quad 7 \times 1 = 7$
Chlorine: $\quad 1 \times 35 = 35$
Total: $\quad 36 + 7 + 35 = 78$

$$\frac{36}{78} = \frac{48}{C_3H_7Cl}$$
$$36C_3H_7Cl = 48(78)$$
$$C_3H_7Cl = \mathbf{104\ grams}$$

6.

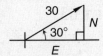

$E = 30 \cos 30° \approx 25.98$

$N = 30 \sin 30° = 15.00$

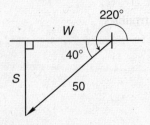

$W = 50 \cos 40° \approx 38.30$

$S = 50 \sin 40° \approx 32.14$

$$\begin{array}{r} 25.98R + 15.00U \\ -38.30R - 32.14U \\ \hline -12.32R - 17.14U \end{array}$$

Running Bear was **12.32 miles west** and **17.14 miles south** of the village.

7.

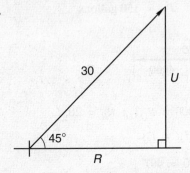

$R = 30 \cos 45° \approx 21.21$

$U = 30 \sin 45° \approx 21.21$

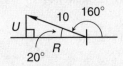

$R = 10 \cos 20° \approx 9.40$

$U = 10 \sin 20° \approx 3.42$

$$\begin{array}{r} 21.21R + 21.21U \\ -9.40R + 3.42U \\ \hline \mathbf{11.81R + 24.63U} \end{array}$$

8.

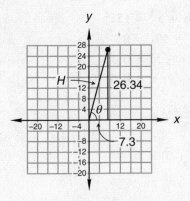

$H = \sqrt{(7.3)^2 + (26.34)^2} \approx 27.33$

$\tan \theta = \dfrac{26.34}{7.3}$

$\theta \approx 74.51°$

27.33 $\underline{/74.51°}$

9. (a) $\dfrac{1}{5}x - \dfrac{5}{2}y = -48$

(b) $0.4x + 0.05y = 5$

(a′) $2x - 25y = -480$

(b′) $40x + 5y = 500$

$$\begin{array}{r} \text{(a′)} \quad 2x - 25y = -480 \\ 5\text{(b′)} \quad 200x + 25y = 2500 \\ \hline 202x \qquad = 2020 \\ x = 10 \end{array}$$

(a′) $2(10) - 25y = -480$

$y = 20$

(10, 20)

10.

$$-x = -2x^2 - 5$$

$$\left(x^2 - \frac{1}{2}x + \right) = -\frac{5}{2}$$

$$x^2 - \frac{1}{2}x + \frac{1}{16} = -\frac{5}{2} + \frac{1}{16}$$

$$\left(x - \frac{1}{4}\right)^2 = -\frac{39}{16}$$

$$x - \frac{1}{4} = \pm\frac{\sqrt{39}}{4}i$$

$$x = \frac{1}{4} \pm \frac{\sqrt{39}}{4}i$$

11.
$$3x^2 = -4 + 2x$$
$$\left(x^2 - \frac{2}{3}x + \quad\right) = -\frac{4}{3}$$
$$x^2 - \frac{2}{3}x + \frac{1}{9} = -\frac{4}{3} + \frac{1}{9}$$
$$\left(x - \frac{1}{3}\right)^2 = -\frac{11}{9}$$
$$x - \frac{1}{3} = \pm\frac{\sqrt{11}}{3}i$$
$$x = \frac{1}{3} \pm \frac{\sqrt{11}}{3}i$$

12. $\text{Mo} = m\text{Zr} + b$

Use the graph to find the slope.

$$m = \frac{-150}{20} = -7.5$$

$$\text{Mo} = -7.5\text{Zr} + b$$

Use the point (116, 500) for Zr and Mo.

$$500 = -7.5(116) + b$$
$$1370 = b$$

$$\mathbf{Mo = -7.5Zr + 1370}$$

13.

$$H^2 = 4^2 + 3^2$$
$$H^2 = 25$$
$$H = 5$$

$$S.A. = \frac{2(6 \times 4)}{2} + 2(20 \times 5) + (20 \times 6)$$
$$= 24 + 200 + 120 = 344 \text{ m}^2$$

$$344 \text{ m}^2 \times \frac{100 \text{ cm}}{1 \text{ m}} \times \frac{100 \text{ cm}}{1 \text{ m}} = \mathbf{3{,}440{,}000 \text{ cm}^2}$$

14.
$$\frac{p + zy}{m} - c = \frac{a}{b}$$
$$bp + bzy - bcm = am$$
$$bzy = am + bcm - bp$$
$$z = \frac{am + bcm - bp}{by}$$

15.
$$\frac{p + zy}{m} - c = \frac{a}{b}$$
$$bp + bzy - bcm = am$$
$$bp + bzy = am + bcm$$
$$\frac{bp + bzy}{a + bc} = m$$

16. $4i^3 - i^5 + 2i^2 - \sqrt{-16}$
$$= 4i(ii) - i(ii)(ii) + 2(ii) - 4i = \mathbf{-2 - 9i}$$

17. $3 - 2i^5 - 3i^4 + \sqrt{-4} - i$
$$= 3 - 2i(ii)(ii) - 3(ii)(ii) + 2i - i = \mathbf{-i}$$

18.
$$\frac{400 \text{ cm}}{\text{min}} \times \frac{1 \text{ in.}}{2.54 \text{ cm}} \times \frac{1 \text{ ft}}{12 \text{ in.}} \times \frac{1 \text{ yd}}{3 \text{ ft}} \times \frac{1 \text{ min}}{60 \text{ s}}$$
$$= \frac{\mathbf{400}}{\mathbf{(2.54)(12)(3)(60)}} \frac{\mathbf{yd}}{\mathbf{s}}$$

19. $4 \text{ mi}^3 \times \dfrac{5280 \text{ ft}}{1 \text{ mi}} \times \dfrac{5280 \text{ ft}}{1 \text{ mi}} \times \dfrac{5280 \text{ ft}}{1 \text{ mi}}$
$$\times \frac{12 \text{ in.}}{1 \text{ ft}} \times \frac{12 \text{ in.}}{1 \text{ ft}} \times \frac{12 \text{ in.}}{1 \text{ ft}}$$
$$\times \frac{2.54 \text{ cm}}{1 \text{ in.}} \times \frac{2.54 \text{ cm}}{1 \text{ in.}} \times \frac{2.54 \text{ cm}}{1 \text{ in.}}$$
$$\times \frac{1 \text{ m}}{100 \text{ cm}} \times \frac{1 \text{ m}}{100 \text{ cm}} \times \frac{1 \text{ m}}{100 \text{ cm}}$$
$$\times \frac{1 \text{ km}}{1000 \text{ m}} \times \frac{1 \text{ km}}{1000 \text{ m}} \times \frac{1 \text{ km}}{1000 \text{ m}}$$
$$= \frac{\mathbf{4(5280)^3 (12)^3 (2.54)^3}}{\mathbf{(100)(100)(100)(1000)(1000)(1000)}} \text{ km}^3$$

20. $\sqrt[5]{3\sqrt[4]{3}} = \left[3(3^{1/4})\right]^{1/5} = 3^{1/5}3^{1/20} = \mathbf{3^{1/4}}$

21. $\sqrt[5]{4\sqrt[4]{2}} = \sqrt[5]{2^2\sqrt[4]{2}} = \left[2^2(2^{1/4})\right]^{1/5} = 2^{2/5}2^{1/20}$
$$= \mathbf{2^{9/20}}$$

22. $\dfrac{4}{(-27)^{-2/3}} = 4\left((-27)^{2/3}\right) = 4\left((-27)^{1/3}\right)^2$
$$= \mathbf{36}$$

23. $\sqrt[4]{xy^2}\sqrt{x^3y} = (xy^2)^{1/4}(x^3y)^{1/2} = x^{1/4}y^{1/2}x^{3/2}y^{1/2}$
$$= \mathbf{x^{7/4}y}$$

24. $3\sqrt{\dfrac{2}{7}} + 5\sqrt{\dfrac{7}{2}} - 3\sqrt{126}$
$$= \frac{3\sqrt{2}}{\sqrt{7}}\frac{\sqrt{7}}{\sqrt{7}} + \frac{5\sqrt{7}}{\sqrt{2}}\frac{\sqrt{2}}{\sqrt{2}} - 9\sqrt{14}$$
$$= \frac{6\sqrt{14}}{14} + \frac{35\sqrt{14}}{14} - \frac{126\sqrt{14}}{14} = \mathbf{-\frac{85\sqrt{14}}{14}}$$

25. $\dfrac{(476{,}158 \times 10^{22})(79{,}318{,}642)}{(983{,}704)(514.0 \times 10^{-14})}$

$\approx \dfrac{(5 \times 10^{27})(8 \times 10^7)}{(1 \times 10^6)(5 \times 10^{-12})} = \mathbf{8 \times 10^{40}}$

26. $\text{Volume}_{\text{Cone}} = \dfrac{1}{3}(\text{Area}_{\text{Base}})(\text{height}) = 12\pi \, \text{m}^3$

$$\dfrac{1}{3}\pi r^2 h = 12\pi \, \text{m}^3$$

$$r^2 = 6 \, \text{m}^2$$

$$r = \mathbf{\sqrt{6} \, \text{m}}$$

27. $12(90 - A) = (180 - A) + 20$

$1080 - 12A = 200 - A$

$-11A = -880$

$A = \mathbf{80°}$

28. Write the equation of the given line in slope-intercept form.

$5x + 4y = 7$

$$y = -\dfrac{5}{4}x + \dfrac{7}{4}$$

Since parallel lines have the same slope,

$$y = -\dfrac{5}{4}x + b$$

$$-7 = -\dfrac{5}{4}(2) + b$$

$$-\dfrac{9}{2} = b$$

$$y = -\dfrac{5}{4}x - \dfrac{9}{2}$$

29. $2 = -2^0 - 2^2 - 2^2(-2 - 1^0)x - 3x - 7x^0y^0 - 4$

$2 = -1 - 4 + 12x - 3x - 7 - 4$

$18 = 9x$

$\mathbf{2} = x$

30. $\dfrac{4x + 5}{3} - \dfrac{x}{7} = 2$

$28x + 35 - 3x = 42$

$25x = 7$

$$x = \mathbf{\dfrac{7}{25}}$$

PRACTICE SET 64

a. $b + \dfrac{1}{\dfrac{1}{z} + 2m} = b + \dfrac{1}{\dfrac{1 + 2mz}{z}}$

$= b + \dfrac{1 \cdot \dfrac{z}{1 + 2mz}}{\dfrac{1 + 2mz}{z} \cdot \dfrac{z}{1 + 2mz}} = b + \dfrac{z}{1 + 2mz}$

$= \dfrac{(1 + 2mz)b}{1 + 2mz} + \dfrac{z}{1 + 2mz} = \dfrac{\mathbf{b + 2bmz + z}}{\mathbf{1 + 2mz}}$

b. $\dfrac{s}{z} + \dfrac{3}{5 + \dfrac{2s}{z}} = \dfrac{s}{z} + \dfrac{3}{\dfrac{5z + 2s}{z}}$

$= \dfrac{s}{z} + \dfrac{3 \cdot \dfrac{z}{5z + 2s}}{\dfrac{5z + 2s}{z} \cdot \dfrac{z}{5z + 2s}} = \dfrac{s}{z} + \dfrac{3z}{5z + 2s}$

$= \dfrac{(5z + 2s)s}{(5z + 2s)z} + \dfrac{(z)3z}{(z)(5z + 2s)}$

$= \dfrac{5sz + 2s^2 + 3z^2}{z(5z + 2s)}$

$= \dfrac{\mathbf{2s^2 + 5sz + 3z^2}}{\mathbf{z(5z + 2s)}} = \dfrac{\mathbf{(2s + 3z)(s + z)}}{\mathbf{z(5z + 2s)}}$

c. $i^4 - 5i^3 - 3\sqrt{-3}\sqrt{-5}$

$= (ii)(ii) - 5i(ii) - 3\sqrt{3}i\sqrt{5}i$

$= (-1)(-1) - 5i(-1) - 3\sqrt{3}\sqrt{5}(ii)$

$= 1 + 5i - 3\sqrt{15}(-1) = 1 + 5i + 3\sqrt{15}$

$= \mathbf{(1 + 3\sqrt{15}) + 5i}$

d. $(3 + 5i)(4 - 5i) = 12 - 15i + 20i - 25i^2$

$= 12 + 5i - 25(-1) = \mathbf{37 + 5i}$

PROBLEM SET 64

1. $C = \dfrac{k}{F}$

$300 = \dfrac{k}{2}$

$k = 600$

$C = \dfrac{600}{0.5} = \mathbf{1200 \text{ grams}}$

2. $\dfrac{P_1}{T_1} = \dfrac{P_2}{T_2}$

$\dfrac{700}{400} = \dfrac{2800}{T_2}$

$T_2 = \mathbf{1600 \text{ K}}$

3. Iodine P_N + Iodine D_N = Iodine Total

$$0.3(P_N) + 0.8(D_N) = 0.4(50)$$

(a) $0.3P_N + 0.8D_N = 20$

(b) $P_N + D_N = 50$

Substitute $D_N = 50 - P_N$ into (a) and get:

(a') $0.3P_N + 0.8(50 - P_N) = 20$

$$-0.5P_N = -20$$

$$P_N = 40$$

(b) $(40) + D_N = 50$

$$D_N = 10$$

40 liters 30%, 10 liters 80%

4.

$R_I T_I = R_O T_O$; $R_I = 400$;

$R_O = 100$; $T_I + T_O = 40$

$400T_I = 100(40 - T_I)$

$500T_I = 4000$

$T_I = 8$ hr

$D_I = 400(8) =$ **3200 kilometers**

5. Carbon: $\quad\quad 1 \times 12 = 12$

Hydrogen: $\quad\quad 3 \times 1 = 3$

Iodine: $\quad\quad 1 \times 127 = 127$

Total: $\quad 12 + 3 + 127 = 142$

Iodine: $\dfrac{127}{142} \times 100\% \approx$ **89.44%**

6. $m + \dfrac{2}{\dfrac{2}{c} + s} = m + \dfrac{2}{\dfrac{2 + cs}{c}}$

$= m + \dfrac{2c}{2 + cs} = \dfrac{\boldsymbol{2m + cms + 2c}}{\boldsymbol{2 + cs}}$

7. $\dfrac{m}{a} + \dfrac{3}{2 + \dfrac{s}{a}} = \dfrac{m}{a} + \dfrac{3}{\dfrac{2a + s}{a}}$

$= \dfrac{m}{a} + \dfrac{3a}{2a + s} = \dfrac{\boldsymbol{2am + ms + 3a^2}}{\boldsymbol{a(2a + s)}}$

8. $\dfrac{m}{c} + \dfrac{8}{2 + \dfrac{m}{c}} = \dfrac{m}{c} + \dfrac{8}{\dfrac{2c + m}{c}}$

$= \dfrac{m}{c} + \dfrac{8c}{2c + m} = \dfrac{\boldsymbol{2cm + m^2 + 8c^2}}{\boldsymbol{c(2c + m)}}$

9. $9i^3 - 3i^4 + 2\sqrt{-4} + \sqrt{-2}\sqrt{-2}$

$= 9i(ii) - 3(ii)(ii) + 4i + \sqrt{2}i\sqrt{2}i$

$= -9i - 3 + 4i - 2 =$ **−5 − 5i**

10. $\sqrt{-4} + \sqrt{-2}\sqrt{-2} - 4^3$

$= 2i + \sqrt{2}i\sqrt{2}i - 64 =$ **−66 + 2i**

11. $i^4 - 3i^2 - 2\sqrt{-2}\sqrt{-3}$

$= (ii)(ii) - 3(ii) - 2\sqrt{2}i\sqrt{3}i =$ **4 + 2$\sqrt{6}$**

12. $2\sqrt{-9} - 3i^4 + 2\sqrt{3}\sqrt{-3} + i$

$= 6i - 3(ii)(ii) + 2\sqrt{3}\sqrt{3}i + i =$ **−3 + 13i**

13. $(2 + 3i)(5 - 3i)$

$= 10 - 6i + 15i - 9i^2 =$ **19 + 9i**

14. $(3i - 5)(2 + 4i)$

$= 6i + 12i^2 - 10 - 20i =$ **−22 − 14i**

15. $(2i - 4)(i + 2) = 2i^2 + 4i - 4i - 8 =$ **−10**

16.

$R = 10 \cos 10° \approx 9.85$

$U = 10 \sin 10° \approx 1.74$

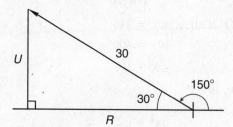

$R = 30 \cos 30° \approx 25.98$

$U = 30 \sin 30° = 15.00$

$\begin{array}{r} 9.85R + 1.74U \\ -25.98R + 15.00U \\ \hline \boldsymbol{-16.13R + 16.74U} \end{array}$

17.

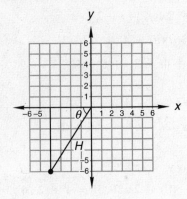

$H = \sqrt{4^2 + 6^2}$

$H = \sqrt{52} = 2\sqrt{13}$

$\tan \theta = \dfrac{6}{4}$

$\theta \approx 56.31°$

Since θ is a third-quadrant angle,

$\theta = 56.31 + 180 = 236.31°$

$2\sqrt{13}/\underline{236.31°}$

18. (a) $\dfrac{3}{2}x - \dfrac{1}{5}y = 28$

(b) $0.02x + 0.4y = 4.4$

(a') $15x - 2y = 280$

(b') $2x + 40y = 440$

$20(a')\ \ 300x - 40y = 5600$

$\ \ (b')\ \ \ \underline{2x + 40y = \ \ 440}$

$\qquad\quad 302x \qquad\quad = 6040$

$\qquad\qquad\qquad\quad x = 20$

(b') $2(20) + 40y = 440$

$\qquad\qquad 40y = 400$

$\qquad\qquad\quad y = 10$

(20, 10)

19. $3x^2 = -2x - 5$

$\left(x^2 + \dfrac{2}{3}x + \quad\right) = -\dfrac{5}{3}$

$x^2 + \dfrac{2}{3}x + \dfrac{1}{9} = -\dfrac{5}{3} + \dfrac{1}{9}$

$\left(x + \dfrac{1}{3}\right)^2 = -\dfrac{14}{9}$

$x + \dfrac{1}{3} = \pm\dfrac{\sqrt{14}}{3}i$

$x = -\dfrac{1}{3} \pm \dfrac{\sqrt{14}}{3}i$

20. $-3x + 2x^2 = -7$

$\left(x^2 - \dfrac{3}{2}x + \quad\right) = -\dfrac{7}{2}$

$x^2 - \dfrac{3}{2}x + \dfrac{9}{16} = -\dfrac{7}{2} + \dfrac{9}{16}$

$\left(x - \dfrac{3}{4}\right)^2 = -\dfrac{47}{16}$

$x - \dfrac{3}{4} = \pm\dfrac{\sqrt{47}}{4}i$

$x = \dfrac{3}{4} \pm \dfrac{\sqrt{47}}{4}i$

21. $W = m\text{Ir} + b$

Use the graph to find the slope.

$m = \dfrac{-35}{250} = -0.14$

$W = -0.14\text{Ir} + b$

Use the point (1850, 50) for Ir and W.

$50 = -0.14(1850) + b$

$309 = b$

$W = -0.14\text{Ir} + 309$

22. $\text{Area} = \text{Area}_{\text{Triangle}} + \text{Area}_{\text{Semicircle}}$

$= \dfrac{1}{2}bH + \dfrac{1}{2}\pi r^2$

$H^2 = 6^2 - \left(\dfrac{5}{2}\right)^2$

$H^2 = 36 - \dfrac{25}{4}$

$H = \dfrac{\sqrt{119}}{2}$

$\text{Area} = \left[\dfrac{1}{2}(5)\left(\dfrac{\sqrt{119}}{2}\right) + \dfrac{1}{2}\pi(3)^2\right]\text{m}^2$

$= \left(\dfrac{5\sqrt{119}}{4} + \dfrac{9}{2}\pi\right)\text{m}^2$

23. $\dfrac{400\text{ cm}^3}{\text{s}} \times \dfrac{1\text{ in.}}{2.54\text{ cm}} \times \dfrac{1\text{ in.}}{2.54\text{ cm}} \times \dfrac{1\text{ in.}}{2.54\text{ cm}}$

$\times \dfrac{60\text{ s}}{1\text{ min}} \times \dfrac{60\text{ min}}{1\text{ hr}}$

$= \dfrac{400(60)(60)}{(2.54)(2.54)(2.54)}\dfrac{\text{in.}^3}{\text{hr}}$

24. $\sqrt[3]{9\sqrt[3]{3}} = \sqrt[3]{3^2\sqrt[3]{3}} = \left[3^2(3^{1/3})\right]^{1/3} = 3^{2/3}3^{1/9}$

$= \mathbf{3^{7/9}}$

25. $2\sqrt{\dfrac{7}{5}} - 3\sqrt{\dfrac{5}{7}} + 2\sqrt{140}$

$= \dfrac{2\sqrt{7}}{\sqrt{5}}\dfrac{\sqrt{5}}{\sqrt{5}} - \dfrac{3\sqrt{5}}{\sqrt{7}}\dfrac{\sqrt{7}}{\sqrt{7}} + 4\sqrt{35}$

$= \dfrac{14\sqrt{35}}{35} - \dfrac{15\sqrt{35}}{35} + \dfrac{140\sqrt{35}}{35} = \mathbf{\dfrac{139\sqrt{35}}{35}}$

26. $\dfrac{a(b+c)}{x} - m = \dfrac{d}{f}$

$abf + acf - fmx = dx$

$abf + acf = dx + fmx$

$\mathbf{\dfrac{abf + acf}{d + fm} = x}$

27. $\dfrac{a(b+c)}{x} - m = \dfrac{d}{f}$

$abf + acf - fmx = dx$

$acf = dx + fmx - abf$

$\mathbf{c = \dfrac{dx + fmx - abf}{af}}$

28. (a) $x - 3y = -6$

$-3y = -x - 6$

$y = \dfrac{1}{3}x + 2$

(b) $2x + 5y = 15$

$5y = -2x + 15$

$y = -\dfrac{2}{5}x + 3$

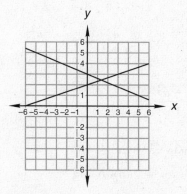

Substitute $x = 3y - 6$ into (b) and get:

(b′) $2(3y - 6) + 5y = 15$

$11y = 27$

$y = \dfrac{27}{11}$

(a) $x = 3\left(\dfrac{27}{11}\right) - 6 = \dfrac{15}{11}$

$\left(\mathbf{\dfrac{15}{11}, \dfrac{27}{11}}\right)$

29.
$$56x = -15x^2 - x^3$$
$$x^3 + 15x^2 + 56x = 0$$
$$x(x + 7)(x + 8) = 0$$
$$x = \mathbf{0, -7, -8}$$

30. $\dfrac{(146{,}842 \times 10^2)(0.0007892)}{(96{,}478 \times 10^{14})(0.000712 \times 10^{42})}$

$\approx \dfrac{(1 \times 10^7)(8 \times 10^{-4})}{(1 \times 10^{19})(7 \times 10^{38})} \approx \mathbf{1 \times 10^{-54}}$

PRACTICE SET 65

$R_P T_P = 288$

$(3R_C)(12 - T_C) = 288$

$36R_C - 3R_C T_C = 288$

$36R_C - 3(108) = 288$

$36R_C - 324 = 288$

$36R_C = 612$

$R_C = \mathbf{17}$

$R_P = 3(17)$

$R_P = \mathbf{51}$

$(51)T_P = 288$

$T_P = \dfrac{288}{51}$

$T_P = \mathbf{\dfrac{96}{17}}$

$\dfrac{96}{17} + T_C = 12$

$T_C = 12 - \dfrac{96}{17}$

$T_C = \mathbf{\dfrac{108}{17}}$

PROBLEM SET 65

1. $Si = kP$

$400 = k(100)$

$4 = k$

$Si = 4(12) = \mathbf{48 \text{ kilograms}}$

2. $P_1 V_1 = P_2 V_2$

$800(2) = P_2(0.1)$

$P_2 = \mathbf{16{,}000 \text{ N/m}^2}$

3. $0.84(500) - (E) = 0.8(500 - E)$

$\qquad 420 - E = 400 - 0.8E$

$\qquad -0.2E = -20$

$\qquad\qquad E = \textbf{100 milliliters}$

4. (a) $N_I = N_E + 400$

(b) $N_I = 4N_E + 100$

Substitute (b) into (a) and get:

(a$'$) $(4N_E + 100) = N_E + 400$

$\qquad\qquad 3N_E = 300$

$\qquad\qquad N_E = 100$

(a) $N_I = (100) + 400 = 500$

100 were erudite while 500 were ignorant.

5. $\dfrac{96}{100} \times T = 1920$

$\qquad T = 1920 \times \dfrac{100}{96} = 2000$

$\text{Phosgene}_{\text{Combined}} = 2000 - 1920$

$\qquad\qquad = \textbf{80 kilograms}$

6. (a) $R_W T_W = 8$

(b) $R_B T_B = 8$

(c) $R_B = 4R_W$

(d) $T_B = 2 - T_W$

Substitute (c) and (d) into (b) and get:

(b$'$) $4R_W(2 - T_W) = 8$

Substitute (a) into (b$'$) and get:

(b$''$) $8R_W - 4(8) = 8$

$\qquad\qquad 8R_W = 40$

$\qquad\qquad R_W = 5$

$R_B = \textbf{20}; \quad T_W = \dfrac{8}{5}; \quad T_B = \dfrac{2}{5}$

7. (a) $R_P T_P = 600$

(b) $R_C T_C = 105$

(c) $R_P = 5R_C$

(d) $T_P + T_C = 15$

Substitute (c) and (d) into (a) and get:

(a$'$) $5R_C(15 - T_C) = 600$

Substitute (b) into (a$'$) and get:

(a$''$) $75R_C - 5(105) = 600$

$\qquad\qquad 75R_C = 1125$

$\qquad\qquad R_C = \textbf{15}$

$R_P = \textbf{75}; \quad T_C = \textbf{7}; \quad T_P = \textbf{8}$

8. (a) $R_1 T_1 = 120$

(b) $R_2 T_2 = 120$

(c) $R_1 = 2R_2$

(d) $T_1 + T_2 = 6$

Substitute (c) and (d) into (a) and get:

(a$'$) $2R_2(6 - T_2) = 120$

Substitute (b) into (a$'$) and get:

(a$''$) $12R_2 - 2(120) = 120$

$\qquad\qquad 12R_2 = 360$

$\qquad\qquad R_2 = \textbf{30}$

$R_1 = \textbf{60}; \quad T_2 = \textbf{4}; \quad T_1 = \textbf{2}$

9. $x + \dfrac{1}{a + \dfrac{b}{c}} = x + \dfrac{1}{\dfrac{ac + b}{c}}$

$\qquad = x + \dfrac{c}{ac + b} = \dfrac{acx + bx + c}{ac + b}$

10. $\dfrac{4}{c} + \dfrac{1}{a + \dfrac{1}{b}} = \dfrac{4}{c} + \dfrac{1}{\dfrac{ab + 1}{b}}$

$\qquad = \dfrac{4}{c} + \dfrac{b}{ab + 1} = \dfrac{4ab + 4 + bc}{c(ab + 1)}$

11. $x + \dfrac{a}{1 + \dfrac{1}{a}} = x + \dfrac{a}{\dfrac{a + 1}{a}} = x + \dfrac{a^2}{a + 1}$

$\qquad = \dfrac{ax + x + a^2}{a + 1}$

12. $\sqrt{-4} - \sqrt{-3}\sqrt{-3} + 2i^5 - 4$

$\qquad = 2i - \sqrt{3}i\sqrt{3}i + 2i(ii)(ii) - 4$

$\qquad = 2i + 3 + 2i - 4 = \textbf{-1 + 4}\boldsymbol{i}$

13. $(5i - 2)(2i - 3)$

$\qquad = 10i^2 - 15i - 4i + 6 = \textbf{-4 - 19}\boldsymbol{i}$

14. $(-i - 3)(-2i + 4)$

$\qquad = 2i^2 - 4i + 6i - 12 = \textbf{-14 + 2}\boldsymbol{i}$

15.

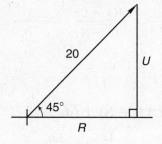

$R = 20 \cos 45° \approx 14.14$

$U = 20 \sin 45° \approx 14.14$

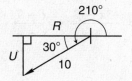

$R = 10 \cos 30° \approx 8.66$

$U = 10 \sin 30° \approx 5.00$

$$14.14R + 14.14U$$
$$\underline{-8.66R - 5.00U}$$
$$\mathbf{5.48R + 9.14U}$$

16.

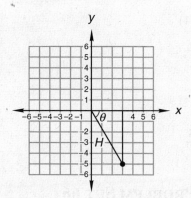

$H = \sqrt{3^2 + 5^2}$

$H = \sqrt{34}$

$\tan \theta = \dfrac{5}{3}$

$\theta \approx 59.04°$

Since θ is a fourth-quadrant angle,

$\theta = 360 - 59.04 = 300.96°$

$\mathbf{\sqrt{34}/300.96°}$

17. (a) $\dfrac{2}{7}x - \dfrac{1}{6}y = 1$

(b) $0.3x + 0.07y = 0.84$

(a′) $12x - 7y = 42$

(b′) $\dfrac{30x + 7y = 84}{42x = 126}$

$x = 3$

(a′) $12(3) - 7y = 42$

$-7y = 6$

$y = -\dfrac{6}{7}$

$\left(3, -\dfrac{6}{7}\right)$

18. $-2 = -3x^2 - 7x$

$\left(x^2 + \dfrac{7}{3}x + \right) = \dfrac{2}{3}$

$x^2 + \dfrac{7}{3}x + \dfrac{49}{36} = \dfrac{2}{3} + \dfrac{49}{36}$

$\left(x + \dfrac{7}{6}\right)^2 = \dfrac{73}{36}$

$x + \dfrac{7}{6} = \pm\dfrac{\sqrt{73}}{6}$

$x = -\dfrac{7}{6} \pm \dfrac{\sqrt{73}}{6}$

19. $2x^2 - 4 = -5x$

$\left(x^2 + \dfrac{5}{2}x + \right) = 2$

$x^2 + \dfrac{5}{2} + \dfrac{25}{16} = 2 + \dfrac{25}{16}$

$\left(x + \dfrac{5}{4}\right)^2 = \dfrac{57}{16}$

$x + \dfrac{5}{4} = \pm\dfrac{\sqrt{57}}{4}$

$x = -\dfrac{5}{4} \pm \dfrac{\sqrt{57}}{4}$

20. K = mRa + b

Use the graph to find the slope.

$m = \dfrac{500}{560} \approx 0.89$

K = 0.89Ra + b

Use the point (2100, 500) for Ra and K.

$500 = 0.89(2100) + b$

$-1369 = b$

K = 0.89Ra − 1369

21. Since the measure of an inscribed angle equals half the measure of the intercepted arc,

$$\frac{m\widehat{AB}}{2} = y°$$

$$m\widehat{AB} = (2y)°$$

Since the measure of an arc of a circle is the same as the measure of the central angle,

$$x° = m\widehat{AB}$$

$$x° = (2y)°$$

22. $\dfrac{600 \text{ ft}^3}{\text{hr}} \times \dfrac{12 \text{ in.}}{1 \text{ ft}} \times \dfrac{12 \text{ in.}}{1 \text{ ft}} \times \dfrac{12 \text{ in.}}{1 \text{ ft}} \times \dfrac{1 \text{ hr}}{60 \text{ min}}$

$$= \frac{600(12)(12)(12)}{(60)} \frac{\text{in.}^3}{\text{min}}$$

23. $\sqrt{x^2 \sqrt{y^3}} = [x^2 y^{3/2}]^{1/2} = xy^{3/4}$

24. $\sqrt[6]{4\sqrt[5]{2}} = \sqrt[6]{2^2 \sqrt[5]{2}} = [2^2(2^{1/5})]^{1/6} = 2^{1/3}2^{1/30}$
$$= 2^{11/30}$$

25. $\sqrt{\dfrac{2}{9}} - 3\sqrt{\dfrac{9}{2}} - 2\sqrt{50}$

$$= \frac{\sqrt{2}}{3} - \frac{9}{\sqrt{2}}\frac{\sqrt{2}}{\sqrt{2}} - 10\sqrt{2}$$

$$= \frac{2\sqrt{2}}{6} - \frac{27\sqrt{2}}{6} - \frac{60\sqrt{2}}{6} = -\frac{85\sqrt{2}}{6}$$

26. $\dfrac{x}{a(b+c)} - m = \dfrac{d}{f}$

$$fx - abfm - acfm = abd + acd$$

$$fx = abd + acd + abfm + acfm$$

$$x = \frac{abd + acd + abfm + acfm}{f}$$

27. $\dfrac{x}{a(b+c)} - m = \dfrac{d}{f}$

$$fx - abfm - acfm = abd + acd$$

$$fx - acfm - acd = abd + abfm$$

$$\frac{fx - acfm - acd}{ad + afm} = b$$

28. $\dfrac{(x-8)(x-4)}{x(x+5)(x-4)} \cdot \dfrac{x(x+5)(x+9)}{(x-8)(x+7)}$

$$= \frac{x+9}{x+7}$$

29. $\dfrac{(47{,}123 \times 10^5)(980)(476)}{(0.00134)(576 \times 10^5)}$

$$\approx \frac{(5 \times 10^9)(1 \times 10^3)(5 \times 10^2)}{(1 \times 10^{-3})(6 \times 10^7)}$$

$$\approx 4 \times 10^{10}$$

30. $\dfrac{4}{x+2} - \dfrac{3}{x^2-4} = \dfrac{4(x-2)}{x^2-4} - \dfrac{3}{x^2-4}$

$$= \frac{4x-11}{x^2-4}$$

PRACTICE SET 66

a. $\dfrac{1}{z-2} - \dfrac{3m}{-z+2} = \dfrac{1}{z-2} + \dfrac{3m}{z-2}$

$$= \frac{1+3m}{z-2}$$

b. $\dfrac{3x+7}{-x-4} + \dfrac{x-7}{x+4} = \dfrac{-3x-7}{x+4} + \dfrac{x-7}{x+4}$

$$= \frac{-3x-7+x-7}{x+4}$$

$$= \frac{-2x-14}{x+4} = -\frac{2x+14}{x+4}$$

c. Since this is a 30°-60°-90° triangle,
$$\sqrt{3}\,\overrightarrow{SF} = 7$$

$$\overrightarrow{SF} = \frac{7}{\sqrt{3}} = \frac{7\sqrt{3}}{3}$$

$$a = \frac{7\sqrt{3}}{3}(1)$$

$$a = \frac{7\sqrt{3}}{3}$$

$$b = \frac{7\sqrt{3}}{3}(2)$$

$$b = \frac{14\sqrt{3}}{3}$$

PROBLEM SET 66

1. $Co = \dfrac{k}{U}$

$$5 = \frac{k}{20}$$

$$100 = k$$

$$Co = \frac{100}{2} = \textbf{50 grams}$$

2. $\dfrac{P_1 V_1}{T_1} = \dfrac{P_2 V_2}{T_2}$

$$\frac{(400)(6)}{200} = \frac{(800)(60)}{T_2}$$

$$T_2 = \textbf{4000 K}$$

3. Arsenic P_N + Arsenic D_N = Arsenic Total
$$0.6(P_N) + 0.2(D_N) = 0.36(200)$$

(a) $0.6P_N + 0.2D_N = 72$

(b) $P_N + D_N = 200$

Substitute $D_N = 200 - P_N$ into (a) and get:

(a') $0.6P_N + 0.2(200 - P_N) = 72$
$$0.4P_N = 32$$
$$P_N = 80$$

(b) $(80) + D_N = 200$
$$D_N = 120$$

80 liters 60%, 120 liters 20%

4.

$$R_C T_C + 10 = R_D T_D; \quad R_C = 4; \quad R_D = 6;$$
$$T_C = T_D$$
$$4T_D + 10 = 6T_D$$
$$10 = 2T_D$$
$$\mathbf{5\ hr} = T_D$$

5. Carbon: $1 \times 12 = 12$
   Hydrogen: $3 \times 1 = 3$
   Bromine: $1 \times 80 = 80$
   Total: $12 + 3 + 80 = 95$

$$\frac{80}{95} = \frac{Br}{950}$$

$$Br = \mathbf{800\ grams}$$

6. $\dfrac{1}{x + 3} - \dfrac{7a}{-x - 3} = \dfrac{1}{x + 3} + \dfrac{7a}{x + 3}$

$$= \mathbf{\dfrac{1 + 7a}{x + 3}}$$

7. $\dfrac{x + 5}{x + 3} + \dfrac{2x - 3}{-3 - x} = \dfrac{x + 5}{x + 3} - \dfrac{2x - 3}{x + 3}$

$$= \mathbf{\dfrac{-x + 8}{x + 3}}$$

8. $\dfrac{4}{x^2 - 4} - \dfrac{2x}{x - 2}$

$$= \dfrac{4}{x^2 - 4} - \dfrac{2x(x + 2)}{x^2 - 4}$$

$$= \mathbf{\dfrac{-2x^2 - 4x + 4}{x^2 - 4}}$$

9. $A_Q = \pi r^2 = 9\pi$ in.^{2}
$$r = 3 \text{ in.}$$

Since the radius of circle Q is 3 in., the radius of each semicircle is 1 in.

$$A_{\text{Shaded}} = \frac{1}{2}A_Q + \frac{\pi r^2}{2} - \frac{2\pi r^2}{2}$$

$$= \frac{1}{2}A_Q - \frac{\pi r^2}{2}$$

$$= \frac{9\pi \text{ in.}^2}{2} - \frac{\pi(1 \text{ in.})^2}{2}$$

$$= \frac{9}{2}\pi \text{ in.}^2 - \frac{1}{2}\pi \text{ in.}^2 = \mathbf{4\pi \text{ in.}^2}$$

10. (a) $R_T T_T = 300$

(b) $R_P T_P = 1200$

(c) $R_P = 8R_T$

(d) $T_T = T_P + 3$

Substitute (c) and (d) into (b) and get:

(b') $8R_T(T_T - 3) = 1200$

Substitute (a) into (b') and get:

(b'') $8(300) - 24R_T = 1200$
$$-24R_T = -1200$$
$$R_T = \mathbf{50}$$

$R_P = \mathbf{400}; \quad T_T = \mathbf{6}; \quad T_P = \mathbf{3}$

11. (a) $R_P T_P = 624$

(b) $R_T T_T = 364$

(c) $T_P = T_T - 4$

(d) $R_P = 4R_T$

Substitute (c) and (d) into (a) and get:

(a') $4R_T(T_T - 4) = 624$

Substitute (b) into (a') and get:

(a'') $4(364) - 16R_T = 624$
$$-16R_T = -832$$
$$R_T = \mathbf{52}$$

$R_P = \mathbf{208}; \quad T_T = \mathbf{7}; \quad T_P = \mathbf{3}$

12. Area = $\pi(3r)^2 - \pi r^2$
$$= 9\pi r^2 - \pi r^2$$
$$= \mathbf{8\pi r^2 \text{ m}^2}$$

13. $ax + \dfrac{1}{a + \dfrac{1}{x}} = ax + \dfrac{1}{\dfrac{ax + 1}{x}}$

$\qquad = ax + \dfrac{x}{ax + 1} = \dfrac{a^2x^2 + ax + x}{ax + 1}$

14. $\dfrac{m}{x} + \dfrac{1}{x + \dfrac{1}{x}} = \dfrac{m}{x} + \dfrac{1}{\dfrac{x^2 + 1}{x}}$

$\qquad = \dfrac{m}{x} + \dfrac{x}{x^2 + 1} = \dfrac{mx^2 + m + x^2}{x(x^2 + 1)}$

15. $-\sqrt{-3}\sqrt{-2} + \sqrt{-4} - \sqrt{-3}\sqrt{-3} - 2i^3$

$\quad = -\sqrt{3}i\sqrt{2}i + 2i - \sqrt{3}i\sqrt{3}i - 2i(ii)$

$\quad = \sqrt{6} + 2i + 3 + 2i = (3 + \sqrt{6}) + 4i$

16. $(4i - 2)(3 + 5i)$

$\quad = 12i + 20i^2 - 6 - 10i = -26 + 2i$

17.

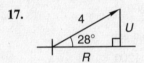

$R = 4\cos 28° \approx 3.53$

$U = 4\sin 28° \approx 1.88$

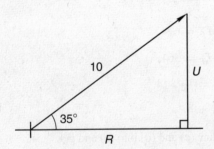

$R = 10\cos 35° \approx 8.19$

$U = 10\sin 35° \approx 5.74$

$\quad \begin{array}{l} 3.53R + 1.88U \\ 8.19R + 5.74U \\ \hline \mathbf{11.72R + 7.62U} \end{array}$

18.

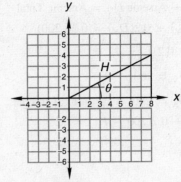

$H = \sqrt{8^2 + 4^2}$

$H = \sqrt{80} = 4\sqrt{5}$

$\tan\theta = \dfrac{4}{8}$

$\theta \approx 26.57°$

$\mathbf{4\sqrt{5} \,/\, 26.57°}$

19. (a) $\dfrac{3}{8}x - \dfrac{1}{4}y = -2$

(b) $0.012x + 0.02y = 0.496$

(a′) $3x - 2y = -16$

(b′) $12x + 20y = 496$

$10(a′)\ \ 30x - 20y = -160$

$\quad \underline{(b′)\ \ 12x + 20y =\ \ \ 496}$

$\qquad\qquad 42x\qquad\quad =\ \ \ 336$

$\qquad\qquad\qquad x = 8$

(a′) $3(8) - 2y = -16$

$\qquad\quad 2y = 40$

$\qquad\quad\ y = 20$

$\mathbf{(8, 20)}$

20. $\qquad\qquad -3 = -2x^2 - 6x$

$\left(x^2 + 3x +\ \ \ \ \right) = \dfrac{3}{2}$

$x^2 + 3x + \dfrac{9}{4} = \dfrac{3}{2} + \dfrac{9}{4}$

$\left(x + \dfrac{3}{2}\right)^2 = \dfrac{15}{4}$

$x + \dfrac{3}{2} = \pm\dfrac{\sqrt{15}}{2}$

$x = -\dfrac{3}{2} \pm \dfrac{\sqrt{15}}{2}$

21.
$$5x^2 - 4 = -5x$$
$$\left(x^2 + x + \right) = \frac{4}{5}$$
$$x^2 + x + \frac{1}{4} = \frac{4}{5} + \frac{1}{4}$$
$$\left(x + \frac{1}{2}\right)^2 = \frac{21}{20}$$
$$x + \frac{1}{2} = \pm\frac{\sqrt{21}}{2\sqrt{5}}$$
$$x = -\frac{1}{2} \pm \frac{\sqrt{105}}{10}$$

22. Since this is a 30°-60°-90° triangle,
$$2\overrightarrow{SF} = 7$$
$$\overrightarrow{SF} = \frac{7}{2}$$
$$x = \frac{7}{2}(\sqrt{3}) = \frac{7\sqrt{3}}{2}$$
$$y = \frac{7}{2}(1) = \frac{7}{2}$$

23. $Mg = mCa + b$

Use the graph to find the slope.

$$m = \frac{1000}{15} \approx 66.67$$

$Mg = 66.67Ca + b$

Use the point (36, 2400) for Ca and Mg.

$$2400 = 36(66.67) + b$$
$$0 \approx b$$

$Mg = 66.67Ca$

24.
$$\frac{10 \text{ in.}^3}{\text{hr}} \times \frac{2.54 \text{ cm}}{1 \text{ in.}} \times \frac{2.54 \text{ cm}}{1 \text{ in.}} \times \frac{2.54 \text{ cm}}{1 \text{ in.}}$$
$$\times \frac{1 \text{ hr}}{60 \text{ min}} = \frac{10(2.54)(2.54)(2.54)}{(60)} \frac{\text{cm}^3}{\text{min}}$$

25. $\sqrt[3]{x^{1/2}\sqrt{x^2}} = [x^{1/2}(x)]^{1/3} = x^{1/6}x^{1/3} = x^{1/2}$

26. $\sqrt[3]{x^{1/5}\sqrt[4]{x}} = [x^{1/5}(x^{1/4})]^{1/3} = x^{1/15}x^{1/12} = x^{3/20}$

27. $3\sqrt{\dfrac{2}{5}} + 7\sqrt{\dfrac{5}{2}} - 6\sqrt{40}$

$$= \frac{3\sqrt{2}}{\sqrt{5}}\frac{\sqrt{5}}{\sqrt{5}} + \frac{7\sqrt{5}}{\sqrt{2}}\frac{\sqrt{2}}{\sqrt{2}} - 12\sqrt{10}$$
$$= \frac{6\sqrt{10}}{10} + \frac{35\sqrt{10}}{10} - \frac{120\sqrt{10}}{10} = -\frac{79\sqrt{10}}{10}$$

28.
$$\frac{px - y}{m} - c = \frac{k}{d}$$
$$dpx - dy - cdm = km$$
$$dpx - cdm - km = dy$$
$$\frac{dpx - cdm - km}{d} = y$$

29.
$$\frac{m}{px - y} + \frac{k}{d} = -c$$
$$dm + kpx - ky = -cdpx + cdy$$
$$kpx + cdpx = cdy + ky - dm$$
$$x = \frac{cdy + ky - dm}{kp + cdp}$$

30.
$$\frac{(40{,}213 \times 10^5)(748{,}609 \times 10^{-30})}{(0.164289)(506{,}217 \times 10^2)}$$
$$\approx \frac{(4 \times 10^9)(7 \times 10^{-25})}{(2 \times 10^{-1})(5 \times 10^7)} \approx 3 \times 10^{-22}$$

PRACTICE SET 67

a. $\dfrac{1}{-3 + \sqrt{7}} \cdot \dfrac{-3 - \sqrt{7}}{-3 - \sqrt{7}} = \dfrac{-3 - \sqrt{7}}{9 - 7} = \dfrac{-3 - \sqrt{7}}{2}$

b. $\dfrac{5}{3\sqrt{2} + \sqrt{3}} \cdot \dfrac{3\sqrt{2} - \sqrt{3}}{3\sqrt{2} - \sqrt{3}} = \dfrac{15\sqrt{2} - 5\sqrt{3}}{9(2) - 3}$

$$= \frac{15\sqrt{2} - 5\sqrt{3}}{15} = \frac{3\sqrt{2} - \sqrt{3}}{3}$$

PROBLEM SET 67

1.
$$R = kA$$
$$2000 = k(12{,}400)$$
$$\frac{5}{31} = k$$
$$3000 = \left(\frac{5}{31}\right)A$$

18,600 Danes $= A$

2.
$$P_1V_1 = P_2V_2$$
$$(800)(300) = (1200)V_2$$
$$V_2 = \mathbf{200 \text{ cm}^3}$$

3.
$$0.2(400) + 0.8(D_N) = 0.32(400 + D_N)$$
$$80 + 0.8D_N = 128 + 0.32D_N$$
$$0.48D_N = 48$$
$$D_N = \mathbf{100 \text{ pounds}}$$

4. (a) $N_N = N_D + 75$

(b) $8N_N = 10N_D + 140$

Substitute (a) into (b) and get:

(b') $8(N_D + 75) = 10N_D + 140$

$$460 = 2N_D$$

230 doctors $= N_D$

(a) $N_N = (230) + 75 = \textbf{305 nurses}$

5. $\dfrac{60}{100} \times T = 240$

$$T = 240 \times \dfrac{100}{60} = 400$$

$NR = 400 - 240 = \textbf{160 grams}$

6. $\dfrac{2}{-4 + \sqrt{5}} \cdot \dfrac{-4 - \sqrt{5}}{-4 - \sqrt{5}}$

$$= \dfrac{-8 - 2\sqrt{5}}{16 - 5} = \dfrac{\textbf{--8} - \textbf{2}\sqrt{\textbf{5}}}{\textbf{11}}$$

7. $\dfrac{1}{2\sqrt{2} + \sqrt{3}} \cdot \dfrac{2\sqrt{2} - \sqrt{3}}{2\sqrt{2} - \sqrt{3}}$

$$= \dfrac{2\sqrt{2} - \sqrt{3}}{8 - 3} = \dfrac{\textbf{2}\sqrt{\textbf{2}} - \sqrt{\textbf{3}}}{\textbf{5}}$$

8. $\dfrac{2}{3\sqrt{5} - 3} \cdot \dfrac{3\sqrt{5} + 3}{3\sqrt{5} + 3} = \dfrac{6\sqrt{5} + 6}{45 - 9}$

$$= \dfrac{\sqrt{\textbf{5}} + \textbf{1}}{\textbf{6}}$$

9. $\dfrac{4x + 2}{x - 2} - \dfrac{3}{2 - x} = \dfrac{4x + 2}{x - 2} + \dfrac{3}{x - 2}$

$$= \dfrac{\textbf{4x} + \textbf{5}}{\textbf{x} - \textbf{2}}$$

10. $\dfrac{4}{x^2 - 9} + \dfrac{2}{x - 3}$

$$= \dfrac{4}{x^2 - 9} + \dfrac{2(x + 3)}{x^2 - 9} = \dfrac{\textbf{2x} + \textbf{10}}{\textbf{x}^2 - \textbf{9}}$$

11. (a) $R_P T_P = 1062$

(b) $R_T T_T = 295$

(c) $T_P = T_T - 2$

(d) $R_P = 6R_T$

Substitute (c) and (d) into (a) and get:

(a') $6R_T(T_T - 2) = 1062$

Substitute (b) into (a') and get:

(a'') $6(295) - 12R_T = 1062$

$$-12R_T = -708$$

$$R_T = \textbf{59}$$

$R_P = \textbf{354}; \ T_T = \textbf{5}; \ T_P = \textbf{3}$

12. $4x + \dfrac{a}{x + \dfrac{a}{b}} = 4x + \dfrac{a}{\dfrac{bx + a}{b}}$

$$= 4x + \dfrac{ab}{bx + a} = \dfrac{\textbf{4bx}^2 + \textbf{4ax} + \textbf{ab}}{\textbf{bx} + \textbf{a}}$$

13. $a + \dfrac{x}{m + \dfrac{1}{x}} = a + \dfrac{x}{\dfrac{mx + 1}{x}}$

$$= a + \dfrac{x^2}{mx + 1} = \dfrac{\textbf{amx} + \textbf{a} + \textbf{x}^2}{\textbf{mx} + \textbf{1}}$$

14. $(5 - i)(6 + 2i)$

$$= 30 + 10i - 6i - 2i^2 = \textbf{32} + \textbf{4i}$$

15. $\sqrt{-4} - \sqrt{-9} + \sqrt{-2}\sqrt{2} - 4i^2$

$$= 2i - 3i + \sqrt{2}i\sqrt{2} - 4(ii)$$

$$= 2i - 3i + 2i + 4 = \textbf{4} + \textbf{i}$$

16.

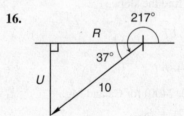

$R = 10\cos 37° \approx 7.99$

$U = 10\sin 37° \approx 6.02$

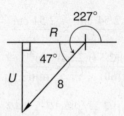

$R = 8\cos 47° \approx 5.46$

$U = 8\sin 47° \approx 5.85$

$$\begin{array}{r} -7.99R - \ \ 6.02U \\ -5.46R - \ \ 5.85U \\ \hline \textbf{--13.45R} - \textbf{11.87U} \end{array}$$

17.

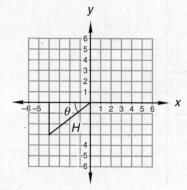

$$H = \sqrt{4^2 + 3^2}$$

$$H = 5$$

$$\tan \theta = \frac{3}{4}$$

$$\theta \approx 36.87°$$

Since θ is a third quadrant angle,

$$\theta = 36.87 + 180 = 216.87°$$

5/216.87°

18. (a) $\frac{2}{7}x - \frac{2}{5}y = 0$

(b) $0.2x - 0.04y = 2.4$

(a') $10x - 14y = 0$

(b') $20x - 4y = 240$

$-2(a')$ $-20x + 28y = 0$

$\underline{(b') 20x - 4y = 240}$

$ 24y = 240$

$ y = 10$

(b') $20x - 4(10) = 240$

$ 20x = 280$

$ x = 14$

(14, 10)

19. $ -x = -1 - 4x^2$

$$\left(x^2 - \frac{1}{4}x + \right) = -\frac{1}{4}$$

$$x^2 - \frac{1}{4}x + \frac{1}{64} = -\frac{1}{4} + \frac{1}{64}$$

$$\left(x - \frac{1}{8}\right)^2 = -\frac{15}{64}$$

$$x - \frac{1}{8} = \pm\frac{\sqrt{15}}{8}i$$

$$x = \frac{1}{8} \pm \frac{\sqrt{15}}{8}i$$

20. $ 3x^2 + 5 = -2x$

$$\left(x^2 + \frac{2}{3}x + \right) = -\frac{5}{3}$$

$$x^2 + \frac{2}{3}x + \frac{1}{9} = -\frac{5}{3} + \frac{1}{9}$$

$$\left(x + \frac{1}{3}\right)^2 = -\frac{14}{9}$$

$$x + \frac{1}{3} = \pm\frac{\sqrt{14}}{3}i$$

$$x = -\frac{1}{3} \pm \frac{\sqrt{14}}{3}i$$

21. Since this is a 30°-60°-90° triangle,

$$\sqrt{3} \times \overrightarrow{SF} = 5$$

$$\overrightarrow{SF} = \frac{5}{\sqrt{3}} = \frac{5\sqrt{3}}{3}$$

$$x = \frac{5\sqrt{3}}{3}(1) = \frac{5\sqrt{3}}{3}$$

$$y = \frac{5\sqrt{3}}{3}(2) = \frac{10\sqrt{3}}{3}$$

22. $\dfrac{400 \text{ cm}^3}{\text{hr}} \times \dfrac{1 \text{ in.}}{2.54 \text{ cm}} \times \dfrac{1 \text{ in.}}{2.54 \text{ cm}} \times \dfrac{1 \text{ in.}}{2.54 \text{ cm}}$

$\times \dfrac{1 \text{ hr}}{60 \text{ min}} = \dfrac{400}{(2.54)(2.54)(2.54)(60)} \dfrac{\text{in.}^3}{\text{min}}$

23. $Ag = mAu + b$

Use the graph to find the slope.

$$m = -\frac{8}{40} = -0.2$$

$$Ag = -0.2Au + b$$

Use the point (120, 2) for Au and Ag.

$$2 = -0.2(120) + b$$

$$26 = b$$

Ag = −0.2Au + 26

24. $\sqrt{2\sqrt[6]{4}} = \sqrt{2\sqrt[6]{2^2}} = \left[2(2^{1/3})\right]^{1/2} = 2^{1/2}2^{1/6}$

$= \mathbf{2^{2/3}}$

25. $\sqrt[5]{x^2 yp}\sqrt[3]{xy^2} = (x^2yp)^{1/5}(xy^2)^{1/3}$

$= x^{2/5}y^{1/5}p^{1/5}x^{1/3}y^{2/3} = \mathbf{x^{11/15}y^{13/15}p^{1/5}}$

26. $4\sqrt{\dfrac{3}{11}} + 2\sqrt{\dfrac{11}{3}} - 2\sqrt{297}$

$= \dfrac{4\sqrt{3}}{\sqrt{11}}\dfrac{\sqrt{11}}{\sqrt{11}} + \dfrac{2\sqrt{11}}{\sqrt{3}}\dfrac{\sqrt{3}}{\sqrt{3}} - 6\sqrt{33}$

$= \dfrac{12\sqrt{33}}{33} + \dfrac{22\sqrt{33}}{33} - \dfrac{198\sqrt{33}}{33} = \mathbf{-\dfrac{164\sqrt{33}}{33}}$

27. $\dfrac{a(b+c)}{x} - \dfrac{m}{y} = p$

$aby + acy - mx = pxy$

$aby + acy = pxy + mx$

$\dfrac{aby + acy}{py + m} = x$

28. $\dfrac{x}{a(b+c)} - \dfrac{y}{m} = p$

$mx - aby - acy = abmp + acmp$

$mx - aby - abmp = acmp + acy$

$\dfrac{mx - aby - abmp}{amp + ay} = c$

29. Graph the line to find the slope.

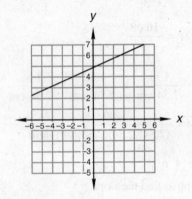

Slope $= \dfrac{3}{7}$

$y = \dfrac{3}{7}x + b$

Use the point $(-2, 4)$ for x and y.

$4 = \dfrac{3}{7}(-2) + b$

$\dfrac{34}{7} = b$

$y = \dfrac{3}{7}x + \dfrac{34}{7}$

30.

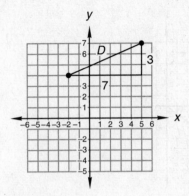

$D^2 = 3^2 + 7^2$
$D^2 = 58$
$D = \sqrt{58}$

PRACTICE SET 68

a. Estimate: $\dfrac{0.00042 \times 10^{-17}}{568,425 \times 10^5} \approx \dfrac{4 \times 10^{-21}}{6 \times 10^{10}}$

$\approx 7 \times 10^{-32}$

Calculator answer $\approx \mathbf{7.39 \times 10^{-32}}$

b. Estimate: $\sqrt[4.2]{156} \longrightarrow 3^4 = 81$ and $4^4 = 256$
so the answer should be between 3 and 4.

Calculator answer $\approx \mathbf{3.33}$

c. Estimate: $(0.00042 \times 10^{-17})(568,425 \times 10^5)$

$\approx (4 \times 10^{-21})(6 \times 10^{10})$

$\approx 2 \times 10^{-10}$

Calculator answer $\approx \mathbf{2.39 \times 10^{-10}}$

d. Estimate: $(1.86)^{-4.86} \longrightarrow 2^{-5} = 0.03125$ and
$1^{-4} = 1$ so the answer should be
between 0.03125 and 1.

Calculator answer $\approx \mathbf{0.049}$

PROBLEM SET 68

1. $D = kP$
$800 = k(9600)$
$\dfrac{1}{12} = k$

$D = \dfrac{1}{12}(24,000) = \mathbf{2000\ dastards}$

2. $P_1 V_1 = P_2 V_2$
$(1200)(200) = (1600)V_2$
$V_2 = \mathbf{150\ mL}$

3. $0.4(800) + 0.2(D_N) = 0.36(800 + D_N)$
    $$320 + 0.2D_N = 288 + 0.36D_N$$
    $$-0.16D_N = -32$$
    $$D_N = \textbf{200 pounds}$$

4. (a) $N_F = 2N_E + 14$

    (b) $2N_F = 20N_E - 100$

    Substitute (a) into (b) and get:

    (b′) $2(2N_E + 14) = 20N_E - 100$
    $$-16N_E = -128$$
    $$N_E = 8$$

    (a) $N_F = 2(8) + 14 = 30$

    8 were ephemeral while 30 were fugacious.

5. $\dfrac{80}{100} \times T = 6720$

    $$T = 6720 \times \dfrac{100}{80}$$

    $$T = \textbf{8400}$$

6. (a) $\dfrac{0.000418 \times 10^{-14}}{501,635 \times 10^6} \approx \dfrac{4 \times 10^{-18}}{5 \times 10^{11}}$
    $$= 8 \times 10^{-30}$$

    Calculator answer $\approx \textbf{8.33} \times \textbf{10}^{-30}$

    (b) $(0.00037 \times 10^{-13})(7231 \times 10^4)$
    $$\approx (4 \times 10^{-17})(7 \times 10^7) = 2.8 \times 10^{-9}$$

    Calculator answer $\approx \textbf{2.68} \times \textbf{10}^{-9}$

7. (a) $\sqrt[3.8]{192} \longrightarrow$ $3^4 = 81$ and $4^4 = 256$

    Answer should be between 3 and 4.

    Calculator answer $\approx \textbf{3.99}$

    (b) $(1.76)^{-3.42} \longrightarrow$ $1^{-3} = 1$ and $2^{-3} = 0.125$

    Answer should be between 1 and 0.125.

    Calculator answer $\approx \textbf{0.14}$

8. Since this is a $30°\text{-}60°\text{-}90°$ triangle,
    $$1 \times \overrightarrow{SF} = 2\sqrt{3}$$
    $$\overrightarrow{SF} = 2\sqrt{3}$$
    $$x = 2\sqrt{3}(2) = \textbf{4}\sqrt{\textbf{3}}$$
    $$y = 2\sqrt{3}(\sqrt{3}) = \textbf{6}$$

9. Since the area of a triangle is equal to half the product of the base and height and since all triangles in the parallelogram whose base is $\overline{AD}$ share the same height, **all have equal areas.**

10. $x + (2x + 10) + 54 + 89 = 360$
    $$3x = 207$$
    $$x = 69°$$

    $x = m\widehat{MN} = \textbf{69}°$

11. $\dfrac{1}{-2 - \sqrt{2}} \cdot \dfrac{-2 + \sqrt{2}}{-2 + \sqrt{2}} = \dfrac{-2 + \sqrt{2}}{4 - 2}$
    $$= \dfrac{-\textbf{2} + \sqrt{\textbf{2}}}{\textbf{2}}$$

12. $\dfrac{4}{3\sqrt{2} - 1} \cdot \dfrac{3\sqrt{2} + 1}{3\sqrt{2} + 1} = \dfrac{12\sqrt{2} + 4}{18 - 1}$
    $$= \dfrac{\textbf{12}\sqrt{\textbf{2}} + \textbf{4}}{\textbf{17}}$$

13. $\dfrac{2}{3\sqrt{3} - 5} \cdot \dfrac{3\sqrt{3} + 5}{3\sqrt{3} + 5} = \dfrac{6\sqrt{3} + 10}{27 - 25}$
    $$= \textbf{3}\sqrt{\textbf{3}} + \textbf{5}$$

14. $\dfrac{-7}{-x + 3} - \dfrac{2x}{x^2 - 9}$
    $$= \dfrac{7(x + 3)}{x^2 - 9} - \dfrac{2x}{x^2 - 9} = \dfrac{\textbf{5x} + \textbf{21}}{x^2 - \textbf{9}}$$

15. $\dfrac{2}{4 - x} - \dfrac{3}{x^2 - 16}$
    $$= \dfrac{-2(x + 4)}{x^2 - 16} - \dfrac{3}{x^2 - 16} = \dfrac{-\textbf{2x} - \textbf{11}}{x^2 - \textbf{16}}$$

16. (a) $R_G T_G = 140$

    (b) $R_B T_B = 140$

    (c) $R_B = 2R_G$

    (d) $T_B = T_G - 7$

    Substitute (c) and (d) into (b) and get:

    (b′) $2R_G(T_G - 7) = 140$

    Substitute (a) into (b′) and get:

    (b″) $2(140) - 14R_G = 140$
    $$-14R_G = -140$$
    $$R_G = \textbf{10}$$

    $R_B = \textbf{20};\ T_G = \textbf{14};\ T_B = \textbf{7}$

17. $4r + \dfrac{m}{x + \dfrac{m}{x}} = 4r + \dfrac{m}{\dfrac{x^2 + m}{x}}$

    $$= 4r + \dfrac{mx}{x^2 + m} = \dfrac{\textbf{4rx}^2 + \textbf{4mr} + \textbf{mx}}{x^2 + \textbf{m}}$$

18. $3a + \dfrac{ax}{a + \dfrac{x}{a}} = 3a + \dfrac{ax}{\dfrac{a^2 + x}{a}}$

$= 3a + \dfrac{a^2 x}{a^2 + x} = \dfrac{3a^3 + 3ax + a^2 x}{a^2 + x}$

19. $(5i - 2)(3i + 4)$

$= 15i^2 + 20i - 6i - 8 = \mathbf{-23 + 14i}$

20. $\sqrt{-2}\sqrt{2} - 3i^2 - \sqrt{-9} + 2i^4 + 4$

$= \sqrt{2}i\sqrt{2} - 3(ii) - 3i + 2(ii)(ii) + 4$

$= 2i + 3 - 3i + 2 + 4 = \mathbf{9 - i}$

21.

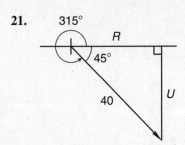

$R = 40 \cos 45° \approx 28.28$

$U = 40 \sin 45° \approx 28.28$

$R = 10 \cos 24° \approx 9.14$

$U = 10 \sin 24° \approx 4.07$

$\quad 28.28R - 28.28U$
$\quad \underline{9.14R + 4.07U}$
$\mathbf{37.42R - 24.21U}$

22. (a) $\dfrac{2}{5}x - \dfrac{2}{3}y = -2$

(b) $-0.06x - 0.4y = -7.2$

(a') $6x - 10y = -30$
(b') $\underline{-6x - 40y = -720}$
$\qquad -50y = -750$
$\qquad\qquad y = 15$

(a') $6x - 10(15) = -30$
$\qquad\quad 6x = 120$
$\qquad\quad\ x = 20$

$(20, 15)$

23. $\qquad -2x = -1 - 4x^2$

$\left(x^2 - \dfrac{1}{2}x + \quad\right) = -\dfrac{1}{4}$

$x^2 - \dfrac{1}{2}x + \dfrac{1}{16} = -\dfrac{1}{4} + \dfrac{1}{16}$

$\left(x - \dfrac{1}{4}\right)^2 = -\dfrac{3}{16}$

$x - \dfrac{1}{4} = \pm\dfrac{\sqrt{3}}{4}i$

$x = \dfrac{1}{4} \pm \dfrac{\sqrt{3}}{4}i$

24. $\qquad -3x^2 + 5 = -2x$

$\left(x^2 - \dfrac{2}{3}x + \quad\right) = \dfrac{5}{3}$

$x^2 - \dfrac{2}{3}x + \dfrac{1}{9} = \dfrac{5}{3} + \dfrac{1}{9}$

$\left(x - \dfrac{1}{3}\right)^2 = \dfrac{16}{9}$

$x - \dfrac{1}{3} = \pm\dfrac{4}{3}$

$x = \dfrac{1}{3} \pm \dfrac{4}{3}$

$x = \dfrac{5}{3}, \mathbf{-1}$

25. $\dfrac{700 \text{ cm}^3}{\text{min}} \times \dfrac{1 \text{ in.}}{2.54 \text{ cm}} \times \dfrac{1 \text{ in.}}{2.54 \text{ cm}} \times \dfrac{1 \text{ in.}}{2.54 \text{ cm}}$

$\times \dfrac{60 \text{ min}}{1 \text{ hr}} = \dfrac{\mathbf{700(60)}}{\mathbf{(2.54)(2.54)(2.54)}} \dfrac{\textbf{in.}^3}{\textbf{hr}}$

26. $\sqrt[7]{3\sqrt[3]{3}} = \left[3(3^{1/3})\right]^{1/7} = 3^{1/7}3^{1/21} = \mathbf{3^{4/21}}$

27. $\sqrt[3]{xy^5}\sqrt{x^5 y} = (xy^5)^{1/3}(x^5 y)^{1/2} = x^{1/3}y^{5/3}x^{5/2}y^{1/2}$

$= \mathbf{x^{17/6}y^{13/6}}$

28. $3\sqrt{\dfrac{2}{3}} - 5\sqrt{\dfrac{3}{2}} + 2\sqrt{24}$

$= \dfrac{3\sqrt{2}}{\sqrt{3}}\dfrac{\sqrt{3}}{\sqrt{3}} - \dfrac{5\sqrt{3}}{\sqrt{2}}\dfrac{\sqrt{2}}{\sqrt{2}} + 4\sqrt{6}$

$= \dfrac{6\sqrt{6}}{6} - \dfrac{15\sqrt{6}}{6} + \dfrac{24\sqrt{6}}{6} = \dfrac{\mathbf{5\sqrt{6}}}{\mathbf{2}}$

29. $\dfrac{m}{x(a + b)} - \dfrac{p}{y} = c$

$my - apx - bpx = acxy + bcxy$

$my - apx - acxy = bcxy + bpx$

$\dfrac{\mathbf{my - apx - acxy}}{\mathbf{cxy + px}} = \mathbf{b}$

30. Graph the line to find the slope.

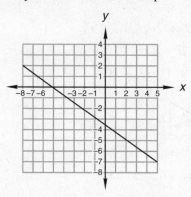

Slope $= -\dfrac{9}{13}$

$y = -\dfrac{9}{13}x + b$

Use the point $(-8, 2)$ for x and y.

$2 = -\dfrac{9}{13}(-8) + b$

$-\dfrac{46}{13} = b$

$y = -\dfrac{9}{13}x - \dfrac{46}{13}$

PRACTICE SET 69

$\dfrac{P_1 V_1}{T_1} = \dfrac{P_2 V_2}{T_2}$

$T_2 P_1 V_1 = T_1 P_2 V_2$

$T_2 = \dfrac{T_1 P_2 V_2}{P_1 V_1}$

$= \dfrac{(300 \times 10^5)(0.00005 \times 10^{14})}{(50 \times 10^3)(0.008 \times 10^{-4})}$

$\times \dfrac{(0.000014 \times 10^{-8})}{(50 \times 10^3)(0.008 \times 10^{-4})}$

$= \textbf{525,000 K}$

PROBLEM SET 69

1. $\dfrac{P_1 V_1}{T_1} = \dfrac{P_2 V_2}{T_2}$

$T_2 = \dfrac{P_2 V_2 T_1}{P_1 V_1}$

$= \dfrac{(0.0008 \times 10^{16})(0.013 \times 10^{-12})(800 \times 10^5)}{(80 \times 10^5)(0.0005 \times 10^{-7})}$

$= \dfrac{(8 \times 10^{12})(1.3 \times 10^{-14})(8 \times 10^7)}{(8 \times 10^6)(5 \times 10^{-11})}$

$T_2 = \textbf{2.08} \times \textbf{10}^{\textbf{10}} \textbf{ K}$

2. Length of side $= \dfrac{7}{\sqrt{2}} = \dfrac{7\sqrt{2}}{2}$ **units**

Area $= s^2 = \left(\dfrac{7\sqrt{2}}{2}\right)^2 = \dfrac{49}{2}$ **units**^{2}

3. $B = \dfrac{k}{T}$

$400 = \dfrac{k}{5}$

$2000 = k$

$B = \dfrac{2000}{25} = \textbf{80 tons}$

4. (a) $0.8(P_N) + 0.4(D_N) = 0.64(2000)$

(b) $P_N + D_N = 2000$

Substitute $D_N = 2000 - P_N$ into (a) and get:

(a′) $0.8(P_N) + 0.4(2000 - P_N) = 1280$

$0.4 P_N = 480$

$P_N = 1200$

(b) $(1200) + D_N = 2000$

$D_N = 800$

1200 mL 80%, 800 mL 40%

5.

$$\overline{\overset{\displaystyle D_B}{}\overset{}{\underset{\displaystyle D_T}{\longrightarrow}}\;40\,|}$$

$R_T T_T + 40 = R_B T_B$; $R_B = 50$; $R_T = 70$;

$T_B = T_T + 2$

$70 T_T + 40 = 50(T_T + 2)$

$20 T_T = 60$

$T_T = 3$ hr

Since the train started at 2 p.m. and took 3 hours to get within 40 miles of the bus, it was **5 p.m.**

6. $\dfrac{1}{x - 5} - \dfrac{2x - 3}{5 - x} = \dfrac{1}{x - 5} + \dfrac{2x - 3}{x - 5}$

$= \dfrac{2x - 2}{x - 5}$

7. $\dfrac{2x + 3}{x - 2} + \dfrac{2x}{2 - x} - \dfrac{3}{-x + 2}$

$= \dfrac{2x + 3}{x - 2} - \dfrac{2x}{x - 2} + \dfrac{3}{x - 2} = \dfrac{6}{x - 2}$

8. $\dfrac{3x + 5}{x - 5} + \dfrac{2}{x^2 - 25}$

$= \dfrac{(3x + 5)(x + 5)}{x^2 - 25} + \dfrac{2}{x^2 - 25}$

$= \dfrac{3x^2 + 15x + 5x + 25 + 2}{x^2 - 25}$

$= \dfrac{\mathbf{3x^2 + 20x + 27}}{\mathbf{x^2 - 25}}$

9. $\dfrac{4}{3 - \sqrt{2}} \cdot \dfrac{3 + \sqrt{2}}{3 + \sqrt{2}} = \dfrac{12 + 4\sqrt{2}}{9 - 2}$

$= \dfrac{\mathbf{12 + 4\sqrt{2}}}{\mathbf{7}}$

10. $\dfrac{2}{5 - 3\sqrt{2}} \cdot \dfrac{5 + 3\sqrt{2}}{5 + 3\sqrt{2}} = \dfrac{10 + 6\sqrt{2}}{25 - 18}$

$= \dfrac{\mathbf{10 + 6\sqrt{2}}}{\mathbf{7}}$

11. $\dfrac{2}{3 - 2\sqrt{8}} \cdot \dfrac{3 + 2\sqrt{8}}{3 + 2\sqrt{8}} = \dfrac{6 + 8\sqrt{2}}{9 - 32}$

$= \dfrac{\mathbf{-6 - 8\sqrt{2}}}{\mathbf{23}}$

12. (a) $R_G T_G = 171$

(b) $R_R T_R = 171$

(c) $R_R = 3R_G$

(d) $T_R = T_G - 6$

Substitute (c) and (d) into (b) and get:

(b′) $3R_G(T_G - 6) = 171$

Substitute (a) into (b′) and get:

(b″) $3(171) - 18R_G = 171$

$-18R_G = -342$

$R_G = \mathbf{19}$

$R_R = \mathbf{57};\ T_G = \mathbf{9};\ T_R = \mathbf{3}$

13. $m + \dfrac{1}{m + \dfrac{1}{m}} = m + \dfrac{1}{\dfrac{m^2 + 1}{m}}$

$= m + \dfrac{m}{m^2 + 1} = \dfrac{\mathbf{m^3 + 2m}}{\mathbf{m^2 + 1}}$

14. $x + \dfrac{a}{x + \dfrac{1}{a}} = x + \dfrac{a}{\dfrac{ax + 1}{a}} = x + \dfrac{a^2}{ax + 1}$

$= \dfrac{\mathbf{ax^2 + x + a^2}}{\mathbf{ax + 1}}$

15. $(4i - 2)(2i - 4) = 8i^2 - 16i - 4i + 8 = \mathbf{-20i}$

16. $-\sqrt{-2}\,\sqrt{-2} + 2i^3 - i^2$

$= -\sqrt{2}i\sqrt{2}i + 2i(ii) - (ii)$

$= 2 - 2i + 1 = \mathbf{3 - 2i}$

17.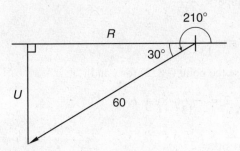

$R = 20 \cos 30° \approx 17.32$

$U = 20 \sin 30° = 10$

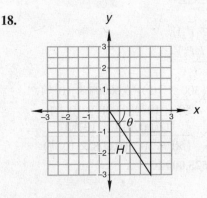

$R = 60 \cos 30° \approx 51.96$

$U = 60 \sin 30° = 30$

$\begin{array}{r} 17.32R + 10U \\ -51.96R - 30U \\ \hline \mathbf{-34.64R - 20U} \end{array}$

18.

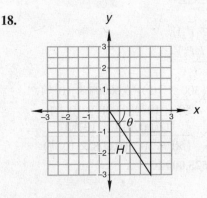

$H = \sqrt{2^2 + 3^2}$

$H = \sqrt{13}$

$\tan \theta = \dfrac{3}{2}$

$\theta \approx 56.31°$

Since θ is a fourth-quadrant angle,

$\theta = -(56.31) + 360 = 303.69°$

$\mathbf{\sqrt{13}\,/\!\underline{303.69°}}$

19. (a) $\dfrac{2}{3}x + \dfrac{2}{5}y = 28$

(b) $-0.05x - 0.2y = -5.5$

(a′) $10x + 6y = 420$

(b′) $-5x - 20y = -550$

$\begin{array}{rl} \text{(a′)} & 10x + 6y = 420 \\ 2\text{(b′)} & \underline{-10x - 40y = -1100} \\ & -34y = -680 \\ & y = 20 \end{array}$

(a′) $10x + 6(20) = 420$

$10x = 300$

$x = 30$

(30, 20)

20. $3x^2 + 8 = 5x$

$\left(x^2 - \dfrac{5}{3}x + \right) = -\dfrac{8}{3}$

$x^2 - \dfrac{5}{3}x + \dfrac{25}{36} = -\dfrac{8}{3} + \dfrac{25}{36}$

$\left(x - \dfrac{5}{6}\right)^2 = -\dfrac{71}{36}$

$x - \dfrac{5}{6} = \pm\dfrac{\sqrt{71}}{6}i$

$x = \dfrac{5}{6} \pm \dfrac{\sqrt{71}}{6}i$

21. $3x^2 + 8 = -5x$

$\left(x^2 + \dfrac{5}{3}x + \right) = -\dfrac{8}{3}$

$x^2 + \dfrac{5}{3}x + \dfrac{25}{36} = -\dfrac{8}{3} + \dfrac{25}{36}$

$\left(x + \dfrac{5}{6}\right)^2 = -\dfrac{71}{36}$

$x + \dfrac{5}{6} = \pm\dfrac{\sqrt{71}}{6}i$

$x = -\dfrac{5}{6} \pm \dfrac{\sqrt{71}}{6}i$

22. Since $\triangle ABC$ is equilateral,

$m\overset{\frown}{BC} = m\overset{\frown}{AB} = m\overset{\frown}{AC} = \mathbf{120°}$ and

$\overline{BC} = \overline{AB} = \overline{AC} = 10$

Use the Pythagorean theorem to find the height.

$10^2 = H^2 + 5^2$

$H^2 = 100 - 25$

$H = 5\sqrt{3}$

Area $= \dfrac{10 \times 5\sqrt{3}}{2} = \mathbf{25\sqrt{3}}$ **units**^{2}

23. $\dfrac{4\,\text{ft}^3}{\text{min}} \times \dfrac{12\,\text{in.}}{1\,\text{ft}} \times \dfrac{12\,\text{in.}}{1\,\text{ft}} \times \dfrac{12\,\text{in.}}{1\,\text{ft}} \times \dfrac{60\,\text{min}}{1\,\text{hr}}$

$= \mathbf{4(12)(12)(12)(60)}\,\dfrac{\textbf{in.}^3}{\textbf{hr}}$

24. $\text{Cr} = m\text{V} + b$

Use the graph to find the slope.

$m = \dfrac{900}{24} = 37.5$

$\text{Cr} = 37.5\text{V} + b$

Use the point (62, 200) for V and Cr.

$200 = 37.5(62) + b$

$-2125 = b$

$\mathbf{Cr = 37.5\,V - 2125}$

25. $\sqrt{27\sqrt[4]{3}} = \sqrt{3^3\sqrt[4]{3}} = \left[3^3(3^{1/4})\right]^{1/2}$

$= 3^{3/2}3^{1/8} = \mathbf{3^{13/8}}$

26. $\sqrt[3]{xm^5}\,\sqrt[4]{xm^2} = (xm^5)^{1/3}(xm^2)^{1/4}$

$= x^{1/3}m^{5/3}x^{1/4}m^{1/2} = \mathbf{x^{7/12}m^{13/6}}$

27. $2\sqrt{\dfrac{9}{2}} + 5\sqrt{\dfrac{2}{9}} - 5\sqrt{50}$

$= \dfrac{6}{\sqrt{2}}\dfrac{\sqrt{2}}{\sqrt{2}} + \dfrac{5\sqrt{2}}{3} - 25\sqrt{2}$

$= \dfrac{18\sqrt{2}}{6} + \dfrac{10\sqrt{2}}{6} - \dfrac{150\sqrt{2}}{6} = \mathbf{-\dfrac{61\sqrt{2}}{3}}$

28. $\dfrac{a(x+y)}{m} - \dfrac{c}{z} = k$

$axz + ayz - cm = kmz$

$axz = kmz + cm - ayz$

$x = \mathbf{\dfrac{kmz + cm - ayz}{az}}$

29. $\dfrac{x+2}{5} - \dfrac{3x-3}{4} = 2$

$4x + 8 - 15x + 15 = 40$

$-11x = 17$

$x = \mathbf{-\dfrac{17}{11}}$

30. (a) $\dfrac{472.2 \times 10^{-26}}{1658.27 \times 10^{10}}$

$\approx \dfrac{5 \times 10^{-24}}{2 \times 10^{13}} \approx 3 \times 10^{-37}$

Calculator answer $\approx \mathbf{2.85 \times 10^{-37}}$

(b) $(1.24)^{-2.73}$

Answer should be between 1 and 0.125.

Calculator answer $\approx \mathbf{0.56}$

PRACTICE SET 70

$$mx = p\left(\frac{z}{x + k} + \frac{2s}{y}\right)$$

$$mx = \frac{pz}{x + k} + \frac{2ps}{y}$$

$$y(x + k)mx = \left(\frac{pz}{(x + k)} + \frac{2ps}{y}\right)y(x + k)$$

$$ymx^2 + ykmx = pyz + 2psx + 2kps$$

$$ykmx - 2kps = pyz + 2psx - ymx^2$$

$$k(ymx - 2ps) = pyz + 2psx - ymx^2$$

$$k = \frac{pyz + 2psx - ymx^2}{ymx - 2ps}$$

PROBLEM SET 70

1. $\dfrac{P_1 V_1}{T_1} = \dfrac{P_2 V_2}{T_2}$

$$T_2 = \frac{P_2 V_2 T_1}{P_1 V_1}$$

$$T_2 = \frac{(0.04 \times 10^5)(500)(4 \times 10^3)}{(0.001 \times 10^{-13})(0.04 \times 10^{14})}$$

$$T_2 = \frac{(4 \times 10^3)(5 \times 10^2)(4 \times 10^3)}{(1 \times 10^{-16})(4 \times 10^{12})}$$

$$T_2 = \mathbf{2 \times 10^{13}\ K}$$

2. $0.2(400) + 0.5(D_N) = 0.26(400 + D_N)$

$$80 + 0.5 D_N = 104 + 0.26 D_N$$

$$0.24 D_N = 24$$

$$D_N = \mathbf{100\ milliliters}$$

3. (a) $50 N_T + 100 N_F = 5000$

(b) $N_T + N_F = 60$

Substitute $N_F = 60 - N_T$ into (a) and get:

(a′) $50 N_T + 100(60 - N_T) = 5000$

$$-50 N_T = -1000$$

$$N_T = \mathbf{20\ people\ flew\ tourist}$$

(b) $N_F = 60 - (20) = \mathbf{40\ people\ flew\ first\text{-}class}$

4. Calcium: $1 \times 40 = 40$

Sulfur: $1 \times 32 = 32$

Oxygen: $4 \times 16 = 64$

Total: $40 + 32 + 64 = 136$

$$\frac{32}{136} = \frac{S}{680}$$

$$S = \mathbf{160\ grams}$$

5. Even integers: N, $N + 2$, $N + 4$

$$4(N)(N + 4) = -10(N + 2 + N + 4) + 28$$

$$4N^2 + 16N = -20N - 32$$

$$4N^2 + 36N + 32 = 0$$

$$N^2 + 9N + 8 = 0$$

$$(N + 8)(N + 1) = 0$$

$$N = -8, -1$$

Since the problem asked for only the even integers, the desired numbers are **−8, −6, −4.**

6. $m = x\left(\dfrac{1}{2p} + \dfrac{3z}{b}\right)$

$$m = \frac{x}{2p} + \frac{3xz}{b}$$

$$2bmp = bx + 6pxz$$

$$2bmp - bx = 6pxz$$

$$b = \frac{6pxz}{2mp - x}$$

7. $ac = x\left(\dfrac{m}{r + s} + \dfrac{t}{z}\right)$

$$ac = \frac{mx}{r + s} + \frac{tx}{z}$$

$$acrz + acsz = mxz + rtx + stx$$

$$acsz - stx = mxz + rtx - acrz$$

$$s = \frac{mxz + rtx - acrz}{acz - tx}$$

8. $\dfrac{3x - 2}{x - 2} - \dfrac{3x}{2 - x} = \dfrac{3x - 2}{x - 2} + \dfrac{3x}{x - 2}$

$$= \frac{6x - 2}{x - 2}$$

9. $\dfrac{4}{x^2 + 8x + 12} + \dfrac{4x - 5}{x + 2}$

$$= \frac{4}{(x + 6)(x + 2)} + \frac{(4x - 5)(x + 6)}{(x + 6)(x + 2)}$$

$$= \frac{4}{x^2 + 8x + 12} + \frac{4x^2 + 19x - 30}{x^2 + 8x + 12}$$

$$= \frac{4x^2 + 19x - 26}{x^2 + 8x + 12}$$

10. $\dfrac{2}{\sqrt{2} - 4} \cdot \dfrac{\sqrt{2} + 4}{\sqrt{2} + 4} = \dfrac{2\sqrt{2} + 8}{2 - 16}$

$$= \frac{-\sqrt{2} - 4}{7}$$

Algebra 2, **Third Edition**

11. $\dfrac{2}{3\sqrt{12} - 2} \cdot \dfrac{3\sqrt{12} + 2}{3\sqrt{12} + 2} = \dfrac{12\sqrt{3} + 4}{108 - 4}$

$= \dfrac{\mathbf{3\sqrt{3} + 1}}{\mathbf{26}}$

12. $\dfrac{2}{2\sqrt{2} - 2} \cdot \dfrac{2\sqrt{2} + 2}{2\sqrt{2} + 2} = \dfrac{4\sqrt{2} + 4}{8 - 4}$

$= \mathbf{\sqrt{2} + 1}$

13. (a) $R_B T_B = 65$

(b) $R_X T_X = 104$

(c) $R_X = 2R_B$

(d) $T_X = T_B - 1$

Substitute (c) and (d) into (b) and get:

(b′) $2R_B(T_B - 1) = 104$

Substitute (a) into (b′) and get:

(b″) $2(65) - 2R_B = 104$

$-2R_B = -26$

$R_B = \mathbf{13}$

$R_X = \mathbf{26};\ T_B = \mathbf{5};\ T_X = \mathbf{4}$

14. $xy + \dfrac{a}{1 + \dfrac{a}{b}} = xy + \dfrac{a}{\dfrac{b + a}{b}}$

$= xy + \dfrac{ab}{b + a} = \dfrac{\boldsymbol{xyb + xya + ab}}{\boldsymbol{b + a}}$

15. $\dfrac{m}{y} + \dfrac{x}{a + \dfrac{1}{y}} = \dfrac{m}{y} + \dfrac{x}{\dfrac{ay + 1}{y}}$

$= \dfrac{m}{y} + \dfrac{xy}{ay + 1} = \dfrac{\boldsymbol{amy + m + xy^2}}{\boldsymbol{y(ay + 1)}}$

16. $(2 - 3i)(5 - 6i)$

$= 10 - 12i - 15i + 18i^2 = \mathbf{-8 - 27i}$

17. $-\sqrt{-4} - \sqrt{-2}\,\sqrt{-3} + \sqrt{-9}$

$= -2i - \sqrt{2}i\sqrt{3}i + 3i$

$= -2i + \sqrt{6} + 3i = \boldsymbol{\sqrt{6} + i}$

18.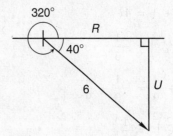

$R = 4\cos 20° \approx 3.76$

$U = 4\sin 20° \approx 1.37$

$R = 6\cos 40° \approx 4.60$

$U = 6\sin 40° \approx 3.86$

$\begin{array}{r} 3.76R - 1.37U \\ 4.60R - 3.86U \\ \hline \mathbf{8.36R - 5.23U} \end{array}$

19.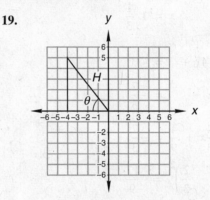

$H = \sqrt{5^2 + 4^2}$

$H = \sqrt{41}$

$\tan\theta = \dfrac{5}{4}$

$\theta \approx 51.34°$

Since θ is a second-quadrant angle,

$\theta = -(51.34) + 180 = 128.66°$

$\boldsymbol{\sqrt{41}\,/128.66°}$

20. (a) $\dfrac{1}{5}x - \dfrac{1}{4}y = -2$

(b) $0.07x + 0.3y = 5.5$

(a′) $4x - 5y = -40$

(b′) $7x + 30y = 550$

$6(a′)\ 24x - 30y = -240$

$\begin{array}{r} (b′)\ \ \ 7x + 30y = \ \ 550 \\ \hline 31x\qquad\quad = \ \ 310 \end{array}$

$x = 10$

(a′) $4(10) - 5y = -40$

$-5y = -80$

$y = 16$

$\mathbf{(10, 16)}$

21.
$$3x^2 + 1 = 4x$$

$$\left(x^2 - \frac{4}{3}x + \right) = -\frac{1}{3}$$

$$x^2 - \frac{4}{3}x + \frac{4}{9} = -\frac{1}{3} + \frac{4}{9}$$

$$\left(x - \frac{2}{3}\right)^2 = \frac{1}{9}$$

$$x - \frac{2}{3} = \pm\frac{1}{3}$$

$$x = \frac{2}{3} \pm \frac{1}{3}$$

$$x = \mathbf{1, \frac{1}{3}}$$

22.
$$-4x + 7 = -3x^2$$

$$\left(x^2 - \frac{4}{3}x + \right) = -\frac{7}{3}$$

$$x^2 - \frac{4}{3}x + \frac{4}{9} = -\frac{7}{3} + \frac{4}{9}$$

$$\left(x - \frac{2}{3}\right)^2 = -\frac{17}{9}$$

$$x - \frac{2}{3} = \pm\frac{\sqrt{17}}{3}i$$

$$x = \mathbf{\frac{2}{3} \pm \frac{\sqrt{17}}{3}i}$$

23. Since this is a 30°-60°-90° triangle,

$$1 \times \overrightarrow{SF} = 4$$

$$\overrightarrow{SF} = 4$$

$$a = 4(\sqrt{3}) = \mathbf{4\sqrt{3}}$$

$$b = 4(2) = \mathbf{8}$$

24. $Co = m\text{Ni} + b$

Use the graph to find the slope.

$$m = \frac{-20}{13} \approx -1.54$$

$$Co = -1.54\text{Ni} + b$$

Use the point (138, 50) for Ni and Co.

$$50 = -1.54(138) + b$$

$$262.52 = b$$

$$\mathbf{Co = -1.54Ni + 262.52}$$

25. (a)
$$\frac{46{,}831 \times 10^{-42}}{9140.26 \times 10^{-33}} \approx \frac{5 \times 10^{-38}}{9 \times 10^{-30}}$$

$$\approx 6 \times 10^{-9}$$

Calculator answer $\approx \mathbf{5.12 \times 10^{-9}}$

(b) $\sqrt[2.7]{146}$

Answer should be between 5 and 7.

Calculator answer $\approx \mathbf{6.33}$

26. $\sqrt[5]{x^4 y^3}\,\sqrt[4]{x^2 y} = (x^4 y^3)^{1/5}(x^2 y)^{1/4}$
$$= x^{4/5}y^{3/5}x^{1/2}y^{1/4} = \mathbf{x^{13/10}y^{17/20}}$$

27. $\sqrt{\dfrac{7}{2}} + 2\sqrt{\dfrac{2}{7}} - 2\sqrt{126}$

$$= \frac{\sqrt{7}}{\sqrt{2}}\frac{\sqrt{2}}{\sqrt{2}} + \frac{2\sqrt{2}}{\sqrt{7}}\frac{\sqrt{7}}{\sqrt{7}} - 6\sqrt{14}$$

$$= \frac{7\sqrt{14}}{14} + \frac{4\sqrt{14}}{14} - \frac{84\sqrt{14}}{14} = \mathbf{-\frac{73\sqrt{14}}{14}}$$

28.
$$\begin{array}{r}
4x^2 + 4x + 4 + \frac{2}{x-1} \\
x - 1 \overline{)\,4x^3 + 0x^2 - 0x - 2} \\
\underline{4x^3 - 4x^2} \\
4x^2 + 0x \\
\underline{4x^2 - 4x} \\
4x - 2 \\
\underline{4x - 4} \\
2
\end{array}$$

29. Write the equation of the given line in slope-intercept form.

$$4x + 3y = 5$$

$$y = -\frac{4}{3}x + \frac{5}{3}$$

Since the slopes of perpendicular lines are negative reciprocals of each other,

$$m_\perp = \frac{3}{4}.$$

$$y = \frac{3}{4}x + b$$

$$5 = \frac{3}{4}(-2) + b$$

$$\frac{13}{2} = b$$

$$\mathbf{y = \frac{3}{4}x + \frac{13}{2}}$$

30. $\dfrac{4x - 2}{5} - \dfrac{3x - 2}{4} = 10$

$$16x - 8 - 15x + 10 = 200$$

$$x = \mathbf{198}$$

PRACTICE SET 71

a.
$$ax^2 + bx + c = 0$$

$$x^2 + \frac{b}{a}x + \frac{c}{a} = 0$$

$$\left(x^2 + \frac{b}{a}x + \quad\right) = -\frac{c}{a}$$

$$\left(x^2 + \frac{b}{a}x + \frac{b^2}{4a^2}\right) = \frac{b^2}{4a^2} - \frac{c}{a}$$

$$\left(x + \frac{b}{2a}\right)^2 = \frac{b^2 - 4ac}{4a^2}$$

$$x + \frac{b}{2a} = \pm\sqrt{\frac{b^2 - 4ac}{4a^2}}$$

$$x = \frac{-b}{2a} \pm \frac{\sqrt{b^2 - 4ac}}{2a}$$

$$x = \frac{-b \pm \sqrt{b^2 - 4ac}}{2a}$$

b. $2x^2 - 6x + 4 = 0$

$a = 2, \ b = -6, \ c = 4$

$$x = \frac{-(-6) \pm \sqrt{(-6)^2 - 4(2)(4)}}{2(2)}$$

$$= \frac{6 \pm \sqrt{36 - 32}}{4} = \frac{6 \pm 2}{4} = \mathbf{1, 2}$$

PROBLEM SET 71

1. $P_1V_1 = P_2V_2$

$$P_2 = \frac{P_1V_1}{V_2}$$

$$P_2 = \frac{(40{,}000 \times 10^{-3})(4000 \times 10^{-2})}{8000 \times 10^{-2}}$$

$$P_2 = \frac{(4 \times 10^1)(4 \times 10^1)}{(8 \times 10^1)} = \mathbf{20 \ N/m^2}$$

2. $F = kP$

$240 = k(4800)$

$$\frac{1}{20} = k$$

$$600 = \left(\frac{1}{20}\right)P$$

12,000 people $= P$

3. (a) $0.1P_N + 0.3D_N = 0.17(200)$

(b) $P_N + D_N = 200$

Substitute $D_N = 200 - P_N$ into (a) and get:

(a') $0.1P_N + 0.3(200 - P_N) = 34$

$$-0.2P_N = -26$$

$$P_N = 130$$

(b) $(130) + D_N = 200$

$$D_N = 70$$

130 mL 10%, 70 mL 30%

4.

$R_RT_R = R_JT_J; \ R_R = 8; \ R_J = 24; \ T_R + T_J = 8$

$8T_R = 24(8 - T_R)$

$32T_R = 192$

$T_R = 6 \text{ hr}$

$D_R = D_J = 6(8) = \mathbf{48 \ miles}$

5.

Hydrogen:	$2 \times 1 = 2$
Carbon:	$1 \times 12 = 12$
Oxygen:	$3 \times 16 = 48$
Total:	$2 + 12 + 48 = 62$

Hydrogen: $\frac{2}{62} \times 100\% \approx \mathbf{3.23\%}$

6. See Lesson 71.

7. $4x^2 - 2x - 6 = 0$

$$x = \frac{-(-2) \pm \sqrt{(-2)^2 - 4(4)(-6)}}{2(4)}$$

$$= \frac{2 \pm \sqrt{100}}{8} = \frac{2 \pm 10}{8} = \mathbf{\frac{3}{2}, -1}$$

8. $2x^2 = -x - 4$

$2x^2 + x + 4 = 0$

$$x = \frac{-1 \pm \sqrt{(1)^2 - 4(2)(4)}}{2(2)} = \frac{-1 \pm \sqrt{-31}}{4}$$

$$x = -\frac{1}{4} \pm \frac{\sqrt{31}}{4}i$$

9. $x = \frac{360 - 280}{2} = \mathbf{40}$

$y = \frac{180 - 80}{2} = \mathbf{50}$

Since the diagonals of a rhombus are perpendicular bisectors of each other, $z = \mathbf{90}$.

10.
$$r = m\left(\frac{1}{x + c} + \frac{3}{y}\right)$$

$$r = \frac{m}{x + c} + \frac{3m}{y}$$

$$rxy + rcy = my + 3mx + 3cm$$

$$rxy - 3mx = my + 3cm - rcy$$

$$x = \frac{my + 3cm - rcy}{ry - 3m}$$

11. $\dfrac{4x + 5}{x - 2} - \dfrac{4}{2 - x} = \dfrac{4x + 5}{x - 2} + \dfrac{4}{x - 2}$

$$= \frac{4x + 9}{x - 2}$$

12. $\dfrac{4}{2 - 3\sqrt{12}} \cdot \dfrac{2 + 3\sqrt{12}}{2 + 3\sqrt{12}} = \dfrac{8 + 24\sqrt{3}}{4 - 108}$

$$= \frac{-1 - 3\sqrt{3}}{13}$$

13. (a) $R_M T_M = 160$

(b) $R_P T_P = 400$

(c) $R_P = 2R_M$

(d) $T_P = T_M + 1$

Substitute (c) and (d) into (b) and get:

(b') $2R_M(T_M + 1) = 400$

Substitute (a) into (b') and get:

(b'') $2(160) + 2R_M = 400$

$$2R_M = 80$$

$$R_M = \mathbf{40}$$

$R_P = \mathbf{80}$; $T_M = \mathbf{4}$; $T_P = \mathbf{5}$

14. $x + \dfrac{x}{1 + \dfrac{1}{x}} = x + \dfrac{x}{\dfrac{x + 1}{x}} = x + \dfrac{x^2}{x + 1}$

$$= \frac{2x^2 + x}{x + 1}$$

15. $a + \dfrac{b}{a + \dfrac{a}{b}} = a + \dfrac{b}{\dfrac{ab + a}{b}}$

$$= a + \frac{b^2}{ab + a} = \frac{a^2 b + a^2 + b^2}{ab + a}$$

16. $-3i^3 + 2\sqrt{-2}\,\sqrt{2} - \sqrt{-9}$

$$= -3i(ii) + 2\sqrt{2}\,\sqrt{2}i - 3i$$

$$= 3i + 4i - 3i = \mathbf{4i}$$

17. $(-i - 1)(-3i + 2) = 3i^2 - 2i + 3i - 2$

$$= \mathbf{-5 + i}$$

18.
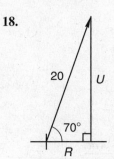

$R = 20\cos 70° \approx 6.84$

$U = 20\sin 70° \approx 18.79$

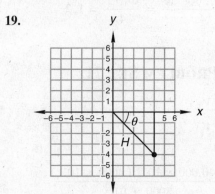

$R = 10\cos 40° \approx 7.66$

$U = 10\sin 40° \approx 6.43$

$$\begin{array}{r} 6.84R + 18.79U \\ 7.66R + 6.43U \\ \hline \mathbf{14.50R + 25.22U} \end{array}$$

19.
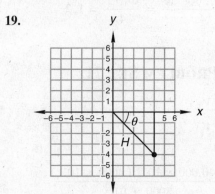

$H = \sqrt{4^2 + 4^2}$

$H = 4\sqrt{2}$

$\tan\theta = \dfrac{4}{4} = 1$

$\theta = 45°$

Since θ is a fourth-quadrant angle,

$\theta = -(45) + 360 = 315°$

$\mathbf{4\sqrt{2}\,/\underline{315°}}$

20. (a) $\dfrac{3}{8}x - \dfrac{1}{2}y = 2$

(b) $0.06x - 0.2y = -0.64$

(a') $3x - 4y = 16$

(b') $6x - 20y = -64$

$-2(a')$ $-6x + 8y = -32$

$\underline{\text{(b')} \quad 6x - 20y = -64}$

$-12y = -96$

$y = 8$

(a') $3x - 4(8) = 16$

$3x = 48$

$x = 16$

(16, 8)

21. $3x^2 - 2x + 5 = 0$

$\left(x^2 - \dfrac{2}{3}x + \quad \right) = -\dfrac{5}{3}$

$x^2 - \dfrac{2}{3}x + \dfrac{1}{9} = -\dfrac{5}{3} + \dfrac{1}{9}$

$\left(x - \dfrac{1}{3}\right)^2 = -\dfrac{14}{9}$

$x - \dfrac{1}{3} = \pm\dfrac{\sqrt{14}}{3}i$

$x = \dfrac{1}{3} \pm \dfrac{\sqrt{14}}{3}i$

22. Since this is a 30°-60°-90° triangle,

$2 \times \overrightarrow{SF} = 11$

$\overrightarrow{SF} = \dfrac{11}{2}$

$a = \dfrac{11}{2}(1) = \dfrac{\mathbf{11}}{\mathbf{2}}$

$b = \dfrac{11}{2}(\sqrt{3}) = \dfrac{\mathbf{11}\sqrt{3}}{\mathbf{2}}$

23. Pb = mB + b

Use the graph to find the slope.

$m = \dfrac{72}{2} = 36$

Pb = 36B + b

Use the point (4, 0) for B and Pb.

$0 = 36(4) + b$

$-144 = b$

Pb = 36B − 144

24. $\sqrt{81\sqrt{3}} = \sqrt{3^4 \sqrt{3}} = \left[3^4(3^{1/2})\right]^{1/2}$

$= 3^2 3^{1/4} = \mathbf{3^{9/4}}$

25. $\sqrt[3]{x^5 y^6}\,\sqrt{xy^3} = (x^5 y^6)^{1/3}(xy^3)^{1/2}$

$= x^{5/3}y^2 x^{1/2}y^{3/2} = \mathbf{x^{13/6}y^{7/2}}$

26. $3\sqrt{\dfrac{2}{5}} + 3\sqrt{\dfrac{5}{2}} - 6\sqrt{40}$

$= \dfrac{3\sqrt{2}}{\sqrt{5}}\dfrac{\sqrt{5}}{\sqrt{5}} + \dfrac{3\sqrt{5}}{\sqrt{2}}\dfrac{\sqrt{2}}{\sqrt{2}} - 12\sqrt{10}$

$= \dfrac{6\sqrt{10}}{10} + \dfrac{15\sqrt{10}}{10} - \dfrac{120\sqrt{10}}{10} = -\dfrac{\mathbf{99}\sqrt{\mathbf{10}}}{\mathbf{10}}$

27. $(x - 2)^3 = (x - 2)(x - 2)(x - 2)$

$= (x^2 - 4x + 4)(x - 2)$

$= x^3 - 2x^2 - 4x^2 + 8x + 4x - 8$

$= \mathbf{x^3 - 6x^2 + 12x - 8}$

28. $\dfrac{x^2 y - \dfrac{1}{y}}{\dfrac{x^2}{y} - 6} = \dfrac{\dfrac{x^2 y^2 - 1}{y}}{\dfrac{x^2 - 6y}{y}} \cdot \dfrac{\dfrac{y}{x^2 - 6y}}{\dfrac{y}{x^2 - 6y}}$

$= \dfrac{\mathbf{x^2 y^2 - 1}}{\mathbf{x^2 - 6y}}$

29. (a) $\dfrac{-471{,}635 \times 10^5}{0.0071893 \times 10^{-14}}$

$\approx \dfrac{-5 \times 10^{10}}{7 \times 10^{-17}} \approx -7 \times 10^{26}$

Calculator answer $\approx \mathbf{-6.56 \times 10^{26}}$

(b) $(2.4)^{-3.06}$

Answer should be between 0.125 and 0.037.

Calculator answer $\approx \mathbf{6.86 \times 10^{-2}}$

30. $\dfrac{b}{z} = \dfrac{x}{y}$

$by = xz$

$\mathbf{b = \dfrac{xz}{y}}$

Practice Set 72

a.

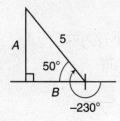

$$\sin 50° = \frac{A}{5}$$

$$5 \sin 50° = A$$

$$3.83 \approx A$$

$$\cos 50° = \frac{B}{5}$$

$$5 \cos 50° = B$$

$$3.21 \approx B$$

$$5\underline{/-230°} = -3.21R + 3.83U$$

b.

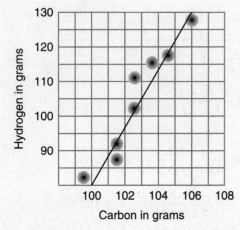

Use the points (100, 80) and (106, 130).

(a) $-80 = -100m - b$

(b) $\dfrac{130 = 106m + b}{50 = 6m}$

$$m = \frac{25}{3} \approx 8.33$$

$$80 = 100 \cdot \frac{25}{3} + b$$

$$b = -\frac{2260}{3} \approx -753.33$$

H = 8.33C − 753.33

Problem Set 72

1. $0.52(500) - (W_R) = 0.4(500 - W_R)$

$$260 - W_R = 200 - 0.4W_R$$

$$-0.6W_R = -60$$

$$W_R = \textbf{100 mL}$$

2. $3.07 \times AP = 31{,}314$

$$AP = \textbf{10,200 things}$$

3. $\dfrac{66}{100} \times M = 5412$

$$M = \textbf{8200 people}$$

4. (a) $N_F = N_J + 160$

(b) $6N_J = N_F + 40$

Substitute (a) into (b) and get:

(b′) $6N_J = (N_J + 160) + 40$

$$5N_J = 200$$

$$N_J = \textbf{40 pieces of jetsam}$$

(a) $N_F = (40) + 160 = \textbf{200 pieces of flotsam}$

5. $\dfrac{P_1}{T_1} = \dfrac{P_2}{T_2}$

$$P_2 = \frac{P_1 T_2}{T_1}$$

$$P_2 = \frac{(500 \times 10^5)(0.002 \times 10^5)}{0.0004 \times 10^7}$$

$$P_2 = \frac{(5 \times 10^7)(2 \times 10^2)}{4 \times 10^3}$$

$$P_2 = \textbf{2.5} \times \textbf{10}^6 \textbf{ N/m}^2$$

6. There is never an exact solution to these problems. One possible solution is given here.

$$S = mC + b$$

Use the graph to find the slope.

$$m = \frac{3}{40} = 0.075$$

$$S = 0.075C + b$$

Use the point (40, 1) for C and S.

$$1 = 0.075(40) + b$$

$$-2 = b$$

S = 0.075C − 2

7.

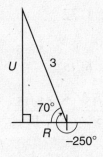

$R = 3 \cos 70° \approx 1.03$

$U = 3 \sin 70° \approx 2.82$

$\mathbf{-1.03R + 2.82U}$

8.

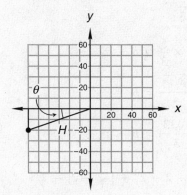

$H = \sqrt{60^2 + 20^2}$

$H = 20\sqrt{10}$

$\tan \theta = \dfrac{20}{60} = \dfrac{1}{3}$

$\theta \approx 18.43°$

Since θ is a third-quadrant angle,

$\theta = 18.43 + 180 = 198.43°$

$\mathbf{20\sqrt{10}\,/\,198.43°}$

9. See Lesson 71.

10.
$$5x^2 = -7 - 2x$$
$$5x^2 + 2x + 7 = 0$$
$$x = \frac{-2 \pm \sqrt{(2)^2 - 4(5)(7)}}{2(5)}$$
$$x = \frac{-2 \pm \sqrt{-136}}{10} = \mathbf{-\frac{1}{5} \pm \frac{\sqrt{34}}{5}i}$$

11.
$$3x^2 + 7x = -3$$
$$3x^2 + 7x + 3 = 0$$
$$x = \frac{-7 \pm \sqrt{7^2 - 4(3)(3)}}{2(3)}$$
$$x = \frac{-7 \pm \sqrt{13}}{6} = \mathbf{-\frac{7}{6} \pm \frac{\sqrt{13}}{6}}$$

12.
$$a = x\left(\frac{1}{m_1} + \frac{y}{m_2}\right)$$
$$a = \frac{x}{m_1} + \frac{xy}{m_2}$$
$$am_1m_2 = m_2x + m_1xy$$
$$am_1m_2 - m_1xy = m_2x$$
$$m_1 = \frac{m_2x}{am_2 - xy}$$

13.
$$\frac{2x + 3}{x^2 - 2x - 8} + \frac{3x - 2}{x - 4}$$
$$= \frac{2x + 3}{(x - 4)(x + 2)} + \frac{(3x - 2)(x + 2)}{(x - 4)(x + 2)}$$
$$= \frac{2x + 3 + 3x^2 + 4x - 4}{x^2 - 2x - 8}$$
$$= \frac{3x^2 + 6x - 1}{x^2 - 2x - 8}$$

14.
$$\frac{3}{2 + 3\sqrt{20}} \cdot \frac{2 - 3\sqrt{20}}{2 - 3\sqrt{20}} = \frac{6 - 18\sqrt{5}}{4 - 180}$$
$$= \frac{-3 + 9\sqrt{5}}{88}$$

15. (a) $R_P T_P = 693$

(b) $R_C T_C = 165$

(c) $R_P = 3R_C$

(d) $T_P = T_C + 2$

Substitute (c) and (d) into (a) and get:

(a') $3R_C(T_C + 2) = 693$

Substitute (b) into (a') and get:

(a'') $3(165) + 6R_C = 693$
$$6R_C = 198$$
$$R_C = 33$$

$R_P = 99; \ T_C = 5; \ T_P = 7$

16. $ab + \dfrac{b}{b + \dfrac{1}{b}} = ab + \dfrac{b}{\dfrac{b^2 + 1}{b}}$

$= ab + \dfrac{b^2}{b^2 + 1} = \dfrac{ab^3 + ab + b^2}{b^2 + 1}$

17. $x^2 + \dfrac{y}{y + \dfrac{1}{xy}} = x^2 + \dfrac{y}{\dfrac{xy^2 + 1}{xy}}$

$= x^2 + \dfrac{xy^2}{xy^2 + 1} = \dfrac{x^3y^2 + x^2 + xy^2}{xy^2 + 1}$

18. $(-3i - 5)(i + 5)$
$= -3i^2 - 15i - 5i - 25 = \mathbf{-22 - 20i}$

19. $-4i^3 - 3i^2 + \sqrt{-9} - \sqrt{-3}\sqrt{-3}$
$= -4i(ii) - 3(ii) + 3i - \sqrt{3}\sqrt{3}(ii)$
$= 4i + 3 + 3i + 3 = \mathbf{6 + 7i}$

20. (a) $\frac{1}{4}x - \frac{1}{5}y = 2$

(b) $0.03x - 0.4y = -1.64$

(a′) $5x - 4y = 40$

(b′) $3x - 40y = -164$

$\begin{array}{l} -10(\text{a}′) \quad -50x + 40y = -400 \\ (\text{b}′) \quad \underline{3x - 40y = -164} \\ \phantom{-10(\text{b}′)\quad} -47x = -564 \\ \phantom{-10(\text{b}′)-47x +40y=} x = 12 \end{array}$

(a′) $5(12) - 4y = 40$
$-4y = -20$
$y = 5$

$\mathbf{(12, 5)}$

21. $2x^2 - x + 4 = 0$
$\left(x^2 - \frac{1}{2}x + \right) = -2$

$x^2 - \frac{1}{2}x + \frac{1}{16} = -2 + \frac{1}{16}$

$\left(x - \frac{1}{4}\right)^2 = -\frac{31}{16}$

$x - \frac{1}{4} = \pm\frac{\sqrt{31}}{4}i$

$x = \mathbf{\frac{1}{4} \pm \frac{\sqrt{31}}{4}i}$

22. (a) $x = \frac{135 + 17}{2} = \mathbf{76°}$

(b) $x = \frac{272 - 40}{2} = \mathbf{116°}$

23. $\sqrt[5]{4\sqrt{2}} = \sqrt[5]{2^2\sqrt{2}} = \left[2^2(2^{1/2})\right]^{1/5}$
$= 2^{2/5}2^{1/10} = \mathbf{2^{1/2}}$

24. $\frac{-2^0}{-8^{-4/3}} = -\left[-(8^{1/3})^4\right] = -[-(16)] = \mathbf{16}$

25. $\sqrt[4]{a^5y}\sqrt{ay^4} = (a^5y)^{1/4}(ay^4)^{1/2}$
$= a^{5/4}y^{1/4}a^{1/2}y^2 = \mathbf{a^{7/4}y^{9/4}}$

26. $2\sqrt{\frac{3}{5}} + 4\sqrt{\frac{5}{3}} - 2\sqrt{135}$

$= \frac{2\sqrt{3}}{\sqrt{5}}\frac{\sqrt{5}}{\sqrt{5}} + \frac{4\sqrt{5}}{\sqrt{3}}\frac{\sqrt{3}}{\sqrt{3}} - 6\sqrt{15}$

$= \frac{6\sqrt{15}}{15} + \frac{20\sqrt{15}}{15} - \frac{90\sqrt{15}}{15} = \mathbf{-\frac{64\sqrt{15}}{15}}$

27. $A^2 = 6^2 + 4^2$
$A = 2\sqrt{13}$

$6 \times \overrightarrow{SF} = 10$

$\overrightarrow{SF} = \frac{5}{3}$

$2\sqrt{13} \times \frac{5}{3} = B + 2\sqrt{13}$

$\frac{10\sqrt{13}}{3} - \frac{6\sqrt{13}}{3} = B$

$\mathbf{\frac{4\sqrt{13}}{3} = B}$

28. $(-2)^0 - 2^2 - 2 - 2^0 - |-2 - 2| - 2^3$
$= -2(-2x - 2)$

$1 - 4 - 2 - 1 - 4 - 8 = 4x + 4$
$-22 = 4x$

$\mathbf{-\frac{11}{2} = x}$

29. Write the equation of the given line in slope-intercept form.

$4y - 3x = 1$

$y = \frac{3}{4}x + \frac{1}{4}$

Since the slopes of perpendicular lines are negative reciprocals of each other,

$m_\perp = -\frac{4}{3}$

$y = -\frac{4}{3}x + b$

$0 = -\frac{4}{3}(-7) + b$

$-\frac{28}{3} = b$

$y = \mathbf{-\frac{4}{3}x - \frac{28}{3}}$

30. (a) $\dfrac{-35{,}123 \times 10^4}{-798 \times 10^{-15}} \approx \dfrac{-4 \times 10^8}{-8 \times 10^{-13}}$

$= 5 \times 10^{20}$

Calculator answer $\approx$ **4.40×10^{20}**

(b) $\sqrt[3.8]{243}$

Answer should be between 3 and 5.

Calculator answer $\approx$ **4.24**

PRACTICE SET 73

a. $\dfrac{5 + \sqrt{3}}{2\sqrt{3}} \cdot \dfrac{2\sqrt{3}}{2\sqrt{3}} = \dfrac{10\sqrt{3} + 2(3)}{4(3)}$

$= \dfrac{10\sqrt{3} + 6}{12} = \dfrac{\mathbf{3} + \mathbf{5}\sqrt{\mathbf{3}}}{\mathbf{6}}$

b. $\dfrac{2\sqrt{12} - 3\sqrt{3}}{2\sqrt{3} - 3\sqrt{2}} \cdot \dfrac{2\sqrt{3} + 3\sqrt{2}}{2\sqrt{3} + 3\sqrt{2}}$

ABOVE

$2\sqrt{12} - 3\sqrt{3}$
$\underline{2\sqrt{3} \quad + 3\sqrt{2}}$
$24 \quad - 18$
$\underline{\quad\quad - 9\sqrt{6} + 12\sqrt{6}}$
$6 + 3\sqrt{6}$

BELOW

$2\sqrt{3} - 3\sqrt{2}$
$\underline{2\sqrt{3} + 3\sqrt{2}}$
$12 - 6\sqrt{6}$
$\underline{\quad\;\; + 6\sqrt{6} - 18}$
$12 \quad\quad - 18 = -6$

$\dfrac{6 + 3\sqrt{6}}{-6} = \dfrac{\mathbf{2} + \sqrt{\mathbf{6}}}{\mathbf{-2}} \text{ or } \dfrac{\mathbf{-2} - \sqrt{\mathbf{6}}}{\mathbf{2}}$

PROBLEM SET 73

1. Carbon: $\quad 2 \times 12 = 24$

Hydrogen: $\quad 5 \times 1 = 5$

Bromine: $\quad 1 \times 80 = 80$

Total: $\quad 24 + 5 + 80 = 109$

$\dfrac{24}{109} = \dfrac{48}{C_2H_5Br}$

C_2H_5Br = **218 grams**

2. (a) $2N_P = 4N_D + 8$

(a') $N_P = 2N_D + 4$

(b) $7N_D = 3N_P - 4$

Substitute (a') into (b) and get:

(b') $7N_D = 3(2N_D + 4) - 4$

N_D = **8 daisies**

(a') $N_P = 2(8) + 4 =$ **20 pansies**

3.
$$\overset{D_L \quad\quad D_T}{\underset{256}{\vert\!\!\longrightarrow\!\!\longrightarrow\!\!\vert}}$$

$R_L T_L + R_T T_T = 256$; $R_L = 16$; $R_T = 12$;

$T_L = T_T + 2$

$16(T_T + 2) + 12T_T = 256$

$28T_T = 224$

$T_T = 8 \text{ hr}$

$D_T = 8(12) =$ **96 miles**

4. $N_F = \dfrac{k}{S_C}$

$50 = \dfrac{k}{50}$

$2500 = k$

$N_F = \dfrac{2500}{25} =$ **100 frangibles**

5. $\dfrac{V_1}{T_1} = \dfrac{V_2}{T_2}$

$T_2 = \dfrac{V_2 T_1}{V_1}$

$T_2 = \dfrac{(0.08)(700 \times 10^5)}{0.0004}$

$T_2 = \dfrac{(8 \times 10^{-2})(7 \times 10^7)}{4 \times 10^{-4}}$

$T_2 =$ **1.4×10^{10} K**

6. $\dfrac{3 + \sqrt{5}}{2 - 2\sqrt{5}} \cdot \dfrac{2 + 2\sqrt{5}}{2 + 2\sqrt{5}}$

$= \dfrac{6 + 6\sqrt{5} + 2\sqrt{5} + 10}{4 - 20} = \dfrac{\mathbf{-2} - \sqrt{\mathbf{5}}}{\mathbf{2}}$

7. $\dfrac{\sqrt{8} - 2\sqrt{2}}{3\sqrt{2} - 2\sqrt{3}} = \dfrac{0}{3\sqrt{2} - 2\sqrt{3}} = \mathbf{0}$

8. Length of side $= \dfrac{7}{\sqrt{2}} = \dfrac{7\sqrt{2}}{2}$ **m**

Area $= s^2 = \left(\dfrac{7\sqrt{2}}{2}\right)^2 = \dfrac{49}{2}$ **m²**

9. There is never an exact solution for these problems. One possible solution is given here.

$H = mC + b$

Use the graph to find the slope.

$m = \dfrac{-40}{5} = -8$

$H = -8C + b$

Use the point (105, 80) for C and H.

$80 = -8(105) + b$

$920 = b$

H = –8C + 920

10.

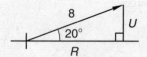

$R = 8 \cos 20° \approx 7.52$

$U = 8 \sin 20° \approx 2.74$

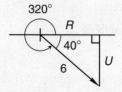

$R = 6 \cos 40° \approx 4.60$

$U = 6 \sin 40° \approx 3.86$

$\begin{array}{r} 7.52R + 2.74U \\ 4.60R - 3.86U \\ \hline \mathbf{12.12R - 1.12U} \end{array}$

11.

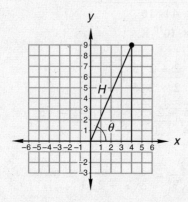

$H = \sqrt{9^2 + 4^2}$

$H = \sqrt{97}$

$\tan \theta = \dfrac{9}{4}$

$\theta \approx 66.04°$

$\mathbf{\sqrt{97}\,\underline{/66.04°}}$

12. See Lesson 71.

13.
$$2x^2 + 5 = -5x$$
$$2x^2 + 5x + 5 = 0$$
$$x = \dfrac{-5 \pm \sqrt{5^2 - 4(2)(5)}}{2(2)} = \dfrac{-5 \pm \sqrt{-15}}{4}$$
$$x = -\dfrac{5}{4} \pm \dfrac{\sqrt{15}}{4}i$$

14.
$$2x^2 - 4 = -5x$$
$$2x^2 + 5x - 4 = 0$$
$$x = \dfrac{-5 \pm \sqrt{5^2 - 4(2)(-4)}}{2(2)} = \dfrac{-5 \pm \sqrt{57}}{4}$$
$$x = -\dfrac{5}{4} \pm \dfrac{\sqrt{57}}{4}$$

15.
$$xc = px\left(\dfrac{1}{km_1} - \dfrac{1}{m_2}\right)$$
$$xc = \dfrac{px}{km_1} - \dfrac{px}{m_2}$$
$$ckm_1m_2x = m_2px - km_1px$$
$$ckm_1m_2x + km_1px = m_2px$$
$$m_1 = \dfrac{m_2 p}{ckm_2 + kp}$$

16. $\dfrac{3x - 2}{x - 2} - \dfrac{4x - 3}{2 - x}$

$= \dfrac{3x - 2}{x - 2} + \dfrac{4x - 3}{x - 2} = \dfrac{\mathbf{7x - 5}}{\mathbf{x - 2}}$

17. (a) $R_A T_A = 160$

(b) $R_B T_B = 240$

(c) $R_B = 2R_A$

(d) $T_A + T_B = 7$

Substitute (c) and (d) into (b) and get:

(b′) $2R_A(7 - T_A) = 240$

Substitute (a) into (b′) and get:

(b″) $14R_A - 2(160) = 240$

$14R_A = 560$

$R_A = \mathbf{40}$

$R_B = \mathbf{80};\ T_A = \mathbf{4};\ T_B = \mathbf{3}$

18. $ax^2 - \dfrac{a}{a - \dfrac{1}{ax}} = ax^2 - \dfrac{a}{\dfrac{a^2x - 1}{ax}}$

$= ax^2 - \dfrac{a^2x}{a^2x - 1} = \dfrac{a^3x^3 - ax^2 - a^2x}{a^2x - 1}$

19. $(3i + 2)(i - 4) - \sqrt{-9}$

$= 3i^2 - 12i + 2i - 8 - 3i = \mathbf{-11 - 13i}$

20. (a) $2x + 3y = 6$

$\qquad y = -\dfrac{2}{3}x + 2$

(b) $x - 2y = 4$

$\qquad y = \dfrac{1}{2}x - 2$

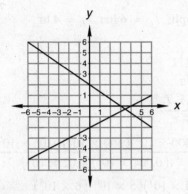

2(a) $4x + 6y = 12$

3(b) $\dfrac{3x - 6y = 12}{7x \qquad\;\; = 24}$

$\qquad\qquad x = \dfrac{24}{7}$

(b) $\left(\dfrac{24}{7}\right) - 2y = 4$

$\qquad\quad -2y = \dfrac{4}{7}$

$\qquad\qquad y = -\dfrac{2}{7}$

$\left(\dfrac{24}{7}, -\dfrac{2}{7}\right)$

21. $\qquad x^2 + 6 = 3x$

$(x^2 - 3x + \quad) = -6$

$\quad x^2 - 3x + \dfrac{9}{4} = -6 + \dfrac{9}{4}$

$\qquad \left(x - \dfrac{3}{2}\right)^2 = -\dfrac{15}{4}$

$\qquad\quad x - \dfrac{3}{2} = \pm\dfrac{\sqrt{15}}{2}i$

$\qquad\qquad x = \dfrac{3}{2} \pm \dfrac{\sqrt{15}}{2}i$

22. $x = \dfrac{80}{2} = \mathbf{40}$

$y = \dfrac{80}{2} = \mathbf{40}$

$a = \dfrac{50}{2} = \mathbf{25}$

$b = \dfrac{50}{2} = \mathbf{25}$

$c = 180 - 40 - 25 = \mathbf{115}$

23. $3\sqrt{9\sqrt{3}} = 3\sqrt{3^2\sqrt{3}} = 3\left[3^2(3^{1/2})\right]^{1/2}$

$= 3 \cdot 3(3^{1/4}) = \mathbf{3^{9/4}}$

24. $\dfrac{-2^2}{-16^{-3/4}} = -\left[-(4)(16^{1/4})^3\right] = \mathbf{32}$

25. $\sqrt{a^2x^0yx^{1/2}y^2} = (a^2x^0yx^{1/2}y^2)^{1/2}$

$= ay^{1/2}x^{1/4}y = \mathbf{ax^{1/4}y^{3/2}}$

26. $2\sqrt{\dfrac{5}{8}} + 3\sqrt{\dfrac{8}{5}} - 2\sqrt{40}$

$= \dfrac{2\sqrt{5}}{\sqrt{8}}\dfrac{\sqrt{8}}{\sqrt{8}} + \dfrac{3\sqrt{8}}{\sqrt{5}}\dfrac{\sqrt{5}}{\sqrt{5}} - 2\sqrt{40}$

$= \dfrac{10\sqrt{40}}{40} + \dfrac{24\sqrt{40}}{40} - \dfrac{80\sqrt{40}}{40}$

$= -\dfrac{46\sqrt{40}}{40} = \mathbf{-\dfrac{23\sqrt{10}}{10}}$

27. $\dfrac{x(x - 8)(x + 2)}{(x - 10)(x + 2)} \cdot \dfrac{(x - 10)(x + 5)}{x(x - 8)(x + 3)}$

$= \mathbf{\dfrac{x + 5}{x + 3}}$

28. $y = -\dfrac{2}{5}x + b$

$2 = -\dfrac{2}{5}(-5) + b$

$0 = b$

$y = -\dfrac{2}{5}x$

29. (a) $\dfrac{4{,}168{,}214 \times 10^{24}}{74.612 \times 10^{-5.34}} \approx \dfrac{4 \times 10^{30}}{7 \times 10^{-4}}$

$\approx 6 \times 10^{33}$

Calculator answer $\approx \mathbf{1.22 \times 10^{34}}$

(b) $(4.01)^{-5.34}$

Answer should be between 9×10^{-4} and 2×10^{-4}.

Calculator answer $\approx \mathbf{6.01 \times 10^{-4}}$

30. $\dfrac{3x - 5}{2} - \dfrac{x}{3} = 6$

$9x - 15 - 2x = 36$

$7x = 51$

$x = \dfrac{51}{7}$

PRACTICE SET 74

D_B
120

D_D
105

$R_B T_B = 120; \quad R_D T_D = 105$

$R_B = 2R_D; \quad T_B = T_D - 3$

$R_B T_B = 120$

$(2R_D)(T_D - 3) = 120$

$2R_D T_D - 6R_D = 120$

$2(105) - 6R_D = 120$

$-6R_D = -90$

$R_D = \mathbf{15 \ mph} \longrightarrow R_B = \mathbf{30 \ mph}$

$(15)T_D = 105$

$T_D = \mathbf{7 \ hours} \longrightarrow T_B = \mathbf{4 \ hours}$

PROBLEM SET 74

1.

D_G

D_B

$R_T T_T = 28; \quad R_B T_B = 28;$

$R_B = 2R_T; \quad T_T + T_B = 12$

$2R_T(12 - T_T) = 28$

$24R_T - 2R_T T_T = 28$

$24R_T - 2(28) = 28$

$24R_T = 84$

$R_T = \mathbf{3.5 \ mph}$

$R_B = \mathbf{7 \ mph}; \quad T_T = \mathbf{8 \ hr}; \quad T_B = \mathbf{4 \ hr}$

2.

D_R
80

D_C
30

$R_R T_R = 80; \quad R_C T_C = 30;$

$R_R = 4R_C; \quad T_R = T_C - 2$

$4R_C(T_C - 2) = 80$

$4R_C T_C - 8R_C = 80$

$4(30) - 8R_C = 80$

$-8R_C = -40$

$R_C = \mathbf{5 \ mph}$

$R_R = \mathbf{20 \ mph}; \quad T_C = \mathbf{6 \ hr}; \quad T_R = \mathbf{4 \ hr}$

3. $\dfrac{P_1 V_1}{T_1} = \dfrac{P_2 V_2}{T_2}$

$T_2 = \dfrac{P_2 V_2 T_1}{P_1 V_1}$

$T_2 = \dfrac{(400 \times 10^5)(500 \times 10^4)(0.06 \times 10^6)}{(0.004 \times 10^5)(0.02 \times 10^4)}$

$T_2 = \dfrac{(4 \times 10^7)(5 \times 10^6)(6 \times 10^4)}{(4 \times 10^2)(2 \times 10^2)}$

$T_2 = \mathbf{1.5 \times 10^{14} \ K}$

4. $0.92(2000) - E_A = 0.8(2000 - E_A)$

$1840 - E_A = 1600 - 0.8E_A$

$-0.2E_A = -240$

$E_A = \mathbf{1200 \ liters}$

5. Odd integers: $N, \ N + 2, \ N + 4$

$4(N + 2)(N + 4) = 20(N + N + 2) + 12$

$4N^2 + 24N + 32 = 40N + 52$

$4N^2 - 16N - 20 = 0$

$4(N^2 - 4N - 5) = 0$

$(N - 5)(N + 1) = 0$

$N = -1, 5$

The desired integers are **–1, 1, 3** and **5, 7, 9.**

6. $\dfrac{2 - \sqrt{3}}{-\sqrt{3} - 2} \cdot \dfrac{-\sqrt{3} + 2}{-\sqrt{3} + 2}$

$= \dfrac{-2\sqrt{3} + 4 + 3 - 2\sqrt{3}}{3 - 4} = \mathbf{-7 + 4\sqrt{3}}$

7. $\dfrac{3\sqrt{2} - 4}{\sqrt{2} - 3} \cdot \dfrac{\sqrt{2} + 3}{\sqrt{2} + 3}$

$= \dfrac{6 + 9\sqrt{2} - 4\sqrt{2} - 12}{2 - 9} = \dfrac{\mathbf{6 - 5\sqrt{2}}}{\mathbf{7}}$

8. $\dfrac{4\sqrt{2} - 5}{2 - 3\sqrt{8}} \cdot \dfrac{2 + 3\sqrt{8}}{2 + 3\sqrt{8}}$

$= \dfrac{8\sqrt{2} + 48 - 10 - 30\sqrt{2}}{4 - 72}$

$= \dfrac{\mathbf{-19 + 11\sqrt{2}}}{\mathbf{34}}$

9. There is never an exact solution for these problems. One possible solution is given here.

$N = mF + b$

Use the graph to find the slope.

$m = \dfrac{350}{5} = 70$

$N = 70F + b$

Use the point (30, 50) for F and N.

$50 = 70(30) + b$

$-2050 = b$

$\mathbf{N = 70F - 2050}$

10.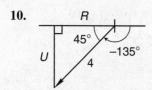

$R = 4 \cos 45° \approx 2.83$

$U = 4 \sin 45° \approx 2.83$

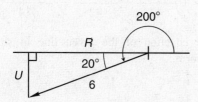

$R = 6 \cos 20° \approx 5.64$

$U = 6 \sin 20° \approx 2.05$

$-2.83R - 2.83U$
$\underline{-5.64R - 2.05U}$
$\mathbf{-8.47R - 4.88U}$

11.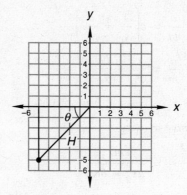

$H = \sqrt{5^2 + 5^2}$

$H = 5\sqrt{2}$

$\tan \theta = \dfrac{5}{5} = 1$

$\theta = 45°$

Since θ is a third-quadrant angle,

$\theta = 45 + 180 = 225°$

$\mathbf{5\sqrt{2}\ /225°}$

12. See Lesson 71.

13. $-3x^2 - x = 4$

$3x^2 + x + 4 = 0$

$x = \dfrac{-1 \pm \sqrt{1^2 - 4(3)(4)}}{2(3)} = \dfrac{-1 \pm \sqrt{-47}}{6}$

$= -\dfrac{\mathbf{1}}{\mathbf{6}} \pm \dfrac{\sqrt{\mathbf{47}}}{\mathbf{6}}\mathbf{i}$

14. $-x - 3x^2 = -4$

$3x^2 + x - 4 = 0$

$x = \dfrac{-1 \pm \sqrt{1^2 - 4(3)(-4)}}{2(3)} = \dfrac{-1 \pm \sqrt{49}}{6}$

$= -\dfrac{1}{6} \pm \dfrac{7}{6} = \mathbf{1, -\dfrac{4}{3}}$

15. $a = m\left(\dfrac{1}{pc} - \dfrac{k}{x}\right)$

$a = \dfrac{m}{pc} - \dfrac{km}{x}$

$acpx = mx - ckmp$

$ckmp = mx - acpx$

$\dfrac{\mathbf{ckmp}}{\mathbf{m - acp}} = x$

16.

$$\frac{a}{m} = c\left(\frac{1}{x_1} + \frac{b}{x_2}\right)$$

$$\frac{a}{m} = \frac{c}{x_1} + \frac{bc}{x_2}$$

$$ax_1x_2 = cmx_2 + bcmx_1$$

$$ax_1x_2 - bcmx_1 = cmx_2$$

$$x_1 = \frac{cmx_2}{ax_2 - bcm}$$

17. $ax - \dfrac{a}{x - \dfrac{x}{a}} = ax - \dfrac{a}{\dfrac{ax - x}{a}}$

$$= ax - \frac{a^2}{ax - x} = \frac{a^2x^2 - ax^2 - a^2}{ax - x}$$

18. $(2i - 3)(i - 3) + \sqrt{-9} + 3i^3$

$$= 2i^2 - 6i - 3i + 9 + 3i + 3i(ii)$$

$$= -2 - 6i - 3i + 9 + 3i - 3i = \mathbf{7 - 9i}$$

19. $\dfrac{3x - 2}{x^2 + 7x + 10} - \dfrac{1}{x + 5}$

$$= \frac{3x - 2}{x^2 + 7x + 10} - \frac{x + 2}{x^2 + 7x + 10}$$

$$= \frac{2x - 4}{x^2 + 7x + 10}$$

20. (a) $\dfrac{3}{2}x - \dfrac{2}{5}y = 2$

(b) $3x + 0.5y = 17$

(a′) $15x - 4y = 20$

(b′) $30x + 5y = 170$

-2(a′) $-30x + 8y = -40$

(b′) $\underline{30x + 5y = 170}$

$$13y = 130$$

$$y = 10$$

(a′) $15x - 4(10) = 20$

$$15x = 60$$

$$x = 4$$

(4, 10)

21.

$$3x^2 - x = -7$$

$$\left(x^2 - \frac{1}{3}x + \right) = -\frac{7}{3}$$

$$x^2 - \frac{1}{3}x + \frac{1}{36} = -\frac{7}{3} + \frac{1}{36}$$

$$\left(x - \frac{1}{6}\right)^2 = -\frac{83}{36}$$

$$x - \frac{1}{6} = \pm\frac{\sqrt{83}}{6}i$$

$$x = \frac{1}{6} \pm \frac{\sqrt{83}}{6}i$$

22. (a) $4x - y = 45$

(b) $3x + 3y = 90$

3(a) $12x - 3y = 135$

(b) $\underline{3x + 3y = 90}$

$$15x = 225$$

$$x = \mathbf{15}$$

(b) $3(15) + 3y = 90$

$$3y = 45$$

$$y = \mathbf{15}$$

23. $2\sqrt{4\sqrt{2}} = 2\sqrt{2^2\sqrt{2}} = 2[2^2 2^{1/2}]^{1/2}$

$$= 2(2)(2^{1/4}) = \mathbf{2^{9/4}}$$

24. $\dfrac{-3^0(-3^0)^2}{-9^{-3/2}} = -[-(9^{1/2})^3] = \mathbf{27}$

25. $\sqrt{4x^2y^5}\,\sqrt[3]{8y^5x} = (4x^2y^5)^{1/2}(8y^5x)^{1/3}$

$$= 2xy^{5/2}2y^{5/3}x^{1/3} = \mathbf{4x^{4/3}y^{25/6}}$$

26. $2\sqrt{\dfrac{6}{7}} + 3\sqrt{\dfrac{7}{6}} - 3\sqrt{42}$

$$= \frac{2\sqrt{6}}{\sqrt{7}}\frac{\sqrt{7}}{\sqrt{7}} + \frac{3\sqrt{7}}{\sqrt{6}}\frac{\sqrt{6}}{\sqrt{6}} - 3\sqrt{42}$$

$$= \frac{12\sqrt{42}}{42} + \frac{21\sqrt{42}}{42} - \frac{126\sqrt{42}}{42} = \mathbf{-\frac{31\sqrt{42}}{14}}$$

27. Write the equation of the given line in slope-intercept form.

$$4x - y = 7$$

$$y = 4x - 7$$

Since parallel lines have the same slopes,

$$y = 4x + b$$

$$0 = 4(-2) + b$$

$$8 = b$$

$$\mathbf{y = 4x + 8}$$

28. $\sqrt{x-5} - 2 = 7$

$\qquad x - 5 = 81$

$\qquad x = \mathbf{86}$

Check: $\sqrt{86-5} - 2 = 7$

$\qquad 9 - 2 = 7$

29. $\dfrac{4x-3}{7} - \dfrac{x-2}{3} = 5$

$12x - 9 - 7x + 14 = 105$

$\qquad 5x = 100$

$\qquad x = \mathbf{20}$

30. Length of side $= \dfrac{9\sqrt{2}}{\sqrt{2}} = \mathbf{9\ m}$

Area $= s^2 = (9\,\text{m})^2 = \mathbf{81\ m^2}$

Practice Set 75

$\dfrac{x-2}{x^2-3x-4} + \dfrac{x+5}{4-x}$

$= \dfrac{x-2}{(x-4)(x+1)} - \dfrac{x+5}{(x-4)} \cdot \dfrac{(x+1)}{(x+1)}$

$= \dfrac{x - 2 - (x^2 + 6x + 5)}{(x-4)(x+1)} = \dfrac{\mathbf{-x^2 - 5x - 7}}{\mathbf{(x-4)(x+1)}}$

Problem Set 75

1.

$\overset{D_D}{\underset{120}{\vdash\!\!\dashv}}$

$\overset{D_E}{\underset{360}{\vdash\!\!\!-\!\!\!-\!\!\!\dashv}}$

$R_D T_D = 120; \quad R_E T_E = 360;$

$R_E = 2R_D; \quad T_E = T_D + 1$

$2R_D(T_D + 1) = 360$

$2R_D T_D + 2R_D = 360$

$2(120) + 2R_D = 360$

$\qquad 2R_D = 120$

$\qquad R_D = \mathbf{60\ mph}$

$R_E = \mathbf{120\ mph};\ T_D = \mathbf{2\ hr};\ T_E = \mathbf{3\ hr}$

2. $\dfrac{P_1}{T_1} = \dfrac{P_2}{T_2}$

$P_2 = \dfrac{P_1 T_2}{T_1}$

$P_2 = \dfrac{(0.0036 \times 10^{-2})(40 \times 10^4)}{50 \times 10^7}$

$P_2 = \dfrac{(3.6 \times 10^{-5})(4 \times 10^5)}{5 \times 10^8}$

$P_2 = \mathbf{2.88 \times 10^{-8}\ N/m^2}$

3. $T = \dfrac{k}{N_M}$

$10 = \dfrac{k}{500}$

$5000 = k$

$T = \dfrac{5000}{200} = \mathbf{25\ days}$

4.

$\overset{D_T}{\underset{D_B}{\xrightarrow{\hspace{4cm}}}} 20$

$R_B T_B + 20 = R_T T_T; \quad R_T = 60;$

$R_B = 40; \quad T_B = T_T + 2$

$40(T_T + 2) + 20 = 60T_T$

$40T_T + 100 = 60T_T$

$\qquad 100 = 20T_T$

$\qquad \mathbf{5\ hr} = T_T$

5. (a) $4N_L + 6N_P = 192$

(b) $N_L = N_P - 2$

Substitute (b) into (a) and get:

(a′) $4(N_P - 2) + 6N_P = 192$

$\qquad\qquad 10N_P = 200$

$\qquad\qquad N_P = \mathbf{20\ poinsettias}$

(b) $N_L = (20) - 2 = \mathbf{18\ lilies}$

6. $\dfrac{x+4}{x^2 + 2x - 3} - \dfrac{2}{1-x}$

$= \dfrac{x+4}{(x+3)(x-1)} + \dfrac{2(x+3)}{(x+3)(x-1)}$

$= \dfrac{\mathbf{3x + 10}}{\mathbf{x^2 + 2x - 3}}$

7. $\dfrac{x-3}{x^2-x-12} - \dfrac{x+2}{-3-x}$

$= \dfrac{x-3}{(x-4)(x+3)} + \dfrac{(x+2)(x-4)}{(x-4)(x+3)}$

$= \dfrac{x-3+x^2-2x-8}{x^2-x-12}$

$= \dfrac{x^2-x-11}{x^2-x-12}$

8. $\dfrac{2-\sqrt{2}}{3+\sqrt{2}} \cdot \dfrac{3-\sqrt{2}}{3-\sqrt{2}}$

$= \dfrac{6-2\sqrt{2}-3\sqrt{2}+2}{9-2} = \dfrac{8-5\sqrt{2}}{7}$

9. $\dfrac{2-3\sqrt{3}}{3-2\sqrt{12}} = \dfrac{2-3\sqrt{3}}{3-4\sqrt{3}} \cdot \dfrac{3+4\sqrt{3}}{3+4\sqrt{3}}$

$= \dfrac{6+8\sqrt{3}-9\sqrt{3}-36}{9-48} = \dfrac{30+\sqrt{3}}{39}$

10. $A_{\text{Circle}} = \pi r^2 = 9\pi \text{ cm}^2$

   $r = \textbf{3 cm}$

   Length of diagonal $= 2r = 2(3 \text{ cm}) = \textbf{6 cm}$

   $A_{\text{Square}} = s^2 = \left(\dfrac{6\sqrt{2}}{2} \text{ cm}\right)^2 = \textbf{18 cm}^2$

11. There is never an exact solution for these problems. One possible solution is given here.

   $V = mK + b$

   Use the graph to find the slope.

   $m = -\dfrac{5}{4} = -1.25$

   $V = -1.25K + b$

   Use the point (95, 27) for K and V.

   $27 = -1.25(95) + b$

   $145.75 = b$

   $\textbf{V} = \textbf{--1.25K} + \textbf{145.75}$

12. See Lesson 71.

13.

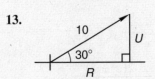

   $R = 10 \cos 30° \approx 8.66$

   $U = 10 \sin 30° = 5$

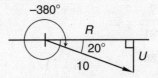

$R = 10 \cos 20° \approx 9.40$

$U = 10 \sin 20° \approx 3.42$

$\begin{array}{r} 8.66R + 5.00U \\ 9.40R - 3.42U \\ \hline \textbf{18.06R} + \textbf{1.58U} \end{array}$

14.

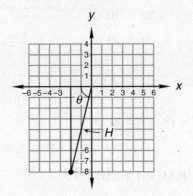

$H = \sqrt{8^2 + 2^2}$

$H = 2\sqrt{17}$

$\tan\theta = \dfrac{8}{2} = 4$

$\theta \approx 75.96°$

Since θ is a third-quadrant angle,

$\theta = 75.96 + 180 = 255.96°$

$\textbf{2}\sqrt{\textbf{17}}\,\underline{/\textbf{255.96°}}$

15. $-2x + 4 = -5x^2$

   $5x^2 - 2x + 4 = 0$

   $x = \dfrac{-(-2) \pm \sqrt{(-2)^2 - 4(5)(4)}}{2(5)}$

   $x = \dfrac{2 \pm \sqrt{-76}}{10} = \dfrac{1}{5} \pm \dfrac{\sqrt{19}}{5}i$

16. $\dfrac{m}{x} = cm\left(\dfrac{a}{x} + \dfrac{b}{y}\right)$

   $\dfrac{m}{x} = \dfrac{acm}{x} + \dfrac{bcm}{y}$

   $my = acmy + bcmx$

   $my - acmy = bcmx$

   $y = \dfrac{bcmx}{m - acm} = \dfrac{bcx}{1 - ac}$

17. Since this is a 30°-60°-90° triangle,

$$\sqrt{3} \cdot \overrightarrow{SF} = 8$$

$$\overrightarrow{SF} = \frac{8\sqrt{3}}{3}$$

$$x = \frac{8\sqrt{3}}{3} \cdot 2 = \frac{16\sqrt{3}}{3}$$

$$y = \frac{8\sqrt{3}}{3} \cdot 1 = \frac{8\sqrt{3}}{3}$$

18. $a^2 y + \dfrac{a^2}{a + \dfrac{a}{y}} = a^2 y + \dfrac{a^2}{\dfrac{ay + a}{y}}$

$$= a^2 y + \frac{a^2 y}{ay + a} = \frac{a^3 y^2 + a^3 y + a^2 y}{ay + a}$$

$$= \frac{a^2 y^2 + a^2 y + ay}{y + 1}$$

19. $(2 + i)(i - 4) - \sqrt{-16}$

$$= 2i - 8 + i^2 - 4i - 4i$$

$$= 2i - 8 - 1 - 4i - 4i = \mathbf{-9 - 6i}$$

20. (a) $\dfrac{1}{4}x + \dfrac{1}{3}y = 15$

(b) $0.02x + 0.2y = 6.4$

(a') $3x + 4y = 180$

(b') $2x + 20y = 640$

$-5(a')\ {-15x - 20y = -900}$

(b') $\underline{\ \ 2x + 20y = \ \ 640}$

$$-13x \qquad = -260$$

$$x = 20$$

(a') $3(20) + 4y = 180$

$$4y = 120$$

$$y = 30$$

(20, 30)

21. $$3x^2 + 2 = -x$$

$$\left(x^2 + \frac{1}{3}x + \quad\right) = -\frac{2}{3}$$

$$x^2 + \frac{1}{3}x + \frac{1}{36} = -\frac{2}{3} + \frac{1}{36}$$

$$\left(x + \frac{1}{6}\right)^2 = -\frac{23}{36}$$

$$x + \frac{1}{6} = \pm\frac{\sqrt{23}}{6}i$$

$$x = -\frac{1}{6} \pm \frac{\sqrt{23}}{6}i$$

22. $A_{\text{Triangle}} = \dfrac{1}{2}bH = 48 \text{ m}^2$

$$H = \frac{48(2) \text{ m}^2}{12 \text{ m}}$$

$$H = \mathbf{8\ m}$$

$A_{\text{Semicircle}} = \dfrac{1}{2}\pi r^2 = 2\pi$

$$r^2 = 4 \text{ m}^2$$

$$r = \mathbf{2\ m}$$

23. $4\sqrt{2\sqrt[3]{2}} = 2^2[2(2^{1/3})]^{1/2} = 2^2 2^{1/2} 2^{1/6} = \mathbf{2^{8/3}}$

24. $\dfrac{-2^0\,(-2^0)}{-4^{-3/2}} = -(4^{1/2})^3 = \mathbf{-8}$

25. $\sqrt[4]{mp^5}\,\sqrt[3]{m^2 p^4} = (mp^5)^{1/4}(m^2 p^4)^{1/3}$

$$= m^{1/4}p^{5/4}m^{2/3}p^{4/3} = \mathbf{m^{11/12}p^{31/12}}$$

26. $3\sqrt{\dfrac{7}{8}} + 2\sqrt{\dfrac{8}{7}} - 2\sqrt{56}$

$$= \frac{3\sqrt{7}}{\sqrt{8}}\frac{\sqrt{8}}{\sqrt{8}} + \frac{2\sqrt{8}}{\sqrt{7}}\frac{\sqrt{7}}{\sqrt{7}} - 2\sqrt{56}$$

$$= \frac{21\sqrt{56}}{56} + \frac{16\sqrt{56}}{56} - \frac{112\sqrt{56}}{56}$$

$$= -\frac{75\sqrt{56}}{56} = -\frac{\mathbf{75\sqrt{14}}}{\mathbf{28}}$$

27. (a) $\dfrac{4813 \times 10^{-14}}{0.01903 \times 10^{-22}} \approx \dfrac{5 \times 10^{-11}}{2 \times 10^{-24}}$

$$\approx 3 \times 10^{13}$$

Calculator answer $\approx \mathbf{2.53 \times 10^{13}}$

(b) $\sqrt[3.6]{198}$

Answer should be between 3 and 5.

Calculator answer $\approx \mathbf{4.34}$

28. Graph the line to find the slope.

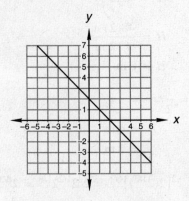

$$m = -\frac{1}{1} = -1$$

Since the slopes of perpendicular lines are negative reciprocals of each other,

$$m_\perp = 1$$

$$y = x + b$$

$$(7) = (5) + b$$

$$2 = b$$

$$\mathbf{y = x + 2}$$

29. $\sqrt{3x - 5} - 2 = 7$

$$3x - 5 = 81$$

$$3x = 86$$

$$x = \frac{86}{3}$$

Check: $\sqrt{3\left(\dfrac{86}{3}\right) - 5} - 2 = 7$

$$9 - 2 = 7$$

30. $\dfrac{4x + 7}{2} - \dfrac{5x}{3} = 4$

$$12x + 21 - 10x = 24$$

$$2x = 3$$

$$x = \frac{3}{2}$$

PRACTICE SET 76

a. $\begin{cases} x = 3y & \text{(a)} \\ x + y + z = 56 & \text{(b)} \\ x - 2y - 3z = -25 & \text{(c)} \end{cases}$

We can substitute (a) into (b) and (c).

(b) $(3y) + y + z = 56$

$\longrightarrow \quad 4y + z = 56 \quad$ (d)

(c) $(3y) - 2y - 3z = -25$

$\longrightarrow \quad y - 3z = -25 \quad$ (e)

$$
\begin{array}{rl}
\text{(d)} & 4y + z = 56 \\
-4\text{(e)} & \underline{-4y + 12z = 100} \\
& 13z = 156 \\
& z = \mathbf{12}
\end{array}
$$

(d) $4y + (12) = 56$

$$4y = 44$$

$$y = \mathbf{11}$$

(a) $x = 3(11)$

$$x = \mathbf{33}$$

b.

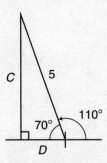

$A = 2 \sin 15° \approx 0.52$

$B = 2 \cos 15° \approx 1.93$

$C = 5 \sin 70° \approx 4.70$

$D = 5 \cos 70° \approx 1.71$

$A + C = 0.52 + 4.70 = 5.22$ up

$B + D = 1.93 + 1.71 = 3.64$ to the left

The solution is $\mathbf{-3.64R + 5.22U}$.

PROBLEM SET 76

1.

$$\begin{array}{c} \overset{D_C}{\vdash\!\!\!-\!\!\!\rightarrow} \\ 32 \end{array}$$

$$\begin{array}{c} \overset{D_T}{\vdash\!\!\!-\!\!\!-\!\!\!-\!\!\!\rightarrow} \\ 72 \end{array}$$

$R_C T_C = 32; \ R_T T_T = 72;$

$R_T = 3R_C; \ T_T = T_C - 2$

$3R_C(T_C - 2) = 72$

$3R_C T_C - 6R_C = 72$

$3(32) - 6R_C = 72$

$-6R_C = -24$

$R_C = \textbf{4 mph}$

$R_T = \textbf{12 mph}; \ T_C = \textbf{8 hr}; \ T_T = \textbf{6 hr}$

2. $\dfrac{P_1 V_1}{T_1} = \dfrac{P_2 V_2}{T_2}$

$V_2 = \dfrac{P_1 V_1 T_2}{P_2 T_1}$

$V_2 = \dfrac{(700 \times 10^5)(700 \times 10^{-7})(8000 \times 10^5)}{(3500 \times 10^4)(56 \times 10^4)}$

$V_2 = \dfrac{(7 \times 10^7)(7 \times 10^{-5})(8 \times 10^8)}{(3.5 \times 10^7)(5.6 \times 10^5)}$

$V_2 = \textbf{2} \times \textbf{10}^{-1} \textbf{ liter}$

3. $0.64(500) - E_A = 0.4(500 - E_A)$

$320 - E_A = 200 - 0.4E_A$

$-0.6E_A = -120$

$E_A = \textbf{200 mL}$

4. Sodium: $\quad 1 \times 23 = 23$

Chlorine: $\quad 1 \times 35 = 35$

Oxygen: $\quad 1 \times 16 = 16$

Total NaO: $23 + 16 = 39$

$\dfrac{35}{39} = \dfrac{280}{\text{NaO}}$

NaO = **312 grams**

5. (a) $4N_B = 3N_R + 14$

(b) $6N_R = N_B + 7$

Substitute $N_B = 6N_R - 7$ into (a) and get:

(a′) $4(6N_R - 7) = 3N_R + 14$

$21N_R = 42$

$N_R = 2$

(b) $N_B = 6(2) - 7 = 5$

A total of **7 chips** were down.

6. (a) $x = 2y$

(b) $x + y + z = -198$

(c) $x - 3y - 2z = 16$

Substitute (a) into (b) and (c) and get:

(b′) $3y + z = -198$

(c′) $-y - 2z = 16$

$\begin{array}{rl} 2(\text{b}′) & 6y + 2z = -396 \\ (\text{c}′) & \underline{-y - 2z = 16} \\ & 5y = -380 \\ & y = -76 \end{array}$

(b′) $3(-76) + z = -198$

$z = 30$

(a) $x = 2(-76) = -152$

(-152, -76, 30)

7. (a) $2x + 2y - z = 81$

(b) $3x - y + 2z = 27$

(c) $x - 3z = 0$

$x = 3z$

Substitute (c) into (a) and (b) and get:

(a′) $2y + 5z = 81$

(b′) $-y + 11z = 27$

$\begin{array}{rl} (\text{a}′) & 2y + 5z = 81 \\ 2(\text{b}′) & \underline{-2y + 22z = 54} \\ & 27z = 135 \\ & z = 5 \end{array}$

(a′) $2y + 5(5) = 81$

$2y = 56$

$y = 28$

(c) $x = 3(5) = 15$

(15, 28, 5)

8.

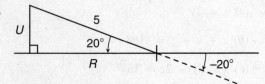

$R = 5 \cos 20° \approx 4.70$

$U = 5 \sin 20° \approx 1.71$

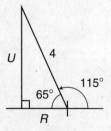

$R = 4 \cos 65° \approx 1.69$

$U = 4 \sin 65° \approx 3.63$

$$\begin{array}{r} -4.70R + 1.71U \\ -1.69R + 3.63U \\ \hline \mathbf{-6.39R + 5.34U} \end{array}$$

9.

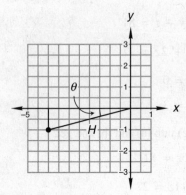

$H = \sqrt{4^2 + 1^2}$

$H = \sqrt{17}$

$\tan \theta = \dfrac{1}{4}$

$\theta \approx 14.04°$

Since θ is a third-quadrant angle,

$\theta = 14.04 + 180 = 194.04°$

$\boldsymbol{\sqrt{17}\,/\,194.04°}$

10. $\dfrac{5x + 2}{x^2 + 3x - 10} - \dfrac{2x}{2 - x}$

$= \dfrac{5x + 2}{(x + 5)(x - 2)} + \dfrac{2x(x + 5)}{(x + 5)(x - 2)}$

$= \dfrac{5x + 2 + 2x^2 + 10x}{x^2 + 3x - 10}$

$= \dfrac{\mathbf{2x^2 + 15x + 2}}{\mathbf{x^2 + 3x - 10}}$

11. $\dfrac{2\sqrt{2} - 1}{1 - \sqrt{2}} \cdot \dfrac{1 + \sqrt{2}}{1 + \sqrt{2}}$

$= \dfrac{2\sqrt{2} + 4 - 1 - \sqrt{2}}{1 - 2} = \mathbf{-3 - \sqrt{2}}$

12. $\dfrac{3 - \sqrt{2}}{4 + 2\sqrt{8}} = \dfrac{3 - \sqrt{2}}{4 + 4\sqrt{2}} \cdot \dfrac{4 - 4\sqrt{2}}{4 - 4\sqrt{2}}$

$= \dfrac{12 - 12\sqrt{2} - 4\sqrt{2} + 8}{16 - 32} = \dfrac{\mathbf{-5 + 4\sqrt{2}}}{\mathbf{4}}$

13. There is never an exact solution to these problems. One possible solution is given here.

Al $= m$B $+ b$

Use the graph to find the slope.

$m = \dfrac{42}{4} = 10.5$

Al $= 10.5$B $+ b$

Use the point (4, 180) for B and Al.

$180 = 10.5(4) + b$

$138 = b$

Al $= 10.5$B $+ 138$

14. See Lesson 71.

15. $\dfrac{a}{c + x} = m\left(\dfrac{1}{r} + \dfrac{1}{t}\right)$

$\dfrac{a}{c + x} = \dfrac{m}{r} + \dfrac{m}{t}$

$art = cmt + mtx + cmr + mrx$

$art - cmt - cmr = mtx + mrx$

$x = \dfrac{\boldsymbol{art - cmt - cmr}}{\boldsymbol{mt + mr}}$

16. $\dfrac{a}{c + x} = m\left(\dfrac{1}{r} + \dfrac{1}{t}\right)$

$\dfrac{a}{c + x} = \dfrac{m}{r} + \dfrac{m}{t}$

$art = cmt + mtx + cmr + mrx$

$art - cmt - mtx = cmr + mrx$

$t = \dfrac{\boldsymbol{cmr + mrx}}{\boldsymbol{ar - cm - mx}}$

17.
$$7x^2 - x - 1 = 0$$

$$\left(x^2 - \frac{1}{7}x + \phantom{\frac{1}{196}}\right) = \frac{1}{7}$$

$$x^2 - \frac{1}{7}x + \frac{1}{196} = \frac{1}{7} + \frac{1}{196}$$

$$\left(x - \frac{1}{14}\right)^2 = \frac{29}{196}$$

$$x - \frac{1}{14} = \pm\frac{\sqrt{29}}{14}$$

$$x = \frac{1}{14} \pm \frac{\sqrt{29}}{14}$$

18.
$$x + \cfrac{a}{a + \cfrac{a}{x}} = x + \cfrac{a}{\cfrac{ax + a}{x}}$$

$$= x + \frac{ax}{ax + a} = \frac{ax^2 + ax + ax}{ax + a}$$

$$= \frac{x^2 + 2x}{x + 1}$$

19. $(3 - i)(2 - i) - 2i^2 - \sqrt{-9}$

$$= 6 - 3i - 2i + i^2 - 2i^2 - 3i$$

$$= 6 - 3i - 2i - 1 + 2 - 3i = \mathbf{7 - 8i}$$

20. (a) $\frac{1}{3}x + \frac{2}{3}y = 31$

(b) $0.02x + 0.7y = 27.6$

(a') $x + 2y = 93$

(b') $2x + 70y = 2760$

$$\begin{array}{r} -2(a') \;\; -2x - 4y = -186 \\ (b') \;\; \underline{2x + 70y = 2760} \\ 66y = 2574 \\ y = 39 \end{array}$$

(a') $x + 2(39) = 93$

$$x = 15$$

(15, 39)

21. The radius of the circle is equal to the diagonal of the rectangle.

$$r = \sqrt{(\sqrt{11})^2 + 5^2}$$

$$r = \mathbf{6}$$

22. $5\sqrt{25\sqrt{5}} = 5\sqrt{5^2\sqrt{5}} = 5[5^2 5^{1/2}]^{1/2}$

$$= 5\left(5\left(5^{1/4}\right)\right) = \mathbf{5^{9/4}}$$

23. $\dfrac{-1^0\,(-1^0)}{-4^{-5/2}} = -(4^{1/2})^5 = \mathbf{-32}$

24. $\sqrt[6]{my^3}\,\sqrt[4]{m^3 y} = (my^3)^{1/6}(m^3 y)^{1/4}$

$$= m^{1/6}y^{1/2}m^{3/4}y^{1/4} = \mathbf{m^{11/12}y^{3/4}}$$

25. $2\sqrt{\dfrac{3}{8}} + 3\sqrt{\dfrac{8}{3}} - 2\sqrt{216}$

$$= \frac{2\sqrt{3}}{\sqrt{8}}\frac{\sqrt{8}}{\sqrt{8}} + \frac{3\sqrt{8}}{\sqrt{3}}\frac{\sqrt{3}}{\sqrt{3}} - 6\sqrt{24}$$

$$= \frac{6\sqrt{24}}{24} + \frac{24\sqrt{24}}{24} - \frac{144\sqrt{24}}{24} = -\frac{114\sqrt{24}}{24}$$

$$= -\frac{\mathbf{19\sqrt{6}}}{\mathbf{2}}$$

26. (a) $\dfrac{0.00842 \times 10^{18}}{4,198,312 \times 10^{-13}} \approx \dfrac{8 \times 10^{15}}{4 \times 10^{-7}}$

$$= 2 \times 10^{22}$$

Calculator answer $\approx \mathbf{2.01 \times 10^{22}}$

(b) $(4.63)^{5.12}$

Answer should be between 1024 and 3125.

Calculator answer $\approx \mathbf{2557.26}$

27.

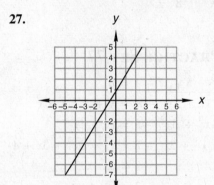

Graph the line to find the slope.

Slope $= \dfrac{11}{7}$

$$y = \frac{11}{7}x + b$$

$$4 = \frac{11}{7}(2) + b$$

$$\frac{6}{7} = b$$

$$y = \frac{\mathbf{11}}{\mathbf{7}}x + \frac{\mathbf{6}}{\mathbf{7}}$$

28. $\sqrt{2x - 2} + 7 = 9$

$2x - 2 = 4$

$2x = 6$

$x = \mathbf{3}$

Check: $\sqrt{2(3) - 2} + 7 = 9$

$2 + 7 = 9$

29. $\dfrac{15x - 2}{3} - \dfrac{2x - 5}{4} = 3$

$60x - 8 - 6x + 15 = 36$

$54x = 29$

$x = \dfrac{\mathbf{29}}{\mathbf{54}}$

30. $A_{\text{Figure}} = \dfrac{1}{2}bH + \dfrac{1}{2}\pi r^2$

$H = \sqrt{(\sqrt{5})^2 - 1^2}$

$H = \sqrt{4} = 2$

$A_{\text{Figure}} = \left[\dfrac{1}{2}(2)(2) + \dfrac{1}{2}\pi\left(\dfrac{\sqrt{5}}{2}\right)^2\right]$ in.^{2}

$= \left(2 + \dfrac{5}{8}\pi\right)$ in.$^2 \approx \mathbf{3.96}$ **in.^{2}**

PRACTICE SET 77

a. $\sqrt[3]{x^3 + 3x^2 - 8} - x - 1 = 0$

$\sqrt[3]{x^3 + 3x^2 - 8} = x + 1$

$x^3 + 3x^2 - 8 = (x + 1)^3$

$x^3 + 3x^2 - 8 = x^3 + 3x^2 + 3x + 1$

$-9 = 3x$

$\mathbf{-3} = x$

Check: $\sqrt[3]{(-3)^3 + 3(-3)^2 - 8} - (-3) - 1 = 0$

$\sqrt[3]{-27 + 27 - 8} + 3 - 1 = 0$

$-2 + 2 = 0$

b. $\sqrt{s - 16} + \sqrt{s} = 4$

$\sqrt{s - 16} = 4 - \sqrt{s}$

$(\sqrt{s - 16})^2 = (4 - \sqrt{s})^2$

$s - 16 = 16 - 8\sqrt{s} + s$

$8\sqrt{s} = 32$

$\sqrt{s} = 4$

$s = \mathbf{16}$

Check: $\sqrt{(16) - 16} + \sqrt{(16)} = 4$

$4 = 4$

PROBLEM SET 77

1.

$$\underset{320}{\overset{D_H}{\vert\!\longrightarrow\!\vert}}$$

$$\underset{240}{\overset{D_S}{\vert\!\longrightarrow\!\vert}}$$

$R_H T_H = 320;\ R_S T_S = 240;$

$R_S = R_H + 20;\ T_H = 2T_S$

$(R_S - 20)2T_S = 320$

$2R_S T_S - 40T_S = 320$

$2(240) - 40T_S = 320$

$-40T_S = -160$

$T_S = \mathbf{4\ hr}$

$T_H = \mathbf{8\ hr};\ R_S = \mathbf{60\ mph};\ R_H = \mathbf{40\ mph}$

2. $E = \dfrac{k}{C}$

$(500) = \dfrac{k}{(10)}$

$5000 = k$

$E = \dfrac{5000}{1} = \mathbf{5000}$

3. $0.7(50) + W_A = 0.97(50 + W_A)$

$35 + W_A = 48.5 + 0.97W_A$

$0.03W_A = 13.5$

$W_A = \mathbf{450\ liters}$

4. Multiples of 7: $7N,\ 7N + 7,\ 7N + 14$

$7N + 4(7N + 14) = 3(7N + 7) + 133$

$35N + 56 = 21N + 154$

$14N = 98$

$N = 7$

The desired integers are **49, 56, 63.**

5.

$$\overset{D_C}{\underset{D_Q}{\vert\!\longrightarrow\!\vert}}$$

$R_C T_C = R_Q T_Q;\ T_C = 6;$

$T_Q = 12;\ R_C = R_Q + 4$

$R_C(6) = (R_C - 4)(12)$

$6R_C = 48$

$R_C = \mathbf{8\ mph}$

6. $\sqrt[3]{x^3 + 9x^2 - 27} = x + 3$

$x^3 + 9x^2 - 27 = x^3 + 9x^2 + 27x + 27$

$-27x = 54$

$x = -2$

Check: $\sqrt[3]{(-2)^3 + 9(-2)^2 - 27} - 1 = 0$

$1 - 1 = 0$

7. $\sqrt{m - 12} - \sqrt{m} + 2 = 0$

$\sqrt{m - 12} = \sqrt{m} - 2$

$m - 12 = m - 4\sqrt{m} + 4$

$-16 = -4\sqrt{m}$

$4 = \sqrt{m}$

$16 = m$

Check: $\sqrt{16 - 12} - \sqrt{16} + 2 = 0$

$2 - 4 + 2 = 0$

8. (a) $2x + y - z = 7$

(b) $x - 2y + z = -2$

(c) $2y + z = 0$

$z = -2y$

Substitute (c) into (a) and (b) and get:

(a′) $2x + 3y = 7$

(b′) $x - 4y = -2$

$\begin{array}{rcl} \text{(a′)} & 2x + 3y = & 7 \\ -2\text{(b′)} & \underline{-2x + 8y = } & \underline{4} \\ & 11y = & 11 \\ & y = & 1 \end{array}$

(b′) $x - 4(1) = -2$

$x = 2$

(c) $z = -2(1) = -2$

(2, 1, −2)

9. (a) $x + y + z = 7$

(b) $2x - y - z = -4$

(c) $z = 2y$

Substitute (c) into (a) and (b) and get:

$\begin{array}{rcl} \text{(a′)} & x + 3y = & 7 \\ \text{(b′)} & \underline{2x - 3y = } & \underline{-4} \\ & 3x = & 3 \end{array}$

$x = 1$

(a′) $(1) + 3y = 7$

$3y = 6$

$y = 2$

(c) $z = 2(2) = 4$

(1, 2, 4)

10. Since this is a 30°-60°-90° triangle,

$2 \times \overline{SF} = 8$

$\overline{SF} = 4$

$r = 4(\sqrt{3}) = \mathbf{4\sqrt{3}}$

$t = 4(1) = \mathbf{4}$

11.

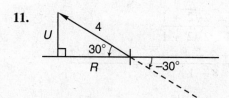

$R = 4 \cos 30° \approx 3.46$

$U = 4 \sin 30° = 2.00$

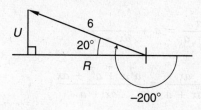

$R = 6 \cos 20° \approx 5.64$

$U = 6 \sin 20° \approx 2.05$

$\begin{array}{r} -3.46R + 2.00U \\ \underline{-5.64R + 2.05U} \\ \mathbf{-9.10R + 4.05U} \end{array}$

12.

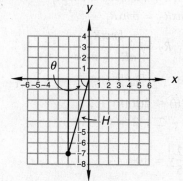

$H = \sqrt{7^2 + 2^2}$

$H = \sqrt{53}$

$\tan \theta = \dfrac{7}{2}$

$\theta \approx 74.05°$

Since θ is a third-quadrant angle,

$\theta = 74.05 + 180 = 254.05°$

$\mathbf{\sqrt{53}/254.05°}$

13. $\dfrac{7x + 2}{x^2 - 2x - 15} - \dfrac{2}{5 - x}$

$= \dfrac{7x + 2}{(x - 5)(x + 3)} + \dfrac{2(x + 3)}{(x - 5)(x + 3)}$

$= \dfrac{7x + 2 + 2x + 6}{x^2 - 2x - 15} = \mathbf{\dfrac{9x + 8}{x^2 - 2x - 15}}$

14. $\dfrac{2 - \sqrt{2}}{2\sqrt{2} - 1} \cdot \dfrac{2\sqrt{2} + 1}{2\sqrt{2} + 1}$

$= \dfrac{4\sqrt{2} + 2 - 4 - \sqrt{2}}{8 - 1} = \mathbf{\dfrac{-2 + 3\sqrt{2}}{7}}$

15. $\dfrac{3 + 2\sqrt{5}}{1 - \sqrt{5}} \cdot \dfrac{1 + \sqrt{5}}{1 + \sqrt{5}}$

$= \dfrac{3 + 3\sqrt{5} + 2\sqrt{5} + 10}{1 - 5} = \mathbf{\dfrac{-13 - 5\sqrt{5}}{4}}$

16. $a + \dfrac{a}{a + \dfrac{a}{x}} = a + \dfrac{a}{\dfrac{ax + a}{x}}$

$= a + \dfrac{ax}{ax + a} = \dfrac{a^2 x + a^2 + ax}{ax + a}$

$= \mathbf{\dfrac{ax + a + x}{x + 1}}$

17. $\dfrac{a}{x} = m\left(\dfrac{a}{R_1} + \dfrac{b}{R_2}\right)$

$\dfrac{a}{x} = \dfrac{am}{R_1} + \dfrac{bm}{R_2}$

$aR_1R_2 = amxR_2 + bmxR_1$

$aR_1R_2 - amxR_2 = bmxR_1$

$R_2 = \mathbf{\dfrac{bmxR_1}{aR_1 - amx}}$

18. $-\sqrt{-9} - 3i^3 - 2i^4 + 2$

$= -3i - 3i(ii) - 2(ii)(ii) + 2$

$= -3i + 3i - 2 + 2 = \mathbf{0}$

19. (a) $\dfrac{3}{7}x + \dfrac{2}{5}y = 10$

(b) $0.03x - 0.2y = -1.58$

(a′) $15x + 14y = 350$

(b′) $3x - 20y = -158$

$\quad$ (a′) $\quad 15x + 14y = 350$

$-5(\text{b′}) \underline{-15x + 100y = 790}$

$\phantom{-5(\text{b′})} \quad\quad 114y = 1140$

$\phantom{-5(\text{b′})} \quad\quad\quad\quad y = 10$

(b′) $3x - 20(10) = -158$

$ x = 14$

$\mathbf{(14, 10)}$

20. $ -7x - 1 = 2x^2$

$\left(x^2 + \dfrac{7}{2}x + \right) = -\dfrac{1}{2}$

$x^2 + \dfrac{7}{2}x + \dfrac{49}{16} = -\dfrac{1}{2} + \dfrac{49}{16}$

$\left(x + \dfrac{7}{4}\right)^2 = \dfrac{41}{16}$

$x + \dfrac{7}{4} = \pm\dfrac{\sqrt{41}}{4}$

$x = \mathbf{-\dfrac{7}{4} \pm \dfrac{\sqrt{41}}{4}}$

21. $ -8x - 1 = 2x^2$

$2x^2 + 8x + 1 = 0$

$x = \dfrac{-8 \pm \sqrt{8^2 - 4(2)(1)}}{2(2)} = \dfrac{-8 \pm \sqrt{56}}{4}$

$= \mathbf{-2 \pm \dfrac{\sqrt{14}}{2}}$

22. $m\angle AOC = 180 - 30 = \mathbf{150°}$

$m\angle OCA = m\angle OAC = \dfrac{180 - 150}{2} = \mathbf{15°}$

Area $= \dfrac{30}{360} \cdot \pi(3)^2 = \mathbf{\dfrac{3\pi}{4}}$ **units**^{2}

23. $A_{\text{Square}} = s^2 = 4 \text{ cm}^2$

$s = \mathbf{2 \text{ cm}}$

Length of diagonal $= \sqrt{2^2 + 2^2} \text{ cm} = \mathbf{2\sqrt{2} \text{ cm}}$

Radius of circle $= \dfrac{s}{2} = \dfrac{2 \text{ cm}}{2} = \mathbf{1 \text{ cm}}$

24. $\dfrac{4000 \text{ cm}^3}{\text{s}} \times \dfrac{1 \text{ in.}}{2.54 \text{ cm}} \times \dfrac{1 \text{ in.}}{2.54 \text{ cm}} \times \dfrac{1 \text{ in.}}{2.54 \text{ cm}}$

$\times \dfrac{1 \text{ ft}}{12 \text{ in.}} \times \dfrac{1 \text{ ft}}{12 \text{ in.}} \times \dfrac{1 \text{ ft}}{12 \text{ in.}} \times \dfrac{60 \text{ s}}{1 \text{ min}}$

$= \mathbf{\dfrac{4000(60)}{(2.54)(2.54)(2.54)(12)(12)(12)}} \dfrac{\mathbf{ft}^3}{\mathbf{min}}$

25. $\sqrt[4]{4\sqrt[3]{2}} = \sqrt[4]{2^2 \sqrt[3]{2}} = [2^2 2^{1/3}]^{1/4} = 2^{1/2}2^{1/12}$

$= \mathbf{2^{7/12}}$

26. $\dfrac{(-3)^0 (-3^0)}{-9^{-3/2}} = -[-(9^{1/2})^3] = \mathbf{27}$

27. $(2\sqrt{5} + 5)(5\sqrt{20} - 1) = (2\sqrt{5} + 5)(10\sqrt{5} - 1)$

$= 100 - 2\sqrt{5} + 50\sqrt{5} - 5 = \mathbf{95 + 48\sqrt{5}}$

28. Write the equation of the given line in slope-intercept form.

$$5x + 4y = 3$$

$$y = -\frac{5}{4}x + \frac{3}{4}$$

Since the slopes of perpendicular lines are negative reciprocals of each other,

$$m_\perp = \frac{4}{5}.$$

$$y = \frac{4}{5}x + b$$

$$4 = \frac{4}{5}(-2) + b$$

$$\frac{28}{5} = b$$

$$y = \frac{4}{5}x + \frac{28}{5}$$

29.

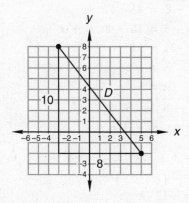

$$D^2 = 10^2 + 8^2$$

$$D^2 = 164$$

$$D = 2\sqrt{41}$$

30. $\dfrac{3x - 1}{4} - \dfrac{x - 5}{7} = 1$

$$21x - 7 - 4x + 20 = 28$$

$$17x = 15$$

$$x = \frac{15}{17}$$

PRACTICE SET 78

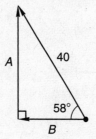

$A = 40 \sin 58° \approx 33.92$

$B = 40 \cos 58° \approx 21.20$

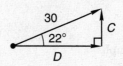

$C = 30 \sin 22° \approx 11.24$

$D = 30 \cos 22° \approx 27.82$

$33.92 + 11.24 = 45.16$ upward

$-21.20 + 27.82 = 6.62$ to the right

The resultant force is **6.62R + 45.16U**.

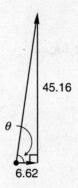

In polar coordinates,

$$\tan \theta = \frac{45.16}{6.62}$$

$$\theta \approx 81.66°$$

$$F = \sqrt{(6.62)^2 + (45.16)^2} \approx 45.64$$

The resultant force is **45.64/81.66°**.

PROBLEM SET 78

1.

$$\underset{135}{\overset{D_R}{\longmapsto}}$$

$$\overset{D_J}{\underset{945}{\longmapsto}}$$

$R_R T_R = 135;\ R_J T_J = 945;$

$T_R = T_J - 4;\ R_J = 3R_R$

$3R_R(T_R + 4) = 945$

$3R_R T_R + 12R_R = 945$

$3(135) + 12R_R = 945$

$12R_R = 540$

$R_R = \mathbf{45\ mph}$

$R_J = \mathbf{135\ mph};\ T_R = \mathbf{3\ hr};\ T_J = \mathbf{7\ hr}$

2. Even integers: $N,\ N + 2,\ N + 4,\ N + 6$

$(N + 2)(N + 6) = -3(N + N + 4) - 16$

$N^2 + 8N + 12 = -6N - 28$

$N^2 + 14N + 40 = 0$

$(N + 10)(N + 4) = 0$

$N = -10, -4$

The desired integers are **–10, –8, –6, –4**
and **–4, –2, 0, 2.**

3. $\dfrac{86}{100} \times T_C = 3440$

$T_C = \mathbf{4000\ grams}$

4. $\dfrac{58}{100} \times C = 232$

$C = \mathbf{400\ chords}$

5. (a) $N_F = 2N_S$

(b) $N_F \cdot N_S = 200$

Substitute (a) into (b) and get:

(b') $2N_S \cdot N_S = 200$

$N_S^2 = 100$

$N_S = \pm 10$

The numbers were either **10, 20** or **–10, –20.**

6. (a) $N = 5D$

(b) $2N = 7D + 6$

Substitute (a) into (b) and get:

(b') $2(5D) = 7D + 6$

$3D = 6$

$D = 2$

(a) $N = 5(2) = 10$

Fraction $= \dfrac{N}{D} = \dfrac{\mathbf{10}}{\mathbf{2}}$

7. $\sqrt{x - 9} + \sqrt{x} = 3$

$\sqrt{x - 9} = 3 - \sqrt{x}$

$x - 9 = 9 - 6\sqrt{x} + x$

$-18 = -6\sqrt{x}$

$3 = \sqrt{x}$

$9 = x$

Check: $\sqrt{9 - 9} + \sqrt{9} = 3$

$0 + 3 = 3$

8. $\sqrt{x - 8} + \sqrt{x} = 4$

$\sqrt{x - 8} = 4 - \sqrt{x}$

$x - 8 = 16 - 8\sqrt{x} + x$

$-24 = -8\sqrt{x}$

$3 = \sqrt{x}$

$\mathbf{9} = x$

Check: $\sqrt{9 - 8} + \sqrt{9} = 4$

$1 + 3 = 4$

9. $\sqrt{k - 24} = 6 - \sqrt{k}$

$k - 24 = 36 - 12\sqrt{k} + k$

$-60 = -12\sqrt{k}$

$5 = \sqrt{k}$

$\mathbf{25} = k$

Check: $\sqrt{25 - 24} = 6 - \sqrt{25}$

$1 = 6 - 5$

10. There is never an exact solution to these problems. One possible solution is given here.

$S = m\text{Fe} + b$

Use the graph to find the slope.

$m = \dfrac{20}{20} = 1$

$S = \text{Fe} + b$

Use the point (140, 50) for Fe and S.

$50 = (140) + b$

$-90 = b$

$\mathbf{S = Fe - 90}$

11. (a) $x - 2y - z = -9$

(b) $2x - y + 2z = 7$

(c) $3x - y = 0$

$y = 3x$

Substitute (c) into (a) and (b) and get:

(a') $-5x - z = -9$

(b') $-x + 2z = 7$

$2(a')\ -10x - 2z = -18$

$\underline{(b')\quad -x + 2z = \quad 7}$

$-11x \quad\quad = -11$

$x = 1$

(b') $-(1) + 2z = 7$

$z = 4$

(c) $y = 3(1) = 3$

(1, 3, 4)

12.

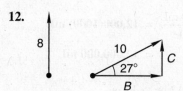

$B = 10 \cos 27° \approx 8.91$

$C = 10 \sin 27° \approx 4.54$

$\begin{array}{l} 0.00R + \ 8.00U \\ \underline{8.91R + \ 4.54U} \\ \mathbf{8.91R + 12.54U} \end{array}$

$\tan \theta = \dfrac{12.54}{8.91}$

$\theta \approx 54.61°$

$F = \sqrt{(8.91)^2 + (12.54)^2} \approx 15.38$

15.38/54.61°

13. $\dfrac{x - 3}{x^2 + 5x - 14} + \dfrac{3x}{2 - x}$

$= \dfrac{x - 3}{(x + 7)(x - 2)} - \dfrac{3x(x + 7)}{(x + 7)(x - 2)}$

$= \dfrac{x - 3 - 3x^2 - 21x}{x^2 + 5x - 14}$

$= \dfrac{\mathbf{-3x^2 - 20x - 3}}{\mathbf{x^2 + 5x - 14}}$

14. $\dfrac{3 - \sqrt{5}}{\sqrt{5} + 2} \cdot \dfrac{\sqrt{5} - 2}{\sqrt{5} - 2}$

$= \dfrac{3\sqrt{5} - 6 - 5 + 2\sqrt{5}}{5 - 4} = \mathbf{-11 + 5\sqrt{5}}$

15. $\dfrac{2 + 2\sqrt{2}}{3 - 3\sqrt{2}} \cdot \dfrac{3 + 3\sqrt{2}}{3 + 3\sqrt{2}}$

$= \dfrac{6 + 6\sqrt{2} + 6\sqrt{2} + 12}{9 - 18} = \dfrac{\mathbf{-6 - 4\sqrt{2}}}{\mathbf{3}}$

16. $\dfrac{4 - 3\sqrt{2}}{1 - \sqrt{2}} \cdot \dfrac{1 + \sqrt{2}}{1 + \sqrt{2}}$

$= \dfrac{4 + 4\sqrt{2} - 3\sqrt{2} - 6}{1 - 2} = \mathbf{2 - \sqrt{2}}$

17. $x^2 = -x - 1$

$x^2 + x + 1 = 0$

$x = \dfrac{-1 \pm \sqrt{1^2 - 4(1)(1)}}{2(1)}$

$x = \dfrac{-1 \pm \sqrt{-3}}{2} = \mathbf{-\dfrac{1}{2} \pm \dfrac{\sqrt{3}}{2}i}$

18. $mc = a\left(\dfrac{1}{x} + \dfrac{1}{R_1}\right)$

$mc = \dfrac{a}{x} + \dfrac{a}{R_1}$

$cmR_1x = aR_1 + ax$

$cmR_1x - aR_1 = ax$

$R_1 = \dfrac{\mathbf{ax}}{\mathbf{cmx - a}}$

19. $mc = a\left(\dfrac{1}{x} + \dfrac{1}{R_1}\right)$

$mc = \dfrac{a}{x} + \dfrac{a}{R_1}$

$cmR_1x = aR_1 + ax$

$c = \dfrac{\mathbf{aR_1 + ax}}{\mathbf{mR_1x}}$

20. $a + \dfrac{a}{a + \dfrac{x}{a}} = a + \dfrac{a}{\dfrac{a^2 + x}{a}}$

$= a + \dfrac{a^2}{a^2 + x} = \dfrac{\mathbf{a^3 + ax + a^2}}{\mathbf{a^2 + x}}$

21. $-5i^3 - \sqrt{-9} + \sqrt{-3}\sqrt{-3} = -5i(ii) - 3i + 3(ii)$

$= 5i - 3i - 3 = \mathbf{-3 + 2i}$

22. Since this is a 30°-60°-90° triangle,

$$2 \cdot \overrightarrow{SF} = \sqrt{5}$$

$$\overrightarrow{SF} = \frac{\sqrt{5}}{2}$$

$$a = \frac{\sqrt{5}}{2} \cdot 1 = \frac{\sqrt{5}}{2}$$

$$b = \frac{\sqrt{5}}{2} \cdot \sqrt{3} = \frac{\sqrt{15}}{2}$$

$$\text{Area} = \frac{bh}{2} = \frac{\frac{\sqrt{5}}{2} \left(\frac{\sqrt{15}}{2} \right)}{2} = \frac{5\sqrt{3}}{8} \text{ units}^2$$

23. $\dfrac{400 \text{ in.}^3}{\text{s}} \times \dfrac{2.54 \text{ cm}}{1 \text{ in.}} \times \dfrac{2.54 \text{ cm}}{1 \text{ in.}} \times \dfrac{2.54 \text{ cm}}{1 \text{ in.}}$

$\times \dfrac{60 \text{ s}}{1 \text{ min}} = \mathbf{400(2.54)(2.54)(2.54)(60)} \dfrac{\mathbf{cm}^3}{\mathbf{min}}$

24. $2\sqrt[5]{4^6 \sqrt{2}} = 2[2^{2 \cdot 6}(2)^{1/2}]^{1/5} = 2[2^{12/5} 2^{1/10}]$

$= 2^{35/10} = \mathbf{2^{7/2}}$

25. $\dfrac{-2^0 (2^{-2})}{4^{-3/2}} = \dfrac{-4^{3/2}}{4} = \dfrac{-(4^{1/2})^3}{4} = \mathbf{-2}$

26. $(2\sqrt{4} - 2)(3\sqrt{9} - 2) = (2)(7) = \mathbf{14}$

27. $4\sqrt{\dfrac{5}{8}} - 3\sqrt{\dfrac{8}{5}} + 2\sqrt{40}$

$= \dfrac{4\sqrt{5}}{\sqrt{8}} \dfrac{\sqrt{8}}{\sqrt{8}} - \dfrac{3\sqrt{8}}{\sqrt{5}} \dfrac{\sqrt{5}}{\sqrt{5}} + 2\sqrt{40}$

$= \dfrac{20\sqrt{40}}{40} - \dfrac{24\sqrt{40}}{40} + \dfrac{80\sqrt{40}}{40} = \dfrac{\mathbf{19\sqrt{10}}}{\mathbf{5}}$

28. (a) $\dfrac{70,218 \times 10^{-4}}{5062 \times 10^5} \approx \dfrac{7 \times 10^0}{5 \times 10^8} \approx 1 \times 10^{-8}$

Calculator answer $\approx \mathbf{1.39 \times 10^{-8}}$

(b) $\sqrt[5.4]{263}$

Answer should be between 2 and 4.

Calculator answer $\approx \mathbf{2.81}$

29. Solve for v:

$$\frac{\sqrt{mv}}{e} = p$$

$$\sqrt{mv} = ep$$

$$mv = e^2 p^2$$

$$v = \frac{e^2 p^2}{m}$$

$$v = \frac{(500)^2 (100 \times 10^{-14})^2}{4 \times 10^7}$$

$$v = \mathbf{6.25 \times 10^{-27}}$$

30. $\dfrac{S}{U} = \dfrac{T}{V}$

$SV = TU$

$S = \dfrac{TU}{V}$

PRACTICE SET 79

a. $12,000 \text{ L} \times \dfrac{1000 \text{ mL}}{1 \text{ L}} = \mathbf{12,000(1000) \text{ mL}}$

$= \mathbf{12,000,000 \text{ mL}}$

b. $10 \text{ ft}^3 \cdot \dfrac{12 \text{ in.}}{1 \text{ ft}} \cdot \dfrac{12 \text{ in.}}{1 \text{ ft}} \cdot \dfrac{12 \text{ in.}}{1 \text{ ft}}$

$\cdot \dfrac{2.54 \text{ cm}}{1 \text{ in.}} \cdot \dfrac{2.54 \text{ cm}}{1 \text{ in.}} \cdot \dfrac{2.54 \text{ cm}}{1 \text{ in.}} \cdot \dfrac{1 \text{ liter}}{1000 \text{ cm}^3}$

$= \dfrac{\mathbf{10(12)(12)(12)(2.54)(2.54)(2.54)}}{\mathbf{(1000)}} \text{ liters}$

c. Since this is a 45°-45°-90° triangle,

$1 \cdot \overrightarrow{SF} = 3$

$\overrightarrow{SF} = 3$

$y = 1 \cdot \overrightarrow{SF}$

$y = \mathbf{3}$

$z = \sqrt{2} \cdot \overrightarrow{SF}$

$z = \mathbf{3\sqrt{2}}$

PROBLEM SET 79

1. $T_C = kN_P$

$2142 = k(3)$

$714 = k$

$T_C = 714(10) = \mathbf{\$7140}$

2.

$R_D T_D = 900$; $\quad T_D = 5T_E$;

$R_E T_E = 120$; $\quad R_D = R_E + 10$

$5T_E(R_E + 10) = 900$

$5R_E T_E + 50T_E = 900$

$5(120) + 50T_E = 900$

$50T_E = 300$

$T_E = \textbf{6 hr}$

$T_D = \textbf{30 hr}; \quad R_E = \textbf{20 kph}; \quad R_D = \textbf{30 kph}$

3. Carbon: $\quad 1 \times 12 = 12$

Oxygen: $\quad 2 \times 16 = 32$

Total: $\quad 12 + 32 = 44$

Carbon: $\dfrac{12}{44} \times 100\% \approx \textbf{27.27\%}$

4. (a) $0.6P_N + 0.9D_N = 0.78(50)$

(b) $P_N + D_N = 50$

Substitute $D_N = 50 - P_N$ into (a) and get:

(a') $0.6P_N + 0.9(50 - P_N) = 39$

$-0.3P_N = -6$

$P_N = 20$

(b) $(20) + D_N = 50$

$D_N = 30$

20 mL 60%, 30 mL 90%

5. (a) $\dfrac{N_{\text{swords}}}{N_{\text{spears}}} = \dfrac{2}{7}$

(a') $7N_{\text{swords}} = 2N_{\text{spears}}$

(b) $5N_{\text{swords}} = N_{\text{spears}} + 120$

(b') $N_{\text{spears}} = 5N_{\text{swords}} - 120$

Substitute (b') into (a') and get:

(a'') $7N_{\text{swords}} = 2(5N_{\text{swords}} - 120)$

$3N_{\text{swords}} = 240$

$N_{\text{swords}} = \textbf{80 swords}$

(b') $N_{\text{spears}} = 5(80) - 120 = \textbf{280 spears}$

6. $50{,}000 \text{ mL} \times \dfrac{1 \text{ liter}}{1000 \text{ mL}} = \textbf{50 liters}$

7. $20 \text{ ft}^3 \times \dfrac{12 \text{ in.}}{1 \text{ ft}} \times \dfrac{12 \text{ in.}}{1 \text{ ft}} \times \dfrac{12 \text{ in.}}{1 \text{ ft}} \times \dfrac{2.54 \text{ cm}}{1 \text{ in.}}$

$\times \dfrac{2.54 \text{ cm}}{1 \text{ in.}} \times \dfrac{2.54 \text{ cm}}{1 \text{ in.}} \times \dfrac{1 \text{ liter}}{1000 \text{ cm}^3}$

$= \dfrac{20(12)(12)(12)(2.54)(2.54)(2.54)}{(1000)} \text{ liters}$

8. $\sqrt{x^2 - 4x + 4} = x + 2$

$x^2 - 4x + 4 = x^2 + 4x + 4$

$-8x = 0$

$x = \textbf{0}$

Check: $\sqrt{0^2 - 4(0) + 4} = 0 + 2$

$2 = 2$

9. $\sqrt{s} = 4 - \sqrt{s + 8}$

$\sqrt{s + 8} = 4 - \sqrt{s}$

$s + 8 = 16 - 8\sqrt{s} + s$

$8 = 8\sqrt{s}$

$1 = \sqrt{s}$

$\textbf{1} = s$

Check: $\sqrt{1} = 4 - \sqrt{1 + 8}$

$1 = 4 - 3$

10. (a) $2x - y + 2z = 3$

(b) $x - y - 2z = -6$

(c) $3x - y = 0$

$y = 3x$

(a) $2x - y + 2z = 3$

(b) $\underline{x - y - 2z = -6}$

(d) $3x - 2y = -3$

Substitute (c) into (d) and get:

(d') $3x - 2(3x) = -3$

$-3x = -3$

$x = 1$

(c) $y = 3(1) = 3$

(b) $(1) - (3) - 2z = -6$

$-2z = -4$

$z = 2$

$(1, 3, 2)$

11.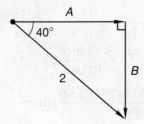

$A = 2 \cos 40° \approx 1.53$

$B = 2 \sin 40° \approx 1.29$

$C = 1 \cos 45° \approx 0.71$

$D = 1 \sin 45° \approx 0.71$

$1.53R - 1.29U$
$\underline{0.71R + 0.71U}$
$\mathbf{2.24R - 0.58U}$

$\tan \theta = -\dfrac{0.58}{2.24}$

$\theta \approx 345.48°$

$F = \sqrt{(2.24)^2 + (0.58)^2} \approx 2.31$

$\mathbf{2.31 / 345.48°}$

12. $\dfrac{4x + 3}{x^2 - 9} - \dfrac{2x}{3 - x}$

$= \dfrac{4x + 3}{x^2 - 9} + \dfrac{2x(x + 3)}{x^2 - 9}$

$= \dfrac{4x + 3 + 2x^2 + 6x}{x^2 - 9}$

$= \dfrac{\mathbf{2x^2 + 10x + 3}}{\mathbf{x^2 - 9}}$

13. $\dfrac{-2 - \sqrt{3}}{2\sqrt{3} + 2} \cdot \dfrac{2\sqrt{3} - 2}{2\sqrt{3} - 2}$

$= \dfrac{-4\sqrt{3} + 4 - 6 + 2\sqrt{3}}{12 - 4} = \dfrac{\mathbf{-1 - \sqrt{3}}}{\mathbf{4}}$

14. $\dfrac{-1 - \sqrt{2}}{-5 - \sqrt{2}} \cdot \dfrac{-5 + \sqrt{2}}{-5 + \sqrt{2}}$

$= \dfrac{5 - \sqrt{2} + 5\sqrt{2} - 2}{25 - 2} = \dfrac{\mathbf{3 + 4\sqrt{2}}}{\mathbf{23}}$

15. See Lesson 71.

16.

$\dfrac{a}{x} = m\left(\dfrac{a}{R_1} + \dfrac{b}{R_2}\right)$

$\dfrac{a}{x} = \dfrac{am}{R_1} + \dfrac{bm}{R_2}$

$aR_1R_2 = amxR_2 + bmxR_1$

$aR_1R_2 - amxR_2 = bmxR_1$

$a = \dfrac{\mathbf{bmxR_1}}{\mathbf{R_1R_2 - mxR_2}}$

17.

$\dfrac{a}{x} = m\left(\dfrac{a}{R_1} + \dfrac{b}{R_2}\right)$

$\dfrac{a}{x} = \dfrac{am}{R_1} + \dfrac{bm}{R_2}$

$aR_1R_2 = amxR_2 + bmxR_1$

$aR_1R_2 - amxR_2 = bmxR_1$

$\dfrac{\mathbf{aR_1R_2 - amxR_2}}{\mathbf{mxR_1}} = b$

18. $ax - \dfrac{ax}{a - \dfrac{a}{x}} = ax - \dfrac{ax}{\dfrac{ax - a}{x}}$

$= ax - \dfrac{ax^2}{ax - a} = \dfrac{a^2x^2 - a^2x - ax^2}{ax - a}$

$= \dfrac{\mathbf{ax^2 - ax - x^2}}{\mathbf{x - 1}}$

19. $\sqrt{-4} - 3i^2 - 2i^4 + 2 - \sqrt{-2}\sqrt{-2}$

$= 2i + 3 - 2 + 2 + 2 = \mathbf{5 + 2i}$

20. (a) $\dfrac{1}{5}x - \dfrac{1}{4}y = -6$

(b) $0.2x + 0.2y = 12$

(a′) $4x - 5y = -120$

(b′) $2x + 2y = 120$

 (a′) $4x - 5y = -120$
$-2(b′)\ \underline{-4x - 4y = -240}$
$-9y = -360$
$y = 40$

(b′) $2x + 2(40) = 120$

$2x = 40$

$x = 20$

(20, 40)

21.
$$3x^2 - 1 = 2x$$
$$3x^2 - 2x - 1 = 0$$
$$x = \frac{-(-2) \pm \sqrt{(-2)^2 - 4(3)(-1)}}{2(3)}$$
$$= \frac{2 \pm \sqrt{16}}{6} = \frac{1}{3} \pm \frac{2}{3} = \mathbf{1, -\frac{1}{3}}$$

22. Since this is a 30°-60°-90° triangle,
$$\sqrt{3} \times \overrightarrow{SF} = 3$$
$$\overrightarrow{SF} = \sqrt{3}$$
$$x = \sqrt{3}(1) = \mathbf{\sqrt{3}}$$
$$y = \sqrt{3}(2) = \mathbf{2\sqrt{3}}$$

23. Since this is a 45°-45°-90° triangle,
$$1 \times \overrightarrow{SF} = \sqrt{3}$$
$$\overrightarrow{SF} = \sqrt{3}$$
$$a = \sqrt{3}(1) = \mathbf{\sqrt{3}}$$
$$b = \sqrt{3}(\sqrt{2}) = \mathbf{\sqrt{6}}$$

24. $\dfrac{40 \text{ mL}}{s} \times \dfrac{1 \text{ cm}^3}{1 \text{ mL}} \times \dfrac{1 \text{ in.}}{2.54 \text{ cm}} \times \dfrac{1 \text{ in.}}{2.54 \text{ cm}}$
$$\times \dfrac{1 \text{ in.}}{2.54 \text{ cm}} \times \dfrac{60 \text{ s}}{1 \text{ min}} \times \dfrac{60 \text{ min}}{1 \text{ hr}}$$
$$= \mathbf{\dfrac{40(60)(60)}{(2.54)(2.54)(2.54)} \dfrac{in.^3}{hr}}$$

25. $3\sqrt{9^2 \sqrt{3}} = 3\sqrt{3^4 \sqrt{3}} = 3[3^4 3^{1/2}]^{1/2}$
$$= 3[3^2 3^{1/4}] = \mathbf{3^{13/4}}$$

26. $2\sqrt{\dfrac{7}{2}} + 3\sqrt{\dfrac{2}{7}} - 2\sqrt{126}$
$$= \dfrac{2\sqrt{7}}{\sqrt{2}}\dfrac{\sqrt{2}}{\sqrt{2}} + \dfrac{3\sqrt{2}}{\sqrt{7}}\dfrac{\sqrt{7}}{\sqrt{7}} - 6\sqrt{14}$$
$$= \dfrac{14\sqrt{14}}{14} + \dfrac{6\sqrt{14}}{14} - \dfrac{84\sqrt{14}}{14} = \mathbf{-\dfrac{32\sqrt{14}}{7}}$$

27. $(4\sqrt{2} + 3)(5\sqrt{2} - 4)$
$$= 40 - 16\sqrt{2} + 15\sqrt{2} - 12$$
$$= \mathbf{28 - \sqrt{2}}$$

28. (a) $\dfrac{41,852 \times 10^{28}}{0.00492 \times 10^{-14}} \approx \dfrac{4 \times 10^{32}}{5 \times 10^{-17}}$
$$= 8 \times 10^{48}$$
Calculator answer $\approx \mathbf{8.51 \times 10^{48}}$

(b) $(194)^{-1.09}$

Answer should be between 5×10^{-3} and 3×10^{-5}.

Calculator answer $\approx \mathbf{3.21 \times 10^{-3}}$

29. $y = \dfrac{1}{5}x + b$
$$7 = \dfrac{1}{5}(5) + b$$
$$6 = b$$
$$\mathbf{y = \dfrac{1}{5}x + 6}$$

30.

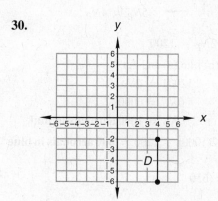

$$D^2 = 0^2 + 4^2$$
$$D^2 = 16$$
$$D = \mathbf{4}$$

PRACTICE SET 80

a. $C = \dfrac{k}{N}$
$$225 = \dfrac{k}{15}$$
$$k = 3375$$
$$C = \dfrac{3375}{42} = \mathbf{\$80.36}$$

b. $B = \dfrac{k}{Y^2}$
$$100 = \dfrac{k}{(3)^2}$$
$$k = 900$$
$$B = \dfrac{900}{(10)^2} = \mathbf{9 \text{ blues}}$$

PROBLEM SET 80

1. $C = kN$

$119 = k(14)$

$k = 8.5$

$C = 8.5(32) = \textbf{\$272}$

2. $\dfrac{B_1}{B_2} = \dfrac{Y_2^2}{Y_1^2}$

$\dfrac{50}{B_2} = \dfrac{(10)^2}{(5)^2}$

$100B_2 = 1250$

$B_2 = \textbf{12.5 blues}$

3. (a) $\dfrac{N_B}{N_P} = \dfrac{4}{5} \longrightarrow 5N_B = 4N_P$

(b) $N_B = 2N_P - 1200$

Substitute (b) into (a) and get:

(a') $5(2N_P - 1200) = 4N_P$

$6N_P = 6000$

$N_P = \textbf{1000 acrobats in pink}$

(b) $N_B = 2(1000) - 1200 = \textbf{800 acrobats in blue}$

4. $3\dfrac{1}{4} \times P = 650$

$P = 650 \times \dfrac{4}{13} = \textbf{200 people}$

5. (a) $40N_D + 2N_C = 820$

(b) $N_D + N_C = 30$

Substitute (b) into (a) and get:

(a') $40N_D + 2(30 - N_D) = 820$

$38N_D = 760$

$N_D = \textbf{20 dogs}$

(b) $N_C = 30 - (20) = \textbf{10 cats}$

6. $\sqrt{x^2 - x - 2} - x + 2 = 0$

$x^2 - x - 2 = x^2 - 4x + 4$

$3x = 6$

$x = \textbf{2}$

Check: $\sqrt{2^2 - 2 - 2} - 2 + 2 = 0$

$0 - 2 + 2 = 0$

7. $\sqrt{p + 20} + \sqrt{p} = 10$

$p + 20 = 100 - 20\sqrt{p} + p$

$20\sqrt{p} = 80$

$\sqrt{p} = 4$

$p = \textbf{16}$

Check: $\sqrt{16 + 20} + \sqrt{16} = 10$

$6 + 4 = 10$

8. $\sqrt{s} - 18 + \sqrt{s - 36} = 0$

$s - 36 = 324 - 36\sqrt{s} + s$

$36\sqrt{s} = 360$

$\sqrt{s} = 10$

$s = \textbf{100}$

Check: $\sqrt{100} - 18 + \sqrt{100 - 36} = 0$

$10 - 18 + 8 = 0$

9. (a) $x + y + z = 8$

(b) $2x - 3y - z = -6$

(c) $2x - z = 0$

$z = 2x$

Substitute (c) into (a) and (b) and get:

(a') $3x + y = 8$

(b') $-3y = -6$

$y = 2$

(a') $3x + (2) = 8$

$3x = 6$

$x = 2$

(c) $z = 2(2) = 4$

(2, 2, 4)

10.

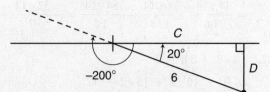

$A = 4\cos 60° = 2.00$

$B = 4\sin 60° \approx 3.46$

$C = 6\cos 20° \approx 5.64$

$D = 6\sin 20° \approx 2.05$

$\begin{array}{r} 2.00R + 3.46U \\ 5.64R - 2.05U \\ \hline \textbf{7.64R + 1.41U} \end{array}$

11.

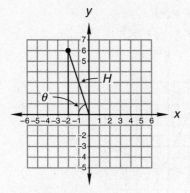

$$H = \sqrt{2^2 + 6^2}$$
$$H = 2\sqrt{10}$$

$$\tan \theta = \frac{6}{2} = 3$$
$$\theta \approx 71.57°$$

Since θ is a second-quadrant angle,

$$\theta \approx -(71.57) + 180 = 108.43°$$

$$\mathbf{2\sqrt{10}\,/108.43°}$$

12. $\dfrac{4x + 2}{x^2 - 6x - 16} - \dfrac{3}{x - 8}$

$$= \frac{4x + 2}{(x - 8)(x + 2)} - \frac{3(x + 2)}{(x - 8)(x + 2)}$$

$$= \frac{\mathbf{x - 4}}{\mathbf{x^2 - 6x - 16}}$$

13. $\dfrac{3\sqrt{2} - 1}{1 + \sqrt{2}} \cdot \dfrac{1 - \sqrt{2}}{1 - \sqrt{2}}$

$$= \frac{3\sqrt{2} - 6 - 1 + \sqrt{2}}{1 - 2} = \mathbf{7 - 4\sqrt{2}}$$

14. $\dfrac{2 - 3\sqrt{2}}{3 - 2\sqrt{2}} \cdot \dfrac{3 + 2\sqrt{2}}{3 + 2\sqrt{2}}$

$$= \frac{6 + 4\sqrt{2} - 9\sqrt{2} - 12}{9 - 8} = \mathbf{-6 - 5\sqrt{2}}$$

15. $A^2 = 3^2 + 4^2$

$$A = 5$$

$$4 \times \overrightarrow{SF} = 8$$

$$\overrightarrow{SF} = 2$$

$$(5)2 = B + 5$$

$$10 = B + 5$$

$$\mathbf{5 = B}$$

16. $$-3x^2 + 2 = -3x$$

$$\left(x^2 - x + \right) = \frac{2}{3}$$

$$x^2 - x + \frac{1}{4} = \frac{2}{3} + \frac{1}{4}$$

$$\left(x - \frac{1}{2}\right)^2 = \frac{11}{12}$$

$$x - \frac{1}{2} = \pm\frac{\sqrt{33}}{6}$$

$$x = \mathbf{\frac{1}{2} \pm \frac{\sqrt{33}}{6}}$$

17. $$a = xm\left(\frac{p}{y} + \frac{q}{c}\right)$$

$$a = \frac{mpx}{y} + \frac{mqx}{c}$$

$$acy = cmpx + mqxy$$

$$acy - mqxy = cmpx$$

$$y = \mathbf{\frac{cmpx}{ac - mqx}}$$

18. $3a - \dfrac{3}{a - \dfrac{3}{a}} = 3a - \dfrac{3}{\dfrac{a^2 - 3}{a}}$

$$= 3a - \frac{3a}{a^2 - 3} = \frac{3a^3 - 9a - 3a}{a^2 - 3}$$

$$= \mathbf{\frac{3a^3 - 12a}{a^2 - 3}}$$

19. (a) Since this is a 45°-45°-90° triangle,

$$\sqrt{2} \times \overrightarrow{SF} = 5$$

$$\overrightarrow{SF} = \frac{5\sqrt{2}}{2}$$

$$m = \frac{5\sqrt{2}}{2}(1) = \mathbf{\frac{5\sqrt{2}}{2}}$$

$$n = \frac{5\sqrt{2}}{2}(1) = \mathbf{\frac{5\sqrt{2}}{2}}$$

(b) Since this is a 30°-60°-90° triangle,

$$2 \times \overrightarrow{SF} = 5$$

$$\overrightarrow{SF} = \frac{5}{2}$$

$$c = \frac{5}{2}(1) = \mathbf{\frac{5}{2}}$$

$$d = \frac{5}{2}(\sqrt{3}) = \mathbf{\frac{5\sqrt{3}}{2}}$$

20. $-\sqrt{-4} + \sqrt{-9} - i^3 + \sqrt{-2}\sqrt{-2} - 4i^4$
$= -2i + 3i - i(ii) + 2(ii) - 4(ii)(ii)$
$= -2i + 3i + i - 2 - 4 = \mathbf{-6 + 2i}$

21. (a) $\dfrac{2}{3}x - \dfrac{1}{4}y = 6$

(b) $0.07x + 0.06y = 1.32$

(a′) $8x - 3y = 72$

(b′) $7x + 6y = 132$

$2(a′)$ $16x - 6y = 144$

$\underline{(b′)\quad 7x + 6y = 132}$
$23x = 276$
$x = 12$

(b′) $7(12) + 6y = 132$
$6y = 48$
$y = 8$

(12, 8)

22. $-x^2 = -x - 5$
$x^2 - x - 5 = 0$

$x = \dfrac{-(-1) \pm \sqrt{(-1)^2 - 4(1)(-5)}}{2(1)}$

$x = \dfrac{1 \pm \sqrt{21}}{2} = \dfrac{\mathbf{1}}{\mathbf{2}} \pm \dfrac{\sqrt{\mathbf{21}}}{\mathbf{2}}$

23. $\dfrac{600 \text{ cm}^3}{\text{min}} \times \dfrac{1 \text{ in.}}{2.54 \text{ cm}} \times \dfrac{1 \text{ in.}}{2.54 \text{ cm}} \times \dfrac{1 \text{ in.}}{2.54 \text{ cm}}$

$\times \dfrac{1 \text{ ft}}{12 \text{ in.}} \times \dfrac{1 \text{ ft}}{12 \text{ in.}} \times \dfrac{1 \text{ ft}}{12 \text{ in.}} \times \dfrac{60 \text{ min}}{1 \text{ hr}}$

$= \dfrac{\mathbf{600(60)}}{\mathbf{(2.54)(2.54)(2.54)(12)(12)(12)}} \dfrac{\mathbf{ft}^3}{\mathbf{hr}}$

24. Volume $= A_{\text{Base}} \times$ height

$= 2\left(\dfrac{\pi r^2}{2}\right) \times h$

$= \pi(6 \text{ in.})^2\left(6 \text{ ft} \times \dfrac{12 \text{ in.}}{1 \text{ ft}}\right)$

$\approx$ **8138.88 1-inch sugar cubes**

25. $\sqrt[4]{x^5 y}\sqrt{xy^3} = (x^5 y)^{1/4}(xy^3)^{1/2}$
$= x^{5/4}y^{1/4}x^{1/2}y^{3/2} = \mathbf{x^{7/4}y^{7/4}}$

26. $\dfrac{-2^0 (-2)^0}{-(4)^{-3/2}} = -[-(4^{1/2})^3] = \mathbf{8}$

27. (a) $x - 3y = 6$

$y = \dfrac{1}{3}x - 2$

(b) $2x + y = -1$

$y = -2x - 1$

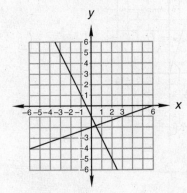

Substitute $y = -2x - 1$ into (a) and get:

(a′) $x - 3(-2x - 1) = 6$
$7x = 3$
$x = \dfrac{3}{7}$

(b) $y = -2\left(\dfrac{3}{7}\right) - 1 = -\dfrac{13}{7}$

$\left(\dfrac{\mathbf{3}}{\mathbf{7}}, -\dfrac{\mathbf{13}}{\mathbf{7}}\right)$

28. $\dfrac{3}{ax} + \dfrac{3x}{a^2 x} + \dfrac{7x}{x + a}$

$= \dfrac{3a(x + a)}{a^2 x(x + a)} + \dfrac{3x(x + a)}{a^2 x(x + a)} + \dfrac{7a^2 x^2}{a^2 x(x + a)}$

$= \dfrac{3ax + 3a^2 + 3x^2 + 3ax + 7a^2 x^2}{a^2 x(x + a)}$

$= \dfrac{\mathbf{3a^2 + 3x^2 + 6ax + 7a^2 x^2}}{\mathbf{a^2 x(x + a)}}$

29. $x^3 = 4x^2 + 32x$
$x^3 - 4x^2 - 32x = 0$
$x(x - 8)(x + 4) = 0$
$x = \mathbf{0, -4, 8}$

30. Write the equation of the given line in slope-intercept form.

$-x - y - 1 = 0$
$y = -x - 1$

Since the slopes of perpendicular lines are negative reciprocals of each other,

$m_\perp = +1$
$y = x + b$
$-3 = -2 + b$
$-1 = b$
$\mathbf{y = x - 1}$

PRACTICE SET 81

a. $\dfrac{2 + 3i}{3 - 3i} \cdot \dfrac{3 + 3i}{3 + 3i}$

ABOVE

$$\begin{array}{r} 2 + 3i \\ 3 + 3i \\ \hline 6 + 9i \\ 6i + 9i^2 \\ \hline \end{array}$$

$6 + 15i - 9 = -3 + 15i$

BELOW

$$\begin{array}{r} 3 - 3i \\ 3 + 3i \\ \hline 9 - 9i \\ 9i - 9i^2 \\ \hline \end{array}$$

$9 \qquad + 9 = 18$

$\dfrac{-3 + 15i}{18} = -\dfrac{1}{6} + \dfrac{5}{6}i$

b. $\dfrac{2 - 2i}{2i - 2} = \dfrac{2 - 2i}{-2 + 2i} \cdot \dfrac{-2 - 2i}{-2 - 2i}$

ABOVE

$$\begin{array}{r} 2 - 2i \\ -2 - 2i \\ \hline -4 + 4i \\ - 4i + 4i^2 \\ \hline \end{array}$$

$-4 \qquad - 4 = -8$

BELOW

$$\begin{array}{r} -2 + 2i \\ -2 - 2i \\ \hline 4 - 4i \\ 4i - 4i^2 \\ \hline \end{array}$$

$4 \qquad + 4 = 8$

$\dfrac{-8}{8} = -1$

PROBLEM SET 81

1. Variation method:

$M = kT^2$

$100 = k(2)^2$

$25 = k$

$M = 25(5^2) =$ **625 monkeys**

Equal ratio method:

$\dfrac{M_1}{M_2} = \dfrac{T_1^2}{T_2^2}$

$\dfrac{100}{M_2} = \dfrac{(2)^2}{(5)^2}$

$4M_2 = 2500$

$M_2 =$ **625 monkeys**

2. $M = \dfrac{k}{A^2}$

$4 = \dfrac{k}{(10)^2}$

$400 = k$

$M = \dfrac{400}{4} =$ **100 macaws**

3.

$$\begin{array}{l} \xrightarrow{\hspace{1.5cm}} D_R \\[-4pt] \xrightarrow{\hspace{2cm}} D_J \end{array}$$

$R_R T_R = 375;\ R_J T_J = 375;$

$R_R = 3R_J;\ T_R = T_J - 10$

$3R_J(T_J - 10) = 375$

$3R_J T_J - 30R_J = 375$

$3(375) - 30R_J = 375$

$-30R_J = -750$

$R_J =$ **25 mph**

$R_R =$ **75 mph**$;\ T_J =$ **15 hr**$;\ T_R =$ **5 hr**

4. (a) $0.1P_N + 0.4D_N = 38$

(b) $P_N + D_N = 200$

Substitute $D_N = 200 - P_N$ into (a) and get:

(a′) $0.1P_N + 0.4(200 - P_N) = 38$

$-0.3P_N = -42$

$P_N = 140$

(b) $(140) + D_N = 200$

$D_N = 60$

140 liters 10%; 60 liters 40%

5. $\dfrac{40}{100} \cdot N_T = 1120$

$N_T = 1120 \cdot \dfrac{100}{40}$

$N_T =$ **2800**

6. $\dfrac{3-i}{2+5i} \cdot \dfrac{2-5i}{2-5i}$

$= \dfrac{6-15i-2i+5i^2}{4-25i^2} = \dfrac{1}{29} - \dfrac{17}{29}i$

7. $\dfrac{3-2i}{2i-4} \cdot \dfrac{2i+4}{2i+4}$

$= \dfrac{6i+12-4i^2-8i}{4i^2-16} = -\dfrac{4}{5} + \dfrac{1}{10}i$

8. $(180-A) = 4(90-A) + 30$

$\quad 180 - A = 360 - 4A + 30$

$\qquad\quad 3A = 210$

$\qquad\quad A = \mathbf{70°}$

9. $\sqrt{x^2 - x + 30} - 3 = x$

$\quad x^2 - x + 30 = x^2 + 6x + 9$

$\qquad\qquad -7x = -21$

$\qquad\qquad\quad x = \mathbf{3}$

Check: $\sqrt{3^2 - 3 + 30} - 3 = 3$

$\qquad\qquad\quad 6 - 3 = 3$

10. $\sqrt{p - 48} = 12 - \sqrt{p}$

$\quad p - 48 = 144 - 24\sqrt{p} + p$

$\quad 24\sqrt{p} = 192$

$\qquad \sqrt{p} = 8$

$\qquad\quad p = \mathbf{64}$

Check: $\sqrt{64 - 48} = 12 - \sqrt{64}$

$\qquad\qquad\quad 4 = 12 - 8$

11. (a) $x + 2y - 3z = 5$

(b) $2x - y - z = 0$

(c) $y - 3z = 0$

$\qquad y = 3z$

Substitute (c) into (a) and (b) and get:

(a′) $x + 3z = 5$

(b′) $2x - 4z = 0$

-2(a′) $-2x - 6z = -10$

$\quad$(b′) $\underline{2x - 4z = 0}$

$\qquad\qquad -10z = -10$

$\qquad\qquad\quad z = 1$

(a′) $x + 3(1) = 5$

$\qquad\qquad x = 2$

(c) $y = 3(1) = 3$

(2, 3, 1)

12.

$A = 8\cos 71° \approx 2.60$

$B = 8\sin 71° \approx 7.56$

$\begin{array}{r} -2.60R + 7.56U \\ 0.00R + 5.00U \\ \hline -2.60R + 12.56U \end{array}$

$\tan\theta = -\dfrac{12.56}{2.60}$

$\quad \theta \approx 101.70°$

$F = \sqrt{(2.60)^2 + (12.56)^2} \approx 12.83$

12.83 / 101.70°

13. $\dfrac{7x-2}{x^2-9} + \dfrac{3x}{3-x}$

$= \dfrac{7x-2}{(x-3)(x+3)} - \dfrac{3x(x+3)}{(x-3)(x+3)}$

$= \dfrac{-3x^2 - 2x - 2}{x^2 - 9}$

14. $\dfrac{\sqrt{2}-5}{\sqrt{2}-2} \cdot \dfrac{\sqrt{2}+2}{\sqrt{2}+2}$

$= \dfrac{2 + 2\sqrt{2} - 5\sqrt{2} - 10}{2 - 4} = \dfrac{8 + 3\sqrt{2}}{2}$

15. $\dfrac{2\sqrt{3}-1}{1-3\sqrt{3}} \cdot \dfrac{1+3\sqrt{3}}{1+3\sqrt{3}}$

$= \dfrac{2\sqrt{3} + 18 - 1 - 3\sqrt{3}}{1 - 27} = \dfrac{-17 + \sqrt{3}}{26}$

16. $\dfrac{1+\sqrt{2}}{3-\sqrt{2}} \cdot \dfrac{3+\sqrt{2}}{3+\sqrt{2}}$

$= \dfrac{3 + \sqrt{2} + 3\sqrt{2} + 2}{9 - 2} = \dfrac{5 + 4\sqrt{2}}{7}$

17. $x = \dfrac{40 + 50}{2} = \mathbf{45}$

$y = \dfrac{140 - 100}{2} = \mathbf{20}$

18. See Lesson 71.

19. $2a^2 - \dfrac{3a}{a + \dfrac{1}{a}} = 2a^2 - \dfrac{3a}{\dfrac{a^2 + 1}{a}}$

$= 2a^2 - \dfrac{3a^2}{a^2 + 1} = \dfrac{\boldsymbol{2a^4 - a^2}}{\boldsymbol{a^2 + 1}}$

20. $\sqrt{-9} - \sqrt{-2}\sqrt{-2} + \sqrt{-2}\sqrt{2} - 3i^3 - 2i^2$

$= 3i - 2(ii) + 2i - 3i(ii) - 2(ii)$

$= 3i + 2 + 2i + 3i + 2 = \boldsymbol{4 + 8i}$

21. (a) $\dfrac{2}{3}x - \dfrac{1}{3}y = 6$

(b) $0.15x + 0.01y = 0.84$

$\begin{aligned}(a')\quad 2x - y &= 18 \\ (b')\quad 15x + y &= 84 \\ \hline 17x &= 102 \\ x &= 6\end{aligned}$

$(a')\quad 2(6) - y = 18$

$y = -6$

$\boldsymbol{(6, -6)}$

22. $\qquad 2 = -2x^2 - 3x$

$2x^2 + 3x + 2 = 0$

$x = \dfrac{-3 \pm \sqrt{3^2 - 4(2)(2)}}{2(2)} = \dfrac{-3 \pm \sqrt{-7}}{4}$

$= \boldsymbol{-\dfrac{3}{4} \pm \dfrac{\sqrt{7}}{4}i}$

23. $\quad x - 4 \overline{)4x^3 + 0x^2 - x + 2}$ with quotient $\boldsymbol{4x^2 + 16x + 63} + \dfrac{254}{x-4}$

$\begin{array}{r} \underline{4x^3 - 16x^2} \\ 16x^2 - x \\ \underline{16x^2 - 64x} \\ 63x + 2 \\ \underline{63x - 252} \\ 254 \end{array}$

24. Since this is a 45°-45°-90° triangle,

$\sqrt{2} \times \overrightarrow{SF} = 17$

$\overrightarrow{SF} = \dfrac{17\sqrt{2}}{2}$

$x = \dfrac{17\sqrt{2}}{2}(1) = \dfrac{\boldsymbol{17\sqrt{2}}}{\boldsymbol{2}}$

$y = \dfrac{17\sqrt{2}}{2}(1) = \dfrac{\boldsymbol{17\sqrt{2}}}{\boldsymbol{2}}$

25. $3\sqrt{9\sqrt[4]{3}} = 3\sqrt{3^2\sqrt[4]{3}} = 3\left[3^2(3^{1/4})\right]^{1/2}$

$= 3 \cdot 3 \cdot 3^{1/8} = \boldsymbol{3^{17/8}}$

26. $2\sqrt{\dfrac{1}{5}} - 3\sqrt{5} + 3\sqrt{20}$

$= \dfrac{2}{\sqrt{5}}\dfrac{\sqrt{5}}{\sqrt{5}} - 3\sqrt{5} + 6\sqrt{5}$

$= \dfrac{2\sqrt{5}}{5} - \dfrac{15\sqrt{5}}{5} + \dfrac{30\sqrt{5}}{5} = \dfrac{\boldsymbol{17\sqrt{5}}}{\boldsymbol{5}}$

27. $\dfrac{x}{x + y} + \dfrac{3}{x^2 y} + \dfrac{2}{xy}$

$= \dfrac{x^3 y}{x^2 y(x + y)} + \dfrac{3(x + y)}{x^2 y(x + y)} + \dfrac{2x(x + y)}{x^2 y(x + y)}$

$= \dfrac{\boldsymbol{x^3 y + 3x + 3y + 2x^2 + 2xy}}{\boldsymbol{x^2 y(x + y)}}$

28. $-4^2 - 3^0 - 2^0(x - x^0) - 3^0(-2x - 5) = 7$

$-16 - 1 - x + 1 + 2x + 5 = 7$

$\boldsymbol{x = 18}$

29.

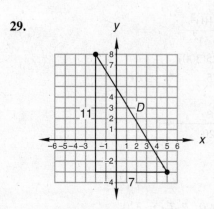

$D^2 = 11^2 + 7^2$

$D^2 = 170$

$D = \boldsymbol{\sqrt{170}}$

30. (a) $\dfrac{0.5061 \times 10^5}{0.0071643 \times 10^{-18}} \approx \dfrac{5 \times 10^4}{7 \times 10^{-21}}$

$\approx 7 \times 10^{24}$

Calculator answer $\approx \boldsymbol{7.06 \times 10^{24}}$

(b) $\sqrt[6.2]{594}$

Answer should be between 2 and 3.

Calculator answer $\approx \boldsymbol{2.80}$

PRACTICE SET 82

a. $\dfrac{1}{3 + \dfrac{x}{3 + \dfrac{3}{a}}} = \dfrac{1}{3 + \dfrac{x}{\dfrac{3a + 3}{a}}} = \dfrac{1}{3 + \dfrac{ax}{3a + 3}}$

$= \dfrac{1}{\dfrac{9a + 9 + ax}{3a + 3}} = \dfrac{3a + 3}{9a + 9 + ax}$

$= \dfrac{3a + 3}{9a + ax + 9}$

b. $\dfrac{m}{x + \dfrac{p}{q + \dfrac{1}{z}}} = \dfrac{m}{x + \dfrac{p}{\dfrac{qz + 1}{z}}} = \dfrac{m}{x + \dfrac{pz}{qz + 1}}$

$= \dfrac{m}{\dfrac{qxz + x + pz}{qz + 1}} = \dfrac{m(qz + 1)}{qxz + x + pz}$

PROBLEM SET 82

1. $\dfrac{Q_1}{Q_2} = \dfrac{S_2^2}{S_1^2}$

$\dfrac{300}{Q_2} = \dfrac{(10)^2}{(5)^2}$

$100Q_2 = 25(300)$

$Q_2 = \mathbf{75}$

2.

$\vdash\!\!\!/\!\!\!\!/\underset{\text{1920}}{\overset{D_P}{\rule{3cm}{0.4pt}\!\!\!\!\!\rightarrow}}\dashv$

$\vdash\underset{\text{320}}{\overset{D_R}{\rule{2cm}{0.4pt}\!\!\!\!\!\rightarrow}}\dashv$

$R_P T_P = 1920;\quad R_R T_R = 320;$

$T_P = T_R + 4;\quad R_P = 3R_R$

$3R_R(T_R + 4) = 1920$

$3R_R T_R + 12R_R = 1920$

$3(320) + 12R_R = 1920$

$12R_R = 960$

$R_R = \mathbf{80\ mph}$

$R_P = \mathbf{240\ mph};\ T_R = \mathbf{4\ hr};\ T_P = \mathbf{8\ hr}$

3. $\dfrac{P_1 V_1}{T_1} = \dfrac{P_2 V_2}{T_2}$

$T_2 = \dfrac{P_2 V_2 T_1}{P_1 V_1}$

$T_2 = \dfrac{(50)(200)(540)}{(5)(250)} = \mathbf{4320\ K}$

4.

$\vdash\underset{\text{60}}{\overset{D_R\qquad D_W}{\rule{3cm}{0.4pt}\!\!\!\!\!\rightarrow}}\dashv$

$R_R T_R + R_W T_W = 60;\ R_R = 10;$

$R_W = 5;\ T_R + T_W = 8$

$10T_R + 5(8 - T_R) = 60$

$5T_R = 20$

$T_R = 4\ hr$

$T_W = 4\ hr$

$D_R = 10(4) = \mathbf{40\ miles}$

$D_W = 5(4) = \mathbf{20\ miles}$

5.

Sodium:	$2 \times 23 =$	46
Hydrogen:	$1 \times 1 =$	1
Phosphorous:	$1 \times 31 =$	31
Oxygen:	$4 \times 16 =$	64
Total:	$46 + 1 + 31 + 64 =$	142

$\dfrac{46}{142} = \dfrac{\text{Na}}{852}$

$142\text{Na} = 46(852)$

$\text{Na} = \mathbf{276\ grams}$

Sodium: $\dfrac{46}{142} \times 100\% \approx \mathbf{32.39\%}$

6. $\dfrac{m}{2 + \dfrac{m}{2 + \dfrac{2}{p}}} = \dfrac{m}{2 + \dfrac{m}{\dfrac{2p + 2}{p}}}$

$= \dfrac{m}{2 + \dfrac{mp}{2p + 2}} = \dfrac{m}{\dfrac{4p + 4 + mp}{2p + 2}}$

$= \dfrac{m(2p + 2)}{4p + 4 + mp}$

7. $\dfrac{p}{a + \dfrac{b}{m + \dfrac{3}{y}}} = \dfrac{p}{a + \dfrac{b}{\dfrac{ym + 3}{y}}}$

$= \dfrac{p}{a + \dfrac{yb}{ym + 3}} = \dfrac{p}{\dfrac{aym + 3a + yb}{ym + 3}}$

$= \dfrac{p(ym + 3)}{aym + 3a + yb}$

8. $V_{\text{Cone}} = \dfrac{\pi r^2 h}{3} = 12\pi\ \text{m}^3$

$h = \dfrac{12(3)\ \text{m}^3}{9\ \text{m}^2} = \mathbf{4\ m}$

9. $\dfrac{2 - 3i}{4 + i} \cdot \dfrac{4 - i}{4 - i} = \dfrac{8 - 2i - 12i - 3}{16 + 1}$

$= \dfrac{5}{17} - \dfrac{14}{17}i$

10. $\dfrac{5 - i}{2 - 3i} \cdot \dfrac{2 + 3i}{2 + 3i} = \dfrac{10 + 15i - 2i + 3}{4 + 9}$

$= \mathbf{1 + i}$

11. $\sqrt{x^2 - x + 47} - 5 = x$

$x^2 - x + 47 = x^2 + 10x + 25$

$11x = 22$

$x = \mathbf{2}$

Check: $\sqrt{4 - 2 + 47} - 5 = 2$

$7 - 5 = 2$

12. $\sqrt{x + 24} + \sqrt{x} = 12$

$x + 24 = 144 - 24\sqrt{x} + x$

$24\sqrt{x} = 120$

$\sqrt{x} = 5$

$x = \mathbf{25}$

Check: $\sqrt{25 + 24} + \sqrt{25} = 12$

$7 + 5 = 12$

13. (a) $2x - 2y - z = 16$

(b) $3x - y + 2z = 5$

(c) $-y + 3z = 0$

$y = 3z$

Substitute (c) into (a) and (b) and get:

(a') $2x - 7z = 16$

(b') $3x - z = 5$

$\begin{array}{r} \text{(a')} \quad 2x - 7z = 16 \\ -7\text{(b')} \quad \underline{-21x + 7z = -35} \\ -19x = -19 \\ x = 1 \end{array}$

(b') $3(1) - z = 5$

$z = -2$

(c) $y = 3(-2) = -6$

$\mathbf{(1, -6, -2)}$

14.

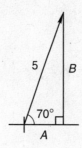

$A = 5 \cos 70° \approx 1.71$

$B = 5 \sin 70° \approx 4.70$

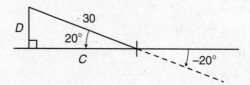

$C = 30 \cos 20° \approx 28.19$

$D = 30 \sin 20° \approx 10.26$

$\begin{array}{r} 1.71R + 4.70U \\ \underline{-28.19R + 10.26U} \\ \mathbf{-26.48R + 14.96U} \end{array}$

15.

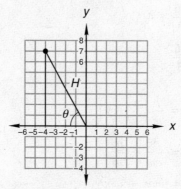

$H = \sqrt{7^2 + 4^2}$

$H = \sqrt{65}$

$\tan \theta = \dfrac{7}{4}$

$\theta \approx 60.26°$

Since θ is a second-quadrant angle,

$\theta = -(60.26) + 180 = 119.74°$

$\mathbf{\sqrt{65} \underline{/119.74°}}$

16. $\dfrac{3x - 2}{x^2 - 9} + \dfrac{x}{3 - x}$

$= \dfrac{3x - 2}{(x - 3)(x + 3)} - \dfrac{x(x + 3)}{(x + 3)(x - 3)}$

$= \dfrac{3x - 2 - x^2 - 3x}{x^2 - 9} = \dfrac{-x^2 - 2}{x^2 - 9}$

17. $\dfrac{3\sqrt{2}-1}{1+\sqrt{2}} \cdot \dfrac{1-\sqrt{2}}{1-\sqrt{2}}$

$= \dfrac{3\sqrt{2}-6-1+\sqrt{2}}{1-2} = \mathbf{7-4\sqrt{2}}$

18. $\dfrac{-2-\sqrt{5}}{2+2\sqrt{5}} \cdot \dfrac{2-2\sqrt{5}}{2-2\sqrt{5}}$

$= \dfrac{-4+4\sqrt{5}-2\sqrt{5}+10}{4-20} = \dfrac{\mathbf{-3-\sqrt{5}}}{\mathbf{8}}$

19. $5^2 = A^2 + 3^2$

$25 = A^2 + 9$

$16 = A^2$

$4 = A$

$5 \times \overrightarrow{SF} = 9$

$\overrightarrow{SF} = \dfrac{9}{5}$

$4 + B = 4 \times \dfrac{9}{5}$

$B = \dfrac{36}{5} - 4$

$B = \dfrac{\mathbf{16}}{\mathbf{5}}$

20. $\dfrac{z}{m^2} = \dfrac{p}{m}\left(\dfrac{x}{a}+y\right)$

$\dfrac{z}{m^2} = \dfrac{px}{am} + \dfrac{py}{m}$

$az = mpx + ampy$

$az - ampy = mpx$

$a = \dfrac{\mathbf{mpx}}{\mathbf{z-mpy}}$

21. $\dfrac{z}{m^2} = \dfrac{p}{m}\left(\dfrac{x}{a}+y\right)$

$\dfrac{z}{m^2} = \dfrac{px}{am} + \dfrac{py}{m}$

$az = mpx + ampy$

$\dfrac{\mathbf{az}}{\mathbf{mx+amy}} = p$

22. Length of side $= \dfrac{\text{diagonal}}{\sqrt{2}} = \dfrac{6\text{ m}}{\sqrt{2}} = \mathbf{3\sqrt{2}\text{ m}}$

Area $= s^2 = (3\sqrt{2}\text{ m})^2 = \mathbf{18\text{ m}^2}$

23. (a) $\dfrac{2}{5}x - \dfrac{1}{3}y = -1$

(b) $0.07x + 0.2y = 2.15$

(a′) $6x - 5y = -15$

(b′) $7x + 20y = 215$

$\quad 4(a′) \;\; 24x - 20y = -60$

$\quad\;\; (b′) \;\;\; 7x + 20y = 215$

$\qquad\qquad\overline{\quad 31x \qquad\quad = 155\quad}$

$\qquad\qquad\qquad x = 5$

(a′) $6(5) - 5y = -15$

$\qquad\quad -5y = -45$

$\qquad\qquad y = 9$

(5, 9)

24. See Lesson 71.

25. $-3x^2 - 2 = 5x$

$3x^2 + 5x + 2 = 0$

$x = \dfrac{-5 \pm \sqrt{5^2 - 4(3)(2)}}{2(3)} = \dfrac{-5 \pm \sqrt{1}}{6}$

$= -\dfrac{5}{6} \pm \dfrac{1}{6} = \mathbf{-\dfrac{2}{3}, -1}$

26. $\sqrt{x^5 y}\sqrt[3]{x^2 y^5} = (x^5 y)^{1/2}(x^2 y^5)^{1/3}$

$= x^{5/2} y^{1/2} x^{2/3} y^{5/3} = \mathbf{x^{19/6} y^{13/6}}$

27. $3\sqrt{\dfrac{2}{9}} + 3\sqrt{\dfrac{9}{2}} - 4\sqrt{50}$

$= \dfrac{3\sqrt{2}}{3} + \dfrac{9}{\sqrt{2}}\dfrac{\sqrt{2}}{\sqrt{2}} - 20\sqrt{2}$

$= \dfrac{6\sqrt{2}}{6} + \dfrac{27\sqrt{2}}{6} - \dfrac{120\sqrt{2}}{6} = \mathbf{-\dfrac{29\sqrt{2}}{2}}$

28. $\dfrac{-2^0}{-4^{-5/2}} = -\left[-(4^{1/2})^5\right] = \mathbf{32}$

29. (a) $4x - 3y = -3$

$\qquad\quad y = \dfrac{4}{3}x + 1$

(b) $4x + 3y = 6$

$\qquad\quad y = -\dfrac{4}{3}x + 2$

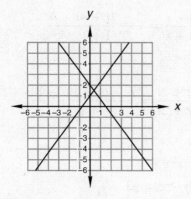

(a) $4x - 3y = -3$

(b) $\dfrac{4x + 3y = 6}{8x = 3}$

$x = \dfrac{3}{8}$

(b) $4\left(\dfrac{3}{8}\right) + 3y = 6$

$3y = \dfrac{9}{2}$

$y = \dfrac{3}{2}$

$\left(\dfrac{3}{8}, \dfrac{3}{2}\right)$

30. $\dfrac{400 \text{ cm}^3}{\text{s}} \times \dfrac{1 \text{ in.}}{2.54 \text{ cm}} \times \dfrac{1 \text{ in.}}{2.54 \text{ cm}} \times \dfrac{1 \text{ in.}}{2.54 \text{ cm}}$

$\times \dfrac{1 \text{ ft}}{12 \text{ in.}} \times \dfrac{1 \text{ ft}}{12 \text{ in.}} \times \dfrac{1 \text{ ft}}{12 \text{ in.}} \times \dfrac{60 \text{ s}}{1 \text{ min}}$

$= \dfrac{400(60)}{(2.54)(2.54)(2.54)(12)(12)(12)} \dfrac{\text{ft}^3}{\text{min}}$

PRACTICE SET 83

a. $x^m a^{3x} x^{m/5} a^{x/2} = a^{3x + x/2} x^{m + m/5} = a^{7x/2} x^{6m/5}$

b. $\dfrac{m^{a-2} p^{a+1}}{m^{a/3} p^{2a}} = m^{a-2} m^{-a/3} p^{a+1} p^{-2a}$

$= m^{a-2-a/3} p^{a+1-2a} = m^{2a/3-2} p^{1-a}$

c. $\dfrac{(m^x)^z (z)^{m+3}}{m^{-x}} = \dfrac{m^{xz} z^{m+3}}{m^{-x}} = m^{xz} m^x z^{m+3}$

$= m^{xz + x} z^{m+3}$

PROBLEM SET 83

1. Equal ratio method:

$\dfrac{R_1}{R_2} = \dfrac{C_1}{C_2}$

$\dfrac{1200}{R_2} = \dfrac{300}{100}$

$300 R_2 = 100(1200)$

$R_2 = $ **400 were resentful**

Variation method:

$R = kC$

$1200 = k(300)$

$4 = k$

$R = 4(100) = $ **400 were resentful**

2.

D_M — 420

D_T — 270

$R_M T_M = 420; \quad R_T T_T = 270;$

$T_M = 2T_T; \quad R_T = R_M + 20$

$(R_T - 20)2T_T = 420$

$2R_T T_T - 40T_T = 420$

$2(270) - 40T_T = 420$

$-40T_T = -120$

$T_T = $ **3 hr**

$T_M = $ **6 hr**; $R_T = $ **90 kph**; $R_M = $ **70 kph**

3.

D_M — 400; D_S

$R_S T_S + 400 = R_M T_M;$

$R_M = 5; \quad T_M = T_S = 400$

$R_S(400) + 400 = 5(400)$

$400 R_S = 1600$

$R_S = $ **4 yd/s**

4. (a) $4N_I = 8N_S + 80$

(a′) $N_I = 2N_S + 20$

(b) $10N_S = N_I + 140$

Substitute (a′) into (b) and get:

(b′) $10N_S = (2N_S + 20) + 140$

$8N_S = 160$

$N_S = $ **20 sedimentary rocks**

(a′) $N_I = 2(20) + 20 = $ **60 igneous rocks**

5. (a) $0.05P_N + 0.2D_N = 64$

(b) $P_N + D_N = 800$

Substitute $D_N = 800 - P_N$ into (a) and get:

(a') $0.05P_N + 0.2(800 - P_N) = 64$

$$-0.15P_N = -96$$

$$P_N = 640$$

(b) $(640) + D_N = 800$

$$D_N = 160$$

640 mL 5%, 160 mL 20%

6. (a) $x + 6y = 40$

(b) $5x + 6y = 80$

-1(a) $-x - 6y = -40$

1(b) $\underline{5x + 6y = 80}$

$$4x \quad\quad = 40$$

$$x = \mathbf{10}$$

(a) $(10) + 6y = 40$

$$6y = 30$$

$$y = \mathbf{5}$$

7. $\dfrac{a^{x-3}m^{x+2}}{a^{x/3}m^{3x}} = a^{x-3-x/3}m^{x+2-3x}$

$$= a^{2x/3-3}m^{-2x+2}$$

8. $\dfrac{(a^x)^m (b^x)^{m+3}}{a^{-m}} = a^{mx+m}b^{mx+3x}$

9. $\dfrac{a}{x + \dfrac{1}{a + \dfrac{1}{x}}} = \dfrac{a}{x + \dfrac{1}{\dfrac{ax+1}{x}}}$

$$= \dfrac{a}{x + \dfrac{x}{ax+1}} = \dfrac{a}{\dfrac{ax^2 + x + x}{ax+1}}$$

$$= \dfrac{a(ax+1)}{ax^2 + 2x}$$

10. $\dfrac{b}{a + \dfrac{b}{a + \dfrac{a}{b}}} = \dfrac{b}{a + \dfrac{b}{\dfrac{ab+a}{b}}}$

$$= \dfrac{b}{a + \dfrac{b^2}{ab+a}} = \dfrac{b}{\dfrac{a^2b + a^2 + b^2}{ab+a}}$$

$$= \dfrac{b(ab+a)}{a^2b + a^2 + b^2}$$

11. $\dfrac{2 - 4i}{1 + i} \cdot \dfrac{1 - i}{1 - i} = \dfrac{2 - 2i - 4i - 4}{1 + 1}$

$$= \mathbf{-1 - 3i}$$

12. $\dfrac{3 + 5i}{2 - 2i} \cdot \dfrac{2 + 2i}{2 + 2i} = \dfrac{6 + 6i + 10i - 10}{4 + 4}$

$$= \mathbf{-\dfrac{1}{2} + 2i}$$

13. (a) $2x + 3y - z = -3$

(b) $x + 2y = 0$

$$x = -2y$$

(c) $x - 2y + z = -2$

Substitute (b) into (a) and (c) and get:

(a') $-y - z = -3$

(c') $\underline{-4y + z = -2}$

$$-5y \quad\quad = -5$$

$$y = 1$$

(a') $-(1) - z = -3$

$$z = 2$$

(b) $x = -2(1) = -2$

(−2, 1, 2)

14. $\sqrt{k} + \sqrt{k + 32} = 8$

$$k + 32 = 64 - 16\sqrt{k} + k$$

$$16\sqrt{k} = 32$$

$$\sqrt{k} = 2$$

$$k = \mathbf{4}$$

Check: $\sqrt{4} + \sqrt{4 + 32} = 8$

$$2 + 6 = 8$$

15.

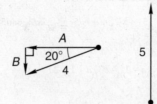

$A = 4 \cos 20° \approx 3.76$

$B = 4 \sin 20° \approx 1.37$

$$-3.76R - 1.37U$$

$$\underline{0.00R + 5.00U}$$

$$\mathbf{-3.76R + 3.63U}$$

$$\tan \theta = -\frac{3.63}{3.76}$$

$$\theta \approx 136.01°$$

$$F = \sqrt{(3.76)^2 + (3.63)^2} \approx 5.23$$

5.23/136.01°

16. $\dfrac{5}{x} + \dfrac{6}{x^2 - 4} - \dfrac{3x}{2 - x}$

$$= \frac{5(x^2 - 4)}{x(x^2 - 4)} + \frac{6x}{x(x^2 - 4)} + \frac{3x^2(x + 2)}{x(x^2 - 4)}$$

$$= \frac{5x^2 - 20 + 6x + 3x^3 + 6x^2}{x(x^2 - 4)}$$

$$= \frac{3x^3 + 11x^2 + 6x - 20}{x(x^2 - 4)}$$

17. $\dfrac{-2\sqrt{2} - 2}{4 + \sqrt{2}} \cdot \dfrac{4 - \sqrt{2}}{4 - \sqrt{2}}$

$$= \frac{-8\sqrt{2} + 4 - 8 + 2\sqrt{2}}{16 - 2} = \frac{-2 - 3\sqrt{2}}{7}$$

18. $\dfrac{-\sqrt{3} - 3}{2 - \sqrt{3}} \cdot \dfrac{2 + \sqrt{3}}{2 + \sqrt{3}}$

$$= \frac{-2\sqrt{3} - 3 - 6 - 3\sqrt{3}}{4 - 3} = -9 - 5\sqrt{3}$$

19. $$p = \frac{a}{x} - c\left(\frac{a}{m} - y\right)$$

$$p = \frac{a}{x} - \frac{ac}{m} + cy$$

$$mpx = am - acx + cmxy$$

$$am + cmxy - mpx = acx$$

$$m = \frac{acx}{a + cxy - px}$$

20. $$p = \frac{a}{x} - c\left(\frac{a}{m} - y\right)$$

$$p = \frac{a}{x} - \frac{ac}{m} + cy$$

$$mpx = am - acx + cmxy$$

$$mpx - am = cmxy - acx$$

$$\frac{mpx - am}{mxy - ax} = c$$

21. Since this is a 30°-60°-90° triangle,

$$\sqrt{3} \times \overrightarrow{SF} = 4$$

$$\overrightarrow{SF} = \frac{4}{\sqrt{3}} = \frac{4\sqrt{3}}{3}$$

$$x = 2\left(\frac{4\sqrt{3}}{3}\right) = \frac{8\sqrt{3}}{3}$$

$$y = 1\left(\frac{4\sqrt{3}}{3}\right) = \frac{4\sqrt{3}}{3}$$

22. Since this is a 45°-45°-90° triangle,

$$1 \times \overrightarrow{SF} = 4$$

$$\overrightarrow{SF} = 4$$

$$m = \sqrt{2}(4) = 4\sqrt{2}$$

$$p = 1(4) = 4$$

23. (a) $x - \dfrac{2}{5}y = 11$

(b) $-0.05x - 0.2y = 1.65$

(a′) $5x - 2y = 55$

(b′) $-5x - 20y = 165$

Solve the equations by elimination:

(a′) $5x - 2y = 55$
(b′) $\underline{-5x - 20y = 165}$
$$-22y = 220$$
$$y = -10$$

(a′) $5x - 2(-10) = 55$
$$5x = 35$$
$$x = 7$$

(7, −10)

24. $$2x^2 - 5x = 5$$

$$\left(x^2 - \frac{5}{2}x + \right) = \frac{5}{2}$$

$$x^2 - \frac{5}{2}x + \frac{25}{16} = \frac{5}{2} + \frac{25}{16}$$

$$\left(x - \frac{5}{4}\right)^2 = \frac{65}{16}$$

$$x - \frac{5}{4} = \pm\frac{\sqrt{65}}{4}$$

$$x = \frac{5}{4} \pm \frac{\sqrt{65}}{4}$$

25. $\sqrt{\dfrac{7}{4}} + 2\sqrt{\dfrac{4}{7}} - 5\sqrt{63}$

$= \dfrac{\sqrt{7}}{2} + \dfrac{4}{\sqrt{7}}\dfrac{\sqrt{7}}{\sqrt{7}} - 15\sqrt{7}$

$= \dfrac{7\sqrt{7}}{14} + \dfrac{8\sqrt{7}}{14} - \dfrac{210\sqrt{7}}{14} = -\dfrac{\mathbf{195}\sqrt{7}}{\mathbf{14}}$

26. $\dfrac{-2^0\,(-3^0)}{-27^{-2/3}} = -\left\{-\left[-(27^{1/3})^2\right]\right\} = \mathbf{-9}$

27. $\left(\sqrt[3]{x^2 y}\right)^4 = \left[(x^2 y)^{1/3}\right]^4 = (x^{2/3} y^{1/3})^4 = \mathbf{x^{8/3} y^{4/3}}$

28. $\dfrac{4 \text{ liters}}{\text{s}} \times \dfrac{1000 \text{ cm}^3}{\text{liter}} \times \dfrac{60 \text{ s}}{\text{min}} \times \dfrac{60 \text{ min}}{1 \text{ hr}}$

$= \mathbf{4(1000)(60)(60)\ \dfrac{cm^3}{hr}}$

29.

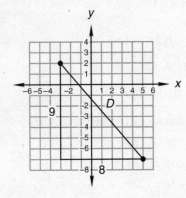

$D^2 = 9^2 + 8^2$

$D^2 = 145$

$D = \mathbf{\sqrt{145}}$

30. Graph the line to find the slope.

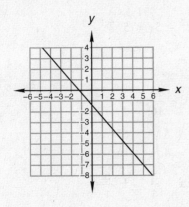

$m = \dfrac{2 - (-7)}{-3 - 5} = -\dfrac{9}{8}$

Use the point (–3, 2) for x and y.

$$y = -\dfrac{9}{8}x + b$$

$$2 = -\dfrac{9}{8}(-3) + b$$

$$-\dfrac{27}{8} + \dfrac{16}{8} = b$$

$$-\dfrac{11}{8} = b$$

$$y = -\dfrac{\mathbf{9}}{\mathbf{8}}x - \dfrac{\mathbf{11}}{\mathbf{8}}$$

PRACTICE SET 84

(b′) $6x - 2y = -5$
2(a) $\underline{6x - 2y = -4}$
$ 0 = -9$ False

Inconsistent and **independent**

PROBLEM SET 84

1. Equal ratio method:

$\dfrac{A_1}{A_2} = \dfrac{B_2}{B_1}$

$\dfrac{20}{A_2} = \dfrac{10}{80}$

$10A_2 = 1600$

$A_2 = \mathbf{160 \text{ were admired}}$

Variation method:

$A = \dfrac{k}{B}$

$20 = \dfrac{k}{80}$

$1600 = k$

$A = \dfrac{1600}{10}$

$A = \mathbf{160 \text{ were admired}}$

2. $50 + 273 = 323$ kelvins

$\dfrac{P_1}{T_1} = \dfrac{P_2}{T_2}$

$\dfrac{4}{323} = \dfrac{8}{T_2}$

$4T_2 = 2584$

$T_2 = 646$ kelvins

$646 - 273 = \mathbf{373°C}$

3. Lithium: $2 \times 7 = 14$

Calcium: $2 \times 40 = 80$

Oxygen: $7 \times 16 = 112$

Total: $14 + 80 + 112 = 206$

$$\frac{14}{206} = \frac{56}{Li_2Ca_2O_7}$$

$14 Li_2Ca_2O_7 = 206(56)$

$Li_2Ca_2O_7 = $ **824 grams**

Lithium: $\frac{14}{206} \cdot 100\% \approx $ **6.80%**

4. $0.1(160) + 0.3P_N = 0.22(160 + P_N)$

$16 + 0.3P_N = 35.2 + 0.22P_N$

$0.08P_N = 19.2$

$P_N = $ **240 mL**

5. $\frac{250}{100} \cdot 140,000 = B_T$

350,000 tons $= B_T$

6. $y^b x^{c+2} y^{b/3} x^{-2-p} = x^{c+2} x^{-2-p} y^b y^{b/3} = x^{c-p} y^{4b/3}$

7. $\frac{y^b x^{c+3}}{y^{b/3} x^{2-p}} = x^{c+3} x^{-2+p} y^b y^{-b/3} = x^{c+p+1} y^{2b/3}$

8. $(x^{a+3})^b x^{-2b+4} = x^{ab+3b} x^{-2b+4} = x^{b+ab+4}$

9. $\frac{(y^a)^{b+2} y^{-ab}}{y^{-2+a}} = y^{ab+2a} y^{-ab} y^{2-a} = y^{a+2}$

10. $\frac{p}{a + \dfrac{m}{1 + \dfrac{1}{am}}} = \frac{p}{a + \dfrac{am^2}{am + 1}}$

$= \frac{p(am + 1)}{a^2 m + a + am^2}$

11. $\frac{1}{p - \dfrac{b}{b - \dfrac{1}{x}}} = \frac{1}{p - \dfrac{bx}{bx - 1}}$

$= \frac{bx - 1}{bpx - p - bx}$

12. $\frac{2 - 3i}{1 + i} \cdot \frac{1 - i}{1 - i} = \frac{2 - 3i - 2i - 3}{1 + 1}$

$= \frac{-1 - 5i}{2} = -\frac{1}{2} - \frac{5}{2}i$

13. $\frac{3 + 4i}{3 - 3i} \cdot \frac{3 + 3i}{3 + 3i} = \frac{9 + 12i + 9i - 12}{9 + 9}$

$= \frac{-3 + 21i}{18} = -\frac{1}{6} + \frac{7}{6}i$

14. $\sqrt{s - 48} + \sqrt{s} = 8$

$s - 48 = 64 - 16\sqrt{s} + s$

$16\sqrt{s} = 112$

$\sqrt{s} = 7$

$s = $ **49**

Check: $\sqrt{49 - 48} + \sqrt{49} = 8$

$1 + 7 = 8$

15. (a) $3x - y - 2z = -6$

(b) $2x - y + z = 2$

(c) $-y + z = 0$

$z = y$

Substitute (c) into (a) and (b) and get:

(a′) $3x - 3y = -6$

(b′) $2x = 2$

$x = 1$

(a′) $3(1) - 3y = -6$

$-3y = -9$

$y = 3$

(b) $2(1) - (3) + z = 2$

$-1 + z = 2$

$z = 3$

(1, 3, 3)

16.

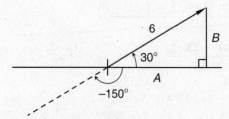

$A = 6 \cos 30° \approx 5.20$

$B = 6 \sin 30° = 3$

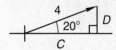

$C = 4 \cos 20° \approx 3.76$

$D = 4 \sin 20° \approx 1.37$

$5.20R + 3.00U$

$3.76R + 1.37U$

$\overline{}$

$8.96R + 4.37U$

17.

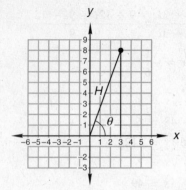

$H = \sqrt{8^2 + 3^2}$

$H = \sqrt{73}$

$\tan \theta = \dfrac{8}{3}$

$\theta \approx 69.44°$

$\sqrt{73} \underline{/69.44°}$

18. $\dfrac{4}{x^2} - \dfrac{2}{-x(x-3)} + \dfrac{5x}{3-x}$

$= \dfrac{4(x-3)}{x^2(x-3)} + \dfrac{2x}{x^2(x-3)} - \dfrac{5x^3}{x^2(x-3)}$

$= \dfrac{4x - 12 + 2x - 5x^3}{x^2(x-3)}$

$= \dfrac{-5x^3 + 6x - 12}{x^2(x-3)}$

19. $\dfrac{4\sqrt{2} - 5}{3\sqrt{2} + 2} \cdot \dfrac{3\sqrt{2} - 2}{3\sqrt{2} - 2}$

$= \dfrac{24 - 15\sqrt{2} - 8\sqrt{2} + 10}{18 - 4}$

$= \dfrac{34 - 23\sqrt{2}}{14}$

20. $(2 + 3\sqrt{20})(4 - 5\sqrt{45})$

$= (2 + 6\sqrt{5})(4 - 15\sqrt{5})$

$= 8 + 24\sqrt{5} - 30\sqrt{5} - 450 = \mathbf{-442 - 6\sqrt{5}}$

21. $\dfrac{m}{c} + x = p\left(\dfrac{1}{x} + \dfrac{b}{y}\right)$

$\dfrac{m}{c} + x = \dfrac{p}{x} + \dfrac{pb}{y}$

$mxy + x^2cy = cpy + cbpx$

$mxy = cpy + cbpx - x^2cy$

$\dfrac{mxy}{py + bpx - x^2y} = c$

22. $\sqrt{-3}\sqrt{3} - \sqrt{2}\sqrt{2} - \sqrt{-4} + 3i^2 - 2i^5$

$= 3i - 2 - 2i - 3 - 2i = \mathbf{-5 - i}$

23. $-2x^2 - x = 3$

$-2x^2 - x - 3 = 0$

$x = \dfrac{1 \pm \sqrt{1 - 4(-3)(-2)}}{2(-2)} = \dfrac{1 \pm \sqrt{-23}}{-4}$

$= -\dfrac{1}{4} \pm \dfrac{\sqrt{23}}{4}i$

24. $A_{\text{Square}} = s^2 = 36 \text{ m}^2$

$s = \mathbf{6\,m}$

$r_{\text{Circle}} = \dfrac{s}{2} = \mathbf{3\,m}$

$A_{\text{Circle}} = \pi r^2 = \pi(3 \text{ m})^2 = \mathbf{9\pi\,m^2}$

25. There is never an exact solution for these problems. One possible solution is given here.

$Y = mB + b$

Use the graph to find the slope.

$m = \dfrac{-300}{6} = -50$

$Y = -50B + b$

Use the point (99, 100) for B and Y.

$100 = -50(99) + b$

$100 = -4950 + b$

$5050 = b$

$\mathbf{Y = -50B + 5050}$

26. (a) $\dfrac{-2.065 \times 10^4}{-500 \times 10^6} \approx \dfrac{-2 \times 10^4}{-5 \times 10^8} = 4 \times 10^{-5}$

Calculator answer $\approx \mathbf{4.13 \times 10^{-5}}$

(b) $(84.9)^{-4.91}$

Answer should be between 3×10^{-10} and 4×10^{-10}.

Calculator answer $\approx \mathbf{3.38 \times 10^{-10}}$

27. $3\sqrt{\dfrac{5}{3}} + 2\sqrt{\dfrac{3}{5}} - 4\sqrt{60}$

$= \dfrac{3\sqrt{5}}{\sqrt{3}} \dfrac{\sqrt{3}}{\sqrt{3}} + \dfrac{2\sqrt{3}}{\sqrt{5}} \dfrac{\sqrt{5}}{\sqrt{5}} - 8\sqrt{15}$

$= \sqrt{15} + \dfrac{2\sqrt{15}}{5} - 8\sqrt{15}$

$= \dfrac{5\sqrt{15}}{5} + \dfrac{2\sqrt{15}}{5} - \dfrac{40\sqrt{15}}{5} = \mathbf{-\dfrac{33\sqrt{15}}{5}}$

28. $\dfrac{40 \text{ cm}}{\text{s}} \times \dfrac{60 \text{ s}}{1 \text{ min}} \times \dfrac{60 \text{ min}}{1 \text{ hr}} \times \dfrac{1 \text{ in.}}{2.54 \text{ cm}}$

$\times \dfrac{1 \text{ ft}}{12 \text{ in.}} \times \dfrac{1 \text{ mi}}{5280 \text{ ft}} = \dfrac{40(60)(60)}{(2.54)(12)(5280)} \dfrac{\text{mi}}{\text{hr}}$

29. $7 - 2(2x + 2)$

$= -2^0\left[-2 - 3(x - 2^2)\right] - 3(2x - 5^0)$

$7 - 4x - 4 = -[-2 - 3x + 12] - 6x + 3$

$-4x + 3 = 3x - 10 - 6x + 3$

$x = \mathbf{10}$

30. $-3\left\{\left[(-2 - 3) - 2\right] - 2\left[-4(-3 - 2^0)\right]\right\}$
$+ 2^0(-3)$

$= -3\left\{[-5 - 2] - 2[16]\right\} - 3$

$= -3(-7 - 32) - 3 = \mathbf{114}$

Practice Set 85

a. (a) $BT_D + 9T_D = 36$

(b) $\dfrac{BT_D - 9T_D = 18}{2BT_D \quad\quad\ = 54}$

(c) $\quad BT_D = 27$

(a) $(27) + 9T_D = 36$

$9T_D = 9$

$T_D = \mathbf{1}$

(b) $B(1) = 27$

$B = \mathbf{27}$

b. $x^2 + y^2 = 25 \quad$ (a)

$2x - y = 5 \quad\quad$ (b)

(b) $y = 2x - 5$

(b') $y^2 = 4x^2 - 20x + 25$

Substitute (b') into (a) to get:

(a) $x^2 + (4x^2 - 20x + 25) = 25$

$5x^2 - 20x + 25 - 25 = 0$

$x(5x - 20) = 0$

$x = 0, 4$

(b) $2(0) - y = 5 \quad\quad 2(4) - y = 5$

$y = -5 \quad\quad\quad\quad y = 3$

There are 2 solutions: **(0, –5)** and **(4, 3)**

Problem Set 85

1. Equal ratio method:

$\dfrac{I_1}{I_2} = \dfrac{T_1}{T_2}$

$\dfrac{800}{I_2} = \dfrac{2400}{9}$

$I_2 = \mathbf{3}$ **were improvident**

Variation method:

$I = kT$

$800 = k(2400)$

$\dfrac{1}{3} = k$

$N_I = \dfrac{1}{3}(9)$

$N_I = \mathbf{3}$ **were improvident**

2.

$\xrightarrow{\hspace{3cm}} D_P$

640

$\xrightarrow{\hspace{1.5cm}} D_B$

280

$R_P T_P = 640; \quad R_B T_B = 280;$

$T_P = 2T_B; \quad R_P = R_B + 20$

$(R_B + 20)2T_B = 640$

$2R_B T_B + 40T_B = 640$

$2(280) + 40T_B = 640$

$40T_B = 80$

$T_B = \mathbf{2 \ hr}$

$T_P = \mathbf{4 \ hr}; \quad R_P = \mathbf{160 \ mph}; \quad R_B = \mathbf{140 \ mph}$

3. (a) $5N_H = N_D + 90$

(b) $3N_D = N_H + 10$

(b') $N_H = 3N_D - 10$

Substitute (b') into (a) and get:

(a') $5(3N_D - 10) = N_D + 90$

$15N_D - 50 = N_D + 90$

$14N_D = 140$

$N_D = \mathbf{10 \ were \ demure}$

(b') $N_H = 3(10) - 10 = \mathbf{20 \ were \ hoydens}$

4. (a) $0.1P_N + 0.5D_N = 136$

(b) $P_N + D_N = 400$

Substitute $D_N = 400 - P_N$ into (a) and get:

(a′) $0.1P_N + 0.5(400 - P_N) = 136$

$$-0.4P_N = -64$$

$$P_N = 160$$

(b) $(160) + D_N = 400$

$$D_N = 240$$

160 ft³ 10%, 240 ft³ 50%

5. Odd integers: $N, N + 2, N + 4$

$$N(N + 4) = 10(-N - 2) - 25$$

$$N^2 + 4N = -10N - 20 - 25$$

$$N^2 + 14N + 45 = 0$$

$$(N + 5)(N + 9) = 0$$

$$N = -5, -9$$

The desired integers are **–9, –7, –5 and –5, –3, –1.**

6. (a) $BT_D + 6T_D = 24$

(b) $\dfrac{BT_D - 6T_D = 12}{2BT_D \qquad = 36}$

$$BT_D = 18$$

(a) $(18) + 6T_D = 24$

$$T_D = \mathbf{1}$$

(b) $B(1) - 6(1) = 12$

$$B = \mathbf{18}$$

7. (a) $x^2 + y^2 = 16$

(b) $2x - y = 4$

$$y = 2x - 4$$

(b′) $y^2 = 4x^2 - 16x + 16$

Substitute (b′) into (a) and get:

(a′) $x^2 + (4x^2 - 16x + 16) = 16$

$$5x^2 - 16x + 16 = 16$$

$$5x^2 - 16x = 0$$

$$x(5x - 16) = 0$$

$$x = 0 \text{ and } x = \frac{16}{5}$$

Substitute these values of x into (b) and solve for y.

(b) $y = 2(0) - 4$

$$y = -4$$

(b) $y = 2\left(\dfrac{16}{5}\right) - 4$

$$y = \frac{12}{5}$$

$\mathbf{(0, -4)}$ and $\left(\dfrac{\mathbf{16}}{\mathbf{5}}, \dfrac{\mathbf{12}}{\mathbf{5}}\right)$

8. $\dfrac{a^x (b^{y-2})^x}{a^{2x}(b^{-2})^x} = \dfrac{a^x b^{xy-2x}}{a^{2x} b^{-2x}}$

$$= a^{x - 2x} b^{xy - 2x + 2x} = \boldsymbol{a^{-x} b^{xy}}$$

9. $\dfrac{a^x b^{x/3} b^{-2}}{a^{x/2}} = a^{x - x/2} b^{x/3 - 2} = \boldsymbol{a^{x/2} b^{x/3 - 2}}$

10. $\dfrac{x}{a + \dfrac{b}{c + \dfrac{x}{m}}} = \dfrac{x}{a + \dfrac{bm}{cm + x}}$

$$= \frac{\boldsymbol{x(cm + x)}}{\boldsymbol{acm + ax + bm}}$$

11. $\dfrac{a}{2 + \dfrac{c}{c + \dfrac{b}{c}}} = \dfrac{a}{2 + \dfrac{c^2}{c^2 + b}}$

$$= \frac{a(c^2 + b)}{2c^2 + 2b + c^2} = \frac{\boldsymbol{a(c^2 + b)}}{\boldsymbol{3c^2 + 2b}}$$

12. $\dfrac{2 - 2i}{3 - 5i} \cdot \dfrac{3 + 5i}{3 + 5i} = \dfrac{6 - 6i + 10i + 10}{9 + 25}$

$$= \frac{16 + 4i}{34} = \frac{\mathbf{8}}{\mathbf{17}} + \frac{\mathbf{2}}{\mathbf{17}}i$$

13. $\dfrac{4 - \sqrt{2}i}{3 + \sqrt{2}i} \cdot \dfrac{3 - \sqrt{2}i}{3 - \sqrt{2}i}$

$$= \frac{12 - 3\sqrt{2}i - 4\sqrt{2}i - 2}{9 + 2} = \frac{\mathbf{10}}{\mathbf{11}} - \frac{\mathbf{7\sqrt{2}}}{\mathbf{11}}i$$

14. $\sqrt{k - 32} + \sqrt{k} = 8$

$$k - 32 = 64 - 16\sqrt{k} + k$$

$$16\sqrt{k} = 96$$

$$\sqrt{k} = 6$$

$$k = \mathbf{36}$$

Check: $\sqrt{36 - 32} + \sqrt{36} = 8$

$$2 + 6 = 8$$

15. (a) $x + 2y + 2z = 6$

(b) $2x - y + 3z = 6$

(c) $y - z = 0$

$\quad\quad y = z$

Substitute (c) into (a) and (b) and get:

(a′) $x + 4z = 6$

(b′) $2x + 2z = 6$

$$\begin{array}{rrr} \text{(a′)} & x + 4z = & 6 \\ -2\text{(b′)} & -4x - 4z = & -12 \\ \hline & -3x = & -6 \\ & x = & 2 \end{array}$$

(a′) $(2) + 4z = 6$

$\quad\quad\quad 4z = 4$

$\quad\quad\quad\ z = 1$

(c) $y = 1$

(2, 1, 1)

16.

$B = 4 \cos 32° \approx 3.39$

$C = 4 \sin 32° \approx 2.12$

$$\begin{array}{r} 0.00R + 6.00U \\ 3.39R - 2.12U \\ \hline \mathbf{3.39R + 3.88U} \end{array}$$

$\tan \theta = \dfrac{3.88}{3.39}$

$\quad \theta \approx 48.86°$

$F = \sqrt{(3.39)^2 + (3.88)^2} \approx 5.15$

5.15 $\underline{/48.86°}$

17. $\dfrac{2x + 3}{x - a} - \dfrac{4}{a - x} = \dfrac{2x + 3 + 4}{x - a}$

$= \dfrac{\mathbf{2x + 7}}{\mathbf{x - a}}$

18. $\dfrac{3 - 2\sqrt{2}}{5 - \sqrt{2}} \cdot \dfrac{5 + \sqrt{2}}{5 + \sqrt{2}}$

$= \dfrac{15 - 10\sqrt{2} + 3\sqrt{2} - 4}{25 - 2} = \dfrac{\mathbf{11 - 7\sqrt{2}}}{\mathbf{23}}$

19. $\dfrac{4 + \sqrt{3}}{2 - 2\sqrt{3}} \cdot \dfrac{2 + 2\sqrt{3}}{2 + 2\sqrt{3}}$

$= \dfrac{8 + 2\sqrt{3} + 8\sqrt{3} + 6}{4 - 12} = \dfrac{14 + 10\sqrt{3}}{-8}$

$= \dfrac{\mathbf{-7 - 5\sqrt{3}}}{\mathbf{4}}$

20. $c = m\left(\dfrac{d}{c} - p\right)$

$c = \dfrac{dm}{c} - mp$

$c^2 = dm - cmp$

$cmp = dm - c^2$

$p = \dfrac{\mathbf{dm - c^2}}{\mathbf{cm}}$

21. $-\sqrt{-2}\sqrt{2} - 3i^3 + 2i + \sqrt{-2}\sqrt{-2} - \sqrt{-9}$

$= -2i + 3i + 2i - 2 - 3i = \mathbf{-2}$

22. (a) $70 = \dfrac{120 + x}{2}$

$\quad 140 = 120 + x$

$\quad\ \ \mathbf{20} = x$

(b) $360 - 120 = 240$

$x = \dfrac{240 - 120}{2} = \mathbf{60}$

23. (a) $\dfrac{1}{9}x + \dfrac{1}{3}y = 3$

(b) $0.3x - 0.04y = 2.46$

(a′) $x + 3y = 27$

(b′) $30x - 4y = 246$

$$\begin{array}{rrr} 30\text{(a′)} & 30x + 90y = & 810 \\ -1\text{(b′)} & -30x + 4y = & -246 \\ \hline & 94y = & 564 \\ & y = & 6 \end{array}$$

(a′) $x + 3(6) = 27$

$\quad\quad\quad\quad x = 9$

(9, 6)

24. See Lesson 71.

25. There is never an exact solution to these problems. One possible solution is given here.

$Na = mMg + b$

Use the graph to find the slope.

$m = \dfrac{-10}{2} = -5$

$Na = -5Mg + b$

Use the point (54, 82) for Mg and Na.

$82 = -5(54) + b$

$352 = b$

$Na = -5Mg + 352$

26. (a) $x - 4y = -8$

$y = \dfrac{1}{4}x + 2$

(b) $3x + y = 6$

$y = -3x + 6$

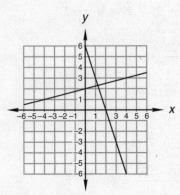

Substitute $y = -3x + 6$ into (a) and get:

(a′) $x - 4(-3x + 6) = -8$

$x + 12x - 24 = -8$

$13x = 16$

$x = \dfrac{16}{13}$

(b) $y = -3\left(\dfrac{16}{13}\right) + 6$

$y = \dfrac{30}{13}$

$\left(\dfrac{16}{13}, \dfrac{30}{13}\right)$

27. $\dfrac{x}{r} = \dfrac{t}{s}$

$x = \dfrac{rt}{s}$

28. $\dfrac{100 \text{ ft}^3}{s} \times \dfrac{60 \text{ s}}{1 \text{ min}} \times \dfrac{12 \text{ in.}}{1 \text{ ft}} \times \dfrac{12 \text{ in.}}{1 \text{ ft}} \times \dfrac{12 \text{ in.}}{1 \text{ ft}}$

$\times \dfrac{2.54 \text{ cm}}{1 \text{ in.}} \times \dfrac{2.54 \text{ cm}}{1 \text{ in.}} \times \dfrac{2.54 \text{ cm}}{1 \text{ in.}}$

$= \mathbf{100(60)(12)(12)(12)(2.54)(2.54)(2.54)\dfrac{cm^3}{min}}$

29. $3\sqrt{\dfrac{5}{12}} + 3\sqrt{\dfrac{12}{5}} + 3\sqrt{240}$

$= \dfrac{3\sqrt{5}}{2\sqrt{3}}\dfrac{\sqrt{3}}{\sqrt{3}} + \dfrac{6\sqrt{3}}{\sqrt{5}}\dfrac{\sqrt{5}}{\sqrt{5}} + 12\sqrt{15}$

$= \dfrac{5\sqrt{15}}{10} + \dfrac{12\sqrt{15}}{10} + \dfrac{120\sqrt{15}}{10} = \mathbf{\dfrac{137\sqrt{15}}{10}}$

30. $\dfrac{-2^0}{-4^{-5/2}} = 4^{5/2} = (4^{1/2})^5 = \mathbf{32}$

PRACTICE SET 86

a. $-x \not\leq 4; \ D = \{\text{Integers}\}$

$-x > 4; \ D = \{\text{Integers}\}$

$x < -4; \ D = \{\text{Integers}\}$

```
◄─────●──●──●──●──┼──►
     -8 -7 -6 -5 -4
```

b. $\begin{cases} x^2 + y^2 = 11 & \text{(a)} \\ y - x = 1 & \text{(b)} \end{cases}$

(b) $y = x + 1$

(b′) $y^2 = x^2 + 2x + 1$

Substitute (b′) into (a) to get:

(a) $x^2 + (x^2 + 2x + 1) = 11$

$2x^2 + 2x - 10 = 0$

$x = \dfrac{-(2) \pm \sqrt{(2)^2 - 4(2)(-10)}}{2(2)}$

$= \dfrac{-2 \pm \sqrt{84}}{4} = -\dfrac{1}{2} \pm \dfrac{\sqrt{21}}{2}$

(b) $y = x + 1$

$$y = \left(-\frac{1}{2} + \frac{\sqrt{21}}{2}\right) + 1$$

$$y = \frac{1}{2} + \frac{\sqrt{21}}{2}$$

$$y = x + 1$$

$$y = \left(-\frac{1}{2} - \frac{\sqrt{21}}{2}\right) + 1$$

$$y = \frac{1}{2} - \frac{\sqrt{21}}{2}$$

$$\left(-\frac{1}{2} + \frac{\sqrt{21}}{2}, \frac{1}{2} + \frac{\sqrt{21}}{2}\right) \text{and}$$

$$\left(-\frac{1}{2} - \frac{\sqrt{21}}{2}, \frac{1}{2} - \frac{\sqrt{21}}{2}\right)$$

PROBLEM SET 86

1. $\dfrac{V_1}{T_1} = \dfrac{V_2}{T_2}$

$$\frac{400}{1273} = \frac{V_2}{2273}$$

$$V_2 = \frac{400(2273)}{1273} \approx \textbf{714.22 liters}$$

2.

$$R_R T_R = R_P T_P; \quad R_R = 20;$$

$$R_P = 2; \quad T_R + T_P = 11$$

$$(20)T_R = 2(11 - T_R)$$

$$20T_R = 22 - 2T_R$$

$$22T_R = 22$$

$$T_R = 1$$

$$D_R = R_R T_R = 20(1) = 20 \text{ miles}$$

Since D_R is only halfway to the swamp, the total distance to the swamp is $2D_R$ or **40 miles.**

3. $0.5(100) + 0.2(D_N) = 0.23(100 + D_N)$

$$50 + 0.2D_N = 23 + 0.23D_N$$

$$27 = 0.03D_N$$

$$\textbf{900 liters} = D_N$$

4.

Hydrogen:	2×1	$= 2$
Carbon:	1×12	$= 12$
Oxygen:	3×16	$= 48$
Total:	$2 + 12 + 48$	$= 62$

$$\frac{12}{62} = \frac{C}{372}$$

$$62C = 12(372)$$

$$C = \textbf{72 grams}$$

5. $RN = 0.14 \cdot 120{,}000$

$$RN = \textbf{16,800 ducks}$$

6. $A_{\text{Circle}} = \pi r^2 = 25\pi \text{ m}^2$

$$r^2 = 25 \text{ m}^2$$

$$r = \textbf{5 m}$$

Length of diagonal $= 2r = 2(5 \text{ m}) = \textbf{10 m}$

Length of side $= \dfrac{10 \text{ m}}{\sqrt{2}} \cdot \dfrac{\sqrt{2}}{\sqrt{2}} = \mathbf{5\sqrt{2} \text{ m}}$

Area of square $= s^2 = (5\sqrt{2} \text{ m})^2 = \textbf{50 m}^2$

7. $x \nleq -2; \quad D = \{\text{Negative integers}\}$

$$x > -2$$

8. $-x + 3 \ngtr 2; \quad D = \{\text{Reals}\}$

$$-x + 3 \leq 2$$

$$-x \leq -1$$

$$x \geq 1$$

9. $-x - 6 \ngeq -3; \quad D = \{\text{Negative integers}\}$

$$-x - 6 < -3$$

$$-x < 3$$

$$x > -3$$

10. (a) $BT_D + 3T_D = 60$

(b) $\dfrac{BT_D - 3T_D = 36}{2BT_D = 96}$

(c) $\qquad BT_D = 48$

(a) $(48) + 3T_D = 60$

$$3T_D = 12$$

$$T_D = \textbf{4}$$

(c) $B(4) = 48$

$$B = \textbf{12}$$

11. (a) $x^2 + y^2 = 4$

(b) $y - x = 1$

$y = x + 1$

(b′) $y^2 = (x + 1)^2 = x^2 + 2x + 1$

Substitute (b′) into (a) and get:

(a′) $x^2 + (x^2 + 2x + 1) = 4$

$2x^2 + 2x - 3 = 0$

Solve this equation by using the quadratic formula.

$x = \dfrac{-2 \pm \sqrt{2^2 - 4(2)(-3)}}{2(2)} = -\dfrac{1}{2} \pm \dfrac{\sqrt{7}}{2}$

Substitute these values of x into (b) and solve for y.

(b) $y = \left(-\dfrac{1}{2} + \dfrac{\sqrt{7}}{2}\right) + 1$

$y = \dfrac{1}{2} + \dfrac{\sqrt{7}}{2}$

(b) $y = \left(-\dfrac{1}{2} - \dfrac{\sqrt{7}}{2}\right) + 1$

$y = \dfrac{1}{2} - \dfrac{\sqrt{7}}{2}$

$\left(-\dfrac{1}{2} + \dfrac{\sqrt{7}}{2}, \dfrac{1}{2} + \dfrac{\sqrt{7}}{2}\right)$ and

$\left(-\dfrac{1}{2} - \dfrac{\sqrt{7}}{2}, \dfrac{1}{2} - \dfrac{\sqrt{7}}{2}\right)$

12. $\dfrac{x^{2a}(y^b)^{2a} x^{a/3}}{y^{ba/3}} = \dfrac{x^{2a} y^{2ab} x^{a/3}}{y^{ab/3}} = x^{7a/3} y^{5ab/3}$

13. $\dfrac{(x^{a+2})^2}{x^{2-a}} = \dfrac{x^{2a+4}}{x^{2-a}} = x^{3a+2}$

14. $\dfrac{1}{x + \dfrac{a}{x + \dfrac{1}{a}}} = \dfrac{1}{x + \dfrac{a^2}{ax + 1}} = \dfrac{1}{\dfrac{ax^2 + x + a^2}{ax + 1}}$

$= \dfrac{ax + 1}{ax^2 + x + a^2}$

15. $\dfrac{2 - 3i}{-5 + i} \cdot \dfrac{-5 - i}{-5 - i} = \dfrac{-10 - 2i + 15i - 3}{25 + 1}$

$= \dfrac{-13 + 13i}{26} = -\dfrac{1}{2} + \dfrac{1}{2}i$

16. $\dfrac{3 + 2i}{5 - i} \cdot \dfrac{5 + i}{5 + i} = \dfrac{15 + 3i + 10i - 2}{25 + 1}$

$= \dfrac{13 + 13i}{26} = \dfrac{1}{2} + \dfrac{1}{2}i$

17. $\dfrac{2 + 1 + 6 + 13 + N}{5} = 9$

$N + 22 = 45$

$N = \mathbf{23}$

18. $\sqrt{p + 48} = 8 - \sqrt{p}$

$p + 48 = 64 - 16\sqrt{p} + p$

$16\sqrt{p} = 16$

$\sqrt{p} = 1$

$p = \mathbf{1}$

Check: $\sqrt{1 + 48} = 8 - \sqrt{1}$

$7 = 8 - 1$

19. (a) $x + 2y - z = 0$

(b) $3x + y - 2z = 3$

(c) $2x - z = 0$

$z = 2x$

Substitute (c) into (a) and (b) and get:

(a′) $-x + 2y = 0$

(b′) $-x + y = 3$

$\begin{array}{r} \text{(a′)} \quad -x + 2y = 0 \\ -1\text{(b′)} \quad \underline{x - y = -3} \\ y = -3 \end{array}$

(a′) $-x + 2(-3) = 0$

$x = -6$

(c) $z = 2(-6) = -12$

$\mathbf{(-6, -3, -12)}$

20.

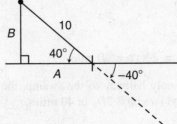

$A = 10 \cos 40° \approx 7.66$

$B = 10 \sin 40° \approx 6.43$

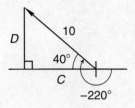

$C = 10 \cos 40° \approx 7.66$

$D = 10 \sin 40° \approx 6.43$

$$\begin{array}{r} -7.66R + 6.43U \\ -7.66R + 6.43U \\ \hline \mathbf{-15.32R + 12.86U} \end{array}$$

21.

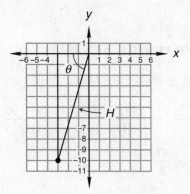

$H = \sqrt{10^2 + 3^2} = \sqrt{109}$

$\tan \theta = \dfrac{10}{3}$

$\theta \approx 73.30°$

Since θ is a third-quadrant angle,

$\theta = 73.30 + 180 = 253.30°$

$\mathbf{\sqrt{109}\ /253.30°}$

22. $\dfrac{-3 - 2\sqrt{3}}{1 - 3\sqrt{3}} \cdot \dfrac{1 + 3\sqrt{3}}{1 + 3\sqrt{3}}$

$= \dfrac{-3 - 9\sqrt{3} - 2\sqrt{3} - 18}{1 - 27} = \dfrac{-21 - 11\sqrt{3}}{-26}$

$= \dfrac{\mathbf{21 + 11\sqrt{3}}}{\mathbf{26}}$

23. $\dfrac{x + 2}{y} - c = m\left(\dfrac{a}{b} + x\right)$

$\dfrac{x + 2}{y} - c = \dfrac{am}{b} + mx$

$bx + 2b - bcy = amy + bmxy$

$bx + 2b - bcy - bmxy = amy$

$\dfrac{\mathbf{amy}}{\mathbf{x + 2 - cy - mxy}} = \mathbf{b}$

24. $-\sqrt{-16} - \sqrt{3}\sqrt{-3} + \sqrt{-3}\sqrt{-3} = -4i - 3i - 3$

$= \mathbf{-3 - 7i}$

25. $5\sqrt{\dfrac{2}{7}} + 3\sqrt{\dfrac{7}{2}} - 2\sqrt{56}$

$= \dfrac{5\sqrt{2}}{\sqrt{7}}\dfrac{\sqrt{7}}{\sqrt{7}} + \dfrac{3\sqrt{7}}{\sqrt{2}}\dfrac{\sqrt{2}}{\sqrt{2}} - 4\sqrt{14}$

$= \dfrac{10\sqrt{14}}{14} + \dfrac{21\sqrt{14}}{14} - \dfrac{56\sqrt{14}}{14} = -\dfrac{\mathbf{25\sqrt{14}}}{\mathbf{14}}$

26. $-3x^2 - 1 = 6x$

$x^2 + 2x + \dfrac{1}{3} = 0$

$(x^2 + 2x + \quad) = -\dfrac{1}{3}$

$x^2 + 2x + 1 = -\dfrac{1}{3} + 1$

$(x + 1)^2 = \dfrac{2}{3}$

$x + 1 = \pm\dfrac{\sqrt{6}}{3}$

$x = \mathbf{-1 \pm \dfrac{\sqrt{6}}{3}}$

27. $\dfrac{40 \text{ in.}^2}{\text{min}} \times \dfrac{1 \text{ ft}}{12 \text{ in.}} \times \dfrac{1 \text{ ft}}{12 \text{ in.}} \times \dfrac{1 \text{ yd}}{3 \text{ ft}} \times \dfrac{1 \text{ yd}}{3 \text{ ft}}$

$\times \dfrac{60 \text{ min}}{1 \text{ hr}} = \dfrac{\mathbf{40(60)}}{\mathbf{(12)(12)(3)(3)}} \dfrac{\mathbf{yd^2}}{\mathbf{hr}}$

28. $-2x^2 - 1 = 6x$

$2x^2 + 6x + 1 = 0$

$x = \dfrac{-6 \pm \sqrt{6^2 - 4(2)(1)}}{2(2)} = \mathbf{-\dfrac{3}{2} \pm \dfrac{\sqrt{7}}{2}}$

29. (a) $2x - 5y = -15$

$$y = \frac{2}{5}x + 3$$

(b) $3x + 4y = -4$

$$y = -\frac{3}{4}x - 1$$

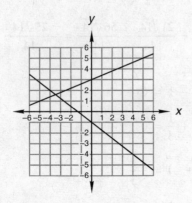

Solve the equations by elimination:

$$-3(a) \quad -6x + 15y = 45$$
$$2(b) \quad \underline{6x + 8y = -8}$$
$$23y = 37$$

$$y = \frac{37}{23}$$

(b) $3x + 4\left(\dfrac{37}{23}\right) = -4$

$$3x = \frac{-240}{23}$$

$$x = -\frac{80}{23}$$

$$\left(-\frac{80}{23}, \frac{37}{23}\right)$$

30. Write the equation of the given line in slope-intercept form.

$$4x - 6y = 25$$

$$-6y = -4x + 25$$

$$y = \frac{2}{3}x - \frac{25}{6}$$

Since the slopes of perpendicular lines are negative reciprocals of each other,

$$m_\perp = -\frac{3}{2}$$

$$y = -\frac{3}{2}x + b$$

$$2 = -\frac{3}{2}(7) + b$$

$$\frac{25}{2} = b$$

$$y = -\frac{3}{2}x + \frac{25}{2}$$

PRACTICE SET 87

$x_1 = -3; \; y_1 = 96; \; x_2 = -11; \; y_2 = 49$

$$m = \frac{y_2 - y_1}{x_2 - x_1} = \frac{(49) - (96)}{(-11) - (-3)} = \frac{49 - 96}{-11 + 3}$$

$$= \frac{-47}{-8} = \frac{47}{8}$$

PROBLEM SET 87

1.

$$D_J$$
$$1440$$

$$D_B$$
$$120$$

$$R_J T_J = 1440; \quad R_B T_B = 120;$$

$$R_J = 4R_B; \quad T_J = T_B + 4$$

$$4R_B(T_B + 4) = 1440$$

$$4(120) + 16R_B = 1440$$

$$16R_B = 960$$

$$R_B = \mathbf{60\ mph}$$

$$R_J = \mathbf{240\ mph}; \quad T_B = \mathbf{2\ hr}; \quad T_J = \mathbf{6\ hr}$$

2. Equal ratio method:

$$\frac{HS_1}{HS_2} = \frac{H_2}{H_1}$$

$$\frac{10}{HS_2} = \frac{200}{400}$$

$$HS_2 = \mathbf{20\ hours}$$

Variation method:

$$HS = \frac{k}{H}$$

$$10 = \frac{k}{400}$$

$$k = 4000$$

$$HS = \frac{4000}{200} = \textbf{20 hours}$$

3. (a) $0.8P_N + 0.3D_N = 240$

(b) $P_N + D_N = 600$

Substitute $D_N = 600 - P_N$ into (a) and get:

(a′) $0.8P_N + 0.3(600 - P_N) = 240$

$$0.5P_N = 60$$

$$P_N = 120$$

(b) $(120) + D_N = 600$

$$D_N = 480$$

120 in.^{3} 80%, 480 in.^{3} 30%

4. (a) $10N_H = N_P - 102$

(b) $100N_H = N_P + 168$

(b′) $N_P = 100N_H - 168$

Substitute (b′) into (a) and get:

(a′) $10N_H = (100N_H - 168) - 102$

$$-90N_H = -270$$

$$N_H = \textbf{3 holographs}$$

(b′) $N_P = 100(3) - 168 = \textbf{132 printed ones}$

5. Potassium (K): $\quad 1 \times 39 = 39$

Chlorine: $\quad 1 \times 35 = 35$

Oxygen: $\quad 3 \times 16 = 48$

Total: $\quad 39 + 35 + 48 = 122$

$$\text{Percent Oxygen} = \frac{\text{Oxygen}}{\text{Total}} \times 100\%$$

$$= \frac{48}{122} \times 100\% \approx \textbf{39.34\%}$$

$$\frac{48}{122} = \frac{576}{KClO_3}$$

$$48 KClO_3 = 122(576)$$

$$KClO_3 = \textbf{1464 grams}$$

6. Refer to Lesson 87.

7. $(x_1, y_1) = (-2, 108); \; (x_2, y_2) = (-21, 47)$

$$m = \frac{y_2 - y_1}{x_2 - x_1} = \frac{47 - 108}{-21 - (-2)} = \frac{-61}{-19} = \frac{\textbf{61}}{\textbf{19}}$$

8. $x \not< -4; \; D = \{\text{Integers}\}$

$x \geq -4$

$$-5 \; -4 \; -3 \; -2 \; -1$$

9. $-x + 2 \leq -3; \; D = \{\text{Positive integers}\}$

$-x \leq -5$

$x \geq 5$

$$4 \; 5 \; 6 \; 7 \; 8$$

10. (a) $BT_D + 4T_D = 36$

(b) $\dfrac{BT_D - 4T_D = 12}{2BT_D \qquad = 48}$

(c) $\qquad BT_D = 24$

(a) $(24) + 4T_D = 36$

$$4T_D = 12$$

$$T_D = 3$$

(c) $B(3) = 24$

$$B = \textbf{8}$$

11. (a) $x^2 + y^2 = 4$

(b) $x - 2y = 1$

$$x = 2y + 1$$

(b′) $x^2 = 4y^2 + 4y + 1$

Substitute (b′) into (a) and get:

(a′) $(4y^2 + 4y + 1) + y^2 = 4$

$$5y^2 + 4y - 3 = 0$$

Solve this equation by using the quadratic formula.

$$y = \frac{-4 \pm \sqrt{4^2 - 4(5)(-3)}}{2(5)} = -\frac{2}{5} \pm \frac{\sqrt{19}}{5}$$

Substitute these values of y into (b) and solve for x.

(b) $x = 2\left(-\dfrac{2}{5} + \dfrac{\sqrt{19}}{5}\right) + 1 = \dfrac{1}{5} + \dfrac{2\sqrt{19}}{5}$

(b) $x = 2\left(-\dfrac{2}{5} - \dfrac{\sqrt{19}}{5}\right) + 1 = \dfrac{1}{5} - \dfrac{2\sqrt{19}}{5}$

$$\left(\frac{1}{5} + \frac{2\sqrt{19}}{5}, -\frac{2}{5} + \frac{\sqrt{19}}{5}\right) \text{ and}$$

$$\left(\frac{1}{5} - \frac{2\sqrt{19}}{5}, -\frac{2}{5} - \frac{\sqrt{19}}{5}\right)$$

12. $\dfrac{m^a m^{2a+2} y^{-b}}{y^{2-b}} = m^{3a+2} y^{-2}$

13. $\dfrac{(m^{a-3})^2 y}{m^a y^{b+1}} = \dfrac{m^{2a-6} y}{m^a y^{b+1}} = m^{a-6} y^{-b}$

14. $\dfrac{a}{a + \dfrac{a}{a + \dfrac{b}{a}}} = \dfrac{a}{a + \dfrac{a^2}{a^2 + b}} = \dfrac{a(a^2+b)}{a^3 + ab + a^2}$

$= \dfrac{a^2 + b}{a^2 + b + a}$

15. $\dfrac{5i-2}{-1-i} \cdot \dfrac{-1+i}{-1+i} = \dfrac{-5i - 5 + 2 - 2i}{1+1}$

$= -\dfrac{3}{2} - \dfrac{7}{2}i$

16. $\dfrac{-3+2i}{-2-i} \cdot \dfrac{-2+i}{-2+i} = \dfrac{6 - 3i - 4i - 2}{4+1}$

$= \dfrac{4}{5} - \dfrac{7}{5}i$

17. (a) $(9315 \times 10^3)(-2.065 \times 10^4)$

   Estimate: $(9 \times 10^6)(-2 \times 10^4)$

   $= -1.8 \times 10^{11}$

   Calculator answer $\approx$ **-1.92×10^{11}**

   (b) $\sqrt[2.7]{1001.94}$

   Answer should be between 10 and 31.

   Calculator answer $\approx$ **12.92**

18. (a) $x + y - 2z = 7$

   (b) $3x - y - z = 3$

   (c) $2x + z = 0$

   $z = -2x$

   Substitute (c) into (a) and (b) and get:

   (a′) $5x + y = 7$

   (b′) $\underline{5x - y = 3}$

   $10x \qquad = 10$

   $x = 1$

   (a′) $5(1) + y = 7$

   $y = 2$

   (c) $z = -2(1) = -2$

   $(1, 2, -2)$

19. $\sqrt{z} - \sqrt{z - 45} = 5$

   $\sqrt{z} - 5 = \sqrt{z - 45}$

   $z - 10\sqrt{z} + 25 = z - 45$

   $10\sqrt{z} = 70$

   $\sqrt{z} = 7$

   $z = \textbf{49}$

   Check: $\sqrt{49} - \sqrt{49 - 45} = 5$

   $7 - 2 = 5$

20.

$A = 5 \cos 72° \approx 1.55$

$B = 5 \sin 72° \approx 4.76$

$-1.55R + 4.76U$

$\underline{8.00R + 0.00U}$

$\textbf{6.45R + 4.76U}$

$\tan \theta = \dfrac{4.76}{6.45}$

$\theta \approx 36.43°$

$F = \sqrt{(4.76)^2 + (6.45)^2} \approx 8.02$

$8.02/\underline{36.43°}$

21. $\dfrac{2 - \sqrt{3}}{\sqrt{3} + 2} \cdot \dfrac{\sqrt{3} - 2}{\sqrt{3} - 2} = \dfrac{2\sqrt{3} - 4 - 3 + 2\sqrt{3}}{3 - 4}$

$= \textbf{7} - \textbf{4}\sqrt{\textbf{3}}$

22. $-3i(ii) - \sqrt{-2}\sqrt{-3} = \sqrt{\textbf{6}} + \textbf{3}i$

23. $3\sqrt{\dfrac{7}{3}} + 3\sqrt{\dfrac{3}{7}} - 4\sqrt{189}$

$= \dfrac{3\sqrt{7}}{\sqrt{3}} \dfrac{\sqrt{3}}{\sqrt{3}} + \dfrac{3\sqrt{3}}{\sqrt{7}} \dfrac{\sqrt{7}}{\sqrt{7}} - 12\sqrt{21}$

$= \dfrac{21\sqrt{21}}{21} + \dfrac{9\sqrt{21}}{21} - \dfrac{252\sqrt{21}}{21} = -\dfrac{\textbf{74}\sqrt{\textbf{21}}}{\textbf{7}}$

24.

$\dfrac{y + 4}{m} = \dfrac{ap}{b} + \dfrac{p}{c}$

$bcy + 4bc = acmp + bmp$

$bcy + 4bc - acmp = bmp$

$c = \dfrac{\textbf{bmp}}{\textbf{by} + \textbf{4b} - \textbf{amp}}$

25. $y = 2(70) - 80 = \mathbf{60}$

$2x = 360 - 2(75)$

$2x = 210$

$x = \mathbf{105}$

26. $-3x^2 - 4 = 2x$

$3x^2 + 2x + 4 = 0$

$x = \dfrac{-2 \pm \sqrt{2^2 - 4(3)(4)}}{2(3)} = -\dfrac{1}{3} \pm \dfrac{\sqrt{11}}{3}i$

27. $\dfrac{10 \text{ km}}{\text{hr}} \times \dfrac{1000 \text{ m}}{1 \text{ km}} \times \dfrac{100 \text{ cm}}{1 \text{ m}} \times \dfrac{1 \text{ in.}}{2.54 \text{ cm}}$

$\times \dfrac{1 \text{ hr}}{60 \text{ min}} \times \dfrac{1 \text{ min}}{60 \text{ s}} = \dfrac{\mathbf{10(1000)(100)}}{\mathbf{(2.54)(60)(60)}} \dfrac{\text{in.}}{\text{s}}$

28. See Lesson 71.

29. $3\sqrt{9\sqrt[4]{3}} = 3\sqrt{3^2 \sqrt[4]{3}} = 3(3)(3^{1/8}) = \mathbf{3^{17/8}}$

30. $\dfrac{-9^{-3/2}}{-(-27)^{-2/3}} = \dfrac{-((-27)^{1/3})^2}{-(9^{1/2})^3} = \dfrac{-9}{-27} = \dfrac{\mathbf{1}}{\mathbf{3}}$

PRACTICE SET 88

a. $x_1 = 4;\ y_1 = -2;\ x_2 = -3;\ y_2 = 1$

$D = \sqrt{(x_1 - x_2)^2 + (y_1 - y_2)^2}$

$= \sqrt{[(4) - (-3)]^2 + [(-2) - (1)]^2}$

$= \sqrt{7^2 + (-3)^2}$

$= \sqrt{\mathbf{58}}$

b. $PV = nRT$

$n = \dfrac{PV}{RT} = \dfrac{(2)(4)}{(0.0821)(159)} \text{ moles} \approx \mathbf{0.61 \text{ mole}}$

PROBLEM SET 88

1. Even integers: $N,\ N + 2,\ N + 4$

$N(N + 4) = 6(-N - 2) + 12$

$N^2 + 4N = -6N$

$N^2 + 10N = 0$

$N(N + 10) = 0$

$N = 0, -10$

The desired integers are **0, 2, 4** and **−10, −8, −6**.

2. Tin (Sn): $1 \times 119 = 119$

Chromate: $1 \times 52 = 52$

Oxygen: $4 \times 16 = 64$

Total: $119 + 52 + 64 = 235$

$\dfrac{119}{235} = \dfrac{595}{\text{SnCrO}_4}$

$\text{SnCrO}_4 = \mathbf{1175 \text{ grams}}$

3.

$R_D T_D = 400;\ R_G T_G = 1120;$

$R_D = R_G - 20;\ T_G = 2T_D$

$(R_D + 20)2T_D = 1120$

$2(400) + 40T_D = 1120$

$40T_D = 320$

$T_D = \mathbf{8 \text{ hr}}$

$T_G = \mathbf{16 \text{ hr}};\ R_D = \mathbf{50 \text{ mph}};\ R_G = \mathbf{70 \text{ mph}}$

4. $\dfrac{P_1 V_1}{T_1} = \dfrac{P_2 V_2}{T_2}$

$V_2 = \dfrac{P_1 V_1 T_2}{T_1 P_2}$

$V_2 = \dfrac{(740)(10)(1473)}{(573)(1480)}$

$V_2 \approx \mathbf{12.85 \text{ liters}}$

5. $PV = nRT$

$\dfrac{PV}{RT} = n$

$n = \dfrac{(1)(5)}{(0.0821)(251)} \text{ mole} \approx \mathbf{0.24 \text{ mole}}$

6. Refer to Section 88.A.

7. $D = \sqrt{(x_1 - x_2)^2 + (y_1 - y_2)^2}$

$= \sqrt{(5 - (-3))^2 + ((-2) - 3)^2}$

$= \sqrt{8^2 + (-5)^2}$

$= \sqrt{64 + 25} = \sqrt{\mathbf{89}}$

8. $-x - 2 \le 4$; $D = \{$Negative integers$\}$

$\qquad -x \le 6$

$\qquad x \ge -6$

9. $-x + 2 \not> 3$; $D = \{$Negative integers$\}$

$\qquad -x + 2 \le 3$

$\qquad -x \le 1$

$\qquad x \ge -1$

10. (a) $BT_D + 6T_D = 22$

(b) $\dfrac{BT_D - 6T_D = 10}{2BT_D \qquad\;\; = 32}$

(c) $\qquad BT_D = 16$

(a) $(16) + 6T_D = 22$

$\qquad\quad 6T_D = 6$

$\qquad\quad T_D = 1$

(c) $B = 16$

11. (a) $x^2 + y^2 = 2$

(b) $x - y = 1$

$\qquad x = y + 1$

(b') $x^2 = (y + 1)^2 = y^2 + 2y + 1$

Substitute (b') into (a) and get:

(a') $(y^2 + 2y + 1) + y^2 = 2$

$\qquad 2y^2 + 2y - 1 = 0$

Solve this equation by using the quadratic formula.

$y = \dfrac{-2 \pm \sqrt{2^2 - 4(2)(-1)}}{2(2)} = -\dfrac{1}{2} \pm \dfrac{\sqrt{3}}{2}$

Substitute these values of y into (b) and solve for x.

(b) $x = \left(-\dfrac{1}{2} + \dfrac{\sqrt{3}}{2}\right) + 1 = \dfrac{1}{2} + \dfrac{\sqrt{3}}{2}$

(b) $x = \left(-\dfrac{1}{2} - \dfrac{\sqrt{3}}{2}\right) + 1 = \dfrac{1}{2} - \dfrac{\sqrt{3}}{2}$

$\left(\dfrac{1}{2} + \dfrac{\sqrt{3}}{2}, -\dfrac{1}{2} + \dfrac{\sqrt{3}}{2}\right)$ and

$\left(\dfrac{1}{2} - \dfrac{\sqrt{3}}{2}, -\dfrac{1}{2} - \dfrac{\sqrt{3}}{2}\right)$

12. $\dfrac{(x^2)^{a+b} x^{-2a+b} y^a}{y^{a/4}} = x^{2a+2b-2a+b} y^{a-a/4}$

$= x^{3b} y^{3a/4}$

13. $\dfrac{(y^{2a+2})^2 y^{a/2} b}{y^a b^{2a}} = y^{4a+4+(a/2)-a} b^{1-2a}$

$= y^{(7a/2)+4} b^{1-2a}$

14. $\dfrac{r}{m + \dfrac{r}{\dfrac{1}{r} + m}} = \dfrac{r}{m + \dfrac{r^2}{1 + rm}} = \dfrac{r(1 + rm)}{m + rm^2 + r^2}$

15. $\dfrac{pc}{p - \dfrac{c^2}{p - \dfrac{1}{pc}}} = \dfrac{cp}{p - \dfrac{c^3 p}{cp^2 - 1}}$

$= \dfrac{cp(cp^2 - 1)}{cp^3 - p - c^3 p} = \dfrac{cp(cp^2 - 1)}{p(cp^2 - c^3 - 1)}$

$= \dfrac{c(cp^2 - 1)}{cp^2 - c^3 - 1}$

16. $\dfrac{4i - 1}{3i - 2} \cdot \dfrac{3i + 2}{3i + 2} = \dfrac{-12 - 3i + 8i - 2}{-9 - 4}$

$= \dfrac{-14 + 5i}{-13} = \dfrac{14}{13} - \dfrac{5}{13}i$

17. (a) $\dfrac{5712 \times 10^{-2}}{0.0416 \times 10^3}$

Estimate: $\dfrac{(6 \times 10^1)}{(4 \times 10^1)} = 1.5$

Calculator answer $\approx$ **1.37**

(b) $(184.3)^{-1.62}$

Answer should be between 5×10^{-3} and 2.5×10^{-5}.

Calculator answer $\approx$ **2.14×10^{-4}**

18. $\sqrt{z - 35} + \sqrt{z} = 7$

$\qquad z - 35 = 49 - 14\sqrt{z} + z$

$\qquad\quad 14\sqrt{z} = 84$

$\qquad\qquad \sqrt{z} = 6$

$\qquad\qquad\; z = 36$

Check: $\sqrt{36 - 35} + \sqrt{36} = 7$

$\qquad\qquad 1 + 6 = 7$

$\qquad\qquad\quad 7 = 7$

19. (a) $2x + 2y - z = 14$

(b) $3x + 3y + z = 16$

(c) $x - 2y = 0$

$\qquad x = 2y$

Substitute (c) into (a) and (b) and get:

(a') $6y - z = 14$

(b') $\underline{9y + z = 16}$

$\qquad 15y \qquad = 30$

$\qquad\qquad y = 2$

(c) $x = 2(2) = 4$

(a) $2(4) + 2(2) - z = 14$

$\qquad\qquad 12 - z = 14$

$\qquad\qquad\qquad z = -2$

(4, 2, -2)

20.

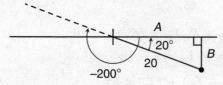

$A = 20 \cos 20° \approx 18.79$

$B = 20 \sin 20° \approx 6.84$

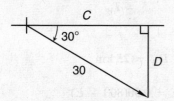

$C = 30 \cos 30° \approx 25.98$

$D = 30 \sin 30° = 15$

$18.79R - 6.84U$

$\underline{25.98R - 15.00U}$

$\mathbf{44.77R - 21.84U}$

21.

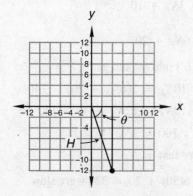

22. $4i^2 - \sqrt{-9} = \mathbf{-4 - 3i}$

23. $4\sqrt{\dfrac{9}{3}} + 3\sqrt{\dfrac{3}{9}} - 5\sqrt{27} = 4\sqrt{3} + \sqrt{3} - 15\sqrt{3}$

$\qquad\qquad = \mathbf{-10\sqrt{3}}$

24. $\dfrac{1 - \sqrt{2}}{3 - 2\sqrt{2}} \cdot \dfrac{3 + 2\sqrt{2}}{3 + 2\sqrt{2}} = \dfrac{3 - 3\sqrt{2} + 2\sqrt{2} - 4}{9 - 8}$

$\qquad\qquad = \mathbf{-1 - \sqrt{2}}$

25. $\dfrac{4 + \sqrt{3}}{1 - \sqrt{3}} \cdot \dfrac{1 + \sqrt{3}}{1 + \sqrt{3}} = \dfrac{4 + \sqrt{3} + 4\sqrt{3} + 3}{1 - 3}$

$\qquad\qquad = \mathbf{\dfrac{-7 - 5\sqrt{3}}{2}}$

26.

$$\frac{x + 2y}{c} = y\left(\frac{1}{x} - \frac{1}{r}\right)$$

$$\frac{x + 2y}{c} = \frac{y}{x} - \frac{y}{r}$$

$$x^2 r + 2xyr = cyr - cxy$$

$$cxy = cyr - 2xyr - x^2 r$$

$$\frac{cxy}{cy - 2xy - x^2} = r$$

27. $-x^2 - 2x - 2 = 0$

$\qquad x^2 + 2x = -2$

$\qquad (x^2 + 2x + 1) = -2 + 1$

$\qquad\qquad (x + 1)^2 = -1$

$\qquad\qquad\quad x + 1 = \pm i$

$\qquad\qquad\qquad x = \mathbf{-1 \pm i}$

28. $\dfrac{10 \text{ mL}}{\text{s}} \times \dfrac{60 \text{ s}}{1 \text{ min}} \times \dfrac{1 \text{ cm}^3}{1 \text{ mL}} \times \dfrac{1 \text{ in.}}{2.54 \text{ cm}} \times \dfrac{1 \text{ in.}}{2.54 \text{ cm}}$

$\times \dfrac{1 \text{ in.}}{2.54 \text{ cm}} = \mathbf{\dfrac{10(60)}{(2.54)(2.54)(2.54)} \dfrac{\text{in.}^3}{\text{min}}}$

The top-right solutions:

$H = \sqrt{12^2 + 4^2} = \sqrt{160} = 4\sqrt{10}$

$\tan \theta = \dfrac{12}{4} = 3$

$\theta \approx 71.57°$

Since θ is a fourth-quadrant angle,

$\theta = 360 - 71.57 = 288.43°$

$\mathbf{4\sqrt{10}\,/\underline{288.43°}}$

29. $\frac{4}{3}\overrightarrow{SF} = \frac{7}{4}$

$\overrightarrow{SF} = \frac{21}{16}$

$x = \frac{7}{3}\overrightarrow{SF}$

$x = \frac{7}{3}\left(\frac{21}{16}\right)$

$x = \dfrac{\mathbf{49}}{\mathbf{16}}$

$y + 83 = 180$

$y = \mathbf{97}$

30. $\dfrac{-3x - 2}{2} - \dfrac{2x - 4}{3} = 7$

$-9x - 6 - 4x + 8 = 42$

$-13x = 40$

$x = -\dfrac{\mathbf{40}}{\mathbf{13}}$

PRACTICE SET 89

a. $-x - 4 \le -1$ and $x - 1 < 1$; $D = \{\text{Integers}\}$

$-x \le 3$

$x \ge -3$ and $\quad x < 2$

b. $-1 < x - 1 \le 3$; $D = \{\text{Reals}\}$

$-1 < x - 1$ and $x - 1 \le 3$

$0 < x \quad$ and $\quad x \le 4$

c. $7x = 3 \cdot 4$

$7x = 12$

$x = \dfrac{\mathbf{12}}{\mathbf{7}}$

d. $4(4 + y) = 6^2$

$16 + 4y = 36$

$4y = 20$

$y = \mathbf{5}$

PROBLEM SET 89

1. Equal ratio method:

$\dfrac{A_1}{A_2} = \dfrac{B_1}{B_2}$

$\dfrac{500}{A_2} = \dfrac{10}{42}$

$A_2 = \mathbf{2100\ altercations}$

Variation method:

$A = kB$

$500 = k(10)$

$50 = k$

$A = 50(42)$

$A = \mathbf{2100\ altercations}$

2.

$R_R T_R + R_W T_W = 65$; $R_R = 10$;

$R_W = 5$; $T_R = 9 - T_W$

$10(9 - T_W) + 5T_W = 65$

$90 - 10T_W + 5T_W = 65$

$25 = 5T_W$

$5 = T_W$

$T_R = 9 - 5 = 4$

$D_R = \mathbf{40\ km}$; $D_W = \mathbf{25\ km}$

3. $0.79(800) - E = 0.30(800 - E)$

$632 - E = 240 - 0.3E$

$392 = 0.7E$

$\mathbf{560\ liters} = E$

4. (a) $10N_F = 2N_S - 140$

(b) $\dfrac{1}{2}N_S = 3N_F + 10$

(b') $N_S = 6N_F + 20$

Substitute (b') into (a) and get:

(a') $\qquad 10N_F = 2(6N_F + 20) - 140$

$10N_F = 12N_F + 40 - 140$

$100 = 2N_F$

$\mathbf{50\ were\ fast} = N_F$

(b') $N_S = 6(50) + 20 = \mathbf{320\ were\ slow}$

5. $\dfrac{740}{100} \times S = 592$

$$S = 592 \times \dfrac{100}{740}$$

$$S = \textbf{80 spotted ones}$$

6. $-x - 5 \le -3$ and $x - 3 < 1$; $D = \{\text{Integers}\}$

$\quad -x \le 2 \quad$ and $\quad x < 4$

$\quad\ \ x \ge -2$ and $\quad x < 4$

7. $-4 < x - 4 \le 1$; $D = \{\text{Reals}\}$

$\quad 0 < x \le 5$

8. $-x \not\ge 2 \quad$ or $\ -x < 1$; $D = \{\text{Reals}\}$

$\quad -x < 2 \quad$ or $\ -x < 1$

$\quad\ \ x > -2$ or $\ \ x > -1$

9. $7x = 2(14)$

$\quad 7x = 28$

$\quad\ \ x = \textbf{4}$

10. $4(10) = 2(y + 2)$

$\quad\ \ 40 = 2y + 4$

$\quad\ \ 36 = 2y$

$\quad\ \ \textbf{18} = y$

11. (a) $BT_D + 5T_D = 57$

$\quad$ (b) $\dfrac{BT_D - 5T_D = 27}{2BT_D \qquad\quad\ = 84}$

$\quad$ (c) $\qquad BT_D = 42$

$\quad$ (a) $(42) + 5T_D = 57$

$\qquad\qquad\ \ 5T_D = 15$

$\qquad\qquad\ \ \ T_D = \textbf{3}$

$\quad$ (c) $B(3) = 42$

$\qquad\quad\ B = \textbf{14}$

12. (a) $x^2 + y^2 = 3$

$\quad$ (b) $x - y = 2$

$\qquad\qquad x = y + 2$

$\quad$ (b′) $x^2 = (y + 2)^2 = y^2 + 4y + 4$

Substitute (b′) into (a) and get:

(a′) $(y^2 + 4y + 4) + y^2 = 3$

$\qquad\quad 2y^2 + 4y + 1 = 0$

Solve this equation by using the quadratic formula.

$$y = \dfrac{-4 \pm \sqrt{4^2 - 4(2)(1)}}{2(2)} = -1 \pm \dfrac{\sqrt{2}}{2}$$

Substitute these values of y into (b) and solve for x.

(b) $x = \left(-1 + \dfrac{\sqrt{2}}{2}\right) + 2 = 1 + \dfrac{\sqrt{2}}{2}$

(b) $x = \left(-1 - \dfrac{\sqrt{2}}{2}\right) + 2 = 1 - \dfrac{\sqrt{2}}{2}$

$$\left(1 + \dfrac{\sqrt{2}}{2}, -1 + \dfrac{\sqrt{2}}{2}\right) \text{ and } \left(1 - \dfrac{\sqrt{2}}{2}, -1 - \dfrac{\sqrt{2}}{2}\right)$$

13. $\dfrac{x^a y^{2b}(x^{a+2})^{1/2}}{y^{3b}} = x^{a+a/2+1}y^{2b-3b}$

$\qquad = x^{3a/2+1}y^{-b}$

14. $\dfrac{(y^{a+2})^a(y^a)^a}{y^{2+a}} = y^{a^2+2a+a^2-2-a}$

$\qquad = y^{2a^2+a-2}$

15. $\dfrac{k}{m + \dfrac{m}{a + \dfrac{1}{m}}} = \dfrac{k}{m + \dfrac{m^2}{am + 1}}$

$\qquad = \dfrac{k(am + 1)}{am^2 + m^2 + m}$

16. $\dfrac{m}{a + \dfrac{x}{b + \dfrac{d}{c}}} = \dfrac{m}{a + \dfrac{cx}{bc + d}} = \dfrac{m(bc + d)}{abc + ad + cx}$

17. $\dfrac{3 - 2i}{i - 4} \cdot \dfrac{i + 4}{i + 4} = \dfrac{3i + 2 + 12 - 8i}{-1 - 16}$

$\qquad = \dfrac{14 - 5i}{-17} = -\dfrac{14}{17} + \dfrac{5}{17}i$

18. $\dfrac{2 - 3i}{4i - 1} \cdot \dfrac{4i + 1}{4i + 1} = \dfrac{8i + 12 + 2 - 3i}{-16 - 1}$

$\qquad = \dfrac{14 + 5i}{-17} = -\dfrac{14}{17} - \dfrac{5}{17}i$

19. (a) $3x + 2y + z = 9$

(b) $x - 2y - 2z = -3$

(c) $2x + z = 0$

$\quad\quad z = -2x$

Substitute (c) into (a) and (b) and get:

(a′) $x + 2y = 9$

(b′) $\dfrac{5x - 2y = -3}{6x \quad\quad = 6}$

$\quad\quad\quad x = 1$

(a′) $(1) + 2y = 9$

$\quad\quad\quad y = 4$

(c) $z = -2(1)$

$\quad\quad z = -2$

(1, 4, −2)

20. $\quad\quad \sqrt{s} = 3 + \sqrt{s - 21}$

$s - 6\sqrt{s} + 9 = s - 21$

$\quad\quad\quad 30 = 6\sqrt{s}$

$\quad\quad\quad\quad 5 = \sqrt{s}$

$\quad\quad\quad \mathbf{25 = s}$

Check: $\sqrt{25} = 3 + \sqrt{25 - 21}$

$\quad\quad\quad 5 = 3 + 2$

21.

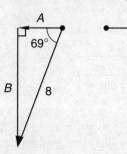

$A = 8 \cos 69° \approx 2.87$

$B = 8 \sin 69° \approx 7.47$

$\dfrac{\begin{array}{c} -2.87R - 7.47U \\ 6.00R + 0.00U \end{array}}{\mathbf{3.13R - 7.47U}}$

$\tan \theta = \dfrac{-7.47}{3.13}$

$\quad \theta \approx -67.27°$

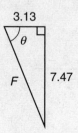

$F = \sqrt{(3.13)^2 + (-7.47)^2}$

$F \approx 8.10$

8.10$\underline{/-67.27°}$

22. $\dfrac{4 + 2\sqrt{3}}{3\sqrt{3} - 2} \cdot \dfrac{3\sqrt{3} + 2}{3\sqrt{3} + 2} = \dfrac{12\sqrt{3} + 18 + 8 + 4\sqrt{3}}{27 - 4}$

$\quad\quad = \dfrac{\mathbf{26 + 16\sqrt{3}}}{\mathbf{23}}$

23. $\dfrac{x}{a + c} = \dfrac{mx}{y} + cm$

$\quad\quad xy = amx + cmx + acmy$

$\quad\quad\quad\quad + c^2 my$

$xy - acmy - c^2 my = amx + cmx$

$\quad\quad y = \dfrac{\mathbf{amx + cmx}}{\mathbf{x - acm - c^2 m}}$

24. $\dfrac{x}{a + c} = \dfrac{mx + mcy}{y}$

$\quad\quad xy = amx + cmx + acmy$

$\quad\quad\quad\quad + c^2 my$

$xy - cmx - c^2 my = amx + acmy$

$\dfrac{\mathbf{xy - cmx - c^2 my}}{\mathbf{mx + cmy}} = a$

25. $3i^3 + 5i - \sqrt{-2}\sqrt{2} = -3i + 5i - 2i = \mathbf{0}$

26. $3\sqrt{\dfrac{3}{8}} + 4\sqrt{\dfrac{8}{3}} - 2\sqrt{24}$

$= \dfrac{3\sqrt{3}}{2\sqrt{2}} \dfrac{\sqrt{2}}{\sqrt{2}} + \dfrac{8\sqrt{2}}{\sqrt{3}} \dfrac{\sqrt{3}}{\sqrt{3}} - 4\sqrt{6}$

$= \dfrac{3\sqrt{6}}{4} + \dfrac{8\sqrt{6}}{3} - 4\sqrt{6}$

$= \dfrac{9\sqrt{6}}{12} + \dfrac{32\sqrt{6}}{12} - \dfrac{48\sqrt{6}}{12} = -\dfrac{\mathbf{7\sqrt{6}}}{\mathbf{12}}$

27. $-7x^2 = -x - 5$

$\quad\quad 0 = 7x^2 - x - 5$

$x = \dfrac{1 \pm \sqrt{1 - 4(7)(-5)}}{2(7)} = \dfrac{\mathbf{1 \pm \sqrt{141}}}{\mathbf{14}}$

28. $\dfrac{10\ \text{ft}^3}{s} \times \dfrac{60\ \text{s}}{1\ \text{min}} \times \dfrac{12\ \text{in.}}{1\ \text{ft}} \times \dfrac{12\ \text{in.}}{1\ \text{ft}} \times \dfrac{12\ \text{in.}}{1\ \text{ft}}$

$= \mathbf{10(60)(12)(12)(12)\ \dfrac{\text{in.}^3}{\text{min}}}$

29. $(6x + 20)° + (4x + 10)° = 180°$

$\qquad 6x + 20 + 4x + 10 = 180$

$\qquad\qquad\qquad\qquad 10x = 150$

$\qquad\qquad\qquad\qquad\quad x = \mathbf{15}$

$(4x + 10)° = A°$

$4(15) + 10 = A$

$\qquad \mathbf{70} = A$

$(6x + 20)° = B°$

$6(15) + 20 = B$

$\qquad \mathbf{110} = B$

30. $(x_1, y_1) = (-2, 3);\ (x_2, y_2) = (8, 4)$

$D = \sqrt{(x_2 - x_1)^2 + (y_2 - y_1)^2}$

$D = \sqrt{(8 - (-2))^2 + (4 - 3)^2}$

$D = \sqrt{100 + 1} = \sqrt{\mathbf{101}}$

PRACTICE SET 90

$\begin{cases} x - 2y + 2z = 2 & \text{(a)} \\ x + y - z = 3 & \text{(b)} \\ 3x - 2y + 2z = 2 & \text{(c)} \end{cases}$

(a) $x - 2y + 2z = 2$

(c) $\dfrac{3x - 2y - 2z = 2}{}$

$\qquad 4x - 4y \qquad\quad = 4$

(d) $\qquad\quad x - y = 1$

(a) $x - 2y + 2z = 2$

2(b) $\dfrac{2x + 2y - 2z = 6}{}$

$\qquad 3x \qquad\qquad = 8$

$\qquad\qquad\qquad x = \dfrac{8}{3}$

(d) $\left(\dfrac{8}{3}\right) - y = 1$

$\qquad\qquad y = \dfrac{8}{3} - 1$

$\qquad\qquad y = \dfrac{5}{3}$

(b) $\left(\dfrac{8}{3}\right) + \left(\dfrac{5}{3}\right) - z = 3$

$\qquad\qquad \dfrac{13}{3} - 3 = z$

$\qquad\qquad\quad \dfrac{4}{3} = z$

$\left(\dfrac{8}{3}, \dfrac{5}{3}, \dfrac{4}{3}\right)$

PROBLEM SET 90

1.

$R_R = R_P + 50;\ R_P T_P = 300;\ R_R T_R = 160;$

$T_P = 5T_R;\ R_P = R_R - 50$

$(R_R - 50)(5T_R) = 300$

$5R_R T_R - 250T_R = 300$

$\qquad 800 - 250T_R = 300$

$\qquad\qquad 500 = 250T_R$

$\qquad\qquad\quad 2 = T_R$

$R_R = \mathbf{80\ mph};\ R_P = \mathbf{30\ mph};$

$T_R = \mathbf{2\ hr};\ T_P = \mathbf{10\ hr}$

2. $PV = nRT$

$V = \dfrac{nRT}{P}$

$V = \dfrac{(0.832)(0.0821)(400)}{3}$ liters $\approx \mathbf{9.11\ liters}$

3. (a) $N_R = 3N_B - 5$

(b) $6N_B = 10N_R - 70$

-2(a) $-2N_R = -6N_B + 10$

(b) $\dfrac{10N_R = \quad 6N_B + 70}{}$

$\qquad 8N_R = \qquad\qquad 80$

$\qquad N_R = \mathbf{10\ red\ boats}$

(a) $\qquad 10 = 3N_B - 5$

$\qquad\qquad 15 = 3N_B$

$\qquad\qquad N_B = \mathbf{5\ blue\ boats}$

4. (a) $0.1P_N + 0.4D_N = 104$

(b) $P_N + D_N = 800$

Substitute $D_N = 800 - P_N$ into (a) and get:

(a′) $0.1P_N + 0.4(800 - P_N) = 104$

$\qquad\qquad\qquad -0.3P_N = -216$

$\qquad\qquad\qquad\qquad P_N = 720$

(b) $(720) + D_N = 800$

$\qquad\qquad D_N = 80$

720 liters 10%, 80 liters 40%

5. $\dfrac{7}{16} \times SP = 672$

$SP = 672 \times \dfrac{16}{7} = \mathbf{1536}$ **spotted ones**

6. (a) $x + y - z = 3$

(b) $-x - 2y - 2z = 0$

(c) $x - 2y - 2z = 4$

(a) $\quad x + y - z = 3$

(b) $\dfrac{-x - 2y - 2z = 0}{}$

(d) $\quad\quad -y - 3z = 3$

(b) $-x - 2y - 2z = 0$

(c) $\dfrac{x - 2y - 2z = 4}{}$

(e) $\quad -4y - 4z = 4$

$4(d)\ -4y - 12z = 12$

$-1(e)\ \dfrac{4y + 4z = -4}{}$

$\quad\quad -8z = 8$

$\quad\quad\quad z = -1$

(d) $-y - 3(-1) = 3$

$\quad -y = 0$

$\quad\quad y = 0$

(a) $x + (0) - (-1) = 3$

$\quad x + 1 = 3$

$\quad\quad x = 2$

$\mathbf{(2, 0, -1)}$

7. (a) $2x - y + z = 2$

(b) $x + 2y + 2z = 3$

(c) $2x - 2y + z = 0$

$2(a)\ 4x - 2y + 2z = 4$

(b) $\dfrac{x + 2y + 2z = 3}{}$

(d) $5x \quad\quad + 4z = 7$

(b) $\quad x + 2y + 2z = 3$

(c) $\dfrac{2x - 2y + z = 0}{}$

(e) $3x \quad\quad + 3z = 3$

$3(d)\ 15x + 12z = 21$

$-4(e)\ \dfrac{-12x - 12z = -12}{}$

$\quad\quad 3x \quad\quad = 9$

$\quad\quad\quad x = 3$

(e) $3(3) + 3z = 3$

$\quad 9 + 3z = 3$

$\quad\quad 3z = -6$

$\quad\quad\quad z = -2$

(c) $2(3) - 2y + (-2) = 0$

$\quad 6 - 2y - 2 = 0$

$\quad\quad 4 = 2y$

$\quad\quad 2 = y$

$\mathbf{(3, 2, -2)}$

8. $-1 \le x - 1 < 4;\ D = \{\text{Integers}\}$

$\quad 0 \le x < 5$

9. $x - 2 \not\ge 0$ or $x - 2 > 2;\ D = \{\text{Reals}\}$

$\quad x - 2 < 0$ or $\quad\quad x > 4$

$\quad\quad x < 2$ or $\quad\quad x > 4$

10. (a) $BT_D + 3T_D = 28$

(b) $\dfrac{BT_D - 3T_D = 16}{}$

$\quad 2BT_D \quad\quad = 44$

(c) $\quad\quad BT_D = 22$

(a) $(22) + 3T_D = 28$

$\quad\quad 3T_D = 6$

$\quad\quad\ T_D = \mathbf{2}$

(c) $B(2) = 22$

$\quad\ B = \mathbf{11}$

11. (a) $x^2 + y^2 = 18$

(b) $y - x = 4$

$\quad x = y - 4$

(b') $x^2 = (y - 4)^2 = y^2 - 8y + 16$

Substitute (b') into (a) and get:

(a') $(y^2 - 8y + 16) + y^2 = 18$

$\quad\quad 2y^2 - 8y - 2 = 0$

$\quad\quad\ y^2 - 4y - 1 = 0$

Solve this equation by using the quadratic formula.

$y = \dfrac{4 \pm \sqrt{16 + 4}}{2} = 2 \pm \sqrt{5}$

Substitute these values of y into (b) and solve for x.

(b) $x = (2 + \sqrt{5}) - 4$

$\quad x = -2 + \sqrt{5}$

(b) $x = (2 - \sqrt{5}) - 4$

$\quad x = -2 - \sqrt{5}$

$\mathbf{(-2 + \sqrt{5}, 2 + \sqrt{5})}$ and $\mathbf{(-2 - \sqrt{5}, 2 - \sqrt{5})}$

12. $\dfrac{a^2 a^{x/2}(a^2)^x}{(a^{-3})^{-x}} = a^{2 + x/2 + 2x - 3x} = a^{2 - x/2}$

13. $\dfrac{y^c(m^{-b})^2}{m^{-b/2}} = y^c m^{-2b + b/2} = \boldsymbol{y^c m^{-3b/2}}$

14. $\dfrac{x}{xm - \dfrac{m}{m - \dfrac{1}{x}}} = \dfrac{x}{mx - \dfrac{mx}{mx - 1}}$

$= \dfrac{x(mx - 1)}{m^2 x^2 - 2mx} = \boldsymbol{\dfrac{mx - 1}{m^2 x - 2m}}$

15. $\dfrac{p}{x - \dfrac{xp}{1 - \dfrac{p}{x}}} = \dfrac{p}{x - \dfrac{px^2}{x - p}} = \boldsymbol{\dfrac{p(x - p)}{x^2 - px - px^2}}$

16. $\dfrac{1 + 2i}{-5 - i} \cdot \dfrac{-5 + i}{-5 + i} = \dfrac{-5 - 10i + i - 2}{25 + 1}$

$= \boldsymbol{-\dfrac{7}{26} - \dfrac{9}{26}i}$

17. Since the $m\overset{\frown}{AC} = 120°$, the $m\overset{\frown}{ABC} = 240°$.

Length of 240° arc $= \dfrac{240}{360} \times 10\pi\,\text{cm} = \boldsymbol{\dfrac{20}{3}\pi\,\text{cm}}$

18. $\sqrt{s} - \sqrt{s - 15} = 3$

$s - 6\sqrt{s} + 9 = s - 15$

$24 = 6\sqrt{s}$

$4 = \sqrt{s}$

$\boldsymbol{16 = s}$

Check: $\sqrt{16} - \sqrt{16 - 15} = 3$

$4 - 1 = 3$

19.

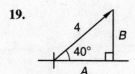

$A = 4\cos 40° \approx 3.06$

$B = 4\sin 40° \approx 2.57$

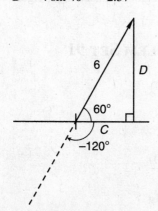

$C = 6\cos 60° = 3$

$D = 6\sin 60° \approx 5.20$

$\begin{array}{r} 3.06R + 2.57U \\ 3.00R + 5.20U \\ \hline \boldsymbol{6.06R + 7.77U} \end{array}$

20. $\tan\theta = \dfrac{-10}{-4}$

$\theta \approx 68.20°$

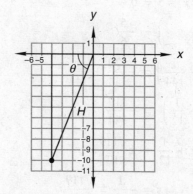

Since θ is a third-quadrant angle,

$\theta = 68.20 + 180 = 248.20°$

$H = \sqrt{(-4)^2 + (-10)^2} = 2\sqrt{29}$

$\boldsymbol{2\sqrt{29}\,\underline{/248.20°}}$

21. $\dfrac{-2 - \sqrt{3}}{2 - 2\sqrt{3}} \cdot \dfrac{2 + 2\sqrt{3}}{2 + 2\sqrt{3}} = \dfrac{-4 - 2\sqrt{3} - 4\sqrt{3} - 6}{4 - 12}$

$= \dfrac{-10 - 6\sqrt{3}}{-8} = \boldsymbol{\dfrac{5 + 3\sqrt{3}}{4}}$

22. $\dfrac{4 + \sqrt{3}}{3 - 2\sqrt{3}} \cdot \dfrac{3 + 2\sqrt{3}}{3 + 2\sqrt{3}} = \dfrac{12 + 3\sqrt{3} + 8\sqrt{3} + 6}{9 - 12}$

$= \dfrac{18 + 11\sqrt{3}}{-3} = \boldsymbol{\dfrac{-18 - 11\sqrt{3}}{3}}$

23. $-2i^2 + \sqrt{-4}\sqrt{4} - \sqrt{-3}\sqrt{-3} - 2i^5$

$= 2 + 4i + 3 - 2i = \boldsymbol{5 + 2i}$

24. $\dfrac{x}{y} - m = p\left(\dfrac{r}{c} - \dfrac{1}{b}\right)$

$\dfrac{x}{y} - m = \dfrac{pr}{c} - \dfrac{p}{b}$

$bcx - bcmy = bpry - cpy$

$bcx - bcmy + cpy = bpry$

$c = \boldsymbol{\dfrac{bpry}{bx - bmy + py}}$

25. $\sqrt[3]{9\sqrt[4]{3}} = (3^2 3^{1/4})^{1/3} = (3^{9/4})^{1/3} = \boldsymbol{3^{3/4}}$

26. (a) $3(12) = 4(4 + x)$

    $36 = 16 + 4x$

    $20 = 4x$

    $\mathbf{5 = x}$

    (b) $6 \cdot 3 = 9 \cdot x$

    $18 = 9x$

    $\mathbf{2 = x}$

27. $-6x^2 - x - 5 = 0$

    $\left(x^2 + \dfrac{x}{6} + \phantom{\dfrac{1}{144}}\right) = -\dfrac{5}{6}$

    $\left(x^2 + \dfrac{x}{6} + \dfrac{1}{144}\right) = -\dfrac{120}{144} + \dfrac{1}{144}$

    $\left(x + \dfrac{1}{12}\right)^2 = -\dfrac{119}{144}$

    $x + \dfrac{1}{12} = \pm\dfrac{\sqrt{119}}{12}i$

    $x = -\dfrac{1}{12} \pm \dfrac{\sqrt{119}}{12}i$

28. $42\ \text{ft}^3 \times \dfrac{12\ \text{in.}}{1\ \text{ft}} \times \dfrac{12\ \text{in.}}{1\ \text{ft}} \times \dfrac{12\ \text{in.}}{1\ \text{ft}}$

    $\times \dfrac{2.54\ \text{cm}}{1\ \text{in.}} \times \dfrac{2.54\ \text{cm}}{1\ \text{in.}} \times \dfrac{2.54\ \text{cm}}{1\ \text{in.}}$

    $= \mathbf{42(12)(12)(12)(2.54)(2.54)(2.54)\ cm^3}$

29. $A = \sqrt{13^2 - 12^2} = \sqrt{25} = 5$

    $13 \times \overrightarrow{SF} = 19$

    $\overrightarrow{SF} = \dfrac{19}{13}$

    $B = 5 \times \overrightarrow{SF} = 5 \times \dfrac{19}{13} = \mathbf{\dfrac{95}{13}}$

30. Write the equation of the given line in slope-intercept form.

    $x + 5y = 7$

    $y = -\dfrac{1}{5}x + \dfrac{7}{5}$

    Since the slopes of perpendicular lines are negative reciprocals of each other,

    $m_\perp = 5$

    $y = 5x + b$

    $7 = 5(-2) + b$

    $17 = b$

    $\mathbf{y = 5x + 17}$

PRACTICE SET 91

a. $\begin{cases} y \ge -x - 2 \\ y \le \dfrac{1}{3}x - 2 \end{cases}$

The first step is to graph the two lines.

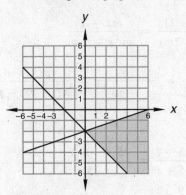

The region we wish to find is on or above the line $y = -x - 2$ and on or below the line $y = \frac{1}{3}x - 2$. This region is shaded in the figure.

b. $\begin{cases} y > x - 3 \\ y \le x + 3 \end{cases}$

The first step is to graph the two lines.

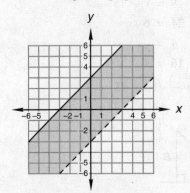

The region we wish to find is above the dashed line $y = x - 3$ and on or below the solid line $y = x + 3$. This region is shaded in the figure.

PROBLEM SET 91

1. $\dfrac{P_1}{T_1} = \dfrac{P_2}{T_2}$

   $P_2 = \dfrac{P_1 T_2}{T_1}$

   $P_2 = \dfrac{(740)(1600)}{400}$

   $P_2 = \mathbf{2960\ mm\ Hg}$

2. (a) $0.6P_N + 0.3D_N = 126$

(b) $P_N + D_N = 300$

Substitute $D_N = 300 - P_N$ into (a) and get:

(a′) $0.6P_N + 0.3(300 - P_N) = 126$

$$0.3P_N = 36$$

$$P_N = 120$$

(b) $(120) + D_N = 300$

$$D_N = 180$$

180 mL 30%, 120 mL 60%

3. Arsenic: $4 \times 75 = 300$

Oxygen: $6 \times 16 = 96$

Total: $300 + 96 = 396$

Arsenic: $\dfrac{300}{396} \times 100\% \approx$ **75.76%**

4.

D_L

$$3000$$

D_S

$$800$$

$T_L = T_S + 1$; $R_L T_L = 3000$; $R_L = 3R_S$;

$R_S T_S = 800$

$3R_S(T_S + 1) = 3000$

$3R_S T_S + 3R_S = 3000$

$2400 + 3R_S = 3000$

$3R_S = 600$

$R_S = 200$

$R_L =$ **600 mph**; $R_S =$ **200 mph**;

$T_L =$ **5 hr**; $T_S =$ **4 hr**

5. Variation method:

$$G = \frac{k}{A}$$

$$35 = \frac{k}{70}$$

$$2450 = k$$

$$G = \frac{2450}{50}$$

$$G = \textbf{49 were glabrous}$$

Equal ratio method:

$$\frac{G_1}{G_2} = \frac{A_2}{A_1}$$

$$\frac{35}{G_2} = \frac{50}{70}$$

$G_2 =$ **49 were glabrous**

6. (a) $y \geq -x - 1$

(b) $y < \dfrac{1}{3}x + 1$

The first step is to graph each of these lines.

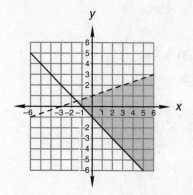

The region we wish to find is on or above the solid line and below the dashed line. This region is shaded in the figure.

7. (a) $y > x - 1$

(b) $y \leq x + 2$

The first step is to graph each of these lines.

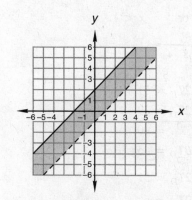

The region we wish to find is on or below the solid line and above the dashed line. This region is shaded in the figure.

8. (a) $x + 2y - z = 1$

(b) $2x - y + 2z = 9$

(c) $x - 2y - 3z = -9$

$$
\begin{array}{r}
\text{(a)} \quad x + 2y - z = 1 \\
\text{2(b)} \quad 4x - 2y + 4z = 18 \\
\hline
\text{(d)} \quad 5x \qquad + 3z = 19
\end{array}
$$

$$
\begin{array}{r}
\text{(a)} \quad x + 2y - z = 1 \\
\text{(c)} \quad x - 2y - 3z = -9 \\
\hline
\text{(e)} \quad 2x \qquad - 4z = -8
\end{array}
$$

$$
\begin{array}{r}
\text{2(d)} \quad 10x + 6z = 38 \\
\text{-5(e)} \quad -10x + 20z = 40 \\
\hline
26z = 78 \\
z = 3
\end{array}
$$

(e) $2x - 4(3) = -8$

$$2x = 4$$

$$x = 2$$

(a) $(2) + 2y - (3) = 1$

$$2y = 2$$

$$y = 1$$

(2, 1, 3)

9. $4 < x + 4 < 6$; $D = \{\text{Integers}\}$

$0 < x < 2$

10. $x + 2 \nleq 5$ or $x + 5 < 6$; $D = \{\text{Reals}\}$

$x + 2 > 5$ or $x + 5 < 6$

$x > 3$ or $\qquad x < 1$

11. (a) $BT_D + 2T_D = 51$

(b) $BT_D - 2T_D = 39$

$$\overline{2BT_D \qquad = 90}$$

(c) $\qquad BT_D = 45$

(a) $(45) + 2T_D = 51$

$$2T_D = 6$$

$$T_D = 3$$

(c) $B(3) = 45$

$$B = 15$$

12. (a) $x^2 + y^2 = 12$

(b) $x + y = 4$

$$x = 4 - y$$

(b') $x^2 = (4 - y)^2 = 16 - 8y + y^2$

Substitute (b') into (a) and get:

(a') $(16 - 8y + y^2) + y^2 = 12$

$$2y^2 - 8y + 4 = 0$$

$$y^2 - 4y + 2 = 0$$

Solve this equation by using the quadratic formula.

$$y = \frac{4 \pm \sqrt{16 - 4(2)(1)}}{2(1)}$$

$$= 2 \pm \frac{\sqrt{8}}{2} = 2 \pm \sqrt{2}$$

Substitute these values of y into (b) and solve for x.

(b) $x = 4 - (2 + \sqrt{2})$

$$x = 4 - 2 - \sqrt{2}$$

$$x = 2 - \sqrt{2}$$

(b) $x = 4 - (2 - \sqrt{2})$

$$x = 4 - 2 + \sqrt{2}$$

$$x = 2 + \sqrt{2}$$

$$(2 - \sqrt{2}, 2 + \sqrt{2}) \text{ and } (2 + \sqrt{2}, 2 - \sqrt{2})$$

13. $\dfrac{(x^b)^2 - a \, x^{ab}}{x^{ab/2}} = x^{2b - ab + ab - ab/2}$

$$= x^{2b - ab/2}$$

14. $\dfrac{a}{b + \dfrac{1}{cx + \dfrac{1}{x}}} = \dfrac{a}{b + \dfrac{x}{cx^2 + 1}}$

$$= \frac{a(cx^2 + 1)}{bcx^2 + b + x}$$

15. $\dfrac{m}{a + \dfrac{ma}{a + \dfrac{m}{a}}} = \dfrac{m}{a + \dfrac{a^2 m}{a^2 + m}}$

$$= \frac{m(a^2 + m)}{a^3 + am + a^2 m}$$

16. $\dfrac{2i + 7}{i + 2} \cdot \dfrac{i - 2}{i - 2} = \dfrac{-2 + 7i - 4i - 14}{-1 - 4}$

$$= \frac{-16 + 3i}{-5} = \frac{16}{5} - \frac{3}{5}i$$

17. $\dfrac{3i - 6}{-2i + 1} \cdot \dfrac{-2i - 1}{-2i - 1}$

$= \dfrac{6 + 12i - 3i + 6}{-4 - 1}$

$= \dfrac{12 + 9i}{-5} = -\dfrac{12}{5} - \dfrac{9}{5}i$

18. $\dfrac{1 - \sqrt{2}}{4 - 5\sqrt{2}} \cdot \dfrac{4 + 5\sqrt{2}}{4 + 5\sqrt{2}}$

$= \dfrac{4 - 4\sqrt{2} + 5\sqrt{2} - 10}{16 - 50} = \dfrac{-6 + \sqrt{2}}{-34}$

$= \dfrac{6 - \sqrt{2}}{34}$

19. $\dfrac{4 + 3\sqrt{2}}{-\sqrt{2}} \cdot \dfrac{\sqrt{2}}{\sqrt{2}} = \dfrac{4\sqrt{2} + 6}{-2} = -3 - 2\sqrt{2}$

20. $\dfrac{x}{my} = d\left(\dfrac{r}{a} + b\right)$

$\dfrac{x}{my} = \dfrac{dr}{a} + db$

$ax = dmry + abdmy$

$ax = y(dmr + abdm)$

$y = \dfrac{ax}{dmr + abdm}$

21. $\dfrac{x}{my} = d\left(\dfrac{r}{a} + b\right)$

$\dfrac{x}{my} = \dfrac{dr}{a} + db$

$ax = dmry + abdmy$

$ax - abdmy = dmry$

$a(x - bdmy) = dmry$

$a = \dfrac{dmry}{x - bdmy}$

22.

$A = 4 \cos 40° \approx 3.06$

$B = 4 \sin 40° \approx 2.57$

$\begin{array}{r} -3.06R + 2.57U \\ 6.00R + 0.00U \\ \hline 2.94R + 2.57U \end{array}$

$\tan \theta = \dfrac{2.57}{2.94}$

$\theta \approx 41.16°$

$F = \sqrt{(2.57)^2 + (2.94)^2} \approx 3.90$

3.90$\underline{/41.16°}$

23. There is never an exact solution to these problems. One possible solution is given here.

$O = mI + b$

Use the graph to find the slope.

$m = \dfrac{100 - 30}{30 - 20} = \dfrac{70}{10} = 7$

$O = 7I + b$

Use the point (20, 30) for I and O.

$30 = 7(20) + b$

$-110 = b$

$O = 7I - 110$

24. $\dfrac{-9^{3/2}}{27^{2/3}} = \dfrac{-(9^{1/2})^3}{(27^{1/3})^2} = \dfrac{-27}{9} = -3$

25. $-2i^5 + 3i^3 - \sqrt{-9} + \sqrt{-4} - \sqrt{-2}\sqrt{-2}$

$= -2i - 3i - 3i + 2i + 2 = 2 - 6i$

26. $2\sqrt{\dfrac{9}{5}} + 3\sqrt{\dfrac{5}{9}} + 3\sqrt{45} = \dfrac{6}{\sqrt{5}} + \sqrt{5} + 9\sqrt{5}$

$= \dfrac{6\sqrt{5}}{5} + \dfrac{5\sqrt{5}}{5} + \dfrac{45\sqrt{5}}{5} = \dfrac{56\sqrt{5}}{5}$

27. See Lesson 71.

28. $\dfrac{400 \text{ mL}}{\text{s}} \times \dfrac{60 \text{ s}}{1 \text{ min}} \times \dfrac{1 \text{ cm}^3}{1 \text{ mL}} \times \dfrac{1 \text{ in.}}{2.54 \text{ cm}}$

$\times \dfrac{1 \text{ in.}}{2.54 \text{ cm}} \times \dfrac{1 \text{ in.}}{2.54 \text{ cm}}$

$= \dfrac{400(60)}{(2.54)(2.54)(2.54)} \dfrac{\text{in.}^3}{\text{min}}$

29. $\begin{array}{r} 3x^2 - 6x + 10 - \frac{18}{x+2} \\ x + 2 \overline{) 3x^3 + 0x^2 - 2x + 2} \\ \underline{3x^3 + 6x^2} \\ -6x^2 - 2x \\ \underline{-6x^2 - 12x} \\ 10x + 2 \\ \underline{10x + 20} \\ -18 \end{array}$

30. (a) $x \cdot x = 3(9 + 3)$

$$x^2 = 36$$

$$x = \mathbf{6}$$

(b) $2(2 + 4) = 1(1 + x)$

$$12 = 1 + x$$

$$\mathbf{11} = x$$

PRACTICE SET 92

a. $(B + W)T_D = D_D$

$(4 + W)T_D = 50$

$4T_D + WT_D = 50$ (a)

$(B - W)T_U = D_U$

$(4 - W)T_D = 30$

$4T_D - WT_D = 30$ (b)

(a) $4T_D + WT_D = 50$

(b) $\dfrac{4T_D - WT_D = 30}{8T_D \qquad\quad = 80}$

$$T_D = \mathbf{10 \ hours} = T_U$$

(a) $4(10) + W(10) = 50$

$$10W = 10$$

$$W = \mathbf{1 \ mph}$$

b. $(B + W)T_D = D_D$

$(B + W)(3) = (33)$

$3B + 3W = 33$

$B + W = 11$ (a)

$(B - W)T_U = D_U$

$(B - W)(4) = (12)$

$4B - 4W = 12$

$B - W = 3$ (b)

(a) $B + W = 11$

(b) $\dfrac{B - W = \ 3}{2B \qquad\ = 14}$

$$B = \mathbf{7 \ mph}$$

(a) $(7) + W = 11$

$$W = \mathbf{4 \ mph}$$

PROBLEM SET 92

1. (a) $(B + W)T_D = D_D$

$(10 + W)T_D = 70$

(b) $(B - W)T_U = D_U$

$(10 - W)T_U = 30$

$T_D = T_U$, so we use T in both equations.

(a′) $10T + WT = \ 70$

(b′) $\dfrac{10T - WT = \ 30}{20T \qquad\quad = 100}$

$$T = \mathbf{5 \ hr}$$

(a′) $10(5) + W(5) = 70$

$$5W = 20$$

$$W = \mathbf{4 \ mph}$$

2. (a) $(B + W)T_D = D_D$

$(B + W)4 = 60$

(a′) $4B + 4W = 60$

(b) $(B - W)T_U = D_U$

$(B - W)5 = 55$

(b′) $5B - 5W = 55$

5(a′) $20B + 20W = 300$

4(b′) $\dfrac{20B - 20W = 220}{40B \qquad\qquad = 520}$

$$B = \mathbf{13 \ mph}$$

(a′) $4(13) + 4W = 60$

$$4W = 8$$

$$W = \mathbf{2 \ mph}$$

3. (a) $(B + W)T_D = D_D$

$(B + 7)T_D = 35$

(b) $(B - W)T_U = D_U$

$(B - 7)T_U = 21$

$TD = T_U$, so we use T in both equations.

(a′) $BT + 7T = 35$

(b′) $\dfrac{BT - 7T = 21}{2BT \qquad\quad = 56}$

(c) $\qquad BT = 28$

(a′) $(28) + 7T = 35$

$$7T = 7$$

$$T = \mathbf{1 \ hr}$$

(c) $B(1) = 28$

$$B = \mathbf{28 \ kph}$$

4. Equal ratio method:

$$\frac{G_1}{G_2} = \frac{C_1}{C_2}$$

$$\frac{500}{1750} = \frac{20}{C_2}$$

$C_2 = $ **70 delicious comestibles**

Variation method:

$G = kC$

$500 = k(20)$

$25 = k$

$$1750 = 25(C)$$

70 delicious comestibles $= C$

5.

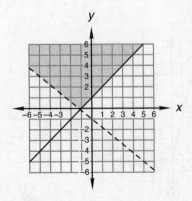

$D_W = R_W T_W = 6T_W;\ D_H = D_W + 50;$

$D_H = R_H T_H = 8T_H;\ T_W = T_H$ so use T

$8T = 6T + 50$

$2T = 50$

$T = $ **25 s**

6. (a) $y \geq x + 1$

(b) $y > -\dfrac{4}{5}x - 1$

The first step is to graph each of these lines.

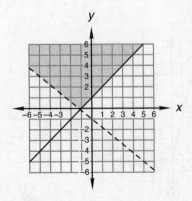

The region we wish to find is on or above the solid line and above the dashed line. This region is shaded in the figure.

7. (a) $y \leq \dfrac{1}{2}x + 2$

(b) $x < 2$

The first step is to graph each of these lines.

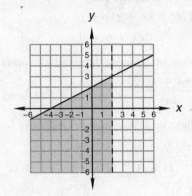

The region we wish to find is on or below the solid line and to the left of the dashed line. This region is shaded in the figure.

8. (a) $x + y + z = 6$

(b) $3x - y + z = 8$

(c) $x - 2y + z = 0$

(a) $\quad x + y + z = 6$
(b) $\underline{3x - y + z = 8}$
(d) $\quad 4x \quad\ + 2z = 14$

2(a) $2x + 2y + 2z = 12$
(c) $\underline{\ x - 2y + z = 0\ }$
(e) $3x \qquad + 3z = 12$

3(d) $12x + 6z = 42$
-2(e) $\underline{-6x - 6z = -24}$
$\qquad 6x \qquad\ = 18$
$\qquad\qquad x = 3$

(e) $3(3) + 3z = 12$

$3z = 3$

$z = 1$

(a) $(3) + y + (1) = 6$

$y = 2$

(3, 2, 1)

9. (a) $x^2 + y^2 = 10$

(b) $x + y = 4$

$y = 4 - x$

(b′) $y^2 = (4 - x)^2 = 16 - 8x + x^2$

Substitute (b′) into (a) and get:

(a′) $x^2 + (16 - 8x + x^2) = 10$

$2x^2 - 8x + 6 = 0$

Solve this equation by using the quadratic formula.

$x = \dfrac{8 \pm \sqrt{64 - 4(12)}}{4} = 2 \pm 1 = 3, 1$

Substitute these values of x into (b) and solve for y.

(b) $y = 4 - (3) = 1$

(b) $y = 4 - (1) = 3$

(3, 1) and **(1, 3)**

10. $-4 \le x - 2 < 2$; $D = \{\text{Reals}\}$

$-2 \le x < 4$

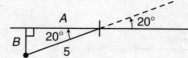

11. $x - 1 \nless 2$ or $x + 2 \ngeq 2$; $D = \{\text{Integers}\}$

$x - 1 \ge 2$ or $x + 2 < 2$

$x \ge 3$ or $x < 0$

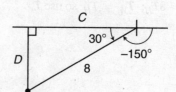

12. $\dfrac{(y^{a+2})^2 x^{2b/3}}{x^b y^{-a}} = y^{2a+4+a} x^{2b/3-b}$

$= y^{3a+4} x^{-b/3}$

13. $\dfrac{x}{y + \dfrac{y}{\dfrac{1}{x} + y}} = \dfrac{x}{y + \dfrac{xy}{1 + xy}}$

$= \dfrac{x(1 + xy)}{y + xy^2 + xy}$

14. $\dfrac{m}{a + \dfrac{a}{1 + \dfrac{a}{m}}} = \dfrac{m}{a + \dfrac{am}{m + a}}$

$= \dfrac{m(m + a)}{2am + a^2}$

15. $\dfrac{i - 5}{7 - i} \cdot \dfrac{7 + i}{7 + i} = \dfrac{7i - 1 - 35 - 5i}{49 + 1}$

$= \dfrac{-36 + 2i}{50} = -\dfrac{18}{25} + \dfrac{1}{25}i$

16. $\dfrac{3i + 2}{2i - 3} \cdot \dfrac{2i + 3}{2i + 3} = \dfrac{-6 + 9i + 4i + 6}{-4 - 9}$

$= \dfrac{13i}{-13} = -i$

17. $\sqrt{-z} - 3 = \sqrt{-z - 27}$

$z - 6\sqrt{z} + 9 = z - 27$

$36 = 6\sqrt{z}$

$6 = \sqrt{z}$

$\mathbf{36} = z$

Check: $\sqrt{36} - 3 = \sqrt{36 - 27}$

$6 - 3 = \sqrt{9}$

18.

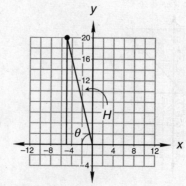

$A = 5\cos 20° \approx 4.70$

$B = 5\sin 20° \approx 1.71$

$C = 8\cos 30° \approx 6.93$

$D = 8\sin 30° = 4$

$\begin{array}{r} -4.70R - 1.71U \\ -6.93R - 4.00U \\ \hline \mathbf{-11.63R - 5.71U} \end{array}$

19.

$\tan \theta = -\dfrac{20}{5}$

$\theta \approx -75.96°$

Since θ is a second-quadrant angle,

$\theta = -75.96 + 180 = 104.04°$

$H = \sqrt{(20)^2 + (-5)^2}$

$H = 5\sqrt{17}$

$\mathbf{5\sqrt{17}\,/104.04°}$

20. $\dfrac{3 - 5\sqrt{2}}{2 - \sqrt{2}} \cdot \dfrac{2 + \sqrt{2}}{2 + \sqrt{2}}$

$= \dfrac{6 + 3\sqrt{2} - 10\sqrt{2} - 10}{4 - 2} = \dfrac{\mathbf{-4 - 7\sqrt{2}}}{\mathbf{2}}$

21. $\dfrac{8 - \sqrt{2}}{4 - \sqrt{8}} = \dfrac{8 - \sqrt{2}}{4 - 2\sqrt{2}} \cdot \dfrac{4 + 2\sqrt{2}}{4 + 2\sqrt{2}}$

$= \dfrac{32 + 16\sqrt{2} - 4\sqrt{2} - 4}{16 - 8} = \dfrac{28 + 12\sqrt{2}}{8}$

$= \dfrac{\mathbf{7 + 3\sqrt{2}}}{\mathbf{2}}$

22. $\sqrt[5]{x^4 y^3}\,\sqrt[3]{x y^2} = x^{4/5}y^{3/5}x^{1/3}y^{2/3} = \mathbf{x^{17/15}y^{19/15}}$

23.
$$\dfrac{a}{by} = x\left(\dfrac{1}{R_1} + \dfrac{1}{R_2}\right)$$
$$\dfrac{a}{by} = \dfrac{x}{R_1} + \dfrac{x}{R_2}$$
$$aR_1R_2 = bxyR_2 + bxyR_1$$
$$bxyR_2 = aR_1R_2 - bxyR_1$$
$$bxyR_2 = R_1(aR_2 - bxy)$$
$$\dfrac{\mathbf{bxyR_2}}{\mathbf{aR_2 - bxy}} = R_1$$

24.
$$\dfrac{a}{by} = x\left(\dfrac{1}{R_1} + \dfrac{1}{R_2}\right)$$
$$\dfrac{a}{by} = \dfrac{x}{R_1} + \dfrac{x}{R_2}$$
$$aR_1R_2 = byxR_2 + byxR_1$$
$$aR_1R_2 = y(bxR_2 + bxR_1)$$
$$\dfrac{\mathbf{aR_1R_2}}{\mathbf{bxR_2 + bxR_1}} = y$$

25. $i^3 - 2i^4 + \sqrt{-9} - \sqrt{-2}\,\sqrt{-2}$

$= -i - 2 + 3i + 2 = \mathbf{2i}$

26. $\sqrt{\dfrac{5}{12}} - 3\sqrt{\dfrac{12}{5}} + 2\sqrt{60}$

$= \dfrac{\sqrt{5}}{2\sqrt{3}}\dfrac{\sqrt{3}}{\sqrt{3}} - \dfrac{6\sqrt{3}}{\sqrt{5}}\dfrac{\sqrt{5}}{\sqrt{5}} + 4\sqrt{15}$

$= \dfrac{\sqrt{15}}{6} - \dfrac{6\sqrt{15}}{5} + 4\sqrt{15}$

$= \dfrac{5\sqrt{15}}{30} - \dfrac{36\sqrt{15}}{30} + \dfrac{120\sqrt{15}}{30} = \dfrac{\mathbf{89\sqrt{15}}}{\mathbf{30}}$

27. $-3x^2 - x = 5$

$-3x^2 - x - 5 = 0$

$x = \dfrac{1 \pm \sqrt{1 - 4(15)}}{-6} = -\dfrac{1}{6} \pm \dfrac{\sqrt{59}}{6}i$

28. $\dfrac{15 \text{ cm}}{\text{s}} \times \dfrac{1 \text{ in.}}{2.54 \text{ cm}} \times \dfrac{1 \text{ ft}}{12 \text{ in.}} \times \dfrac{1 \text{ yd}}{3 \text{ ft}} \times \dfrac{60 \text{ s}}{1 \text{ min}}$

$= \dfrac{\mathbf{15(60)}}{\mathbf{(2.54)(12)(3)}} \dfrac{\mathbf{yd}}{\mathbf{min}}$

29. $\dfrac{4}{x^2 - 9} - \dfrac{3x}{-3 + x}$

$= \dfrac{4}{(x + 3)(x - 3)} - \dfrac{3x(x + 3)}{(x - 3)(x + 3)}$

$= \dfrac{4 - 3x^2 - 9x}{(x + 3)(x - 3)} = \dfrac{\mathbf{-3x^2 - 9x + 4}}{\mathbf{x^2 - 9}}$

30. $x = \dfrac{100 + 20}{2} = \mathbf{60}$

$3 \cdot 7 = 4 \cdot y$

$21 = 4y$

$\dfrac{\mathbf{21}}{\mathbf{4}} = y$

PRACTICE SET 93

a. $\qquad x^2 = -3x + 2$

$x^2 + 3x - 2 = 0$

$a = 1,\ b = 3,\ c = -2$

$b^2 - 4ac = (3)^2 - 4(1)(-2) = 9 + 8 = 17$

The discriminant is a positive number, so **there are two real number solutions.**

b. $\qquad -4x = -3x^2 - 3$

$3x^2 - 4x + 3 = 0$

$a = 3,\ b = -4,\ c = 3$

$b^2 - 4ac = (-4)^2 - 4(3)(3) = 16 - 36 = -20$

The discriminant is a negative number, so **there are two complex solutions that are conjugates.**

PROBLEM SET 93

1. Downstream: $(B + W)T_D = D_D$ (a)

Upstream: $(B - W)T_U = D_U$ (b)

Since $T_D = T_U$, we use T_D in both equations.

(a') $BT_D + 5T_D = 45$

(b') $\dfrac{BT_D - 5T_D = 15}{2BT_D \qquad\quad = 60}$

(c) $\qquad BT_D = 30$

(a') $(30) + 5T_D = 45$

$\qquad\quad 5T_D = 15$

$\qquad\qquad T_D = 3$

(c) $B(3) = 30$

$\quad B = \textbf{10 mph}$

2. Downstream: $(B + W)T_D = D_D$ (a)

Upstream: $(B - W)T_U = D_U$ (b)

(a') $4B + 4W = 48$

(b') $8B - 8W = 64$

2(a') $8B + 8W = 96$

 (b') $\dfrac{8B - 8W = 64}{16B \qquad\quad = 160}$

$\qquad\qquad B = \textbf{10 mph}$

(a') $4(10) + 4W = 48$

$\qquad\qquad 4W = 8$

$\qquad\qquad W = \textbf{2 mph}$

3. Downstream: $(B + W)T_D = D_D$ (a)

Upstream: $(B - W)T_U = D_U$ (b)

Since $T_U = 2T_D$, we substitute and get:

(a') $40T_D + WT_D = 210$

(b') $80T_D - 2WT_D = 380$

2(a') $80T_D + 2WT_D = 420$

 (b') $\dfrac{80T_D - 2WT_D = 380}{160T_D \qquad\qquad = 800}$

$\qquad\qquad T_D = 5$

(a') $40(5) + W(5) = 210$

$\qquad\qquad 5W = 10$

$\qquad\qquad W = \textbf{2 mph}$

4.

$$\begin{array}{c} \xrightarrow{\hspace{3cm}} \\[-4pt] D_C \\[-10pt] \end{array}$$

D_C

40

D_R

48

$R_C T_C = 40; \quad T_R = T_C - 4;$

$R_R T_R = 48; \quad R_R = 2R_C$

$2R_C(T_C - 4) = 48$

$2R_C T_C - 8R_C = 48$

$2(40) - 8R_C = 48$

$\qquad\quad 32 = 8R_C$

$\qquad\quad 4 = R_C$

$R_C = \textbf{4 mph}; \quad R_R = \textbf{8 mph};$

$T_C = \textbf{10 hr}; \quad T_R = \textbf{6 hr}$

5. $\dfrac{P_1}{T_1} = \dfrac{P_2}{T_2}$

$T_2 = \dfrac{P_2 T_1}{P_1}$

$T_2 = \dfrac{(1)(4000)}{5} = \textbf{800 K}$

6. $\qquad\qquad x^2 = -5x + 1$

$x^2 + 5x - 1 = 0$

$b^2 - 4ac = (5)^2 - 4(1)(-1) = 25 + 4 = 29$

$b^2 - 4ac > 0$

There are two real number solutions.

7. $\qquad\qquad -3x = -2x^2 - 5$

$2x^2 - 3x + 5 = 0$

$b^2 - 4ac = (-3)^2 - 4(2)(5) = 9 - 40 = -31$

$b^2 - 4ac < 0$

There are two complex number solutions that are conjugates.

8. (a) $x + 2y < 2$

$\qquad\qquad 2y < -x + 2$

$\qquad\qquad y < -\dfrac{1}{2}x + 1$

(b) $y \geq -1$

The next step is to graph each of these lines.

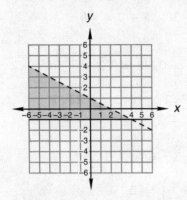

The region we wish to find is on or above the solid line and below the dashed line. This region is shaded in the figure.

9. $-3 < x - 4 < 2; \quad D = \{\text{Integers}\}$

$1 < x < 6$

10. (a) $x + y - 2z = -3$

(b) $2x + y + z = 7$

(c) $3x - y - z = 13$

(b) $2x + y + z = 7$

(c) $\underline{3x - y - z = 13}$

$5x = 20$

$x = 4$

-1(a) $-x - y + 2z = 3$

(b) $2x + y + z = 7$

(d) $\underline{x + 3z = 10}$

(d) $(4) + 3z = 10$

$3z = 6$

$z = 2$

(a) $(4) + y - 2(2) = -3$

$y = -3$

(4, –3, 2)

11. (a) $x^2 + y^2 = 1$

(b) $x - 2y = 2$

$x = 2y + 2$

(b′) $x^2 = (2y + 2)^2 = 4y^2 + 8y + 4$

Substitute (b′) into (a) and get:

(a′) $(4y^2 + 8y + 4) + y^2 = 1$

$5y^2 + 8y + 3 = 0$

Solve this equation by using the quadratic formula.

$$y = \frac{-8 \pm \sqrt{8^2 - 4(3)(5)}}{2(5)} = -\frac{4}{5} \pm \frac{1}{5}$$

$$y = -\frac{3}{5}, 1$$

Substitute these values of y into (b) and solve for x.

(b) $x = 2\left(-\dfrac{3}{5}\right) + \dfrac{10}{5} = \dfrac{4}{5}$

(b) $x = 2(-1) + 2 = 0$

$(\mathbf{0, -1})$ and $\left(\dfrac{\mathbf{4}}{\mathbf{5}}, -\dfrac{\mathbf{3}}{\mathbf{5}}\right)$

12. $(y^{a+2})^2 y^{a/3} y^2 = y^{2a+4+a/3+2} = \mathbf{y^{7a/3+6}}$

13. $\dfrac{x}{1 + \dfrac{a}{b + \dfrac{1}{c}}} = \dfrac{x}{1 + \dfrac{ac}{bc + 1}}$

$$= \frac{x(bc + 1)}{bc + 1 + ac}$$

14. $\dfrac{m}{2x + \dfrac{3}{3 + \dfrac{1}{m}}} = \dfrac{m}{2x + \dfrac{3m}{3m + 1}}$

$$= \frac{m(3m + 1)}{6mx + 2x + 3m}$$

15. $\dfrac{3i - 5}{i - 7} \cdot \dfrac{i + 7}{i + 7} = \dfrac{-3 - 5i + 21i - 35}{-1 - 49}$

$$= \frac{-38 + 16i}{-50} = \frac{19}{25} - \frac{8}{25}i$$

16. $\dfrac{2i + 4}{3i + 2} \cdot \dfrac{3i - 2}{3i - 2} = \dfrac{-6 + 12i - 4i - 8}{-9 - 4}$

$$= \frac{-14 + 8i}{-13} = \frac{14}{13} - \frac{8}{13}i$$

17. $\sqrt{p} = 5 + \sqrt{p - 35}$

$\sqrt{p} - 5 = \sqrt{p - 35}$

$p - 10\sqrt{p} + 25 = p - 35$

$-10\sqrt{p} = -60$

$\sqrt{p} = 6$

$p = \mathbf{36}$

Check: $\sqrt{36} = 5 + \sqrt{36 - 35}$

$6 = 5 + 1$

18.

$A = 12 \cos 32° \approx 10.18$

$B = 12 \sin 32° \approx 6.36$

$\begin{array}{r} -10.18R - 6.36U \\ \underline{15.00R + 0.00U} \\ \mathbf{4.82R - 6.36U} \end{array}$

$\tan \theta = \dfrac{-6.36}{4.82}$

$\theta \approx -52.84°$

$H = \sqrt{(-6.36)^2 + (4.82)^2} \approx 7.98$

$\mathbf{7.98\underline{/-52.84°}}$

19. $\dfrac{3 + 4\sqrt{2}}{3\sqrt{2} - 4} \cdot \dfrac{3\sqrt{2} + 4}{3\sqrt{2} + 4}$

$= \dfrac{9\sqrt{2} + 24 + 12 + 16\sqrt{2}}{18 - 16}$

$= \dfrac{\mathbf{36 + 25\sqrt{2}}}{\mathbf{2}}$

20. $\dfrac{5 + \sqrt{5}}{5 + 2\sqrt{5}} \cdot \dfrac{5 - 2\sqrt{5}}{5 - 2\sqrt{5}}$

$= \dfrac{25 + 5\sqrt{5} - 10\sqrt{5} - 10}{25 - 20} = \dfrac{15 - 5\sqrt{5}}{5}$

$= \mathbf{3 - \sqrt{5}}$

21. $\sqrt[3]{4^5 \sqrt{2}} = \left(2^2(2^{1/5})\right)^{1/3} = 2^{2/3}2^{1/15} = \mathbf{2^{11/15}}$

22. $\sqrt[4]{xy^6}\sqrt{x^3 y^5} = x^{1/4}y^{3/2}x^{3/2}y^{5/2} = \mathbf{x^{7/4}y^4}$

23. $\dfrac{a + c}{m} = m\left(\dfrac{1}{x} + \dfrac{b}{d}\right)$

$\dfrac{a + c}{m} = \dfrac{m}{x} + \dfrac{mb}{d}$

$adx + cdx = dm^2 + m^2bx$

$adx = dm^2 + m^2bx - cdx$

$a = \dfrac{\mathbf{dm^2 + m^2bx - cdx}}{\mathbf{dx}}$

24. $\dfrac{a + c}{m} = m\left(\dfrac{1}{x} + \dfrac{b}{d}\right)$

$\dfrac{a + c}{m} = \dfrac{m}{x} + \dfrac{mb}{d}$

$adx + cdx = dm^2 + m^2bx$

$adx + cdx - m^2bx = dm^2$

$x = \dfrac{\mathbf{dm^2}}{\mathbf{ad + cd - m^2b}}$

25. $i^3 - 2i^2 - \sqrt{-9} + \sqrt{-4}\sqrt{-4} + 2$

$= -i + 2 - 3i - 4 + 2 = \mathbf{-4i}$

26. $3\sqrt{\dfrac{2}{9}} + \sqrt{\dfrac{9}{2}} - 3\sqrt{18} = \sqrt{2} + \dfrac{3\sqrt{2}}{2} - 9\sqrt{2}$

$= \dfrac{2\sqrt{2}}{2} + \dfrac{3\sqrt{2}}{2} - \dfrac{18\sqrt{2}}{2} = -\dfrac{\mathbf{13\sqrt{2}}}{\mathbf{2}}$

27. $\qquad 3x^2 = -x - 2$

$\left(3x^2 + x + \quad\right) = -2$

$x^2 + \dfrac{1}{3}x + \dfrac{1}{36} = -\dfrac{24}{36} + \dfrac{1}{36}$

$\left(x + \dfrac{1}{6}\right)^2 = -\dfrac{23}{36}$

$x + \dfrac{1}{6} = \pm\dfrac{\sqrt{23}}{6}i$

$x = -\dfrac{1}{6} \pm \dfrac{\sqrt{23}}{6}i$

28. $\dfrac{10\text{ m}}{\text{s}} \times \dfrac{60\text{ s}}{1\text{ min}} \times \dfrac{100\text{cm}}{1\text{ m}} \times \dfrac{1\text{ in.}}{2.54\text{ cm}} \times \dfrac{1\text{ ft}}{12\text{ in.}}$

$= \dfrac{\mathbf{10(60)(100)}}{\mathbf{(2.54)(12)}}\ \dfrac{\mathbf{ft}}{\mathbf{min}}$

29.

$$x + 3 \overline{\smash{\big)}\ x^3 - 3x^2 + 0x - 2} \quad\quad x^2 - 6x + 18 - \dfrac{56}{x+3}$$

$\underline{x^3 + 3x^2}$

$-6x^2 + 0x$

$\underline{-6x^2 - 18x}$

$18x - 2$

$\underline{18x + 54}$

-56

30. $\dfrac{90 - x}{2} = 25$

$90 - x = 50$

$x = \mathbf{40}$

$5(5 + y) = 4(11)$

$25 + 5y = 44$

$5y = 19$

$y = \dfrac{\mathbf{19}}{\mathbf{5}}$

PRACTICE SET 94

a. Function

b. Function

c. Function

d. Not a function

e. $p(-5) = (-5)^2 - 5(-5) = 25 + 25 = \mathbf{50}$

PROBLEM SET 94

1. $PV = nRT$

$$n = \frac{PV}{RT}$$

$$n = \frac{(2)(10)}{(0.0821)(473)} = \mathbf{0.52\ mole}$$

2. $0.2(40) + 0.6A = 0.44(40 + A)$

$$8 + 0.6A = 17.6 + 0.44A$$

$$0.16A = 9.6$$

$$A = \mathbf{60\ gallons}$$

3. Downstream: $(B + W)T_D = D_D$ (a)

Upstream: $(B - W)T_U = D_U$ (b)

Since $T_D = T_U$, we use T_D in both equations.

(a′) $10T_D + WT_D = 48$

(b′) $\underline{10T_D - WT_D = 32}$

$\ \ 20T_D = 80$

$$T_D = 4$$

(a′) $10(4) + W(4) = 48$

$$4W = 8$$

$$W = \mathbf{2\ mph}$$

4. $P_1V_1 = P_2V_2$

$$(700)(1400) = (2800)V_2$$

$$V_2 = \frac{(700)(1400)}{2800} = \mathbf{350\ mL}$$

5. $P = \dfrac{k}{R^2}$

$$4 = \frac{k}{10^2}$$

$$400 = k$$

$$P = \frac{400}{5^2} = \mathbf{16\ purples}$$

6. Sets **(a)**, **(b)**, and **(d)** are functions.

Set (c) is not a function, because 6 has two images.

7. $p(x) = x^2 - 2x$

$$p(-2) = (-2)^2 - 2(-2)$$

$$p = 4 + 4$$

$$p = \mathbf{8}$$

8. $-x^2 = 4x + 4$

$$0 = x^2 + 4x + 4$$

$$b^2 - 4ac = 4^2 - 4(1)(4) = 16 - 16 = 0$$

There is one real number solution.

9. (a) $2x + 3y > -6$

$$3y > -2x - 6$$

$$y > -\frac{2}{3}x - 2$$

(b) $x - 3y \geq -6$

$$-3y \geq -x - 6$$

$$y \leq \frac{1}{3}x + 2$$

The next step is to graph each of these lines.

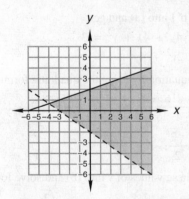

The region we wish to find is on or below the solid line and above the dashed line. This region is shaded in the figure.

10. $-x + 3 \not< -2$ or $-x + 3 < -5$; $D = \{\text{Integers}\}$

$$-x + 3 \geq -2 \quad \text{or} \quad -x + 3 < -5$$

$$-x \geq -5 \quad \text{or} \quad -x < -8$$

$$x \leq 5 \quad \text{or} \quad x > 8$$

11. (a) $x + 2y - z = 2$

(b) $2x - y + z = 2$

(c) $3x - y + 2z = 4$

(a) $x + 2y - z = 2$

(b) $\underline{2x - y + z = 2}$

(d) $3x + y \qquad = 4$

2(a) $2x + 4y - 2z = 4$

(c) $\underline{3x - y + 2z = 4}$

(e) $5x + 3y \qquad = 8$

3(d) $9x + 3y = 12$

−1(e) $\underline{-5x - 3y = -8}$

$4x \qquad = 4$

$x = 1$

(d) $3(1) + y = 4$

$y = 1$

(b) $2(1) - (1) + z = 2$

$1 + z = 2$

$z = 1$

(1, 1, 1)

12. (a) $x^2 + y^2 = 3$

(b) $x - y = 2$

$x = y + 2$

(b′) $x^2 = (y + 2)^2 = y^2 + 4y + 4$

Substitute (b′) into (a) and get:

(a′) $(y^2 + 4y + 4) + y^2 = 3$

$2y^2 + 4y + 1 = 0$

Solve this equation by using the quadratic formula.

$y = \dfrac{-4 \pm \sqrt{16 - 8}}{4} = -1 \pm \dfrac{\sqrt{2}}{2}$

$y = -1 + \dfrac{\sqrt{2}}{2}, -1 - \dfrac{\sqrt{2}}{2}$

Substitute these values of y into (b) and solve for x.

(b) $x = \left(-1 + \dfrac{\sqrt{2}}{2}\right) + 2 = 1 + \dfrac{\sqrt{2}}{2}$

(b) $x = \left(-1 - \dfrac{\sqrt{2}}{2}\right) + 2 = 1 - \dfrac{\sqrt{2}}{2}$

$\left(\mathbf{1 + \dfrac{\sqrt{2}}{2}, -1 + \dfrac{\sqrt{2}}{2}}\right)$ **and**

$\left(\mathbf{1 - \dfrac{\sqrt{2}}{2}, -1 - \dfrac{\sqrt{2}}{2}}\right)$

13. $\dfrac{x^{a/3} y^2}{x^{3a/2} (y^2)^a} = x^{a/3 - 3a/2} y^{2 - 2a} = x^{-7a/6} y^{2 - 2a}$

14. $\dfrac{p}{m + \dfrac{m}{p - \dfrac{1}{mp}}} = \dfrac{p}{m + \dfrac{m^2 p}{mp^2 - 1}}$

$= \dfrac{p(mp^2 - 1)}{m^2 p^2 - m + m^2 p}$

15. $\dfrac{x}{a + \dfrac{b}{ab - \dfrac{1}{b}}} = \dfrac{x}{a + \dfrac{b^2}{ab^2 - 1}}$

$= \dfrac{x(ab^2 - 1)}{a^2 b^2 - a + b^2}$

16. $\dfrac{2i + 7}{-3i} \cdot \dfrac{3i}{3i} = \dfrac{-6 + 21i}{9} = -\dfrac{2}{3} + \dfrac{7}{3}i$

17. $\dfrac{-5i - 2}{-2i + 5} \cdot \dfrac{-2i - 5}{-2i - 5}$

$= \dfrac{-10 + 4i + 25i + 10}{-4 - 25} = \dfrac{29i}{-29} = -i$

18. $\sqrt{k} + \sqrt{k - 21} = 7$

$\sqrt{k - 21} = 7 - \sqrt{k}$

$k - 21 = 49 - 14\sqrt{k} + k$

$14\sqrt{k} = 70$

$\sqrt{k} = 5$

$k = \mathbf{25}$

Check: $\sqrt{25} + \sqrt{25 - 21} = 7$

$5 + 2 = 7$

19.

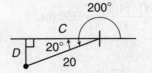

$A = 20 \cos 20° \approx 18.79$

$B = 20 \sin 20° \approx 6.84$

$C = 20 \cos 20° \approx 18.79$

$D = 20 \sin 20° \approx 6.84$

$18.79R + 6.84U$

$\underline{-18.79R - 6.84U}$

$\mathbf{0.00R + 0.00U}$

20.

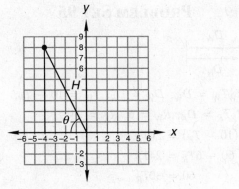

$$\tan \theta = -\frac{8}{4}$$

$$\theta \approx -63.43°$$

Since θ is a second-quadrant angle,

$$\theta = -63.43 + 180 = 116.57°$$

$$H = \sqrt{8^2 + (-4)^2}$$

$$H = 4\sqrt{5}$$

$$4\sqrt{5}\,\underline{/116.57°}$$

21. $\dfrac{2 - 5\sqrt{2}}{3\sqrt{2} - 2} \cdot \dfrac{3\sqrt{2} + 2}{3\sqrt{2} + 2}$

$= \dfrac{6\sqrt{2} - 30 + 4 - 10\sqrt{2}}{18 - 4}$

$= \dfrac{-26 - 4\sqrt{2}}{14} = \dfrac{-13 - 2\sqrt{2}}{7}$

22. $4\sqrt{\dfrac{5}{12}} + 3\sqrt{\dfrac{12}{5}} - 2\sqrt{240}$

$= \dfrac{2\sqrt{5}}{\sqrt{3}} + \dfrac{6\sqrt{3}}{\sqrt{5}} - 8\sqrt{15}$

$= \dfrac{2\sqrt{15}}{3} + \dfrac{6\sqrt{15}}{5} - 8\sqrt{15}$

$= \dfrac{10\sqrt{15}}{15} + \dfrac{18\sqrt{15}}{15} - \dfrac{120\sqrt{15}}{15} = -\dfrac{92\sqrt{15}}{15}$

23.
$$\frac{a + b}{x} = \left(\frac{1}{R_1} + \frac{c}{R_2}\right)$$

$$aR_1R_2 + bR_1R_2 = xR_2 + cxR_1$$

$$aR_1R_2 + bR_1R_2 - xR_2 = cxR_1$$

$$\frac{aR_1R_2 + bR_1R_2 - xR_2}{xR_1} = c$$

24.
$$\frac{a + b}{x} = \frac{1}{R_1} + \frac{c}{R_2}$$

$$aR_1R_2 + bR_1R_2 = xR_2 + cxR_1$$

$$aR_1R_2 + bR_1R_2 - cxR_1 = xR_2$$

$$R_1 = \frac{xR_2}{aR_2 + bR_2 - cx}$$

25. $3i^2 + 2i^5 - 2i + \sqrt{-9} - \sqrt{-2}\sqrt{2}$

$= -3 + 2i - 2i + 3i - 2i = \mathbf{-3 + i}$

26. (a) Since this is a 30°-60°-90° triangle,

$$\sqrt{3} \times \overrightarrow{SF} = 4$$

$$\overrightarrow{SF} = \frac{4\sqrt{3}}{3}$$

$$M = 1 \times \frac{4\sqrt{3}}{3} = \frac{\mathbf{4\sqrt{3}}}{\mathbf{3}}$$

$$N = 2 \times \frac{4\sqrt{3}}{3} = \frac{\mathbf{8\sqrt{3}}}{\mathbf{3}}$$

(b) Since this is a 45°-45°-90° triangle

$$1 \times \overrightarrow{SF} = 4$$

$$\overrightarrow{SF} = 4$$

$$C = 1 \times 4 = \mathbf{4}$$

$$D = \sqrt{2} \times 4 = \mathbf{4\sqrt{2}}$$

27. $-2x^2 = -7 + x$

$$0 = 2x^2 + x - 7$$

$$x = \frac{-1 \pm \sqrt{1 + 56}}{4} = -\frac{\mathbf{1}}{\mathbf{4}} \pm \frac{\sqrt{\mathbf{57}}}{\mathbf{4}}$$

28. $\dfrac{20 \text{ liters}}{\text{s}} \times \dfrac{1000 \text{ cm}^3}{1 \text{ liter}} \times \dfrac{1 \text{ in.}}{2.54 \text{ cm}} \times \dfrac{1 \text{ in.}}{2.54 \text{ cm}}$

$\times \dfrac{1 \text{ in.}}{2.54 \text{ cm}} \times \dfrac{60 \text{ s}}{1 \text{ min}}$

$= \dfrac{\mathbf{20(1000)(60)}}{\mathbf{(2.54)(2.54)(2.54)}} \dfrac{\text{in.}^3}{\text{min}}$

29. There is never an exact solution to these problems. One possible solution is given here.

$$N = mR + b$$

Use the graph to find the slope.

$$m = \frac{70 - 0}{120 - 180} \approx -1.17$$

$$N = (-1.17)R + b$$

Use the point (120, 70) for R and N.

$$70 = (-1.17)(120) + b$$

$$210.4 = b$$

$$N = \mathbf{-1.17R + 210.4}$$

30. $\dfrac{3}{a^4x^3} + \dfrac{4}{x^2 - 9} - \dfrac{3x}{-3 + x}$

$= \dfrac{\mathbf{3(x^2 - 9) + 4a^4x^3 - 3a^4x^4(x + 3)}}{\mathbf{a^4x^3(x^2 - 9)}}$

PRACTICE SET 95

a. $\begin{cases} 3x - y = 4 & \text{(a)} \quad \text{(straight line)} \\ xy = 7 & \text{(b)} \quad \text{(hyperbola)} \end{cases}$

(b) $xy = 7$

$$x = \frac{7}{y}$$

(a) $\quad 3\left(\dfrac{7}{y}\right) - y = 4$

$$\frac{21}{y} - y = 4$$

$$21 - y^2 = 4y$$

$$y^2 + 4y - 21 = 0$$

$$(y + 7)(y - 3) = 0$$

$$y = -7, 3$$

(b) $x(-7) = 7$

$$x = -1$$

(b) $x(3) = 7$

$$x = \frac{7}{3}$$

There are two solutions for this system: **(-1, -7)** and **$\left(\frac{7}{3}, 3\right)$**.

b. $\begin{cases} x^2 + y^2 = 10 & \text{(a)} \quad \text{(circle)} \\ 3x^2 - y^2 = -2 & \text{(b)} \quad \text{(hyperbola)} \end{cases}$

(a) $\quad x^2 + y^2 = 10$

(b) $\dfrac{3x^2 - y^2 = -2}{4x^2 \qquad\;\; = 8}$

$$x^2 = 2$$

$$x = \pm\sqrt{2}$$

(a) $(\sqrt{2})^2 + y^2 = 10$

$$2 + y^2 = 10$$

$$y^2 = 8$$

$$y = \pm\sqrt{8} = \pm2\sqrt{2}$$

(a) $(-\sqrt{2})^2 + y^2 = 10$

$$2 + y^2 = 10$$

$$y^2 = 8$$

$$y = \pm\sqrt{8} = \pm2\sqrt{2}$$

There are four solutions for this system:
$(\sqrt{2}, 2\sqrt{2})$, $(\sqrt{2}, -2\sqrt{2})$, $(-\sqrt{2}, 2\sqrt{2})$, and
$(-\sqrt{2}, -2\sqrt{2})$.

PROBLEM SET 95

1.

$R_W T_W = D_W; \; D_W = D_R; \; T_W = 10 - T_R;$
$R_R T_R = D_R; \; R_W = 6; \; R_R = 24$

$$6(10 - T_R) = 24T_R$$

$$60 - 6T_R = 24T_R$$

$$60 = 30T_R$$

$$2 = T_R$$

$$D_R = 2(24) = \textbf{48 km}$$

2. $0.6A + 0.2(200) = 0.52(A + 200)$

$$0.6A + 40 = 0.52A + 104$$

$$0.08A = 64$$

$$A = \frac{64}{0.08}$$

$$A = \textbf{800 mL}$$

3. $\dfrac{V_1}{T_1} = \dfrac{V_2}{T_2}$

$$V_2 = \frac{V_1 T_2}{T_1}$$

$$V_2 = \frac{(400)(873)}{473} = \textbf{738.27 mL}$$

4. $R_R T_R = 360; \; R_J T_J = 480;$
$T_J = 4T_R; \; R_J = R_R - 60$
$(R_R - 60)(4T_R) = 480$
$4(360) - 240T_R = 480$
$\qquad\qquad -240T_R = -960$
$\qquad\qquad\quad\; T_R = 4$

$T_R = \textbf{4 hr}; \; T_J = \textbf{16 hr};$
$R_R = \textbf{90 mph}; \; R_J = \textbf{30 mph}$

5. Downstream: $(B + W)T_D = D_D \quad$ (a)
Upstream: $(B - W)T_U = D_U \qquad$ (b)

(a′) $4B + 4W = 60$
(b′) $8B - 8W = 72$
2(a′) $8B + 8W = 120$
(b′) $\dfrac{8B - 8W = \;\; 72}{16B \qquad\;\; = 192}$

$$B = \textbf{12 mph}$$

(a′) $4(12) + 4W = 60$

$$4W = 12$$

$$W = \textbf{3 mph}$$

6. (a) $4x - y = 3$

(b) $xy = 6$

$$x = \frac{6}{y}$$

Substitute (b) into (a) and get:

(a′) $4\left(\dfrac{6}{y}\right) - y = 3$

$$\frac{24}{y} - y = 3$$

$$24 - y^2 = 3y$$

$$y^2 + 3y - 24 = 0$$

Solve this equation by using the quadratic formula.

$$y = \frac{-3 \pm \sqrt{9 - 4(-24)}}{2} = -\frac{3}{2} \pm \frac{\sqrt{105}}{2}$$

Substitute these values of y into (a) and solve for x.

(a) $4x = \left(-\dfrac{3}{2} + \dfrac{\sqrt{105}}{2}\right) + 3$

$$x = \frac{3}{8} + \frac{\sqrt{105}}{8}$$

(a) $4x = \left(-\dfrac{3}{2} - \dfrac{\sqrt{105}}{2}\right) + 3$

$$x = \frac{3}{8} - \frac{\sqrt{105}}{8}$$

$\left(\dfrac{3}{8} + \dfrac{\sqrt{105}}{8}, -\dfrac{3}{2} + \dfrac{\sqrt{105}}{2}\right)$ and

$\left(\dfrac{3}{8} - \dfrac{\sqrt{105}}{8}, -\dfrac{3}{2} - \dfrac{\sqrt{105}}{2}\right)$

7. (a) $x^2 + y^2 = 16$

(b) $\dfrac{2x^2 - y^2 = -1}{3x^2 \qquad = 15}$

$$x^2 = 5$$

$$x = \pm\sqrt{5}$$

(a) $(\sqrt{5})^2 + y^2 = 16$

$$y^2 = 11$$

$$y = \pm\sqrt{11}$$

(a) $(-\sqrt{5})^2 + y^2 = 16$

$$y^2 = 11$$

$$y = \pm\sqrt{11}$$

$(\sqrt{5}, \pm\sqrt{11})$ and $(-\sqrt{5}, \pm\sqrt{11})$

8. (a) $x + 2y - z = 4$

(b) $2x - y + z = -3$

(c) $x - y + z = -4$

(a) $x + 2y - z = 4$

(b) $\dfrac{2x - y + z = -3}{}$

(d) $3x + y \qquad = 1$

(a) $x + 2y - z = 4$

(c) $\dfrac{x - y + z = -4}{}$

(e) $2x + y \qquad = 0$

$$y = -2x$$

(d) $3x + (-2x) = 1$

$$x = 1$$

(e) $y = -2(1) = -2$

(b) $2 + 2 + z = -3$

$$z = -7$$

$(1, -2, -7)$

9. Systems (**a**) and (**d**) are functions. System (b) is not a function, because 5 has two images. System (c) is not a function because m has no image.

10. $3x^2 - x + 5 = 0$

$$b^2 - 4ac = 1 - 60 = -59$$

The quadratic has two complex number solutions that are conjugates.

11. (a) $x > -2$

(b) $2x + 3y > -3$

$$3y > -2x - 3$$

$$y > -\frac{2}{3}x - 1$$

The next step is to graph each of these lines.

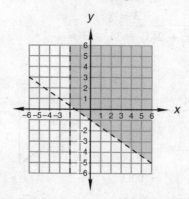

The region we wish to find is to the right of the vertical dashed line and above the slanted dashed line. This region is shaded in the figure.

12. $-2 < -x - 2 < 0$; $D = \{\text{Integers}\}$
$0 < -x < 2$
$0 > x > -2$

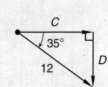

-3 -2 -1 0 1

13. $\dfrac{(a^{x+2})^{1/2}\,x^{2a}}{a^x x^a} = a^{x/2+1-x} x^{2a-a}$
$= a^{-x/2+1} x^a$

14. $\dfrac{x}{4 + \dfrac{4}{1 + \dfrac{x}{4}}} = \dfrac{x}{4 + \dfrac{16}{4+x}}$

$= \dfrac{x(4+x)}{16 + 4x + 16} = \dfrac{x(4+x)}{32 + 4x}$

15. $\dfrac{5}{2 + \dfrac{1}{2 + \dfrac{2}{x}}} = \dfrac{5}{2 + \dfrac{x}{2x+2}}$

$= \dfrac{5(2x+2)}{4x + 4 + x} = \dfrac{5(2x+2)}{5x+4} = \dfrac{10(x+1)}{5x+4}$

16. $\dfrac{3i-5}{3-5i} \cdot \dfrac{3+5i}{3+5i}$

$= \dfrac{9i - 15 - 15 - 25i}{9 + 25} = \dfrac{-30 - 16i}{34}$

$= -\dfrac{15}{17} - \dfrac{8}{17}i$

17. $\dfrac{4+i}{-i} \cdot \dfrac{i}{i} = \dfrac{4i-1}{1} = -1 + 4i$

18. $\sqrt{x^2 + 2x + 34} - x = 4$
$\quad \sqrt{x^2 + 2x + 34} = x + 4$
$\quad x^2 + 2x + 34 = x^2 + 8x + 16$
$\quad\quad\quad\quad\quad 18 = 6x$
$\quad\quad\quad\quad\quad\; 3 = x$
Check: $\sqrt{3^2 + 2(3) + 34} - 3 = 4$
$\quad\quad\quad\quad \sqrt{49} - 3 = 4$
$\quad\quad\quad\quad\quad 7 - 3 = 4$

19.

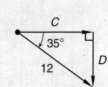

$C = 12 \cos 35° \approx 9.83$
$D = 12 \sin 35° \approx 6.88$
$\quad 14.00R + 0.00U$
$\quad \underline{\;9.83R - 6.88U}$
$\quad 23.83R - 6.88U$

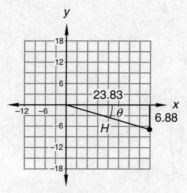

$\tan \theta = -\dfrac{6.88}{23.83}$
$\quad \theta \approx -16.10°$
$H = \sqrt{(-6.88)^2 + (23.83)^2} \approx 24.80$
24.80/−16.10°

20. $\dfrac{2\sqrt{2} - 5}{2\sqrt{2} + 3} \cdot \dfrac{2\sqrt{2} - 3}{2\sqrt{2} - 3}$

$= \dfrac{8 - 10\sqrt{2} - 6\sqrt{2} + 15}{8 - 9} = \dfrac{23 - 16\sqrt{2}}{-1}$

$= -23 + 16\sqrt{2}$

21. $\dfrac{3 - \sqrt{2}}{\sqrt{2} + 4} \cdot \dfrac{\sqrt{2} - 4}{\sqrt{2} - 4}$

$= \dfrac{3\sqrt{2} - 2 - 12 + 4\sqrt{2}}{2 - 16}$

$= \dfrac{-14 + 7\sqrt{2}}{-14} = \dfrac{2 - \sqrt{2}}{2}$

22. $\dfrac{m(a+b)}{x} = \left(\dfrac{1}{p} + \dfrac{r}{q}\right)$
$mapq + mbpq = qx + prx$
$mapq + mbpq - qx = prx$
$\dfrac{ampq + bmpq - qx}{px} = r$

23. $\dfrac{m(a+b)}{x} = \left(\dfrac{1}{p} + \dfrac{r}{q}\right)$
$mapq + mbpq = qx + prx$
$mapq + mbpq - prx = qx$
$p = \dfrac{qx}{amq + bmq - rx}$

24. $4 - 3i^2 + \sqrt{-9} + \sqrt{-3}\sqrt{-3}$
$= 4 + 3 + 3i - 3 = 4 + 3i$

25. $2\sqrt{\dfrac{7}{3}} - 3\sqrt{\dfrac{3}{7}} - 2\sqrt{84}$

$= \dfrac{2\sqrt{21}}{3} - \dfrac{3\sqrt{21}}{7} - 4\sqrt{21}$

$= \dfrac{14\sqrt{21}}{21} - \dfrac{9\sqrt{21}}{21} - \dfrac{84\sqrt{21}}{21} = -\dfrac{79\sqrt{21}}{21}$

26.
$$-x = x^2 - 3x - 4$$
$$4 = x^2 - 2x$$
$$4 + 1 = (x^2 - 2x + 1)$$
$$5 = (x - 1)^2$$
$$\pm\sqrt{5} = x - 1$$
$$\mathbf{1 \pm \sqrt{5}} = x$$

27. $PV = nRT$

$V = \dfrac{nRT}{P}$

$V = \dfrac{(1.32)(0.0821)(600)}{5} \approx \mathbf{13.00 \ liters}$

28. Write the equation of the given line in slope-intercept form.

$3y - 2x = 5$

$3y = 2x + 5$

$y = \dfrac{2}{3}x + \dfrac{5}{3}$

Since the slopes of perpendicular lines are negative reciprocals of each other,

$m_{\perp} = -\dfrac{3}{2}$

$y = -\dfrac{3}{2}x + b$

$2 = -\dfrac{3}{2}(4) + b$

$8 = b$

$y = -\dfrac{3}{2}x + 8$

29.
$$4(4 + x) = 5(12)$$
$$16 + 4x = 60$$
$$4x = 44$$
$$x = \mathbf{11}$$
$$6(6) = 4(4 + y)$$
$$36 = 16 + 4y$$
$$20 = 4y$$
$$\mathbf{5} = y$$

30. $\dfrac{30 \ mi}{hr} \times \dfrac{5280 \ ft}{1 \ mi} \times \dfrac{12 \ in.}{1 \ ft} \times \dfrac{2.54 \ cm}{1 \ in.}$

$\times \dfrac{1 \ hr}{60 \ min} \times \dfrac{1 \ min}{60 \ s}$

$= \dfrac{30(5280)(12)(2.54)}{(60)(60)} \dfrac{cm}{s}$

Practice Set 96

a. $\begin{cases} x - 3y = 5 & \text{(a)} \\ xy = 3 & \text{(b)} \end{cases}$

(b) $xy = 3$

$x = \dfrac{3}{y}$

(a) $\left(\dfrac{3}{y}\right) - 3y = 5$

$3 - 3y^2 = 5y$

$3y^2 + 5y - 3 = 0$

$y = \dfrac{-b \pm \sqrt{b^2 - 4ac}}{2a}$

$= \dfrac{-5 \pm \sqrt{5^2 - 4(3)(-3)}}{2(3)}$

$= -\dfrac{5}{6} \pm \dfrac{\sqrt{61}}{6}$

(a) $x - 3\left(-\dfrac{5}{6} + \dfrac{\sqrt{61}}{6}\right) = 5$

$x + \dfrac{5}{2} - \dfrac{\sqrt{61}}{2} = 5$

$x = \dfrac{5}{2} + \dfrac{\sqrt{61}}{2}$

(a) $x - 3\left(-\dfrac{5}{6} - \dfrac{\sqrt{61}}{6}\right) = 5$

$x + \dfrac{5}{2} + \dfrac{\sqrt{61}}{2} = 5$

$x = \dfrac{5}{2} - \dfrac{\sqrt{61}}{2}$

There are two solutions to this system:

$\left(\dfrac{5}{2} + \dfrac{\sqrt{61}}{2}, -\dfrac{5}{6} + \dfrac{\sqrt{61}}{6}\right)$ and

$\left(\dfrac{5}{2} - \dfrac{\sqrt{61}}{2}, -\dfrac{5}{6} - \dfrac{\sqrt{61}}{6}\right)$

b. Variation method:

$$E = \frac{kA}{D}$$

$$(75) = \frac{k(15)}{(85)}$$

$$6375 = 15k$$

$$425 = k$$

$$(20) = \frac{425(30)}{D}$$

$$20D = 12{,}750$$

$$D = \textbf{637 deer}$$

Note that half a deer is not considered as part of the population.

Equal ratio method:

$$\frac{E_1}{E_2} = \frac{A_1 D_2}{A_2 D_1}$$

$$\frac{(75)}{(20)} = \frac{(15)D_2}{(30)(85)}$$

$$D_2 = \textbf{637 deer}$$

Problem Set 96

1. Variation method:

$$N_G = \frac{kN_T}{N_B}$$

$$65 = \frac{k(15)}{3}$$

$$k = 13$$

$$5 = \frac{13(100)}{N_B}$$

$$N_B = \textbf{260 boys}$$

Equal ratio method:

$$\frac{N_{G1}}{N_{G2}} = \frac{N_{T1} N_{B2}}{N_{T2} N_{B1}}$$

$$\frac{65}{5} = \frac{(15)N_{B2}}{100(3)}$$

$$N_{B2} = \textbf{260 boys}$$

2. Variation method:

$$S = kRM$$

$$100 = k(4)(5)$$

$$k = 5$$

$$20 = 5(2)R$$

$$R = \textbf{2 ratchets}$$

Equal ratio method:

$$\frac{S_1}{S_2} = \frac{R_1 M_1}{R_2 M_2}$$

$$\frac{100}{20} = \frac{4(5)}{R(2)}$$

$$R = \textbf{2 ratchets}$$

3. Downstream: $(B + W)T_D = D_D$ (a)

Upstream: $(B - W)T_U = D_U$ (b)

Since $T_U = 2T_D$, we substitute and get:

(a′) $BT_D + 6T_D = 80$

(b) $2BT_D - 12T_D = 40$

2(a′) $2BT_D + 12T_D = 160$

$$\begin{array}{r} \text{(b′)} \quad 2BT_D - 12T_D = 40 \\ \hline 4BT_D = 200 \end{array}$$

(c) $BT_D = 50$

(a′) $(50) + 6T_D = 80$

$$6T_D = 30$$

$$T_D = 5$$

(c) $B(5) = 50$

$$B = \textbf{10 kph}$$

4. $R_G T_G = R_B T_B = 300;$

$T_G = T_B + 5;$ $R_B = 2R_G$

$$2R_G(T_G - 5) = 300$$

$$2R_G T_G - 10R_G = 300$$

$$300 = 10R_G$$

$$30 = R_G$$

$R_G = \textbf{30 mph};$ $R_B = \textbf{60 mph};$

$T_G = \textbf{10 hr};$ $T_B = \textbf{5 hr}$

5. (a) $0.2P_N + 0.6D_N = 160$

(b) $P_N + D_N = 500$

Substitute $D_N = 500 - P_N$ into (a) and get:

(a′) $0.2P_N + 0.6(500 - P_N) = 160$

$$-0.4P_N = -140$$

$$P_N = 350$$

(b) $(350) + D_N = 500$

$$D_N = 150$$

350 mL 20%, 150 mL 60%

6. (a) $x - 3y = 2$

(b) $xy = 4$

$$x = \frac{4}{y}$$

Substitute (b) into (a) and get:

(a′) $\left(\dfrac{4}{y}\right) - 3y = 2$

$$4 - 3y^2 = 2y$$

$$0 = 3y^2 + 2y - 4$$

Solve this equation by using the quadratic formula.

$$y = \frac{-2 \pm \sqrt{4 + 48}}{6} = -\frac{1}{3} \pm \frac{\sqrt{13}}{3}$$

Substitute these values of y into (a) and solve for x.

(a) $x - 3\left(-\dfrac{1}{3} + \dfrac{\sqrt{13}}{3}\right) = 2$

$$x + 1 - \sqrt{13} = 2$$

$$x = 1 + \sqrt{13}$$

(a) $x - 3\left(-\dfrac{1}{3} - \dfrac{\sqrt{13}}{3}\right) = 2$

$$x + 1 + \sqrt{13} = 2$$

$$x = 1 - \sqrt{13}$$

$$\left(1 + \sqrt{13}, -\frac{1}{3} + \frac{\sqrt{13}}{3}\right) \text{ and}$$

$$\left(1 - \sqrt{13}, -\frac{1}{3} - \frac{\sqrt{13}}{3}\right)$$

7. (a) $x^2 + y^2 = 4$

(b) $\dfrac{4x^2 - y^2 = -4}{5x^2 \qquad = 0}$

$$x^2 = 0$$

$$x = 0$$

(a) $(0)^2 + y^2 = 4$

$$y^2 = 4$$

$$y = \pm 2$$

(0, 2) and **(0, –2)**

8. (a) $x + 3y - z = 2$

(b) $x + y + 2z = 6$

(c) $2x + 2y - z = 2$

2(a) $2x + 6y - 2z = 4$

(b) $\dfrac{x + y + 2z = 6}{}$

(d) $3x + 7y = 10$

(b) $x + y + 2z = 6$

2(c) $\dfrac{4x + 4y - 2z = 4}{}$

(e) $5x + 5y = 10$

5(d) $15x + 35y = 50$

(–3)(e) $\dfrac{-15x - 15y = -30}{20y = 20}$

$$y = 1$$

(e) $5x + 5(1) = 10$

$$5x = 5$$

$$x = 1$$

(b) $(1) + (1) + 2z = 6$

$$2z = 4$$

$$z = 2$$

(1, 1, 2)

9. Sets **(a)** and **(b)** are functions. Set (c) is not a function, because 4 has two images.

10. $g(x) = x^2 - 4;\ D = \{\text{Integers}\}$

$g(-2) = (-2)^2 - 4 = 4 - 4 = \mathbf{0}$

11. (a) $x - y < -2$

$$-y < -x - 2$$

$$y > x + 2$$

(b) $y \geq -2$

The next step is to graph each of these lines.

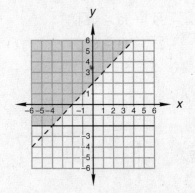

The region we wish to find is on or above the solid line and above the dashed line. This region is shaded in the figure.

12. $x + 4 \not> 2$ or $4 > -1;\ D = \{\text{Reals}\}$

$x + 4 \leq 2$ or $x - 4 > -1$

$x \leq -2$ or $x > 3$

13. $\dfrac{\left(a^{x+4}\right)^{1/2} b^{2x}}{a^{3/2} b^x} = a^{x/2 + 2 - 3/2} b^{2x-x}$

$= a^{x/2 + 1/2} b^x$

14. $\dfrac{x}{a + \dfrac{b}{a^2 + \dfrac{1}{ab}}} = \dfrac{x}{a + \dfrac{ab^2}{a^3b + 1}}$

$= \dfrac{x(a^3b + 1)}{a^4b + a + ab^2}$

15. $2\sqrt{8\sqrt[3]{2}} = 2\left(2^3(2^{1/3})\right)^{1/2} = 2(2^{10/3})^{1/2}$

$= 2(2^{5/3}) = \mathbf{2^{8/3}}$

16. $\dfrac{2i - 8}{4 - 6i} \cdot \dfrac{4 + 6i}{4 + 6i} = \dfrac{8i - 32 - 12 - 48i}{16 + 36}$

$= \dfrac{-44 - 40i}{52} = \mathbf{-\dfrac{11}{13} - \dfrac{10}{13}i}$

17. $\dfrac{i - i^2}{i} = \dfrac{i(1 - i)}{i} = \mathbf{1 - i}$

18. $\sqrt{s - 39} = 13 - \sqrt{s}$

$s - 39 = 169 - 26\sqrt{s} + s$

$26\sqrt{s} = 208$

$\sqrt{s} = 8$

$s = \mathbf{64}$

Check: $\sqrt{64 - 39} = 13 - \sqrt{64}$

$\sqrt{25} = 13 - 8$

$5 = 5$

19.

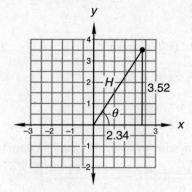

$A = 6\cos 67° \approx 2.34$

$B = 6\sin 67° \approx 5.52$

$2.34R + 5.52U$
$\underline{0.00R - 2.00U}$
$\mathbf{2.34R + 3.52U}$

$\tan\theta = \dfrac{3.52}{2.34}$

$\theta \approx 56.39°$

$H = \sqrt{(3.52)^2 + (2.34)^2}$

$H \approx 4.23$

4.23 / 56.39°

20. $\dfrac{3\sqrt{5} - 1}{1 - \sqrt{5}} \cdot \dfrac{1 + \sqrt{5}}{1 + \sqrt{5}}$

$= \dfrac{3\sqrt{5} - 1 + 15 - \sqrt{5}}{1 - 5} = \dfrac{14 + 2\sqrt{5}}{-4}$

$= \dfrac{\mathbf{-7 - \sqrt{5}}}{\mathbf{2}}$

21. $\dfrac{2 - \sqrt{7}}{1 + \sqrt{7}} \cdot \dfrac{1 - \sqrt{7}}{1 - \sqrt{7}}$

$= \dfrac{2 - \sqrt{7} - 2\sqrt{7} + 7}{1 - 7} = \dfrac{9 - 3\sqrt{7}}{-6}$

$= \dfrac{\mathbf{-3 + \sqrt{7}}}{\mathbf{2}}$

22. $c = m\left(\dfrac{a + d}{p} - r\right)$

$c = \dfrac{am + dm}{p} - mr$

$cp = am + dm - mpr$

$cp + mpr = am + dm$

$p = \dfrac{\mathbf{am + dm}}{\mathbf{c + mr}}$

23. $c = m\left(\dfrac{a + d}{p} - r\right)$

$c = \dfrac{am + dm}{p} - mr$

$cp = am + dm - mpr$

$cp - dm + mpr = am$

$\dfrac{\mathbf{cp - dm + mpr}}{\mathbf{m}} = a$

24. $2i^4 - i^2 - \sqrt{-16} - \sqrt{-4}\sqrt{-4}$

$= 2 + 1 - 4i + 4 = \mathbf{7 - 4i}$

25. $PV = nRT$

$n = \dfrac{PV}{RT}$

$n = \dfrac{5(20)}{(0.0821)(673)} \approx \mathbf{1.81\ moles}$

26. $4x^2 + 6 = -x$

$4x^2 + x + 6 = 0$

$x = \dfrac{-1 \pm \sqrt{1 - 4(4)(6)}}{2(4)} = -\dfrac{1}{8} \pm \dfrac{\sqrt{95}}{8}i$

27. (a) $x + 2y = 6$

$2y = -x + 6$

$y = -\dfrac{1}{2}x + 3$

(b) $2x - 5y = -10$

$-5y = -2x - 10$

$y = \dfrac{2}{5}x + 2$

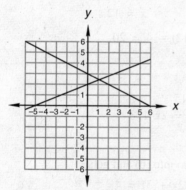

2(a) $2x + 4y = 12$

(-1)(b) $\underline{-2x + 5y = 10}$

$9y = 22$

$y = \dfrac{22}{9}$

(a) $x + 2\left(\dfrac{22}{9}\right) = \dfrac{54}{9}$

$x = \dfrac{10}{9}$

$\left(\dfrac{10}{9}, \dfrac{22}{9}\right)$

28. $\dfrac{40\ \text{in.}}{\text{hr}} \times \dfrac{2.54\ \text{cm}}{1\ \text{in.}} \times \dfrac{1\ \text{m}}{100\ \text{cm}} \times \dfrac{1\ \text{km}}{1000\ \text{m}}$

$\times \dfrac{1\ \text{hr}}{60\ \text{min}} = \dfrac{\mathbf{40(2.54)}}{\mathbf{(100)(1000)(60)}}\ \dfrac{\mathbf{km}}{\mathbf{min}}$

29. $A = \sqrt{8^2 - 6^2} = 2\sqrt{7}$

$8 \times \overrightarrow{SF} = 12$

$\overrightarrow{SF} = \dfrac{3}{2}$

$C = 2\sqrt{7} \times \dfrac{3}{2} = \mathbf{3\sqrt{7}}$

30. $A_{\text{Circle}} = \pi r^2 = 100\pi\ \text{m}^2$

$r = 10\ \text{m}$

Side of square $= 2r = 20\ \text{m}$

$A_{\text{Square}} = (20\ \text{m})^2 = \mathbf{400\ m^2}$

PRACTICE SET 97

$\begin{cases} 3x - 5y = 11 & \text{(a)} \\ 2x - 4y = -6 & \text{(b)} \end{cases}$

(a) $3x - 5y = 11$

$-5y = 11 - 3x$

$y = \dfrac{3}{5}x - \dfrac{11}{5}$

(b) $2x - 4\left(\dfrac{3}{5}x - \dfrac{11}{5}\right) = -6$

$2x(5) - 4\left(\dfrac{3}{5}x - \dfrac{11}{5}\right)(5) = -6(5)$

$10x - 12x + 44 = -30$

$-2x = -74$

$x = 37$

(b) $2(37) - 4y = -6$

$-4y = -80$

$y = 20$

The solution is the ordered pair **(37, 20)**.

PROBLEM SET 97

1. (a) $2N_T = 3N_U + 12$

(b) $4N_U = 3N_T - 48$

3(a) $6N_T = 9N_U + 36$

(-2)(b) $\underline{-6N_T = -8N_U - 96}$

$0 = N_U - 60$

$N_U = \mathbf{60\ were\ untalented}$

(a) $2N_T = 3(60) + 12$

$2N_T = 192$

$N_T = \mathbf{96\ were\ talented}$

2. $0.3A + 0.2(300) = 0.24(300 + A)$

$\qquad 0.3A + 60 = 72 + 0.24A$

$\qquad\qquad 0.06A = 12$

$\qquad\qquad\quad A = \textbf{200 mL}$

3. $\dfrac{P_1}{T_1} = \dfrac{P_2}{T_2}$

$T_2 = \dfrac{P_2 T_1}{P_1} = \dfrac{30(500)}{10} = \textbf{1500 K}$

4. Variation method:

$B = \dfrac{kG}{W^2}$

$4 = \dfrac{k3}{2^2}$

$k = \dfrac{16}{3}$

$2 = \dfrac{\left(\dfrac{16}{3}\right)G}{4^2}$

$32 = \dfrac{16}{3}G$

$G = \textbf{6 greens}$

Equal ratio method:

$\dfrac{B_1}{B_2} = \dfrac{G_1 W_2^2}{G_2 W_1^2}$

$\dfrac{4}{2} = \dfrac{3(4^2)}{G_2(2^2)}$

$G_2 = \textbf{6 greens}$

5. Variation method:

$C = kFJ^2$

$1000 = k(100)(4)^2$

$k = 0.625$

$C = (0.625)(10)(20)^2 = \textbf{2500 cheers}$

Equal ratio method:

$\dfrac{C_1}{C_2} = \dfrac{F_1 J_1^2}{F_2 J_2^2}$

$\dfrac{1000}{C_2} = \dfrac{100(4^2)}{10(20^2)}$

$C_2 = \textbf{2500 cheers}$

6. (a) $2x + 3y = -7$

(b) $3x - 3y = 12$

$\qquad\quad y = x - 4$

Substitute (b) into (a) and get:

(a′) $2x + 3(x - 4) = -7$

$\qquad 2x + 3x - 12 = -7$

$\qquad\qquad\qquad 5x = 5$

$\qquad\qquad\qquad\; x = 1$

(b) $y = (1) - 4 = -3$

(1, –3)

7. (a) $4x - 2y = 8$

$\qquad -2y = -4x + 8$

$\qquad\quad y = 2x - 4$

(b) $3x - 2y = -4$

Substitute (a) into (b) and get:

(b) $3x - 2(2x - 4) = -4$

$\qquad 3x - 4x + 8 = -4$

$\qquad\qquad\quad -x = -12$

$\qquad\qquad\qquad x = 12$

(a) $y = 2(12) - 4 = 20$

(12, 20)

8. (a) $y - 2x = 3$

$\qquad\quad y = 2x + 3$

(b) $xy = 4$

Substitute (a) into (b) and get:

(b′) $\qquad x(2x + 3) = 4$

$\qquad\qquad 2x^2 + 3x = 4$

$\qquad 2x^2 + 3x - 4 = 0$

Solve this equation by using the quadratic formula.

$x = \dfrac{-3 \pm \sqrt{3^2 - 4(-4)(2)}}{2(2)} = -\dfrac{3}{4} \pm \dfrac{\sqrt{41}}{4}$

Substitute these values of x into (a) and solve for y.

(a) $y = 2\left(-\dfrac{3}{4} + \dfrac{\sqrt{41}}{4}\right) + 3 = \dfrac{3}{2} + \dfrac{\sqrt{41}}{2}$

(a) $y = 2\left(-\dfrac{3}{4} - \dfrac{\sqrt{41}}{4}\right) + 3 = \dfrac{3}{2} - \dfrac{\sqrt{41}}{2}$

$\left(-\dfrac{3}{4} + \dfrac{\sqrt{41}}{4}, \dfrac{3}{2} + \dfrac{\sqrt{41}}{2}\right)$ and

$\left(-\dfrac{3}{4} - \dfrac{\sqrt{41}}{4}, \dfrac{3}{2} - \dfrac{\sqrt{41}}{2}\right)$

9. (a) $x^2 + y^2 = 11$

(b) $\dfrac{2x^2 - y^2 = -2}{3x^2 \qquad = 9}$

$$x^2 = 3$$

$$x = \pm\sqrt{3}$$

(a) $(\sqrt{3})^2 + y^2 = 11$

$$3 + y^2 = 11$$

$$y^2 = 8$$

$$y = \pm 2\sqrt{2}$$

(a) $(-\sqrt{3})^2 + y^2 = 11$

$$3 + y^2 = 11$$

$$y^2 = 8$$

$$y = \pm 2\sqrt{2}$$

$(\sqrt{3}, \pm 2\sqrt{2})$ and $(-\sqrt{3}, \pm 2\sqrt{2})$

10. (a) $3x + y + z = 2$

(b) $2x - y - z = 3$

(c) $x + 2y - z = 8$

(a) $3x + y + z = 2$

(b) $\dfrac{2x - y - z = 3}{5x \qquad = 5}$

$$x = 1$$

(a) $3x + y + z = 2$

(c) $x + 2y - z = 8$

(d) $4x + 3y \qquad = 10$

(d) $4(1) + 3y = 10$

$$3y = 6$$

$$y = 2$$

(a) $3(1) + (2) + z = 2$

$$z = -3$$

$(1, 2, -3)$

11. $g(x) = x^2 - 2x + 2;\ D = \{\text{Reals}\}$

$g(5) = 5^2 - 2(5) + 2 = \mathbf{17}$

12. (a) $x - 2y < 2$

$$-2y < -x + 2$$

$$y > \frac{1}{2}x - 1$$

(b) $y \geq 0$

The next step is to graph each of these lines.

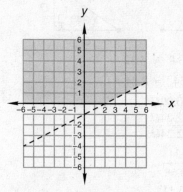

The region we wish to find is on or above the *x*-axis and above the dashed line. This region is shaded in the figure.

13. $4 \not> x + 3 < 7;\ D = \{\text{Integers}\}$

$$4 \leq x + 3 < 7$$

$$1 \leq x < 4$$

14. $\dfrac{(x^{a+2})^{1/2}\,x^{3a/2}y^b}{y^{-b/2}} = x^{a/2 + 1 + 3a/2}y^{b + b/2}$

$$= x^{2a+1}y^{3b/2}$$

15. $\dfrac{p}{mx - \dfrac{m}{x + \dfrac{1}{mx}}} = \dfrac{p}{mx - \dfrac{m^2 x}{mx^2 + 1}}$

$$= \dfrac{p(mx^2 + 1)}{m^2 x^3 + mx - m^2 x}$$

16. $\dfrac{5i - i^2}{2i^2 + i^3} = \dfrac{i(5 - i)}{i(2i + i^2)} = \dfrac{5 - i}{2i - 1} \cdot \dfrac{2i + 1}{2i + 1}$

$$= \dfrac{10i + 2 + 5 - i}{-4 - 1} = \dfrac{7 + 9i}{-5} = -\dfrac{7}{5} - \dfrac{9}{5}i$$

17. $\sqrt[6]{8\sqrt{2}} = \left(2^3(2^{1/2})\right)^{1/6} = 2^{1/2}2^{1/12} = \mathbf{2^{7/12}}$

18. $\dfrac{5i - 2i^2}{-i} = \dfrac{i(5 - 2i)}{i(-1)} = \dfrac{5 - 2i}{-1} = \mathbf{-5 + 2i}$

19. $\sqrt{z - 33} + \sqrt{z} = 11$

$$\sqrt{z - 33} = 11 - \sqrt{z}$$

$$z - 33 = 121 - 22\sqrt{z} + z$$

$$22\sqrt{z} = 154$$

$$\sqrt{z} = 7$$

$$z = \mathbf{49}$$

Check: $\sqrt{49 - 33} + \sqrt{49} = 11$

$$\sqrt{16} + 7 = 11$$

$$4 + 7 = 11$$

20.

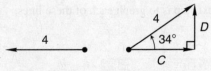

$C = 4 \cos 34° \approx 3.32$

$D = 4 \sin 34° \approx 2.24$

$$\begin{array}{r} -4.00R + 0.00U \\ 3.32R + 2.24U \\ \hline \mathbf{-0.68R + 2.24U} \end{array}$$

$\tan \theta = \dfrac{2.24}{-0.68}$

$\quad \theta \approx -73.11°$

Since θ is a second-quadrant angle,

$\theta = -73.11 + 180 = 106.89°$

$H = \sqrt{(-0.68)^2 + (2.24)^2}$

$H \approx 2.34$

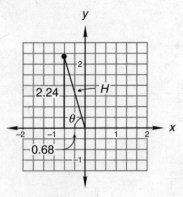

$\mathbf{2.34\underline{/106.89°}}$

21. $\dfrac{3 - 2\sqrt{2}}{4 + 2\sqrt{2}} \cdot \dfrac{4 - 2\sqrt{2}}{4 - 2\sqrt{2}} = \dfrac{12 - 8\sqrt{2} - 6\sqrt{2} + 8}{16 - 8}$

$= \dfrac{20 - 14\sqrt{2}}{8} = \dfrac{\mathbf{10 - 7\sqrt{2}}}{\mathbf{4}}$

22. $\dfrac{3 - \sqrt{7}}{-\sqrt{7}} \cdot \dfrac{\sqrt{7}}{\sqrt{7}} = \dfrac{3\sqrt{7} - 7}{-7} = \dfrac{\mathbf{7 - 3\sqrt{7}}}{\mathbf{7}}$

23. $\sqrt{\dfrac{9}{3}} + 2\sqrt{\dfrac{3}{9}} - 5\sqrt{27} = \sqrt{3} + \dfrac{2\sqrt{3}}{3} - 15\sqrt{3}$

$= \dfrac{3\sqrt{3}}{3} + \dfrac{2\sqrt{3}}{3} - \dfrac{45\sqrt{3}}{3} = -\dfrac{\mathbf{40\sqrt{3}}}{\mathbf{3}}$

24. $-4i^2 - \sqrt{-9} - \sqrt{2}\sqrt{-2} - 5i^5$

$= 4 - 3i - 2i - 5i = \mathbf{4 - 10i}$

25. $\dfrac{a}{x + y} - c = \dfrac{1}{r^2}$

$ar^2 - cr^2x - cr^2y = x + y$

$ar^2 - x - cr^2x = y + cr^2y$

$\dfrac{\mathbf{ar^2 - x - cr^2x}}{\mathbf{1 + cr^2}} = \mathbf{y}$

26. $\dfrac{p}{x} = my\left(\dfrac{1}{a} + \dfrac{1}{c}\right)$

$\dfrac{p}{x} = \dfrac{my}{a} + \dfrac{my}{c}$

$pac = cmxy + amxy$

$pac - amxy = cmxy$

$a = \dfrac{\mathbf{cmxy}}{\mathbf{cp - mxy}}$

27. $A_{\text{Circle}} = \pi r^2 = 49\pi \text{ cm}^2$

$r = 7 \text{ cm}$

Diagonal of square $= 2r = 14 \text{ cm}$

Side of square $= \dfrac{14}{\sqrt{2}} \text{ cm} = 7\sqrt{2} \text{ cm}$

$A_{\text{Square}} = (7\sqrt{2} \text{ cm})^2 = \mathbf{98 \text{ cm}^2}$

28. See Lesson 71.

29. $\dfrac{400 \text{ mL}}{\text{s}} \times \dfrac{1 \text{ cm}^3}{1 \text{ mL}} \times \dfrac{1 \text{ in.}}{2.54 \text{ cm}} \times \dfrac{1 \text{ in.}}{2.54 \text{ cm}}$

$\times \dfrac{1 \text{ in.}}{2.54 \text{ cm}} \times \dfrac{60 \text{ s}}{1 \text{ min}} \times \dfrac{60 \text{ min}}{1 \text{ hr}}$

$= \dfrac{\mathbf{400(60)(60)}}{\mathbf{(2.54)(2.54)(2.54)}} \dfrac{\mathbf{in.}^3}{\mathbf{hr}}$

30. $\dfrac{x - 4}{2} - \dfrac{x - 6}{3} = 7$

$3x - 12 - 2x + 12 = 42$

$x = \mathbf{42}$

PRACTICE SET 98

$N = 3\dfrac{1}{2} + \dfrac{1}{8}\left(5\dfrac{1}{6} - 3\dfrac{1}{2}\right)$

$= \dfrac{7}{2} + \dfrac{1}{8}\left(\dfrac{31}{6} - \dfrac{7}{2}\right)$

$= \dfrac{7}{2} + \dfrac{1}{8}\left(\dfrac{31}{6} - \dfrac{21}{6}\right)$

$= \dfrac{7}{2} + \dfrac{1}{8}\left(\dfrac{10}{6}\right)$

$= \dfrac{7}{2} + \dfrac{5}{24}$

$= \dfrac{84}{24} + \dfrac{5}{24}$

$= \dfrac{\mathbf{89}}{\mathbf{24}}$

PROBLEM SET 98

1.

$$\begin{array}{c} \overset{D_R}{\longmapsto} \quad \overset{D_W}{\longmapsto} \\ \underset{96}{\longmapsto} \end{array}$$

$96 = R_W T_W + R_R T_R; \quad T_W = 12 - T_R;$

$R_R = 12; \quad R_W = 6$

$96 = 6(12 - T_R) + 12T_R$

$96 = 72 - 6T_R + 12T_R$

$24 = 6T_R$

$4 = T_R$

$T_W = 8$

$D_R = 12(4) = \mathbf{48\ miles}$

$D_W = 6(8) = \mathbf{48\ miles}$

2. (a) $0.1P_N + 0.6D_N = 90$

(b) $P_N + D_N = 600$

Substitute $D_N = 600 - P_N$ into (a) and get:

(a') $0.1P_N + 0.6(600 - P_N) = 90$

$\qquad\qquad\qquad -0.5P_N = -270$

$\qquad\qquad\qquad\qquad P_N = 540$

(b) $(540) + D_N = 600$

$\qquad\qquad D_N = 60$

540 mL 10%, 60 mL 60%

3.

$$\begin{array}{c} \overset{D_C}{\longmapsto} \\ \underset{1200}{\longmapsto} \end{array}$$

$$\begin{array}{c} \overset{D_M}{\longmapsto} \\ \underset{360}{} \end{array}$$

$1200 = R_C T_C; \quad R_M = R_C + 10;$

$R_C = R_M - 10; \quad 360 = R_M T_M; \quad T_C = 4T_M$

$(R_M - 10)(4T_M) = 1200$

$4R_M T_M - 40T_M = 1200$

$\qquad\qquad -40T_M = -240$

$\qquad\qquad\qquad T_M = 6$

$T_C = \mathbf{24\ hr}; \quad T_M = \mathbf{6\ hr};$

$R_C = \mathbf{50\ mph}; \quad R_M = \mathbf{60\ mph}$

4. Downstream: $(B + W)T_D = D_D$ (a)

Upstream: $(B - W)T_U = D_U$ (b)

(a') $(B + W)4 = 28$

(b') $(B - W)8 = 40$

2(a') $8B + 8W = 56$

(b') $\underline{8B - 8W = 40}$

$16B \qquad\quad = 96$

$\qquad\qquad B = \mathbf{6\ mph}$

(a') $4(6) + 4W = 28$

$\qquad\quad 4W = 4$

$\qquad\quad\ W = \mathbf{1\ mph}$

5. Variation method:

R = rabbits; S = squirrels; r = raccoons

$R = \dfrac{kS}{r}$

$10 = \dfrac{k(40)}{2}$

$k = 0.5$

$5 = \dfrac{(0.5)(20)}{r}$

$r = \mathbf{2\ raccoons}$

Equal ratio method:

$\dfrac{R_1}{R_2} = \dfrac{S_1 r_2}{S_2 r_1}$

$\dfrac{10}{5} = \dfrac{(40)r_2}{20(2)}$

$r_2 = \mathbf{2\ raccoons}$

6. $N = \dfrac{1}{4} + \dfrac{1}{2}\left(\dfrac{7}{12} - \dfrac{1}{4}\right)$

$= \dfrac{1}{4} + \dfrac{1}{2}\left(\dfrac{7}{12} - \dfrac{3}{12}\right)$

$= \dfrac{1}{4} + \dfrac{1}{2}\left(\dfrac{4}{12}\right)$

$= \dfrac{3}{12} + \dfrac{2}{12}$

$= \dfrac{\mathbf{5}}{\mathbf{12}}$

7. $N = 1\dfrac{1}{5} + \dfrac{2}{5}\left(2\dfrac{5}{6} - 1\dfrac{1}{5}\right)$

$= \dfrac{6}{5} + \dfrac{2}{5}\left(\dfrac{17}{6} - \dfrac{6}{5}\right)$

$= \dfrac{6}{5} + \dfrac{2}{5}\left(\dfrac{85}{30} - \dfrac{36}{30}\right)$

$= \dfrac{6}{5} + \dfrac{2}{5}\left(\dfrac{49}{30}\right)$

$= \dfrac{90}{75} + \dfrac{49}{75}$

$= \dfrac{\mathbf{139}}{\mathbf{75}}$

8. (a) $3x + 2y = 5$

(b) $5x + 6y = 7$

$$6y = -5x + 7$$

$$y = \frac{-5x + 7}{6}$$

Substitute (b) into (a) and get:

(a') $3x + 2\left(\dfrac{-5x + 7}{6}\right) = 5$

$$9x + (-5x + 7) = 15$$

$$4x = 8$$

$$x = 2$$

(b) $y = \dfrac{-5(2) + 7}{6} = -\dfrac{3}{6} = -\dfrac{1}{2}$

$$\left(2, -\frac{1}{2}\right)$$

9. (a) $y - 3x = 5$

$$y = 3x + 5$$

(b) $xy = 6$

Substitute (a) into (b) and get:

(b') $x(3x + 5) = 6$

$$3x^2 + 5x - 6 = 0$$

Solve this equation by using the quadratic formula.

$$x = \frac{-5 \pm \sqrt{25 - 4(-18)}}{6} = -\frac{5}{6} \pm \frac{\sqrt{97}}{6}$$

Substitute these values of x into (a) and solve for y.

(a) $y = 3\left(-\dfrac{5}{6} + \dfrac{\sqrt{97}}{6}\right) + 5 = \dfrac{5}{2} + \dfrac{\sqrt{97}}{2}$

(a) $y = 3\left(-\dfrac{5}{6} - \dfrac{\sqrt{97}}{6}\right) + 5 = \dfrac{5}{2} - \dfrac{\sqrt{97}}{2}$

$$\left(-\frac{5}{6} + \frac{\sqrt{97}}{6}, \frac{5}{2} + \frac{\sqrt{97}}{2}\right) \text{ and }$$

$$\left(-\frac{5}{6} - \frac{\sqrt{97}}{6}, \frac{5}{2} - \frac{\sqrt{97}}{2}\right)$$

10. (a) $x^2 + y^2 = 16$

(b) $\dfrac{2x^2 - y^2 = -4}{3x^2 \qquad = 12}$

$$x^2 = 4$$

$$x = \pm 2$$

(a) $(2)^2 + y^2 = 16$

$$y^2 = 12$$

$$y = \pm 2\sqrt{3}$$

(a) $(-2)^2 + y^2 = 16$

$$y^2 = 12$$

$$y = \pm 2\sqrt{3}$$

$$(2, \pm 2\sqrt{3}) \text{ and } (-2, \pm 2\sqrt{3})$$

11. Sets **(a)**, **(b)**, and **(c)** are all functions.

12. (a) $x + 2y > 4$

$$y > -\frac{1}{2}x + 2$$

(b) $y \geq 1$

The next step is to graph each of these lines.

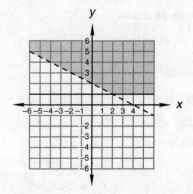

The region we wish to find is on or above the solid line and above the dashed line. This region is shaded in the figure.

13. $4 \not< -x + 2$ or $x + 3 < -1$; $D = \{\text{Integers}\}$

$$4 \geq -x + 2 \text{ or } x + 3 < -1$$

$$-2 \leq x \qquad \text{or} \qquad x < -4$$

14. $\dfrac{(x^{2a})^{1/3} x^{2a}}{x^{a/2}} = x^{2a/3 + 2a - a/2}$

$$= x^{4a/6 + 12a/6 - 3a/6} = \mathbf{x^{13a/6}}$$

15. $\dfrac{xy}{x + \dfrac{xy}{x + \dfrac{1}{y}}} = \dfrac{xy}{x + \dfrac{xy^2}{xy + 1}}$

$$= \frac{xy(xy + 1)}{x^2y + x + xy^2} = \frac{y(xy + 1)}{xy + 1 + y^2}$$

16. $\sqrt[7]{4\sqrt[3]{2}} = \left(2^2(2^{1/3})\right)^{1/7} = 2^{2/7}2^{1/21} = \mathbf{2^{1/3}}$

17. $\dfrac{2i - 3i^2}{-i} = \mathbf{-2 + 3i}$

18. $\dfrac{2i^4 - i^3}{-2i} = \dfrac{2i^3 - i^2}{-2} = \mathbf{-\dfrac{1}{2} + i}$

19. There is never an exact solution to these problems. One possible solution is given here.

$S = mP + b$

$m = \dfrac{25 - 175}{7 - 4} = \dfrac{-150}{3} = -50$

$S = -50P + b$

Use the point (4, 175) for P and S.

$175 = -50(4) + b$

$375 = b$

$S = -50P + 375$

20.

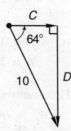

$C = 10 \cos 64° \approx 4.38$

$D = 10 \sin 64° \approx 8.99$

$12.00R + 0.00U$
$4.38R - 8.99U$
$\overline{16.38R - 8.99U}$

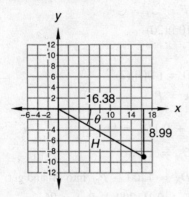

$\tan \theta = \dfrac{-8.99}{16.38}$

$\theta \approx -28.76°$

$H = \sqrt{(-8.99)^2 + (16.38)^2}$

$H \approx 18.68$

$18.68\underline{/-28.76°}$

21. $\dfrac{5 - \sqrt{2}}{2 - 5\sqrt{2}} \cdot \dfrac{2 + 5\sqrt{2}}{2 + 5\sqrt{2}}$

$= \dfrac{10 - 2\sqrt{2} + 25\sqrt{2} - 10}{4 - 50}$

$= \dfrac{23\sqrt{2}}{-46} = -\dfrac{\sqrt{2}}{2}$

22. $\dfrac{3 - \sqrt{3}}{3 - 2\sqrt{3}} \cdot \dfrac{3 + 2\sqrt{3}}{3 + 2\sqrt{3}}$

$= \dfrac{9 - 3\sqrt{3} + 6\sqrt{3} - 6}{9 - 12}$

$= \dfrac{3 + 3\sqrt{3}}{-3} = \mathbf{-1 - \sqrt{3}}$

23. $\dfrac{a}{x + y} = z\left(\dfrac{1}{m} + \dfrac{1}{n}\right)$

$\dfrac{a}{x + y} = \dfrac{z}{m} + \dfrac{z}{n}$

$amn = nxz + nyz + mxz + myz$

$amn - mxz - myz = nxz + nyz$

$m = \dfrac{nxz + nyz}{an - xz - yz}$

24. $\dfrac{a}{x + y} = z\left(\dfrac{1}{m} + \dfrac{1}{n}\right)$

$\dfrac{a}{x + y} = \dfrac{z}{m} + \dfrac{z}{n}$

$nxz + nyz + mxz + myz = amn$

$amn - nxz - mxz = nyz + myz$

$\dfrac{amn - mxz - nxz}{mz + nz} = y$

25. $-\sqrt{-9} - \sqrt{-2}\sqrt{-2} + 3i^2 - 2i^3 + 4$

$= -3i + 2 - 3 + 2i + 4 = \mathbf{3 - i}$

26. $\sqrt{\dfrac{7}{3}} - 2\sqrt{\dfrac{3}{7}} + 5\sqrt{84} = \dfrac{\sqrt{21}}{3} - \dfrac{2\sqrt{21}}{7} + 10\sqrt{21}$

$= \dfrac{7\sqrt{21}}{21} - \dfrac{6\sqrt{21}}{21} + \dfrac{210\sqrt{21}}{21} = \mathbf{\dfrac{211\sqrt{21}}{21}}$

27. $-5x^2 - x - 5 = 0$

$5x^2 + x = -5$

$\left(x^2 + \dfrac{1}{5}x + \right) = -1$

$x^2 + \dfrac{1}{5}x + \dfrac{1}{100} = -\dfrac{100}{100} + \dfrac{1}{100}$

$\left(x + \dfrac{1}{10}\right)^2 = -\dfrac{99}{100}$

$x + \dfrac{1}{10} = \pm\dfrac{3\sqrt{11}}{10}i$

$x = -\dfrac{1}{10} \pm \dfrac{3\sqrt{11}}{10}i$

28. $\dfrac{60 \text{ in.}}{\text{s}} \times \dfrac{2.54 \text{ cm}}{1 \text{ in.}} \times \dfrac{60 \text{ s}}{1 \text{ min}} = \mathbf{60(2.54)(60)} \dfrac{\textbf{cm}}{\textbf{min}}$

29.
$$\dfrac{\dfrac{a}{xy} - \dfrac{x}{y^2}}{\dfrac{4}{x} - \dfrac{3}{xy^2}} = \dfrac{\dfrac{ay - x^2}{xy^2}}{\dfrac{4y^2 - 3}{xy^2}} = \dfrac{ay - x^2}{4y^2 - 3}$$

30. (a) $\dfrac{47{,}162 \times 10^{-12}}{50{,}132 \times 10^{5}}$

Estimate: $\dfrac{5 \times 10^{-8}}{5 \times 10^{9}} = 1 \times 10^{-17}$

Calculator answer $\approx$ **9.41 $\times$ 10^{-18}**

(b) $\sqrt[3.4]{311}$

Estimate: $310^{1/3} \approx 6.77$

Calculator answer: $\sqrt[3.4]{311} \approx$ **5.41**

PRACTICE SET 99

$-|x| + 3 < -2; \ D = \{\text{Integers}\}$

$\quad -|x| < -5$

$\quad\quad |x| > 5$

PROBLEM SET 99

1. Silver (Ag): $\quad 2 \times 108 = 216$

Sulfur: $\quad\quad\ \ 1 \times 32 = 32$

Total: $\quad\quad\ \ \ 216 + 32 = 248$

Silver: $\dfrac{216}{248} \times 100\% \approx$ **87.10%**

2. (a) $2N_P = 10N_M + 16$

(b) $13N_M = N_P + 8$

(b′) $N_P = 13N_M - 8$

Substitute (b′) into (a) and get:

(a′) $2(13N_M - 8) = 10N_M + 16$

$\quad\quad 26N_M - 16 = 10N_M + 16$

$\quad\quad\quad 16N_M = 32$

$\quad\quad\quad\quad N_M = $ **2 maunderers**

(b′) $N_P = $ **18 purposeful walkers**

3. Downstream: $(B + W)T_D = D_D$ (a)

Upstream: $(B - W)T_U = D_U$ (b)

Since $T_D = 2T_U$, we substitute and get:

(a′) $(B + 8)2T_U = 280$

(b′) $(B - 8)T_U = 60$

$\quad$ (a′) $\quad 2BT_U + 16T_U = 280$

2(b′) $\quad \underline{2BT_U - 16T_U = 120}$

$\quad\quad\quad\quad\quad 4BT_U \quad\quad\ = 400$

$\quad$ (c) $\quad\quad\quad BT_U = 100$

(a′) $\quad 2(100) + 16T_U = 280$

$\quad\quad\quad\quad\quad\quad T_U = 5$

(c) $B(5) = 100$

$\quad\ B = $ **20 mph**

4. Equal ratio method:

$$\dfrac{W_1}{W_2} = \dfrac{P_1 F_1}{P_2 F_2}$$

$$\dfrac{8{,}000}{16{,}000} = \dfrac{100(20)}{P_2(2)}$$

$\quad P_2 = $ **2000 people**

Variation method:

$\quad W = kPF$

$8000 = k(100)(20)$

$\quad\quad 4 = k$

$\quad 16{,}000 = (4)(P)(2)$

2000 people $= P$

5. (a) $0.05P_N + 0.1D_N = 96$

(b) $P_N + D_N = 1200$

Substitute $D_N = 1200 - P_N$ into (a) and get:

(a′) $0.05P_N + 0.1(1200 - P_N) = 96$

$\quad\quad\quad\quad\quad\quad -0.05P_N = -24$

$\quad\quad\quad\quad\quad\quad\quad\quad P_N = 480$

(b) $(480) + D_N = 1200$

$\quad\quad\quad\quad D_N = 720$

480 mL 5%, 720 mL 10%

6. $-|x| + 5 > 0; \ D = \{\text{Integers}\}$

$\quad -|x| > -5$

$\quad\quad |x| < 5$

$x > -5$ and $x < 5$

7. $-|x| + 1 < -3; \ D = \{\text{Reals}\}$

$$-|x| < -4$$
$$|x| > 4$$

$x > 4 \ \text{or} \ x < -4$

8. (a) Since this is a 30°-60°-90° triangle,

$$2 \times \overrightarrow{SF} = 124$$
$$\overrightarrow{SF} = 62$$
$$m = \sqrt{3}(62) = \mathbf{62\sqrt{3}}$$
$$n = 1(62) = \mathbf{62}$$

(b) Since this is a 45°-45°-90° triangle,

$$\sqrt{2} \times \overrightarrow{SF} = 5\sqrt{2}$$
$$\overrightarrow{SF} = 5$$
$$p = 1(5) = \mathbf{5}$$
$$q = 1(5) = \mathbf{5}$$

9. $N = \dfrac{1}{2} + \dfrac{2}{7}\left(2\dfrac{1}{3} - \dfrac{1}{2}\right)$

$$= \dfrac{1}{2} + \dfrac{2}{7}\left(\dfrac{11}{6}\right)$$

$$= \dfrac{21}{42} + \dfrac{22}{42} = \mathbf{\dfrac{43}{42}}$$

10. (a) $3x + 3y = 9$

$$y = -x + 3$$

(b) $4x - 6y = -8$

Substitute (a) into (b) and get:

(b') $4x - 6(-x + 3) = -8$

$$4x + 6x - 18 = -8$$
$$10x = 10$$
$$x = 1$$

(a) $y = -(1) + 3 = 2$

(1, 2)

11. (a) $x - 3y = 2$

$$y = \dfrac{1}{3}x - \dfrac{2}{3}$$

(b) $xy = 8$

$$y = \dfrac{8}{x}$$

Substitute (b) into (a) and get:

(a') $\qquad x - 3\left(\dfrac{8}{x}\right) = 2$

$$x^2 - 24 = 2x$$
$$x^2 - 2x - 24 = 0$$
$$(x - 6)(x + 4) = 0$$
$$x = 6, -4$$

Substitute these values of x into (a) and solve for y.

(a) $y = \dfrac{1}{3}(6) - \dfrac{2}{3} = \dfrac{4}{3}$

(a) $y = \dfrac{1}{3}(-4) - \dfrac{2}{3} = -2$

$\left(\mathbf{6, \dfrac{4}{3}}\right)$ and **(−4, −2)**

12. (a) $x^2 + y^2 = 8$

(b) $\dfrac{2x^2 - y^2 = 7}{3x^2 \qquad\ = 15}$

$$x^2 = 5$$
$$x = \pm\sqrt{5}$$

(a) $y^2 = 8 - (\sqrt{5})^2$

$$y^2 = 3$$
$$y = \pm\sqrt{3}$$

(a) $y^2 = 8 - (-\sqrt{5})^2$

$$y^2 = 3$$
$$y = \pm\sqrt{3}$$

$(\mathbf{\sqrt{5}, \pm\sqrt{3}})$ and $(\mathbf{-\sqrt{5}, \pm\sqrt{3}})$

13. (a) $3x + 2y - z = 1$

(b) $x + y - z = -1$

(c) $5x + 2y + 2z = 8$

(a) $3x + 2y - z = 1$

−1(b) $\dfrac{-x - \ \ y + z = 1}{}$

(d) $\overline{2x + \ \ y \qquad\ \ = 2}$

2(b) $2x + 2y - 2z = -2$

(c) $\dfrac{5x + 2y + 2z = \ \ 8}{}$

(e) $\overline{7x + 4y \qquad\ \ = 6}$

−4(d) $-8x - 4y = -8$

(e) $\dfrac{7x + 4y = \ \ 6}{}$

$$\overline{-x \qquad\ \ = -2}$$

$$x = 2$$

(d) $2(2) + y = 2$

$$y = -2$$

(b) $(2) + (-2) - z = -1$

$$z = 1$$

(2, −2, 1)

14. The solution is $\varnothing$ **or** { } because 4 is not in the domain of $h(x)$.

15. (a) $x - y < -2$

$$y > x + 2$$

(b) $3x + 5y \le -5$

$$y \le -\frac{3}{5}x - 1$$

The next step is to graph each of these lines.

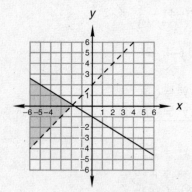

The region we wish to find is on or below the solid line and above the dashed line. This region is shaded in the figure.

16. $x + 4 \le 3$ or $x + 1 > 2$; $D =$ {Reals}

$$x \le -1 \text{ or } \qquad x > 1$$

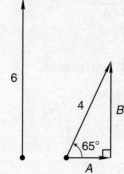

17. $(x^{2-a})^2 x^{a/4} = x^{4-2a} x^{a/4} = x^{\mathbf{4-7a/4}}$

18. $\dfrac{ab}{a + \dfrac{b}{1 + \dfrac{a}{b^2}}} = \dfrac{ab}{a + \dfrac{b^3}{b^2 + a}}$

$$= \frac{ab(b^2 + a)}{ab^2 + a^2 + b^3}$$

19. $2\sqrt[5]{16\sqrt[3]{2}} = 2\sqrt[5]{2^4\sqrt[3]{2}} = 2(2^{4/5})(2^{1/15}) = 2^{\mathbf{28/15}}$

20. $\dfrac{2 - 3i}{2i^3} = \dfrac{2 - 3i}{-2i} \cdot \dfrac{2i}{2i} = \dfrac{4i + 6}{4} = \dfrac{\mathbf{3}}{\mathbf{2}} + \mathbf{i}$

21. $\dfrac{2i - i^3}{-i} = \dfrac{2i + i}{-i} \cdot \dfrac{i}{i} = \dfrac{-2 - 1}{1} = \mathbf{-3}$

22. $O = mI + b$

Use the graph to find the slope.

$$m = \frac{200}{50} = 4$$

$$O = 4I + b$$

Use the point (45, 0) for I and O.

$$0 = 4(45) + b$$

$$-180 = b$$

$$\mathbf{O = 4I - 180}$$

23.

$$A = 4 \cos 65° \approx 1.69$$

$$B = 4 \sin 65° \approx 3.63$$

$$\begin{array}{r} 0.00R + 6.00U \\ 1.69R + 3.63U \\ \hline \mathbf{1.69R + 9.63U} \end{array}$$

$$\tan \theta = \frac{9.63}{1.69}$$

$$\theta \approx 80.05°$$

$$F = \sqrt{(1.69)^2 + (9.63)^2} \approx 9.78$$

$$\mathbf{9.78\underline{/80.05°}}$$

24. $\dfrac{3 - \sqrt{2}}{\sqrt{2} + 3} \cdot \dfrac{\sqrt{2} - 3}{\sqrt{2} - 3} = \dfrac{3\sqrt{2} - 9 - 2 + 3\sqrt{2}}{2 - 9}$

$$= \frac{\mathbf{11 - 6\sqrt{2}}}{\mathbf{7}}$$

25. $\dfrac{4 - 2\sqrt{3}}{-\sqrt{3}} \cdot \dfrac{\sqrt{3}}{\sqrt{3}} = \dfrac{4\sqrt{3} - 6}{-3} = \dfrac{\mathbf{-4\sqrt{3} + 6}}{\mathbf{3}}$

26. $\dfrac{m}{c} = \dfrac{p}{a} + \dfrac{p}{b}$

$$abm = bcp + acp$$

$$\dfrac{abm}{bp + ap} = c$$

27. $-\sqrt{-9} - 3i^3 + 2i - \sqrt{-4}\sqrt{4} + 3\sqrt{-4}$

$$= -3i + 3i + 2i - 4i + 6i = \mathbf{4i}$$

28. $-\sqrt{\dfrac{3}{10}} + 4\sqrt{\dfrac{10}{3}} - \sqrt{120}$

$= -\dfrac{\sqrt{3}}{\sqrt{10}} + \dfrac{4\sqrt{10}}{\sqrt{3}} - \sqrt{120}$

$= -\dfrac{\sqrt{30}}{10} + \dfrac{4\sqrt{30}}{3} - 2\sqrt{30}$

$= -\dfrac{3\sqrt{30}}{30} + \dfrac{40\sqrt{30}}{30} - \dfrac{60\sqrt{30}}{30} = \mathbf{-\dfrac{23\sqrt{30}}{30}}$

29. $PV = nRT$

$V = \dfrac{nRT}{P}$

$V = \dfrac{(0.0163)(0.0821)(870)}{10} \approx \mathbf{0.12\ liter}$

30. $\dfrac{40\ cm}{s} \times \dfrac{1\ in.}{2.54\ cm} \times \dfrac{1\ ft}{12\ in.} \times \dfrac{1\ mi}{5280\ ft}$

$\times \dfrac{60\ s}{1\ min} \times \dfrac{60\ min}{1\ hr} = \mathbf{\dfrac{40(60)(60)}{(2.54)(12)(5280)}}\ \dfrac{\mathbf{mi}}{\mathbf{hr}}$

PRACTICE SET 100

a. $y = x^2 - 2x + 3$

$y = (x^2 - 2x\quad\ ) + 3$

$y = (x^2 - 2x + 1) + 3 - 1$

$y = (x - 1)^2 + 2$

From this we see:

(a) Opens upward

(b) Axis of symmetry is $x = 1$

(c) y-coordinate of vertex is $+2$

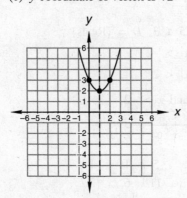

b. $y = -x^2 - 4x - 3$

$-y = (x^2 + 4x\quad\ ) + 3$

$-y = (x^2 + 4x + 4) + 3 - 4$

$-y = (x + 2)^2 - 1$

$y = -(x + 2)^2 + 1$

From this we see:

(a) Opens downward

(b) Axis of symmetry is $x = -2$

(c) y-coordinate of vertex is $+1$

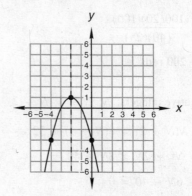

PROBLEM SET 100

1.

$\begin{array}{c}D_B \\ \overline{\qquad\qquad} \\ 320\end{array}$

$\begin{array}{c}D_S \\ \overline{\qquad\quad} \\ 240\end{array}$

$R_B T_B = 320;\ R_S T_S = 240;$

$R_B = 2R_S;\ T_B = T_S - 2$

$2R_S(T_S - 2) = 320$

$2(240) - 4R_S = 320$

$4R_S = 160$

$R_S = \mathbf{40\ mph}$

$R_B = \mathbf{80\ mph};\ T_S = \mathbf{6\ hr};\ T_B = \mathbf{4\ hr}$

2. $0.68(600) - 1(D_N) = 0.2(600 - D_N)$

$408 - D_N = 120 - 0.2D_N$

$0.8D_N = 288$

$D_N = \mathbf{360\ mL}$

3. (a) $10N_S = 6N_C + 40$

(b) $4N_C = 2N_S + 160$

(b') $N_S = 2N_C - 80$

Substitute (b') into (a) and get:

(a') $10(2N_C - 80) = 6N_C + 40$

$20N_C - 800 = 6N_C + 40$

$14N_C = 840$

$N_C = \mathbf{60\ coruscated}$

(b') $N_S = 2(60) - 80$

$N_S = \mathbf{40\ sparkled}$

4. $\dfrac{R_1}{R_2} = \dfrac{Y_1 G_2^2}{Y_2 G_1^2}$

$\dfrac{100}{R_2} = \dfrac{40(5)^2}{20(10)^2}$

$R_2 = \dfrac{100(20)(100)}{(40)(25)}$

$R_2 = \textbf{200 reds}$

5. Consecutive integers: $N,\ N+1,\ N+2$

$N(N+2) = 8(N+1) + 32$

$N^2 + 2N = 8N + 40$

$N^2 - 6N - 40 = 0$

$(N+4)(N-10) = 0$

$N = -4, 10$

The desired integers are **–4, –3, –2** and **10, 11, 12.**

6. $y = x^2 - 6x + 1$

$y = (x^2 - 6x + 9) + 1 - 9$

$y = (x - 3)^2 - 8$

From this we see:

(a) Opens upward

(b) Axis of symmetry is $x = 3$

(c) y-coordinate of vertex is –8

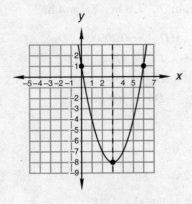

7. $y = -x^2 + 4x + 4$

$-y = (x^2 - 4x + 4) - 4 - 4$

$-y = (x - 2)^2 - 8$

$y = -(x - 2)^2 + 8$

From this we see:

(a) Opens downward

(b) Axis of symmetry is $x = 2$

(c) y-coordinate of vertex is +8

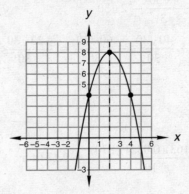

8. (a) Since this is a 30°-60°-90° triangle,

$\sqrt{3} \times \overrightarrow{SF} = 5$

$\overrightarrow{SF} = \dfrac{5\sqrt{3}}{3}$

$m = \dfrac{5\sqrt{3}}{3}(2) = \dfrac{10\sqrt{3}}{3}$

$n = \dfrac{5\sqrt{3}}{3}(1) = \dfrac{5\sqrt{3}}{3}$

(b) Since this is a 45°-45°-90° triangle,

$1 \times \overrightarrow{SF} = 7$

$\overrightarrow{SF} = 7$

$p = 7(1) = \textbf{7}$

$q = 7(\sqrt{2}) = \textbf{7}\sqrt{\textbf{2}}$

9. $-|x| + 5 \nleq 3;\ D = \{\text{Reals}\}$

$-|x| > -2$

$|x| < 2$

$x < 2 \text{ and } x > -2$

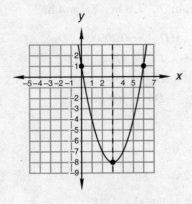

10. $N = 2\dfrac{1}{3} + \dfrac{5}{11}\left(3\dfrac{1}{6} - 2\dfrac{1}{3}\right)$

$= \dfrac{7}{3} + \dfrac{5}{11}\left(\dfrac{19}{6} - \dfrac{14}{6}\right)$

$= \dfrac{7}{3} + \dfrac{25}{66}$

$= \dfrac{154}{66} + \dfrac{25}{66} = \dfrac{\textbf{179}}{\textbf{66}}$

11. (a) $2x - 2y = -1$

$$x = y - \frac{1}{2}$$

(b) $4x + 3y = 5$

Substitute (a) into (b) and get:

(b') $4\left(y - \frac{1}{2}\right) + 3y = 5$

$$4y - 2 + 3y = 5$$

$$7y = 7$$

$$y = 1$$

(a) $x = (1) - \frac{1}{2} = \frac{1}{2}$

$$\left(\frac{1}{2}, 1\right)$$

12. (a) $x - y = 5$

(b) $xy = 2$

$$y = \frac{2}{x}$$

Substitute (b) into (a) and get:

(a') $x - \left(\frac{2}{x}\right) = 5$

$$x^2 - 2 = 5x$$

$$x^2 - 5x - 2 = 0$$

Solve this equation by using the quadratic formula.

$$x = \frac{-(-5) \pm \sqrt{(-5)^2 - 4(1)(-2)}}{2(1)}$$

$$x = \frac{5}{2} \pm \frac{\sqrt{33}}{2}$$

Substitute these values of x into (a) and solve for y.

(a) $y = \left(\frac{5}{2} + \frac{\sqrt{33}}{2}\right) - 5 = -\frac{5}{2} + \frac{\sqrt{33}}{2}$

(a) $y = \left(\frac{5}{2} - \frac{\sqrt{33}}{2}\right) - 5 = -\frac{5}{2} - \frac{\sqrt{33}}{2}$

$$\left(\frac{5}{2} + \frac{\sqrt{33}}{2}, -\frac{5}{2} + \frac{\sqrt{33}}{2}\right) \text{ and }$$

$$\left(\frac{5}{2} - \frac{\sqrt{33}}{2}, -\frac{5}{2} - \frac{\sqrt{33}}{2}\right)$$

13. (a) $x^2 + y^2 = 5$

(b) $\dfrac{2x^2 - y^2 = 4}{3x^2 \qquad = 9}$

$$x^2 = 3$$

$$x = \pm\sqrt{3}$$

(a) $(\sqrt{3})^2 + y^2 = 5$

$$y^2 = 2$$

$$y = \pm\sqrt{2}$$

(a) $(-\sqrt{3})^2 + y^2 = 5$

$$y^2 = 2$$

$$y = \pm\sqrt{2}$$

$$(\sqrt{3}, \pm\sqrt{2}) \text{ and } (-\sqrt{3}, \pm\sqrt{2})$$

14. (a) $2x + 2y - z = 0$

(b) $x + y - 2z = -12$

(c) $2x - y + z = 10$

$$\begin{array}{r} \text{(a)} \quad 2x + 2y - z = 0 \\ -2\text{(b)} \quad \underline{-2x - 2y + 4z = 24} \\ 3z = 24 \\ z = 8 \end{array}$$

(b) $x + y - 2z = -12$

(c) $\dfrac{2x - y + z = 10}{}$

(d) $\overline{3x \qquad - z = -2}$

(d) $3x - (8) = -2$

$$3x = 6$$

$$x = 2$$

(a) $2(2) + 2y - (8) = 0$

$$2y = 4$$

$$y = 2$$

(2, 2, 8)

15. None of the sets are functions.

Set (a) is not a function, because 2 has two images.

Set (b) is not a function, because 2 has two images.

Set (c) is not a function, because –3 has two images.

16. (a) $y \leq -3$

(b) $4x + y < -2$

$\quad y < -4x - 2$

The next step is to graph each of these lines.

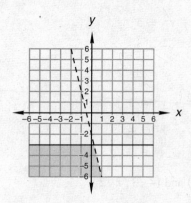

The region we wish to find is on or below the solid line and below the dashed line. This region is shaded in the figure.

17. $x + 2 \not\leq 5$ or $x + 3 < 3$; $D = \{\text{Integers}\}$

$\quad x > 3$ or $\quad x < 0$

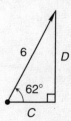

18. $\dfrac{a^{2x+4}a^{b/2}}{a^{1-b/2}} = a^{2x+4}a^{-1+b} = \mathbf{a^{2x+3+b}}$

19. $\dfrac{x}{x^2y - \dfrac{1}{1 + \dfrac{1}{xy}}} = \dfrac{x}{x^2y - \dfrac{xy}{xy + 1}}$

$\quad = \dfrac{x(xy + 1)}{x^3y^2 + x^2y - xy} = \dfrac{\mathbf{xy + 1}}{\mathbf{x^2y^2 + xy - y}}$

20. $3\sqrt{9\sqrt{3}} = 3\sqrt{3^2\sqrt{3}} = 3 \cdot 3 \cdot 3^{1/4} = \mathbf{3^{9/4}}$

21. $\dfrac{2 - i^3}{-i} = \dfrac{2 + i}{-i} \cdot \dfrac{i}{i} = \dfrac{2i - 1}{-(-1)} = \mathbf{-1 + 2i}$

22. $\dfrac{3 - i}{i^2 - 3i} = \dfrac{3 - i}{-1 - 3i} \cdot \dfrac{-1 + 3i}{-1 + 3i}$

$\quad = \dfrac{-3 + 9i + i + 3}{1 + 9} = \mathbf{i}$

23.

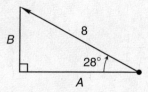

$A = 8\cos 28° \approx 7.06$

$B = 8\sin 28° \approx 3.76$

$C = 6\cos 62° \approx 2.82$

$D = 6\sin 62° \approx 5.30$

$\begin{array}{r} -7.06R + 3.76U \\ 2.82R + 5.30U \\ \hline \mathbf{-4.24R + 9.06U} \end{array}$

$\tan\theta = \dfrac{9.06}{-4.24}$

$\quad \theta \approx -64.92°$

Since θ is a second-quadrant angle,

$\theta = (-64.92) + 180 = 115.08°$

$F = \sqrt{(-4.24)^2 + (9.06)^2} \approx 10.00$

$\mathbf{10.00/\underline{115.08°}}$

24. $\dfrac{5 - 2\sqrt{2}}{\sqrt{2}} \cdot \dfrac{\sqrt{2}}{\sqrt{2}} = \dfrac{\mathbf{-4 + 5\sqrt{2}}}{\mathbf{2}}$

25. $\dfrac{3 - 4\sqrt{5}}{\sqrt{5} - 1} \cdot \dfrac{\sqrt{5} + 1}{\sqrt{5} + 1}$

$\quad = \dfrac{3\sqrt{5} + 3 - 20 - 4\sqrt{5}}{5 - 1} = \dfrac{\mathbf{-17 - \sqrt{5}}}{\mathbf{4}}$

26. $\sqrt{\dfrac{2}{13}} + 3\sqrt{\dfrac{13}{2}} - 2\sqrt{104}$

$\quad = \dfrac{\sqrt{2}}{\sqrt{13}}\dfrac{\sqrt{13}}{\sqrt{13}} + \dfrac{3\sqrt{13}}{\sqrt{2}}\dfrac{\sqrt{2}}{\sqrt{2}} - 4\sqrt{26}$

$\quad = \dfrac{2\sqrt{26}}{26} + \dfrac{39\sqrt{26}}{26} - \dfrac{104\sqrt{26}}{26} = -\dfrac{\mathbf{63\sqrt{26}}}{\mathbf{26}}$

27. $-\sqrt{-7}\sqrt{-7} + 2\sqrt{-16} - 3i^5 + 2i^2$

$\quad = 7 + 8i - 3i - 2 = \mathbf{5 + 5i}$

28. $\dfrac{a}{k+c} = \dfrac{mx}{y} + md$

$ay = kmx + cmx + mdky + mdcy$

$ay - mdky - mdcy = kmx + cmx$

$y = \dfrac{kmx + cmx}{a - mdk - mdc}$

29. $\dfrac{400\ \text{ft}^3}{\text{min}} \times \dfrac{12\ \text{in.}}{1\ \text{ft}} \times \dfrac{12\ \text{in.}}{1\ \text{ft}} \times \dfrac{12\ \text{in.}}{1\ \text{ft}} \times \dfrac{1\ \text{min}}{60\ \text{s}}$

$= \dfrac{400(12)(12)(12)}{60} \dfrac{\text{in.}^3}{\text{s}}$

30. (a) Estimate: $\dfrac{2 \times 10^{-6}}{-5 \times 10^6} = -4 \times 10^{-13}$

Calculator answer $\approx$ **-3.92×10^{-13}**

(b) Estimate: some number between
$(4)^{-5} \approx 10 \times 10^{-4}$ and $(5)^{-5} = 3.2 \times 10^{-4}$

Calculator answer $\approx$ **7.46×10^{-4}**

PRACTICE SET 101

Selling price = purchase price + markup

$16{,}295 = P_P + 0.25P_P$

$16{,}295 = 1.25P_P$

$13,036 $= P_P$

PROBLEM SET 101

1. Selling price = purchase price + markup

$78 = P_P + 0.3P_P$

$78 = 1.3P_P$

$60 $= P_P$

Markup $= 0.3(\$60) =$ **$18**

2. Selling price = purchase price + markup

$S_P = 2100 + 0.6S_P$

$0.4S_P = 2100$

$S_P =$ **$5250**

3. Selling price = purchase price + markup

$16{,}535 = P_P + 0.25P_P$

$16{,}535 = 1.25P_P$

$13,228 $= P_P$

4. $0.6(400) + 0.8(D_N) = 0.72(400 + D_N)$

$240 + 0.8D_N = 288 + 0.72D_N$

$0.08D_N = 48$

$D_N =$ **600 liters**

5. Downstream: $(B + W)T_D = D_D$ (a)

Upstream: $(B - W)T_U = D_U$ (b)

Since $T_D = T_U$, we use T in both equations.

(a') $(20 + W)T = 104$

(b') $(20 - W)T = 56$

(a') $20T + WT = 104$

(b') $\underline{20T - WT = \ \ 56}$

$40T \quad\quad = 160$

$T = 4$

(a') $20(4) + 4W = 104$

$4W = 24$

$W =$ **6 mph**

6. $y = -x^2 - 4x - 5$

$-y = (x^2 + 4x + 4) + 5 - 4$

$-y = (x + 2)^2 + 1$

$y = -(x + 2)^2 - 1$

From this we see:

(a) Opens downward

(b) Axis of symmetry is $x = -2$

(c) y-coordinate of vertex is -1

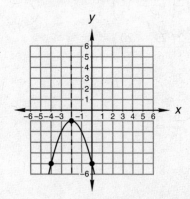

7. $y = x^2 + 2x + 2$

$y = (x^2 + 2x + 1) + 2 - 1$

$y = (x + 1)^2 + 1$

From this we see:

(a) Opens upward

(b) Axis of symmetry is $x = -1$

(c) y-coordinate of vertex is $+1$

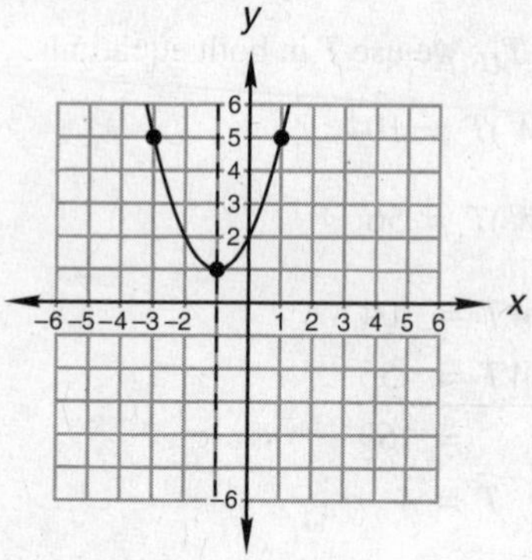

8. $V_{\text{Cone}} = \frac{1}{3}\pi r^2 h = 60\pi \text{ cm}^3$

$h = \frac{60\pi(3) \text{ cm}^3}{(3 \text{ cm})^2 \pi}$

$h = \frac{180\pi \text{ cm}^3}{9\pi \text{ cm}^2} = \mathbf{20 \text{ cm}}$

9. $-|x| + 3 \nless 2$; $D = \{\text{Integers}\}$

$-|x| \geq -1$

$|x| \leq 1$

$x \leq 1$ and $x \geq -1$

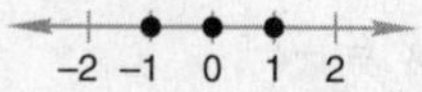

10. $N = 3\frac{1}{3} + \frac{2}{5}\left(4\frac{5}{6} - 3\frac{1}{3}\right)$

$= \frac{10}{3} + \frac{2}{5}\left(\frac{29}{6} - \frac{20}{6}\right)$

$= \frac{10}{3} + \frac{3}{5}$

$= \frac{50}{15} + \frac{9}{15} = \mathbf{\frac{59}{15}}$

11. (a) $6x + 5y = 8$

(b) $4x + 2y = 3$

$y = -2x + \frac{3}{2}$

Substitute (b) into (a) and get:

(a′) $6x + 5\left(-2x + \frac{3}{2}\right) = 8$

$6x - 10x + \frac{15}{2} = 8$

$-8x + 15 = 16$

$-8x = 1$

$x = -\frac{1}{8}$

(b) $y = -2\left(-\frac{1}{8}\right) + \frac{3}{2}$

$y = \frac{1}{4} + \frac{6}{4} = \frac{7}{4}$

$\mathbf{\left(-\frac{1}{8}, \frac{7}{4}\right)}$

12. (a) $3x - y = 4$

(b) $xy = 5$

$y = \frac{5}{x}$

Substitute (b) into (a) and get:

(a′) $3x - \left(\frac{5}{x}\right) = 4$

$3x^2 - 5 = 4x$

$3x^2 - 4x - 5 = 0$

Solve this equation by using the quadratic formula.

$x = \frac{-(-4) \pm \sqrt{(-4)^2 - 4(3)(-5)}}{2(3)}$

$x = \frac{2}{3} \pm \frac{\sqrt{19}}{3}$

Substitute these values of x into (a) and solve for y.

(a) $y = 3\left(\frac{2}{3} + \frac{\sqrt{19}}{3}\right) - 4 = -2 + \sqrt{19}$

(a) $y = 3\left(\frac{2}{3} - \frac{\sqrt{19}}{3}\right) - 4 = -2 - \sqrt{19}$

$\mathbf{\left(\frac{2}{3} + \frac{\sqrt{19}}{3}, -2 + \sqrt{19}\right)}$ and

$\mathbf{\left(\frac{2}{3} - \frac{\sqrt{19}}{3}, -2 - \sqrt{19}\right)}$

13. (a) $x^2 + y^2 = 16$

(b) $\dfrac{2x^2 - y^2 = 2}{3x^2 \quad\;\; = 18}$

$x^2 = 6$

$x = \pm\sqrt{6}$

(a) $y^2 = 16 - (\sqrt{6})^2$

$y^2 = 10$

$y = \pm\sqrt{10}$

(a) $y^2 = 16 - (-\sqrt{6})^2$

$y^2 = 10$

$y = \pm\sqrt{10}$

$\mathbf{(\sqrt{6}, \pm\sqrt{10})}$ **and** $\mathbf{(-\sqrt{6}, \pm\sqrt{10})}$

14. (a) $3x + y + z = 7$

(b) $x - 2y - z = 2$

(c) $-x + y - z = -5$

(a) $3x + y + z = 7$

(b) $\dfrac{x - 2y - z = 2}{}$

(d) $\overline{4x - y \quad\;\; = 9}$

(a) $3x + y + z = 7$

(c) $\dfrac{-x + y - z = -5}{}$

(e) $\overline{2x + 2y \quad\;\; = 2}$

2(d) $8x - 2y = 18$

(e) $\dfrac{2x + 2y = 2}{10x \quad\quad = 20}$

$x = 2$

(e) $2(2) + 2y = 2$

$y = -1$

(c) $-(2) + (-1) - z = -5$

$z = 2$

$\mathbf{(2, -1, 2)}$

15. $p(x) = x^2 - 4;\; D = \{\text{Reals}\}$

$p\!\left(\dfrac{1}{2}\right) = \left(\dfrac{1}{2}\right)^2 - 4 = -\dfrac{15}{4}$

16. (a) $3y - 2x > -3$

$y > \dfrac{2}{3}x - 1$

(b) $x \geq -2$

The next step is to graph each of these lines.

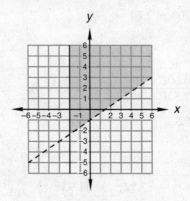

The region we wish to find is on or to the right of the solid line and above the dashed line. This region is shaded in the figure.

17. $-10 < x + 2 < -4;\; D = \{\text{Reals}\}$

$-12 < x < -6$

18. $\dfrac{(a^{x+2})^{1/2}\, y}{(y^2)^a} = \dfrac{a^{x/2+1}y}{y^{2a}} = a^{x/2+1}y^{1-2a}$

19. $\dfrac{m}{my - \dfrac{1}{1 - \dfrac{1}{my}}} = \dfrac{m}{my - \dfrac{my}{my - 1}}$

$= \dfrac{m(my - 1)}{m^2 y^2 - my - my} = \dfrac{my - 1}{my^2 - 2y}$

20. $7\sqrt{49\sqrt[3]{7}} = 7\sqrt{7^2\sqrt[3]{7}} = 7(7^2)^{1/2}(7^{1/6}) = 7^{13/6}$

21. $\dfrac{-2 - 3i}{3 + 2i} \cdot \dfrac{3 - 2i}{3 - 2i} = \dfrac{-6 + 4i - 9i - 6}{9 + 4}$

$= -\dfrac{12}{13} - \dfrac{5}{13}i$

22. $\dfrac{i}{2i - 3} \cdot \dfrac{2i + 3}{2i + 3} = \dfrac{-2 + 3i}{-4 - 9}$

$= \dfrac{2}{13} - \dfrac{3}{13}i$

23.

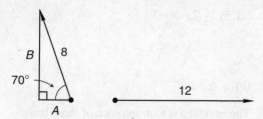

$A = 8 \cos 70° \approx 2.74$

$B = 8 \sin 70° \approx 7.52$

$-2.74R + 7.52U$
$\underline{12.00R + 0.00U}$
$\mathbf{9.26R + 7.52U}$

$\tan \theta = \dfrac{7.52}{9.26}$

$\theta \approx 39.08°$

$F = \sqrt{(9.26)^2 + (7.52)^2} \approx 11.93$

$\mathbf{11.93\underline{/39.08°}}$

24. $\dfrac{2\sqrt{2} - \sqrt{3}}{\sqrt{6}} \cdot \dfrac{\sqrt{6}}{\sqrt{6}} = \dfrac{\mathbf{4\sqrt{3} - 3\sqrt{2}}}{\mathbf{6}}$

25. $\dfrac{3 - \sqrt{2}}{\sqrt{2} + 2} \cdot \dfrac{\sqrt{2} - 2}{\sqrt{2} - 2} = \dfrac{3\sqrt{2} - 6 - 2 + 2\sqrt{2}}{2 - 4}$

$= \dfrac{\mathbf{8 - 5\sqrt{2}}}{\mathbf{2}}$

26. $2\sqrt{\dfrac{2}{5}} - 4\sqrt{\dfrac{5}{2}} + 2\sqrt{40}$

$= \dfrac{2\sqrt{2}}{\sqrt{5}}\dfrac{\sqrt{5}}{\sqrt{5}} - \dfrac{4\sqrt{5}}{\sqrt{2}}\dfrac{\sqrt{2}}{\sqrt{2}} + 4\sqrt{10}$

$= \dfrac{4\sqrt{10}}{10} - \dfrac{20\sqrt{10}}{10} + \dfrac{40\sqrt{10}}{10} = \dfrac{\mathbf{12\sqrt{10}}}{\mathbf{5}}$

27. $-3i^2 - 2i^3 + 4 - i^5 + \sqrt{-9}$

$= 3 + 2i + 4 - i + 3i = \mathbf{7 + 4i}$

28. $\dfrac{m}{x} - c = \dfrac{1}{R_1} + \dfrac{1}{R_2}$

$mR_1R_2 - cR_1R_2x = R_2x + R_1x$

$mR_1R_2 - cR_1R_2x - R_1x = R_2x$

$R_1 = \dfrac{R_2x}{mR_2 - cR_2x - x}$

29. $\qquad -2x^2 = x + 4$

$2x^2 + x + 4 = 0$

$x = \dfrac{-1 \pm \sqrt{(1)^2 - 4(2)(4)}}{2(2)} = \mathbf{-\dfrac{1}{4} \pm \dfrac{\sqrt{31}}{4}i}$

30. $\dfrac{2x^0 y^{-2} p^{-4} yp^4 m}{x^2 p^{-4} x^{-2}} - \dfrac{6x^0 y^{-2} p^{-4} xy^0}{x^2 p^{-4}}$

$= \dfrac{2y^{-1}m}{p^{-4}} - \dfrac{6xy^{-2}p^{-4}}{x^2 p^{-4}} = \mathbf{2mp^4 y^{-1} - 6x^{-1}y^{-2}}$

PRACTICE SET 102

a. $h(x) = x + 1$

$\underline{g(x) = x^2 - 1}$

$(h + g)(x) = x^2 + x$

$(h + g)(5) = (5)^2 + (5) = \mathbf{30}$

b. $\quad h(x) = x + 2$

$h(-2) = (-2) + 2 = 0$

$\quad g(x) = x^2 - 7$

$g(-2) = (-2)^2 - 7 = -3$

$hg(-2) = 0 \cdot -3 = \mathbf{0}$

c. $\quad f(x) = x + 6; \ g(x) = x - 4$

$fg(x) = (x + 6)(x - 4)$

$fg(x) = \mathbf{x^2 + 2x - 24; \ D = \{Positive\ integers\}}$

PROBLEM SET 102

1.

$$D_S$$
$$40 \bullet \longrightarrow$$
$$D_{JR}$$

$R_S T_S + 40 = R_{JR}T_{JR}; \ R_S = 46;$

$R_{JR} = 50; \ T_S = T_{JR}$

$46(T_S) + 40 = 50(T_S)$

$\qquad 4T_S = 40$

$\qquad T_S = 10 \text{ hr}$

$D_S = R_S T_S = 46(10) = \mathbf{460\ miles}$

2. Downstream: $(B + W)T_D = D_D$ (a)

Upstream: $(B - W)T_U = D_U$ (b)

(a') $(10 + W)T = 78$

(b') $(10 - W)T = 42$

(a') $10T + WT = 78$

(b') $\underline{10T - WT = 42}$

$\quad 20T \qquad\quad = 120$

$\qquad T = 6$

(a') $10(6) + 6W = 78$

$\qquad 6W = 18$

$\qquad W = \mathbf{3\ mph}$

3. $\dfrac{H_1}{H_2} = \dfrac{G_1(P_2)^2}{G_2(P_1)^2}$

$\dfrac{5}{10} = \dfrac{2(6)^2}{G_2(4)^2}$

$G_2 = \dfrac{2(36)(10)}{5(16)} = \textbf{9 goats}$

4. Selling price = purchase price + markup

$1666 = P_P + 0.7P_P$

$1666 = 1.7P_P$

$\textbf{\$980} = P_P$

5. Selling price = purchase price + markup

$1680 = P_P + 0.4P_P$

$1680 = 1.4P_P$

$\textbf{\$1200} = P_P$

6. $\dfrac{V_1}{T_1} = \dfrac{V_2}{T_2}$

$\dfrac{450}{776} = \dfrac{V_2}{1016}$

$V_2 = \textbf{589.18 mL}$

7. $h(x) = x + 1; \ D = \{\text{Reals}\}$

$g(x) = x^2 - 6; \ D = \{\text{Negative integers}\}$

$h(-5) = -5 + 1 = -4$

$g(-5) = (-5)^2 - 6 = 19$

$hg(-5) = -4(19) = \textbf{-76}$

8. $f(x) = x + 4; \ D = \{\text{Reals}\}$

$g(x) = x - 1; \ D = \{\text{Positive integers}\}$

$f(x)g(x) = (x + 4)(x - 1)$

$fg(x) = x^2 + 3x - 4$

We cannot use this function to find $fg(-3)$, because -3 is not a member of the domain of $g(x)$, so it is not a member of the domain of $fg(x)$. Therefore, the answer is either $\varnothing$ or $\{ \ \}$.

9. $y = x^2 + 4x + 2$

$y = (x^2 + 4x + 4) + 2 - 4$

$y = (x + 2)^2 - 2$

From this we see:

(a) Opens upward

(b) Axis of symmetry is $x = -2$

(c) y-coordinate of vertex is -2

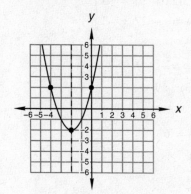

10. $y = -x^2 - 4x - 2$

$-y = (x^2 + 4x + 4) + 2 - 4$

$y = -(x + 2)^2 + 2$

From this we see:

(a) Opens downward

(b) Axis of symmetry is $x = -2$

(c) y-coordinate of vertex is $+2$

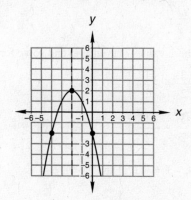

11. $-|x| - 2 \le -5; \ D = \{\text{Integers}\}$

$-|x| \le -3$

$|x| \ge 3$

$x \ge 3 \text{ or } x \le -3$

12. (a) $2x + 3y = -3$

(b) $4x - 2y = 18$

$y = 2x - 9$

Substitute (b) into (a) and get:

(a′) $2x + 3(2x - 9) = -3$

$2x + 6x - 27 = -3$

$8x = 24$

$x = 3$

(b) $y = 2(3) - 9 = -3$

(3, –3)

13. (a) $2x - y = 6$

(b) $xy = 4$

$y = \dfrac{4}{x}$

Substitute (b) into (a) and get:

(a′) $2x - \left(\dfrac{4}{x}\right) = 6$

$2x^2 - 4 = 6x$

$x^2 - 3x - 2 = 0$

Solve this equation by using the quadratic formula.

$x = \dfrac{-(-3) \pm \sqrt{(-3)^2 - 4(1)(-2)}}{2(1)}$

$x = \dfrac{3}{2} \pm \dfrac{\sqrt{17}}{2}$

Substitute these values of x into (a) and solve for y.

(a) $y = 2\left(\dfrac{3}{2} + \dfrac{\sqrt{17}}{2}\right) - 6 = -3 + \sqrt{17}$

(a) $y = 2\left(\dfrac{3}{2} - \dfrac{\sqrt{17}}{2}\right) - 6 = -3 - \sqrt{17}$

$\left(\dfrac{3}{2} + \dfrac{\sqrt{17}}{2}, -3 + \sqrt{17}\right)$ and

$\left(\dfrac{3}{2} - \dfrac{\sqrt{17}}{2}, -3 - \sqrt{17}\right)$

14. (a) $x^2 + y^2 = 12$

(b) $\dfrac{3x^2 - y^2 = 4}{4x^2 = 16}$

$x^2 = 4$

$x = \pm 2$

(a) $y^2 = 12 - (2)^2$

$y^2 = 8$

$y = \pm 2\sqrt{2}$

(a) $y^2 = 12 - (-2)^2$

$y^2 = 8$

$y = \pm 2\sqrt{2}$

$(2, \pm 2\sqrt{2})$ and $(-2, \pm 2\sqrt{2})$

15. (a) $x + y + z = 8$

(b) $x + y - z = 0$

(c) $2x - y + z = 3$

(a) $x + y + z = 8$

(b) $\dfrac{x + y - z = 0}{2x + 2y = 8}$

(d) $ x + y = 4$

(b) $x + y - z = 0$

(c) $\dfrac{2x - y + z = 3}{3x = 3}$

$x = 1$

(d) $(1) + y = 4$

$y = 3$

(a) $(1) + (3) + z = 8$

$z = 4$

(1, 3, 4)

16. (a) $3x - 5y < 10$

$y > \dfrac{3}{5}x - 2$

(b) $y \geq -2$

The next step is to graph each of these lines.

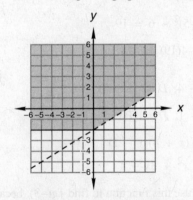

The region we wish to find is on or above the solid line and above the dashed line. This region is shaded in the figure.

17. $x + 2 < 0$ or $x + 3 \nleq 3$; $D = \{\text{Integers}\}$

$x < -2$ or $ x > 0$

18. $N = \dfrac{1}{5} + \dfrac{1}{8}\left(2\dfrac{1}{3} - \dfrac{1}{5}\right)$

$\quad = \dfrac{1}{5} + \dfrac{1}{8}\left(\dfrac{35}{15} - \dfrac{3}{15}\right)$

$\quad = \dfrac{1}{5} + \dfrac{32}{120}$

$\quad = \dfrac{24}{120} + \dfrac{32}{120} = \dfrac{7}{15}$

19. $\dfrac{x^{a/2}\,y^{2a}}{x^{3a}\,y^{-2a/3}} = x^{-5a/2}y^{8a/3}$

20. $\dfrac{kx}{x - \dfrac{kx}{k - \dfrac{1}{x}}} = \dfrac{kx}{x - \dfrac{kx^2}{kx - 1}}$

$\quad = \dfrac{kx(kx - 1)}{kx^2 - x - kx^2} = -k(kx - 1) = k - k^2x$

21. $\sqrt[3]{x^5 y}\,\sqrt[4]{xy^2} = x^{5/3}y^{1/3}x^{1/4}y^{1/2} = x^{23/12}y^{5/6}$

22. $\dfrac{3i + 4}{-i^2 - i^5} = \dfrac{3i + 4}{1 - i} \cdot \dfrac{1 + i}{1 + i}$

$\quad = \dfrac{3i + 3i^2 + 4 + 4i}{1 - i^2}$

$\quad = \dfrac{1 + 7i}{2} = \dfrac{1}{2} + \dfrac{7}{2}i$

23. $\dfrac{4i - 3}{i^3 - 2i^2} = \dfrac{4i - 3}{-i + 2} \cdot \dfrac{-i - 2}{-i - 2}$

$\quad = \dfrac{4 - 8i + 3i + 6}{i^2 - 4}$

$\quad = \dfrac{10 - 5i}{-5} = -2 + i$

24.

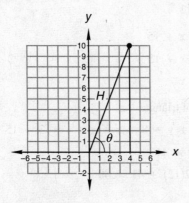

$H = \sqrt{10^2 + 4^2}$

$H = 2\sqrt{29}$

$\tan \theta = \dfrac{10}{4}$

$\theta \approx 68.20°$

$2\sqrt{29}\,\underline{/68.20°}$

25. $\dfrac{a}{x} + \dfrac{b}{m + c} = ax$

$am + ac + bx = amx^2 + acx^2$

$ac - acx^2 = amx^2 - am - bx$

$c = \dfrac{amx^2 - am - bx}{a - ax^2}$

26. $\dfrac{2 - 2\sqrt{2}}{3\sqrt{2} - 2} \cdot \dfrac{3\sqrt{2} + 2}{3\sqrt{2} + 2}$

$\quad = \dfrac{6\sqrt{2} + 4 - 12 - 4\sqrt{2}}{18 - 4} = \dfrac{-8 + 2\sqrt{2}}{14}$

$\quad = \dfrac{-4 + \sqrt{2}}{7}$

27. $3i + 2 + 3i - 3i = 2 + 3i$

28. $4\sqrt{\dfrac{5}{12}} + 3\sqrt{\dfrac{12}{5}} - 3\sqrt{60}$

$\quad = \dfrac{4\sqrt{5}}{\sqrt{12}} + \dfrac{3\sqrt{12}}{\sqrt{5}} - 3\sqrt{60}$

$\quad = \dfrac{4\sqrt{60}}{12} + \dfrac{3\sqrt{60}}{5} - 3\sqrt{60}$

$\quad = \dfrac{20\sqrt{60}}{60} + \dfrac{36\sqrt{60}}{60} - \dfrac{180\sqrt{60}}{60}$

$\quad = -\dfrac{124\sqrt{60}}{60} = -\dfrac{62\sqrt{15}}{15}$

29. See Lesson 71.

30. $\angle AED$ and $\angle CEA$ are supplementary angles and need not be equal.

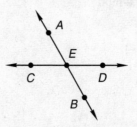

Choice (**c**) is correct.

PRACTICE SET 103

a.

$$
\begin{array}{r}
4x^2 - 8xy + 16y^2 \\
2x + 4y\,\overline{)8x^3 \qquad\qquad + 64y^3} \\
\underline{8x^3 + 16x^2y} \\
-16x^2y \\
\underline{-16x^2y - 32xy^2} \\
32xy^2 + 64y^3 \\
\underline{32xy^2 + 64y^3} \\
0
\end{array}
$$

b.

$$
\begin{array}{r}
4x^2 + 8xy + 16y^2 \\
2x - 4y\,\overline{)8x^3 \qquad\qquad - 64y^3} \\
\underline{8x^3 - 16x^2y} \\
16x^2y \\
\underline{16x^2y - 32xy^2} \\
32xy^2 - 64y^3 \\
\underline{32xy^2 - 64y^3} \\
0
\end{array}
$$

PROBLEM SET 103

1. Selling price = purchase price + markup

$$1424 = P_P + 0.6P_P$$
$$1424 = 1.6P_P$$
$$\mathbf{\$890} = P_P$$

2. Downstream: $(B + W)T_D = D_D$ (a)

Upstream: $(B - W)T_U = D_U$ (b)

(a') $(18 + W)T = 132$

(b') $(18 - W)T = 84$

(a') $18T + WT = 132$

(b') $\dfrac{18T - WT =\ \ 84}{36T \qquad\quad = 216}$

$$T = 6$$

(a') $(18 + W)6 = 132$

$$6W = 24$$
$$W = \mathbf{4\ mph}$$

3.

$$
\begin{array}{c}
\xleftrightarrow{\hspace{2cm}} \\
D_D \\
720
\end{array}
$$

$$
\begin{array}{c}
\xleftrightarrow{\hspace{0.8cm}} \\
D_M \\
200
\end{array}
$$

$$R_D T_D = 720; \quad R_M T_M = 200;$$
$$T_D = 2T_M; \quad R_D = R_M + 40$$

$$(R_M + 40)2T_M = 720$$
$$2R_M T_M + 80T_M = 720$$
$$2(200) + 80T_M = 720$$
$$80T_M = 320$$
$$T_M = \mathbf{4\ hr}$$

$$T_D = \mathbf{8\ hr}; \quad R_M = \mathbf{50\ mph}; \quad R_D = \mathbf{90\ mph}$$

4.

$$\frac{P_1}{T_1} = \frac{P_2}{T_2}$$
$$\frac{400}{300} = \frac{600}{T_2}$$
$$T_2 = \mathbf{450\ K}$$

5. Multiples of 11: $11N,\ 11(N + 1),\ 11(N + 2)$

$$4(11N + 11N + 22) = 10(11N + 11) - 66$$
$$88N + 88 = 110N + 44$$
$$44 = 22N$$
$$2 = N$$

The desired integers are **22, 33,** and **44.**

6.

$$
\begin{array}{r}
9x^2 - 6xy + 4y^2 \\
3x + 2y\,\overline{)27x^3 \qquad\qquad + 8y^3} \\
\underline{27x^3 + 18x^2y} \\
-18x^2y \\
\underline{-18x^2y - 12xy^2} \\
12xy^2 + 8y^3 \\
\underline{12xy^2 + 8y^3} \\
0
\end{array}
$$

7. Since the lengths of tangent segments drawn to a circle from a point outside the circle are equal,

$$y + 3 = 15$$
$$y = \mathbf{12}$$

$$y + 8 = x + 15$$
$$12 + 8 = x + 15$$
$$5 = x$$

Perimeter of triangle

$$= x + 15 + y + 8 + x + x + y + 3 + 15$$
$$= 3x + 2y + 41$$
$$= 3(5) + 2(12) + 41 = \mathbf{80}$$

8. Since 2 is not a member of the domain of $b(x)$, it is not a member of the domain of $ab(x)$. Therefore, the answer is either $\varnothing$ or { }.

9. $y = x^2 + 4x + 6$

$y = (x^2 + 4x + 4) + 6 - 4$

$y = (x + 2)^2 + 2$

From this we see:

(a) Opens upward

(b) Axis of symmetry is $x = -2$

(c) y-coordinate of vertex is $+2$

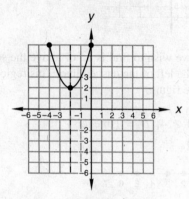

10. $y = -x^2 + 4x - 6$

$-y = (x^2 - 4x + 4) + 6 - 4$

$-y = (x - 2)^2 + 2$

$y = -(x - 2)^2 - 2$

From this we see:

(a) Opens downward

(b) Axis of symmetry is $x = 2$

(c) y-coordinate of vertex is -2

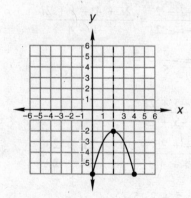

11. $x + 3 \geq 5$; $D = \{\text{Reals}\}$

$x \geq 2$

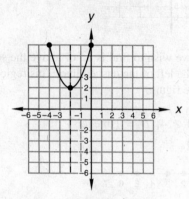

12. $N = \dfrac{1}{4} + \dfrac{2}{3}\left(2\dfrac{1}{2} - \dfrac{1}{4}\right)$

$= \dfrac{1}{4} + \dfrac{2}{3}\left(\dfrac{10}{4} - \dfrac{1}{4}\right)$

$= \dfrac{1}{4} + \dfrac{3}{2}$

$= \dfrac{1}{4} + \dfrac{6}{4} = \dfrac{\mathbf{7}}{\mathbf{4}}$

13. (a) $4x + 3y = 17$

(b) $2x - 3y = -5$

$y = \dfrac{2}{3}x + \dfrac{5}{3}$

Substitute (b) into (a) and get:

(a′) $4x + 3\left(\dfrac{2}{3}x + \dfrac{5}{3}\right) = 17$

$4x + 2x + 5 = 17$

$6x = 12$

$x = 2$

(b) $y = \dfrac{2}{3}(2) + \dfrac{5}{3}$

$y = \dfrac{4}{3} + \dfrac{5}{3} = 3$

(2, 3)

14. (a) $x^2 + y^2 = 6$

(b) $x - y = 2$

$y = x - 2$

Substitute (b) into (a) and get:

(a′) $\quad x^2 + (x - 2)^2 = 6$

$x^2 + x^2 - 4x + 4 = 6$

$2x^2 - 4x - 2 = 0$

$x^2 - 2x - 1 = 0$

Solve this equation by using the quadratic formula.

$x = \dfrac{-(-2) \pm \sqrt{(-2)^2 - 4(1)(-1)}}{2(1)} = 1 \pm \sqrt{2}$

Substitute these values of x into (b) and solve for y.

(b) $y = (1 + \sqrt{2}) - 2 = -1 + \sqrt{2}$

(b) $y = (1 - \sqrt{2}) - 2 = -1 - \sqrt{2}$

$(\mathbf{1 + \sqrt{2}, -1 + \sqrt{2}})$ and $(\mathbf{1 - \sqrt{2}, -1 - \sqrt{2}})$

15. (a) $x^2 + y^2 = 10$

$$y^2 = 10 - x^2$$

(b) $2x^2 - 2y^2 = 5$

Substitute (a) into (b) and get:

(b') $2x^2 - 2(10 - x^2) = 5$

$$2x^2 - 20 + 2x^2 = 5$$

$$4x^2 = 25$$

$$x^2 = \frac{25}{4}$$

$$x = \pm\frac{5}{2}$$

Substitute these values of x into (a) and solve for y.

(a) $y^2 = 10 - \left(\frac{5}{2}\right)^2 = \pm\frac{\sqrt{15}}{2}$

(a) $y^2 = 10 - \left(-\frac{5}{2}\right)^2 = \pm\frac{\sqrt{15}}{2}$

$\left(\frac{5}{2}, \pm\frac{\sqrt{15}}{2}\right)$ and $\left(-\frac{5}{2}, \pm\frac{\sqrt{15}}{2}\right)$

16. (a) $x + 2y + z = -1$

(b) $3x - y + z = 6$

(c) $2x - 3y - z = 8$

(b) $3x - y + z = 6$
(c) $\underline{2x - 3y - z = 8}$
(d) $5x - 4y = 14$

(a) $x + 2y + z = -1$
(c) $\underline{2x - 3y - z = 8}$
$ 3x - y = 7$

(e) $ y = 3x - 7$

Substitute (e) into (d) and get:

(d') $5x - 4(3x - 7) = 14$

$$5x - 12x + 28 = 14$$

$$7x = 14$$

$$x = 2$$

(e) $y = 3(2) - 7 = -1$

(a) $(2) + 2(-1) + z = -1$

$$z = -1$$

(2, -1, -1)

17. (a) $x - 4y \le -4$

$$y \ge \frac{1}{4}x + 1$$

(b) $x < 3$

The next step is to graph each of these lines.

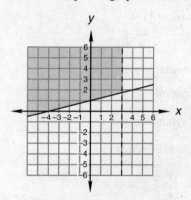

The region we wish to find is on or above the solid line and to the left of the dashed line. This region is shaded in the figure.

18. $-3 \le x - 3 \not\ge 4;\ D = \{\text{Integers}\}$

$$0 \le x < 7$$

19. $\dfrac{x^{2ab - 2b}}{x^{b/2}} = x^{2ab - 5b/2}$

20. $\dfrac{m}{m^2 + \dfrac{m}{m^2 + \dfrac{1}{m}}} = \dfrac{m}{m^2 + \dfrac{m^2}{m^3 + 1}}$

$$= \frac{m(m^3 + 1)}{m^5 + m^2 + m^2} = \frac{m^3 + 1}{m^4 + 2m}$$

21. $\sqrt[5]{x^2 y^3}\ \sqrt[4]{xy} = x^{2/5}y^{3/5}x^{1/4}y^{1/4} = x^{13/20}y^{17/20}$

22. $\dfrac{-2 - i}{-i + 2} \cdot \dfrac{-i - 2}{-i - 2} = \dfrac{2i + 4 - 1 + 2i}{-1 - 4}$

$$= \frac{3 + 4i}{-5} = -\frac{3}{5} - \frac{4}{5}i$$

23. $\dfrac{2i - 5}{-5 - 2i} \cdot \dfrac{-5 + 2i}{-5 + 2i}$

$$= \frac{-10i - 4 + 25 - 10i}{25 + 4} = \frac{21}{29} - \frac{20}{29}i$$

24. $\dfrac{3 + 2\sqrt{5}}{5 - 2\sqrt{5}} \cdot \dfrac{5 + 2\sqrt{5}}{5 + 2\sqrt{5}}$

$$= \frac{15 + 6\sqrt{5} + 10\sqrt{5} + 20}{25 - 20}$$

$$= \frac{35 + 16\sqrt{5}}{5}$$

25.

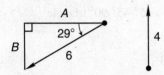

$A = 6 \cos 29° \approx 5.25$

$B = 6 \sin 29° \approx 2.91$

$$\begin{array}{r} -5.25R - 2.91U \\ 0.00R + 4.00U \\ \hline -5.25R + 1.09U \end{array}$$

$\tan \theta = -\dfrac{1.09}{5.25}$

$\theta \approx -11.73°$

Since θ is a second-quadrant angle,

$\theta = (-11.73) + 180 = 168.27°$

$F = \sqrt{(-5.25)^2 + (1.09)^2} \approx 5.36$

5.36$\underline{/168.27°}$

26. $a\left(\dfrac{b}{c} - \dfrac{1}{x}\right) = \dfrac{m}{p}$

$\dfrac{ab}{c} - \dfrac{a}{x} = \dfrac{m}{p}$

$abpx - acp = cmx$

$abpx - cmx = acp$

$x = \dfrac{acp}{abp - cm}$

27. $\sqrt{z} + \sqrt{z + 33} = 11$

$\sqrt{z + 33} = 11 - \sqrt{z}$

$z + 33 = 121 - 22\sqrt{z} + z$

$22\sqrt{z} = 88$

$\sqrt{z} = 4$

$z = \mathbf{16}$

Check: $\sqrt{16} + \sqrt{16 + 33} = 11$

$4 + 7 = 11$

28. $3\sqrt{\dfrac{4}{3}} - 2\sqrt{\dfrac{3}{4}} + 5\sqrt{48} = \dfrac{6}{\sqrt{3}} - \sqrt{3} + 5\sqrt{48}$

$= \dfrac{6\sqrt{3}}{3} - \sqrt{3} + 20\sqrt{3} = \mathbf{21\sqrt{3}}$

29. $4i - 2i(-3) - i = 4i + 6i - i = \mathbf{9i}$

30. Since there are 180° in a triangle,

$\angle ABD + \angle BDA + \angle BAD = 180°$

$\angle ABD + 90° + 40° = 180°$

$\angle ABD = 50°$

Since $\triangle ABC$ is isosceles,

$\angle DBC + \angle ABD = 70°$

$\angle DBC + 50° = 70°$

$\angle DBC = \mathbf{20°}$

PRACTICE SET 104

a. $0.00000513 \times \dfrac{10^8}{10^8} = \dfrac{513}{100,000,000}$

b. $\begin{array}{r} 100N = 1.524\ 24\ 24\ 24\ \ldots \\ N = 0.015\ 24\ 24\ 24\ \ldots \\ \hline 99N = 1.509 \end{array}$

$N = \dfrac{1.509}{99} = \dfrac{\mathbf{1509}}{\mathbf{99,000}}$

PROBLEM SET 104

1. (a) $2N_D = 24N_G - 6$

(a′) $N_D = 12N_G - 3$

(b) $10N_G = N_D - 5$

Substitute (a′) into (b) and get:

(b′) $10N_G = (12N_G - 3) - 5$

$2N_G = 8$

$N_G = \mathbf{4\ geese}$

(a′) $N_D = 12(4) - 3 = \mathbf{45\ ducks}$

2.

$R_U T_U = R_B T_B;\ R_U = 240;$

$R_B = 360;\ T_B = T_U - 4$

$240T_U = 360(T_U - 4)$

$120T_U = 1440$

$T_U = 12$

$D_U = R_U T_U = 240(12) = \mathbf{2880\ miles}$

3. (a) $0.1P_N + 0.2D_N = 44$

(b) $P_N + D_N = 400$

Substitute $D_N = 400 - P_N$ into (a) and get:

(a') $0.1P_N + 0.2(400 - P_N) = 44$

$$-0.1P_N = -36$$

$$P_N = 360$$

(b) $(360) + D_N = 400$

$$D_N = 40$$

360 mL 10%, 40 mL 20%

4. Downstream: $(B + W)T_D = D_D$ (a)

Upstream: $(B - W)T_U = D_U$ (b)

(a') $12B + 12W = 168$

(b') $9B - 9W = 54$

3(a') $36B + 36W = 504$

4(b') $\dfrac{36B - 36W = 216}{72B \qquad = 720}$

$$B = 10 \text{ mph}$$

(a') $12(10) + 12W = 168$

$$12W = 48$$

$$W = 4 \text{ mph}$$

5. Selling price = purchase price + markup

$$2400 = 400 + M_U$$

$$\$2000 = M_U$$

% of cost $= \dfrac{2000}{400} \times 100\% = \mathbf{500\%}$

% of $S_P = \dfrac{2000}{2400} \times 100\% = \mathbf{83.33\%}$

6. $0.00000512 \times \dfrac{10^8}{10^8} = \dfrac{\mathbf{512}}{\mathbf{100,000,000}}$

7. $N = 0.01432|32|32 \ldots$

$100N = 1.432\ 32\ 32\ 32 \ldots$

$\dfrac{N = 0.014\ 32\ 32\ 32 \ldots}{99N = 1.418}$

$$N = \dfrac{\mathbf{1418}}{\mathbf{99,000}}$$

8. $A_{\text{Triangle}} = \dfrac{1}{2}BH$

$H = \sqrt{(4\sqrt{3})^2 - (2\sqrt{3})^2}$

$H = \sqrt{48 - 12} = \sqrt{36} = 6$ cm

$A_{\text{Triangle}} = \dfrac{1}{2}(4\sqrt{3}\text{ cm})(6\text{ cm}) = \mathbf{12\sqrt{3}\ cm^2}$

9. (a) Since this is a 45°-45°-90° triangle,

$$1 \times \overrightarrow{SF} = 3$$

$$\overrightarrow{SF} = 3$$

$$m = \sqrt{2}(3) = \mathbf{3\sqrt{2}}$$

$$n = 1(3) = \mathbf{3}$$

(b) Since this is a 30°-60°-90° triangle,

$$1 \times \overrightarrow{SF} = 4$$

$$\overrightarrow{SF} = 4$$

$$x = \sqrt{3}(4) = \mathbf{4\sqrt{3}}$$

$$y = 2(4) = \mathbf{8}$$

10.
$$
\begin{array}{r}
m^2 + mp + p^2 \\
m - p \overline{) m^3 \qquad\qquad - p^3} \\
\underline{m^3 - m^2p} \\
m^2p \\
\underline{m^2p - mp^2} \\
mp^2 - p^3 \\
\underline{mp^2 - p^3} \\
0
\end{array}
$$

11. Sets **(a)** and **(c)** are functions. Set **(b)** is not a function, because −2 has two images.

12. $y = -x^2 + 4x - 2$

$-y = (x^2 - 4x + 4) + 2 - 4$

$-y = (x - 2)^2 - 2$

$y = -(x - 2)^2 + 2$

From this we see:

(a) Opens downward

(b) Axis of symmetry is $x = 2$

(c) y-coordinate of vertex is 2

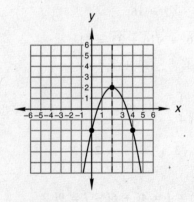

13. $-|x| + 2 > -2; \; D = \{$Integers$\}$

$$-|x| > -4$$
$$|x| < 4$$

$x < 4$ and $x > -4$

```
——●——●——●——●——●——●——●——●——
  -4 -3 -2 -1  0  1  2  3  4
```

14. $N = \dfrac{1}{8} + \dfrac{3}{7}\left(3\dfrac{1}{4} - \dfrac{1}{8}\right)$

$$= \dfrac{1}{8} + \dfrac{3}{7}\left(\dfrac{26}{8} - \dfrac{1}{8}\right)$$

$$= \dfrac{1}{8} + \dfrac{3}{7}\left(\dfrac{25}{8}\right)$$

$$= \dfrac{7}{56} + \dfrac{75}{56} = \mathbf{\dfrac{41}{28}}$$

15. (a) $\dfrac{1}{3}x - \dfrac{2}{5}y = -5$

(b) $0.005x - 0.04y = -0.755$

(a') $5x - 6y = -75$

(b') $5x - 40y = -755$

$$\begin{array}{rl} \text{(a')} & 5x - 6y = -75 \\ -1\text{(b')} & -5x + 40y = 755 \\ \hline & 34y = 680 \\ & y = 20 \end{array}$$

(a') $5x - 6(20) = -75$

$$5x = 45$$
$$x = 9$$

(9, 20)

16. (a) $4x - y = 2$

(b) $xy = 3$

$$y = \dfrac{3}{x}$$

Substitute (b) into (a) and get:

(a') $\quad 4x - \left(\dfrac{3}{x}\right) = 2$

$$4x^2 - 3 = 2x$$
$$4x^2 - 2x - 3 = 0$$

Solve this equation by using the quadratic formula.

$$x = \dfrac{-(-2) \pm \sqrt{(-2)^2 - 4(4)(-3)}}{2(4)}$$

$$x = \dfrac{1}{4} \pm \dfrac{\sqrt{13}}{4}$$

Substitute these values of x into (a) and solve for y.

(a) $y = 4\left(\dfrac{1}{4} + \dfrac{\sqrt{13}}{4}\right) - 2 = -1 + \sqrt{13}$

(a) $y = 4\left(\dfrac{1}{4} - \dfrac{\sqrt{13}}{4}\right) - 2 = -1 - \sqrt{13}$

$$\left(\mathbf{\dfrac{1}{4} + \dfrac{\sqrt{13}}{4}, \; -1 + \sqrt{13}}\right) \text{ and}$$

$$\left(\mathbf{\dfrac{1}{4} - \dfrac{\sqrt{13}}{4}, \; -1 - \sqrt{13}}\right)$$

17. (a) $x - y - 2z = -14$

(b) $2x + y - z = 2$

(c) $-x + y - z = -4$

$$\begin{array}{rl} \text{(a)} & x - y - 2z = -14 \\ \text{(b)} & 2x + y - z = 2 \\ \hline & 3x \qquad - 3z = -12 \end{array}$$

(d) $\qquad x - z = -4$

$$\begin{array}{rl} \text{(a)} & x - y - 2z = -14 \\ \text{(c)} & -x + y - z = -4 \\ \hline & -3z = -18 \\ & z = 6 \end{array}$$

(d) $x - (6) = -4$

$$x = 2$$

(a) $(2) - y - 2(6) = -14$

$$y = 4$$

(2, 4, 6)

18. (a) $x - 3y \le -6$

$$y \ge \dfrac{1}{3}x + 2$$

(b) $x \ge -2$

The next step is to graph each of these lines.

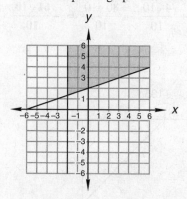

The region we wish to find is on or above the solid slanted line and on or to the right of the solid vertical line. This region is shaded in the figure.

19. $0 < x + 2 \not> 4; \ D = \{\text{Reals}\}$

$-2 < x \le 2$

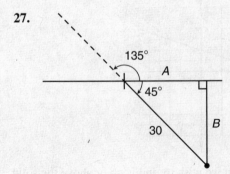

20. $\dfrac{(x^{-2})^{a+2} \ y^{-3a}}{y^{-a/2}} = \dfrac{x^{-2a-4} y^{-3a}}{y^{-a/2}}$

$\quad = x^{-2a-4} y^{-5a/2}$

21. $\dfrac{k}{k^2 x \ - \ \dfrac{1}{x \ - \ \dfrac{1}{k^2}}} = \dfrac{k}{k^2 x \ - \ \dfrac{k^2}{k^2 x - 1}}$

$\quad = \dfrac{k(k^2 x - 1)}{k^4 x^2 - k^2 x - k^2} = \dfrac{k^2 x - 1}{k^3 x^2 - kx - k}$

22. $\sqrt[5]{4\sqrt[3]{2}} = (2^2)^{1/5} 2^{1/15} = 2^{2/5} 2^{1/15} = 2^{7/15}$

23. $\dfrac{6i - i^2}{-i^3 + 3} = \dfrac{6i + 1}{i + 3} \cdot \dfrac{i - 3}{i - 3}$

$\quad = \dfrac{-6 - 18i + i - 3}{-1 - 9} = \dfrac{9}{10} + \dfrac{17}{10}i$

24. $\dfrac{2 + 3\sqrt{2}}{4 - \sqrt{18}} = \dfrac{2 + 3\sqrt{2}}{4 - 3\sqrt{2}} \cdot \dfrac{4 + 3\sqrt{2}}{4 + 3\sqrt{2}}$

$\quad = \dfrac{8 + 6\sqrt{2} + 12\sqrt{2} + 18}{16 - 18} = -13 - 9\sqrt{2}$

25. $-i^5 + \sqrt{-4}\sqrt{4} - 3\sqrt{-9} + 2i^4$

$\quad = -i + 4i - 9i + 2 = \mathbf{2 - 6i}$

26. $3\sqrt{\dfrac{5}{2}} + 2\sqrt{\dfrac{2}{5}} - 4\sqrt{40}$

$\quad = \dfrac{3\sqrt{5}}{\sqrt{2}} + \dfrac{2\sqrt{2}}{\sqrt{5}} - 4\sqrt{40}$

$\quad = \dfrac{3\sqrt{10}}{2} + \dfrac{2\sqrt{10}}{5} - 8\sqrt{10}$

$\quad = \dfrac{15\sqrt{10}}{10} + \dfrac{4\sqrt{10}}{10} - \dfrac{80\sqrt{10}}{10} = -\dfrac{61\sqrt{10}}{10}$

27.

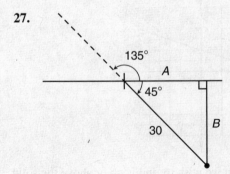

$A = 30 \cos 45° \approx 21.21$

$B = 30 \sin 45° \approx 21.21$

$C = 20 \cos 20° \approx 18.79$

$D = 20 \sin 20° \approx 6.84$

$\begin{array}{r} 21.21R - 21.21U \\ 18.79R - 6.84U \\ \hline \mathbf{40.00R - 28.05U} \end{array}$

$\tan \theta = -\dfrac{28.05}{40.00}$

$\quad \theta \approx -35.04°$

$F = \sqrt{(40)^2 + (-28.05)^2} \approx 48.85$

$\mathbf{48.85 /\!\!-\!35.04°}$

28. $\qquad \dfrac{m}{x} + \dfrac{m}{y} = \dfrac{1}{c} + \dfrac{a}{b}$

$bcmy + bcmx = bxy + acxy$

$bcmy + bcmx - axcy = bxy$

$\qquad\qquad c = \dfrac{bxy}{bmy + bmx - axy}$

29. $\qquad -4x^2 = x - 5$

$\qquad 4x^2 + x - 5 = 0$

$\qquad x^2 + \dfrac{1}{4}x - \dfrac{5}{4} = 0$

$\left(x^2 + \dfrac{1}{4}x + \dfrac{1}{64}\right) = \dfrac{5}{4} + \dfrac{1}{64}$

$\qquad \left(x + \dfrac{1}{8}\right)^2 = \dfrac{81}{64}$

$\qquad\quad x + \dfrac{1}{8} = \pm\dfrac{9}{8}$

$\qquad\qquad x = -\dfrac{1}{8} \pm \dfrac{9}{8}$

$\qquad\qquad x = \mathbf{1, -\dfrac{5}{4}}$

30. $\dfrac{4000 \text{ mL}}{\text{s}} \times \dfrac{1 \text{ cm}^3}{1 \text{ mL}} \times \dfrac{1 \text{ in.}}{2.54 \text{ cm}} \times \dfrac{1 \text{ in.}}{2.54 \text{ cm}}$

$\times \dfrac{1 \text{ in.}}{2.54 \text{ cm}} \times \dfrac{1 \text{ ft}}{12 \text{ in.}} \times \dfrac{1 \text{ ft}}{12 \text{ in.}} \times \dfrac{1 \text{ ft}}{12 \text{ in.}} \times \dfrac{60 \text{ s}}{1 \text{ min}}$

$= \dfrac{4000(60)}{(2.54)(2.54)(2.54)(12)(12)(12)} \dfrac{\text{ft}^3}{\text{min}}$

PRACTICE SET 105

a. $-5x - 12 + 2x^2 = 0$

$2x^2 - 5x - 12 = 0$

$2 \cdot -12 = -24$

FACTORS OF -24		SUM OF FACTORS
$(-24)(1)$	$\longrightarrow$	-23
$(-12)(2)$	$\longrightarrow$	-10
$(-8)(3)$	$\longrightarrow$	-5

$2x^2 - 8x + 3x - 12 = 0$

$2x(x - 4) + 3(x - 4) = 0$

$(2x + 3)(x - 4) = 0$

$2x + 3 = 0 \qquad x - 4 = 0$

$x = -\dfrac{3}{2} \qquad x = 4$

b. $\qquad -7x - 6 = -3x^2$

$3x^2 - 7x - 6 = 0$

$3 \cdot -6 = -18$

FACTORS OF -18		SUM OF FACTORS
$(-18)(1)$	$\longrightarrow$	-17
$(-9)(2)$	$\longrightarrow$	-7

$3x^2 - 9x + 2x - 6 = 0$

$3x(x - 3) + 2(x - 3) = 0$

$(3x + 2)(x - 3) = 0$

$3x + 2 = 0 \qquad x - 3 = 0$

$x = -\dfrac{2}{3} \qquad x = 3$

PROBLEM SET 105

1. Carbon: $\qquad 3 \times 12 = 36$

Hydrogen: $\qquad 3 \times 1 = 3$

Chlorine: $\qquad 5 \times 35 = 175$

Total: $\qquad 36 + 3 + 175 = 214$

$\dfrac{175}{214} = \dfrac{1050}{C_3H_3Cl_5}$

$C_3H_3Cl_5 = \textbf{1284 grams}$

2.

$R_T T_T + R_W T_W = 64; \ R_T = 10;$

$R_W = 6; \ T_T + T_W = 8$

$10(8 - T_W) + 6T_W = 64$

$\qquad\qquad 4T_W = 16$

$\qquad\qquad T_W = 4$

$T_T = 8 - (4) = 4$

$D_W = R_W T_W = 6(4) = \textbf{24 miles}$

$D_T = R_T T_T = 10(4) = \textbf{40 miles}$

3. $0.2(140) + (D_N) = 0.44(140 + D_N)$

$\qquad 28 + D_N = 61.6 + 0.44D_N$

$\qquad\quad 0.56D_N = 33.6$

$\qquad\qquad D_N = \textbf{60 mL}$

4. $\dfrac{P_1}{P_2} = \dfrac{M_1(F_1)^2}{M_2(F_2)^2}$

$\dfrac{750}{P_2} = \dfrac{5(5)^2}{10(10)^2}$

$P_2 = \textbf{6000 potatoes}$

5. Selling price = purchase price + markup

$\qquad S_P = 2400 + 800$

$\qquad S_P = \$3200$

% of $S_P = \dfrac{800}{3200} \times 100\% = \textbf{25\%}$

% of cost $= \dfrac{800}{2400} \times 100\% = \textbf{33.33\%}$

6. $(g + h)(x) = g(x) + h(x)$

$\qquad\qquad = x^2 + 1 + x - 5$

$\qquad\qquad = x^2 + x - 4$

$(g + h)(2) = (2)^2 + (2) - 4 = \textbf{2}$

7. $hg(x) = h(x) \cdot g(x)$

$\qquad = (x - 5)(x^2 + 1)$

$\qquad = x^3 + x - 5x^2 - 5$

$\qquad = \boldsymbol{x^3 - 5x^2 + x - 5}; \ D = \textbf{\{Integers\}}$

8. $N = 0.0001234|234|234 \ldots$

$1000N = 0.1234 \ 234 \ 234 \ldots$

$\underline{\quad N = 0.0001 \ 234 \ 234 \ldots}$

$999N = 0.1233$

$N = \dfrac{\textbf{1233}}{\textbf{9,990,000}}$

9. $N = 0.01651|651|651 \ldots$

$$1000N = 16.51651\ 651\ 651\ \ldots$$
$$\underline{N = \ \ 0.01651\ 651\ 651\ \ldots}$$
$$999N = 16.5$$
$$N = \frac{\mathbf{165}}{\mathbf{9990}}$$

10.

$$\begin{array}{r} m^2 - mp + p^2 \\ m+p\overline{)m^3 \qquad\qquad + p^3} \\ \underline{m^3 + m^2p} \\ -m^2p \\ \underline{-m^2p - mp^2} \\ mp^2 + p^3 \\ \underline{mp^2 + p^3} \\ 0 \end{array}$$

11.

$$\begin{array}{r} x^2 - xy + y^2 \\ x+y\overline{)x^3 \qquad\qquad + y^3} \\ \underline{x^3 + x^2y} \\ -x^2y \\ \underline{-x^2y - xy^2} \\ xy^2 + y^3 \\ \underline{xy^2 + y^3} \\ 0 \end{array}$$

12. $y = x^2 + 6x + 8$

$y = (x^2 + 6x + 9) + 8 - 9$

$y = (x + 3)^2 - 1$

From this we see:

(a) Opens upward

(b) Axis of symmetry is $x = -3$

(c) y-coordinate of vertex is -1

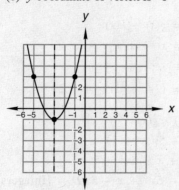

13. $-|x| + 2 > 1; \ D = \{\text{Integers}\}$

$\qquad -|x| > -1$

$\qquad\quad |x| < 1$

$x < 1$ and $x > -1$

14. $N = 2\frac{1}{4} + \frac{3}{5}\left(4\frac{1}{2} - 2\frac{1}{4}\right)$

$\quad = \frac{9}{4} + \frac{3}{5}\left(\frac{18}{4} - \frac{9}{4}\right)$

$\quad = \frac{9}{4} + \frac{3}{5}\left(\frac{9}{4}\right) = \frac{45}{20} + \frac{27}{20} = \frac{\mathbf{18}}{\mathbf{5}}$

15. (a) $\frac{2}{7}x - \frac{1}{4}y = -6$

(b) $0.07x + 0.14y = 6.58$

(a$'$) $8x - 7y = -168$

(b$'$) $7x + 14y = 658$

$\begin{array}{r} 2(a')\ \ 16x - 14y = -336 \\ (b')\ \ \underline{7x + 14y = \ \ 658} \\ 23x \qquad\quad = \ \ 322 \\ x = 14 \end{array}$

(a$'$) $8(14) - 7y = -168$

$\qquad\qquad -7y = -280$

$\qquad\qquad\quad y = 40$

(14, 40)

16. (a) $5x - y = 2$

(b) $xy = 6$

$\qquad y = \frac{6}{x}$

Substitute (b) into (a) and get:

(a$'$) $\qquad 5x - \left(\frac{6}{x}\right) = 2$

$\qquad\qquad 5x^2 - 6 = 2x$

$\qquad\qquad 5x^2 - 2x - 6 = 0$

Solve this equation by using the quadratic formula.

$x = \dfrac{-(-2) \pm \sqrt{(-2)^2 - 4(5)(-6)}}{2(5)}$

$x = \dfrac{1}{5} \pm \dfrac{\sqrt{31}}{5}$

Substitute these values of x into (a) and solve for y.

(a) $y = 5\left(\dfrac{1}{5} + \dfrac{\sqrt{31}}{5}\right) - 2 = -1 + \sqrt{31}$

(a) $y = 5\left(\dfrac{1}{5} - \dfrac{\sqrt{31}}{5}\right) - 2 = -1 - \sqrt{31}$

$\left(\dfrac{1}{5} + \dfrac{\sqrt{31}}{5}, -1 + \sqrt{31}\right)$ and

$\left(\dfrac{1}{5} - \dfrac{\sqrt{31}}{5}, -1 - \sqrt{31}\right)$

17. (a) $x^2 + y^2 = 8$

(b) $x - y = 2$

$$y = x - 2$$

Substitute (b) into (a) and get:

(a') $\quad x^2 + (x - 2)^2 = 8$

$$x^2 + x^2 - 4x + 4 = 8$$

$$x^2 - 2x - 2 = 0$$

Solve this equation by using the quadratic formula.

$$x = \frac{-(-2) \pm \sqrt{(-2)^2 - 4(1)(-2)}}{2(1)} = 1 \pm \sqrt{3}$$

Substitute these values of x into (b) and solve for y.

(b) $y = (1 + \sqrt{3}) - 2 = -1 + \sqrt{3}$

(b) $y = (1 - \sqrt{3}) - 2 = -1 - \sqrt{3}$

$(1 + \sqrt{3}, -1 + \sqrt{3})$ and $(1 - \sqrt{3}, -1 - \sqrt{3})$

18. (a) $2x - y - 2z = 2$

(b) $x + y - z = 7$

(c) $2x - y - z = 0$

(a) $2x - y - 2z = 2$

(b) $\underline{x + y - z = 7}$

$3x - 3z = 9$

(d) $\quad\quad\quad x - z = 3$

(a) $\quad 2x - y - 2z = 2$

-1(c) $\underline{-2x + y + z = 0}$

$ -z = 2$

$ z = -2$

(d) $x - (-2) = 3$

$\quad\quad x = 1$

(b) $(1) + y - (-2) = 7$

$\quad\quad\quad y = 4$

$(1, 4, -2)$

19. (a) $3x + 5y = 4$

(b) $10x - 15y = -50$

$$y = \frac{2}{3}x + \frac{10}{3}$$

Substitute (b) into (a) and get:

(a') $3x + 5\left(\frac{2}{3}x + \frac{10}{3}\right) = 4$

$$3x + \frac{10}{3}x + \frac{50}{3} = 4$$

$$\frac{19}{3}x = -\frac{38}{3}$$

$$x = -\frac{38}{3}\left(\frac{3}{19}\right) = -2$$

(b) $y = \frac{2}{3}(-2) + \frac{10}{3}$

$$y = -\frac{4}{3} + \frac{10}{3} = 2$$

(–2, 2)

20. (a) $x - 3y \geq 6$

$$y \leq \frac{1}{3}x - 2$$

(b) $x \geq -3$

The next step is to graph each of these lines.

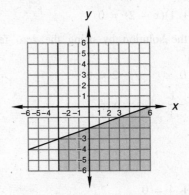

The region we wish to find is on or below the solid slanted line and on or to the right of the solid vertical line. This region is shaded in the figure.

21. $3x^3 - 5x^2 - 2x = 0$

$$x(3x^2 - 5x - 2) = 0$$

Now we multiply the coefficient of x^2 by the constant term.

$$3(-2) = -6$$

Find the factors of -6 whose sum is -5.

$$1(-6) = -6$$

$$1 + (-6) = -5$$

Replace $-5x$ with $-6x + x$ and get:

$$x(3x^2 - 6x + x - 2) = 0$$

$$x(3x(x - 2) + 1(x - 2)) = 0$$

$$x(3x + 1)(x - 2) = 0$$

Complete the solution by using the zero factor theorem.

$x = 0 \quad\quad 3x + 1 = 0 \quad\quad x - 2 = 0$

$\quad\quad\quad\quad\quad\quad x = -\frac{1}{3} \quad\quad\quad x = 2$

$0, -\dfrac{1}{3}, 2$

22. $6x^2 - 10x - 4 = 0$

$2(3x^2 - 5x - 2) = 0$

Now we multiply the coefficient of x^2 by the constant term.

$3(-2) = -6$

Find the factors of -6 whose sum is -5.

$1(-6) = -6$

$1 + (-6) = -5$

Replace $-5x$ with $-6x + x$ and get:

$3x^2 - 6x + x - 2 = 0$

$3x(x - 2) + 1(x - 2) = 0$

$(3x + 1)(x - 2) = 0$

Complete the solution by using the zero factor theorem.

$3x + 1 = 0 \qquad x - 2 = 0$

$x = -\dfrac{1}{3} \qquad x = 2$

$-\dfrac{1}{3}, 2$

23. $3x^2 + 8x + 4 = 0$

Now we multiply the coefficient of x^2 by the constant term.

$3(4) = 12$

Find the factors of 12 whose sum is 8.

$6(2) = 12$

$6 + 2 = 8$

Replace $8x$ with $6x + 2x$ and get:

$3x^2 + 6x + 2x + 4 = 0$

$3x(x + 2) + 2(x + 2) = 0$

$(3x + 2)(x + 2) = 0$

Complete the solution by using the zero factor theorem.

$3x + 2 = 0 \qquad x + 2 = 0$

$x = -\dfrac{2}{3} \qquad x = -2$

$-\dfrac{2}{3}, -2$

24. $9x^3 + 24x^2 + 12x = 0$

$3x(3x^2 + 8x + 4) = 0$

Now we multiply the coefficient of x^2 by the constant term.

$3(4) = 12$

Find the factors of 12 whose sum is 8.

$6(2) = 12$

$6 + 2 = 8$

Replace $8x$ with $6x + 2x$ and get:

$3x(3x^2 + 6x + 2x + 4) = 0$

$3x(3x(x + 2) + 2(x + 2)) = 0$

$3x(3x + 2)(x + 2) = 0$

Complete the solution by using the zero factor theorem.

$3x = 0 \qquad 3x + 2 = 0 \qquad x + 2 = 0$

$x = 0 \qquad x = -\dfrac{2}{3} \qquad x = -2$

$0, -\dfrac{2}{3}, -2$

25. $2p^2 - 3p - 5 = 0$

Now we multiply the coefficient of p^2 by the constant term.

$2(-5) = -10$

Find the factors of -10 whose sum is -3.

$2(-5) = -10$

$2 + (-5) = -3$

Replace $-3p$ with $2p - 5p$ and get:

$2p^2 + 2p - 5p - 5 = 0$

$2p(p + 1) - 5(p + 1) = 0$

$(2p - 5)(p + 1) = 0$

Complete the solution by using the zero factor theorem.

$2p - 5 = 0 \qquad p + 1 = 0$

$p = \dfrac{5}{2} \qquad p = -1$

$\dfrac{5}{2}, -1$

26. $4x^2 + 18x + 8 = 0$

$2(2x^2 + 9x + 4) = 0$

Now we multiply the coefficient of x^2 by the constant term.

$2(4) = 8$

Find the factors of 8 whose sum is 9.

$8(1) = 8$

$8 + 1 = 9$

Replace $9x$ with $8x + x$ and get:

$$2x^2 + 8x + x + 4 = 0$$

$$2x(x + 4) + 1(x + 4) = 0$$

$$(2x + 1)(x + 4) = 0$$

Complete the solution by using the zero factor theorem.

$$2x + 1 = 0 \qquad x + 4 = 0$$

$$x = -\frac{1}{2} \qquad x = -4$$

$$\mathbf{-\frac{1}{2}, -4}$$

27. $\dfrac{x^a(x^{a/2+4})^2 \, y^b}{y^{b/3} x^{a/6}} = \dfrac{x^a x^{a+8} y^b}{y^{b/3} x^{a/6}}$

   $= \dfrac{x^{2a+8} y^b}{y^{b/3} x^{a/6}} = x^{11a/6} + 8 y^{2b/3}$

28. $\dfrac{2 - 3i^3}{i + 2i^2 + 3i^3} = \dfrac{2 + 3i}{-2i - 2} \cdot \dfrac{-2i + 2}{-2i + 2}$

   $= \dfrac{-4i + 4 + 6 + 6i}{-4 - 4} = -\dfrac{5}{4} - \dfrac{1}{4}i$

29. $\dfrac{4 + 2\sqrt{5}}{5 - 3\sqrt{5}} \cdot \dfrac{5 + 3\sqrt{5}}{5 + 3\sqrt{5}}$

   $= \dfrac{20 + 12\sqrt{5} + 10\sqrt{5} + 30}{25 - 45}$

   $= \dfrac{-25 - 11\sqrt{5}}{10}$

30. Area of circles $= 2(\pi(1)^2) + \pi(2)^2$

   $= 2\pi + 4\pi = 6\pi$ units^2

   Area of circles = Area of triangle

   $$6\pi = \frac{3(H)}{2}$$

   $$\mathbf{4\pi \text{ units}} = H$$

PRACTICE SET 106

$\begin{cases} 3x + 2y = 6 & \text{(a)} \\ 2x - z = 9 & \text{(b)} \\ 3y - z = 10 & \text{(c)} \end{cases}$

$\begin{array}{ll} \text{(b)} & 2x \qquad - z = 9 \\ -\text{(c)} & \underline{\qquad - 3y + z = -10} \\ \text{(d)} & 2x - 3y \qquad = -1 \end{array}$

2(a) $\quad 6x + 4y = 12$

-3(d) $\dfrac{-6x + 9y = 3}{13y = 15}$

$$y = \frac{15}{13}$$

(a) $3x + 2\left(\dfrac{15}{13}\right) = 6$

$$3x = 6 - \frac{30}{13}$$

$$3x = \frac{48}{13}$$

$$x = \frac{16}{13}$$

(b) $2\left(\dfrac{16}{13}\right) - z = 9$

$$\frac{32}{13} - 9 = z$$

$$-\frac{85}{13} = z$$

PROBLEM SET 106

1. Selling price = purchase price + markup

   $$715 = P_P + 0.3P_P$$

   $$715 = 1.3\,P_P$$

   $$\mathbf{\$550} = P_P$$

2.
   $$\overset{D_P}{\underset{1200}{\longmapsto}}$$

   $$\overset{D_C}{\underset{250}{\longmapsto}}$$

   $R_P T_P = 1200; \quad R_C T_C = 250;$

   $R_P = 6R_C; \quad T_P = T_C - 1$

   $6R_C(T_C - 1) = 1200$

   $6(250) - 6R_C = 1200$

   $6R_C = 300$

   $R_C = \mathbf{50 \text{ mph}}; \quad R_P = \mathbf{300 \text{ mph}};$

   $T_C = \mathbf{5 \text{ hr}}; \quad T_P = \mathbf{4 \text{ hr}}$

3. Downstream: $(B + W)T_D = D_D$ (a)

   Upstream: $(B - W)T_U = D_U$ (b)

   (a') $(B + 2)T_D = 56$

   (b') $(B - 2)2T_D = 80$

   2(a') $2BT_D + 4T_D = 112$

   (b') $\dfrac{2BT_D - 4T_D = 80}{4BT_D = 192}$

   (c) $BT_D = 48$

   (a') $(48) + 2T_D = 56$

   $T_D = 4$

   (c) $B(4) = 48$

   $B = \textbf{12 mph}$

4. $P_1V_1 = P_2V_2$

   $700(500) = P_2(1000)$

   $P_2 = \textbf{350 torr}$

5. (a) $3x - 3y = 9$

   (b) $4x + z = 5$

   (c) $4y + 2z = -10$

   −2(b) $-8x - 2z = -10$

   (c) $\dfrac{ 4y + 2z = -10}{-8x + 4y = -20}$

   (d) $ -2x + y = -5$

   3(d) $-6x + 3y = -15$

   (a) $\dfrac{ 3x - 3y = 9}{-3x = -6}$

   $ x = 2$

   (d) $-2(2) + y = -5$

   $ y = -1$

   (c) $4(-1) + 2z = -10$

   $ z = -3$

   (2, −1, −3)

6. (a) $2x - 2y - z = 9$

   (b) $3x + 3y - z = 6$

   (c) $x + y + z = -2$

   (a) $2x - 2y - z = 9$

   (c) $\dfrac{x + y + z = -2}{3x - y = 7}$

   (d)

   (b) $3x + 3y - z = 6$

   (c) $\dfrac{x + y + z = -2}{4x + 4y = 4}$

   (e) $ x + y = 1$

   (d) $3x - y = 7$

   (e) $\dfrac{x + y = 1}{4x = 8}$

   $ x = 2$

   (e) $(2) + y = 1$

   $ y = -1$

   (c) $(2) + (-1) + z = -2$

   $ z = -3$

   (2, −1, −3)

7. $A_{\text{Triangle}} = \dfrac{bH}{2}$

   $H = \sqrt{(7\pi)^2 - (4\pi)^2} = \sqrt{49\pi^2 - 16\pi^2}$

   $ = \sqrt{33}\,\pi$

   $A_{\text{Triangle}} = \dfrac{8\pi(\sqrt{33}\,\pi)}{2} = \mathbf{4\sqrt{33}\,\pi^2 \ cm^2}$

8. (a) Since this is a 45°-45°-90° triangle,

   $\sqrt{2} \times \overrightarrow{SF} = 3$

   $\overrightarrow{SF} = \dfrac{3\sqrt{2}}{2}$

   $m = 1\left(\dfrac{3\sqrt{2}}{2}\right) = \dfrac{3\sqrt{2}}{2}$

   $n = 1\left(\dfrac{3\sqrt{2}}{2}\right) = \dfrac{3\sqrt{2}}{2}$

   (b) Since this is a 30°-60°-90° triangle,

   $1 \times \overrightarrow{SF} = 7$

   $\overrightarrow{SF} = 7$

   $p = \sqrt{3}(7) = \mathbf{7\sqrt{3}}$

   $q = 2(7) = \textbf{14}$

9. $1000N = 0.7013\ 013\ 013 \ldots$

   $\dfrac{N = 0.0007\ 013\ 013 \ldots}{999N = 0.7006}$

   $N = \dfrac{\textbf{7006}}{\textbf{9,990,000}}$

10. $100N = 410.26\ 26\ 26 \ldots$

   $\dfrac{N = 4.10\ 26\ 26\ 26 \ldots}{99N = 406.16}$

   $N = \dfrac{\textbf{40,616}}{\textbf{9900}}$

11. $-y = x^2 + 2x + 3$

$-y = (x^2 + 2x + 1) + 3 - 1$

$-y = (x + 1)^2 + 2$

$y = -(x + 1)^2 - 2$

From this we see:

(a) Opens downward

(b) Axis of symmetry is $x = -1$

(c) y-coordinate of vertex is -2

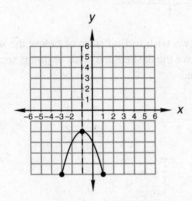

12. $-|x| - 4 \leq 0$; $D = \{$Integers$\}$

$-|x| \leq 4$

$|x| \geq -4$

All integers satisfy this inequality because any integer (even zero) has an absolute value greater than -4.

13. $N = 3\frac{1}{3} + \frac{1}{10}\left(6\frac{1}{2} - 3\frac{1}{3}\right)$

$= \frac{10}{3} + \frac{1}{10}\left(\frac{13}{2} - \frac{10}{3}\right)$

$= \frac{10}{3} + \frac{1}{10}\left(\frac{19}{6}\right)$

$= \frac{200}{60} + \frac{19}{60} = \frac{73}{20}$

14. (a) $\frac{3}{5}x - \frac{1}{4}y = 5$

(b) $0.012x + 0.07y = 2.20$

(a') $12x - 5y = 100$

(b') $12x + 70y = 2200$

$-1(a')\ -12x + 5y = -100$

$\underline{(b')\quad 12x + 70y = 2200}$

$75y = 2100$

$y = 28$

(a') $12x - 5(28) = 100$

$x = 20$

(20, 28)

15. (a) $5x - y = 3$

(b) $xy = 4$

$y = \frac{4}{x}$

Substitute (b) into (a) and get:

(a') $5x - \left(\frac{4}{x}\right) = 3$

$5x^2 - 4 = 3x$

$5x^2 - 3x - 4 = 0$

Solve this equation by using the quadratic formula.

$x = \frac{-(-3) \pm \sqrt{(-3)^2 - 4(5)(-4)}}{2(5)}$

$x = \frac{3}{10} \pm \frac{\sqrt{89}}{10}$

Substitute these values of x into (a) and solve for y.

(a) $y = 5\left(\frac{3}{10} + \frac{\sqrt{89}}{10}\right) - 3 = -\frac{3}{2} + \frac{\sqrt{89}}{2}$

(a) $y = 5\left(\frac{3}{10} - \frac{\sqrt{89}}{10}\right) - 3 = -\frac{3}{2} - \frac{\sqrt{89}}{2}$

$\left(\frac{3}{10} + \frac{\sqrt{89}}{10}, -\frac{3}{2} + \frac{\sqrt{89}}{2}\right)$ and

$\left(\frac{3}{10} - \frac{\sqrt{89}}{10}, -\frac{3}{2} - \frac{\sqrt{89}}{2}\right)$

16. (a) $x^2 + y^2 = 7$

(b) $2x - y = 2$

$$y = 2x - 2$$

Substitute (b) into (a) and get:

(a′) $\quad x^2 + (2x - 2)^2 = 7$

$$x^2 + 4x^2 - 8x + 4 = 7$$

$$5x^2 - 8x - 3 = 0$$

Solve this equation by using the quadratic formula.

$$x = \frac{-(-8) \pm \sqrt{(-8)^2 - 4(5)(-3)}}{2(5)}$$

$$x = \frac{4}{5} \pm \frac{\sqrt{31}}{5}$$

Substitute these values of x into (b) and solve for y.

(b) $y = 2\left(\dfrac{4}{5} + \dfrac{\sqrt{31}}{5}\right) - 2 = -\dfrac{2}{5} + \dfrac{2\sqrt{31}}{5}$

(b) $y = 2\left(\dfrac{4}{5} - \dfrac{\sqrt{31}}{5}\right) - 2 = -\dfrac{2}{5} - \dfrac{2\sqrt{31}}{5}$

$$\left(\mathbf{\frac{4}{5} + \frac{\sqrt{31}}{5}, -\frac{2}{5} + \frac{2\sqrt{31}}{5}}\right) \text{ and}$$

$$\left(\mathbf{\frac{4}{5} - \frac{\sqrt{31}}{5}, -\frac{2}{5} - \frac{2\sqrt{31}}{5}}\right)$$

17. (a) $5x - 3y = 27$

$$y = \frac{5}{3}x - 9$$

(b) $2x - 5y = 26$

Substitute (a) into (b) and get:

(b′) $2x - 5\left(\dfrac{5}{3}x - 9\right) = 26$

$$\frac{6}{3}x - \frac{25}{3}x + 45 = 26$$

$$\frac{19}{3}x = 19$$

$$x = 19\left(\frac{3}{19}\right) = 3$$

(a) $y = \dfrac{5}{3}(3) - 9 = -4$

(3, −4)

18. (a) $3x - 4y \geq 8$

$$y \leq \frac{3}{4}x - 2$$

(b) $y > -2$

The next step is to graph each of these lines.

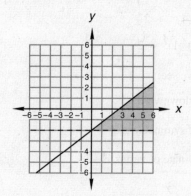

The region we wish to find is on or below the solid line and above the dashed line. This region is shaded in the figure.

19. $\dfrac{3 - 2i^2 - i}{3i^3 + 3i + 2} = \dfrac{5 - i}{2} = \mathbf{\dfrac{5}{2} - \dfrac{1}{2}i}$

20.
$$x^2 - \frac{1}{3}x = \frac{7}{3}$$

$$\left(x^2 - \frac{1}{3}x + \frac{1}{36}\right) = \frac{84}{36} + \frac{1}{36}$$

$$\left(x - \frac{1}{6}\right)^2 = \frac{85}{36}$$

$$x - \frac{1}{6} = \pm\frac{\sqrt{85}}{6}$$

$$x = \mathbf{\frac{1}{6} \pm \frac{\sqrt{85}}{6}}$$

21.

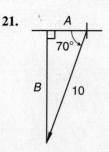

$A = 10 \cos 70° \approx 3.42$

$B = 10 \sin 70° \approx 9.40$

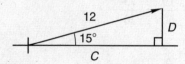

$C = 12 \cos 15° \approx 11.59$

$D = 12 \sin 15° \approx 3.11$

$$-3.42R - 9.40U$$
$$\underline{11.59R + 3.11U}$$
$$\mathbf{8.17R - 6.29U}$$

$$\tan \theta = -\frac{6.29}{8.17} \longrightarrow \theta \approx -37.59°$$

$$F = \sqrt{(8.17)^2 + (6.29)^2} \approx 10.31$$

$$\mathbf{10.31\underline{/-37.59°}}$$

22. **Yes,** the set designates a function, because no two pairs have the same first element and different second elements.

23. Since $\frac{1}{2}$ is not a member of the domain of $\theta(x)$, it is not a member of the domain of $\Psi\theta(x)$. Therefore, the answer is either $\varnothing$ or $\{\ \}$.

24.
$$\begin{array}{r} m^2 + mp + p^2 \\ m - p \overline{)\ m^3 \qquad\qquad - p^3} \\ \underline{m^3 - m^2p} \\ m^2p \\ \underline{m^2p - mp^2} \\ mp^2 - p^3 \\ \underline{mp^2 - p^3} \\ 0 \end{array}$$

25.
$$3x^2 + 7x + 2 = 0$$
$$3x^2 + 6x + x + 2 = 0$$
$$3x(x + 2) + 1(x + 2) = 0$$
$$(3x + 1)(x + 2) = 0$$
$$3x + 1 = 0 \qquad x + 2 = 0$$
$$x = -\frac{1}{3} \qquad x = -2$$

$$-\frac{1}{3}, -2$$

26.
$$3x^2 + x - 2 = 0$$
$$3x^2 + 3x - 2x - 2 = 0$$
$$3x(x + 1) - 2(x + 1) = 0$$
$$(3x - 2)(x + 1) = 0$$
$$3x - 2 = 0 \qquad x + 1 = 0$$
$$x = \frac{2}{3} \qquad x = -1$$

$$\frac{2}{3}, -1$$

27.
$$2z^2 + 13z + 15 = 0$$
$$2z^2 + 10z + 3z + 15 = 0$$
$$2z(z + 5) + 3(z + 5) = 0$$
$$(2z + 3)(z + 5) = 0$$
$$2z + 3 = 0 \qquad z + 5 = 0$$
$$z = -\frac{3}{2} \qquad z = -5$$

$$-\frac{3}{2}, -5$$

28.
$$6p^3 + 33p^2 + 45p = 0$$
$$3p(2p^2 + 11p + 15) = 0$$
$$3p(2p^2 + 6p + 5p + 15) = 0$$
$$3p(2p(p + 3) + 5(p + 3)) = 0$$
$$3p(2p + 5)(p + 3) = 0$$
$$3p = 0 \qquad 2p + 5 = 0 \qquad p + 3 = 0$$
$$p = 0 \qquad p = -\frac{5}{2} \qquad p = -3$$

$$0, -\frac{5}{2}, -3$$

29.
$$3p^2 - 13p - 10 = 0$$
$$3p^2 - 15p + 2p - 10 = 0$$
$$3p(p - 5) + 2(p - 5) = 0$$
$$(3p + 2)(p - 5) = 0$$
$$3p + 2 = 0 \qquad p - 5 = 0$$
$$p = -\frac{2}{3} \qquad p = 5$$

$$-\frac{2}{3}, 5$$

30.
$$2a^2 - 11a + 15 = 0$$
$$2a^2 - 6a - 5a + 15 = 0$$
$$2a(a - 3) - 5(a - 3) = 0$$
$$(2a - 5)(a - 3) = 0$$
$$2a - 5 = 0 \qquad a - 3 = 0$$
$$a = \frac{5}{2} \qquad a = 3$$

$$\frac{5}{2}, 3$$

PRACTICE SET 107

T = tens digit

U = units digit

$10T + U$ = original number

$10U + T$ = reversed number

$T + U = 7$

$$10U + T = 10T + U - 27$$
$$10(7 - T) + T = 10T + (7 - T) - 27$$
$$70 - 10T + T = 10T + 7 - T - 27$$
$$-10T + T - 10T + T = -70 + 7 - 27$$
$$-18T = -90$$
$$T = 5$$

$$(5) + U = 7$$
$$U = 2$$

Thus the original number was **52**.

PROBLEM SET 107

1. (a) $0.3P_N + 0.6D_N = 144$

(b) $P_N + D_N = 400$

Substitute $D_N = 400 - P_N$ into (a) and get:

(a') $0.3P_N + 0.6(400 - P_N) = 144$
$$-0.3P_N = -96$$
$$P_N = 320$$

(b) $(320) + D_N = 400$
$$D_N = 80$$

320 mL 30%, 80 mL 60%

2. Carbon: $1 \times 12 = 12$

Hydrogen: $3 \times 1 = 3$

Bromine: $1 \times 80 = 80$

Total: $12 + 3 + 80 = 95$

Bromine: $\dfrac{80}{95} \times 100\% \approx$ **84.21%**

3. T = tens digit

U = units digit

$10T + U$ = original number

$10U + T$ = reversed number

(a) $T + U = 15$
$$T = 15 - U$$

(b) $10U + T = 10T + U + 9$

Substitute (a) into (b) and get:

(b') $10U + (15 - U) = 10(15 - U) + U + 9$
$$9U + 15 = -9U + 159$$
$$18U = 144$$
$$U = 8$$

(a) $T = 15 - (8) = 7$

Original number = **78**

4. T = tens digit

U = units digit

$10T + U$ = original number

$10U + T$ = reversed number

(a) $T + U = 13$
$$T = 13 - U$$

(b) $10U + T = 10T + U - 9$

Substitute (a) into (b) and get:

(b') $10U + (13 - U) = 10(13 - U) + U - 9$
$$9U + 13 = -9U + 121$$
$$18U = 108$$
$$U = 6$$

(a) $T = 13 - (6) = 7$

Original number = **76**

5. $S_P = P_P + M_U$
$$1400 = P_P + 0.7(1400)$$
$$\$420 = P_P$$
$$M_U = 0.7(1400) = \$980$$

6. (a) $2x - y = -6$

(b) $3y + 2z = 12$

(c) $x - 3z = -11$

$$\begin{array}{rl}
\text{(a)} & 2x - y \qquad\quad = -6 \\
-2\text{(c)} & \underline{-2x \qquad + 6z = 22} \\
\text{(d)} & \quad -y + 6z = 16
\end{array}$$

$$\begin{array}{rl}
\text{(b)} & 3y + 2z = 12 \\
3\text{(d)} & \underline{-3y + 18z = 48} \\
& \quad\quad 20z = 60 \\
& \quad\quad\quad z = 3
\end{array}$$

(d) $-y + 6(3) = 16$
$$y = 2$$

(a) $2x - (2) = -6$
$$x = -2$$

$(-2, 2, 3)$

7. (a) $5x - y - z = 2$

(b) $x - 5y + z = -2$

(c) $-x + y - z = -2$

(b) $x - 5y + z = -2$

(c) $\underline{-x + y - z = -2}$

$ -4y = -4$

$ y = 1$

(a) $5x - y - z = 2$

(b) $\underline{x - 5y + z = -2}$

(d) $6x - 6y = 0$

(d) $6x - 6(1) = 0$

$ x = 1$

(c) $-(1) + (1) - z = -2$

$ z = 2$

(1, 1, 2)

8. $1000N = 1.213\ 213\ 213\ \ldots$

$\underline{N = 0.001\ 213\ 213\ \ldots}$

$\ 999N = 1.212$

$N = \dfrac{\mathbf{1212}}{\mathbf{999{,}000}}$

9.

$$
\begin{array}{r}
x^2 - xy + y^2 \\
x + y \overline{\smash{)}\,x^3 + y^3} \\
\underline{x^3 + x^2 y} \\
-x^2 y \\
\underline{-x^2 y - xy^2} \\
xy^2 + y^3 \\
\underline{xy^2 + y^3} \\
0
\end{array}
$$

10. $-y = x^2 - 2x - 1$

$-y = (x^2 - 2x + 1) - 1 - 1$

$-y = (x - 1)^2 - 2$

$y = -(x - 1)^2 + 2$

From this we see:

(a) Opens downward

(b) Axis of symmetry is $x = 1$

(c) y-coordinate of vertex is 2

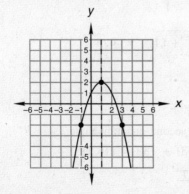

11. $x - 5 \geq -4;\ D = \{\text{Reals}\}$

$x \geq 1$

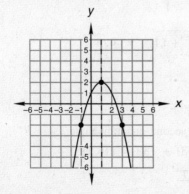

12. $N = 2 + \dfrac{3}{4}\left(6\dfrac{2}{3} - 2\right) = 2 + \dfrac{3}{4}\left(\dfrac{14}{3}\right)$

$= \dfrac{4}{2} + \dfrac{7}{2} = \dfrac{\mathbf{11}}{\mathbf{2}}$

13. (a) $2x - y = 15$

$y = 2x - 15$

(b) $-6x - 40y = -432$

Substitute (a) into (b) and get:

(b′) $-6x - 40(2x - 15) = -432$

$86x = 1032$

$x = 12$

(a) $y = 2(12) - 15 = 9$

(12, 9)

14. (a) $4y - x = 2$

(b) $xy = 5$

$x = \dfrac{5}{y}$

Substitute (b) into (a) and get:

(a′) $\quad 4y - \left(\dfrac{5}{y}\right) = 2$

$4y^2 - 5 = 2y$

$4y^2 - 2y - 5 = 0$

Solve this equation by using the quadratic formula.

$y = \dfrac{-(-2) \pm \sqrt{(-2)^2 - 4(4)(-5)}}{2(4)}$

$y = \dfrac{1}{4} \pm \dfrac{\sqrt{21}}{4}$

Substitute these values of y into (a) and solve for x.

(a) $x = 4\left(\dfrac{1}{4} + \dfrac{\sqrt{21}}{4}\right) - 2 = -1 + \sqrt{21}$

(a) $x = 4\left(\dfrac{1}{4} - \dfrac{\sqrt{21}}{4}\right) - 2 = -1 - \sqrt{21}$

$\left(\mathbf{-1 + \sqrt{21},\ \dfrac{1}{4} + \dfrac{\sqrt{21}}{4}}\right)$ and

$\left(\mathbf{-1 - \sqrt{21},\ \dfrac{1}{4} - \dfrac{\sqrt{21}}{4}}\right)$

15. (a) $x^2 + y^2 = 4$

(b) $x - 2y = 1$

$$x = 2y + 1$$

Substitute (b) into (a) and get:

(a') $\quad (2y + 1)^2 + y^2 = 4$

$$4y^2 + 4y + 1 + y^2 = 4$$

$$5y^2 + 4y - 3 = 0$$

Solve this equation by using the quadratic formula.

$$y = \frac{-(4) \pm \sqrt{(4)^2 - 4(5)(-3)}}{2(5)} = -\frac{2}{5} \pm \frac{\sqrt{19}}{5}$$

Substitute these values of y into (b) and solve for x.

(b) $x = 2\left(-\dfrac{2}{5} + \dfrac{\sqrt{19}}{5}\right) + 1 = \dfrac{1}{5} + \dfrac{2\sqrt{19}}{5}$

(b) $x = 2\left(-\dfrac{2}{5} - \dfrac{\sqrt{19}}{5}\right) + 1 = \dfrac{1}{5} - \dfrac{2\sqrt{19}}{5}$

$\left(\dfrac{1}{5} + \dfrac{2\sqrt{19}}{5}, -\dfrac{2}{5} + \dfrac{\sqrt{19}}{5}\right)$ and

$\left(\dfrac{1}{5} - \dfrac{2\sqrt{19}}{5}, -\dfrac{2}{5} - \dfrac{\sqrt{19}}{5}\right)$

16. (a) $5x - 3y = 32$

(b) $2x - 2y = 16$

$$y = x - 8$$

Substitute (b) into (a) and get:

(a') $5x - 3(x - 8) = 32$

$$2x = 8$$

$$x = 4$$

(b) $y = (4) - 8 = -4$

(4, −4)

17. (a) $3x - 8y > -x$

$$-8y > -4x$$

$$y < \frac{1}{2}x$$

(b) $x \leq y$

$$y \geq x$$

The next step is to graph each of these lines.

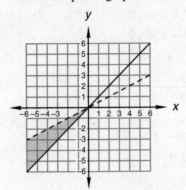

The region we wish to find is on or above the solid line and below the dashed line. This region is shaded in the figure.

18. $\dfrac{2i^3 - i + 2}{3 + 4i} = \dfrac{-3i + 2}{3 + 4i} \cdot \dfrac{3 - 4i}{3 - 4i}$

$$= \dfrac{-9i - 12 + 6 - 8i}{9 + 16} = -\dfrac{6}{25} - \dfrac{17}{25}i$$

19. $\sqrt[3]{x^5 y^2} \sqrt[4]{xy^3} = x^{5/3}y^{2/3}x^{1/4}y^{3/4} = x^{23/12}y^{17/12}$

20. $\sqrt{s - 48} = 8 - \sqrt{s}$

$$s - 48 = 64 - 16\sqrt{s} + s$$

$$16\sqrt{s} = 112$$

$$\sqrt{s} = 7$$

$$s = \mathbf{49}$$

Check: $\sqrt{49 - 48} = 8 - \sqrt{49}$

$$1 = 1$$

21.

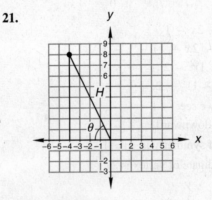

$H = \sqrt{(8)^2 + (4)^2} = 4\sqrt{5}$

$\tan \theta = \dfrac{8}{4}$

$\theta \approx 63.43°$

Since θ is a second-quadrant angle,

$\theta = -(63.43) + 180 = 116.57°$

$4\sqrt{5}\ /\underline{116.57°}$

22. Write the equation of the given line in slope-intercept form.

$$5x - 3y = 4$$

$$y = \frac{5}{3}x - \frac{4}{3}$$

Since the slopes of perpendicular lines are negative reciprocals of each other,

$$m_\perp = -\frac{3}{5}$$

$$y = -\frac{3}{5}x + b$$

$$3 = -\frac{3}{5}(-2) + b$$

$$\frac{9}{5} = b$$

$$y = -\frac{3}{5}x + \frac{9}{5}$$

23.
$$mx = \frac{1}{mr} + \frac{1}{mp}$$

$$m^2rpx = p + r$$

$$m^2rpx - r = p$$

$$r = \frac{p}{m^2px - 1}$$

24.
$$\frac{800 \text{ liters}}{\text{min}} \times \frac{1000 \text{ mL}}{1 \text{ liter}} \times \frac{1 \text{ cm}^3}{1 \text{ mL}}$$

$$\times \frac{1 \text{ in.}}{2.54 \text{ cm}} \times \frac{1 \text{ in.}}{2.54 \text{ cm}} \times \frac{1 \text{ in.}}{2.54 \text{ cm}}$$

$$\times \frac{1 \text{ ft}}{12 \text{ in.}} \times \frac{1 \text{ ft}}{12 \text{ in.}} \times \frac{1 \text{ ft}}{12 \text{ in.}} \times \frac{1 \text{ min}}{60 \text{ s}}$$

$$= \frac{800(1000)}{(2.54)(2.54)(2.54)(12)(12)(12)(60)} \frac{\text{ft}^3}{\text{s}}$$

25. Area of rectangle = Area of right triangle

$$10(5) = \frac{10(H)}{2}$$

$$10 \text{ m} = H$$

$$FG = \sqrt{(10)^2 + (10)^2} = \mathbf{10\sqrt{2} \text{ m}}$$

26. Area of circle = Area of square

$$\pi(2\sqrt{\pi})^2 = s^2$$

$$4\pi^2 = s^2$$

$$\mathbf{2\pi \text{ cm}} = s$$

27.
$$4x^3 + 2x^2 - 30x = 0$$

$$2x(2x^2 + x - 15) = 0$$

$$2x(2x^2 + 6x - 5x - 15) = 0$$

$$2x(2x(x + 3) - 5(x + 3)) = 0$$

$$2x(2x - 5)(x + 3) = 0$$

$$2x = 0 \qquad 2x - 5 = 0 \qquad x + 3 = 0$$

$$x = 0 \qquad x = \frac{5}{2} \qquad x = -3$$

$$\mathbf{0, \frac{5}{2}, -3}$$

28.
$$8x^2 + 12x + 4 = 0$$

$$4(2x^2 + 3x + 1) = 0$$

$$2x^2 + 2x + x + 1 = 0$$

$$2x(x + 1) + 1(x + 1) = 0$$

$$(2x + 1)(x + 1) = 0$$

$$2x + 1 = 0 \qquad x + 1 = 0$$

$$x = -\frac{1}{2} \qquad x = -1$$

$$\mathbf{-\frac{1}{2}, -1}$$

29.
$$1000N = 74{,}213.213 \; 213 \; 213 \ldots$$
$$\underline{N = \qquad 74.213 \; 213 \; 213 \ldots}$$
$$999N = 74{,}139$$

$$N = \frac{\mathbf{74{,}139}}{\mathbf{999}}$$

30.
$$(h + g)(x) = (x + 2) + (x^3 + 2)$$

$$(h + g)(x) = x^3 + x + 4$$

$$(h + g)(-3) = (-3)^3 + (-3) + 4$$

$$(h + g)(-3) = \mathbf{-26}$$

Practice Set 108

$$64p^6a^9 - x^3y^{12} = (4p^2a^3)^3 - (xy^4)^3$$

This expression is a difference of 2 cubes and can be factored as

$$\mathbf{(4p^2a^3 - xy^4)(16p^4a^6 + 4p^2a^3xy^4 + x^2y^8)}$$

PROBLEM SET 108

1.
$$S_P = P_P + M_U$$
$$6400 = P_P + 0.4(6400)$$
$$\$3840 = P_P$$

2. T = tens digit
U = units digit
$10T + U$ = original number
$10U + T$ = reversed number

(a) $T + U = 6$
$$T = 6 - U$$

(b) $10U + T = 10T + U - 18$

Substitute (a) into (b) and get:

(b') $10U + (6 - U) = 10(6 - U) + U - 18$
$$9U + 6 = -9U + 42$$
$$18U = 36$$
$$U = 2$$

(a) $T = 6 - (2) = 4$

Original number = **42**

3. T = tens digit
U = units digit
$10T + U$ = original number
$10U + T$ = reversed number

(a) $T + U = 15$
$$T = 15 - U$$

(b) $10U + T = 10T + U - 27$

Substitute (a) into (b) and get:

(b') $10U + (15 - U) = 10(15 - U) + U - 27$
$$9U + 15 = -9U + 123$$
$$18U = 108$$
$$U = 6$$

(a) $T = 15 - (6) = 9$

Original number = **96**

4. Equal ratio method:
$$\frac{Y_1}{Y_2} = \frac{(G_1)^2 B_2}{(G_2)^2 B_1}$$
$$\frac{100}{10} = \frac{(1)^2 B_2}{(10)^2 5}$$
$$B_2 = \textbf{5000 blues}$$

Variation method:
$$Y = k\frac{G^2}{B}$$
$$k = \frac{100(5)}{(1)^2} = 500$$
$$B = \frac{500(10)^2}{10}$$
$$B = \textbf{5000 blues}$$

5. Downstream: $(B + W)T_D = D_D$ (a)

Upstream: $(B - W)T_U = D_U$ (b)

(a') $(B + 3)T = 92$

(b') $(B - 3)T = 68$

$$
\begin{array}{rl}
(a')\; & BT + 3T = 92 \\
(b')\; & \underline{BT - 3T = 68} \\
& 2BT = 160
\end{array}
$$

(c) $\quad BT = 80$

(a') $(80) + 3T = 92$
$$T = 4 \text{ hr}$$

(c) $B(4) = 80$
$$B = \textbf{20 mph}$$

$$T_D = T_U = \textbf{4 hr}$$

6. $27a^6p^{12} + y^3 = (3a^2p^4)^3 + (y)^3$
$$= (3a^2p^4 + y)(9a^4p^8 - 3a^2p^4y + y^2)$$

7. $8x^{12}z^6 - m^3y^9 = (2x^4z^2)^3 - (my^3)^3$
$$= (2x^4z^2 - my^3)(4x^8z^4 + 2mx^4y^3z^2 + m^2y^6)$$

8. $m^6y^9 - z^6 = (m^2y^3)^3 - (z^2)^3$
$$= (m^2y^3 - z^2)(m^4y^6 + m^2y^3z^2 + z^4)$$

9.
$$\sqrt{13^2 - 12^2} = \sqrt[n]{125}$$
$$\sqrt{25} = \sqrt[n]{125}$$
$$5 = \sqrt[n]{125}$$
$$5^n = 125$$
$$n = \textbf{3}$$

10.
$$
\begin{array}{r}
10N = 41.23\;3\;3\ldots \\
\underline{N = 4.12\;3\;3\ldots} \\
9N = 37.11
\end{array}
$$
$$N = \frac{\textbf{3711}}{\textbf{900}}$$

11. $y = x^2 - 2x - 1$

$y = (x^2 - 2x + 1) - 1 - 1$

$y = (x - 1)^2 - 2$

From this we see:

(a) Opens upward

(b) Axis of symmetry is $x = 1$

(c) y-coordinate of vertex is -2

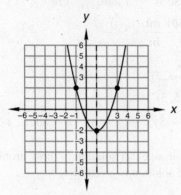

12. $-|x| - 3 < -5$; $D = \{$Reals$\}$

$-|x| < -2$

$|x| > 2$

$x > 2$ or $x < -2$

13. (a) $\dfrac{2}{5}x - \dfrac{1}{4}y = 2$

(b) $-0.008x - 0.2y = -1.68$

(a') $8x - 5y = 40$

(b') $\underline{-8x - 200y = -1680}$

$-205y = -1640$

$y = 8$

(a') $8x - 5(8) = 40$

$8x = 80$

$x = 10$

(10, 8)

14. (a) $x^2 + y^2 = 5$

(b) $y - 2x = 2$

$y = 2x + 2$

Substitute (b) into (a) and get:

(a') $x^2 + (2x + 2)^2 = 5$

$x^2 + 4x^2 + 8x + 4 = 5$

$5x^2 + 8x - 1 = 0$

Solve this equation by using the quadratic formula.

$x = \dfrac{-(8) \pm \sqrt{(8)^2 - 4(5)(-1)}}{2(5)} = -\dfrac{4}{5} \pm \dfrac{\sqrt{21}}{5}$

Substitute these values of x into (b) and solve for y.

(b) $y = 2\left(-\dfrac{4}{5} + \dfrac{\sqrt{21}}{5}\right) + 2 = \dfrac{2}{5} + \dfrac{2\sqrt{21}}{5}$

(b) $y = 2\left(-\dfrac{4}{5} - \dfrac{\sqrt{21}}{5}\right) + 2 = \dfrac{2}{5} - \dfrac{2\sqrt{21}}{5}$

$\left(-\dfrac{4}{5} + \dfrac{\sqrt{21}}{5}, \dfrac{2}{5} + \dfrac{2\sqrt{21}}{5}\right)$ and

$\left(-\dfrac{4}{5} - \dfrac{\sqrt{21}}{5}, \dfrac{2}{5} - \dfrac{2\sqrt{21}}{5}\right)$

15. (a) $4x + 2y = 8$

(b) $3x - 3z = -9$

(c) $-3x + z = 1$

(b) $3x - 3z = -9$

(c) $\underline{-3x + z = 1}$

$-2z = -8$

$z = 4$

(c) $-3x + (4) = 1$

$x = 1$

(a) $4(1) + 2y = 8$

$y = 2$

(1, 2, 4)

16. (a) $x - y - 3z = -2$

(b) $3x + y + z = 12$

(c) $2x - y + z = 5$

(a) $x - y - 3z = -2$

(b) $\underline{3x + y + z = 12}$

(d) $4x - 2z = 10$

(b) $3x + y + z = 12$

(c) $\underline{2x - y + z = 5}$

(e) $5x + 2z = 17$

(d) $4x - 2z = 10$

(e) $\underline{5x + 2z = 17}$

$9x = 27$

$x = 3$

(d) $4(3) - 2z = 10$

$z = 1$

(a) $(3) - y - 3(1) = -2$

$y = 2$

(3, 2, 1)

17. (a) $-x - 3y \geq -9$

$$y \leq -\frac{1}{3}x + 3$$

(b) $y < 2x$

The next step is to graph each of these lines.

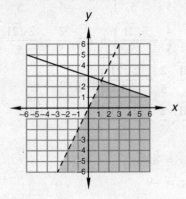

The region we wish to find is on or below the solid line and below the dashed line. This region is shaded in the figure.

18. $\dfrac{-i^3 - \sqrt{-2}\sqrt{-2}}{i^2 - 2i} = \dfrac{i + 2}{-1 - 2i} \cdot \dfrac{-1 + 2i}{-1 + 2i}$

$$= \dfrac{-i - 2 - 2 + 4i}{1 + 4} = -\dfrac{4}{5} + \dfrac{3}{5}i$$

19. $\dfrac{4 + 3\sqrt{5}}{2 + \sqrt{5}} \cdot \dfrac{2 - \sqrt{5}}{2 - \sqrt{5}}$

$$= \dfrac{8 - 4\sqrt{5} + 6\sqrt{5} - 15}{4 - 5}$$

$$= 7 - 2\sqrt{5}$$

20. $\sqrt[6]{9\sqrt[3]{3}} = (3^2)^{1/6}3^{1/18} = 3^{1/3}3^{1/18} = 3^{7/18}$

21. $\dfrac{5\sqrt{3}}{\sqrt{5}} + \dfrac{2\sqrt{5}}{\sqrt{3}} - \sqrt{60}$

$$= \dfrac{5\sqrt{15}}{5} + \dfrac{2\sqrt{15}}{3} - 2\sqrt{15}$$

$$= \dfrac{15\sqrt{15}}{15} + \dfrac{10\sqrt{15}}{15} - \dfrac{30\sqrt{15}}{15} = -\dfrac{\sqrt{15}}{3}$$

22.

y-axis graph with θ and H labeled, x-axis from -12 to 12, y-axis from -16 to 8.

$H = \sqrt{(4)^2 + (14)^2} = 2\sqrt{53}$

$\tan \theta = \dfrac{14}{4}$

$\theta \approx -74.05°$

$2\sqrt{53}\,\underline{/-74.05°}$

23. $\dfrac{40 \text{ ft}}{\text{s}} \times \dfrac{1 \text{ mi}}{5280 \text{ ft}} \times \dfrac{60 \text{ s}}{1 \text{ min}} \times \dfrac{60 \text{ min}}{1 \text{ hr}}$

$$= \dfrac{40(60)(60)}{(5280)} \dfrac{\text{mi}}{\text{hr}}$$

24. $(x_1, y_1) = (-3, 7)$

$(x_2, y_2) = (5, 3)$

$D = \sqrt{(-3 - 5)^2 + (7 - 3)^2} = \sqrt{80} = 4\sqrt{5}$

25. There is never an exact solution to these problems. One possible solution is given here.

$W = mE + b$

Use the graph to find the slope.

$m = \dfrac{150}{10} = 15$

$W = 15E + b$

Use the point $(40, 100)$ for E and W.

$100 = 15(40) + b$

$-500 = b$

$W = 15E - 500$

26. $\dfrac{ab}{a^2 + \dfrac{ab^2}{a^3 + 1}} = \dfrac{ab(a^3 + 1)}{a^5 + a^2 + ab^2}$

$$= \dfrac{b(a^3 + 1)}{a^4 + a + b^2}$$

27. See Lesson 71.

28. $\quad 2x^2 + 9x + 9 = 0$

$\quad 2x^2 + 6x + 3x + 9 = 0$

$\quad 2x(x + 3) + 3(x + 3) = 0$

$\quad\quad (2x + 3)(x + 3) = 0$

$2x + 3 = 0 \qquad x + 3 = 0$

$\quad\quad x = -\dfrac{3}{2} \qquad\quad x = -3$

$-\dfrac{3}{2}, -3$

29.
$$2b(3b^2 + 10b + 3) = 0$$
$$2b(3b^2 + 9b + b + 3) = 0$$
$$2b(3b(b + 3) + 1(b + 3)) = 0$$
$$2b(3b + 1)(b + 3) = 0$$

$$2b = 0 \qquad 3b + 1 = 0 \qquad b + 3 = 0$$

$$b = 0 \qquad b = -\frac{1}{3} \qquad b = -3$$

$$\mathbf{0, -\frac{1}{3}, -3}$$

30. $(h + p)(x) = x^2 + x^3$
$(h + p)(-3) = (-3)^2 + (-3)^3 = \mathbf{-18}$

PRACTICE SET 109

a.
$$\begin{array}{r} m^{1/2} + a^{1/2} \\ m^{1/2} + a^{1/2} \\ \hline m + m^{1/2}a^{1/2} \\ m^{1/2}a^{1/2} + a \\ \hline \mathbf{m + 2m^{1/2}a^{1/2} + a} \end{array}$$

b.
$$\begin{array}{r} z^{1/2} + p^{1/3} \\ z^{1/2} + p^{1/3} \\ \hline z + z^{1/2}p^{1/3} \\ z^{1/2}p^{1/3} + p^{2/3} \\ \hline \mathbf{z + 2z^{1/2}p^{1/3} + a^{2/3}} \end{array}$$

PROBLEM SET 109

1. T = tens digit

U = units digit

$10T + U$ = original number

(a) $10T + U = 8(T + U)$

(b) $6U = T + 5$

$T = 6U - 5$

Substitute (b) into (a) and get:

(a′) $10(6U - 5) + U = 8(6U - 5) + 8U$

$$61U - 50 = 56U - 40$$
$$5U = 10$$
$$U = 2$$

(b) $T = 6(2) - 5 = 7$

Original number = **72**

2. T = tens digit

U = units digit

$10T + U$ = original number

$10U + T$ = reversed number

(a) $T + U = 11$

$T = 11 - U$

(b) $10U + T = 10T + U - 27$

Substitute (a) into (b) and get:

(b′) $10U + (11 - U) = 10(11 - U) + U - 27$

$$9U + 11 = -9U + 83$$
$$18U = 72$$
$$U = 4$$

(a) $T = 11 - (4) = 7$

Original number = **74**

3.

$$\begin{array}{c} D_L \\ \vdash\!\!\longrightarrow \\ 63 \end{array}$$

$$\begin{array}{c} D_C \\ \vdash\!\!\longrightarrow \\ 60 \end{array}$$

$R_L T_L = 63$; $R_C T_C = 60$;

$T_L = T_C + 11$; $R_C = 2R_L$

$$2R_L(T_L - 11) = 60$$
$$2(63) - 22R_L = 60$$
$$-22R_L = -66$$
$$R_L = 3$$

R_L = **3 mph**; R_C = **6 mph**; T_L = **21 hr**;
T_C = **10 hr**

4.
$$\frac{P_1}{T_1} = \frac{P_2}{T_2}$$
$$\frac{800}{400} = \frac{P_2}{1200}$$
$$P_2 = \mathbf{2400\ torr}$$

5. $0.46(600) - 1(D_N) = 0.4(600 - D_N)$
$$276 - D_N = 240 - 0.4D_N$$
$$0.6D_N = 36$$
$$D_N = \mathbf{60\ mL}$$

6. Apply the power rule and get:
$\mathbf{27x^{3/4}y^{3/2}m^3}$

7.
$$\begin{array}{r} x^{1/4} + y^{1/4} \\ x^{1/4} + y^{1/4} \\ \hline x^{1/2} + x^{1/4}y^{1/4} \\ x^{1/4}y^{1/4} + y^{1/2} \\ \hline \mathbf{x^{1/2} + 2x^{1/4}y^{1/4} + y^{1/2}} \end{array}$$

8. $x^{1/4} + y^{-1/4}$
$$\frac{x^{1/4} + y^{-1/4}}{x^{1/2} + x^{1/4}y^{-1/4}}$$
$$\frac{x^{1/4}y^{-1/4} + y^{-1/2}}{x^{1/2} + 2x^{1/4}y^{-1/4} + y^{-1/2}}$$

9. $x^3y^6 - 27m^3 = (xy^2)^3 - (3m)^3$
$= (xy^2 - 3m)(x^2y^4 + 3mxy^2 + 9m^2)$

10. $64x^9y^6 + p^{12}z^3 = (4x^3y^2)^3 + (p^4z)^3$
$= (4x^3y^2 + p^4z)(16x^6y^4 - 4p^4x^3y^2z + p^8z^2)$

11. $100N = 102.342\ 42\ 42\ ...$
$N = 1.023\ 42\ 42\ ...$
$\overline{99N = 101.319}$

$$N = \frac{101{,}319}{99{,}000}$$

12. $-y = x^2 - 4x + 1$
$-y = (x^2 - 4x + 4) + 1 - 4$
$-y = (x - 2)^2 - 3$
$y = -(x - 2)^2 + 3$

From this we see:

(a) Opens downward

(b) Axis of symmetry is $x = 2$

(c) y-coordinate of vertex is 3

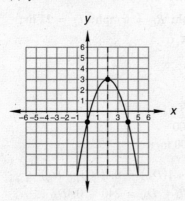

13. $-2 \geq x + 2 > -4$; $D = \{\text{Reals}\}$
$-4 \geq x > -6$

14. (a) $\dfrac{2}{5}x - \dfrac{1}{3}y = 1$

(b) $0.3x - 0.05y = 2.55$

(a') $6x - 5y = 15$

(b') $30x - 5y = 255$

-1(a') $-6x + 5y = -15$

(b') $\underline{30x - 5y = 255}$
$24x = 240$
$x = 10$

(a') $6(10) - 5y = 15$
$y = 9$

(10, 9)

15. (a) $x - 2y = 5$

(b) $xy = 3$

$x = \dfrac{3}{y}$

Substitute (b) into (a) and get:

(a') $\left(\dfrac{3}{y}\right) - 2y = 5$

$3 - 2y^2 = 5y$

$2y^2 + 5y - 3 = 0$

Solve this equation by using the quadratic formula.

$$y = \frac{-(5) \pm \sqrt{(5)^2 - 4(2)(-3)}}{2(2)}$$

$$y = -\frac{5}{4} \pm \frac{7}{4} = \frac{1}{2}, -3$$

Substitute these values of y into (a) and solve for x.

(a) $x = 2\left(\dfrac{1}{2}\right) + 5 = 6$

(a) $x = 2(-3) + 5 = -1$

$\left(6, \dfrac{1}{2}\right)$ and $(-1, -3)$

16. (a) $x + y - z = 7$

(b) $4x + y + z = 4$

(c) $3x + y - z = 9$

(a) $x + y - z = 7$
(b) $\underline{4x + y + z = 4}$
(d) $5x + 2y = 11$

(b) $4x + y + z = 4$
(c) $\underline{3x + y - z = 9}$
(e) $7x + 2y = 13$

-1(d) $-5x - 2y = -11$

(e) $\underline{7x + 2y = 13}$
$2x = 2$
$x = 1$

(d) $5(1) + 2y = 11$

$\qquad y = 3$

(a) $(1) + (3) - z = 7$

$\qquad z = -3$

(1, 3, −3)

17. (a) $2x + 3y = 15$

(b) $x - 2z = -3$

(c) $3y - z = 6$

$\qquad z = 3y - 6$

Substitute (c) into (b) and get:

(b′) $x - 2(3y - 6) = -3$

$\qquad x - 6y = -15$

2(a) $4x + 6y = 30$

(b′) $\underline{x - 6y = -15}$

$\qquad 5x \qquad = 15$

$\qquad\quad x = 3$

(a) $2(3) + 3y = 15$

$\qquad\qquad y = 3$

(c) $z = 3(3) - 6 = 3$

(3, 3, 3)

18. (a) $2x - 5y \geq 15$

$\qquad y \leq \dfrac{2}{5}x - 3$

(b) $y \leq -x$

The next step is to graph each of these lines.

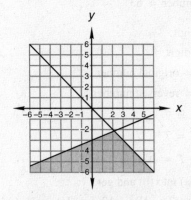

The region we wish to find is on or below the solid lines. This region is shaded in the figure.

19. $\dfrac{2i^2 - \sqrt{-9} + 2}{3 - \sqrt{-2}\sqrt{2}} = \dfrac{-3i}{3 - 2i} \cdot \dfrac{3 + 2i}{3 + 2i}$

$= \dfrac{-9i + 6}{9 + 4} = \dfrac{6}{13} - \dfrac{9}{13}i$

20. $\dfrac{3 + 2\sqrt{2}}{5\sqrt{2} - 2} \cdot \dfrac{5\sqrt{2} + 2}{5\sqrt{2} + 2}$

$= \dfrac{15\sqrt{2} + 6 + 20 + 4\sqrt{2}}{50 - 4} = \dfrac{26 + 19\sqrt{2}}{46}$

21. $\sqrt[3]{27}\,\sqrt[3]{3} = (3^3)^{1/3}3^{1/3} = 3(3^{1/3}) = \mathbf{3^{4/3}}$

22. $\sqrt{x^5 y}\,\sqrt{x^2 y} = x^{5/2}y^{1/2}xy^{1/2} = \mathbf{x^{7/2}y}$

23. $\dfrac{x^{a/3 - 2/3}y^{b/2}}{x^{2a}y^{-b}} = \mathbf{x^{-5a/3 - 2/3}y^{3b/2}}$

24. $\dfrac{\sqrt{2}}{\sqrt{3}} + \dfrac{4\sqrt{3}}{\sqrt{2}} - 6\sqrt{24} = \dfrac{\sqrt{6}}{3} + \dfrac{4\sqrt{6}}{2} - 12\sqrt{6}$

$= \dfrac{2\sqrt{6}}{6} + \dfrac{12\sqrt{6}}{6} - \dfrac{72\sqrt{6}}{6} = -\dfrac{\mathbf{29\sqrt{6}}}{\mathbf{3}}$

25. $\dfrac{ka^2}{ka - \dfrac{a^3}{k^2 a - 1}} = \dfrac{ka^2(k^2 a - 1)}{k^3 a^2 - ka - a^3}$

$= \dfrac{\mathbf{ka(k^2 a - 1)}}{\mathbf{k^3 a - k - a^2}}$

26.

$A = 15\cos 47° \approx 10.23$

$B = 15\sin 47° \approx 10.97$

$\begin{array}{r} -10.23R + 10.97U \\ 20.00R + 0.00U \\ \hline \mathbf{9.77R + 10.97U} \end{array}$

$\tan\theta = \dfrac{10.97}{9.77}$

$\theta \approx 48.31°$

$F = \sqrt{(9.77)^2 + (10.97)^2} \approx 14.69$

14.69 ⁄ 48.31°

27. $\dfrac{1000 \text{ liters}}{\text{min}} \times \dfrac{1000 \text{ mL}}{1 \text{ liter}} \times \dfrac{1 \text{ min}}{60 \text{ s}}$

$= \dfrac{\mathbf{1000(1000)}}{\mathbf{(60)}} \dfrac{\text{mL}}{\text{s}}$

28.
$$6p^2 - 3p - 30 = 0$$
$$3(2p^2 - p - 10) = 0$$
$$2p^2 + 4p - 5p - 10 = 0$$
$$2p(p + 2) - 5(p + 2) = 0$$
$$(2p - 5)(p + 2) = 0$$
$$2p - 5 = 0 \qquad p + 2 = 0$$
$$p = \frac{5}{2} \qquad p = -2$$

$$\frac{5}{2}, -2$$

29.
$$4x^3 - 14x^2 - 8x = 0$$
$$2x(2x^2 - 7x - 4) = 0$$
$$2x(2x^2 - 8x + x - 4) = 0$$
$$2x(2x(x - 4) + 1(x - 4)) = 0$$
$$2x(2x + 1)(x - 4) = 0$$
$$2x = 0 \qquad 2x + 1 = 0 \qquad x - 4 = 0$$
$$x = 0 \qquad x = -\frac{1}{2} \qquad x = 4$$

$$0, -\frac{1}{2}, 4$$

30.
$$3x^2 - 7x - 6 = 0$$
$$3x^2 - 9x + 2x - 6 = 0$$
$$3x(x - 3) + 2(x - 3) = 0$$
$$(3x + 2)(x - 3) = 0$$
$$3x + 2 = 0 \qquad x - 3 = 0$$
$$x = -\frac{2}{3} \qquad x = 3$$

$$-\frac{2}{3}, 3$$

PRACTICE SET 110

a. $(x + 1)(x - 2) > 0; \ D = \{\text{Reals}\}$

$(\text{Pos})(\text{Pos}) > 0$

$x + 1 > 0 \quad$ and $\quad x - 2 > 0$

$\qquad x > -1 \quad$ and $\qquad x > 2$

$(\text{Neg})(\text{Neg}) > 0$

$x + 1 < 0 \quad$ and $\quad x - 2 < 0$

$\qquad x < -1 \quad$ and $\qquad x < 2$

Thus, the solution is $x > 2$ or $x < -1$.

b. $x^2 - 3x \ge 4; \ D = \{\text{Integers}\}$

$$x^2 - 3x - 4 \ge 0$$
$$(x - 4)(x + 1) \ge 0$$

$(\text{Pos})(\text{Pos}) \ge 0$

$x - 4 \ge 0 \quad$ and $\quad x + 1 \ge 0$

$\qquad x \ge 4 \quad$ and $\qquad x \ge -1$

$(\text{Neg})(\text{Neg}) \ge 0$

$x - 4 \le 0 \quad$ and $\quad x + 1 \le 0$

$\qquad x \le 4 \quad$ and $\qquad x \le -1$

Thus, the solution is $x \ge 4$ or $x \le -1$.

PROBLEM SET 110

1. $T = $ tens digit

$U = $ units digit

$10T + U = $ original number

$10U + T = $ reversed number

(a) $T + U = 9$

$\qquad T = 9 - U$

(b) $10U + T = 10T + U - 27$

Substitute (a) into (b) and get:

(b') $10U + (9 - U) = 10(9 - U) + U - 27$

$\qquad\qquad 9U + 9 = -9U + 63$

$\qquad\qquad\quad 18U = 54$

$\qquad\qquad\qquad U = 3$

(a) $T = 9 - (3) = 6$

Original number = **63**

2. $T = $ tens digit

$U = $ units digit

$10T + U = $ original number

$10U + T = $ reversed number

(a) $T + U = 7$

$\qquad T = 7 - U$

(b) $10U + T = 10T + U + 45$

Substitute (a) into (b) and get:

(b') $10U + (7 - U) = 10(7 - U) + U + 45$

$\qquad\qquad 9U + 7 = -9U + 115$

$\qquad\qquad\quad 18U = 108$

$\qquad\qquad\qquad U = 6$

(a) $T = 7 - (6) = 1$

Original number = **16**

3. Potassium (K): $1 \times 39 = 39$

   Chromium (Cr): $2 \times 52 = 104$

   Oxygen: $7 \times 16 = 112$

   Total: $39 + 104 + 112 = 255$

$$\frac{112}{255} = \frac{336}{KCr_2O_7}$$

$KCr_2O_7 = $ **765 grams**

4. Downstream: $(B + W)TD = D_D$ (a)

   Upstream: $(B - W)T_U = D_U$ (b)

   (a′) $(B + W)8 = 120$

   (b′) $(B - W)9 = 63$

   9(a′) $72B + 72W = 1080$

   8(b′) $\underline{72B - 72W = 504}$

   $144B = 1584$

   $ B = $ **11 mph**

   (a′) $8(11) + 8W = 120$

   $ W = $ **4 mph**

5. $S_P = P_P + M_U$

   $S_P = 1400 + 700$

   $S_P = \$2100$

   % of $S_P = \dfrac{700}{2100} \times 100\% = $ **33.33%**

   % of cost $= \dfrac{700}{1400} \times 100\% = $ **50%**

6. $(x + 2)(x - 4) > 0$; $D = \{\text{Reals}\}$

   (Pos)(Pos) > 0

   $x + 2 > 0$ and $x - 4 > 0$

   $ x > -2$ and $ x > 4$

   (Neg)(Neg) > 0

   $x + 2 < 0$ and $x - 4 < 0$

   $ x < -2$ and $ x < 4$

   Thus, the solution is $x > 4$ or $x < -2$.

   ← |——⊙——|——|——|——|——⊙——| →
   $-3 \;\; -2 \;\; -1 \quad 0 \quad 1 \quad 2 \quad 3 \quad 4 \quad 5$

7. $x^2 - 4x - 5 \geq 0$; $D = \{\text{Integers}\}$

   $(x - 5)(x + 1) \geq 0$

   (Pos)(Pos) ≥ 0

   $x - 5 \geq 0$ and $x + 1 \geq 0$

   $ x \geq 5$ and $ x \geq -1$

(Neg)(Neg) ≥ 0

$x - 5 \leq 0$ and $x + 1 \leq 0$

$ x \leq 5$ and $ x \leq -1$

Thus, the solution is $x \geq 5$ or $x \leq -1$.

← |—•—•——|——|——|——|——•——•—| →
$-2 \;\; -1 \quad 0 \quad 1 \quad 2 \quad 3 \quad 4 \quad 5 \quad 6$

8. Apply the power rule and get $4x^6y^4z^6$.

9. $\begin{array}{l} x^{1/2} - y^{1/4} \\ \underline{x^{1/2} - y^{1/4}} \\ x - x^{1/2}y^{1/4} \\ \underline{ - x^{1/2}y^{1/4} + y^{1/2}} \\ x - 2x^{1/2}y^{1/4} + y^{1/2} \end{array}$

10. $\begin{array}{l} x^{1/2} + y^{1/2} \\ \underline{x^{1/2} - y^{1/2}} \\ x + x^{1/2}y^{1/2} \\ \underline{- x^{1/2}y^{1/2} - y} \\ x \phantom{+ x^{1/2}y^{1/2}} - y = x - y \end{array}$

11. $8x^9 - y^6p^3 = (2x^3)^3 - (y^2p)^3$

$= (2x^3 - y^2p)(4x^6 + 2x^3y^2p + y^4p^2)$

12. $27x^{12}y^9 + p^6m^{15} = (3x^4y^3)^3 + (p^2m^5)^3$

$= (3x^4y^3 + p^2m^5)(9x^8y^6 - 3x^4y^3p^2m^5 + p^4m^{10})$

13. $1000N = 13.62 \; 362 \; 362 \ldots$

$\underline{N = 0.01 \; 362 \; 362 \ldots}$

$999N = 13.61$

$N = \dfrac{\textbf{1361}}{\textbf{99,900}}$

14. $y = x^2 - 4x + 3$

$y = (x^2 - 4x + 4) + 3 - 4$

$y = (x - 2)^2 - 1$

From this we see:

(a) Opens upward

(b) Axis of symmetry is $x = 2$

(c) y-coordinate of vertex is -1

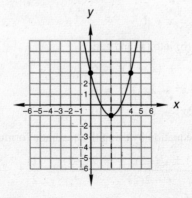

15. $3 > x + 2$ or $x + 5 \geq 8$; $D = \{\text{Reals}\}$

$1 > x$ or $x \geq 3$

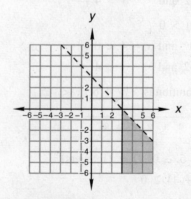

Number line showing points 0 1 2 3 4 with open circle at 1 and closed circle at 3.

16. (a) $\dfrac{2}{7}x - \dfrac{1}{5}y = 2$

(b) $0.03x + 0.07y = 1.12$

(a') $10x - 7y = 70$

(b') $\dfrac{3x + 7y = 112}{}$

$\quad 13x \quad\quad = 182$

$\quad\quad\quad x = 14$

(a') $10(14) - 7y = 70$

$\quad\quad\quad y = 10$

(14, 10)

17. (a) $x + y + z = 1$

(b) $4x - 2y - z = 6$

(c) $3x - y + z = -1$

(a) + (b): $5x - y = 7$ (d)

(b) + (c): $7x - 3y = 5$ (e)

$-3(d)$ $-15x + 3y = -21$

(e) $\dfrac{7x - 3y = \quad 5}{}$

$\quad -8x \quad\quad = -16$

$\quad\quad\quad x = 2$

(d) $5(2) - y = 7$

$\quad\quad\quad y = 3$

(a) $(2) + (3) + z = 1$

$\quad\quad\quad\quad z = -4$

(2, 3, –4)

18. (a) $x^2 + y^2 = 6$

(b) $x - y = 1$

$\quad\quad y = x - 1$

Substitute (b) into (a) and get:

(a') $\quad x^2 + (x - 1)^2 = 6$

$x^2 + x^2 - 2x + 1 = 6$

$2x^2 - 2x - 5 = 0$

Solve this equation by using the quadratic formula.

$x = \dfrac{-(-2) \pm \sqrt{(-2)^2 - 4(2)(-5)}}{2(2)} = \dfrac{1}{2} \pm \dfrac{\sqrt{11}}{2}$

Substitute these values of x into (b) and solve for y.

(b) $y = \left(\dfrac{1}{2} + \dfrac{\sqrt{11}}{2}\right) - 1 = -\dfrac{1}{2} + \dfrac{\sqrt{11}}{2}$

(b) $y = \left(\dfrac{1}{2} - \dfrac{\sqrt{11}}{2}\right) - 1 = -\dfrac{1}{2} - \dfrac{\sqrt{11}}{2}$

$\left(\dfrac{1}{2} + \dfrac{\sqrt{11}}{2}, -\dfrac{1}{2} + \dfrac{\sqrt{11}}{2}\right)$ and

$\left(\dfrac{1}{2} - \dfrac{\sqrt{11}}{2}, -\dfrac{1}{2} - \dfrac{\sqrt{11}}{2}\right)$

19. (a) $x - z = 3$

(b) $x + 2y = 5$

(c) $y + z = 0$

(a) + (c): $x + y = 3$ (d)

$-2(d)$ $-2x - 2y = -6$

(e) $\dfrac{x + 2y = \quad 5}{}$

$\quad -x \quad\quad = -1$

$\quad\quad\quad x = 1$

(b) $(1) + 2y = 5$

$\quad\quad\quad y = 2$

(a) $(1) - z = 3$

$\quad\quad\quad z = -2$

(1, 2, –2)

20. (a) $2x \geq 6$

$\quad x \geq 3$

(b) $x + y < 3$

$\quad y < -x + 3$

The next step is to graph each of these lines.

Graph with x and y axes, gridlines from -6 to 6, showing a dashed line and a solid vertical line, with a shaded region in the lower right.

The region we wish to find is on and to the right of the solid line and below the dashed line. This region is shaded in the figure.

21. $\dfrac{2i^2 - 2i + 2}{\sqrt{-9} - \sqrt{-3}\sqrt{-3}} = \dfrac{-2i}{3i + 3} \cdot \dfrac{3i - 3}{3i - 3}$

$= \dfrac{6 + 6i}{-9 - 9} = -\dfrac{1}{3} - \dfrac{1}{3}i$

22. $\dfrac{3 + 4\sqrt{5}}{1 - \sqrt{5}} \cdot \dfrac{1 + \sqrt{5}}{1 + \sqrt{5}}$

$= \dfrac{3 + 3\sqrt{5} + 4\sqrt{5} + 20}{1 - 5} = \dfrac{-23 - 7\sqrt{5}}{4}$

23. $\dfrac{a^{4 - 2b}x^2}{x^{b/2}a^{b/2}} = a^{4 - 5b/2}x^{2 - b/2}$

24. $\sqrt[4]{8\sqrt{2}} = (2^3)^{1/4}2^{1/8} = 2^{3/4}2^{1/8} = 2^{7/8}$

25. $\dfrac{\sqrt{2}}{\sqrt{3}} - \dfrac{5\sqrt{3}}{\sqrt{2}} + 3\sqrt{24} = \dfrac{\sqrt{6}}{3} - \dfrac{5\sqrt{6}}{2} + 6\sqrt{6}$

$= \dfrac{2\sqrt{6}}{6} - \dfrac{15\sqrt{6}}{6} + \dfrac{36\sqrt{6}}{6} = \dfrac{23\sqrt{6}}{6}$

26. $\sqrt{k} - 6 = \sqrt{k - 48}$

$k - 12\sqrt{k} + 36 = k - 48$

$12\sqrt{k} = 84$

$\sqrt{k} = 7$

$k = \mathbf{49}$

Check: $\sqrt{49} - 6 = \sqrt{49 - 48}$

$1 = 1$

27.

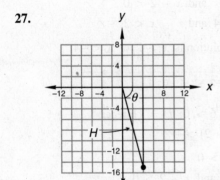

$H = \sqrt{(15)^2 + (4)^2} = \sqrt{241}$

$\tan \theta = \dfrac{15}{4}$

$\theta \approx -75.07°$

$\sqrt{241}\,\underline{/-75.07°}$

28. $3s^2 + 11s + 10 = 0$

$3s^2 + 6s + 5s + 10 = 0$

$3s(s + 2) + 5(s + 2) = 0$

$(3s + 5)(s + 2) = 0$

$3s + 5 = 0 \qquad s + 2 = 0$

$s = -\dfrac{5}{3} \qquad s = -2$

$-\dfrac{5}{3}, -2$

29. $8x^3 + 6x^2 - 2x = 0$

$2x(4x^2 + 3x - 1) = 0$

$2x(4x^2 + 4x - x - 1) = 0$

$2x(4x(x + 1) - 1(x + 1)) = 0$

$2x(4x - 1)(x + 1) = 0$

$2x = 0 \qquad 4x - 1 = 0 \qquad x + 1 = 0$

$x = 0 \qquad x = \dfrac{1}{4} \qquad x = -1$

$0, \dfrac{1}{4}, -1$

30. Since –2 is not a member of the domain of $g(x)$, it is not a member of the domain of $(h + g)(x)$. Therefore, the answer is either $\varnothing$ or { }.

PRACTICE SET 111

$N + D + Q = 35 \qquad \text{(a)}$

$5N + 10D + 25Q = 500 \quad \text{(b)}$

$2N = Q \qquad\qquad \text{(c)}$

(a) $N + D + (2N) = 35$

(a′) $3N + D = 35$

(b) $5N + 10D + 25(2N) = 500$

(b′) $55N + 10D = 500$

$-10(\text{a}′) \quad -30N - 10D = -350$

$(\text{b}′) \quad \underline{55N + 10D = 500}$

$\qquad\qquad 25N = 150$

$\qquad\qquad\qquad N = 6$

(c) $Q = 2N = 12$

(a) $(6) + D + (12) = 35$

$D = 17$

There were **6 nickels, 17 dimes,** and **12 quarters.**

PROBLEM SET 111

1. (a) $N_N + N_D + N_Q = 28$

    (b) $5N_N + 10N_D + 25N_Q = 250$

    (c) $N_N = 5N_Q$

    Substitute (c) into (a) and (b) and get:

    (a') $N_D + 6N_Q = 28$

    (b') $10N_D + 50N_Q = 250$

    -10(a') $-10N_D - 60N_Q = -280$

    (b') $\underline{10N_D + 50N_Q = 250}$

    $-10N_Q = -30$

    $N_Q = \textbf{3 quarters}$

    (c) $N_N = 5(3) = \textbf{15 nickels}$

    (a) $(15) + N_D + (3) = 28$

    $N_D = \textbf{10 dimes}$

2. (a) $N_B + N_G + N_Y = 10$

    (b) $N_B + 4N_G + 5N_Y = 39$

    (c) $N_Y = N_G + 2$

    Substitute (c) into (a) and (b) and get:

    (a') $N_B + 2N_G = 8$

    (b') $N_B + 9N_G = 29$

    -1(a') $-N_B - 2N_G = -8$

    (b') $\underline{N_B + 9N_G = 29}$

    $7N_G = 21$

    $N_G = \textbf{3 greens}$

    (c) $N_Y = (3) + 2 = \textbf{5 yellows}$

    (a) $N_B + (3) + (5) = 10$

    $N_B = \textbf{2 blues}$

3. T = tens digit

    U = units digit

    $10T + U$ = original number

    (a) $10T + U = 4(T + U)$

    (b) $U = T + 1$

    Substitute (b) into (a) and get:

    (a') $10T + (T + 1) = 4T + 4(T + 1)$

    $11T + 1 = 8T + 4$

    $3T = 3$

    $T = 1$

    (b) $U = (1) + 1 = 2$

    Original number = **12**

4. Consecutive integers: $N,\ N + 1,\ N + 2$

    $N(N + 2) = 5(N + 1) + 35$

    $N^2 + 2N = 5N + 40$

    $N^2 - 3N - 40 = 0$

    Solve this equation by factoring.

    $(N + 5)(N - 8) = 0$

    $N = -5, 8$

    The desired integers are **–5, –4, –3** and **8, 9, 10.**

5. Equal ratio method:

    $$\frac{S_1}{S_2} = \frac{T_1(A_1)^2}{T_2(A_2)^2}$$

    $$\frac{1000}{S_2} = \frac{5(2)^2}{8(1)^2}$$

    $$S_2 = \textbf{400 students}$$

    Variation method:

    $S = kTA^2$

    $1000 = k(5)(2)^2$

    $50 = k$

    $S = (50)(8)(1)^2$

    $S = \textbf{400 students}$

6. $(x + 4)(x - 2) > 0;\ D = \{\text{Integers}\}$

    $(\text{Pos})(\text{Pos}) > 0$

    $x + 4 > 0\quad$ and $\ x - 2 > 0$

    $x > -4$ and $x > 2$

    $(\text{Neg})(\text{Neg}) > 0$

    $x + 4 < 0\quad$ and $\ x - 2 < 0$

    $x < -4$ and $x < 2$

    Thus, the solution is $x > 2$ or $x < -4$.

7. $x^2 - 5x + 6 > 0;\ D = \{\text{Integers}\}$

    $(x - 3)(x - 2) > 0$

    $(\text{Pos})(\text{Pos}) > 0$

    $x - 3 > 0$ and $x - 2 > 0$

    $x > 3$ and $x > 2$

    $(\text{Neg})(\text{Neg}) > 0$

    $x - 3 < 0$ and $x - 2 < 0$

    $x < 3$ and $x < 2$

    Thus, the solution is $x > 3$ or $x < 2$.

8. $(x^{1/2} + y^{1/4})^2$

$$x^{1/2} + y^{1/4}$$
$$\underline{x^{1/2} + y^{1/4}}$$
$$x + x^{1/2}y^{1/4}$$
$$\underline{\quad\quad x^{1/2}y^{1/4} + y^{1/2}}$$
$$\boldsymbol{x + 2x^{1/2}y^{1/4} + y^{1/2}}$$

9. $(x^{1/2} - y^{-1/2})^2$

$$x^{1/2} - y^{-1/2}$$
$$\underline{x^{1/2} - y^{-1/2}}$$
$$x - x^{1/2}y^{-1/2}$$
$$\underline{\quad\quad - x^{1/2}y^{-1/2} + y^{-1}}$$
$$\boldsymbol{x - 2x^{1/2}y^{-1/2} + y^{-1}}$$

10. Apply the power rule and get $\boldsymbol{xy^{-1}}$.

11. $x^3 - m^6y^6 = (x)^3 - (m^2y^2)^3$
$\quad = (x - m^2y^2)(x^2 + m^2xy^2 + m^4y^4)$

12. $8x^6y^3 - 27m^3p^{12} = (2x^2y)^3 - (3mp^4)^3$
$\quad = (2x^2y - 3mp^4)(4x^4y^2 + 6x^2ymp^4 + 9m^2p^8)$

13.
$$100N = 102.13\ 13\ 13\ \dots$$
$$\underline{\quad N = \quad 1.02\ 13\ 13\ \dots}$$
$$99N = 101.11$$
$$N = \frac{\boldsymbol{10{,}111}}{\boldsymbol{9900}}$$

14. $-y = x^2 + 4x + 1$
$-y = (x^2 + 4x + 4) + 1 - 4$
$-y = (x + 2)^2 - 3$
$\quad y = -(x + 2)^2 + 3$

From this we see:

(a) Opens downward

(b) Axis of symmetry is $x = -2$

(c) y-coordinate of vertex is 3

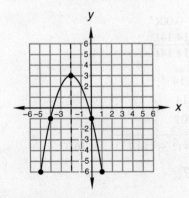

15. $-|x| - 3 \geq -7;\ D = \{\text{Reals}\}$
$\quad\quad -|x| \geq -4$
$\quad\quad\ |x| \leq 4$

$x \leq 4$ and $x \geq -4$

16. $-2 \leq x + 5 < 4;\ D = \{\text{Integers}\}$
$-7 \leq x < -1$

17. (a) $\dfrac{3}{5}x - \dfrac{2}{5}y = -10$

(b) $0.003x + 0.2y = 1.97$

(a') $3x - 2y = -50$

(b') $3x + 200y = 1970$

$-1(a')\ -3x + \quad 2y = \quad 50$
$\ \ (b')\ \ \underline{\ 3x + 200y = 1970}$
$\quad\quad\quad\quad\quad\quad 202y = 2020$
$\quad\quad\quad\quad\quad\quad\ \ y = 10$

(a') $3x - 2(10) = -50$
$\quad\quad\quad\quad\ x = -10$

(−10, 10)

18. (a) $x + 2y = 10$

(b) $x - 3z = -16$

(c) $y + 2z = 16$

$2(b) + 3(c):\ 2x + 3y = 16$ (d)

$-2(a) + (d):\ -y = -4$
$\quad\quad\quad\quad\quad\quad y = 4$

(a) $x + 2(4) = 10$
$\quad\quad\quad\quad x = 2$

(c) $(4) + 2z = 16$
$\quad\quad\quad\quad z = 6$

(2, 4, 6)

19. (a) $x^2 + y^2 = 4$

    (b) $x - y = 1$

    $y = x - 1$

    Substitute (b) into (a) and get:

    (a') $x^2 + (x - 1)^2 = 4$

    $x^2 + x^2 - 2x + 1 = 4$

    $2x^2 - 2x - 3 = 0$

    Solve this equation by using the quadratic formula.

    $x = \dfrac{-(-2) \pm \sqrt{(-2)^2 - 4(2)(-3)}}{2(2)} = \dfrac{1}{2} \pm \dfrac{\sqrt{7}}{2}$

    Substitute these values of x into (b) and solve for y.

    (b) $y = \left(\dfrac{1}{2} + \dfrac{\sqrt{7}}{2} \right) - 1 = -\dfrac{1}{2} + \dfrac{\sqrt{7}}{2}$

    (b) $y = \left(\dfrac{1}{2} - \dfrac{\sqrt{7}}{2} \right) - 1 = -\dfrac{1}{2} - \dfrac{\sqrt{7}}{2}$

    $\left(\dfrac{1}{2} + \dfrac{\sqrt{7}}{2}, -\dfrac{1}{2} + \dfrac{\sqrt{7}}{2} \right)$ and

    $\left(\dfrac{1}{2} - \dfrac{\sqrt{7}}{2}, -\dfrac{1}{2} - \dfrac{\sqrt{7}}{2} \right)$

20. $2x^2 - 3x - 5 = 0$

    $x^2 - \dfrac{3}{2}x = \dfrac{5}{2}$

    $\left(x^2 - \dfrac{3}{2}x + \dfrac{9}{16} \right) = \dfrac{40}{16} + \dfrac{9}{16}$

    $\left(x - \dfrac{3}{4} \right)^2 = \dfrac{49}{16}$

    $x - \dfrac{3}{4} = \pm\dfrac{7}{4}$

    $x = \dfrac{3}{4} \pm \dfrac{7}{4}$

    $x = \dfrac{5}{2}, -1$

21. $\dfrac{40 \text{ in.}}{\text{s}} \times \dfrac{2.54 \text{ cm}}{1 \text{ in.}} \times \dfrac{1 \text{ m}}{100 \text{ cm}} \times \dfrac{60 \text{ s}}{1 \text{ min}} \times \dfrac{60 \text{ min}}{1 \text{ hr}}$

    $= \dfrac{40(2.54)(60)(60)}{(100)} \dfrac{\text{m}}{\text{hr}}$

22. $\dfrac{2i^3 - \sqrt{-3}\sqrt{-3}}{4 - 3i^2} = \dfrac{-2i + 3}{7} = \dfrac{3}{7} - \dfrac{2}{7}i$

23. $\dfrac{2\sqrt{3} + 2}{3 - \sqrt{3}} \cdot \dfrac{3 + \sqrt{3}}{3 + \sqrt{3}} = \dfrac{6\sqrt{3} + 6 + 6 + 2\sqrt{3}}{9 - 3}$

    $= \dfrac{6 + 4\sqrt{3}}{3}$

24. $\dfrac{a^{x/2}y^{1 - x/2}}{a^{3x}y^{-2x}} = a^{-5x/2}y^{1 + 3x/2}$

25. $\sqrt{xy}\,\sqrt{x^2 y} = x^{1/2}y^{1/2}xy^{1/2} = x^{3/2}y$

26. $\dfrac{\sqrt{2}}{\sqrt{7}} - \dfrac{3\sqrt{7}}{\sqrt{2}} + 2\sqrt{126} = \dfrac{\sqrt{14}}{7} - \dfrac{3\sqrt{14}}{2} + 6\sqrt{14}$

    $= \dfrac{2\sqrt{14}}{14} - \dfrac{21\sqrt{14}}{14} + \dfrac{84\sqrt{14}}{14} = \dfrac{65\sqrt{14}}{14}$

27. (a) $-y < 3$

    $y > -3$

    (b) $3x + y \le 3$

    $y \le -3x + 3$

    The next step is to graph each of these lines.

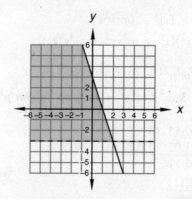

    The region we wish to find is on and below the solid line and above the dashed line. This region is shaded in the figure.

28.

    $A = 20 \cos 45° \approx 14.14$

    $B = 20 \sin 45° \approx 14.14$

    $\begin{array}{r} -6.00R + 0.00U \\ 14.14R + 14.14U \\ \hline \mathbf{8.14R} + \mathbf{14.14U} \end{array}$

    $\tan \theta = \dfrac{14.14}{8.14}$

    $\theta \approx 60.07°$

    $F = \sqrt{(8.14)^2 + (14.14)^2} \approx 16.32$

    16.32 $\underline{/60.07°}$

29.
$$2x^2 - x - 10 = 0$$
$$2x^2 + 4x - 5x - 10 = 0$$
$$2x(x + 2) - 5(x + 2) = 0$$
$$(2x - 5)(x + 2) = 0$$
$$2x - 5 = 0 \qquad x + 2 = 0$$
$$x = \frac{5}{2} \qquad x = -2$$

$$\frac{5}{2}, -2$$

30.
$$2x^3 - 7x^2 - 15x = 0$$
$$x(2x^2 - 7x - 15) = 0$$
$$x(2x^2 - 10x + 3x - 15) = 0$$
$$x(2x(x - 5) + 3(x - 5)) = 0$$
$$x(2x + 3)(x - 5) = 0$$
$$x = 0 \qquad 2x + 3 = 0 \qquad x - 5 = 0$$
$$x = -\frac{3}{2} \qquad x = 5$$

$$0, -\frac{3}{2}, 5$$

PRACTICE SET 112

a. $(x + 4)(x - 1) < 0;\ D = \{\text{Reals}\}$

$(\text{Neg})(\text{Pos}) < 0$

$x + 4 < 0 \quad$ and $\quad x - 1 > 0$

$\qquad x < -4$ and $\qquad x > 1$

$(\text{Pos})(\text{Neg}) < 0$

$x + 4 > 0 \quad$ and $\quad x - 1 < 0$

$\qquad x > -4$ and $\qquad x < 1$

There are no real numbers that satisfy the first conjunction, so the solution must be **$-4 < x < 1$.**

b. $x^2 - 3x - 10 < 0;\ D = \{\text{Integers}\}$

$(x - 5)(x + 2) < 0$

$(\text{Neg})(\text{Pos}) < 0$

$x - 5 < 0$ and $x + 2 > 0$

$\qquad x < 5$ and $\qquad x > -2$

$(\text{Pos})(\text{Neg}) < 0$

$x - 5 > 0$ and $x + 2 < 0$

$\qquad x > 5$ and $\qquad x < -2$

There are no integers that satisfy the second conjunction, so the solution must be **$-2 < x < 5$.**

PROBLEM SET 112

1. (a) $N_N + N_D + N_Q = 20$

(b) $5N_N + 10N_D + 25N_Q = 325$

(c) $N_Q = 2N_D$

Substitute (c) into (a) and (b) and get:

(a') $N_N + 3N_D = 20$

(b') $5N_N + 60N_D = 325$

$$\begin{array}{r} -5(\text{a'}) \quad -5N_N - 15N_D = -100 \\ (\text{b'}) \quad \underline{5N_N + 60N_D = 325} \\ 45N_D = 225 \\ N_D = \textbf{5 dimes} \end{array}$$

(c) $N_Q = 2(5) = $ **10 quarters**

(a) $N_N + (5) + (10) = 20$

$$N_N = \textbf{5 nickels}$$

2. $T = $ tens digit

$U = $ units digit

$10T + U = $ original number

$10U + T = $ reversed number

(a) $T + U = 7$

$\qquad T = 7 - U$

(b) $10U + T = 10T + U - 9$

Substitute (a) into (b) and get:

(b') $10U + (7 - U) = 10(7 - U) + U - 9$

$$9U + 7 = -9U + 61$$
$$18U = 54$$
$$U = 3$$

(a) $T = 7 - (3) = 4$

Original number = **43**

3. $S_P = P_P + M_U$

$$1800 = P_P + 0.2(1800)$$
$$P_P = 1800 - 360$$
$$P_P = \textbf{\$1440}$$

4. Downstream: $(B + W)T_D = D_D$ (a)

Upstream: $(B - W)T_U = D_U$ (b)

$T_D = 2T_U$

(a') $(B + 3)2T_U = 230$

(b') $(B - 3)T_U = 85$

$\begin{array}{r} \text{(a')} \quad 2BT_U + 6T_U = 230 \\ 2\text{(b')} \quad 2BT_U - 6T_U = 170 \\ \hline 4BT_U \qquad\quad = 400 \end{array}$

(c) $\qquad\quad BT_U = 100$

(a') $2(100) + 6T_U = 230$

$\qquad\qquad 6T_U = 30$

$\qquad\qquad T_U = \textbf{5 hr}; \ T_D = \textbf{10 hr}$

(c) $B(5) = 100$

$\qquad B = \textbf{20 mph}$

5.

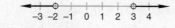

$R_F T_F = 1800; \ R_H T_H = 1200;$

$R_H = R_F + 200; \ T_F = 3T_H$

$(R_H - 200)3T_H = 1800$

$3(1200) - 600T_H = 1800$

$\qquad -600T_H = -1800$

$\qquad\qquad T_H = \textbf{3 hr}$

$T_F = \textbf{9 hr}; \ R_H = \textbf{400 mph}; \ R_F = \textbf{200 mph}$

6. $(x + 3)(x - 4) < 0; \ D = \{\text{Reals}\}$

$(\text{Neg})(\text{Pos}) < 0$

$x + 3 < 0 \quad \text{and} \ x - 4 > 0$

$\quad x < -3 \ \text{and} \qquad x > 4$

$(\text{Pos})(\text{Neg}) < 0$

$x + 3 > 0 \quad \text{and} \ x - 4 < 0$

$\quad x > -3 \ \text{and} \qquad x < 4$

There are no real numbers that satisfy the first conjunction, so the solution must be $-3 < x < 4$.

7. $(x - 6)(x + 1) < 0; \ D = \{\text{Integers}\}$

$(\text{Neg})(\text{Pos}) < 0$

$x - 6 < 0 \ \text{and} \ x + 1 > 0$

$\quad x < 6 \ \text{and} \qquad x > -1$

$(\text{Pos})(\text{Neg}) < 0$

$x - 6 > 0 \ \text{and} \ x + 1 < 0$

$\quad x > 6 \ \text{and} \qquad x < -1$

There are no integers that satisfy the second conjunction, so the solution must be $-1 < x < 6$.

8. $(x + 2)(x - 3) > 0; \ D = \{\text{Reals}\}$

$(\text{Pos})(\text{Pos}) > 0$

$x + 2 > 0 \quad \text{and} \ x - 3 > 0$

$\quad x > -2 \ \text{and} \qquad x > 3$

$(\text{Neg})(\text{Neg}) > 0$

$x + 2 < 0 \quad \text{and} \ x - 3 < 0$

$\quad x < -2 \ \text{and} \qquad x < 3$

Thus, the solution is $x > 3$ or $x < -2$.

9. $x^{1/2} + y^{1/2}$

$\dfrac{x^{1/2} - y^{-1/4}}{}$

$x + x^{1/2}y^{1/2}$

$\dfrac{\quad - x^{1/2}y^{-1/4} - y^{1/4}}{x + x^{1/2}y^{1/2} - x^{1/2}y^{-1/4} - y^{1/4}}$

10. $p^6x^6 - k^3 = (p^2x^2)^3 - (k)^3$

$= (p^2x^2 - k)(p^4x^4 + kp^2x^2 + k^2)$

11. $100N = 401.43 \ 43 \ 43 \dots$

$\dfrac{N = \quad 4.01 \ 43 \ 43 \dots}{99N = 397.42}$

$N = \dfrac{\textbf{39,742}}{\textbf{9900}}$

12. $y = x^2 + 2x + 3$

$y = (x^2 + 2x + 1) + 3 - 1$

$y = (x + 1)^2 + 2$

From this we see:

(a) Opens upward

(b) Axis of symmetry is $x = -1$

(c) y-coordinate of vertex is 2

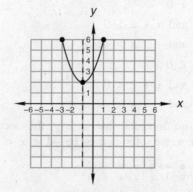

13. $-|x| + 3 \leq 0$; $D = \{\text{Reals}\}$

$$-|x| \leq -3$$
$$|x| \geq 3$$

$x \geq 3$ or $x \leq -3$

14. $x - 2 \leq 0$ or $x + 4 > 8$; $D = \{\text{Integers}\}$

$x \leq 2$ or $\quad x > 4$

15. Sets **(a)** and **(b)** are functions. Set (c) is not a function, because -4 has two images.

16. $N = 2\dfrac{1}{8} + \dfrac{1}{3}\left(5 - 2\dfrac{1}{8}\right) = \dfrac{17}{8} + \dfrac{1}{3}\left(\dfrac{40}{8} - \dfrac{17}{8}\right)$

$\qquad = \dfrac{51}{24} + \dfrac{23}{24} = \mathbf{\dfrac{37}{12}}$

17. $5x^2 + x + 4 = 0$

$$x = \frac{-(1) \pm \sqrt{(1)^2 - 4(5)(4)}}{2(5)}$$

$$x = -\frac{1}{10} \pm \frac{\sqrt{79}}{10}i$$

18. Write the equation of the given line in slope-intercept form.

$x + 3y - 4 = 0$

$$y = -\frac{1}{3}x + \frac{4}{3}$$

Since the slopes of perpendicular lines are negative reciprocals of each other,

$m_\perp = 3$

$y = 3x + b$

$-7 = 3(5) + b$

$-22 = b$

$\mathbf{y = 3x - 22}$

19. (a) $2x + y = 28$

$\qquad y = 28 - 2x$

(b) $70x - 2y = 536$

Substitute (a) into (b) and get:

(b′) $70x - 2(28 - 2x) = 536$

$\qquad\qquad\qquad\quad 74x = 592$

$\qquad\qquad\qquad\qquad x = 8$

(a) $y = 28 - 2(8) = 12$

(8, 12)

20. (a) $x - 2y = 10$

(b) $3x - z = 11$

(c) $2y - 3z = -9$

(a) + (c): $x - 3z = 1$ (d)

-3(d) + (b): $8z = 8$

$\qquad\qquad\qquad z = 1$

(d) $x - 3(1) = 1$

$\qquad\quad x = 4$

(a) $(4) - 2y = 10$

$\qquad\qquad y = -3$

(4, −3, 1)

21. (a) $2x - y = 7$

(b) $xy = 4$

$$y = \frac{4}{x}$$

Substitute (b) into (a) and get:

(a′) $\quad 2x - \left(\dfrac{4}{x}\right) = 7$

$\qquad\qquad 2x^2 - 4 = 7x$

$\qquad 2x^2 - 7x - 4 = 0$

Solve this equation by using the quadratic formula.

$$x = \frac{-(-7) \pm \sqrt{(-7)^2 - 4(2)(-4)}}{2(2)}$$

$$x = \frac{7}{4} \pm \frac{9}{4} = 4, -\frac{1}{2}$$

Substitute these values of x into (a) and solve for y.

(a) $y = 2(4) - 7 = 1$

(a) $y = 2\left(-\dfrac{1}{2}\right) - 7 = -8$

$\mathbf{(4, 1)}$ **and** $\mathbf{\left(-\dfrac{1}{2}, -8\right)}$

22. (a) $x + y + z = 1$

(b) $2x - y + z = -5$

(c) $3x + y + z = 5$

(a) + (b): $3x + 2z = -4$ (d)

(b) + (c): $5x + 2z = 0$ (e)

-1(d) + (e): $2x = 4$

$\qquad\qquad\qquad x = 2$

(d) $3(2) + 2z = -4$

$\qquad\qquad\quad z = -5$

(a) $(2) + y + (-5) = 1$

$\qquad\qquad\qquad y = 4$

(2, 4, −5)

23. $\dfrac{-3i^2 - 2i^3}{\sqrt{-3}\sqrt{-3} - \sqrt{-9}} = \dfrac{3 + 2i}{-3 - 3i} \cdot \dfrac{-3 + 3i}{-3 + 3i}$

$= \dfrac{-9 + 9i - 6i - 6}{9 + 9} = -\dfrac{5}{6} + \dfrac{1}{6}i$

24. $\dfrac{a^{x/2 - 1}y^2}{y^{x/2}a^{x/2}} = a^{-1}y^{2 - x/2}$

25. $\sqrt[3]{x^5 y}\sqrt{x^5 y^2} = x^{5/3}y^{1/3}x^{5/2}y = x^{25/6}y^{4/3}$

26. $\dfrac{\sqrt{2}}{\sqrt{7}} + \dfrac{\sqrt{7}}{\sqrt{2}} - 3\sqrt{56} = \dfrac{\sqrt{14}}{7} + \dfrac{\sqrt{14}}{2} - 6\sqrt{14}$

$= \dfrac{2\sqrt{14}}{14} + \dfrac{7\sqrt{14}}{14} - \dfrac{84\sqrt{14}}{14} = -\dfrac{75\sqrt{14}}{14}$

27. $\dfrac{3\sqrt{2} - 2}{7\sqrt{2} - 3} \cdot \dfrac{7\sqrt{2} + 3}{7\sqrt{2} + 3}$

$= \dfrac{42 + 9\sqrt{2} - 14\sqrt{2} - 6}{98 - 9} = \dfrac{36 - 5\sqrt{2}}{89}$

28. $\qquad 3x^3 + 5x^2 + 2x = 0$

$\qquad x(3x^2 + 5x + 2) = 0$

$\qquad x(3x^2 + 3x + 2x + 2) = 0$

$\qquad x(3x(x + 1) + 2(x + 1)) = 0$

$\qquad x(3x + 2)(x + 1) = 0$

$\quad x = 0 \qquad 3x + 2 = 0 \qquad x + 1 = 0$

$\qquad\qquad\qquad x = -\dfrac{2}{3} \qquad x = -1$

$0, -\dfrac{2}{3}, -1$

29. $\qquad 2x^2 - 3x - 2 = 0$

$\qquad 2x^2 - 4x + x - 2 = 0$

$\quad 2x(x - 2) + 1(x - 2) = 0$

$\qquad\quad (2x + 1)(x - 2) = 0$

$\quad 2x + 1 = 0 \qquad x - 2 = 0$

$\qquad x = -\dfrac{1}{2} \qquad x = 2$

$-\dfrac{1}{2}, 2$

30. $\qquad 3x^2 + 8x + 4 = 0$

$\qquad 3x^2 + 6x + 2x + 4 = 0$

$\quad 3x(x + 2) + 2(x + 2) = 0$

$\qquad\quad (3x + 2)(x + 2) = 0$

$\quad 3x + 2 = 0 \qquad x + 2 = 0$

$\qquad x = -\dfrac{2}{3} \qquad x = -2$

$-\dfrac{2}{3}, -2$

PRACTICE SET 113

a. $x = \ln 0.0052 \approx -5.26$

b. $e^x = 51.4$

$x = \boxed{\text{INV}}\, e^x = \ln e^x = \ln(51.4) \approx \mathbf{3.94}$

c. $\ln x = -4.16$

$x = \boxed{\text{INV}}\, \ln x = e^{\ln x} = e^{-4.16} \approx 0.0156$

$= \mathbf{1.56 \times 10^{-2}}$

d. $\log x = -4.16$

$x = \boxed{\text{INV}}\, \log x = 10^{\log x} = 10^{-4.16}$

$\approx \mathbf{6.92 \times 10^{-5}}$

e. $\dfrac{(0.000612)(576)}{0.0512 \times 10^{-14}} = \dfrac{\ln(0.000612)\ln(576)}{\ln(0.0512 \times 10^{-14})}$

$= \dfrac{e^{-7.40}e^{6.36}}{e^{-35.21}} = e^{-7.40}e^{6.36}e^{+35.21} = e^{34.17}$

$\approx \mathbf{6.92 \times 10^{14}}$

PROBLEM SET 113

1. (a) $N_N + N_D + N_Q = 19$

   (b) $5N_N + 10N_D + 25N_Q = 200$

   (c) $N_N = 2N_D$

   Substitute (c) into (a) and (b) and get:

   (a') $3N_D + N_Q = 19$

   $\qquad\qquad N_Q = 19 - 3N_D$

   (b') $20N_D + 25N_Q = 200$

   Substitute (a') into (b') and get:

   (b'') $20N_D + 25(19 - 3N_D) = 200$

   $\qquad\qquad\qquad -55N_D = -275$

   $\qquad\qquad\qquad\quad N_D = \mathbf{5\ dimes}$

   (a') $N_Q = 19 - 3(5) = \mathbf{4\ quarters}$

   (a) $N_N + (5) + (4) = 19$

   $\qquad\qquad N_N = \mathbf{10\ nickels}$

2. $\dfrac{R_1}{R_2} = \dfrac{B_1(M_2)^2}{B_2(M_1)^2}$

   $\dfrac{10}{3} = \dfrac{4(20)^2}{B_2(2)^2}$

   $B_2 = \mathbf{120\ blues}$

3. (a) $0.7P_N + 0.6D_N = 126$

(b) $P_N + D_N = 200$

Substitute $D_N = 200 - P_N$ into (a) and get:

(a′) $0.7P_N + 0.6(200 - P_N) = 126$

$$0.1P_N = 6$$
$$P_N = 60$$

(b) $(60) + D_N = 200$

$$D_N = 140$$

60 mL 70%, 140 mL 60%

4.

$R_C T_C = R_D T_D$; $T_C = 8$; $T_D = 12$;

$R_D = R_C - 20$

$R_C(8) = (R_C - 20)12$

$8R_C = 12R_C - 240$

$-4R_C = -240$

$R_C =$ **60 mph**

$R_D =$ **40 mph**; $D_C = D_D =$ **480 miles**

5. $\dfrac{V_1}{T_1} = \dfrac{V_2}{T_2}$

$\dfrac{1000}{1700} = \dfrac{2000}{T_2}$

$T_2 =$ **3400 K**

6. (a) **−4.68**

(b) **4.14**

7. (a) e^{5163}

(b) **136.77**

8. $AE \times \overrightarrow{SF} = AB$

$6 \times \overrightarrow{SF} = 24$

$\overrightarrow{SF} = 4$

$AC = AD \times \overrightarrow{SF}$

$AC = 4(4) =$ **16 meters**

9. $(x + 2)(x - 3) < 0$; $D = \{\text{Reals}\}$

(Neg)(Pos) < 0

$x + 2 < 0$ and $x - 3 > 0$

$x < -2$ and $\quad x > 3$

(Pos)(Neg) < 0

$x + 2 > 0$ and $x - 3 < 0$

$x > -2$ and $\quad\quad x < 3$

There are no real numbers that satisfy the first conjunction, so the solution must be $-2 < x < 3$.

10. $(x - 3)(x + 2) \geq 0$; $D = \{\text{Integers}\}$

(Pos)(Pos) ≥ 0

$x - 3 \geq 0$ and $x + 2 \geq 0$

$x \geq 3$ and $\quad\quad x \geq -2$

(Neg)(Neg) ≥ 0

$x - 3 \leq 0$ and $x + 2 \leq 0$

$x \leq 3$ and $\quad\quad x \leq -2$

Thus the solution is $x \geq 3$ or $x \leq -2$.

11. $(x - 4)(x + 2) \leq 0$; $D = \{\text{Integers}\}$

(Neg)(Pos) ≤ 0

$x - 4 \leq 0$ and $x + 2 \geq 0$

$x \leq 4$ and $\quad\quad x \geq -2$

(Pos)(Neg) ≤ 0

$x - 4 \geq 0$ and $x + 2 \leq 0$

$x \geq 4$ and $\quad\quad x \leq -2$

There are no integers that satisfy the second conjunction, so the solution must be $-2 \leq x \leq 4$.

12. $|x| - 1 > 0$; $D = \{\text{Integers}\}$

$|x| > 1$

$x > 1$ or $x < -1$

13. $7 \leq x - 2 < 10$; $D = \{\text{Reals}\}$

$9 \leq x < 12$

14.

$$\dfrac{x^{1/3} + y^{2/3}}{x + x^{2/3}y^{2/3}}$$

$$\dfrac{x^{2/3} + y^{1/3}}{+ x^{1/3}y^{1/3} + y}$$

$$x + x^{1/3}y^{1/3} + x^{2/3}y^{2/3} + y$$

15. $8p^6k^{15} - x^3m^6 = (2p^2k^5)^3 - (xm^2)^3$
$= (2p^2k^5 - xm^2)(4p^4k^{10} + 2p^2k^5xm^2 + x^2m^4)$

16. $100N = 0.316\ 16\ 16\ \ldots$
$N = 0.003\ 16\ 16\ \ldots$

$\overline{99N = 0.313}$

$N = \dfrac{\mathbf{313}}{\mathbf{99,000}}$

17. $-y = x^2 - 4x + 1$
$-y = (x^2 - 4x + 4) + 1 - 4$
$-y = (x - 2)^2 - 3$
$y = -(x - 2)^2 + 3$

From this we see:

(a) Opens downward

(b) Axis of symmetry is $x = 2$

(c) y-coordinate of vertex is 3

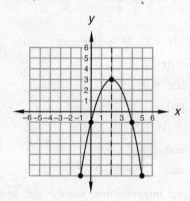

18. $N = 2 + \dfrac{2}{11}\left(4\dfrac{1}{6} - 2\right)$

$= 2 + \dfrac{2}{11}\left(\dfrac{25}{6} - \dfrac{12}{6}\right)$

$= \dfrac{66}{33} + \dfrac{13}{33} = \dfrac{\mathbf{79}}{\mathbf{33}}$

19. $3x^2 - x - 7 = 0$

$x^2 - \dfrac{1}{3}x = \dfrac{7}{3}$

$\left(x^2 - \dfrac{1}{3}x + \dfrac{1}{36}\right) = \dfrac{84}{36} + \dfrac{1}{36}$

$\left(x - \dfrac{1}{6}\right)^2 = \dfrac{85}{36}$

$x - \dfrac{1}{6} = \pm\dfrac{\sqrt{85}}{6}$

$x = \dfrac{1}{6} \pm \dfrac{\sqrt{85}}{6}$

20. (a) $1\dfrac{1}{5}x + \dfrac{2}{3}y = 30$

(b) $-0.18x - 0.02y = -3.78$

(a$'$) $18x + 10y = 450$

(b$'$) $\underline{-18x - 2y = -378}$

$ 8y = 72$

$ y = 9$

(a$'$) $18x + 10(9) = 450$

$ 18x = 360$

$ x = 20$

(20, 9)

21. (a) $x^2 + y^2 = 4$

(b) $3x - y = 2$

$ y = 3x - 2$

Substitute (b) into (a) and get:

(a$'$) $ x^2 + (3x - 2)^2 = 4$

$x^2 + 9x^2 - 12x + 4 = 4$

$ 10x^2 - 12x = 0$

$ 2x(5x - 6) = 0$

$ x = 0,\ \dfrac{6}{5}$

Substitute these values of x into (b) and solve for y.

(b) $y = 3(0) - 2$

$ y = -2$

(b) $y = 3\left(\dfrac{6}{5}\right) - 2$

$ y = \dfrac{8}{5}$

(0, –2) and $\left(\dfrac{\mathbf{6}}{\mathbf{5}}, \dfrac{\mathbf{8}}{\mathbf{5}}\right)$

22. (a) $x - 4y = -15$

(b) $3x + z = 20$

(c) $2y - z = 5$

(b) + (c): $3x + 2y = 25$ (d)

$2(d) + (a): 7x = 35$

$ x = 5$

(d) $3(5) + 2y = 25$

$ y = 5$

(b) $3(5) + z = 20$

$ z = 5$

(5, 5, 5)

23. (a) $x - 2y - z = -8$

(b) $3x - y - 2z = -5$

(c) $x + y + z = 9$

(a) + (c): $2x - y = 1$ (d)

(b) + 2(c): $\dfrac{5x + y = 13}{7x \quad\ \ = 14}$ (e)

$\qquad\qquad\qquad x = 2$

(e) $5(2) + y = 13$

$\qquad\qquad y = 3$

(c) $(2) + (3) + z = 9$

$\qquad\qquad\qquad z = 4$

(2, 3, 4)

24. $\dfrac{2i^3 - i}{-\sqrt{-3}\sqrt{-3} + 3} = -\dfrac{3i}{6} = -\dfrac{1}{2}i$

25. $\dfrac{\sqrt{2} - 5}{2\sqrt{2} - 4} \cdot \dfrac{2\sqrt{2} + 4}{2\sqrt{2} + 4}$

$= \dfrac{4 + 4\sqrt{2} - 10\sqrt{2} - 20}{8 - 16}$

$= \dfrac{-16 - 6\sqrt{2}}{-8} = \dfrac{\mathbf{8 + 3\sqrt{2}}}{\mathbf{4}}$

26. $\sqrt[6]{xy^3}\sqrt[3]{xy^2} = x^{1/6}y^{1/2}x^{1/3}y^{2/3} = \mathbf{x^{1/2}y^{7/6}}$

27. $\dfrac{2}{\sqrt{3}} + \dfrac{2\sqrt{3}}{2} - 3\sqrt{48} = \dfrac{2\sqrt{3}}{3} + \sqrt{3} - 12\sqrt{3}$

$= \dfrac{2\sqrt{3}}{3} + \dfrac{3\sqrt{3}}{3} - \dfrac{36\sqrt{3}}{3} = \mathbf{-\dfrac{31\sqrt{3}}{3}}$

28. $\qquad 2x^3 + x^2 - 3x = 0$

$\qquad x(2x^2 + x - 3) = 0$

$\qquad x(2x^2 - 2x + 3x - 3) = 0$

$\qquad x(2x(x - 1) + 3(x - 1)) = 0$

$\qquad\qquad x(2x + 3)(x - 1) = 0$

$x = 0 \qquad 2x + 3 = 0 \qquad x - 1 = 0$

$\qquad\qquad x = -\dfrac{3}{2} \qquad\quad x = 1$

$\mathbf{0, -\dfrac{3}{2}, 1}$

29. $\qquad 3x^2 - x - 2 = 0$

$\qquad 3x^2 - 3x + 2x - 2 = 0$

$\qquad 3x(x - 1) + 2(x - 1) = 0$

$\qquad\qquad (3x + 2)(x - 1) = 0$

$3x + 2 = 0 \qquad x - 1 = 0$

$\quad x = -\dfrac{2}{3} \qquad\qquad x = 1$

$\mathbf{-\dfrac{2}{3}, 1}$

30. $\qquad 3x^3 + 7x^2 + 2x = 0$

$\qquad x(3x^2 + 7x + 2) = 0$

$\qquad x(3x^2 + 6x + x + 2) = 0$

$\qquad x(3x(x + 2) + 1(x + 2)) = 0$

$\qquad\qquad x(3x + 1)(x + 2) = 0$

$x = 0 \quad 3x + 1 = 0 \qquad x + 2 = 0$

$\qquad\qquad x = -\dfrac{1}{3} \qquad\quad x = -2$

$\mathbf{0, -\dfrac{1}{3}, -2}$

Practice Set 114

Region A (This region includes all points on or above the line that lie outside the circle.)

Problem Set 114

1. Consecutive even integers: $N,\ N + 2,\ N + 4$

$\qquad N(N + 4) = 8(N + 2) + 16$

$\qquad N^2 + 4N = 8N + 32$

$\quad N^2 - 4N - 32 = 0$

$\quad (N + 4)(N - 8) = 0$

$\qquad\qquad\qquad N = -4, 8$

The desired integers are **–4, –2, 0** and **8, 10, 12.**

2. $0.2(240) + 1(D_N) = 0.52(240 + D_N)$

$\qquad 48 + D_N = 124.8 + 0.52D_N$

$\qquad 0.48D_N = 76.8$

$\qquad\qquad D_N = \mathbf{160\ mL}$

3.

$$\overrightarrow{\underset{4800}{D_F}}$$

$$\overset{D_S}{\underset{2000}{\vdash\dashv}}$$

$R_F T_F = 4800; \quad R_S T_S = 2000;$

$T_F = T_S + 1; \quad R_F = 2R_S$

$2R_S(T_S + 1) = 4800$

$2(2000) + 2R_S = 4800$

$\quad\quad\quad 2R_S = 800$

$\quad\quad\quad\quad R_S = \textbf{400 mph}$

$R_F = \textbf{800 mph}; \quad T_S = \textbf{5 hr}; \quad T_F = \textbf{6 hr}$

4. Downstream: $(B + W)T_D = D_D$ (a)

Upstream: $(B - W)T_U = D_U$ (b)

$T_U = 3T_D$

(a′) $BT_D + 4T_D = 34$

(b′) $3BT_D - 12T_D = 54$

$3(\text{a}') + (\text{b}'): 6BT_D = 156$

$\quad\quad\quad\quad\quad BT_D = 26$ (c)

(a′) $(26) + 4T_D = 34$

$\quad\quad\quad\quad T_D = 2$

(c) $B(2) = 26$

$\quad\quad B = \textbf{13 mph}$

5. $T = $ tens digit

$U = $ units digit

$10T + U = $ original number

$10U + T = $ reversed number

(a) $T + U = 8$

$\quad\quad T = 8 - U$

(b) $10U + T = 10T + U + 54$

Substitute (a) into (b) and get:

(b′) $10U + (8 - U) = 10(8 - U) + U + 54$

$\quad\quad\quad 9U + 8 = -9U + 134$

$\quad\quad\quad\quad\quad 18U = 126$

$\quad\quad\quad\quad\quad\quad U = 7$

(a) $T = 8 - (7) = 1$

Original number = **17**

6. **Region A** (This region includes all points on or above both the line and the parabola.)

7. **Region A** (This region includes all points on or above the parabola and all points below the line.)

8. **Region B** (This region includes all points on or inside the circle and all points on or above the line.)

9. (a) **−4.77**

(b) **4.47**

10. (a) e^{9185}

(b) **1541.70**

11. $A_{\text{Square}} = s^2 = 9 \text{ cm}^2$

$\quad\quad\quad\quad s = 3 \text{ cm}$

$AB = 3 \text{ cm} + \sqrt{7^2 - 3^2} \text{ cm} = \left(\mathbf{3 + 2\sqrt{10}}\right) \textbf{ cm}$

12. $\quad 7.15 \times 10^{-8} = \mathbf{10^{-7.15}}$

$\log 7.15 \times 10^{-8} = \textbf{−7.15}$

13. $\quad S_P = P_P + M_U$

$\quad 140 = P_P + 0.2(140)$

$\quad \mathbf{\$112} = P_P$

14. $(x + 4)(x - 1) \geq 0; \quad D = \{\text{Integers}\}$

(Pos)(Pos) ≥ 0

$x + 4 \geq 0 \quad$ and $\quad x - 1 \geq 0$

$\quad x \geq -4 \quad$ and $\quad\quad x \geq 1$

(Neg)(Neg) ≥ 0

$x + 4 \leq 0 \quad$ and $\quad x - 1 \leq 0$

$\quad x \leq -4 \quad$ and $\quad\quad x \leq 1$

Thus, the solution is $x \geq 1$ or $x \leq -4$.

$$\xleftarrow{\quad}\overset{\bullet\quad\bullet\quad\,|\quad\,|\quad\,|\quad\,|\quad\bullet\quad\bullet}{\underset{-5\;-4\;-3\;-2\;-1\;\;0\;\;1\;\;2}{\xrightarrow{\quad\quad\quad\quad\quad\quad\quad}}}$$

15. $(x - 4)(x + 1) \leq 0; \quad D = \{\text{Integers}\}$

(Neg)(Pos) ≤ 0

$x - 4 \leq 0$ and $x + 1 \geq 0$

$\quad x \leq 4 \quad$ and $\quad\quad x \geq -1$

(Pos)(Neg) ≤ 0

$x - 4 \geq 0$ and $x + 1 \leq 0$

$\quad x \geq 4 \quad$ and $\quad\quad x \leq -1$

There are no integers that satisfy the second conjunction, so the solution must be $-1 \leq x \leq 4$.

$$\xleftarrow{\quad}\overset{|\quad\bullet\quad\bullet\quad\bullet\quad\bullet\quad\bullet\quad\bullet\quad|}{\underset{-2\;-1\;\;0\;\;1\;\;2\;\;3\;\;4\;\;5}{\xrightarrow{\quad\quad\quad\quad\quad\quad\quad}}}$$

16. $-|x| - 3 > -7; \quad D = \{\text{Integers}\}$

$\qquad -|x| > -4$

$\qquad |x| < 4$

$\qquad x < 4 \text{ and } x > -4$

```
<———+——•——•——•——•——•——•——•——+———>
   -4 -3 -2 -1  0  1  2  3  4
```

17. $6 \leq x - 4 < 8; \quad D = \{\text{Integers}\}$

$\qquad 10 \leq x < 12$

```
<———+——+——•——•——+———>
    8  9 10 11 12
```

18. $100N = 0.1056\ 56\ 56 \ldots$

$\qquad \underline{N = 0.0010\ 56\ 56 \ldots}$

$\qquad 99N = 0.1046$

$\qquad N = \dfrac{1046}{990{,}000}$

19. $y = x^2 - 4x + 7$

$\qquad y = (x^2 - 4x + 4) + 7 - 4$

$\qquad y = (x - 2)^2 + 3$

From this we see:

(a) Opens upward

(b) Axis of symmetry is $x = 2$

(c) y-coordinate of vertex is 3

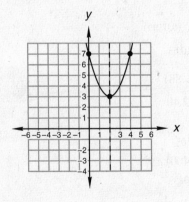

20. $N = 4\dfrac{1}{2} + \dfrac{3}{8}\left(6\dfrac{1}{4} - 4\dfrac{1}{2}\right)$

$\qquad = \dfrac{9}{2} + \dfrac{3}{8}\left(\dfrac{25}{4} - \dfrac{18}{4}\right)$

$\qquad = \dfrac{9}{2} + \dfrac{21}{32}$

$\qquad = \dfrac{144}{32} + \dfrac{21}{32} = \dfrac{165}{32}$

21. (a) $2\dfrac{1}{3}x + \dfrac{1}{5}y = 10$

(b) $0.03x - 0.03y = -0.36$

(a') $35x + 3y = 150$

(b') $\underline{3x - 3y = -36}$

$\qquad 38x \qquad = 114$

$\qquad\qquad x = 3$

(b') $3(3) - 3y = -36$

$\qquad\qquad y = 15$

(3, 15)

22. (a) $3x - z = 8$

(b) $2x - 2y = -4$

(c) $2y + 3z = 2$

(b) + (c): $2x + 3z = -2$ (d)

3(a) + (d): $11x = 22$

$\qquad\qquad x = 2$

(d) $2(2) + 3z = -2$

$\qquad\qquad z = -2$

(c) $2y + 3(-2) = 2$

$\qquad\qquad y = 4$

(2, 4, –2)

23. (a) $x + y = 6$

(b) $xy = -1$

$\qquad y = -\dfrac{1}{x}$

Substitute (b) into (a) and get:

(a') $\quad x + \left(-\dfrac{1}{x}\right) = 6$

$\qquad\qquad x^2 - 1 = 6x$

$\qquad\qquad x^2 - 6x - 1 = 0$

Solve this equation by using the quadratic formula.

$x = \dfrac{-(-6) \pm \sqrt{(-6)^2 - 4(1)(-1)}}{2(1)} = 3 \pm \sqrt{10}$

Substitute these values of x into (a) and solve for y.

(a) $y = 6 - (3 + \sqrt{10}) = 3 - \sqrt{10}$

(a) $y = 6 - (3 - \sqrt{10}) = 3 + \sqrt{10}$

$\mathbf{(3 + \sqrt{10},\ 3 - \sqrt{10})} \text{ and } \mathbf{(3 - \sqrt{10},\ 3 + \sqrt{10})}$

24. (a) $x - y + z = 3$

(b) $2x - y + 2z = 9$

(c) $-x + y + z = 1$

-1(a) + (b): $x + z = 6$ (d)

(b) + (c): $x + 3z = 10$ (e)

$-$(d) $\quad -x - z = -6$

(e) $\quad \underline{x + 3z = 10}$

$\qquad\qquad 2z = 4$

$\qquad\qquad z = 2$

(d) $x + (2) = 6$

$\qquad x = 4$

(a) $(4) - y + (2) = 3$

$\qquad\qquad y = 3$

(4, 3, 2)

25. There is never an exact solution to these problems. One possible solution is given here.

$O = mI + b$

Use the graph to find the slope.

$m = \dfrac{225}{10} = 22.5$

$O = 22.5I + b$

Use the point (85, 400) for I and O.

$400 = 22.5(85) + b$

$-1513 = b$

$O = 22.5I - 1513$

26. $\dfrac{i^3 - i^2}{i^5 + 2} = \dfrac{-i + 1}{i + 2} \cdot \dfrac{i - 2}{i - 2}$

$= \dfrac{1 + 2i + i - 2}{-1 - 4} = \dfrac{1}{5} - \dfrac{3}{5}i$

27. $\dfrac{\sqrt{5}}{2\sqrt{2}} + \dfrac{4\sqrt{2}}{\sqrt{5}} - 3\sqrt{40}$

$= \dfrac{\sqrt{10}}{4} + \dfrac{4\sqrt{10}}{5} - 6\sqrt{10}$

$= \dfrac{5\sqrt{10}}{20} + \dfrac{16\sqrt{10}}{20} - \dfrac{120\sqrt{10}}{20}$

$= -\dfrac{\mathbf{99\sqrt{10}}}{\mathbf{20}}$

28. $\sqrt{x - 15} = 5 - \sqrt{x}$

$x - 15 = 25 - 10\sqrt{x} + x$

$-40 = -10\sqrt{x}$

$4 = \sqrt{x}$

$16 = x$

Check: $\sqrt{16 - 15} = 5 - \sqrt{16}$

$1 = 1$

29. $\qquad 5x^3 + 7x^2 + 2x = 0$

$x(5x^2 + 7x + 2) = 0$

$x(5x^2 + 5x + 2x + 2) = 0$

$x[5x(x + 1) + 2(x + 1)] = 0$

$x(5x + 2)(x + 1) = 0$

$x = 0 \qquad 5x + 2 = 0 \qquad x + 1 = 0$

$\qquad\qquad x = -\dfrac{2}{5} \qquad x = -1$

$\mathbf{0, -\dfrac{2}{5}, -1}$

30. $x^{1/2} - y^{-1/2}$

$\dfrac{x^{1/2} - y^{-1/2}}{x - x^{1/2}y^{-1/2}}$

$\underline{\quad - x^{1/2}y^{-1/2} + y^{-1}\quad}$

$\mathbf{x - 2x^{1/2}y^{-1/2} + y^{-1}}$

Practice Set 115

a. $\quad 27 = 10^{x + 5}$

$10^{1.43} = 10^{x + 5}$

$1.43 = x + 5$

$-3.57 = x$

b. $A_t = Pe^{rt}$

$A_9 = (980)e^{(0.07)(9)}$

$A_9 = 980\, e^{0.63}$

$A_9 \approx 980(1.88)$

$A_9 = \mathbf{\$1842.40}$

c. $\quad A_t = A_0 e^{kt}$

$(1600) = (400)\, e^{k(3)}$

$4 = e^{3k}$

$e^{1.39} = e^{3k}$

$1.39 = 3k$

$0.46 \approx k$

$A_{10} = 400\, e^{0.46(10)}$

$A_{10} = 400\, e^{4.6}$

$A_{10} \approx 400(99.48)$

$A_{10} = \mathbf{39{,}792\ rabbits}$

PROBLEM SET 115

1. Potassium: $\qquad 1 \times 39 = 39$

Manganese (Mn): $\qquad 1 \times 55 = 55$

Oxygen: $\qquad 4 \times 16 = 64$

Total: $\qquad 39 + 55 + 64 = 158$

$$\frac{\text{Oxygen}}{790} = \frac{64}{158}$$

Oxygen = **320 grams**

2.

$R_B T_B + R_S T_S = 280$; $R_B = 20$;

$R_S = 45$; $T_B + T_S = 9$

$20T_B + 45(9 - T_B) = 280$

$\qquad -25T_B = -125$

$\qquad\qquad T_B = 5$

$T_S = 9 - (5) = 4$

$D_B = R_B T_B = 20(5) =$ **100 miles**

$D_S = R_S T_S = 45(4) =$ **180 miles**

3.

$R_H T_H = 1200$; $R_B T_B = 480$;

$T_H = T_B + 1$; $R_H = 2R_B$

$2R_B(T_B + 1) = 1200$

$2(480) + 2R_B = 1200$

$\qquad\quad 2R_B = 240$

$\qquad\quad\ R_B =$ **120 mph**

$R_H =$ **240 mph**; $T_B =$ **4 hr**; $T_H =$ **5 hr**

4. (a) $N_N + N_D + N_Q = 14$

(b) $5N_N + 10N_D + 25N_Q = 105$

(c) $N_D = 3N_Q$

Substitute (c) into (a) and (b) and get:

(a') $N_N + 4N_Q = 14$

(b') $5N_N + 55N_Q = 105$

$-5(a') + (b')$: $35N_Q = 35$

$\qquad\qquad\qquad N_Q =$ **1 quarter**

(a') $N_N + 4(1) = 14$

$\qquad\qquad N_N =$ **10 nickels**

(a) $(10) + N_D + (1) = 14$

$\qquad\qquad\qquad N_D =$ **3 dimes**

5. T = tens digit

U = units digit

$10T + U$ = original number

(a) $10T + U = 4(T + U)$

(b) $4U = T + 14$

$\qquad T = 4U - 14$

Substitute (b) into (a) and get:

(a') $10(4U - 14) + U = 4(4U - 14) + 4U$

$\qquad\quad 41U - 140 = 20U - 56$

$\qquad\qquad\quad 21U = 84$

$\qquad\qquad\qquad U = 4$

(b) $T = 4(4) - 14 = 2$

Original number = **24**

6. **−4.88**

7. **4.53**

8. $10^{1.53} = 10^{x + 3}$

$\quad 1.53 = x + 3$

$-1.47 = x$

9. $10^{3.412} \approx$ **2582.26**

10. $\dfrac{(e^{-7.89})(e^{6.18})}{(e^{-39.63})} = e^{-7.89 + 6.18 + 39.63}$

$= e^{37.92} \approx$ **2.94 × 10^{16}**

11. $A_t = Pe^{rt}$

$A_9 = 100e^{0.09(9)}$

$A_9 =$ **\$224.79**

12. $\qquad A_t = A_0 e^{kt}$

$60{,}000 = 16{,}000e^{k(3)}$

$\qquad 3.75 = e^{3k}$

$\qquad 1.32 \approx 3k$

$\qquad 0.44 = k$

$A_{10} = 16{,}000e^{0.44(10)} \approx$ **1,303,214 inhabitants**

13. $H = \sqrt{\left(\dfrac{s}{2}\right)^2 + \left(\dfrac{s}{2}\right)^2} = \dfrac{s\sqrt{2}}{2}$ **units**

$A_{HEFG} = H^2 = \left(\dfrac{s\sqrt{2}}{2}\right)^2 = \dfrac{s^2}{2}$ **units^2**

14. **Region C** (This region includes all points on or inside the circle and on or below the parabola.)

15. $(x + 5)(x - 2) > 0$; $D = \{\text{Reals}\}$

(Pos)(Pos) > 0

$x + 5 > 0$ and $x - 2 > 0$

$\quad x > -5$ and $\quad\quad x > 2$

(Neg)(Neg) > 0

$x + 5 < 0$ and $x - 2 < 0$

$\quad x < -5$ and $\quad\quad x < 2$

Thus, the solution is $x > 2$ or $x < -5$.

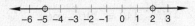

16. $(x + 5)(x + 2) < 0$; $D = \{\text{Reals}\}$

(Neg)(Pos) < 0

$x + 5 < 0$ and $x + 2 > 0$

$\quad x < -5$ and $\quad\quad x > -2$

(Pos)(Neg) < 0

$x + 5 > 0$ and $x + 2 < 0$

$\quad x > -5$ and $\quad\quad x < -2$

There are no real numbers that satisfy the first conjunction, so the solution must be $-5 < x < -2$.

17. $|x| + 2 \le 4$; $D = \{\text{Integers}\}$

$\quad |x| \le 2$

$x \le 2$ and $x \ge -2$

18. $6 < x - 5 < 10$; $D = \{\text{Integers}\}$

$\quad 11 < x < 15$

19. $(x^{1/4} - y^{-1/4})^2$

$\quad x^{1/4} - y^{-1/4}$

$\quad x^{1/4} - y^{-1/4}$

$\overline{\quad x^{1/2} - x^{1/4}y^{-1/4}}$

$\quad\quad - x^{1/4}y^{-1/4} + y^{-1/2}$

$\overline{x^{1/2} - 2x^{1/4}y^{-1/4} + y^{-1/2}}$

20. $x^3m^{15} - 8p^3y^6 = (xm^5)^3 - (2py^2)^3$
$\quad = (xm^5 - 2py^2)(x^2m^{10} + 2xm^5py^2 + 4p^2y^4)$

21. $100N = 104.747\ 47\ 47\ \ldots$

$\quad\underline{\quad N = \quad\ 1.047\ 47\ 47\ \ldots}$

$\quad 99N = 103.7$

$\quad\quad N = \dfrac{1037}{990}$

22. $y = x^2 + 2x + 1$

$y = (x^2 + 2x + 1) + 1 - 1$

$y = (x + 1)^2$

From this we see:

(a) Opens upward

(b) Axis of symmetry is $x = -1$

(c) y-coordinate of vertex is 0

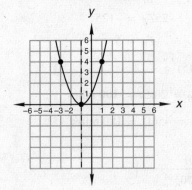

23. $N = 5\dfrac{2}{3} + \dfrac{1}{10}\left(6\dfrac{1}{2} - 5\dfrac{2}{3}\right)$

$\quad = \dfrac{17}{3} + \dfrac{1}{10}\left(\dfrac{39}{6} - \dfrac{34}{6}\right)$

$\quad = \dfrac{68}{12} + \dfrac{1}{12} = \dfrac{23}{4}$

24. (a) $1\dfrac{2}{3}x - 2\dfrac{1}{4}y = -7$

(b) $-0.2x + 0.05y = -1.8$

(a') $\quad 20x - 27y = -84$

(b') $\underline{-20x + \ 5y = -180}$

$\quad\quad\quad\quad -22y = -264$

$\quad\quad\quad\quad\quad\quad y = 12$

(b') $-20x + 5(12) = -180$

$\quad\quad\quad\quad -20x = -240$

$\quad\quad\quad\quad\quad\ x = 12$

$(12, 12)$

25. (a) $4x - z = 12$

(b) $x - 3y = -10$

(c) $3y + z = 8$

(a) + (c): $4x + 3y = 20$ (d)

(b) + (d): $5x = 10$

$x = 2$

(d) $4(2) + 3y = 20$

$y = 4$

(c) $3(4) + z = 8$

$z = -4$

(2, 4, –4)

26. (a) $x + y - z = 4$

(b) $2x + y + z = 10$

(c) $3x + y + z = 14$

(a) + (b): $3x + 2y = 14$ (d)

(a) + (c): $4x + 2y = 18$ (e)

-1(d) + (e): $x = 4$

(d) $3(4) + 2y = 14$

$y = 1$

(b) $2(4) + (1) + z = 10$

$z = 1$

(4, 1, 1)

27. $-3 - 2i - (-2) + (-1) - 3i + 2i - 6$

$= \mathbf{-8 - 3i}$

28. $\dfrac{4\sqrt{2} + 1}{1 - 3\sqrt{2}} \cdot \dfrac{1 + 3\sqrt{2}}{1 + 3\sqrt{2}}$

$= \dfrac{4\sqrt{2} + 24 + 1 + 3\sqrt{2}}{1 - 18} = \dfrac{\mathbf{-25 - 7\sqrt{2}}}{\mathbf{17}}$

29. $3x^2 - x - 6 = 0$

$x^2 - \dfrac{1}{3}x = 2$

$\left(x^2 - \dfrac{1}{3}x + \dfrac{1}{36}\right) = \dfrac{72}{36} + \dfrac{1}{36}$

$\left(x - \dfrac{1}{6}\right)^2 = \dfrac{73}{36}$

$x - \dfrac{1}{6} = \pm\dfrac{\sqrt{73}}{6}$

$x = \dfrac{1}{6} \pm \dfrac{\sqrt{73}}{6}$

30. $3x^2 + 2x - 8 = 0$

$3x^2 + 6x - 4x - 8 = 0$

$3x(x + 2) - 4(x + 2) = 0$

$(3x - 4)(x + 2) = 0$

$3x - 4 = 0 \qquad x + 2 = 0$

$x = \dfrac{4}{3} \qquad x = -2$

$\dfrac{4}{3}, \mathbf{-2}$

PRACTICE SET 116

a. $\boxed{7\ |\ 6\ |\ 5} = 7 \cdot 6 \cdot 5 = \mathbf{210}$

b. There are 36 possible outcomes in the sample space when rolling two dice. Six of these outcomes add to 7. Thus,

$$P(7) = \dfrac{6}{36} = \dfrac{1}{6}$$

There are also only 6 outcomes with a total greater than nine, so the probability of rolling a total greater than nine is equal to

$$P(>9) = \dfrac{6}{36} = \dfrac{1}{6}$$

Thus, the probability for the given sequence of events is

$$P(7) \cdot P(>9) = \dfrac{1}{6} \cdot \dfrac{1}{6} = \dfrac{\mathbf{1}}{\mathbf{36}}$$

PROBLEM SET 116

1. Multiples of 6: $6N,\ 6(N + 1),\ 6(N + 2)$

$6(6N + 6N + 12) = 10(6N + 6) - 84$

$72N + 72 = 60N - 24$

$12N = -96$

$N = -8$

The desired integers are **–48, –42,** and **–36.**

2. $\dfrac{V_1}{T_1} = \dfrac{V_2}{T_2}$

$\dfrac{400}{800} = \dfrac{200}{T_2}$

$T_2 = \mathbf{400\ K}$

3. Downstream: $(B + W)T_D = D_D$ (a)

Upstream: $(B - W)T_U = D_U$ (b)

(a') $(B + W)5 = 65$

(b') $(B - W)8 = 56$

$8(a') + 5(b')$: $80B = 800$

$$B = \textbf{10 mph}$$

(a') $(50) + 5W = 65$

$$W = \textbf{3 mph}$$

4. Equal ratio method:

$$\frac{T_1}{T_2} = \frac{R_1(F_1)^2}{R_2(F_2)^2}$$

$$\frac{1000}{T_2} = \frac{2(1)^2}{1(2)^2}$$

$$T_2 = \textbf{2000 tomatoes}$$

Variation method:

$$T = kRF^2$$

$$1000 = k(2)(1)^2$$

$$500 = k$$

$$T = 500(1)(2)^2$$

$$T = \textbf{2000 tomatoes}$$

5. T = tens digit

U = units digit

$10T + U$ = original number

(a) $10T + U = 2(T + U) + 7$

(b) $U = 3T + 3$

Substitute (b) into (a) and get:

(a') $10T + (3T + 3) = 2T + 2(3T + 3) + 7$

$$13T + 3 = 8T + 13$$

$$5T = 10$$

$$T = 2$$

(b) $U = 3(2) + 3 = 9$

Original number = **29**

6. (a) **−4.95**

(b) $\textbf{5.86} \times \textbf{10}^{-3}$

(c) $10^{1.92} \approx 10^{x+4}$

$$1.92 = x + 4$$

$$\textbf{−2.08} = x$$

7. $\dfrac{(e^{-7.40})(e^{6.36})}{(e^{-35.21})} = e^{-7.40 + 6.36 + 35.21}$

$= e^{34.17} \approx \textbf{6.92} \times \textbf{10}^{14}$

8. (a) pH $= -\log H^+$

pH $= -\log 0.00204$

pH $\approx \textbf{2.69}$

(b) pH $= -\log H^+$

$$10^{-pH} = H^+$$

$$10^{-3.2} = H^+$$

$$H^+ \approx \textbf{6.31} \times \textbf{10}^{-4} \, \frac{\textbf{mole}}{\textbf{liter}}$$

9. $A_t = Pe^{rt}$

$A_7 = 1400e^{0.11(7)} = \textbf{\$3023.67}$

10. $A_t = A_0 e^{kt}$

$$1{,}200{,}000 = 400{,}000e^{k(3)}$$

$$3 = e^{3k}$$

$$1.10 \approx 3k$$

$$0.37 = k$$

$A_8 = 400{,}000e^{0.37(8)} = \textbf{7,719,188 paramecia}$

11. $\boxed{9 \mid 8 \mid 7 \mid 6 \mid 5} = \textbf{15,120}$

12. $\boxed{9 \mid 9 \mid 9 \mid 10 \mid 10 \mid 10 \mid 10} = \textbf{7,290,000}$

13. $m\angle BAC = 180 - 35 - 35 = 110°$

$$m\angle 3 = 180 - 110 = 70°$$

$$m\angle 4 = 180 - 35 = 145°$$

$$m\angle 3 + m\angle 4 = 70 + 145 = \textbf{215°}$$

14. **Region A** (This region includes all points on or above the line and on or above the parabola.)

15. $x^2 + 2x - 3 \geq 0$; D = {Integers}

$(x + 3)(x - 1) \geq 0$

(Pos)(Pos) ≥ 0

$x + 3 \geq 0$ and $x - 1 \geq 0$

$x \geq -3$ and $x \geq 1$

(Neg)(Neg) ≥ 0

$x + 3 \leq 0$ and $x - 1 \leq 0$

$x \leq -3$ and $x \leq 1$

Thus, the solution is $x \geq 1$ or $x \leq -3$.

16. $x^2 + 2x - 3 < 0$; $D = \{\text{Integers}\}$

$(x + 3)(x - 1) < 0$

$(\text{NEG})(\text{POS}) < 0$

$x + 3 < 0 \quad \text{and} \quad x - 1 > 0$

$\quad x < -3 \quad \text{and} \quad x > 1$

$(\text{POS})(\text{NEG}) < 0$

$x + 3 > 0 \quad \text{and} \quad x - 1 < 0$

$\quad x > -3 \quad \text{and} \quad x < 1$

There are no integers that satisfy the first conjunction, so the solution must be $-3 < x < 1$.

$$\underset{-3\;-2\;-1\;\;0\;\;1}{\bullet\;\bullet\;\bullet}$$

17. $-|x| + 2 > -1$; $D = \{\text{Integers}\}$

$\quad -|x| > -3$

$\quad\;\; |x| < 3$

$x < 3 \quad \text{and} \quad x > -3$

$$\underset{-3\;-2\;-1\;\;0\;\;1\;\;2\;\;3}{\bullet\;\bullet\;\bullet\;\bullet\;\bullet}$$

18. $100N = 104.76\;76\;76\ldots$

$\underline{\quad N = \quad\; 1.04\;76\;76\ldots}$

$99N = 103.72$

$\quad N = \dfrac{\mathbf{10{,}372}}{\mathbf{9900}}$

19. $-y = x^2 + 4x + 6$

$-y = (x^2 + 4x + 4) + 6 - 4$

$-y = (x + 2)^2 + 2$

$\;\; y = -(x + 2)^2 - 2$

From this we see:

(a) Opens downward

(b) Axis of symmetry is $x = -2$

(c) y-coordinate of vertex is -2

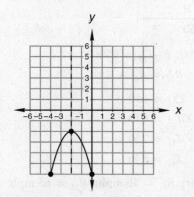

20. $(x^{1/2} - y^{3/4})^2$

$x^{1/2} - y^{3/4}$

$\underline{x^{1/2} - y^{3/4}}$

$x - x^{1/2}y^{3/4}$

$\underline{\quad\; - x^{1/2}y^{3/4} + y^{3/2}}$

$x - 2x^{1/2}y^{3/4} + y^{3/2}$

21. $27m^9p^3 - x^{12}y^3 = (3m^3p)^3 - (x^4y)^3$

$= (3m^3p - x^4y)(9m^6p^2 + 3m^3px^4y + x^8y^2)$

22. $N = \dfrac{1}{4} + \dfrac{2}{9}\left(3\dfrac{1}{2} - \dfrac{1}{4}\right)$

$= \dfrac{1}{4} + \dfrac{2}{9}\left(\dfrac{14}{4} - \dfrac{1}{4}\right)$

$= \dfrac{1}{4} + \dfrac{26}{36}$

$= \dfrac{9}{36} + \dfrac{26}{36} = \dfrac{\mathbf{35}}{\mathbf{36}}$

23. (a) $\dfrac{3}{5}x - \dfrac{1}{7}y = 6$

(b) $-0.21x + 0.02y = -2.73$

(a′) $21x - 5y = 210$

(b′) $\underline{-21x + 2y = -273}$

$\quad\quad -3y = -63$

$\quad\quad\quad\; y = 21$

(a′) $21x - 5(21) = 210$

$\quad\quad\quad 21x = 315$

$\quad\quad\quad\quad x = 15$

(15, 21)

24. (a) $x - 2z = 7$

(b) $y + 2z = -9$

(c) $-x + 2y = -7$

(a) + (b): $x + y = -2$ (d)

(d) + (c): $3y = -9$

$\quad\quad\quad y = -3$

(d) $x + (-3) = -2$

$\quad\quad\quad x = 1$

(b) $(-3) + 2z = -9$

$\quad\quad\quad z = -3$

(1, -3, -3)

25. (a) $2x - y + 2z = -9$

(b) $2x + 2y + z = -15$

(c) $x - 2y + z = 0$

(b) + (c): $3x + 2z = -15$ (d)

$2(a) + (b)$: $6x + 5z = -33$ (e)

$-2(d) + (e)$: $z = -3$

(d) $3x + 2(-3) = -15$

$x = -3$

(c) $(-3) - 2y + (-3) = 0$

$y = -3$

$(-3, -3, -3)$

26. $\dfrac{2i^3 - 3}{1 - \sqrt{-4}\sqrt{4}} = \dfrac{-2i - 3}{1 - 4i} \cdot \dfrac{1 + 4i}{1 + 4i}$

$= \dfrac{-2i + 8 - 3 - 12i}{1 + 16} = \dfrac{5}{17} - \dfrac{14}{17}i$

27. $\dfrac{3 - 2\sqrt{6}}{2 - \sqrt{6}} \cdot \dfrac{2 + \sqrt{6}}{2 + \sqrt{6}}$

$= \dfrac{6 + 3\sqrt{6} - 4\sqrt{6} - 12}{4 - 6} = \dfrac{6 + \sqrt{6}}{2}$

28. $\dfrac{a^{x-4}m^x}{m^{x/2}a^{x/2}} = a^{x/2 - 4}m^{x/2}$

29. $\sqrt{p - 45} = 9 - \sqrt{p}$

$p - 45 = 81 - 18\sqrt{p} + p$

$-126 = -18\sqrt{p}$

$7 = \sqrt{p}$

$49 = p$

Check: $\sqrt{49 - 45} = 9 - \sqrt{49}$

$2 = 2$

30. $3x^3 - x^2 - 2x = 0$

$x(3x^2 - x - 2) = 0$

$x(3x^2 - 3x + 2x - 2) = 0$

$x(3x(x - 1) + 2(x - 1)) = 0$

$x(3x + 2)(x - 1) = 0$

$x = 0 \qquad 3x + 2 = 0 \qquad x - 1 = 0$

$x = -\dfrac{2}{3} \qquad x = 1$

$0, -\dfrac{2}{3}, 1$

PRACTICE SET 117

$\{x \in \mathbb{Z} \mid x + 3 > 5\}$

$x + 3 > 5$

$x > 2$; x is an integer.

PROBLEM SET 117

1. (a) $N_N + N_D + N_Q = 16$

(b) $5N_N + 10N_D + 25N_Q = 150$

(c) $N_D = 3N_Q$

Substitute (c) into (a) and (b) and get:

(a′) $N_N + 4N_Q = 16$

(b′) $5N_N + 55N_Q = 150$

$N_N + 11N_Q = 30$

$-1(a′) + (b′)$: $7N_Q = 14$

$N_Q =$ **2 quarters**

(a′) $N_N + 4(2) = 16$

$N_N =$ **8 nickels**

(a) $(8) + N_D + (2) = 16$

$N_D =$ **6 dimes**

2. $S_P = P_P + M_U$

$5000 = 4000 + M_U$

$\$1000 = M_U$

% of $P_P = \dfrac{1000}{4000} \times 100\% =$ **25%**

% of $S_P = \dfrac{1000}{5000} \times 100\% =$ **20%**

3.

$R_G T_G = 200$; $R_M T_M = 650$;

$T_M = 2T_G$; $R_M = R_G + 25$

$2T_G(R_G + 25) = 650$

$2(200) + 50T_G = 650$

$50T_G = 250$

$T_G =$ **5 hr**

$T_M =$ **10 hr**; $R_G =$ **40 mph**; $R_M =$ **65 mph**

4. (a) $0.3P_N + 0.6D_N = 234$

   (b) $P_N + D_N = 600$

   Substitute $D_N = 600 - P_N$ into (a) and get:

   (a') $0.3P_N + 0.6(600 - P_N) = 234$

   $$-0.3P_N = -126$$

   $$P_N = 420$$

   (b) $(420) + D_N = 600$

   $$D_N = 180$$

   420 mL 30%, 180 mL 60%

5. $M_U = 0.8(4320) =$ **\$3456**

   $$S_P = P_P + M_U$$

   $$4320 = P_P + 3456$$

   $$\textbf{\$864} = P_P$$

6. $\boxed{8\ |\ 7\ |\ 6\ |\ 5\ |\ 4} =$ **6720**

7. $\dfrac{4}{36} \cdot \dfrac{26}{36} = \dfrac{\textbf{13}}{\textbf{162}}$

8. $x = 3(-5.50) =$ **−16.50**

9. $4e^x = 24$

   $$e^x = 6$$

   $$x = \ln 6$$

   $$x = \textbf{1.79}$$

10. (a) $\text{pH} = -\log \text{H}^+$

    $$10^{-\text{pH}} = \text{H}^+$$

    $$10^{-5.34} = \text{H}^+$$

    $$\text{H}^+ \approx \textbf{4.57} \times \textbf{10}^{-6} \ \frac{\textbf{mole}}{\textbf{liter}}$$

    (b) $\text{pH} = -\log \text{H}^+$

    $$10^{-\text{pH}} = \text{H}^+$$

    $$10^{-0.00263} = \text{H}^+$$

    $$\text{H}^+ \approx \textbf{0.994} \ \frac{\textbf{mole}}{\textbf{liter}}$$

11. $A_t = Pe^{rt}$

    $$A_{11} = 1260e^{0.08(11)}$$

    $$A_{11} = \textbf{\$3037.73}$$

12. $A_t = A_0 e^{kt}$

    $$1700 = 85e^{k(12)}$$

    $$20 = e^{12k}$$

    $$3.00 = 12k$$

    $$0.25 = k$$

    $$A_{130} \approx 85e^{0.25(130)} \approx \textbf{1.11} \times \textbf{10}^{16} \ \textbf{rabbits}$$

13. **Region E** (This region includes all points on or outside the circle and on or below the parabola.)

14. $V = A_{\text{Base}} \times \text{height}$

    $$= \left[\frac{270}{360}\left(\pi(2 \text{ m})^2\right) + \frac{1}{2}(2 \text{ m})(2 \text{ m})\right] \times 10\text{m}$$

    $$= (3\pi + 2)(10) \text{ m}^3$$

    $$\approx \frac{114.25(100)(100)(100)}{(2.54)(2.54)(2.54)(12)(12)(12)} \text{ ft}^3$$

    $$\approx \textbf{4034.70 ft}^3$$

15. $6 \times \overrightarrow{SF} = 9$

    $$\overrightarrow{SF} = \frac{3}{2}$$

    $$B \times \overrightarrow{SF} = 7$$

    $$B \times \frac{3}{2} = 7$$

    $$B = \frac{14}{3}$$

    $$A = \sqrt{(6)^2 - \left(\frac{14}{3}\right)^2} = \frac{8\sqrt{2}}{3}$$

    $$\frac{8\sqrt{2}}{3} \times \overrightarrow{SF} = A + C$$

    $$\frac{8\sqrt{2}}{3} \times \frac{3}{2} = \frac{8\sqrt{2}}{3} + C$$

    $$\frac{24\sqrt{2}}{6} = \frac{8\sqrt{2}}{3} + C$$

    $$\frac{\textbf{4}\sqrt{\textbf{2}}}{\textbf{3}} = C$$

16. $x + 1 > 1; D = \{\text{Integers}\}$

    $$x > 0$$

17. $x^2 + 4x + 3 \geq 0; D = \{\text{Reals}\}$

    $$(x + 3)(x + 1) \geq 0$$

    $$(\text{Pos})(\text{Pos}) \geq 0$$

    $$x + 3 \geq 0 \quad \text{and} \quad x + 1 \geq 0$$

    $$x \geq -3 \quad \text{and} \quad x \geq -1$$

    $$(\text{Neg})(\text{Neg}) \geq 0$$

    $$x + 3 \leq 0 \quad \text{and} \quad x + 1 \leq 0$$

    $$x \leq -3 \quad \text{and} \quad x \leq -1$$

    Thus the solution is $x \geq -1$ or $x \leq -3$.

18. $x^2 + 4x + 3 < 0$; $D = \{\text{Reals}\}$

$(x + 3)(x + 1) < 0$

$(\text{NEG})(\text{POS}) < 0$

$x + 3 < 0$ and $x + 1 > 0$

$x < -3$ and $x > -1$

$(\text{POS})(\text{NEG}) < 0$

$x + 3 > 0$ and $x + 1 < 0$

$x > -3$ and $x < -1$

There are no real numbers that satisfy the first conjunction, so the solution must be $-3 < x < -1$.

19. (a) $y > x + 3$

(b) $y < -x$

The first step is to graph each of these lines.

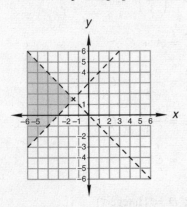

The region we wish to find is below the negatively sloped dashed line and above the positively sloped dashed line. This region is shaded in the figure.

20. $100N = 204.25\ 25\ 25\ \ldots$

$N = 2.04\ 25\ 25\ \ldots$

$99N = 202.21$

$N = \dfrac{20{,}221}{9900}$

21. $-y = x^2 - 4x + 2$

$-y = (x^2 - 4x + 4) + 2 - 4$

$-y = (x - 2)^2 - 2$

$y = -(x - 2)^2 + 2$

From this we see:

(a) Opens downward

(b) Axis of symmetry is $x = 2$

(c) y-coordinate of vertex is 2

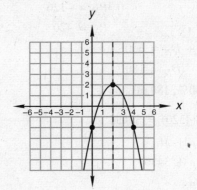

22. $\dfrac{\begin{array}{l} x^{1/2} - y^{-1/2} \\ \underline{x^{1/2} - y^{-1/2}} \\ x - x^{1/2}y^{-1/2} \\ \underline{ - x^{1/2}y^{-1/2} + y^{-1}} \end{array}}{x - 2x^{1/2}y^{-1/2} + y^{-1}}$

23. $m^3 - 8p^6k^9 = (m)^3 - (2p^2k^3)^3$

$= (m - 2p^2k^3)(m^2 + 2mp^2k^3 + 4p^4k^6)$

24. $N = \dfrac{3}{5} + \dfrac{4}{9}\left(1\dfrac{2}{5} - \dfrac{3}{5}\right)$

$= \dfrac{3}{5} + \dfrac{4}{9}\left(\dfrac{4}{5}\right) = \dfrac{27}{45} + \dfrac{16}{45} = \dfrac{\mathbf{43}}{\mathbf{45}}$

25. (a) $\dfrac{5}{8}x - \dfrac{2}{3}y = 4$

(b) $-0.15x + 0.2y = -0.6$

(a′) $15x - 16y = 96$

(b′) $\dfrac{-15x + 20y = -60}{4y = 36}$

$y = 9$

(a′) $15x - 16(9) = 96$

$x = 16$

(16, 9)

26. (a) $3x + y = 2$

(b) $2x - z = 0$

(c) $2y + z = -4$

(b) + (c): $2x + 2y = -4$ (d)

$-2(a) + (d): -4x = -8$

$x = 2$

(d) $2(2) + 2y = -4$

$y = -4$

(c) $2(-4) + z = -4$

$z = 4$

(2, -4, 4)

27. $\dfrac{\sqrt{-2}\sqrt{-2} - 3i^3}{i + 2} = \dfrac{-2 + 3i}{i + 2} \cdot \dfrac{i - 2}{i - 2}$

$= \dfrac{-2i + 4 - 3 - 6i}{-1 - 4} = -\dfrac{1}{5} + \dfrac{8}{5}i$

28. $\dfrac{2\sqrt{2} - 4}{4 - \sqrt{2}} \cdot \dfrac{4 + \sqrt{2}}{4 + \sqrt{2}}$

$= \dfrac{8\sqrt{2} + 4 - 16 - 4\sqrt{2}}{16 - 2} = \dfrac{-6 + 2\sqrt{2}}{7}$

29. $\sqrt[3]{x^5}\sqrt[4]{x^3 y} = x^{5/3}x^{3/4}y^{1/4} = x^{29/12}y^{1/4}$

30. $2x^2 - 11x - 6 = 0$

$2x^2 - 12x + x - 6 = 0$

$2x(x - 6) + 1(x - 6) = 0$

$(2x + 1)(x - 6) = 0$

$2x + 1 = 0 \qquad x - 6 = 0$

$x = -\dfrac{1}{2} \qquad x = 6$

$-\dfrac{1}{2}, 6$

PRACTICE SET 118

a. $\log_5(x + 8) + \log_5 4 = \log_5 80$

$\log_5(x + 8)(4) = \log_5 80$

$4x + 32 = 80$

$4x = 48$

$x = \mathbf{12}$

b. $\log_7(x + 7) - \log_7(x - 2) = \log_7 10$

$\log_7 \dfrac{x + 7}{x - 2} = \log_7 10$

$\dfrac{x + 7}{x - 2} = 10$

$x + 7 = 10x - 20$

$27 = 9x$

$\mathbf{3} = x$

c. $2\log_3 x = \log_3 16$

$\log_3 x^2 = \log_3 16$

$x^2 = 16$

$x = +\sqrt{16}$

$x = \mathbf{4}$

PROBLEM SET 118

1. $\dfrac{9}{16} \times T = 6399$

$T = 11,376$

$S = 11,376 - 6399 = \mathbf{4977 \; squatted}$

2. Carbon: $2 \times 12 = 24$

Hydrogen: $4 \times 1 = 4$

Oxygen: $1 \times 16 = 16$

Total: $24 + 4 + 16 = 44$

$\dfrac{4}{44} = \dfrac{H}{396}$

$H = \mathbf{36 \; grams}$

3. (a) $N_N + N_Q = 18$

(b) $5N_N + 25N_Q = 270$

$-5(a) + (b): 20N_Q = 180$

$N_Q = \mathbf{9 \; quarters}$

(a) $N_N + (9) = 18$

$N_N = \mathbf{9 \; nickels}$

4. Downstream: $(B + W)T_D = D_D$ (a)

Upstream: $(B - W)T_U = D_U$ (b)

$T_D = 2T_U$

(a') $(B + 5)2T_U = 160$

(b') $(B - 5)T_U = 40$

(a') + 2(b'): $4BT_U = 240$

$BT_U = 60$ (c)

(b') $(60) - 5T_U = 40$

$T_U = \mathbf{4 \; hr}; \; T_D = \mathbf{8 \; hr}$

(c) $B(4) = 60$

$B = \mathbf{15 \; mph}$

5. T = tens digit

U = units digit

$10T + U$ = original number

(a) $10T + U = 8(T + U) + 1$

(b) $3T = U + 11$

$U = 3T - 11$

Substitute (b) into (a) and get:

(a') $10T + (3T - 11) = 8T + 8(3T - 11) + 1$

$13T - 11 = 32T - 87$

$76 = 19T$

$4 = T$

(b) $U = 3(4) - 11 = 1$

Original number = **41**

6. $A_t = Pe^{rt}$

$A_{10} = 15,000e^{0.095(10)} = \textbf{\$38,785.64}$

7. | 11 | 10 | 9 | 8 | 7 | 6 | = **332,640**

8. $\dfrac{3}{36} \cdot \dfrac{21}{36} = \dfrac{\textbf{7}}{\textbf{144}}$

9. $\ln x = 0.0144$

$x \approx \textbf{1.01}$

10. $\dfrac{(e^{-1.45})(e^{19.94})}{(e^{10.47})} = e^{-1.45 + 19.94 - 10.47}$

$= e^{8.02} \approx \textbf{3041.18}$

11. $A_t = A_0 e^{kt}$

$20 = 4e^{k5}$

$5 = e^{5k}$

$1.61 = 5k$

$0.322 = k$

$A_{40} = 4e^{0.322(40)} \approx \textbf{1,569,542}$

12. $pH = -\log H^+$

$pH = -\log 3.14 \times 10^{-3}$

$pH \approx \textbf{2.5}$

13. $H^+ = 10^{-pH}$

$H^+ = 10^{-5.042}$

$H^+ \approx \textbf{9.08} \times \textbf{10}^{-6} \ \dfrac{\textbf{mole}}{\textbf{liter}}$

14. Since $ABCD$ is a rhombus,

$m\angle ABC = m\angle ADC$

$m\angle ABD = m\angle CBD = m\angle BDA = m\angle BDC$

$2(m\angle ABD) + 34 = 180$

$2(m\angle ABD) = 146$

$m\angle ABD = 73°$

$m\angle BDA = m\angle ABD = \textbf{73°}$

15. $\log_7 (x + 5) + \log_7 3 = \log_7 60$

$\log_7 (x + 5)(3) = \log_7 60$

$3x + 15 = 60$

$3x = 45$

$x = \textbf{15}$

16. $4 \log_6 x = \log_6 64$

$\log_6 x^4 = \log_6 64$

$x^4 = 64$

$x = \sqrt[4]{64} = \textbf{2}\sqrt{\textbf{2}} \approx \textbf{2.83}$

17. $100N = 0.163 \ 63 \ 63 \ ...$

$\underline{\quad N = 0.001 \ 63 \ 63 \ ...}$

$99N = 0.162$

$N = \dfrac{\textbf{162}}{\textbf{99,000}}$

18. $-y = x^2 + 6x + 10$

$-y = (x^2 + 6x + 9) + 10 - 9$

$-y = (x + 3)^2 + 1$

$y = -(x + 3)^2 - 1$

From this we see:

(a) Opens downward

(b) Axis of symmetry is $x = -3$

(c) y-coordinate of vertex is -1

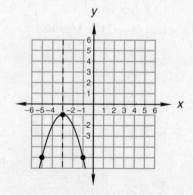

19. $|x| - 3 > -7$; $D = $ {Integers}

$\qquad |x| > -4$

The solution consists of all integers because any integer (even zero) has an absolute value greater than -4.

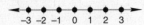

20. (a) $x + y \geq -3$

$\qquad\qquad y \geq -x - 3$

(b) $x - 2y < -4$

$\qquad\qquad y > \dfrac{1}{2}x + 2$

The next step is to graph each of these lines.

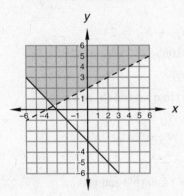

The region we wish to find is on or above the solid line and above the dashed line. This region is shaded in the figure.

21. $\quad x^2 - 2x - 3 \geq 0$; $D = $ {Integers}

$(x - 3)(x + 1) \geq 0$

$(\text{POS})(\text{POS}) \geq 0$

$x - 3 \geq 0$ and $x + 1 \geq 0$

$\qquad x \geq 3$ and $\qquad x \geq -1$

$(\text{NEG})(\text{NEG}) \geq 0$

$x - 3 \leq 0$ and $x + 1 \leq 0$

$\qquad x \leq 3$ and $\qquad x \leq -1$

Thus, the solution is $x \geq 3$ or $x \leq -1$.

22. $\quad x^2 - 2x - 3 < 0$; $D = $ {Integers}

$(x - 3)(x + 1) < 0$

$(\text{NEG})(\text{POS}) < 0$

$x - 3 < 0$ and $x + 1 > 0$

$\qquad x < 3$ and $\qquad x > -1$

$(\text{POS})(\text{NEG}) < 0$

$x - 3 > 0$ and $x + 1 < 0$

$\qquad x > 3$ and $\qquad x < -1$

There are no integers that satisfy the second conjunction, so the solution must be $-1 < x < 3$.

23. $\quad x^2 + 6x + 10 = 0$

$(x^2 + 6x + 9) = -10 + 9$

$\qquad (x + 3)^2 = -1$

$\qquad\quad x + 3 = \pm i$

$\qquad\qquad x = \mathbf{-3 \pm i}$

24. $\dfrac{x^{1/4} - y^{1/4}}{}$

$\dfrac{x^{1/4} - y^{1/4}}{\begin{array}{l} x^{1/2} - x^{1/4}y^{1/4} \\[4pt] \underline{\quad - x^{1/4}y^{1/4} + y^{1/2}} \\[4pt] \mathbf{x^{1/2} - 2x^{1/4}y^{1/4} + y^{1/2}} \end{array}}$

25. $x^6y^3 - 27p^6m^9 = (x^2y)^3 - (3p^2m^3)^3$

$\qquad = (x^2y - 3p^2m^3)(x^4y^2 + 3x^2yp^2m^3 + 9p^4m^6)$

26. $N = 4\dfrac{1}{5} + \dfrac{3}{8}\left(6\dfrac{1}{10} - 4\dfrac{1}{5}\right)$

$\quad = \dfrac{21}{5} + \dfrac{3}{8}\left(\dfrac{61}{10} - \dfrac{42}{10}\right)$

$\quad = \dfrac{21}{5} + \dfrac{57}{80}$

$\quad = \dfrac{336}{80} + \dfrac{57}{80} = \dfrac{\mathbf{393}}{\mathbf{80}}$

27. (a) $3x - y - z = 9$

(b) $2x + y - z = 12$

(c) $2x - y + z = 0$

(a) + (b): $5x - 2z = 21$ (d)

(b) + (c): $4x = 12$

$\qquad\qquad x = 3$

(d) $5(3) - 2z = 21$

$\qquad\qquad z = -3$

(b) $2(3) + y - (-3) = 12$

$\qquad\qquad\qquad y = 3$

$(\mathbf{3, 3, -3})$

28. $\dfrac{2i + 2}{i + 1} \cdot \dfrac{i - 1}{i - 1} = \dfrac{-2 - 2i + 2i - 2}{-1 - 1}$

$\qquad = \mathbf{2}$

29. $\sqrt[5]{27\sqrt{3}} = 3^{3/5}3^{1/10} = \mathbf{3^{7/10}}$

30. $\dfrac{\sqrt{2} - 5}{3 - 2\sqrt{2}} \cdot \dfrac{3 + 2\sqrt{2}}{3 + 2\sqrt{2}}$

$\qquad = \dfrac{3\sqrt{2} + 4 - 15 - 10\sqrt{2}}{9 - 8} = \mathbf{-11 - 7\sqrt{2}}$

PRACTICE SET 119

a. $\{x \in \mathbb{R} \mid |x - 3| < 5\}$

$\quad x - 3 > -5$ and $x - 3 < 5$

$\qquad x > -2$ and $\qquad x < 8$

b. $\{x \in \mathbb{Z} \mid |x + 3| \le 2\}$

$\quad x + 3 \ge -2$ and $x + 3 \le 2$

$\qquad x \ge -5$ and $\qquad x \le -1$

PROBLEM SET 119

1. $\dfrac{V_1}{T_1} = \dfrac{V_2}{T_2}$

$\dfrac{500}{700} = \dfrac{V_2}{2100}$

$V_2 = \mathbf{1500 \ mL}$

2.

$R_G T_G = 250; \ R_T T_T = 400;$

$T_T = 2T_G; \ R_G = R_T + 10$

$2T_G(R_G - 10) = 400$

$2(250) - 20T_G = 400$

$\qquad -20T_G = -100$

$\qquad\qquad T_G = \mathbf{5 \ hr}$

$T_T = \mathbf{10 \ hr}; \ R_G = \mathbf{50 \ mph}; \ R_T = \mathbf{40 \ mph}$

3. Equal ratio method:

$\dfrac{P_1}{P_2} = \dfrac{(B_2)^2 \, W_1}{(B_1)^2 \, W_2}$

$\dfrac{2}{P_2} = \dfrac{(1)^2 \, 4}{(10)^2 \, 20}$

$P_2 = \mathbf{1000 \ pinks}$

Variation method:

$P = \dfrac{kW}{B^2}$

$2 = \dfrac{k(4)}{(10)^2}$

$50 = k$

$P = \dfrac{50(20)}{(1)^2} = \mathbf{1000 \ pinks}$

4. (a) $N_N + N_D + N_Q = 24$

(b) $5N_N + 10N_D + 25N_Q = 425$

(c) $N_N = N_D$

Substitute (c) into (a) and (b) and get:

(a') $2N_D + N_Q = 24$

$\qquad\qquad N_Q = 24 - 2N_D$

(b') $15N_D + 25N_Q = 425$

Substitute (a') into (b') and get:

(b'') $15N_D + 25(24 - 2N_D) = 425$

$\qquad\qquad -35N_D = -175$

$\qquad\qquad\qquad N_D = \mathbf{5 \ dimes}$

(c) $N_N = N_D = \mathbf{5 \ nickels}$

(a) $(5) + (5) + N_Q = 24$

$\qquad\qquad N_Q = \mathbf{14 \ quarters}$

5. $T =$ tens digit

$U =$ units digit

$10T + U =$ original number

$10U + T =$ reversed number

(a) $T + U = 5$

$\qquad T = 5 - U$

(b) $10U + T = 10T + U - 27$

Substitute (a) into (b) and get:

(b') $10U + (5 - U) = 10(5 - U) + U - 27$

$\qquad\qquad 9U + 5 = -9U + 23$

$\qquad\qquad\qquad 18U = 18$

$\qquad\qquad\qquad\quad U = 1$

(a) $T = 5 - (1) = 4$

Original number $= \mathbf{41}$

6. $A_t = A_0 e^{kt}$

$640 = 40e^{k(3)}$

$16 = e^{3k}$

$2.77 = 3k$

$0.923 = k$

$A_{20} = 40e^{0.923(20)} \approx$ **4,160,409,959 amoebae**

7. $|x + 1| \le 3$; $D = \{\text{Integers}\}$

$x + 1 \ge -3$ and $x + 1 \le 3$

$x \ge -4$ and $\quad x \le 2$

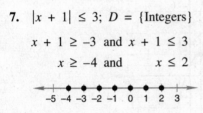

8. $|x - 3| > 5$; $D = \{\text{Reals}\}$

$x - 3 > 5$ or $x - 3 < -5$

$x > 8$ or $\quad x < -2$

9. $\ln(x + 3) + \ln 4 = \ln 40$

$\ln(x + 3)(4) = \ln 40$

$4x + 12 = 40$

$4x = 28$

$x = 7$

10. $3\log_{15} x = \log_{15} 27$

$\log_{15} x^3 = \log_{15} 27$

$x^3 = 27$

$x = 3$

11. $N = 6\dfrac{1}{10} + \dfrac{4}{5}\left(12\dfrac{3}{20} - 6\dfrac{1}{10}\right)$

$= \dfrac{61}{10} + \dfrac{4}{5}\left(\dfrac{243}{20} - \dfrac{122}{20}\right)$

$= \dfrac{61}{10} + \dfrac{484}{100}$

$= \dfrac{610}{100} + \dfrac{484}{100} = \dfrac{\mathbf{547}}{\mathbf{50}}$

12.

$x^{1/2} - y^{1/2}$

$\underline{x^{1/2} - y^{1/2}}$

$x - x^{1/2}y^{1/2}$

$\underline{\quad - x^{1/2}y^{1/2} + y}$

$x - 2x^{1/2}y^{1/2} + y$

13. $x^3y^9 - 64p^{12}m^9 = (xy^3)^3 - (4p^4m^3)^3$

$= (xy^3 - 4p^4m^3)(x^2y^6 + 4xy^3p^4m^3 + 16p^8m^6)$

14. (a) -5.45

(b) $e^{-4.13} \approx$ **1.61×10^{-2}**

15. $\dfrac{(e^{-7.78})(e^{6.07})}{(e^{-42.29})} = e^{-7.78 + 6.07 + 42.29}$

$= e^{40.58} \approx$ **4.20×10^{17}**

16. $m\angle CBD = 180 - 130 = 50°$

$m\angle CDB = 180 - 90 - 50 = 40°$

$m\angle x = 180 - 40 =$ **$140°$**

17. **Region B** (This region includes all points on or above the line and on or below the parabola.)

18. $\text{pH} = -\log \text{H}^+$

$\text{pH} = -\log 9.52 \times 10^{-12}$

$\text{pH} \approx$ **11.02**

19. $\text{H}^+ = 10^{-\text{pH}}$

$\text{H}^+ = 10^{-2.23}$

$\text{H}^+ \approx$ **$5.89 \times 10^{-3} \dfrac{\text{mole}}{\text{liter}}$**

20. $\dfrac{5000 \text{ L}}{\text{min}} \times \dfrac{1000 \text{ mL}}{1 \text{ L}} \times \dfrac{1 \text{ cm}^3}{1 \text{ mL}} \times \dfrac{1 \text{ in.}}{2.54 \text{ cm}}$

$\times \dfrac{1 \text{ in.}}{2.54 \text{ cm}} \times \dfrac{1 \text{ in.}}{2.54 \text{ cm}} \times \dfrac{1 \text{ min}}{60 \text{ s}}$

$= \dfrac{\mathbf{5000(1000)}}{\mathbf{(2.54)(2.54)(2.54)(60)}} \dfrac{\text{in.}^3}{\text{s}}$

21. $(-3 - \sqrt{2}, 4)$

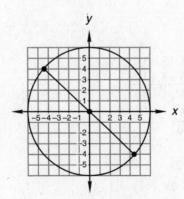

22. $A_{\text{Shaded}} = A_{\text{Sector } AOE} - A_{\text{Triangle } POE}$

$A_{\text{Sector } AOE} = \dfrac{30}{360}(\pi(3 \text{ cm})^2) = \dfrac{3\pi}{4} \text{ cm}^2$

ΔDOE is equilateral because
$\angle DOE = \angle OED = \angle EDO = 60°$. It follows that
$PE = \frac{3}{2}$, since $\overline{OA}$ is the bisector of $\angle DOE$ and,
therefore, the bisector of $\overline{DE}$.

Since triangles POE and POD are 30°-60°-90°
triangles,

$2 \times \overrightarrow{SF} = 3$

$\overrightarrow{SF} = \dfrac{3}{2}$

$PO = \sqrt{3}\left(\dfrac{3}{2}\right) = \dfrac{3\sqrt{3}}{2} \text{ cm}$

$A_{\text{Triangle } POE} = \dfrac{1}{2}\left(\dfrac{3}{2} \text{ cm}\right)\left(\dfrac{3\sqrt{3}}{2} \text{ cm}\right)$

$= \dfrac{9\sqrt{3}}{8} \text{ cm}^2$

$A_{\text{Shaded}} = \left(\dfrac{3\pi}{4} - \dfrac{9\sqrt{3}}{8}\right) \text{cm}^2$

23. (a) $2x - y - z = 8$

(b) $3x + y - z = 9$

(c) $6x - y + z = 0$

(a) + (b): $5x - 2z = 17$ (d)

(b) + (c): $9x = 9$

$x = 1$

(d) $5(1) - 2z = 17$

$z = -6$

(b) $3(1) + y - (-6) = 9$

$y = 0$

(1, 0, –6)

24. $100N = 1.3\ 13\ 13\ ...$

$\underline{\quad N = 0.0\ 13\ 13\ ...}$

$99N = 1.3$

$N = \dfrac{\mathbf{13}}{\mathbf{990}}$

25. $-y = x^2 + 2x - 1$

$-y = (x^2 + 2x + 1) - 1 - 1$

$-y = (x + 1)^2 - 2$

$y = -(x + 1)^2 + 2$

From this we see:

(a) Opens downward

(b) Axis of symmetry is $x = -1$

(c) y-coordinate of vertex is 2

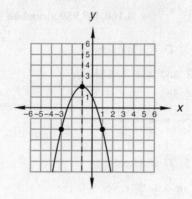

26. See Lesson 71.

27. $N = 3\dfrac{1}{3} + \dfrac{1}{5}\left(5\dfrac{2}{5} - 3\dfrac{1}{3}\right)$

$= \dfrac{10}{3} + \dfrac{1}{5}\left(\dfrac{81}{15} - \dfrac{50}{15}\right)$

$= \dfrac{10}{3} + \dfrac{31}{75}$

$= \dfrac{250}{75} + \dfrac{31}{75} = \dfrac{\mathbf{281}}{\mathbf{75}}$

28. $\dfrac{2i^3 - 2}{3 - \sqrt{-2}\sqrt{2}} = \dfrac{-2i - 2}{3 - 2i} \cdot \dfrac{3 + 2i}{3 + 2i}$

$= \dfrac{-6i + 4 - 6 - 4i}{9 + 4} = -\dfrac{\mathbf{2}}{\mathbf{13}} - \dfrac{\mathbf{10}}{\mathbf{13}}i$

29. $\dfrac{a^b x^b}{a^{b/2} x^{b/2}} = a^{b/2} x^{b/2}$

30. $3x^3 - 3x^2 - 6x = 0$

$3x(x^2 - x - 2) = 0$

$3x(x^2 - 2x + x - 2) = 0$

$3x(x(x - 2) + 1(x - 2)) = 0$

$3x(x + 1)(x - 2) = 0$

$3x = 0 \qquad x + 1 = 0 \qquad x - 2 = 0$

$x = 0 \qquad x = -1 \qquad x = 2$

0, –1, 2

PRACTICE SET 120

	Now	5 Years Ago	10 Years From Now
Ben:	B	$B - 5$	$B + 10$
Kris:	K	$K - 5$	$K + 10$

$$B - 5 = \frac{2}{3}(K - 5) \quad \text{(a)}$$

$$B + 10 = \frac{5}{6}(K + 10) \quad \text{(b)}$$

3(a) $3B - 15 = 2K - 10$

(a′) $3B - 2K = 5$

6(b) $6B + 60 = 5K + 50$

(b′) $6B - 5K = -10$

−2(a′) $-6B + 4K = -10$

(b′) $\underline{6B - 5K = -10}$

$$-K = -20$$

$$K = 20$$

(a′) $3B - 2(20) = 5$

$$3B - 40 = 5$$

$$B = 15$$

PROBLEM SET 120

1. $0.76(300) - (D_N) = 0.2(300 - D_N)$

$$228 - D_N = 60 - 0.2D_N$$

$$168 = 0.8D_N$$

210 liters $= D_N$

2. $T = $ tens digit

$U = $ units digit

$10T + U = $ original number

$10U + T = $ reversed number

(a) $T + U = 11$

$$T = 11 - U$$

(b) $10U + T = 3(10T + U) + 5$

Substitute (a) into (b) and get:

(b′) $10U + (11 - U) = 30(11 - U) + 3U + 5$

$$9U + 11 = -27U + 335$$

$$36U = 324$$

$$U = 9$$

(a) $T = 11 - (9) = 2$

Original number = **29**

3.

	Now	+ 15 Years
Man:	M_N	$M_N + 15$
Son:	S_N	$S_N + 15$

(a) $M_N = 18S_N$

(b) $M_N + 15 = 3(S_N + 15)$

Substitute (a) into (b) and get:

(b′) $(18S_N) + 15 = 3S_N + 45$

$$15S_N = 30$$

$$S_N = \mathbf{2}$$

(a) $M_N = 18(2) = \mathbf{36}$

4. Since the triangle is equilateral, each side must equal 8 meters.

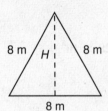

$$H = \sqrt{(8\text{ m})^2 - (4\text{ m})^2} = 4\sqrt{3}\text{ m}$$

$$A = \frac{1}{2}(8\text{ m})(4\sqrt{3}\text{ m}) = \mathbf{16\sqrt{3}\text{ m}^2}$$

5.

	Now	−6 Years	−20 Years
Lucie:	L_N	$L_N - 6$	$L_N - 20$
Myrna:	M_N	$M_N - 6$	$M_N - 20$

(a) $L_N - 20 = 2(M_N - 20) + 2$

(b) $M_N - 6 = \frac{3}{4}(L_N - 6)$

(a′) $L_N - 2M_N = -18$

(b′) $3L_N - 4M_N = -6$

−2(a′) $-2L_N + 4M_N = 36$

(b′) $\underline{3L_N - 4M_N = -6}$

$$L_N \qquad = 30$$

(a′) $(30) - 2M_N = -18$

$$M_N = 24$$

$L_N = \mathbf{30}$; $M_N = \mathbf{24}$

6. $|x - 3| < 2$; $D = \{\text{Integers}\}$

$$x - 3 > -2 \text{ and } x - 3 < 2$$

$$x > 1 \quad \text{and} \quad x < 5$$

7. $|x + 3| \leq 2$; $D = \{Reals\}$

$x + 3 \geq -2$ and $x + 3 \leq 2$

$x \geq -5$ and $\qquad x \leq -1$

18. $(-3 + \sqrt{2}, 4 - \sqrt{2})$

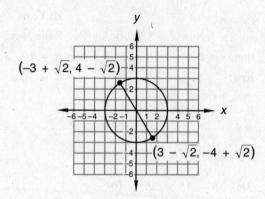

8. $A_t = Pe^{rt}$

$A_8 = 2000e^{0.06(8)} = \mathbf{\$3232.15}$

9. | 26 | 25 | 24 | 10 | 9 | 8 | $= \mathbf{11,232,000}$

10. $\dfrac{e^{-15.91}}{e^{12.83}} = e^{-15.91 - 12.83} = e^{\mathbf{-28.74}}$

$\approx \mathbf{3.30 \times 10^{-13}}$

11. $(e^{7.11})^{1.5} = e^{10.665} \approx \mathbf{4.28 \times 10^4}$

12. $4x = 3 \ln 0.0037$

$x = \dfrac{3 \ln 0.0037}{4} \approx \mathbf{-4.20}$

13. $3 \ln x = -4.13$

$\ln x = -\dfrac{4.13}{3}$

$x \approx \mathbf{0.25}$

14. $\text{pH} = -\log \text{H}^+$

$\text{pH} = -\log 0.062$

$\text{pH} \approx \mathbf{1.21}$

15. $\text{H}^+ = 10^{-\text{pH}}$

$\text{H}^+ = 10^{-3.13}$

$\text{H}^+ \approx \mathbf{7.41 \times 10^{-4} \dfrac{mole}{liter}}$

16. $\dfrac{40 \text{ ft}^3}{\min} \times \dfrac{12 \text{ in.}}{1 \text{ ft}} \times \dfrac{12 \text{ in.}}{1 \text{ ft}} \times \dfrac{12 \text{ in.}}{1 \text{ ft}} \times \dfrac{1 \min}{60 \text{ s}}$

$= \dfrac{\mathbf{40(12)(12)(12)}}{\mathbf{(60)}} \dfrac{\mathbf{in.}^3}{\mathbf{s}}$

17. $1000N = 21.63 \ 163 \ 163 \ldots$

$\underline{N = 0.02 \ 163 \ 163 \ldots}$

$999N = 21.61$

$N = \dfrac{\mathbf{2161}}{\mathbf{99,900}}$

19. $-y = x^2 - 2x + 3$

$-y = (x^2 - 2x + 1) + 3 - 1$

$-y = (x - 1)^2 + 2$

$y = -(x - 1)^2 - 2$

From this we see:

(a) Opens downward

(b) Axis of symmetry is $x = 1$

(c) y-coordinate of vertex is -2

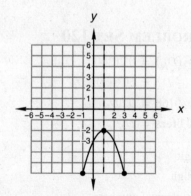

20. $5x^2 + 2x - 1 = 0$

$x^2 + \dfrac{2}{5}x = \dfrac{1}{5}$

$\left(x^2 + \dfrac{2}{5}x + \dfrac{1}{25}\right) = \dfrac{5}{25} + \dfrac{1}{25}$

$\left(x + \dfrac{1}{5}\right)^2 = \dfrac{6}{25}$

$x + \dfrac{1}{5} = \pm \dfrac{\sqrt{6}}{5}$

$x = -\dfrac{1}{5} \pm \dfrac{\sqrt{6}}{5}$

21. (a) $\dfrac{3}{2}x + y = 13$

(b) $0.2x - 0.02y = 1.12$

(a') $3x + 2y = 26$

(b') $\dfrac{20x - 2y = 112}{23x\qquad\ = 138}$

$x = 6$

(a') $3(6) + 2y = 26$

$y = 4$

(6, 4)

22.

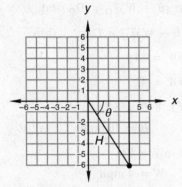

$H = \sqrt{(6)^2 + (4)^2} = 2\sqrt{13}$

$\tan \theta = \dfrac{6}{4}$

$\theta \approx -56.31°$

$2\sqrt{13}\,/\underline{-56.31°}$

23.

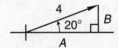

$A = 4 \cos 20° \approx 3.76$

$B = 4 \sin 20° \approx 1.37$

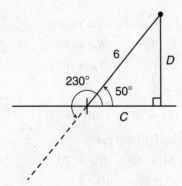

$C = 6 \cos 50° \approx 3.86$

$D = 6 \sin 50° \approx 4.60$

$3.76R + 1.37U$

$\dfrac{3.86R + 4.60U}{7.62R + 5.97U}$

$F = \sqrt{(7.62)^2 + (5.97)^2} \approx 9.68$

$\tan \theta = \dfrac{5.97}{7.62}$

$\theta \approx 38.08°$

$9.68\,/\underline{38.08°}$

24.
$$5x^3 + 9x^2 - 2x = 0$$
$$x(5x^2 + 9x - 2) = 0$$
$$x(5x^2 + 10x - x - 2) = 0$$
$$x(5x(x + 2) - 1(x + 2)) = 0$$
$$x(5x - 1)(x + 2) = 0$$
$$x = 0 \qquad 5x - 1 = 0 \qquad x + 2 = 0$$
$$x = \dfrac{1}{5} \qquad x = -2$$

$0, \dfrac{1}{5}, -2$

25. $\log_4 (x - 3) - \log_4 7 = \log_4 31$

$\log_4 \dfrac{(x - 3)}{7} = \log_4 31$

$x - 3 = 217$

$x = 220$

26. $\ln (x + 5) + \ln 5 = \ln 65$

$\ln (5)(x + 5) = \ln 65$

$5x + 25 = 65$

$5x = 40$

$x = 8$

27. $(x^{3/2} - y^{3/2})^2$

$x^{3/2} - y^{3/2}$

$\dfrac{x^{3/2} - y^{3/2}}{x^3 - x^{3/2}y^{3/2}}$

$\dfrac{\quad - x^{3/2}y^{3/2} + y^3}{x^3 - 2x^{3/2}y^{3/2} + y^3}$

28. $m^6p^{12} - 8y^3z^{15} = (m^2p^4)^3 - (2yz^5)^3$
$= (m^2p^4 - 2yz^5)(m^4p^8 + 2m^2p^4yz^5 + 4y^2z^{10})$

29. $OB = \frac{1}{2}BC = 6$

$AB = \sqrt{(12)^2 + (9)^2} = 15$

Since $\triangle BPO$ and $\triangle BCA$ are similar triangles,

$6 \times \overrightarrow{SF} = 15$

$\overrightarrow{SF} = \frac{15}{6}$

$OP \times \frac{15}{6} = 9$

$OP = \frac{18}{5}$

30. $m\angle B = \frac{1}{2}(180) = 90°$

$m\angle BAD = 180 - 90 - 54 = 36°$

$\frac{1}{2}m\angle BAO = \frac{1}{2}(36) = 18°$

$x = \frac{1}{2}m\angle BAO = 18°$

PRACTICE SET 121

$1 < \dfrac{-2}{x - 3}$; $D = \{\text{Reals}\}$

The value $x = 3$ cannot be a solution, because division by zero is not allowed. Multiply both sides by $(x - 3)^2$.

$(x - 3)^2 < \dfrac{-2(x - 3)(x - 3)}{x - 3}$

$x^2 - 6x + 9 < -2x + 6$

$x^2 - 4x + 3 < 0$

$(x - 3)(x - 1) < 0$

$(\text{Pos})(\text{Neg}) < 0$

$x - 3 > 0$ and $x - 1 < 0$

$\quad x > 3$ and $\quad\quad x < 1$

$(\text{Neg})(\text{Pos}) < 0$

$x - 3 < 0$ and $x - 1 > 0$

$\quad x < 3$ and $\quad\quad x > 1$

No real numbers satisfy the first inequality, so the solution is given by $1 < x < 3$.

PROBLEM SET 121

1. $0.4(80) + (D_N) = 0.52(80 + D_N)$

$32 + D_N = 41.6 + 0.52D_N$

$0.48D_N = 9.6$

$D_N = \mathbf{20 \text{ liters}}$

2. $\dfrac{P_1}{T_1} = \dfrac{P_2}{T_2}$

$\dfrac{10}{600} = \dfrac{20}{T_2}$

$T_2 = \mathbf{1200 \text{ K}}$

3. Downstream: $(B + W)T_D = D_D$ (a)

Upstream: $(B - W)T_U = D_U$ (b)

(a') $6B + 6W = 84$

(b') $7B - 7W = 42$

$7(a') + 6(b')$: $84B = 840$

$\quad\quad\quad\quad\quad\quad B = \mathbf{10 \text{ mph}}$

(a') $6(10) + 6W = 84$

$\quad\quad\quad\quad W = \mathbf{4 \text{ mph}}$

4.
	Now	+ 10 Years
Garfunkel:	G_N	$G_N + 10$
Spot:	S_N	$S_N + 10$

(a) $G_N = 2S_N$

(b) $4(G_N + 10) = 3(S_N + 10) + 15$

Substitute (a) into (b) and get:

(b') $4(2S_N) + 40 = 3S_N + 45$

$\quad\quad\quad 5S_N = 5$

$\quad\quad\quad\quad S_N = \mathbf{1}$

(a) $G_N = 2(1) = \mathbf{2}$

5.
	Now	+ 10 Years
Rover Boy:	R_N	$R_N + 10$
Yolanda:	Y_N	$Y_N + 10$

(a) $R_N = Y_N + 5$

(b) $4(R_N + 10) = 2(Y_N + 10) + 50$

Substitute (a) into (b) and get:

(b') $4(Y_N + 5) + 40 = 2Y_N + 70$

$\quad\quad\quad\quad 2Y_N = 10$

$\quad\quad\quad\quad\quad Y_N = \mathbf{5}$

(a) $R_N = (5) + 5 = \mathbf{10}$

6. $\boxed{9}\ \boxed{8}\ \boxed{7}\ \boxed{6} = 3024$

7. $\dfrac{3}{36} \times \dfrac{26}{36} = \dfrac{13}{216}$

8. $A_t = Pe^{rt}$
$A_7 = 1,000,000\, e^{0.13(7)} = \$2,484,322.53$

9. $A_t = A_0 e^{kt}$
$140 = 40 e^{k(5)}$
$3.5 = e^{5k}$
$1.25 = 5k$
$0.25 = k$
$A_{10} = 40 e^{0.25(10)} \approx 487$

10. $|x + 2| \le 3;\ D = \{\text{Reals}\}$
$x + 2 \ge -3$ and $x + 2 \le 3$
$x \ge -5$ and $\quad x \le 1$

11. Multiply both sides by $(m + 3)^2$
$(m + 3)(m - 3) \le 2(m + 3)^2$
$m^2 - 9 \le 2m^2 + 12m + 18$
$m^2 + 12m + 27 \ge 0$
$(m + 9)(m + 3) \ge 0$

$m = -3$ cannot be a solution, because division by zero is not defined.

(Pos)(Pos) ≥ 0
$m + 9 \ge 0$ and $m + 3 > 0$
$m \ge -9$ and $\quad m > -3$

(Neg)(Neg) ≥ 0
$m + 9 \le 0$ and $m + 3 < 0$
$m \le -9$ and $\quad m < -3$

Thus, the solution is $m > -3$ or $m \le -9$.

12. $\ln (x + 2) + \ln 6 = \ln 36$
$\ln (6)(x + 2) = \ln 36$
$6x + 12 = 36$
$6x = 24$
$x = 4$

13. $3 \log_{11} x = \log_{11} 27$
$\log_{11} x^3 = \log_{11} 27$
$x^3 = 27$
$x = 3$

14. $x = 6 \ln 0.003 \approx \mathbf{-34.85}$

15. $6 \ln x = -2.78$
$\ln x = -\dfrac{2.78}{6}$
$x \approx \mathbf{0.63}$

16. $\dfrac{e^{11.62}}{e^{-8.11}} = e^{11.62 + 8.11} = e^{\mathbf{19.73}} \approx \mathbf{3.70 \times 10^8}$

17. $\angle PQR + \angle PRQ = 180 - 80$
$\angle PQR + \angle PRQ = \mathbf{100°}$
$\dfrac{1}{2}(\angle PQR + \angle PRQ) = \dfrac{1}{2}(100°) = \mathbf{50°}$
$m\angle QSR = 180 - 50 = \mathbf{130°}$

18. $\text{pH} = -\log \text{H}^+$
$\text{pH} = -\log 0.053$
$\text{pH} \approx \mathbf{1.28}$

19. $\text{H}^+ = 10^{-\text{pH}}$
$\text{H}^+ = 10^{-7.24 \times 10^{-5}}$
$\text{H}^+ \approx \mathbf{1.00}\ \dfrac{\textbf{mole}}{\textbf{liter}}$

20. $P = 2 \times 62 = \mathbf{124}$
$x = 180 - 62 = \mathbf{118}$
$y = 180 - 28 - 118 = \mathbf{34}$
$m\overarc{BD} = 124 - 2(34) = \mathbf{56°}$
$m\angle A = \dfrac{1}{2}(56) = \mathbf{28°}$
$m\angle BDA = 180 - 62 - 28 = \mathbf{90°}$

21. $A_{\text{Triangle}} = \dfrac{1}{2}bh$

Since $\triangle OAB$ is equilateral,
$b = 8$ cm
$h = \sqrt{8^2 - 4^2} = 4\sqrt{3}$ cm
$A_{\text{Triangle}} = \dfrac{1}{2}(8\text{ cm})(4\sqrt{3}\text{ cm}) = \mathbf{16\sqrt{3}\ cm^2}$
$A_{\text{Hexagon}} = 6(A_{\text{Triangle}}) = 6(16\sqrt{3}\text{ cm}^2)$
$\quad = \mathbf{96\sqrt{3}\ cm^2}$

22. **Region B** (This region includes all points above the line and below the parabola.)

23. $-y = x^2 - 4x + 7$

$-y = (x^2 - 4x + 4) + 7 - 4$

$-y = (x - 2)^2 + 3$

$y = -(x - 2)^2 - 3$

From this we see:

(a) Opens downward

(b) Axis of symmetry is $x = 2$

(c) y-coordinate of vertex is -3

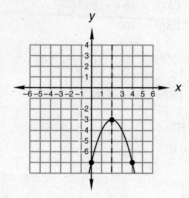

24.

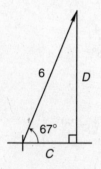

$B = 4 \sin 15° \approx 1.04$

$A = 4 \cos 15° \approx 3.86$

$D = 6 \sin 67° \approx 5.52$

$C = 6 \cos 67° \approx 2.34$

$-3.86R - 1.04U$

$\underline{2.34R + 5.52U}$

$\mathbf{-1.52R + 4.48U}$

$F = \sqrt{(-1.52)^2 + (4.48)^2} \approx 4.73$

$\tan \theta = -\dfrac{4.48}{1.52}$

$\theta \approx -71.26 + 180 = 108.74°$

$\mathbf{4.73\underline{/108.74°}}$

25. (a) $3x - y + z = 1$

(b) $x - y - z = 1$

(c) $x - 2y - z = -2$

(a) + (b): $4x - 2y = 2$ (d)

(a) + (c): $4x - 3y = -1$ (e)

(d) + (-1)(e): $y = 3$

(d) $4x - 2(3) = 2$

$x = 2$

(b) $(2) - (3) - z = 1$

$z = -2$

(2, 3, -2)

26. (a) $\dfrac{1}{2}x + \dfrac{1}{3}y = 5$

(b) $0.4x - 0.2y = -0.2$

(a') $3x + 2y = 30$

(b') $\dfrac{4x - 2y = -2}{7x \qquad = 28}$

$x = 4$

(a') $3(4) + 2y = 30$

$y = 9$

(4, 9)

27. (a) $5x + y = 7$

(b) $2x - z = -1$

(c) $y + z = 5$

(b) + (c): $2x + y = 4$ (d)

-1(d) + (a): $3x = 3$

$x = 1$

(a) $5(1) + y = 7$

$y = 2$

(c) $(2) + z = 5$

$z = 3$

(1, 2, 3)

28. $\dfrac{4 - \sqrt{5}}{\sqrt{5} + 2} \cdot \dfrac{\sqrt{5} - 2}{\sqrt{5} - 2}$

$= \dfrac{4\sqrt{5} - 8 - 5 + 2\sqrt{5}}{5 - 4} = -13 + 6\sqrt{5}$

29.
$$3x^3 - 4x^2 - 7x = 0$$
$$x(3x^2 - 4x - 7) = 0$$
$$x(3x^2 + 3x - 7x - 7) = 0$$
$$x(3x(x + 1) - 7(x + 1)) = 0$$
$$x(3x - 7)(x + 1) = 0$$

$$x = 0 \qquad 3x - 7 = 0 \qquad x + 1 = 0$$
$$x = \frac{7}{3} \qquad x = -1$$

$$\mathbf{0, \frac{7}{3}, -1}$$

30. (a) $\mathbf{1.74 \times 10^4}$

(b) $\mathbf{4.84 \times 10^{-3}}$

PRACTICE SET 122

a. $M \cap P$

The points that are members of both M and P

b. $M \cap X$

The points that are members of both M and X

c. $X \cup M$

The points that are members of either X or M

d. $X \cup P$

The points that are members of either X or P

PROBLEM SET 122

1. (a) $5N_N + 10N_D = 455$

(b) $N_N = N_D + 25$

Substitute (b) into (a) and get:

(a′) $5(N_D + 25) + 10N_D = 455$
$$15N_D = 330$$
$$N_D = \mathbf{22 \ dimes}$$

(b) $N_N = (22) + 25 = \mathbf{47 \ nickels}$

2. Equal ratio method:
$$\frac{M_1}{M_2} = \frac{A_1(V_1)^2}{A_2(V_2)^2}$$
$$\frac{400}{1600} = \frac{2(2)^2}{A_2\left(\frac{1}{2}\right)^2}$$
$$A_2 = \mathbf{128 \ apes}$$

Variation method:
$$M = kA(V)^2$$
$$400 = k(2)(2)^2$$
$$50 = k$$
$$1600 = (50)(A)\left(\frac{1}{2}\right)^2$$
$$A = \mathbf{128 \ apes}$$

3. T = tens digit

U = units digit

$10T + U$ = original number

(a) $10T + U = 2(T + U) + 8$

(b) $4U = T + 30$
$$T = 4U - 30$$

Substitute (b) into (a) and get:

(a′) $10(4U - 30) + U = 2(4U - 30) + 2U + 8$
$$41U - 300 = 10U - 52$$
$$31U = 248$$
$$U = 8$$

(b) $T = 4(8) - 30 = 2$

Original number = **28**

4.

	Now	+ 10 Years
Yehudi:	Y_N	$Y_N + 10$
Mohab:	M_N	$M_N + 10$

(a) $Y_N = M_N + 4$

(b) $2(Y_N + 10) = M_N + 10 + 24$

Substitute (a) into (b) and get:

(b′) $2(M_N + 4) + 20 = M_N + 34$

$2M_N + 28 = M_N + 34$

$M_N = \mathbf{6}$

(a) $Y_N = (6) + 4 = \mathbf{10}$

5.

	Now	+ 10 Years
Petunia:	P_N	$P_N + 10$
Daisy:	D_N	$D_N + 10$

(a) $P_N = 2D_N$

(b) $2(P_N + 10) = D_N + 10 + 25$

Substitute (a) into (b) and get:

(b′) $2(2D_N) + 20 = D_N + 35$

$3D_N = 15$

$D_N = \mathbf{5}$

(a) $P_N = 2(5) = \mathbf{10}$

6.
$$A_t = A_0 e^{kt}$$
$$1{,}500{,}000 = 1000\, e^{k(3)}$$
$$1500 = e^{3k}$$
$$2.44 = k$$
$$A_8 = 1000 e^{2.44(8)} \approx \mathbf{3.00 \times 10^{11}}\ \textbf{euglenae}$$

7. $\boxed{7\ 6\ 5\ 4} = \mathbf{840}$

8. $\boxed{3\ 3\ 3\ 3\ 3\ 3} = \mathbf{729}$

9. (a) $\log MN = \log M + \log N$

(b) $\log \dfrac{M}{N} = \log M - \log N$

(c) $\log M^N = N \log M$

10. $(x - 2)^2(2) \le -2(x - 2)$

$2x^2 - 8x + 8 \le -2x + 4$

$x^2 - 3x + 2 \le 0$

$(x - 2)(x - 1) \le 0$

$x = 2$ cannot be a solution, because division by zero is not defined.

(Neg)(Pos) ≤ 0

$x - 2 < 0$ and $x - 1 \ge 0$

$x < 2$ and $x \ge 1$

(Pos)(Neg) ≤ 0

$x - 2 > 0$ and $x - 1 \le 0$

$x > 2$ and $x \le 1$

There are no real numbers that satisfy the second conjunction, so the solution must be $1 \le x < 2$.

11. $(m - 3)(m + 3) \le 1(m - 3)^2$

$m^2 - 9 \le m^2 - 6m + 9$

$-18 \le -6m$

$3 \ge m$

$m = 3$ cannot be a solution, because division by zero is not defined. Thus, the solution is $m < 3$.

12. $|x - 2| < 1$; $D = \{\text{Reals}\}$

$x - 2 > -1$ and $x - 2 < 1$

$x > 1$ and $x < 3$

13. $|x + 3| \le 4$; $D = \{\text{Integers}\}$

$x + 3 \ge -4$ and $x + 3 \le 4$

$x \ge -7$ and $x \le 1$

14. $\dfrac{10^{9.71}}{10^{-7.15}} = 10^{9.71 + 7.15} \approx \mathbf{7.24 \times 10^{16}}$

15. $(10^{5.51})^{2/7} = 10^{1.57} \approx \mathbf{37.15}$

16. $(10^{14.66})(10^{-19.52}) = 10^{14.66 - 19.52}$
$$= 10^{-4.86} \approx \mathbf{1.38 \times 10^{-5}}$$

17. $\text{pH} = -\log \text{H}^+$

$\text{pH} = -\log 3.26 \times 10^{-9}$

$\text{pH} \approx \mathbf{8.49}$

18. $\text{pH} = -\log \text{H}^+$

$\text{pH} = -\log 7.04 \times 10^{-5}$

$\text{pH} \approx \mathbf{4.15}$

19. $\text{pH} = -\log \text{H}^+$

$\text{pH} = -\log 0.0016$

$\text{pH} \approx \mathbf{2.80}$

20. $\text{H}^+ = 10^{-\text{pH}}$

$\text{H}^+ = 10^{-4.02}$

$\text{H}^+ \approx \mathbf{9.55 \times 10^{-5}} \dfrac{\mathbf{mole}}{\mathbf{liter}}$

21. $\text{H}^+ = 10^{-\text{pH}}$

$\text{H}^+ = 10^{-8.23}$

$\text{H}^+ \approx \mathbf{5.89 \times 10^{-9}} \dfrac{\mathbf{mole}}{\mathbf{liter}}$

22. $\text{H}^+ = 10^{-\text{pH}}$

$\text{H}^+ = 10^{-10.13}$

$\text{H}^+ \approx \mathbf{7.41 \times 10^{-11}} \dfrac{\mathbf{mole}}{\mathbf{liter}}$

23. $A_{\text{Shaded}} = A_{\text{Big Circle}} - 2A_{\text{Small Circle}}$

$= \pi(12 \text{ yd})^2 - 2(\pi(6 \text{ yd})^2)$

$= 72\pi \text{ yd}^2 \approx 226.08 \text{ yd}^2$

$226.08 \text{ yd}^2 = \mathbf{226.08(3)(3)(12)(12)} \text{ in.}^2$

24. $\dfrac{1000 \text{ in.}}{\text{s}} \times \dfrac{2.54 \text{ cm}}{1 \text{ in.}} \times \dfrac{1 \text{ m}}{100 \text{ cm}} \times \dfrac{1 \text{ km}}{1000 \text{ m}}$

$\times \dfrac{60 \text{ s}}{1 \text{ min}} \times \dfrac{60 \text{ min}}{1 \text{ hr}}$

$= \dfrac{\mathbf{1000(2.54)(60)(60)}}{\mathbf{(100)(1000)}} \dfrac{\mathbf{km}}{\mathbf{hr}}$

25. $100N = 0.168\ 68\ 68\ \ldots$

$\underline{N = 0.001\ 68\ 68\ \ldots}$

$99N = 0.167$

$N = \dfrac{\mathbf{167}}{\mathbf{99,000}}$

26. $5x^2 + x + 4 = 0$

$x^2 + \dfrac{1}{5}x = -\dfrac{4}{5}$

$\left(x^2 + \dfrac{1}{5}x + \dfrac{1}{100}\right) = -\dfrac{80}{100} + \dfrac{1}{100}$

$\left(x + \dfrac{1}{10}\right)^2 = -\dfrac{79}{100}$

$x + \dfrac{1}{10} = \pm\dfrac{\sqrt{79}}{10}i$

$x = \mathbf{-\dfrac{1}{10} \pm \dfrac{\sqrt{79}}{10}i}$

27. $\dfrac{\sqrt{-3}\sqrt{-3} - i^3}{2 - \sqrt{-2}\sqrt{2}} = \dfrac{-3 + i}{2 - 2i} \cdot \dfrac{2 + 2i}{2 + 2i}$

$= \dfrac{-6 - 6i + 2i - 2}{4 + 4} = \mathbf{-1 - \dfrac{1}{2}i}$

28. $\dfrac{4\sqrt{2} - 5}{1 - \sqrt{2}} \cdot \dfrac{1 + \sqrt{2}}{1 + \sqrt{2}}$

$= \dfrac{4\sqrt{2} + 8 - 5 - 5\sqrt{2}}{1 - 2} = \mathbf{-3 + \sqrt{2}}$

29. $\sqrt[4]{xy^5}\ \sqrt[6]{x^3y} = x^{1/4}y^{5/4}x^{1/2}y^{1/6} = \mathbf{x^{3/4}y^{17/12}}$

30. (a) $P \cap Z$

The points that are members of both P and Z

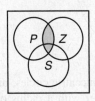

(b) $P \cap S$

The points that are members of both P and S

(c) $Z \cup P$

The points that are members of either Z or P or both

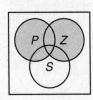

(d) $Z \cup S$

The points that are members of either Z or S or both

PRACTICE SET 123

a.

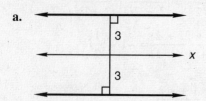

The locus is a pair of parallel lines that are 6 feet apart. (Each is 3 feet from the given line.)

b.

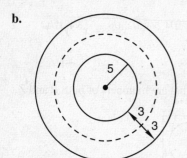

The locus is a pair of concentric circles, one with a radius of 5 cm, the other with a radius of 11 cm. (Both circles are also concentric with the given circle.)

PROBLEM SET 123

1. See Lesson 123.

2. See Lesson 123.

3. See Lesson 123.

4. See Lesson 123.

5. See Lesson 123.

6. See Lesson 123.

7. Consecutive odd integers: N, $N + 2$, $N + 4$

$$N(N + 4) = 10(N + 2) - 13$$
$$N^2 + 4N = 10N + 7$$
$$N^2 - 6N - 7 = 0$$
$$(N + 1)(N - 7) = 0$$
$$N = -1, 7$$

The desired integers are **−1, 1, 3** and **7, 9, 11.**

8.

D_M
800

D_O
650

$R_M T_M = 800$; $R_O T_O = 650$;
$T_M = 2T_O$; $R_M = R_O - 50$
$(R_O - 50)2T_O = 800$
$2(650) - 100T_O = 800$
$-100T_O = -500$
$T_O = $ **5 hr**

$T_M = $ **10 hr**; $R_O = $ **130 mph**; $R_M = $ **80 mph**

9.

D_H
D_W

$R_H T_H = R_W T_W$; $R_H = 16$;
$R_W = 10$; $T_H + T_W = 13$
$16(T_H) = 10(13 - T_H)$
$26T_H = 130$
$T_H = 5$

Distance $= R_H T_H = 16(5) = $ **80 miles**

10. $T = $ tens digit
$U = $ units digit
$10T + U = $ original number

(a) $10T + U = 3(T + U) + 13$

(b) $U = T + 1$

Substitute (b) into (a) and get:

(a′) $10T + (T + 1) = 3T + 3(T + 1) + 13$
$11T + 1 = 6T + 16$
$5T = 15$
$T = 3$

(b) $U = 4$

Original number $= $ **34**

11.

	Now	+5 Years
Man:	M_N	$M_N + 5$
Son:	S_N	$S_N + 5$

(a) $M_N = 6S_N$

(b) $M_N + 5 = 3(S_N + 5) + 2$

Substitute (a) into (b) and get:

(b′) $(6S_N) + 5 = 3S_N + 17$
$3S_N = 12$
$S_N = $ **4**

(a) $M_N = $ **24**

12. $P \cap K = \{5, 7, 13\}$

13. $A \cup B = \{1, 3, 5, 7, 8, 10\}$

14. $P \cup K = \{2, 3, 5, 7, 8, 9, 10, 11, 13, 15\}$

15. $(x - 1)^2(1) \le -1(x - 1)$

$x^2 - 2x + 1 \le -x + 1$

$x^2 - x \le 0$

$x(x - 1) \le 0$

$x = 1$ cannot be a solution, because division by zero is not defined.

(NEG)(POS) ≤ 0

$x \le 0$ and $x > 1$

(POS)(NEG) ≤ 0

$x \ge 0$ and $x < 1$

There are no real numbers that satisfy the first conjunction, so the solution must be $0 \le x < 1$.

```
  |──●──○──|──|──
 -1  0  1  2  3
```

16. $(m - 1)(m + 1) \le 1(m - 1)^2$

$m^2 - 1 \le m^2 - 2m + 1$

$-2 \le -2m$

$1 \ge m$

$m = 1$ cannot be a solution, because division by zero is not defined. Thus, the solution is $1 > m$.

```
 ──|──|──|──○──|──
 -2 -1  0  1  2
```

17. $|x + 3| \le 3;\ D = \{\text{Reals}\}$

$x + 3 \ge -3$ and $x + 3 \le 3$

$x \ge -6$ and $\quad x \le 0$

```
◄──|──●──|──|──|──|──|──●──|──►
  -7 -6 -5 -4 -3 -2 -1  0  1
```

18. $\text{pH} = -\log \text{H}^+$

$\text{pH} = -\log 1.42 \times 10^{-11}$

$\text{pH} \approx \mathbf{10.85}$

19. $\text{H}^+ = 10^{-\text{pH}}$

$\text{H}^+ = 10^{-3.97}$

$\text{H}^+ \approx \mathbf{1.07 \times 10^{-4} \ \dfrac{mole}{liter}}$

20. $A_t = A_0 e^{kt}$

$480 = 240 e^{k(10)}$

$2 = e^{10k}$

$0.069 \approx k$

$A_{18} = 240 e^{0.069(18)} \approx \mathbf{831\ bacteria}$

21. **Region C** (This region includes all points on or below the line and inside the circle.)

22. $\log_7 (x + 2) + \log_7 3 = \log_7 15$

$\log_7 3(x + 2) = \log_7 15$

$3x + 6 = 15$

$3x = 9$

$x = \mathbf{3}$

23. $\ln (x - 9) + \ln 2 = \ln 45$

$\ln 2(x - 9) = \ln 45$

$2x - 18 = 45$

$2x = 63$

$x = \dfrac{\mathbf{63}}{\mathbf{2}}$

24.
$$
\begin{array}{r}
x^{4/5} - y^{4/5} \\
x^{4/5} - y^{4/5} \\
\hline
x^{8/5} - x^{4/5}y^{4/5} \\
- x^{4/5}y^{4/5} + y^{8/5} \\
\hline
x^{8/5} - 2x^{4/5}y^{4/5} + y^{8/5}
\end{array}
$$

25. $a^3 m^{27} - p^6 y^{36} = (am^9)^3 - (p^2 y^{12})^3$

$= (am^9 - p^2 y^{12})(a^2 m^{18} + am^9 p^2 y^{12} + p^4 y^{24})$

26.
$$
\begin{array}{r}
1000N = 1.2352\ 352\ 352\ \ldots \\
N = 0.0012\ 352\ 352\ \ldots \\
\hline
999N = 1.234
\end{array}
$$

$N = \dfrac{\mathbf{1234}}{\mathbf{999,000}}$

27. $-y = x^2 - 4x + 1$

$-y = (x^2 - 4x + 4) + 1 - 4$

$-y = (x - 2)^2 - 3$

$y = -(x - 2)^2 + 3$

From this we see:

(a) Opens downward

(b) Axis of symmetry is $x = 2$

(c) y-coordinate of vertex is 3

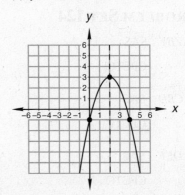

28. $3x^2 + 5x + 2 = 0$

$$x = \frac{-(5) \pm \sqrt{(5)^2 - 4(3)(2)}}{2(3)}$$

$$x = \frac{-(5) \pm 1}{6} = -\frac{2}{3}, -1$$

29. $3 - 6i + 2i - 2i + 2i = \mathbf{3 - 4i}$

30. (a) Since this is a 30°-60°-90° triangle,

$$2 \times \overrightarrow{SF} = 14$$
$$\overrightarrow{SF} = 7$$
$$m = 1(7) = \mathbf{7}$$
$$n = \sqrt{3}(7) = \mathbf{7\sqrt{3}}$$

(b) Since this is a 45°-45°-90° triangle,

$$1 \times \overrightarrow{SF} = 3$$
$$\overrightarrow{SF} = 3$$
$$c = \sqrt{2}(3) = \mathbf{3\sqrt{2}}$$
$$d = 1(3) = \mathbf{3}$$

PRACTICE SET 124

a. The conditions of congruence are **SSS, AAAS, SAS,** and **HL.**

b. Since $\angle E \cong \angle H$, $\triangle EDH$ is isoceles.

$ED \cong HD$ Definition of isoceles triangle

$\triangle EDF \cong \triangle HDG$ SAS

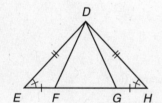

PROBLEM SET 124

1. $\triangle WAX \cong \triangle ZBY$ SAS

    $\angle W \cong \angle Z$ CPCTC

2. $\triangle ABD \cong \triangle CBD$ SAS

    $\overline{AD} \cong \overline{DC}$ CPCTC

3. $\triangle BAG \cong \triangle DEF$ SAS

    $\overline{BG} \cong \overline{DF}$ CPCTC

4. $\triangle DCB \cong \triangle DAB$ SSS

    $\angle CBD \cong \angle ABD$ CPCTC

    $\overline{BD} \perp \overline{CA}$

Two equal adjacent angles whose sum is 180° are right angles.

5. $\triangle EAB \cong \triangle EDC$ SAS

    $\overline{BE} \cong \overline{CE}$ CPCTC

6. See Lesson 123.

7. See Lesson 123.

8. See Lesson 123.

9. $(m - 3)(m + 3) \geq 1(m - 3)^2$

$$m^2 - 9 \geq m^2 - 6m + 9$$
$$-18 \geq -6m$$
$$3 \leq m$$

$m = 3$ cannot be a solution, because division by zero is not defined. Thus, the solution is $3 < m$.

<< number line: 2 3 4 5 6, open circle at 3 >>

10. $$2(x - 1)^2 \leq -2(x - 1)$$
$$2x^2 - 4x + 2 \leq -2x + 2$$
$$2x^2 - 2x \leq 0$$
$$2x(x - 1) \leq 0$$

$x = 1$ cannot be a solution, because division by zero is not defined.

(NEG)(POS) ≤ 0

$x \leq 0$ and $x > 1$

(POS)(NEG) ≤ 0

$x \geq 0$ and $x < 1$

There are no integers that satisfy the first conjunction, so the solution must be $0 \leq x < 1$.

<< number line: -2 -1 0 1 2, filled dot at 0 >>

11. $|x + 2| < 3$; $D = \{\text{Reals}\}$

$x + 2 > -3$ and $x + 2 < 3$

     $x > -5$ and $x < 1$

<< number line: -6 -5 -4 -3 -2 -1 0 1 2, open circles at -5 and 1 >>

12.
$$38 = 10^{x+3}$$
$$10^{1.58} \approx 10^{x+3}$$
$$1.58 = x + 3$$
$$\mathbf{-1.42 = x}$$

13.
$$\ln(x + 2) + \ln 3 = \ln 39$$
$$\ln 3(x + 2) = \ln 39$$
$$3x + 6 = 39$$
$$x = \mathbf{11}$$

14.
$$4 \log_8 x = \log_8 48$$
$$\log_8 x^4 = \log_8 48$$
$$x^4 = 48$$
$$x = \sqrt[4]{\mathbf{48}}$$

15. (a) $\log MN = \log M + \log N$

(b) $\log \dfrac{M}{N} = \log M - \log N$

(c) $\log M^N = N \log M$

16.

	Now	+ 12 Years
Man:	M_N	$M_N + 12$
Son:	S_N	$S_N + 12$

(a) $M_N = 11 S_N$

(b) $M_N + 12 = 3(S_N + 12)$

Substitute (a) into (b) and get:

(b') $(11S_N) + 12 = 3S_N + 36$
$$8S_N = 24$$
$$S_N = \mathbf{3}$$

(a) $M_N = \mathbf{33}$

17. $\boxed{5\,|\,5\,|\,5\,|\,5} = \mathbf{625}$

18. $\boxed{6\,|\,6\,|\,6} = \mathbf{216}$

19. $N = \dfrac{3}{8} + \dfrac{2}{7}\left(2\dfrac{1}{5} - \dfrac{3}{8}\right)$

$= \dfrac{3}{8} + \dfrac{2}{7}\left(\dfrac{88}{40} - \dfrac{15}{40}\right)$

$= \dfrac{3}{8} + \dfrac{2}{7}\left(\dfrac{73}{40}\right)$

$= \dfrac{3}{8} + \dfrac{73}{140}$

$= \dfrac{105}{280} + \dfrac{146}{280} = \dfrac{\mathbf{251}}{\mathbf{280}}$

20.
$$-y = x^2 - 2x + 4$$
$$-y = (x^2 - 2x + 1) + 4 - 1$$
$$-y = (x - 1)^2 + 3$$
$$y = -(x - 1)^2 - 3$$

From this we see:

(a) Opens downward

(b) Axis of symmetry is $x = 1$

(c) y-coordinate of vertex is -3

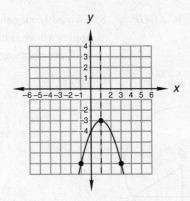

PRACTICE SET 125

a.

1.	Circle O	1. Given
2.	$\angle OAP = 90°$	2. Given
3.	$\angle OBP = 90°$	3. Given
4.	$\overline{OA} \cong \overline{OB}$	4. All radii of circle O are congruent.
5.	$\overline{OP} \cong \overline{OP}$	5. Reflexive
6.	$\triangle AOP \cong \triangle BOP$	6. HL (4, 5)
7.	$\overline{AP} \cong \overline{BP}$	7. CPCTC

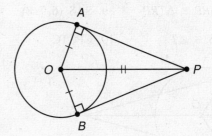

b.

1. Circle O	1. Given
2. $\overline{EG} \cong \overline{FG}$	2. Given
3. Line segment $\overline{EF}$	3. Given
4. $\overline{OG} \cong \overline{OG}$	4. Reflexive
5. $\overline{OE} \cong \overline{OF}$	5. All radii of circle O are congruent.
6. $\triangle OEG \cong \triangle OFG$	6. SSS (2, 4, 5)
7. $\angle OGE \cong \angle OGF$	7. CPCTC
8. $\angle OGE \cong \angle OGF$ $= 90°$	8. Two adjacent equal angles whose sum is $180°$ are right angles.
9. $\overline{OH} \perp \overline{EF}$	9. QED

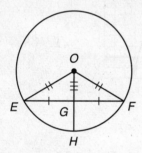

c.

1. Circle Q	1. Given
2. $\overline{PR} \perp \overline{ST}$	2. Given
3. $\overline{SQ} \cong \overline{TQ}$	3. All radii of circle Q are congruent.
4. $\overline{RQ} \cong \overline{RQ}$	4. Reflexive
5. $\triangle SRQ \cong \triangle TRQ$	5. HL (3, 4)
6. $\overline{SR} \cong \overline{TR}$	6. CPCTC
7. $\angle SRQ \cong \angle TRQ$	7. CPCTC
8. $\overline{RP} \cong \overline{RP}$	8. Reflexive
9. $\triangle SRP \cong \triangle TRP$	9. SAS (6, 7, 8)
10. $\angle S \cong \angle T$	10. CPCTC

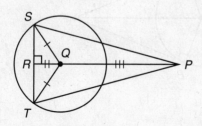

PROBLEM SET 125

1.

1. Circle Q	1. Given
2. $\overline{PR} \perp \overline{ST}$	2. Given
3. $\overline{QS} \cong \overline{QT}$	3. Radii of same circle
4. $\overline{QR} \cong \overline{QR}$	4. Reflexive property
5. $\triangle QRS \cong \triangle QRT$	5. HL (3, 4)
6. $\overline{RS} \cong \overline{RT}$	6. CPCTC
7. $\angle PRS \cong \angle PRT$	7. CPCTC
8. $\overline{PR} \cong \overline{PR}$	8. Reflexive property
9. $\triangle PRS \cong \triangle PRT$	9. SAS (6, 7, 8)
10. $\angle S \cong \angle T$	10. CPCTC

2. $\angle BED \cong \angle BDE$ Given

$\angle AEB \cong \angle CDB$ Given

$\angle AEB + \angle BED \cong \angle CDB + \angle BDE$

$\angle AED \cong \angle CDE$

3. $\triangle ABE \cong \triangle CBE$ AAAS

$\overline{CE} \cong \overline{AE}$ CPCTC

4. $\triangle OAM \cong \triangle OBM$ SSS

$\angle AMO \cong \angle BMO$ CPCTC

$\overline{OM} \perp \overline{AB}$

Two equal adjacent angles whose sum is $180°$ are right angles.

5. Begin by drawing $\overline{OA}$, $\overline{OB}$, and $\overline{OP}$.

$\triangle OAP \cong \triangle OBP$ HL

$\overline{AP} \cong \overline{BP}$ CPCTC

6. See Lesson 123.

7. See Lesson 123.

8. See Lesson 123.

9. See Lesson 123.

10. $A_t = Pe^{rt}$

$A_{11} = 1150e^{0.08(11)} \approx \mathbf{\$2773}$

11. $A_t = A_0 e^{kt}$

$1600 = 1000 e^{k(3)}$

$1.6 = e^{3k}$

$0.157 \approx k$

$A_{10} = 1000 e^{0.157(10)} \approx$ **4791 synaptic reactions**

12. $5x = 3 \ln 0.0035$

$x = \dfrac{3 \ln 0.0035}{5}$

$x \approx$ **−3.39**

13. $\ln x = -\dfrac{5.13}{3}$

$x \approx$ **0.18**

14. $|x - 5| < 3$; $D = \{\text{Integers}\}$

$x - 5 > -3$ and $x - 5 < 3$

$x > 2$ and $x < 8$

15. $x^2 - 6x + 9 > 0$; $D = \{\text{Reals}\}$

$(x - 3)(x - 3) > 0$

$(\text{Pos})(\text{Pos}) > 0$

$x > 3$

$(\text{Neg})(\text{Neg}) > 0$

$x < 3$

Thus, the solution is $3 < x < 3$.

16.

	Now	−6 Years	−20 Years
Melvina:	M_N	$M_N - 6$	$M_N - 20$
Beula:	B_N	$B_N - 6$	$B_N - 20$

(a) $M_N - 20 = 2(B_N - 20) + 4$

(b) $B_N - 6 = \dfrac{3}{5}(M_N - 6)$

(a′) $M_N - 2B_N = -16$

(b′) $-3M_N + 5B_N = 12$

$3(\text{a′}) + (\text{b′})$: $B_N = 36$

$B_N = $ **36**

(a′) $M_N = $ **56**

17. $\boxed{2\,|\,2\,|\,2\,|\,2\,|\,2\,|\,2\,|\,2\,|\,2\,|\,2\,|\,2\,|\,2\,|\,2}$ = **4096**

18. $\boxed{4\,|\,3\,|\,2\,|\,1}$ = **24**

19. $\dfrac{(e^{-7.56})(e^{6.82})}{(e^{-27.89})} = e^{-7.56 + 6.82 + 27.89}$

$= e^{27.15} \approx$ **6.18 × 10^{11}**

20. $1000N = 31.54\ 154\ 154 \ldots$

$\underline{\quad N = \ 0.03\ 154\ 154 \ldots}$

$999N = 31.51$

$N = \dfrac{3151}{99{,}900}$

PROBLEM SET 126

1. $\triangle BCE \cong \triangle DCE$ SAS

$\overline{BE} \cong \overline{ED}$ CPCTC

2. Draw radii OX and OW.

$\triangle OXY \cong \triangle OWY$ SSS

$\angle XYZ \cong \angle WYZ$ CPCTC

$\angle XZY \cong \angle WZY$ AA $\longrightarrow$ AAA

$\overline{OY} \perp \overline{WX}$

Two equal adjacent angles whose sum is 180° are right angles.

3. Draw radii AP, BP, CP, and DP.

$\triangle AXP \cong \triangle BXP \cong \triangle DYP \cong \triangle CYP$ HL

$\overline{AX} \cong \overline{BX} \cong \overline{CY} \cong \overline{DY}$ CPCTC

$\triangle APB \cong \triangle CPD$ SSS

$\overline{AB} \cong \overline{CD}$ CPCTC

4. $\triangle BED \cong \triangle BFD$ SAS

$\triangle BAE \cong \triangle BCF$ AAAS

5. $\triangle AFD \cong \triangle ABD$ SSS

$\angle 3 \cong \angle 4$ CPCTC

$\triangle DEF \cong \triangle DCE$ SAS

$\overline{EF} \cong \overline{BC}$ CPCTC

6. See Lesson 123.

7. See Lesson 123.

8. See Lesson 123.

9. See Lesson 123.

10. $\boxed{9}\ \boxed{8}\ \boxed{7}\ \boxed{6}\ \boxed{5}$ = **15,120**

11. $\boxed{3}\ \boxed{3}\ \boxed{3}\ \boxed{3}\ \boxed{3}\ \boxed{3}\ \boxed{3}\ \boxed{3}$ = **6561**

12. (a) $\log MN = \log M + \log N$

(b) $\log \dfrac{M}{N} = \log M - \log N$

(c) $\log M^N = N \log M$

13. $x = \dfrac{3}{4} \ln 0.0069 \approx$ **-3.73**

14. $\ln x = -\dfrac{4.98}{4}$

$x \approx$ **0.29**

15. $pH = -\log H^+$

$pH = -\log 0.0053$

$pH \approx$ **2.28**

16. $H^+ = 10^{-pH}$

$H^+ = 10^{-6.19}$

$H^+ \approx$ **6.46 × 10⁻⁷** $\dfrac{\text{mole}}{\text{liter}}$

17. $(p - 2)(p + 2) \le 2(p - 2)^2$

$p^2 - 4 \le 2p^2 - 8p + 8$

$p^2 - 8p + 12 \ge 0$

$(p - 2)(p - 6) \ge 0$

$p = 2$ cannot be a solution, because division by zero is not defined.

(Pos)(Pos) ≥ 0

$p - 2 > 0$ and $p - 6 \ge 0$

$p > 2$ and $p \ge 6$

(Neg)(Neg) ≥ 0

$p - 2 < 0$ and $p - 6 \le 0$

$p < 2$ and $p \le 6$

Thus, the solution is $p \ge 6$ or $p < 2$.

18. $x^2 - 5x + 4 \le 0;\ D = \{\text{Reals}\}$

$(x - 4)(x - 1) \le 0$

(Neg)(Pos) ≤ 0

$x \le 4$ and $x \ge 1$

(Pos)(Neg) ≤ 0

$x \ge 4$ and $x \le 1$

There are no real numbers that satisfy the second conjunction, so the solution must be $1 \le x \le 4$.

19. $T = $ tens digit

$U = $ units digit

$10T + U = $ original number

$10U + T = $ reversed number

(a) $T + U = 14$

$T = 14 - U$

(b) $10U + T = 2(10T + U) - 23$

Substitute (a) into (b) and get:

(b′) $10U + (14 - U)$

$= 20(14 - U) + 2U - 23$

$9U + 14 = -18U + 257$

$27U = 243$

$U = 9$

(a) $T = 5$

Original number = **59**

20. $y = x^2 - 6x + 3$

$y = (x^2 - 6x + 9) + 3 - 9$

$y = (x - 3)^2 - 6$

From this we see:

(a) Opens upward

(b) Axis of symmetry is $x = 3$

(c) y-coordinate of vertex is -6

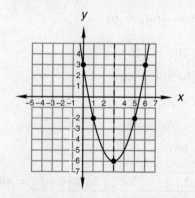

PRACTICE SET 127

a. $\overline{PF} \cong \overline{PF}$ — Reflexive

$\triangle PFG \cong \triangle PFH$ — HL

$\angle G \cong \angle H$ — CPCTC

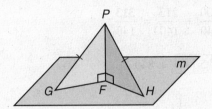

b. $\overline{DE} \cong \overline{CE}$ — Definition of bisector

$\overline{BE} \cong \overline{BE}$ — Reflexive

$\angle CEB \cong \angle DEB$ — All right angles are congruent.

$\triangle BDE \cong \triangle BCE$ — SAS

$\overline{BC} \cong \overline{BD}$ — CPCTC

$\overline{AB} \cong \overline{AB}$ — Reflexive

$\angle ABD \cong \angle ABC$ — All right angles are congruent.

$\overline{AD} \cong \overline{AC}$ — CPCTC

$\triangle ADC$ is isoceles — Definition of isoceles triangle.

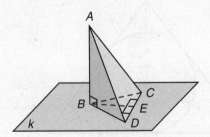

PROBLEM SET 127

1. $\triangle APB \cong \triangle CPB$ — Given

$\overline{AB} \cong \overline{CB}$ — CPCTC

2. $\triangle BAP \cong \triangle CAP$ — HL

$\overline{AB} \cong \overline{CB}$ — CPCTC

Thus, A is equidistant from B and C.

3. $\angle BYZ \cong \angle C$ — Corresponding angles are equal.

$\angle C \cong \angle YAC$ — Definition of isosceles triangle

$\angle YAC \cong \angle AYZ$ — Alternate interior angles are equal.

$\angle BYZ \cong \angle AYZ$ — Reflexive property

$\overline{YZ}$ bisects $\angle AYB$ — Definition of angle bisector

4. $\overline{EZ}$ is a perpendicular bisector of $\overline{XY}$.

Therefore, $\overline{EZ} \perp \overline{XY}$

5. $\triangle ABE \cong \triangle ACE$ — HL

$\overline{BE} \cong \overline{CE}$ — CPCTC

$\overline{AE}$ bisects $\overline{BC}$ — Definition of bisector

6. See Lesson 123.

7. See Lesson 123.

8. See Lesson 123.

9. See Lesson 123.

10. $A_t = Pe^{rt}$

$A_9 = 1460e^{0.09(9)} \approx$ **\$3282**

11. $A_t = A_0e^{kt}$

$560 = 40e^{k(3)}$

$0.88 \approx k$

$A_9 = 40e^{0.88(9)} \approx$ **110,070 incidents**

12. $pH = -\log H^+$

$pH = -\log 0.081$

$pH \approx$ **1.09**

13. $H^+ = 10^{-pH}$

$H^+ = 10^{-5.11}$

$H^+ \approx$ **7.76 $\times$ 10^{-6} $\dfrac{\text{mole}}{\text{liter}}$**

14. $91 = 10^{x+2}$

$10^{1.96} = 10^{x+2}$

$1.96 = x + 2$

$\mathbf{-0.04} = x$

15. $\dfrac{e^{-20.49}}{e^{13.16}} = e^{-20.49 - 13.16}$

$= e^{-33.65} \approx$ **2.43 $\times$ 10^{-15}**

16. (a) $|x + 1| \le 3$; $D = \{\text{Reals}\}$

$$x + 1 \ge -3 \text{ and } x + 1 \le 3$$
$$x \ge -4 \text{ and } \quad x \le 2$$

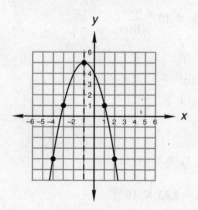

(b) $(p + 3)(p - 3) \ge 2(p + 3)^2$

$$p^2 - 9 \ge 2p^2 + 12p + 18$$
$$p^2 + 12p + 27 \le 0$$
$$(p + 9)(p + 3) \le 0$$

$p = -3$ cannot be a solution, because division by zero is not defined.

$(\text{Neg})(\text{Pos}) \le 0$

$p \le -9$ and $p > -3$

$(\text{Pos})(\text{Neg}) \le 0$

$p \ge -9$ and $p < -3$

There are no real numbers that satisfy the first conjunction, so the solution must be $-9 \le p < -3$.

17. $-y = x^2 + 2x - 4$

$$-y = (x^2 + 2x + 1) - 4 - 1$$
$$-y = (x + 1)^2 - 5$$
$$y = -(x + 1)^2 + 5$$

From this we see:

(a) Opens downward

(b) Axis of symmetry is $x = -1$

(c) y-coordinate of vertex is 5

18. $N = \dfrac{5}{7} + \dfrac{3}{5}\left(3\dfrac{1}{4} - \dfrac{5}{7}\right)$

$$= \dfrac{5}{7} + \dfrac{3}{5}\left(\dfrac{91}{28} - \dfrac{20}{28}\right)$$
$$= \dfrac{5}{7} + \dfrac{213}{140}$$
$$= \dfrac{100}{140} + \dfrac{213}{140} = \mathbf{\dfrac{313}{140}}$$

19. $\boxed{7 \mid 6 \mid 5 \mid 4} = \mathbf{840}$

20. $A_{\text{Triangle}} = \dfrac{1}{2}bh$

$$h = \sqrt{(5)^2 - \left(\dfrac{5}{2}\right)^2} = \dfrac{5\sqrt{3}}{2} \text{ cm}$$

$$A_{\text{Triangle}} = \dfrac{1}{2}(5 \text{ cm})\left(\dfrac{5\sqrt{3}}{2} \text{ cm}\right) = \dfrac{25\sqrt{3}}{4} \text{ cm}^2$$

$$A_{\text{Shaded}} = A_{\text{Circle}} - A_{\text{Triangle}}$$
$$= \pi(5 \text{ cm})^2 - \dfrac{25\sqrt{3}}{4} \text{ cm}^2$$
$$= \left(25\pi - \dfrac{25\sqrt{3}}{4}\right) \text{ cm}^2$$

PRACTICE SET 128

a.

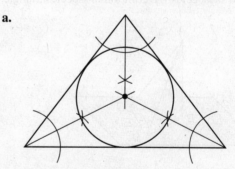

b.

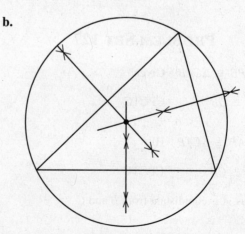

PROBLEM SET 128

1. $\triangle CBD \cong \triangle ABD$ SAS

$\angle ADB \cong \angle CDB$ CPCTC

2.

1. $\overline{AB} \cong \overline{BC}$	1. Given
2. $\overline{BD} \perp \overline{CA}$	2. Given
3. $\angle CBD \cong \angle ABD$	3. Perpendicular angles are equal (2).
4. $\overline{BD} \cong \overline{BD}$	4. Reflexive property
5. $\triangle CBD \cong \triangle ABD$	5. SAS (1, 3, 4)
6. $\angle ADB \cong \angle CDB$	6. CPCTC

3. $\triangle XDA \cong \triangle YCB$ SAS

$\angle AXD \cong \angle BYC$ CPCTC

Therefore, by definition, $\triangle OXY$ is isosceles.

4.

1. $ABCD$ is a rectangle.	1. Given
2. $\overline{XD} \cong \overline{CY}$	2. Given
3. $\angle XDA \cong \angle YCB$	3. From 1
4. $\overline{AD} \cong \overline{BC}$	4. From 1
5. $\triangle XDA \cong \triangle YCB$	5. SAS (2, 3, 4)
6. $\triangle OXY$ is isosceles.	6. From 5

5. $\triangle KNL \cong \triangle MNL$ SAS

6. $\triangle SOT \cong \triangle POT$ SAS

$\overline{ST} \cong \overline{PT}$ CPCTC

Therefore, by definition, $\triangle STP$ is isosceles.

7.

1. $NPRS$ is a parallelogram.	1. Given
2. $\overline{SO} \cong \overline{OP}$	2. Given
3. $\angle SOT \cong \angle POT$	3. Given
4. $\overline{TO} \cong \overline{TO}$	4. Reflexive property
5. $\triangle SOT \cong \triangle POT$	5. SAS (2, 3, 4)
6. $\overline{ST} \cong \overline{PT}$	6. CPCTC
7. $\triangle STP$ is isosceles.	7. From 6

8. $\triangle BXP \cong \triangle AXP \cong \triangle CYP \cong \triangle DYP$ HL

$\triangle BPA \cong \triangle CPD$ SAS

$\overline{AB} \cong \overline{CD}$ CPCTC

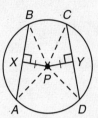

9. $\triangle AOP \cong \triangle BOP$ HL

$\overline{AP} \cong \overline{BP}$ CPCTC

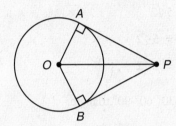

10. $\triangle ADB \cong \triangle BCA$ SSS

$\angle ADB \cong \angle BCA$ CPCTC

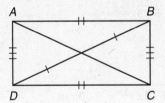

11.
$$PQ = RS$$
$$2x + 6 = x + 8$$
$$x = 2$$
$$P_{PQRS} = 2(8) + (2x + 6) + (x + 8)$$
$$P_{PQRS} = 16 + 3x + 14$$
$$P_{PQRS} = 3x + 30$$
$$P_{PQRS} = 3(2) + 30 = \mathbf{36}$$

12.
$$AC = DB$$
$$x - 12 = 0.2x$$
$$-12 = -0.8x$$
$$15 = x$$
$$DB = 0.2(15) = \mathbf{3}$$

13.
$$x + 60 = 90$$
$$x = 30$$
$$P_{DEFG} = 4(30 + 1) = \mathbf{124}$$

14. $V = \pi r^2 h$

$250\pi \text{ cm}^3 = \pi r^2 (1000 \text{ cm})$

$\dfrac{250 \text{ cm}^3}{1000 \text{ cm}} = r^2$

$\mathbf{0.5 \text{ cm}} = r$

15. $A = \pi r^2$

$4\pi^2 \text{ cm}^2 = \pi r^2$

$\mathbf{2\sqrt{\pi} \text{ cm}} = r$

16. Since this is a 45°-45°-90° triangle,

$\sqrt{2} \times \overrightarrow{SF} = 10$

$\overrightarrow{SF} = 5\sqrt{2}$

$A = 1(5\sqrt{2}) = \mathbf{5\sqrt{2}}$

$B = 1(5\sqrt{2}) = \mathbf{5\sqrt{2}}$

17. Since this is a 30°-60°-90° triangle,

$1 \times \overrightarrow{SF} = 5$

$\overrightarrow{SF} = 5$

$C = 2(5) = \mathbf{10}$

$D = \sqrt{3}(5) = \mathbf{5\sqrt{3}}$

18. $A = \dfrac{1}{2}bh$

$h = \sqrt{(4\pi)^2 - (2\pi)^2} = 2\sqrt{3}\pi \text{ in.}$

$A = \dfrac{1}{2}(4\pi \text{ in.})(2\sqrt{3}\pi \text{ in.}) = \mathbf{4\sqrt{3}\pi^2 \text{ in.}^2}$

19. $x = \dfrac{40 + 80}{2} = \mathbf{60}$

20. $y = \dfrac{120 - 40}{2} = \mathbf{40}$

21. $7x = 4(5)$

$x = \dfrac{\mathbf{20}}{\mathbf{7}}$

22. $6(y + 6) = 7 \cdot 7$

$6y + 36 = 49$

$6y = 13$

$y = \dfrac{13}{6}$

23. $4 \times \overrightarrow{SF} = 10$

$\overrightarrow{SF} = \dfrac{5}{2}$

$7\left(\dfrac{5}{2}\right) = x + 7$

$\dfrac{\mathbf{21}}{\mathbf{2}} = x$

$y = 9\left(\dfrac{5}{2}\right) = \dfrac{\mathbf{45}}{\mathbf{2}}$

24. $4 \times \overrightarrow{SF} = 6$

$\overrightarrow{SF} = \dfrac{3}{2}$

$M \times \dfrac{3}{2} = 7$

$M = \dfrac{\mathbf{14}}{\mathbf{3}}$

$N = 3 \times \dfrac{3}{2} = \dfrac{\mathbf{9}}{\mathbf{2}}$

25. $\overparen{ABC} = \dfrac{300}{360}(2\pi(6 \text{ cm}))$

$\overparen{ABC} = \mathbf{10\pi \text{ cm}}$

PRACTICE SET 129

	STEM	LEAF
a.	4	8, 9, 7
	5	2
	6	3, 8, 2, 8, 0, 7, 1, 5, 3, 3, 6
	7	0, 2, 4, 4, 0, 7, 4, 7, 5, 5, 4, 3, 9, 7, 4
	8	6, 8, 6, 7, 0, 9, 1, 4, 3, 8, 9, 3, 7
	9	8, 0, 9, 8, 2, 6, 7

Range: $99 - 47 = \mathbf{52}$

b. 2, 3, 4, 5, 5, 8, 10, 15

Mean $= \dfrac{(2 + 3 + 4 + 5 + 5 + 8 + 10 + 15)}{8}$

Mean $= \mathbf{6.5}$

Median $= \dfrac{5 \cdot 5}{2} = \mathbf{5}$

Mode $= \mathbf{5}$

Range $= 15 - 2 = \mathbf{13}$

c. Mean $= \dfrac{(5 + 7 + 9 + 14 + 8 + 5)}{6} = 8$

DISTANCE FROM MEAN	SQUARED DISTANCE FROM MEAN
5: $8 - 5 = 3$	9
7: $8 - 7 = 1$	1
9: $9 - 8 = 1$	1
14: $14 - 8 = 6$	36
8: $8 - 8 = 0$	0
5: $8 - 5 = 3$	$\dfrac{9}{56}$

Standard deviation $= \sqrt{\dfrac{1}{6}(56)} \approx \mathbf{3.06}$

PROBLEM SET 129

1. $A = \dfrac{1}{2}bh$

$h = \sqrt{(\sqrt{13})^2 - \left(\dfrac{\sqrt{7}}{2}\right)^2} = \dfrac{3\sqrt{5}}{2}$ cm

$A = \dfrac{1}{2}(\sqrt{7} \text{ cm})\left(\dfrac{3\sqrt{5}}{2} \text{ cm}\right)$

$\quad = \dfrac{\mathbf{3\sqrt{35}}}{\mathbf{4}}$ **cm²**

2. $x + 2 = 3x - 6$

$\quad 8 = 2x$

$\quad 4 = x$

$p = (4 + 1) + (4 + 2) + [3(4) - 6] = \mathbf{17 \text{ cm}}$

3. $x = \dfrac{110 + 20}{2} = \mathbf{65}$

4. $4x = 5(3)$

$\quad x = \dfrac{\mathbf{15}}{\mathbf{4}}$

5. $z = \dfrac{140 - 40}{2} = \mathbf{50}$

6. $4 \times \overrightarrow{SF} = 11$

$\quad \overrightarrow{SF} = \dfrac{11}{4}$

$x \times \dfrac{11}{4} = 9$

$\quad x = \dfrac{\mathbf{36}}{\mathbf{11}}$

7. $6 \times \dfrac{11}{4} = y + 6$

$\quad y = \dfrac{\mathbf{21}}{\mathbf{2}}$

7. $2 \times \overrightarrow{SF} = 5$

$\quad \overrightarrow{SF} = \dfrac{5}{2}$

$P \times \dfrac{5}{2} = 8$

$\quad P = \dfrac{\mathbf{16}}{\mathbf{5}}$

$4 \times \dfrac{5}{2} = Q$

$\quad \mathbf{10} = Q$

8. $A = \dfrac{40}{360}\pi(5 \text{ cm})^2 = \dfrac{\mathbf{25\pi}}{\mathbf{9}}$ **cm²**

9. Since this is a 45°-45°-90° triangle,

$\sqrt{2} \times \overrightarrow{SF} = \sqrt{6}$

$\quad \overrightarrow{SF} = \sqrt{3}$

$x = 1(\sqrt{3}) = \mathbf{\sqrt{3}}$

$y = 1(\sqrt{3}) = \mathbf{\sqrt{3}}$

10. Since this is a 30°-60°-90° triangle,

$2 \times \overrightarrow{SF} = \sqrt{7}$

$\quad \overrightarrow{SF} = \dfrac{\sqrt{7}}{2}$

$P = 1 \times \dfrac{\sqrt{7}}{2} = \dfrac{\mathbf{\sqrt{7}}}{\mathbf{2}}$

$Q = \sqrt{3} \times \dfrac{\sqrt{7}}{2} = \dfrac{\mathbf{\sqrt{21}}}{\mathbf{2}}$

11. $A_{\text{Trapezoid}} = \dfrac{1}{2}(4)(3) + \dfrac{1}{2}(2)(3) = 9 \text{ units}^2$

$A_{\text{Circle}} = \pi r^2 = 9 \text{ units}^2$

$\quad r = \dfrac{\mathbf{3\sqrt{\pi}}}{\mathbf{\pi}}$ **units**

12. See Lesson 123.

13. See Lesson 123.

14. See Lesson 123.

15. $\triangle ABX \cong \triangle CBX$ SAS

    $\overline{AX} \cong \overline{CX}$ CPCTC

    $\overline{BX} \perp$ bisector $\overline{AC}$

    Points (B and X) equidistant from the ends of a line segment ($\overline{AC}$) lie on the perpendicular bisector of the segment.

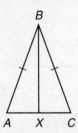

16. $LSA = 2\pi rh$

    $6\pi^2 \text{ cm}^2 = 2\pi(3 \text{ cm})h$

    $\pi \text{ cm} = h$

17. $\pi r^2 = 25\pi^2 \text{ cm}^2$

    $r^2 = 25\pi \text{ cm}^2$

    $r = 5\sqrt{\pi} \text{ cm}$

    $d = 2r = \mathbf{10\sqrt{\pi} \text{ cm}}$

18. $PQ = RS$

    $2x + 4 = 6x - 2$

    $6 = 4x$

    $\dfrac{3}{2} = x$

    $P_{PQRS} = 2(7) + \left(2\left(\dfrac{3}{2}\right) + 4\right) + \left(6\left(\dfrac{3}{2}\right) - 2\right)$

    $P_{PQRS} = \mathbf{28}$

19. $2x + 40 = 90$

    $x = 25$

    $P_{ABCD} = 4(25 - 15) = \mathbf{40}$

20. $A_t = Pe^{rt}$

    $A_5 = 1400e^{0.09(5)} = \mathbf{\$2195.64}$

21. $A_t = A_0e^{kt}$

    $400 = 50e^{3k}$

    $0.69 \approx k$

    $A_{12} = 50e^{0.69(12)} \approx \mathbf{197{,}209 \text{ bugs}}$

22. $75 = 10^{x+4}$

    $10^{1.88} \approx 10^{x+4}$

    $1.88 = x + 4$

    $\mathbf{-2.12} = x$

23. $\dfrac{e^{-24.27}}{e^{13.34}} = e^{-24.27 - 13.34}$

    $= e^{-37.61} \approx \mathbf{4.64 \times 10^{-17}}$

24. $x + 3 \geq 2$; $D = \{\text{Reals}\}$

    $x \geq -1$

    ![number line from -2 to 2 with closed dot at -1]

25. $y = x^2 - 2x - 2$

    $y = (x^2 - 2x + 1) - 2 - 1$

    $y = (x - 1)^2 - 3$

    From this we see:

    (a) Opens upward

    (b) Axis of symmetry is $x = 1$.

    (c) y-coordinate of vertex is -3.

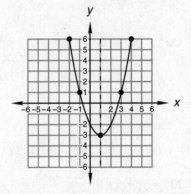